D0125205

Eliot Ness
AND THE
MAD
BUTCHER

MAX ALLAN COLLINS AND A. BRAD SCHWARTZ

ELIOT NESS AND THE MAD BUTCHER. Copyright © 2020 by Max Allan Collins and A. Brad Schwartz. All rights reserved. Printed in the United States of America. No part of this book may be used or reproduced in any manner whatsoever without written permission except in the case of brief quotations embodied in critical articles and reviews. For information, address HarperCollins Publishers, 195 Broadway, New York, NY 10007.

HarperCollins books may be purchased for educational, business, or sales promotional use. For information, please email the Special Markets Department at SPsales@harpercollins.com.

A hardcover edition of this book was published in 2020 by William Morrow, an imprint of HarperCollins Publishers.

FIRST WILLIAM MORROW PAPERBACK EDITION PUBLISHED 2021.

Designed by Elina Cohen

Photograph on the title page courtesy of The Cleveland Police Historical Society, Inc.
Part title page photograph courtesy of Buffalo State College Archives & Special Collections, Courier-Express Collection.
Newspaper front page image used throughout © 1936 The Plain Dealer. All rights reserved. Reprinted/used with permission.

Library of Congress Cataloging-in-Publication Data has been applied for.

ISBN 978-0-06-288198-4

21 22 23 24 25 LSC 10 9 8 7 6 5 4 3 2 1

ALSO BY MAX ALLAN COLLINS AND A. BRAD SCHWARTZ

Scarface and the Untouchable: Al Capone, Eliot Ness, and the Battle for Chicago

Hunting a Serial Killer at the Dawn of Modern Criminology

wm

WILLIAM MORROW
An Imprint of HarperCollinsPublishers

For Rabbi Matt Green

A gentleman and a scholar
(There aren't too many of those left these days . . .)

IF THERE WERE ENOUGH LIKE HIM,
THE WORLD WOULD BE A VERY SAFE PLACE TO LIVE IN,
WITHOUT BECOMING TOO DULL TO BE WORTH LIVING IN.

—*Raymond Chandler*

CONTENTS

Contents

All quotations come from sources cited in the endnotes. A few minor liberties were taken with quotes from newspapers and other print sources of the day, occasionally (not always) correcting spelling and punctuation to avoid a plethora of *sics* that might cause readers to stumble.

Eliot Ness
AND THE
Mad Butcher

Eliot Ness in the 1950s.

Cleveland Public Library Photograph Collection

Untouchable

1956

They made a strange pair—the broken-down businessman, honest to a fault, and his sportswriter acquaintance, bullshitter to the core.

The locals would see them wandering the streets of the mountain-bound Pennsylvania hamlet, the writer—younger, thinner, sandy hair receding—hustling to keep up while his companion charged ahead. Even in middle age, the businessman retained the broad shoulders of an athletic youth. A neat, careful dresser since childhood, he wore tailored suits when his bank balance advised buying off the rack.

The writer's tattered sport jacket was about as fancy as he got. Why he'd come to town got around quick; his syndicated column carried his name even to this corner of western Pennsylvania. But the idea of writing a book about his new pal—who had moved here to prop up a failing paper company—struck some as "an attempt to make a fast buck."

The sportswriter could use the cash. A gambler and a womanizer, he invented charming tales to cloak the darkness in his past. When he heard this aging executive's story—a real adventure that sounded like fiction—the old pro just knew it could sell. Properly spun into a book, the yarn might even make them both rich.

If only this guy could remember it all.

The two would stroll the picture-perfect town square, with its elegant Victorian courthouse, lofty cupola topped by a gilded statue of Lady Justice. She carried her trademark scales but lacked her usual blindfold—a reminder American justice was anything but blind.

The businessman seemed to know everyone; locals greeted him warmly. People up in the Alleghenies often nursed suspicion of outsiders, like this city boy here less than a year. Yet the sportswriter marveled at how they seemed to welcome his companion, and not because of his past.

The locals had heard the tales Eliot Ness shared over drinks in a nearby tavern—stories of gangsters and G-men, writ large across the colorful canvas of Prohibition-era Chicago. Some refused to believe any of it. Why would somebody like that ever end up here? Others thought the newcomer chose this out-of-the-way spot to hide from the mob.

The sportswriter, Oscar Fraley, nursed his own doubts. Having learned what this guy did before entering the paper business, Fraley had stared at the older man, trying to find the gangbuster.

Ness looked a decade older than his fifty-three years. A once-boyish yet sharp-featured face had gone bloated and soft, youthful freckles still littering a complexion mottled from years of drinking. His eyebrows drooped, heavy bags under his eyes, brown hair thick as ever, parted off center now—no longer straight down the middle, time perhaps teaching him nothing in life was so evenly parsed.

Twenty-five years before, Eliot Ness had inspired the creation of the most square-jawed detective in popular culture. Now his own firm chin was disappearing into the folds of his neck.

Yet the former G-man's old iron will and stubborn determination remained just below the surface. Although he'd moved where deer hunting was a way of life, he wanted nothing to do with guns, wouldn't even permit one in his house.

"I've seen too much of shooting and killing," he'd say.

Eliot Ness remembered the violence of the old days—when a friend and comrade wound up on a slab, shot in the eye. Ness had never liked guns and often went unarmed, even when any other cop would have packed heat.

But he'd had plenty of reasons to fear for his life back when gangsters had threatened and followed him. They tried to pay him off, too, but he refused to be bribed, as did most of his men. In a city where everyone seemed to be for sale, these incorruptible Prohibition agents soon earned a new name.

The Untouchables.

Memories of those days stayed with Ness—the thrill of raiding illegal breweries, crashing in with a battering-ram truck and rousting the workers before they knew what hit them. Waiting at the base of a telephone pole, watching out for armed thugs, as an Untouchable put in a wiretap. Alerting the city's most powerful gangster that a parade of confiscated beer trucks would soon rattle past his headquarters in broad daylight.

And he remembered May 3, 1932, when twenty-nine-year-old Prohibition agent Eliot Ness helped escort Alphonse "Scarface Al" Capone from the Cook County Jail to Chicago's Dearborn Station and a train headed for federal prison. Press photographers and newsreel cameramen captured the two men marching through the train shed, surrounded by onlookers—the only time Ness met the man newspapers called his "nemesis."

On the platform, watching the train roll away, the young federal agent reflected on years of raids and stakeouts, wiretaps and paperwork. He and his men had crippled Capone's bootleg empire, smashing the breweries that financed the gangster's rise to wealth and power. But they hadn't been the ones to defeat him in court—that fell to the Treasury Department's Intelligence Unit, which built the income tax evasion case that sent Scarface away on an eleven-year sentence, while Ness's conspiracy case took a backseat. Only privately would the Untouchable admit disappointment.

"We did our part, of course," he told the press. "But the real work of sending Capone to prison was done by the tax investigators. Our job was more spectacular, that was all."

The sportswriter needed more than a few scattered anecdotes to weave a compelling narrative, and Ness struggled to give Fraley what he wanted, names and details eluding him. The two men puzzled over scrapbooks of newspaper clippings, wiretap transcripts, letters, and other documents, trying to assemble the pieces of a life lived long ago.

They holed up in Fraley's room at the run-down hotel on the town square, drinking and talking. Ness paced, a caged animal, a fist to his forehead, scolding himself for his faulty memory.

"The hell with it," he'd snarl.

But the former federal agent sorely *needed* a success, because years of bad business decisions had left him drowning in debt. He had a wife to support and a son with no college fund. Then there was Eliot's heart condition—how long could he expect to provide for them both? He had no insurance, nothing to leave them.

Except for his story.

So he kept at it—going along with Fraley wanting to jazz things up to make the book sell. At times he found himself talking about what happened *after* the Capone days, when he'd gone on to Cleveland—a crime-ridden town battered by the Depression, where the new mayor placed him in charge of the police and fire departments. Another corrupt city, with a host of challenges surpassing anything he'd faced in Chicago.

Vice and incompetence plagued the police force. Gangsters shook down legitimate industry and made fortunes from illegal gambling, killing anyone in their way. In the city's poorer neighborhoods, kids born without hope found themselves caught in a cycle of crime and incarceration. Clevelanders in cars slaughtered each other on the streets, turning their town into one of America's deadliest. Strikes rocked the city, sparking pitched battles between workers and police.

The Untouchable—youngest police executive the city had ever had—confronted each problem with creativity, vigor, and determination. He battled his own police force—employing cutting-edge reforms, rooting out corruption, turning the department into one of the nation's most progressive. He led raids on illicit gambling and built airtight cases against Cleveland's top racketeers. Disturbed by rising juvenile delinquency, he gave these kids a second chance. Saving countless lives with his innovative traffic safety programs, he earned nationwide renown and became a local hero. Still a young man, he left the city safer, cleaner, and far better than he'd found it.

But there was one case he could never publicly close—the monster who emerged to prey on the city's weakest and most vulnerable even as Eliot Ness began cleaning up their town, a killer who made Capone seem benign by comparison, branded in the press a "Butcher" for what he did to his victims: cutting off their heads while they still breathed, chopping up their bodies like cuts of meat, leaving the pieces scattered around town. This faceless murderer—only later recognized as a serial killer—terrorized the city just when it seemed poised for a more promising future.

Cleveland turned to its young top cop, hoping he might end the horror. The Untouchable duly joined the investigation, helping pioneer some of the techniques—including criminal profiling—still used to hunt serial killers today. But this man so adept at catching criminals, whose methods and motives he could understand, faltered when faced with one he could not fathom—a killer who preyed on strangers, for reasons incomprehensible outside his own twisted pathology.

The Butcher remained as anonymous as his victims, and when the killing stopped, his shadow remained, looming over the legacy of Cleveland's law enforcement icon—the one criminal he could never catch.

Only he *had* caught the bastard. He was certain he had! But, he told Fraley, he'd had to keep it a secret. . . .

As they worked on their Capone book, Ness broke his silence, revealing the secret investigation that turned up a promising suspect: a man who fit their profile and knew things only the Butcher could have known. This person of interest had taunted his pursuers, all but daring them to catch him. Yet they couldn't build a case that would hold up in court, and so the Untouchable skirted the law's limits, dealing with his suspect by other means.

The story might have seemed improbable, unverifiable—an attempt to save face by slapping a satisfying ending on an unsolved case. But Fraley saw the proof, tucked away among Ness's scrapbooks: chilling, threatening postcards, one of which bore the full name of the secret suspect.

Fraley left Pennsylvania with the beginnings of the book that would turn his friend into an American legend. The resulting television series and films would paint Eliot Ness as "the man who got Capone," something the Untouchable himself never claimed.

Ness would go to his grave having covered up, by necessity, the resolution of his greatest case—the mad killer he believed he had identified and stopped. Yet the Butcher became a symbol of the Untouchable's failure, eclipsing so many of his triumphs.

Post-Capone, Ness faced problems that would plague the criminal justice system into the twenty-first century: police corruption and abuse of power, systemic prejudice and racism, the linkage between poverty and incarceration. This lawman—most remembered for one high-profile case in Chicago—offered up in Cleveland a transformative vision, all but forgotten today, for more humane law enforcement, which every crisis he confronted—especially the Butcher—put to the test.

Seeing promise in the Cleveland story, Fraley went on to write his version of it—how Eliot Ness had cleaned up a dark city while hunting the monster who, even more than Capone, deserved to be called his nemesis. As with his previous Ness book, Fraley embellished and exaggerated, further obscuring this lesser-known chapter in the Untouchable's life.

But even that incorrigible bullshit artist recognized a simple truth that Hollywood almost erased.

For Eliot Ness, Al Capone was only the beginning.

ife Identified a
ler; Head Found

of Grisly Discovery on Lonely Country Road

PART ONE

PUBLIC SAFETY

Eliot Ness in the 1930s.

The Cleveland Police Historical Society, Inc.

ONE

The Dark City

1934

On April 19, 1934, Eliot Ness turned thirty-one amid the wreckage of a once promising, even heralded career.

Eight years earlier, not long out of college, Ness had taken his oath of office as a Prohibition agent, swearing to battle the bootleggers ruling his hometown. His decision distressed and mystified his Norwegian immigrant parents, who'd struggled and sacrificed so their youngest son could enjoy a better life.

Why would such a bright, hardworking young man—with a University of Chicago degree—choose to join the ranks of the notorious Prohibition Unit, whose agents were known for shooting innocent citizens and taking bribes from gangsters?

Peter and Emma Ness's son, unlike most Prohibition agents, had no interest in lining his pockets; for him, a friend recalled, "honesty amounted to almost a fetish." Nor did Eliot consider Prohibition an especially worthy cause. Any law so widely disdained and disregarded was both doomed to failure and damaging to law enforcement. If cops or federal agents took a bribe to ignore Volstead Act violations, what other crimes might they learn to overlook?

Even so, the Prohibition Unit offered Ness entrée into his

chosen field. Growing up on the South Side of Chicago, Ness had idolized his much older brother-in-law, Alexander Jamie, a Scottish immigrant who joined the embryonic Bureau of Investigation (not yet the FBI) when Eliot was still a teenager.

Jamie and his fellow federal agents—forerunners of the G-men who would one day become America's heroes—represented a new breed of lawmen so unlike old-school beat cops, inspiring young Eliot to make a career in law enforcement. He would serve the public while feeding his appetite for danger and excitement, and perhaps achieve a professional standing reserved for doctors and lawyers.

As a child, Ness had read Sir Arthur Conan Doyle's Sherlock Holmes stories; the famous detective's scientific acumen and mastery of martial arts became his model for an ideal investigator. Ness trained body and mind to emulate his literary hero—learning jujitsu, mastering marksmanship, and studying under famed police reformer August Vollmer.

After Eliot's brother-in-law clashed with new boss J. Edgar Hoover, Ness followed Jamie into the Prohibition Unit, where they could rise through the ranks together, the older agent serving as protector and patron. Although Ness might have preferred joining Hoover's Bureau, he couldn't help but stand out in the dry force amid a crowd of grafters, crooks, and blunderers.

Ness's dedication and drive soon won his superiors' respect. In late 1930, they tapped him to lead a crucial part of the federal assault on the Capone Outfit, assigning him to build a small squad of agents who couldn't be bribed. While smashing the mob's bootleg operations and drying up its immense income, the team gathered evidence for a massive conspiracy indictment linking Capone and dozens of others to five thousand Prohibition violations.

The groundbreaking case they built would never go to trial; federal officials chose instead to seek Capone's conviction on income tax charges. But Ness and his raiders crippled the Outfit financially, receiving much public credit for Capone's downfall and winning nationwide fame as "the Untouchables."

Ness became a local—and, briefly, national—celebrity. When

author Sax Rohmer, creator of Dr. Fu Manchu, visited Chicago in 1932, he sought time with just three prominent lawmen: Police Commissioner James Allman, forensic scientist Calvin Goddard, and Eliot Ness. Local cartoonist Chester Gould modeled the iconic comic-strip detective Dick Tracy on Ness.

But the real man seemed hardly the hard-boiled stereotype come to life.

"He stood just under six feet," Fletcher Knebel reported, "weighed 172 pounds and owned thick brown hair that refused to stay parted. His blue-gray eyes, shy smile and uncreased features gave him a boyish appearance. His manners were correct, his voice so low as to be inaudible at times. He was courteous, gentlemanly."

Many might have exploited this sudden celebrity—as did Chicago G-man Melvin Purvis, a few years later. Famed as the FBI agent who got John Dillinger, then forced from the Bureau for loving the limelight, Purvis became a radio announcer, Hollywood personality, and breakfast cereal pitchman. No such path tempted Eliot Ness.

After Capone's conviction, Ness kept up his assault on the Outfit, while other federal men moved on. But with Scarface in jail, the American people and their government showed little interest in pursuing Capone's associates. And with Franklin Roosevelt elected president in 1932, Prohibition wouldn't last long.

Ness found himself trapped in a shrinking agency soon to be obsolete. He'd battled the Outfit to the brink of bankruptcy, but he couldn't finish the job alone. His moment had passed, and with it his chance to climb the federal ladder.

Back in 1929, he'd married Edna Stahle, a petite brunette three years his junior. Quiet, reserved, Edna came from his old South Side neighborhood; although they'd known each other as kids, their romance only began when she reentered Eliot's life as Jamie's secretary. For a while, their personal and professional lives were entwined, but after Edna left the federal service they grew apart. By 1933, Edna had taken to waiting outside Eliot's office for her husband to come off duty, as whispered gossip of their shaky marriage traveled through the federal bureaucracy.

Then Ness made an ill-advised attempt to shore up his career. Hoping to win a job with Hoover's Bureau—even to replace Melvin Purvis as Chicago's Special Agent in Charge—he curried favor with the staff of an Illinois politician. Along the way, Ness encountered another constituent seeking a favor: a party man trying to get protection for an illicit still.

Ness did nothing to help the man but didn't report him, either. The federal government, anticipating repeal, had abolished the Prohibition Bureau and replaced it with a new Alcoholic Beverage Unit, to which Ness now reported—there seemed little urgency in busting yet another small-time, independent bootlegger. But Ness's superiors found out and investigated. Finding no further evidence of misconduct, they transferred Ness to Cincinnati, Ohio, almost certainly as punishment.

Banished from Chicago, Ness sought to return by continuing his efforts to join Hoover's Bureau, now known as the Division of Investigation. But Purvis shared the reasons behind Ness's transfer with the Director.

Hoover personally rejected Ness's application, regarding him with suspicion and disdain from then on.

In early 1934, Ness found himself in a hostile work environment, surrounded by agents he didn't trust, enforcing a moribund law.

"Our Unit has been passing through a rather unsettled period," Ness wrote to a colleague that April, "due to the fact that many men were dismissed."

Despite the end of national Prohibition in December 1933, bootleggers kept plying their trade. The government taxed legal liquor heavily, largely to pay for President Roosevelt's new relief and recovery programs. This created a thriving black market for cheap, rotgut booze, prompting another crackdown. In May 1934, Ness and other dry agents transferred into a new Alcohol Tax Unit of the Treasury Department.

Ness now faced a different, more dangerous bootlegger than the Chicago breed. The Cincinnati ATU office oversaw Michigan, Ohio, Kentucky, and Tennessee; Ness's assignment took him south into rough, rural country—the "Moonshine Mountains."

Families there had been brewing white lightning for generations, but Prohibition turned the practice into "a backwoods industry of menacing proportions." Fearful of raids, the locals didn't hesitate to shoot the hats off anyone who wandered too close.

"Those mountain men and their squirrel rifles," Ness remembered, "gave me almost as many chills as the Capone mob."

Ness's stint as a "revenooer" didn't last long. Treasury officials soon realized the Cincinnati office covered too much ground, and that Appalachian moonshiners posed a different problem than Prohibition-style bootleggers in Michigan and Ohio. Cleveland remained riddled with illicit stills, whose profits fueled the growth of a powerful crime syndicate.

That August, the ATU cut the Cincinnati district in two, making Ness the acting investigator in charge of northern Ohio. Whatever his sins in Chicago, he had more than paid for them in the Moonshine Mountains. Now he decamped for Cleveland, the headquarters of the new district, and got back to the work he knew best.

NESS ARRIVED TO find a wounded beast of a city, ravaged by the Great Depression. Cleveland had ridden high in the 1920s, rising to a level of prosperity it would never see again. Its prime location on the shores of Lake Erie, between New York and Chicago, helped make it an industrial epicenter. Factories and steel mills—along the banks of the Cuyahoga, the greasy, snaky river slicing through the center of the city—thrummed day and night, giant blast furnaces blotting out the sky with smoke and fire. Workers swarmed in from all over, swelling Cleveland to America's fifth largest city—third, if you included the suburbs.

Civic leaders expressed their optimism in stone and steel, erecting monumental public buildings along the grassy mall near the lakefront. In 1923, they broke ground for a massive train station complex, a "city within a city" overseen by the town's first skyscraper. Planned for twenty-five stories, the neo-Gothic Terminal Tower rose to fifty-two, its 708 feet perched on a ridge overlooking the Cuyahoga and the industrial valley that spawned it—the tallest building in the world outside New York.

But when this $150 million monument opened in 1930, Cleveland had already begun to slide into despair and decay. In April 1930, one in seven Clevelanders was out of work; within nine months, the jobless rate rose to one-third. A legion of unemployed and underemployed sought refuge among factories in "the Flats," the low-lying region near the Cuyahoga. Amid smokestacks and naked wrought-iron bridges, they built cities of their own—clusters of shanties, cobbled from whatever was at hand, offering poor protection from Cleveland's bitter, brutal winters. Other down-and-outers disappeared into the disease-ridden warren of East Side slums—the "Roaring Third" police precinct, where crime flourished as cops looked the other way.

Faced with an unprecedented crisis, Cleveland's city government buckled under the strain. In 1933, voters ousted their well-meaning mayor and replaced him with Harry L. Davis, a slick, ineffectual politician who filled City Hall with corrupt cronies. The Cleveland Police Department, already rife with Prohibition-era graft, degenerated even further. Gambling parlors and bookie joints ran unhindered in the Roaring Third and the suburbs, funneling whatever cash their patrons could spare into the pockets of organized crime.

Among America's criminal class, Cleveland became known as a "safe" city—where even the most notorious hoods could hide. Bank robber Alvin Karpis, last of the "public enemies" to remain on the run, found refuge there from the Division of Investigation.

"The fix was really in in Cleveland," he recalled.

That tolerance for grafters, gamblers, and gangsters made fertile ground for crime. Robbery and murder grew commonplace, blackening the pages of Cleveland's papers. With police little more than a public joke, even minor criminals felt free to operate with brazen self-assurance—as three men did one day in June 1932, when they walked into an East Side tailor shop and walked off with a suit they hadn't paid for. The owner, sixty-year-old Lithuanian immigrant Michel Siegel, died trying to stop them.

After police did little to solve the crime, Siegel's seventeen-year-old son, Jerry, began to envision a hero who would set things right—an invulnerable do-gooder, immensely strong and impervious to bullets. Jerry brainstormed with a young friend, artist Joe Shuster. They called their character Superman.

But not even Superman could drag Cleveland from the mire. The city's mood had plunged right along with the stock market, the Depression killing its heady optimism, throwing the city deeper into despair.

Terminal Tower, potentially the start of a glorious new skyline, now stood proud and alone, a shantytown sprawling in its shadow. You could see the skyscraper from practically anywhere in town—stark against slate-gray skies filled with heavy clouds and the soot of industry, blotting out the sun and giving Cleveland a new nickname: "The Dark City."

IN A TOWN starved for good news, reporters took whatever silver linings they could get. For Charles "Wes" Lawrence of the *Cleveland Plain Dealer*, the arrival of Capone's onetime nemesis qualified.

When Lawrence met the unassuming young federal agent—hardly the brash lawman he'd expected—he knew he'd found something unusual.

Ness told him of the Untouchables but refused to take credit for Capone's conviction. Lawrence had rarely met a public figure so modest, so determined to talk about his team and not himself.

"I am just finding my way around Cleveland now," Ness said, "and would rather talk about what we can do here after we have accomplished it."

By the end of October, Ness and his men had shut down seventy-two stills, cutting Cleveland's bootleg liquor supply nearly in half.

The ATU moved on to shuttering speakeasies, including the luxurious Blackstone Club on the city's northeast side. Ness raided the place in mid-November, ordering his agents to confiscate any possible collateral against unpaid tax.

"They took not only the bartender, but the bar also," a reporter wrote. "They took the chairs, the tables, and the elegant red-and-black Japanese hangings and decorations."

Not even those cooking up home brew for their own use could rest easy.

"The federal laws make no provision for the home manufacture of liquor, beer or wine," Ness said. "The government is entitled to its cut on every gallon of alcoholic beverage made."

But once that tax was paid, Ness saw no reason not to slake his own thirst. He hadn't been a drinker before joining the Prohibition Bureau, but alcohol came with the job. Agents often gathered evidence by going undercover to patronize suspected speakeasies, and they sometimes developed a taste.

After long days spent busting up stills and nightclubs, Ness often unwound by going out for a few beers with Lawrence and other reporters. They became his friends and some of his biggest boosters, giving his exploits good coverage.

Ness began to put down roots. He rented a lakefront cottage in Bay Village, a quiet suburb far west. Little more than a guesthouse for a larger property, not much larger than a two-car garage, it nonetheless offered the childless young couple a garden, a Lake Erie view, and a secluded getaway from downtown bustle.

Edna came from Chicago to join Eliot there. Together they seemed to repair the rift in their marriage.

The Nesses rented the cottage from a former assistant attorney general, whose son, Robert West Chamberlin, became a close friend. A lawyer and a captain in the Ohio National Guard, Chamberlin looked every bit the military man, with a long face, high forehead, and trimmed mustache. He shared Ness's passion for athletics, having played football at the University of Michigan.

"I told him once that I hardly called [his job] work," Chamberlin recalled. "So we went out on a raid together. And I'll never forget the way he pushed open the door. He didn't know what was behind it, and he didn't seem to care. He just doesn't know what fear is."

Having survived Chicago and the Moonshine Mountains, Ness saw little reason to fear Cleveland's bootleggers. But this new city had its own demons, of a kind Ness had never encountered.

One, in particular, would soon remind him what it meant to be afraid.

EMIL FRONEK COULDN'T remember, exactly, when he encountered the doctor.

He was pretty sure it was in the latter part of 1934. In years past, a strapping stevedore like Fronek could easily have found work in Cleveland, whose bustling lakefront always needed strong men. But after the Great Depression robbed Fronek of his livelihood, he fell into a tramp's life, roaming streets and shantytowns, just scraping by.

One evening, Fronek wandered up Broadway, a major thoroughfare cutting through Cleveland's industrial center, in search of a pair of shoes. This working-class neighborhood of mostly Central European immigrants might include a countryman who'd take pity on Fronek's aching feet. But the man who answered his knock at the back door of a two-story house, somewhere between East Fiftieth and East Fifty-Fifth Streets, was neither a fellow immigrant nor of the working class.

Fronek's middle-aged, smooth-faced host, with sandy hair going gray at the temples, had strange, almost colorless eyes, which he trained on his visitor before escorting him upstairs into what seemed to be a doctor's office.

"He said he would give me some shoes," Fronek recalled. "He told me first he would give me something to eat."

The apparent doctor stepped into another room and returned soon after with a large steak, French fries, coleslaw, and coffee. Famished, Fronek didn't stop to question the generous handout. He just dove in, as the doctor watched.

When Fronek grew sick to his stomach, and told his host, the doctor promised to get his guest some whiskey. But the nausea kept building, and so did dizziness—had the food been drugged?

"All I could see was the door," Fronek recalled, "and I jumped up and ran out. The doctor said: 'Wait a minute, wait a minute, let's have some more to drink.' But I kept going until I found an empty boxcar on some railroad tracks near there and I crawled in and went to sleep."

He came to three days later, after some tramps roused him, thinking he was drunk. When he'd come to his senses, an enraged Fronek set out to settle with the "doctor" who'd poisoned him. But by day, the street looked different, and Fronek couldn't find the house he'd wandered into. He cut his losses and jumped another train.

Fronek later told his story to another man riding the rails.

"That's funny," his listener said, "I almost got cut up in that house, too."

The fellow traveler told his own tale of meeting the doctor, of being welcomed into his home and given a meal. After that, the man's memory went blank till he woke up in what appeared to be "a private hospital" with slashes in his chest and abdomen. He'd panicked and fled, vaulting over a fence to get away.

The man displayed the scars on his chest, but Fronek didn't need convincing—he'd already resolved to give Cleveland a wide berth, where a visit to a certain doctor could kill you.

OTHERS WEREN'T SO lucky.

In August 1934, when Ness first arrived in Cleveland, pieces of a woman's body began littering the Lake Erie shore—first her ribs, then part of her backbone, thirty miles east of town. On September 5, the lower half of her torso, its rotted flesh looking barely human, turned up at Euclid Beach on Cleveland's East Side. The woman's spine had been sliced as if by a butcher knife, her legs severed at the knees with surgical precision. When this discovery made the papers, other reports came in of body parts floating in the lake.

One fourteen-year-old girl said she'd stumbled over two legs five or six weeks earlier. Another claimed a hand waved at her from underwater, four weeks after that. Her father had seen it, too.

"I'm sure it was a human hand," he told the *Cleveland Press*.

But police only ever found the upper arm, not nearly enough to identify the woman's body. Denied a face or a name, she became "the Lady of the Lake."

Cuyahoga County Coroner Arthur J. Pearse placed her at around forty and estimated she had died back in March. She'd been cut up by someone with a fair amount of anatomical knowledge, who expertly separated her spine and unhooked her knees. In removing her right arm, however, the killer slipped up or got careless—sawing it off instead of making a clean slice. This, Pearse believed, ruled out surgeons as potential suspects.

"No surgeon ever would have used a saw," Pearse insisted. "He would have known how to manipulate a knife around the joint."

A chemical preservative had apparently been applied to the body, reddening and toughening its skin. But why would the killer keep his corpus delicti around and not get rid of it as soon as possible? Had he slipped up again, mistaking slacked lime, which preserved the corpse, for quicklime, which would've destroyed it? No one could say for sure.

Lake Erie's unpredictable currents might have carried the pieces from just about anywhere in Cleveland, or even as far away as Canada. With no identity to go on, and no solid leads or suspects, police found themselves stymied. Asked whether this was a perfect crime, the lead detective on the case claimed it was not.

But, he added, it was "so close to being perfect that we don't know what to do next."

Kingsbury Run in the mid-1930s.
Cleveland Press Collection, Cleveland State University

Ness (third from left) with Mayor Harold Burton (far left) and
Police Chief George Matowitz (far right).
Authors' Collection

TWO

An Impossible Mission

1935

The locals called it Kingsbury Run.

Amid the industrial sprawl of Cleveland's southeast side, this stretch of land remained rugged, untamed, and feral. An ancient gully, carved by a river since forced underground, the Run sliced through a region of factories and slums, leaving a deep, curved gash, too large to fill in, its walls too steep for any kind of development. You couldn't even drive a car close to the edge without risking the ground giving way. Weedy thickets clung to its sides; heaps of garbage littered its floor. The occasional sunflower, fighting through the snarl, offered a rare splash of color.

"The Run's ugliness is worse in the winter," wrote a reporter, "when the sumacs and willows are naked and the fresher wounds of dumps and excavations lie uncovered. A wild tangle of greenery helps hide those sores in the summer."

Night hid them, too, in silent blackness, cutting the Run off from the modern world.

Yet somehow this wilderness had long been a conduit for wealth. As early as 1857, the railroads used Kingsbury Run as a fast route into the city, their tracks drawing industry as if magnetized. During the Civil War, John D. Rockefeller built his first oil refinery on the Run's edge. More sprang up, their noxious drainage saturating the ground and seeping into the Cuyahoga, turning it oily and flammable.

Decades later, two homegrown tycoons, the Van Sweringen brothers, ran a new Rapid Transit line for suburban commuters through the ravine. At one end, they built the bedroom community of Shaker Heights, an affluent, exclusive "Garden City" laid out like the campus of an elite university. At the other, they erected Terminal Tower, a monument to their own ambition. The brothers promoted both as paradise on earth, ignoring the industrial hell between them.

The Van Sweringens' empire, built on a rickety latticework of holding companies and overblown loans, could not withstand the Great Depression. By 1935, they had lost their fortune, taking the city's economy down with them. They left behind Shaker Heights and Terminal Tower, along with the Rapid Transit connecting the two. As prosperous passengers cut through Kingsbury Run, traveling eight miles in just twenty-one minutes, they could see hoboes making their camps and kids hurrying to hop a freight.

The evening commute had just begun on Monday, September 23, 1935, when two boys dashed after a softball into the Run. They'd been playing catch atop Jackass Hill, which sloped sixty steep feet to the tracks on the ravine floor. Sixteen-year-old James Wagner got there first, outpacing his twelve-year-old friend. But as he searched the weeds for the missing ball, Wagner saw something stark white against the brush—something unexpected, something horrible. . . .

He froze for a moment, then bolted back up, shouting he'd seen "a dead man with no head down there."

Police found the relatively fresh corpse of a man in his mid to late twenties, resting on its side as if in slumber, wearing only a pair of black socks. His head had been cut cleanly off at the neck, his genitals slashed away. The search for the head produced, thirty feet away, another dead body, also naked, emasculated, and decapitated—a middle-aged man, dead for up to several weeks, skin tough and discolored, like the Lady of the Lake found almost exactly a year before.

This time, investigators couldn't decide whether the body had also been treated with a chemical preservative or whether fire had singed it. The missing heads were found buried apart in shallow graves; a few strands of the younger man's hair poking above the surface, human sprouts indicating a grotesque crop awaiting harvest. No attempt had been made to hide the genitals, which were piled nearby, conveniently if not neatly.

Autopsies revealed both men had died of decapitation, hearts still beating when their heads were cut off.

"That's odd," a detective observed. "Usually a murderer kills by other means—stabbing, shooting, strangulation, poison. Sometimes, not often, the heads are removed to prevent identification, but almost never to kill. It's a hell of a job to remove a human head anyway."

No blood had been found at the scene, although (as an officer pointed out) "the jugular vein is a snaky thing, it splatters blood everywhere when you cut it." Both corpses seemed to have been washed and drained of blood before consignment to the Run.

But the ghastly remains hadn't just been dumped—the positioning and condition of the bodies suggested their killer conveyed them, one by one, down steep Jackass Hill, probably in the dark. Police assumed they were dealing with at least two murderers who'd split the heavy lifting between them. Only later did they come to see this as the work of a single individual—a man of immense physical strength and an almost theatrical flair. The odd composition of the crime scene, and the lack of any effort to conceal the bodies, suggested a killer proud of his work.

Investigators couldn't lift fingerprints from the rough, rotting skin of the older victim, who—despite police efforts—would never be identified. The younger man's fingers, however, yielded a clean set of prints identifying him as Edward Andrassy, twenty-eight, a West Side resident. Finally, police seemed to catch a break—the devilishly handsome young victim provided plenty of possible motives for his murder.

An off-and-on employee in the mental ward at Cleveland's City Hospital, Andrassy had a reputation in the Roaring Third Precinct as a drunken brawler who sold pornography, marijuana, and women. Shortly before Andrassy's death, a jilted husband had sworn "to get him for playing around with my wife." Others spoke of same-sex liaisons; evidence suggested Andrassy made money as a procurer of young men. A gang of Italians, he'd told relatives, was seeking revenge over him stabbing one of theirs in a fight. So many leads for the police to check out—so many dead ends.

Both the cops and the press saw these murders as crimes of passion. Emasculated victims indicated vengeance, whether sexual or otherwise. Andrassy had earned the killer's special scorn, dying with rope burns on his wrists, suggesting he'd fought to free himself, likely conscious when castrated.

As darkness took Kingsbury Run and the bodies were carted off, Detective Orley May—in that coldly understated way of a seasoned cop—admitted never having seen the like.

"I've got a bad feeling," he said, "about this one."

ELIOT NESS'S FIRST year in Cleveland passed in a whirlwind of raids, arrests, and painstaking detective work.

He and a small team of Alcohol Tax Unit agents spent their days and nights scouring northern Ohio for illicit stills and the bottling plants where legal liquor containers were refilled with everything from pure grain alcohol to radiator fluid. They hit without mercy—smashing equipment and scattering booze until "the place looked as though a small tornado had struck." Before long, word that Ness's raiders had brought their axes to the Dark City was enough to send bootleggers scurrying.

Ness's biggest success came late in 1934 when he broke up "a miniature liquor empire" in Akron. While ATU agents raided stills in and around the city, Ness gathered evidence that Summit County Sheriff Ray Potts had routinely shaken down local bootleggers. Rumor had the deputies selling liquor out of the county jail.

Using a trick from his Chicago days, Ness placed an under-cover agent behind bars with orders to buy booze. After Potts's chief deputy took the bait, Ness hauled him in and grilled him until he cracked. The deputy's testimony led to conspiracy indict-ments against the sheriff and thirty-two others, landing Potts in the penitentiary.

Agent George Mulvanity said Ness had "a real eagle eye"—an uncanny knack for spotting smugglers and bootleggers. Once, as they were driving back to Cleveland from Toledo, Ness ordered Mulvanity to follow a car for no apparent reason. When they pulled it over, they found the vehicle's trunk crammed with illicit booze.

Another time, Ness learned of a "haunted house" on Cleve-land's northeast side, where a woman had been murdered months earlier. Neighborhood kids steered clear, claiming it gave off "strange noises" and "funny smells." What seemed straight out of a Dead End Kids movie was nonetheless a story Ness took seriously enough to raid the place. In the basement was a two-hundred-gallon still.

These stills kept getting more elaborate, regularly described by newspapers as "the largest ever confiscated in Eastern Ohio" or "the biggest 'still' capture since prohibition days." Reports came in of gangsters cooking huge quantities of liquor in Ohio for ship-ment to New York and New Jersey. Such a large, industrial opera-tion required massive amounts of cash and high-level organization surpassing even the old Capone mob.

ATU agents followed leads to a massive three-story brick building on the outskirts of Zanesville, Ohio. Supposedly a fac-tory turning grain into cattle feed, the building gave off sweet-smelling fumes—a telltale sign of liquor cooked from molasses. But when Ness and several other agents crashed in they searched the place for almost an hour. Nothing.

Then Ness saw a man dash into a side room, hurried after him into a bathroom—and found no one in it! Ness grabbed an ax and hacked away at a wall, convinced the suspect had slipped through a secret passage.

Ness's boss remarked, "I believe you're seeing things."

"I thought I saw a man," Ness said. "But I guess I didn't."

Other agents climbed to the roof, broke in through a sky-light, and slid down a fire hose into a well-concealed chamber, the air thick with sweet fumes. They found a combination still and brewery, worth some $250,000, capable of turning out 5,000 gallons of alcohol and more than 36,000 gallons of beer per day. The operation required tremendous amounts of water, which the bootleggers stole by tapping directly into the nearest water main. They shipped the product by truck and boxcar, using a rail siding next to the plant.

Ness and his men found electric alarms and a complex system of escape tunnels. One led up to a certain bathroom, its entrance hidden behind a fake toilet. Yet all these precautions weren't enough to save the men inside the plant. The still was so large and so well hidden, the bootleggers didn't know the feds had broken in. Many kept working until their arrest.

Of the twenty-three indicted after the raid, twelve pleaded guilty. But the feds knew these were "just flunkies," as the *Cleveland Plain Dealer* put it. Further investigation linked the plant to a growing criminal syndicate based in Cleveland, run by slight, predatory Moe Dalitz and his three partners.

Dalitz rose to power during Prohibition, prospering after repeal by investing in legitimate business. The strength of his syndicate lay in diversification; unlike Capone's Chicago Outfit, the loss of a single big moneymaker could not cripple a criminal combine that stayed out of the public eye even as it spread across several states and built ties with East Coast gangsters.

On March 12, Ness grasped the scope of Dalitz's operation after raiding a bottling plant and sales office on Cleveland's East Side. The ATU agents hit the phones for four hours, tracking down customers by taking orders and making deliveries. They also seized purchase records of almost one thousand nightclubs, restaurants, and private citizens. The buyers included wealthy residents of Shaker Heights, cheapskates who bought watered-down moonshine rather than pay an affordable tax.

Ness marveled at the detailed records, with some buyers paying by check—he'd never seen anything like it in Chicago. Post-Prohibition, bootlegging remained, as the *Cleveland Press* said, "more widespread than almost anyone imagined."

But the ATU was built to collect taxes, not take down a budding criminal empire like the Cleveland Syndicate. And while the FBI's war on bank-robbing bandits grabbed the headlines, Treasury got little support for its own crime fighting. Ness struggled with a lack of manpower and resources.

Additional ATU funding from Congress came with a new round of civil service tests ordered by a Democrat seeking to purge the unit of Republicans. Ness passed, but half his small force didn't. Several stayed on without pay, on a promise that "special dispensation" might be coming.

Their dedication speaks both to Ness's leadership and a dismal Depression job market. Though Ness would come down hard on any agents shirking their duty, his ATU team adored him. Mulvanity, who went on to a long and decorated ATU career, said Ness taught him much about the job. Other agents regularly put in fifteen- or eighteen-hour days.

Ness could only wonder if it was all worthwhile—for every still he smashed, three more seemed to crop up. The ATU focused on squeezing as much revenue from the drinking public as possible, while the courts remained locked in a post-Prohibition hangover, not really interested in bootlegging convictions.

At a bar in their off-hours, Ness shared his frustrations with Mulvanity, talking openly about a career change.

MOST OF CLEVELAND shared Eliot Ness's desire for change. The Republican administration of Mayor Harry L. Davis seemed unable, or unwilling, to help the tens of thousands of out-of-work Clevelanders clamoring for relief. City government was flat broke; grafting and politicking infested the police department. Meanwhile, Davis grew scarce, taking "long mysterious trips."

To serve as director of public safety, in charge of Cleveland's police and fire departments, the mayor had chosen Martin Lavelle, a former police captain who drove a Rolls-Royce. Lavelle enjoyed cozy, enduring relationships with gangsters and saw no reason to abandon old friends over his new job.

In late June, Lavelle joined bootlegger Marty O'Boyle for "a speedboat liquor party" on Lake Erie. A young woman from City Hall fell overboard and drowned; the safety director neglected to report her death.

The newspapers plastered the scandal on their front pages, but Lavelle refused to step down, and Mayor Davis stood by him. The city's outrage built into a determination to oust Davis at the polls.

In the Republican primary, Davis faced a stiff challenge from Harold Hitz Burton, forty-seven, a Harvard-educated attorney prominent in civic affairs. Stocky and square-jawed, Burton was a hero of the Great War, recipient of the Purple Heart and Croix de Guerre. He'd settled in Cleveland as a young lawyer seeking a less class-conscious climate than his native Boston.

Admirers spoke of Burton's "rock-ribbed New England conscience, stiff geared and in good working order." Despite dark, heavy bags under his eyes, Burton seemed physically tireless, working twelve-hour days, never taking sick leave. He didn't smoke or drink, and stayed in shape. To a city drowning in corruption, he seemed a human life preserver.

Though a lifelong Republican, Burton opposed Davis's powerful political machine by running as an independent. Neither rousing speaker nor showman, Burton lacked the charisma of a political pro like Davis, possessing no gift for shaking hands and slapping backs. But he put in sixteen-hour days on the campaign trail.

"It is absolutely necessary," Burton declared, "that there be no politics, political pressure or political groups having control over any individual in the police department."

After defeating Davis in the primary, Burton trounced his Democratic opponent in the general.

The success or failure of the new administration now hinged

on who Burton chose to replace Lavelle as director of public safety. Picking another political hack would brand Burton's speeches as so much talk, ensuring more of the same from the city's crooked cops.

"Ness would be just the kind of guy Burton needs," reporter Wes Lawrence told his editor the day after the election. "But it seems impossible that Burton would offer him the job. . . . Harold tries to be independent, but he's still a Republican. I don't think Ness has any politics."

The foreman of a federal grand jury, impressed by Ness's Akron cleanup, began drumming up support from prominent businessmen, bombarding Burton and his staff with praise for the young ATU chief. The new mayor sent out feelers to reporters to find out "who this guy Ness was."

"Ness is a public official dear to the hearts of reporters," wrote *Plain Dealer* editor Philip Porter. "They admire his courage and his skill, and they like him personally."

But Burton already had a man in mind: his old law school classmate, Joseph B. Keenan. A prominent former Clevelander, Keenan had been the federal special prosecutor in Franklin Roosevelt's war on crime. Burton went to Washington to woo him back, even meeting with the president to try to pry Keenan loose.

When Keenan turned his old friend down, Burton was left with a trio of second choices: the head of Cleveland's Secret Service office, an assistant U.S. district attorney, and dark horse Ness.

The mayor arranged interviews with all three, meeting with the ATU agent for the first time on December 7. Ness had given so little thought to local politics—he was not even a registered voter—he needed directions to City Hall. Friends warned him not to take the job, seeing it as "an impossible mission," but that only sharpened Ness's resolve.

"I will accept the position if it is offered," he told the *Cleveland Press*. "It would be an opportunity to do some real work, but it would be a tough assignment."

Ness sat with the mayor for almost an hour and a half—he would only take the job, he said, if it came with no political strings attached. He wanted the freedom to run his own investigations, and the funds to hire a secret squad of operatives—a new set of Untouchables—who could gather the necessary evidence.

Burton said that wouldn't be a problem; he had many deep-pocketed friends, sick of being extorted by gangsters, who would gladly help out. Although Ness had become "quite cynical about government," meeting Burton proved "a revelation." The mayor seemed genuine and willing to grant him a free hand.

The *Plain Dealer* gave Ness the "inside track" for the job. But Burton held off until December 11, when he received a phone call from Joe Keenan. Burton's onetime top pick now endorsed Ness, saying Dwight Green, assistant prosecutor on the Capone tax case, credited the Untouchable as key in sending Scarface to prison. Burton called Green, who confirmed it.

Shortly after noon, Ness strode into the cavernous lobby of City Hall wearing a topcoat over his gray pin-striped, double-breasted suit and red tie. He passed between the immense Doric columns and headed up to the mayor's office on the second floor, where he waited among a crowd of job seekers. A few reporters recognized him when the mayor called him inside. After a meeting so brief he didn't remove his coat, Ness was sworn in as the man in charge of Cleveland's 2,400 cops and firefighters.

At just thirty-two, he was the youngest Safety Director the city had ever had.

Ness left the mayor's office to find a crowd clogging the doorway and the marble hall beyond, straining to "get a look" and offer their congratulations. On the street, Cleveland's afternoon papers already had the story. The new Safety Director told reporters he would be as "conservative as possible" until he had the lay of the land.

"After that I don't know what I'll do," Ness said, then added, "but I hope to take necessary action first and talk about it later."

Cleveland's three major newspapers fawned over Ness like a movie star. They presented him as the city's answer to Sherlock Holmes—"a scientific policeman of the type which has become famous in modern European cities."

The political elite looked on, aghast. Ness's selection had been "a real bombshell," as Phil Porter put it, because no insiders expected Burton to pick someone who hadn't lifted a finger in his election.

And that made it the canniest decision of Burton's political career. The mayor needed someone both competent and exciting, a Safety Director who could bring the right kind of attention to his department. No other candidate for the job, not even Keenan, could rile the press up quite like the Untouchable.

Still, the more cynical politicos didn't take Ness seriously. He seemed too young and inexperienced to pose a threat. They sat back and waited for him to make the kind of mistake that would halt Burton's half-baked crusade.

At the police department, many officers feared the days of benign neglect and plentiful graft had ended. Others had no idea what to make of their new boss.

"Policemen have seen safety directors come and safety directors go," a veteran reporter observed, "and things don't usually change much under the surface. . . . A police department is nothing but a vegetable, or a set of vegetables. You don't get any sharp reactions from vegetables."

No one fit that description better than Police Chief George J. Matowitz.

He had been a good cop once, a dogged detective with "a fist like a sack of cement" and unquestioned integrity. But early on he'd learned not to upset the politically powerful.

While Matowitz issued empty orders and watered his beloved potted plants, a shadow organization arose within the department, making sure the wrong people didn't get busted. An "inside chief" gave political marching orders to an "outside chief," who passed them along to the rank and file. The actual chief did his best to stay blissfully ignorant.

Matowitz, serving as his own acting Safety Director before Ness's appointment, hoped to hold on to the position. Now he feared Ness's department-wide purge would leave him with no job at all.

But the new Safety Director had no intention of dismissing Matowitz. Until he earned the department's trust, Ness needed a police chief the rank and file liked and respected. Matowitz's record proved he'd do as told, if it meant hanging on to his job.

"I found Mr. Ness very sincere and impressive," Matowitz gushed to the *Press* after their first meeting. "What we discussed, I would rather have come from him. But he gave me full authority over the Police Department, placing responsibility of policing the city in my hands."

Ness no doubt agreed. The chief could keep giving the orders and watering his plants, but everyone would know who was really in charge of the hothouse.

S TORSO KILLER NEW INSAN

Couzens Trails in Rep⸺an Ra

MAINE VOTE IS BAD NEWS TO NEW DEAL

Buel Says Election Shows Threat of Republican Victory in November.

ROOSEVELT JUST SMILES

Indicates Result Was About What He Expected.

BY WALKER S. BUEL
Plain Dealer Bureau
813 Albee Bldg.
WASHINGTON, Sept 15.

Maine's election is very bad news for the New Deal and President Roosevelt.

If it is a certain indication of a Republican trend, a definite threat of Republican victory in November, a definite forerunner of a downturn in Democratic membership in Congress, a definite indication of a Republican revival, especially in the agricultural

When it has so superlatized factors in the campaign, the Maine vote might be regarded as a final news-alarm history.

For Maine votes, except that she has several votes again the late hope that the days of the New and 1934 Democratic landslides added, and that makes President Roosevelt can hold the seat much as he, is headed for ...

Woodrow Wilson won in 1916 in a election, without a vote of any here data except New Hampshire by a ten margin. But Wilson of the vote and told Roosevelt, as she went and his needs. Only exponents to overcome the main raised by the Maine vote, somewhat put the best face possible ...

To confirm the snake position, the analysis confidence, but tonight there sentiments general made by the and expected ...

that the election in Maine will be one of the places in recent history.

... and, that it will be more than national elections in the past, vote between the urban industrial, supporting President work, and the small towns and rural regions, backing Gov. Land ...

that exception, the held toward either rather up large majorities by the Democratic candidate, but tonight these accumulating was not than offset by the tide of plain failing from the agri ...

No. 20 for Allen

Allen injured his back in the fifth inning but was given credit for his twentieth victory yesterday as the Indianapolis Wooton, 15 to 2. Indians finished the game. Tuesday hit his 19th and 40th homers.

New York defeated Chicago, 5 to 1; Detroit trimmed Philadelphia, 6 to 5, and Washington took a double header from St. Louis, 15 to 7 and 6 to 3.

Weather stopped the National League.

(Details in Sport Pages)

WPA WORKERS TO BE EXPO GUESTS

Families, Also, to Attend Saturday as Honor to Garden Builders.

Today's Events.

United Rubber Workers Day.
United States Patriots Day.
Boy's Knighthood of America Day.
National Society of Patriots Day.
City Club Day.
Maton (B.) Day.
Garden Club of Michigan Day.

Attendance yesterday 78,882
Attendance for 89 days 5,973,443
Days in Expo ....

The WPA will have its day at the Great Lakes Exposition.

Some of the civic officials thought that, since everybody was having his act at the big show, it would be altogether unfair to forget the WPA, source of whose 37,000 laborers built the first new Multicultural Gardens on the ground.

So the boys who stayed the shovels and the boys who swing the picks have been invited to attend the exposition Saturday. They will have music furnished by their own WPA bands.

They will have the whole stadium as a dance salon. Arrangements have been made with exposition concessionaires to sell their hot dogs at prices they can afford.

Such a celebration has been in mind for weeks because numerous employees have said they wanted to see the WPA-built gardens," Joseph M. Alexander, WPA district director, said. "The present are one of out first projects."

The invitation, which include members of the workers' families will be in the form of identification ...

Louis Bight is Dynamite Blast.
BARNESVILLE, O., Sept. 15. —Charles Gallagher, 65, a WPA worker, was permanently blinded in a dynamite explosion here today. Other debris resulted in the explosion may cost him his life.

BUY YOUR OWN MEALS, NESS TELLS ROOKIES

Ten New Patrolmen Told Appointments Are Based on Own Merits.

"DON'T BE OBLIGATED"

Warns "You'll Get No Great Reward for Honesty."

Ten new patrolmen were sworn into office yesterday by Safety Director Eliot Ness in his office in City Hall with the revolutionary advice that their patrolman are expected to pay for their own meals.

"You have been appointed on your own merits and because you are good for the top of the civil service list and for no other reasons," Ness told the recruits. "I expect you fellows to pay that he will responsible for your appointments, pay no solicitor.

"Your appointment is up to you.

"You are expected to be honest and to know that you will get no great rewards for being honest. Don't be obligated to anyone even in small things.

"When you walk into a restaurant for a meal pay for it. When you get any marketable commodity useful to you, pay for it. If people have been accustomed to giving you things or holding prior to your ordering a policeman, I suppose it is all right for you to continue to do all right those things.

Three Win Promotions.

"However, if people who never gave you anything run before now want to give you something without charge, you can conclude that they are buying your badge and your business.

In addition to appointing the ten new policemen, Ness promoted Sergt. Augustus F.Y. Foley to a lieutenancy and Patrolman Herbert Eberle and William M. Miller to sergeancies.

(the recruits were:)

ELMER A. BARNIKER, 3375 Topeka...
...
ADELBERT R GRAHL 2759 Denison...
...
EDWARD FRINDT, 28, 3070 West...
Road E K
...
WESLYN I. STANLEY, 4613 W. 179th Street.
...
FRANK R CADEN, 29, 4609 A Cloth-bound St.
ROY F THOMBACH, 8975 Tram Ave...
...
EDWARD R. NEIDER, 3557 E. 149th...
...
CLARENCE D. TRIBBIE, 7357 Fairy Av-...
...
JOHN E. WILSON, 5471 ... a ship-...
...
ELMER J PAINE, 3441 Jones Road
...

Ocdeh, the nephew of former Capt. Louis J. Cadek, was appointed in the department a month ago by John H. Flynn, executive secretary to Mayor Burton. His appointment was the second of that kind, for News because Flynn had except the candidate as the son of the film.

Says Fight With Richman Nearly Sank Ocean Plane

NEW YORK, Sept. 15.—(AP) —The Daily News, in a copyrighted dispatch from a staff correspondent at Musgrave Harbor, Newfoundland, says a quarrel amid the Atlantic between the trans-oceanic flyers Harry Richman and Dick Merrill [almost ended with the plane, H. Davey Jones' locker.

Merrill and Richman landed at that isolated village yesterday after a record flight from England.
In the ...

... the decisions, it's big flight—the most. All my arguments for different strategies were thrown aside. As Richman approached during the conversation, he and Merrill broke into opposite directions, the paper said ...

Newspaper Plane Damaged.
ST. JOHN'S, Newfoundland, Sept. 15.—(I.P.) —A newspaper plane owned by the New York Daily News

Youth, 16, I[n t]atens Shirley Ter[ple]

ATLANTA Press Wirephoto.
Robert Edward Simpson, sixteen-year old Atlanta boy, (arrest)ed at Atlanta yesterday. He was "charged" with sending an extortion letter to the mother of Shirley Temple child film star. He is shown between two federal agents as he was moved from the Atlanta police station to the Federal Building.

ATLANTA, Ga., Sept 15.—A mildmannered youth who said he spent six of his 16 years in a reform school calmly told federal authorities today of sending a $35,000 extortion letter to the mother of Shirley Temple.

Another schoolmate pointed boy Simpson, of W. Donald, is under bond of $3,000 at Great Neck, on a charge of attempting to extort $25,000 from the child star last May. He will be tried next year.

The youth caught today, booked as Frank Edward Simpson, was arrested by Federal Detain having preset operatives and ordered to his own recognizance after a hearing before United States Commissioner L. S. Griffith.

Simpson, taken into custody as a restaurant where he worked part-time, signed his own bond of $350, in requesting said it would mean pending the situation of the boy's story that he is in custody from the Alabama Boys Industrial School at Birmingham.

Records of the Alabama institution said avail the records but could not the name given.

Fow boys have written only hit not used only.

OUTLAW SITDOWN, PLEA IS UP TO URW

Strikes Hit Akron Plants as Rubber International Weighs Policy Issue.

Plain Dealer Bureau.
233 Ohio Building.
AKRON, O., Sept 15.

The issue of the sitdown strike is might loomed as the most important question before the United Rubber Workers of America at their first international convention, in session here.

Resolutions before the convention tonight are asking that the undertake to undertake to outlawed and another they calls the sitdown "one of the most powerful weapons of organized labor" and asks the incorporation into URW policies.

"Direct Violation," Is Ware.

"I told them that sitdowns were a direct violation of your policies and your principles," Germer said.
...

SHAKER EXTE[N] TO RUN CARS

Shuttle Service May Go to Rich

BY JAMES G. MINN
First extension of the trolley in Shaker Heights circomplete in this new available... the will be started after what has been from track east of WarrensbRoad on the Shaker line is to be tracked as far west... Work on starting shuttle trolley cars... along line it. Just this will be a new-track se... here it is said to be a... ... shuttle near to Warrens ... the next future, into... focus of the Cleveland Railway, ... the first last stage always certainly of Aviation Green lead...

It is learned by corporate service between Green Shaker Square B., to a... time and the Shaker south being service. At... the east-bank one... had been served ... They

The Harvard Club raid, January 10, 1936.
Cleveland Public Library Photograph Collection

Ness stands at center, between John Flynn and Frank Cullitan.
Cleveland Press Collection, Cleveland State University

THREE

Showdown

December 1935–January 1936

Cloistered in the tiny Bay Village cottage, Edna Ness remained a nearly invisible presence in her husband's life. Describing the new Safety Director, one headline mistakenly referred to him as YOUNG AND SINGLE. After all, who but a bachelor could throw himself so fully into his work?

If Mrs. Eliot Ness had any hopes this new job would mean shorter hours and more time at home, Mr. Ness shattered them soon. The evening of his second day on duty, Eliot took his wife and some friends out for dinner, only to be interrupted by a report of a nearby break-in. The Safety Director's responsibilities didn't include catching burglars, but he scurried off anyway.

At the Williamson Building on Public Square, as cops with revolvers and machine guns combed the premises, Ness joined in. They didn't find the burglars, who had botched the job, cracking a safe filled with papers while another nearby held the cash. But Ness got a chance to see how his men worked under pressure.

Then reports of a five-alarm factory fire sent Ness heading southwest. He watched for over an hour as Fire Chief James Granger and his men—making do with the department's clunky, antiquated equipment—battled the blaze. Doubling back toward downtown, Ness joined two patrolmen on an impromptu tour of the Roaring Third, speeding past more than a dozen brothels and gambling joints, each quieter than usual.

Around midnight, they stumbled onto some action—a brothel on Orange Avenue, where hookers hawked themselves from windows. Ness raided the place, only to find it empty, the prostitutes apparently slipping out the back.

"That was a quick getaway," Ness said.

More likely, a friendly cop had tipped them off.

Shortly before dawn, Ness came home to find Edna waiting. She told her husband just how much his abrupt departure had hurt and embarrassed her.

The incident embarrassed Ness, too, in a different way. He'd hoped to keep the inspection tour a secret, but the *Plain Dealer* had it on the next day's front page. Ness warned the press not to expect more late-night adventures.

"I'm certainly not going to chase robbers," he told a reporter, probably repeating a promise he'd made to his wife.

THE NEW SAFETY Director soon realized his department's problems extended beyond simple corruption. Clevelanders were accustomed to seeing slovenly cops slip into a bar for a quick on-duty drink. And instead of working as one cohesive unit, the various police bureaus refused to cooperate.

"A traffic officer," Ness recalled, "might shrug his shoulders at a purse snatcher."

The city did have its share of honest, dedicated policemen, but they were marginalized and demoralized. Promotions went to those who could pay hundreds of dollars, allowing inept and ignorant officers to rise through the ranks. The worst of the worst ended up in the Detective Bureau, home not to the department's best but a nest of political hacks, the refuse of Mayor Davis's old regime.

Ness couldn't make a dent in Cleveland's crime picture with

this motley crew. He needed to "clean the enemy out of our own camp first."

His cleanup started small, with two policemen caught drunk on duty. Ness presided over their disciplinary hearing on December 17. Both officers had been up on charges multiple times. The most flagrant offender had already received a demotion to traffic duty. This time, he wouldn't get off so easily.

Ness asked each cop's superior if either officer had given "distinguished service of any kind, which might be taken into consideration." Neither had. Both tried to appeal to Ness's sympathies by pouring out their personal problems.

Unmoved, Ness fired them both.

"Other officers," he said, "testified that the first thing they did in handling these men when they were found to be intoxicated was to disarm them, take their revolvers away. In London, where policemen are not armed, drunkenness on duty is sufficient cause for immediate dismissal. Here a drunken policeman is a menace because he is armed."

Ness's decision shouldn't have been news—but in Cleveland, it was. The *Plain Dealer* announced the verdict with a banner headline.

Soon after, a columnist for the *Press* reported "a troubled gaze" in the eyes of the average officer on the beat. "It's getting so a poor cop will hardly dare stand up to a bar in uniform for a shot these cold nights without finding himself on the carpet," he wrote.

The next blow fell two days before Christmas. Ness had Chief Matowitz shuffle 122 policemen, several of high rank, around the city's various precincts. He also removed the head of the Detective Bureau—a "fair-haired boy" of Mayor Davis—and assigned him to conduct a traffic survey.

Only someone with the "highest technical intelligence," Ness said with a straight face, could be trusted with arranging the city's stop signs and traffic lights.

For a new Detective Bureau chief, Ness chose Joseph Sweeney, a cunning cop with a photographic memory and no political interest. Of the officers who received promotions, fifteen were rookies—"men who have not fallen into the rut of routine police procedure," noted the *Plain Dealer*, "whose faces are not familiar to racketeers, and who have youth and other assets that fit them for training in crime detection."

Ness's intent was obvious—to remake the department in his own image.

Later that month, the young Safety Director again broke precedent by hiring an "executive assistant": John Flynn, a six-foot-four-inch attorney with a close-cropped military mustache. A graduate of Notre Dame and a gridiron veteran, Flynn possessed Ness's qualifications for an ideal investigator: brains and brawn.

Although the press speculated that Ness had tapped Flynn to "police the police department," the appointment was really the Safety Director's one concession to politics. The executive assistant position had been created to give the local Republican Party and other special interests someone they could talk to when Ness ignored them.

Early in the new year, Ness unveiled a seven-point program for an overhaul of the police department. Too many malcontents, Ness believed, had taken up policing because they couldn't get jobs during the Depression. He urged stiffer entrance exams, testing a recruit's temperament and mental fitness, and sought funds to establish the city's first police academy.

The plan was ambitious—even fanciful in a cash-strapped city with such a low opinion of its cops. First, Ness needed to dramatically change the image of policing in Cleveland. He would soon get his opportunity.

NOTHING MARKED CLEVELAND as a wide-open town more than its many gambling parlors, illegal lotteries, and bookie joints. While the inner-city suckers dropped a few coins on numbers or the ponies, the swells headed out to the suburbs, where a legion of

classy casinos catered to fat wallets. These gambling dens sat comfortably outside city limits, where police couldn't touch them, not
that they'd ever shown much inclination.

That made closing these casinos the job of Cuyahoga County's
silver-haired sheriff, "Honest John" Sulzmann, who adhered to a
"home rule policy," acting only when a mayor asked for help. The
gambling barons made sure that rarely happened.

"Take care of the locals and the locals will take care of you,"
declared Sam "Gameboy" Miller, manager of the Thomas Club
in Maple Heights. Like other casinos, the Thomas Club did its
best to be an upstanding member of the community. Get past
the armed guard at the door, and you'd find "a clean-cut place,"
offering roulette, blackjack, slot machines, and more.

"You never had any riff-raff out there, no stabbings, no crime
and no bombings like you see all the time these days," a patron
recalled.

Moe Dalitz's syndicate controlled the club, which opened its
doors to bank robbers looking to launder their loot. The massive
Harvard Club, not far away in Newburgh Heights, proved just
as accommodating. Its chief proprietors—slim, fair-haired Art
Hebebrand and portly, pugnacious James "Shimmy" Patton—
entertained five hundred or more gamblers a night in what might
be the biggest casino between Chicago and New York. These and
other casinos were fast becoming the syndicate's biggest revenue
source.

With the sheriff benching himself, County Prosecutor Frank
T. Cullitan set about trying to close the Thomas and Harvard
Clubs by any means necessary. A stout, broad-shouldered Irishman, Cullitan was known for his honesty and determination. In
the fall of 1935, the prosecutor won the convictions of six "big
shots" from the Thomas and Harvard Clubs; but the judge gave
each defendant a month or less behind bars, with Sulzmann se-
questering them in his finest cells.

Cullitan planned a second assault in early 1936; he would raid
the clubs himself, deputizing twenty private detectives as special

constables and renting two moving vans to haul off everything not bolted down. And he would keep Sulzmann in the dark, showing the locals how little their sheriff actually did.

That year, Sulzmann planned to run for Congress, mounting a primary challenge against the Democratic incumbent, a powerful firebrand named Martin L. Sweeney. Some speculated that Cullitan, also a Democrat, planned the raids to squelch Sulzmann's bid and save Sweeney's seat.

The prosecutor secured search warrants on January 10, 1936. At 4 P.M., his raiding party split into two groups, Cullitan taking the Thomas Club while his chief assistant, Charles McNamee, headed for the Harvard.

Cullitan presented his search warrant to a lookout, who told them to wait while he checked with those in charge. After ten minutes, the prosecutor grew impatient, ordering his constables to bust down the door with a nearby bench. Someone let them inside before they finished breaking in, and they found the casino filled with about five hundred patrons, who were shuttled out before Cullitan's men dismantled the place, seizing slot machines, roulette wheels, craps tables, chuck-a-luck cages, and $1,000 in coins. They also found several account books and what the *Cleveland Press* described as "a small arsenal."

For the benefit of press photographers, the prosecutor smilingly pointed to the hole his raiders had smashed in the front door. But his pride evaporated when he went over to the Harvard Club, where the other raid had not gone so smoothly.

Around 5 P.M., McNamee had led his raiders up to the casino at 3111 Harvard Avenue. Their knock brought Shimmy Patton to the door. Hard-eyed, beetle-browed, Patton looked the constables over.

"You come in," he told McNamee. "Alone."

McNamee entered the spacious casino. He could see roughly a thousand people crowding a room about ninety feet square, with a racing blackboard and green baize tables, a machine gun nest behind bulletproof glass near the door.

After McNamee said he had a warrant, Patton demanded profanely to see Cullitan. McNamee told him the prosecutor was busy raiding the Thomas Club.

Patton gestured to several heavily armed men in the balcony. "You just step aside," their host said, "and let the fellows you've got with you try to come in. We'll mow them down."

Outside, a club "executive," apparently drunk and wearing a shoulder holster, approached Assistant Prosecutor Frank Celebrezze.

"You have your job," he told Celebrezze, "and I have mine."

One of the exec's own people took his gun away. "You're talking to a man from the prosecutor's office," he said, defusing the situation.

The Harvard Club had been raided many times, but never had its operators responded with such defiance. McNamee would later claim Patton refused entry to the raiders because the FBI's "most wanted" fugitive, Alvin Karpis, was within, buying time for his escape.

Wanting to avoid a massacre, McNamee tried to be diplomatic, telling Patton he would give the patrons half an hour to leave. Then he went back out and assembled his men.

While the men inside emptied the club of anything valuable, Patton hurled obscenities at the raiders.

"We don't want any bloodshed," McNamee said.

"The hell with that," Patton shot back. "You aren't coming in. If you do, you'll get killed."

When Cullitan arrived around seven, he found Patton cavorting like a maniac outside the entrance, sporting a green hat and black topcoat, white scarf whipping in the wind. The gangster spotted Cullitan and hurried over, yelling threats and cursing.

"I've tried to go about this as decently as I could," Cullitan said wearily, "and we're going to see it through."

At a gas station half a block away, Cullitan called the Cleveland Police, asking for "two emergency squads" of detectives to assist him. But the new Detective Bureau head, Joseph Sweeney—unsure if the law allowed sending his men outside city limits—put Culli-tan's request on hold. A Harvard Club employee arrived at the gas station, promising to let the raiders inside "as soon as we get our money counted."

The club's parking lot lights were off, but the stalled raiders could see cars filled with gambling equipment pulling out, "a steady line of men with bulging overcoats" exiting the club. Cul-litan could do nothing to stop them. His search warrant covered only the inside of the building.

Despite the twenty-eight-degree chill, more than three hun-dred people gathered to watch—reporters among them, ready to record Cullitan's humiliation.

Desperate, Cullitan phoned the mayor of Newburgh Heights, who could force the sheriff to join the raid, but the prosecutor couldn't reach His Honor. Then he called the Central Police Sta-tion, asking for Matowitz. The chief wasn't in either.

McNamee and Celebrezze were in conference with Patton.

"You ain't going to make a pinch here," Patton told the prose-cutors. "No pinches! Understand?"

At the gas station, Cullitan rang the county jail and asked for the sheriff. The chief jailer answered: Sulzmann was home, sick in bed.

"We're in trouble at the Harvard Club," Cullitan said. "Send ten, twenty deputies, all you can get."

The jailer promised to pass the message along, then hung up. While Cullitan waited, he told reporters about the call. At least, if the raiders did have to retreat, everyone would know Sulzmann shared the blame.

A few minutes later, the phone rang.

"The sheriff says he stands on his home rule policy," the jailer told Cullitan. "He says that if Mayor Sticha will call and request—"

Cullitan slammed down the receiver. He'd run out of peo-ple to ask for help, yet he couldn't back down. That might end his career, and it would certainly prove gangsters really did rule Cuyahoga County. What avenue was left open to him?

He called Eliot Ness. Cullitan found the Safety Director in a city council meeting. When Ness picked up the phone, Cullitan gave him a rundown.

"We need help," the prosecutor said.

"Hold everything," Ness replied. "I'll be there."

Cullitan hung up and settled in. Reporters badgered him, asking what he thought he'd find if he ever got inside the club.

"This is the most brazen defiance of law and order I have heard of anywhere," Cullitan said. "This is going to be a showdown."

NESS HAD PLENTY of reasons to stay away.

He'd be crossing city limits, leaving his authority behind, to wade into a situation poised to spiral into violence. Though hardly risk averse, he did everything he could to minimize danger—meticulously planning his raids, anticipating how everything might go down. Going off half-cocked simply wasn't his style.

Despite Cullitan's plea, Ness remained reluctant "to inject myself in a problem outside my domain." He called the county jail.

"Prosecutor Cullitan is out at the Harvard Club with several of his staff and their lives are endangered," Ness said. "As a citizen I am calling on you to send deputies out there to protect the prosecutor."

The jailer said, "We can't send men out there without a call from the mayor of Newburgh."

"The mayor cannot be reached. Will you go out, or won't you?"

"I'll have to call the sheriff and call you back."

"To hell with this calling back. I'll wait on the phone."

The jailer put him on hold. Ness steamed till he finally came back on.

"No," the man said, "we won't go out there."

That did it.

Ness hated the idea of criminals defying officers of the law, holding the raiders back until they had time to destroy evidence and move money.

Still, he took time to see Mayor Burton and discuss the situation with the city's law director. The Safety Director, they concluded, couldn't legally take part in the raid, but he could offer to guard Cullitan "as a private citizen."

And he could bring policemen with him—each acting as a private citizen, but armed with tear gas guns, should they see a felony take place.

"You know," Ness said, "an old law gives any citizen the right to make an arrest if a felony is committed in his presence."

He went to the Central Police Station for backup, arriving around 9 P.M.—shift change. As officers came off duty, Ness asked for volunteers.

"I told the men the city's responsibility for them ended when they crossed the boundary line," Ness remembered. "I told them if they were killed out there, their families might be cut off the pensions rolls."

Left unsaid, perhaps, was they were being given the opportunity to prove Cleveland really did have some decent, honest cops.

"I told them I wouldn't hold it against them if they didn't go," Ness recalled. "Without an exception, they all agreed to go."

At least thirty-three officers still in uniform piled into squad cars and climbed aboard motorcycles, following Ness to Newburgh Heights. They reached the Harvard Club shortly after ten, where a throng—including what Ness described as "many tough-looking 'birds'"—blocked their path in the street.

"I told our driver to open up his siren," Ness remembered, "and split a way through the crowd."

Witnesses said it looked like the cavalry riding to the rescue. The lead car rolled to a stop. Ness sprang out and dashed into the gas station with John Flynn at his side.

Cullitan hadn't expected such a show of force and didn't know quite how to take it—he wasn't after a fight. Nor was Ness, though he seemed unusually aggressive.

"If this affair had been within the territorial limits of Cleveland, where we have authority," Ness recalled, "we would have fought it out."

But Ness and his men came as guards, not raiders.

"We are here to protect you," he told the prosecutor, "and to do that we must go where you go."

That was good enough for Cullitan. They prepared to rush the place.

"About the time we got ready," Ness remembered, "a newspaper man came bouncing out and told us the tough babies inside were ready for trouble."

Ness stepped out of the gas station wearing a dark fedora and a tan camel's hair topcoat, his gold Safety Director's badge glinting from a lapel as he surveyed the darkened parking lot.

"Let's have a light here," Ness said. "All right? Let's go."

Then he marched, at the head of some sixty cops and county officials, toward the Harvard Club. The men behind him carried riot guns, revolvers, and sawed-off shotguns; Ness, as usual, went unarmed. His tan overcoat stood out starkly against the pack of bluecoats. If anyone started shooting, he'd be the natural target.

But no one opened fire as they crossed the parking lot. When they reached the front door, Ness shoved it open and turned to Cullitan.

"All right," he said, "let your men go in there and serve their warrants. We'll back them up."

Cullitan and his constables went in and found nothing.

The place had practically been picked clean. Only a few tables, scraps of paper, and the racing board remained from the once-bustling casino. The county men scoured the club while Ness remained outside, careful not to overstep. Patton was nowhere to be found, but a Cleveland cop cornered the club owner's partner, Art Hebebrand.

"Don't try to slug me," Hebebrand roared. "If you do, you won't get out of this place alive. Act like gentlemen while you're in here or you'll wish the hell you had."

When the constables tried to serve him their warrant, Hebebrand slipped into an office. Cullitan and his men waited half an hour for him to come out, then called Ness over to have the cops force their way in.

Ness squinted through a hole in the wall and saw a group of

men, including one apparently carrying a gun. The Safety Director prepared to have his unofficial raiders fire tear gas into the office; but before he could give the order, the door opened and the men walked out, single file. Hebebrand was not among them—he'd climbed on a chair and out a window.

Ness noted the machine-gun nest near the door. "I don't think there is any doubt," he told a reporter, "but that if Cullitan had gone into the Harvard earlier in the evening, he would have been murdered."

Outside, Cullitan found two moving vans—hauling gambling equipment. Since his warrant only covered the club itself, the prosecutor let both vehicles leave.

"We have achieved our purpose," Cullitan told the press, "to put both the Harvard and Thomas Clubs out of business."

Actually, the prosecutor had only chased them out of their current locations. The Harvard Club would soon reopen with the same equipment, proprietors, and clientele. Patton and Hebebrand had escaped, and so it seemed had Karpis, though the FBI would catch up with him later that year.

The Harvard Club raid might be judged a law enforcement fiasco.

Yet Eliot Ness reaped a public relations triumph. The press praised him and Cullitan "as public officials true to their duty and courageous to carry it out," while excoriating the sheriff.

Sulzmann would never make it to Congress now—the raid "cooked his political goose," wrote Phil Porter, while giving his opponent, Martin Sweeney, "a new lease on life." Only later, when Sweeney emerged as one of Ness's fiercest critics, would a bitter irony reveal itself.

Ness celebrated the officers who'd followed him outside the city, telling the *Plain Dealer* their actions would show "the city and the county that the police department wants to clean up and intends to clean up." That department, meanwhile, had learned not to underestimate their new Safety Director.

"Some cops may have been puzzled by this young boss," Phil Porter wrote, "but they all admire guts."

• • •

TWO WEEKS AND two days after the Harvard Club raid, on the bitterly cold morning of January 26, a barking dog roused residents of the Roaring Third near the north end of Kingsbury Run. When a woman went to investigate, she found a pair of half-bushel baskets in the snowy yard behind a factory. She opened one, looked inside, then walked to a nearby butcher shop, telling the proprietor "some meat was in a basket" nearby.

The butcher took a look for himself, then called police. He knew human flesh when he saw it.

The baskets held pieces of a woman's body—the thighs, one arm, and the lower torso—carefully wrapped in newspaper and covered in burlap. Most of the missing pieces turned up several days later, sectioned and scattered in a yard not far from the basket. Police now had a complete corpse from the neck down; they would never find the head. Fingerprints identified the woman as Florence Polillo, a middle-aged prostitute. Investigators pieced together a sordid story, leaving them no closer to finding her killer.

She'd been a nice tenant, her landlady said, and friendly, when she hadn't been drinking. She collected dolls, owning more than ten or twelve—named them, dressed them, left them posed about her room. Sometimes she'd let the landlady's children play with them.

As with Edward Andrassy and his unidentified companion, Polillo's autopsy revealed that she'd probably died from decapitation. But after quickly removing her head, her killer took his time cutting up the rest of her. She'd been dismembered violently, even crudely—her limbs "wrenched . . . from the socket," her groin gashed where the killer's knife seemingly slipped.

Her torso had been bisected in precisely the same manner as 1934's Lady of the Lake.

And the placement of the baskets recalled the staging of the earlier two victims—left where they could easily be found, wrapped like presents to be opened. Yet police refused to consider the possibility that these deaths might be linked.

"At first we thought it was a 'nationality case,'" a detective recalled. "It's not unusual for a Hungarian or Bohemian to cut up people, they learn to butcher in the old country. So we figured what the hell, we'll send a couple detectives up on Jackass Hill that can speak the language, ask a few questions, and that's it."

The effort got them nowhere. Cleveland police had no idea they were dealing with a phenomenon few had ever recognized before: a serial murderer.

TORSO KILLER NEW INSANE T

zens Trails in Rep... ...an Race

VOTE
NEWS
DEAL

n Shows
blican
ber.

SMILES

s About
ted.

No. 20 for Allen

Allen injured his back in the fifth inning, but was given credit for his twentieth victory yesterday as the Indians walloped Boston, 13 to 2. Hildebrand finished the game. Trotsky hit his 29th and 40th homers. New York defeated Chicago, 7 to 3; Detroit trimmed Philadelphia, 8 to 5, and Washington took a double header from St. Louis, 13 to 7 and 8 to 1.

Weather stopped the National League.

(Details on Sport Pages)

WPA WORKERS TO BE EXPO GUESTS

Families, Also, to Attend Saturday as Honor to Garden Builders.

Today's Events.

United Rubber Workers Day.
United States PostalBox Day.
Royal Neighbors of America Day.
National Society of Patriots Day.
City Club Day.
Huron (O.) Day.
Garden Club of Michigan Day.

Attendance yesterday 29,890
Attendance for 90 days ... 3,273,419
Days left...2.

The WPA will have its day at the Great Lakes Exposition.

BUY YOUR OWN MEALS, NESS TELLS ROOKIES

Ten New Patrolmen Told Appointments Are Based on Own Merits.

"DON'T BE OBLIGATED"

Warns "You'll Get No Great Reward for Honesty."

Ten new patrolmen were sworn into office yesterday by Safety Director Eliot Ness in his office at City Hall with the revolutionary admonition that policemen are expected to pay for their own meals.

"You have been appointed on your own merits now because you stood at the top of the civil service lists and for no other reasons," Ness told the recruits. "If anyone made claims to you that he was responsible for your appointment, pay no attention.

"Your advancement is up to you.

Youth, 16, T...atens Shirley Temple

Associated Press Wirephoto.

Frank Edward Stephens, sixteen-year-old Atlanta boy, arrested at Atlanta yesterday and charged with sending an extortion letter to the mother of Shirley Temple, child film star, is shown between two federal agents as he was moved from the Atlanta police station to the Federal Building.

ATLANTA, Ga., Sept 15.—A sandy-haired youth who said he spent six of his 16 years in a reform school calmly told federal authorities today of sending a $15,000 extortion letter to the mother of Shirley Temple.

OUTLAW SITDOWN, PLEA IS UP TO URW

Strikes Hit Akron Plants as Rubber International Weighs Policy Issue.

Plain Dealer Bureau,
122 Ohio Building.

AKRON O., Sept. 15.—

SHAKER EXTENSION TO RUN CARS SOON

Shuttle Service to Green Rd. Expected in 2 Weeks; May Go to Richmond.

By JAMES C. MONNETT, JR.

...ays Fight With Richman Nearly Sank Ocean Plane

NEW YORK, Sept. 15.—(AP)—The story of Harry Richman's and Dick Merrill's fight from the ocean.

Ness demonstrates his martial arts skills by disarming an opponent, 1936.

Cleveland Public Library Photograph Collection

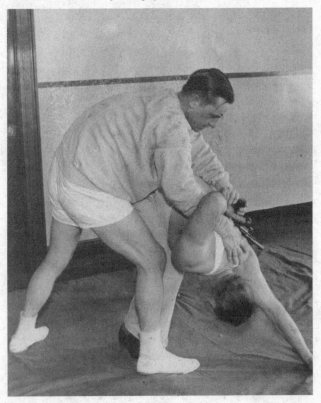

FOUR

The Mad Butcher

January–June 1936

Despite failing eyesight, August Vollmer could see—out his front window, across San Francisco Bay—Alcatraz Island, now home to Al Capone. Whenever he did, Vollmer thought of a former student.

In 1929 Eliot Ness had taken Vollmer's graduate course in police administration at the University of Chicago and found a perfect role model. Simply pursuing and jailing offenders, Vollmer believed, would never address the social problems that created crime. Instead, college-educated policemen should enter communities as social workers, steering potential juvenile delinquents away from crime.

"Boy gangs," he wrote, "may be transformed into juvenile police and taught to be friendly helpers. . . . Wayward girls may be saved from taking the final plunge into a life of evil."

As police chief of Berkeley, California, Vollmer had led the way in professionalizing American law enforcement, putting radios in squad cars and establishing a crime lab. As chief of the Los Angeles Police Department, he forced bent cops to resign, put detectives on wheels, and established a police academy. But Vollmer's battle against corruption found him forced from his job by L.A.'s rich and powerful.

Now he encouraged his former protégé's "attempts to put Cleveland on a sound police foundation" and "[rid] the ranks of the service of those who are stupid or otherwise unfit for the responsibilities of the office." But he knew from bitter experience that Eliot would need his community's backing.

"The situation here is in a sense similar to that of Chicago in the early thirties," Ness wrote his mentor, "when the businessmen organized the Secret Six." That vigilante organization, formed by Chicago's wealthiest citizens, helped fund both Ness's Untouchables and the Treasury agents in "getting" Capone. But the group devolved into a private police force for the wealthy, only to collapse in scandal.

"I am going to receive some help along a similar line here," Ness told Vollmer, though he would take care not to "become associated with any movement which may prove embarrassing or binding upon the work I hope to do as a whole."

Cautious or not, Ness's swagger shone through.

"Racketeering here is rampant," he wrote, "and the racketeers have virtual control of business and industry, much more so than is apparent on the surface. . . . This angle, of course, is old stuff to me and will probably be one of the simplest."

NESS MOVED QUICKLY against gambling. Many downtown casinos had shuttered after the election, waiting to see whether this new administration was serious. The Safety Director, resolved to keep them closed, ordered raids on betting parlors and casinos, warning police officials he would hold precinct captains responsible for any wide-open gambling on their watch.

The crackdown had a chilling effect within city limits. One week after the Harvard Club raid, a Cleveland lingerie manufacturer complained to Ness that a slowdown had him laying off several workers. Professional gamblers, it seemed, were his best customers.

Personally, Ness had no moral objections to gambling.

"I am inclined to be liberal in my views of amusements," he

said in a speech at Cleveland College, "and I do not want to intrude my opinions on others, but as a safety director I must recognize everything which contributes to a lawless situation."

Profits from such illegal enterprises, Ness knew, would corrupt and corrode the workings of government. Gangsters, empowered by gambling money, could operate with impunity, creating "a situation in which the policeman on the beat, and perhaps his captain, doesn't know what laws to enforce, what persons to arrest, and what persons to avoid."

Asked his thoughts on proposed laws, from gun control to traffic regulation, Ness always returned to the dry decade's lessons. "In passing any law," he said, "there is always the question of what the people want. We had our experience with Prohibition."

Yet once a law was on the books, Ness insisted on enforcement without fear or favor. He believed "that cities which have the lid most tightly on have the least crime," a conviction that informed everything he did as Safety Director. All illegal activity was of a piece; you couldn't arrest some lawbreakers while winking at others and expect the situation to improve.

"A policeman," Ness said, "must be able to do police work without having to find out the family background, the connections, of every individual he comes across in his work."

Ness sought a delicate balance between repressing crime and preserving personal freedom. Put too few cops on the streets, and reap a crime wave; too many, and create a police state.

But he would always err on the side of the latter if it meant keeping people safe.

AFTER THAT FIRST round of raids, Ness's crackdown quieted enough to convince Cleveland's gamblers the danger had passed. The all clear went out in early February, and the city's betting parlors began to reopen, their owners installing hookups to the wire services with race results, something they did only when they felt confident of no raids. But the *Cleveland Press* gave them an unwelcome valentine on February 14 by publishing the names, addresses, and descriptions of twenty-three wide-open gambling joints.

Before, bookies might have welcomed such an exposé as free advertising. Now they had Ness to worry about, and the *Press* made sure he saw the story, sending an advance copy to his apartment at 10017 Lake Avenue, which he'd rented to establish a residence within city limits. The Bay Village cottage he shared with Edna was now a weekend getaway.

Bedridden with a cold, Ness ordered raids on every address the *Press* provided. Seven squads went to shutter each place, finding evidence of gambling in only one. And of the ten men arrested there, nine had to be released.

Had someone warned the bookies? The raiders, the *Press* noted, took their time before busting a joint run by Julius Finkle, brother of a city councilman who helped get Mayor Burton elected. But Ness's assistant, John Flynn, said the plan swung into action too fast for Finkle to get a "tipoff."

Still, rumors of police protection persisted until March 7, when Ness ordered another surprise raid on Finkle's place. This time the cops found the joint in operation and filled seven paddy wagons with patrons and employees.

The message was clear: Not even Burton's friends could expect protection from Ness's department.

In early April, Ness received a call from the "Ghost Reporter," anonymous star of a new muckraking radio program on station WJAY. The Ghost gave Ness the locations of fifteen downtown bookie joints he planned to reveal on air that night, and Ness ordered them raided.

Again, someone tipped the bookies off. By the time police arrived, each place had already shut down. Ness told Flynn to find the leak and plug it.

Five days later, a bomb rocked the home of station WJAY's owner, nearly killing him and his wife. No one could fix responsibility for the blast, but the owner took it as retaliation for Ness's raids. He ordered his station manager to fire the employees who'd gone digging into gamblers' affairs.

"I've got three children," he told the *Press*. "I don't want them hurt."

The Ghost Reporter went off the air the following night.

WHILE NESS SHOWED little interest in publicity for its own sake—preferring to do his job well and quietly—he needed headlines to win public support. He kept up relationships with reporters, staying friendly by feeding them copy. Some cops would wryly recall Ness's habit of calling photographers before he called for backup.

Newspapers ate these leads up and reciprocated by extolling Ness's work. Their stories attracted the interest of out-of-town papers, which ran their own glowing profiles of Cleveland's Safety Director. Each served to broadcast Ness's ideas to an ever-widening audience.

"Not naturally a gabby guy," wrote Phil Porter of the *Plain Dealer*, "[Ness] made the mistake of accepting a couple of luncheon invitations, under the naive theory that the newspapers wouldn't cover them."

Before the Cuyahoga County League of Women Voters on January 29, he spoke of the need for a police academy: "A successful police officer must be a marksman, a boxer, a wrestler, a diplomat, [and a] two fisted go-getter at the same time."

He went out of his way to praise the department. Despite a lack of manpower and funds, they "responded marvelously," he said, "and have cheerfully and efficiently performed their duties." The remarks were inspirational and aspirational—also unobjectionable.

But two days later, before a closed-door meeting of the Cleveland Advertising Club, Ness spoke candidly of a force he described as "inadequate and demoralized." He told of hearing a bulletin about a burglary over his car's police radio, with enough time passing "to commit six or seven other burglaries" before a squad car answered the call.

Perhaps he should've been grateful the officers made it there at all, given the department's outdated rattletraps. At least one vehicle still in use was so old, Ness said, the factory had stopped making parts for it.

The next day, Ness's "off the record" comments got front-page attention. The opinion around City Hall, according to the *Cleveland News*, was that the Safety Director should "make no more speeches." Not only had he hurt the department's image, he'd described details of his early probes into gambling and racketeering—information he'd hoped to keep confidential.

After that, Ness would keep the press at bay, even as he socialized with reporters and angled for good coverage. He rarely granted interviews, preferring to let his work speak for itself.

"Ness is an enigma to police, to politicians, to underworld contact men and even to his closest associates," observed the *News*. "He takes no one into his confidence and this is especially true in respect to ranking police officials. No one knows his mind, what he will do next, where he will strike."

The short list of people Ness trusted included Burton, Flynn, and precious few others.

"Anything I whisper to a friend," he said, "comes out in the papers the next day as if I'd shouted it from a megaphone on Public Square."

He still gave speeches, limiting himself to harmless topics, and grew into the role of local dignitary. When the African-American aviator John Robinson, who'd fought fascists in Ethiopia, visited Cleveland while Burton was away, Ness served as official greeter and gave "the Brown Condor" a key to the city.

Above all, Ness sought to preserve the upright, all-knowing image the press had painted of him, both to shield himself from criticism and help him do his job. Ness's Untouchable reputation remained his best asset in cleaning up Cleveland, giving the cops an ideal to live up to while satisfying the public's hunger for a hero.

Unhappy with the poor physical condition of many Cleveland cops and disappointed that the department offered no workout facilities of its own, Ness presented himself as a model of fitness. He scorned cigarettes (if enjoying the occasional cigar) and, at a moment's notice, might drop to the floor for some pushups. Three times a week, he brushed up on his jujitsu at a downtown health club in the Standard Building till (according to his trainer) he could "throw a man . . . in 30 different ways."

In gym shorts and a sweatshirt, Ness posed for pictures, sub-duing an armed opponent—grabbing the man's wrist, twisting it behind his back, forcing him to the mat. The *Press* ran these side by side, like a how-to self-defense manual. Ness didn't usually show off like this; his message was that every officer should be able to do the same.

But the *Press* made the story about him: the super sleuth "quick as a cat," who could break your arm if you threatened him with a gun. Before long, the whole city seemed to want to emulate their dashing Safety Director.

In early April, Ness helped the *News* inaugurate a crimestop-per club for kids: the "Dick Tracy Detective Squad." The program echoed Vollmer's suggestion to turn youth gangs "into juvenile police," while letting the *News* promote Chester Gould's comic strip, which ran in their pages.

On April 4, nearly one thousand children showed up at the *News* building to meet a real G-man and be fingerprinted in ex-change for a genuine Dick Tracy badge. Ness spent fifteen min-utes quieting this "howling, yelling, whistling crowd" before he launched into stories of his Untouchables days. The youngsters listened, "spellbound," entirely unaware those exploits inspired their favorite comic strip.

"You have a badge just like mine," Ness said to a chorus of cheers and shouts. "Only maybe yours is a little smaller. . . . When you grow up to be a man with long pants perhaps your badge will grow up with you. . . . And when that time comes I'd like to have you all working for me as real detectives."

The children's "enthusiasm," reported the *News*, "was uncon-trollable."

• • •

FOR THE FIRST time in years, Cleveland began to dream big again.

A certain optimism, even excitement, permeated the city. Burton's election seemed to mark a turning point; with the economic outlook brighter, Clevelanders faced the busiest, most exciting summer in their history.

In March, Burton broke ground for the Great Lakes Exposition, Cleveland's lavish answer to Chicago's 1933 Century of Progress. The Windy City had taken years to mount its world's fair, but Cleveland would build its Expo in just 110 days. As the temperature rose and snow melted, "Tin Can Plaza," a trash-strewn wasteland and former shantytown site, was transformed into a sprawling "city of ivory," 125 acres of amusements, exhibits, and technological marvels.

"Incredible," wrote the *Press*, "to pass a dump one day and the next to find it a garden, complete with rolling lawns and flowering shrubs."

With City Hall sitting near the Expo's entrance, Ness could watch this growth up close. The fair meant more work for the Safety Director struggling to keep order amid an influx of tourists and traffic.

Cleveland would play host to four political conventions that summer, even as the city celebrated its centennial. First the Socialists and then the Republicans would come to nominate candidates to take on FDR. Then supporters of Francis Townsend, a California doctor who'd built a mass movement around his plan for a system of old-age pensions, would meet to endorse another third-party candidate, as would the National Union for Social Justice—the populist political organization led by Father Charles Coughlin. Though their views stretched from the far left to the far right, each group shared a desire to dethrone Franklin Roosevelt—and an apparent conviction that the road to the White House ran through Cleveland.

The president and two of his cabinet members would also visit the city that summer; so would the American Legion, which chose Cleveland as the site of its annual meeting. Looking ahead on New Year's Day, the *Plain Dealer* asserted that 1936 "ought to be, and can be made, the best and happiest [year] Cleveland has ever had."

Under a national spotlight, civic leaders hoped to prove their city, like the Expo itself, had risen from ruin to greatness.

"Now the country is getting out of the depression," declared the *News*, "and Cleveland should show the whole United States in 1936 that it is leading the procession."

Before the Republican National Convention opened June 8, one party leader—eager to give the delegates a good time—visited Ness seeking an end to the attacks on gambling. Ness refused—the Republicans could only stop him, he said, if they managed to get him fired.

As the convention approached, Ness cracked down harder, promising to scrub the city clean of vice throughout the summer—to the dismay of Cleveland's "bookie and gambling operators, all of whom had been looking forward to making a killing," according to the *Press*.

"It's going to be tough," a gambler said. "They're not 'taking' at City Hall."

Meanwhile, Ness set up a special squad to catch pickpockets. Police patrolled the streets in a new fleet of bright white Oldsmobiles dubbed "Voice of Safety" cars, each with a loudspeaker on its roof for directing traffic.

Politicians remained among Ness's least favorite people, but the convention nonetheless found him an official greeter, welcoming a delegation of Chicago Republicans. These included an old friend from the Capone case, prosecutor Dwight Green. Others were politicos looking to bend Eliot's ear for a favor.

Ness offered them all a smile, then confided to a reporter that he was "thinking of a short vacation to Bermuda or somewhere." Still, he played along, doing his best to help his city shine.

• • •

THE NEXT DAY, June 5, two young boys playing hooky on the southeast side headed out in fine weather to go fishing. Cutting through Kingsbury Run, they spied a brown pair of pants wadded at the foot of a tree. One kid poked the bundle with his fishing rod, hoping to find cash.

The pants unraveled on a man's face—eyes shut, mouth open as if for a kiss.

The head belonged to a white male in his mid-twenties—handsome, with shaggy dark hair. The matching body turned up the following day, naked and facedown less than a thousand feet away, dead for about two days. His arms and legs bore several tattoos; perhaps the man had been a sailor.

With distinctive marks, a set of fingerprints, and an intact, sensitive face, the body seemed to stand an excellent chance of identification. Police photographed the head for the newspapers and let the curious view it in the morgue. More than two thousand took a look; no one admitted recognizing it. As the head wouldn't keep forever, Coroner Arthur Pearse made a plaster mold.

At last, police could see a pattern among the beheaded bodies strewn about the East Side. The latest head had been left near Jackass Hill, where the corpses of Edward Andrassy and his still-unidentified companion had been found less than nine months earlier. An autopsy indicated the tattooed man—like Andrassy, his companion, and Flo Polillo—died from decapitation. Coroner Pearse told the *Press* "that the workmanship in all four cases is similar."

Acting Detective Inspector Charles O. Nevel proclaimed that a "maniac with a lust to kill" had murdered all four people. Nevel told the *Plain Dealer* the latest victim had probably been a hobo who hopped off a freight before making the mistake of bedding down in Kingsbury Run.

"While he was sleeping," Nevel said, "this maniac attacked

him. First he cut his throat. Then he hacked away at the neck. Then he undressed the victim."

Why, the *Plain Dealer* asked, had the killer bothered to disrobe the dead man?

"That's a maniac's trick," Nevel replied, with no further explanation.

For a city intent on making a good impression, the timing couldn't have been worse. Republican visitors who picked up a newspaper saw stories of the convention competing with lurid headlines of the MANIAC and FIEND now stalking the city.

"Somewhere in the countless byways of the crowded Southeast Side," announced the *Press*, ". . . is the grisly workshop of a human butcher who in the last 10 months has carved up and decapitated four persons."

The paper cited "the opinion of Detective Sergeant James Hogan, head of the homicide squad, who believes a crazed killer with a flair for butchery is at work."

The murderer would pick up a host of sobriquets, from "Head Hunter" to "Torso Killer." But the *Press*'s description of him as a deranged butcher on the prowl really stuck with Clevelanders— "the Mad Butcher of Kingsbury Run."

The severed head of the Butcher victim known only as the "Tattooed Man," found in Kingsbury Run on June 5, 1936.

Cleveland Press Collection, Cleveland State University

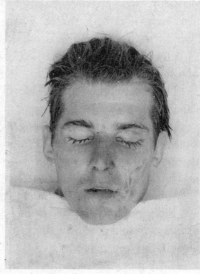

The Great Lakes Exposition, with City Hall at left and Terminal Tower in the background.

General Photograph Collection, Michael Schwartz Library, Cleveland State University

FIVE

This Is a Raid!

On the same day the *Press* christened Cleveland's homicidal maniac, Eliot Ness made his own headlines with a daring East Side raid.

A week earlier, Ness had received a visit from Anton Vehovec, crusading city councilman from the Collinwood neighborhood. Vehovec brought the names of bookie joints and brothels the police had failed to close, a list Ness passed along to local precinct captain Michael Harwood. Harwood let the matter slide.

"Vehovec has made a mountain out of a molehill," the captain told the *Plain Dealer*. "This vice stuff is greatly exaggerated."

On June 6, Vehovec tried again. This time—with a handful of cops and two reporters, Ralph Kelly of the *Plain Dealer* and Clayton Fritchey of the *Press*—the councilman escorted Ness to the Black Hawk Inn, a nightclub just off Euclid Avenue. Ness found what "was plainly a gambling joint"—a bookmaking operation offering blackjack on the side.

When Vehovec said Captain Harwood's son, Edward, owned the building, Ness decided to raid it at once. He didn't have a search warrant, because he hadn't known where Vehovec was taking him, but he ordered a detective to bust down the door anyway.

As the detective smashed in, "about 35 men and women," according to Vehovec, "nearly broke their necks trying to get away." Most patrons escaped, but the cops arrested twelve who admitted they'd seen or participated in gambling.

About ten minutes later, Edward Harwood showed up, shocked to see the Safety Director, and denied any knowledge of the gambling, insisting he rented the room to a "Joe" whose last name he didn't know. Shortly after Harwood exercised his right to a phone call, a self-identified Joe McCarthy arrived and said he ran the place.

"Didn't Harwood telephone you to come down here?" Ness demanded. ". . . You're quite sure you want to take the rap on this?"

McCarthy said he did, but still couldn't convince Ness. Finding keys on both Harwood and McCarthy, police began trying them in the locks around the Black Hawk. Harwood's "fitted every door," McCarthy's none.

Ness called Chief Matowitz and ordered him to suspend Captain Harwood.

"The matter has now gone far beyond the operation of a single bookmaking establishment," Ness told the *Plain Dealer*. "It is a question of police efficiency, discipline and honesty in the Fourteenth Precinct, and every officer in it is going to be called on for a recital of everything that is known."

Captain Harwood didn't let the suspension get him down. In twenty years on the force, he'd often run afoul of chiefs and safety directors, always managing to survive and come back stronger. Most bent cops tried to hide their corruption, but Harwood— burly and bellicose—all but advertised his.

"He consorted openly with important politicians," reported the *Press*, "he financed and operated notorious night spots in his own precincts and he ruled a small bootleg kingdom with an iron hand."

"Big Mike," "Czar of the 14th," became a legend among the ranks. The average beat cop took it for granted that "Mike Harwood can't be broken."

Gathering evidence on Harwood wouldn't be easy; criminals who paid police protection rarely talked, fearing retaliation. But Ness knew he could make it work because of what two newfound allies, Clayton Fritchey and Frank Cullitan, had accomplished earlier that year.

Working on an investment scam story, reporter Fritchey had learned Police Captain Louis J. Cadek had far more money in the bank than any honest cop should. Fritchey passed his discovery along to Prosecutor Cullitan, who pried into Cadek's past, locating thirty-four witnesses who said Cadek had regularly demanded bribes from bootleggers during Prohibition. With the dry law a memory, Cadek's victims no longer had to make a living outside the law, and many still resented his constant demands for cash and gifts.

Cullitan won indictments charging Cadek with accepting at least $26,000 in bribes. After a short trial, Cadek was convicted and sentenced to two to twenty years.

Following Cullitan's example, Ness went after evidence of Prohibition payoffs—stories dated enough to protect their tellers, yet recent enough to point Ness in the right direction.

Graft from the dry decade, Ness said, had "worked down through the years. If the police have been paid off for one thing, they naturally didn't move against the gangs for anything else. And if a bootlegger turned vice czar, or policy slip vendor, he usually kept his same 'contacts' with the police department."

Unable to trust anyone in his own department, Ness turned to Fritchey. The two, about the same age, hit it off. Ohio-born but raised in Baltimore, Fritchey—forehead high, narrow blue eyes crinkling with a lopsided grin—had been a newspaperman since nineteen. After cracking the Cadek case, Fritchey had been digging into police corruption himself, and readily agreed to join forces.

Fritchey's editor—small, foulmouthed Louis B. Seltzer—approved him working with the Safety Director full-time, if the *Press* got an exclusive.

"For three months," Fritchey recalled, "we turned the city inside out for elusive witnesses."

They targeted bar owners who'd kept serving during Prohibition by paying off police. Former ATU agent Ness knew just where to find potential witnesses, going down some of Cleveland's meanest streets and up some of its richest. The Safety Director and the reporter focused first on Harwood, but their search kept broadening as they turned up evidence against other crooked cops. Ness did much of the legwork, disappearing from his office for days, leaving only cryptic explanations.

At first, no one in the rough parts of town trusted Ness enough to talk. Some didn't believe this mild individual—so unlike the belligerent cops they usually encountered—could really be who he claimed.

But Ness and Fritchey kept at it, meeting with witnesses again and again, gently but firmly urging them to go on record. Few bootleggers had tasted the riches of Prohibition, and much of what the barkeeps, brewers, and alky cookers made went into police pockets. Ness and Fritchey played on their resentments, offering a different kind of protection—and a shot at getting even.

Among the first to turn state's evidence was fifty-three-year-old saloonkeeper Casper Korce, who'd regularly bribed Harwood.

Ness "treated me decent," Korce recalled. "He didn't act as if I were dirt. They're a lot of poor foreign-born people out my way and he treated them the same way. No threats, no rough stuff, and he never acted as if he owned the town just because he was safety director."

Soon others began to fall in line.

When word of Ness's investigation began to leak out, "a severe attack of jitters [went] up and down a number of blue-coated spines," according to the *Plain Dealer*.

On June 22, Ness accepted the resignation of a deputy inspector tight with the politicians. Reporters believed the inspector, a thirty-year veteran, had gotten out while the getting was good.

All summer, Ness kept the heat on. One night, he and Fritchey walked into a bar on Cleveland's far East Side where a uniformed officer was enjoying a drink. Ness seemed not to notice as the cop fled up the back stairs to find a locked door barring his way. The officer huddled against the wall, hoping Ness hadn't seen him.

Apparently oblivious, Ness struck up a conversation with the bartender. When he gave the man his name, another patron laughed.

"Oh, yeah?" the customer said. "I suppose you're the safety director, too!"

"That's right," Ness said.

"Listen, buddy, go peddle that stuff somewhere else. It just happens the director's a personal friend of mine."

"I see," Ness said. "OK, buddy, but if you've got any doubts about who I am, just ask that officer who's hiding up there on the landing!"

At that, Ness walked out, an amused Fritchey right behind him.

BY SCARING OFF bent cops, Ness made way for the kind of officer who could change the force. Cash-strapped Cleveland could afford a police department only half the size of similar cities. Every cop who retired, resigned, or lost his job created a precious opening that Ness sought to fill with recruits as honest, educated, and professional as himself.

"In Cleveland, the rookie has been Mr. Ness' pride and joy," a reporter observed, "and he takes them right into his bosom at the City Hall and seldom lets them out of his sight."

Ness held them on a short leash, hoping to keep them pure and "prevent their 'pollution' by the veterans." Those who made the cut became the only officers he trusted to carry out his orders and keep his secrets—fresh faces, unfamiliar both to crooks and crooked cops, suited for undercover work.

In late June, Ness swore in a large contingent of new recruits, advising them to "be courteous and don't expect to get rich."

While these rookies personified Ness's reforms, the *Call & Post*, Cleveland's leading black newspaper, noted a conspicuous absence: "Not a one of these men was colored. Thus, this city continues as one of the few large communities in this country without a representative number of Negroes on its police force."

Despite a growing African-American population of perhaps eighty thousand, Cleveland employed only a relative handful of black cops, which struck the *Call & Post* as shameful. The paper—whose publisher, William O. Walker, was racially progressive but otherwise conservative—did not blame Ness or the Burton administration. Rather, it urged its readers to answer the police department's calls for new recruits, taking Ness at his word that these jobs would be filled on merit.

"The blame for this situation," declared the *Call & Post*, "rests entirely on the young men who are too trifling to take the civil service examination. . . . These examinations are open to all citizens alike. Why so few of our group take them is unexplainable."

Of course, young black men's reluctance to seek employment as cops was hardly unexplainable. Pervasive if unspoken racism blocked the hiring and promotion of black men and women who should have advanced on their own merits. City officials knew how to use the very civil service tests Ness championed to prevent black people from serving as cops, pointing toward applicants' allegedly poor scores as justification for passing them over.

Despite these barriers, members of Cleveland's black community kept volunteering to serve and protect their fellow citizens. On the civil service test results that fall, the first two names eligible for the city's Policewomen's Bureau belonged to African Americans: Virginia Houston and Charlotte Clark.

Houston, whose score of 83.80 matched that of the current captain of the bureau, lived up to Ness's image of the police officer as social worker.

Originally from Detroit, Houston graduated summa cum laude from Wayne University and earned a master's in social service from the University of Chicago, Ness's alma mater. Her graduate studies focused on issues of juvenile justice, and her résumé included service in the Detroit court system and charity work in Chicago. She'd spent more than eight years in Cleveland working for the Negro Welfare Association, an organization helping black citizens find jobs and livable housing, before she joined the police department on a temporary basis in 1936. Her outstanding civil service score qualified her for a permanent position.

But would Ness grant it?

After all, Ness had to make two provisional posts permanent; giving the jobs to Houston and Clark meant dismissing a white policewoman currently occupying one of those temporary spots.

"The question now," asked the *Call & Post*, "is will Director Ness, the champion of civil service and merit, continue to follow the custom he inaugurated when he took over the office, or will he bow to those who are already busy demanding that the present list be ignored?"

Ness did not disappoint.

With no fanfare, he gave the jobs to Houston and Clark—the women who had earned them. They joined two other black officers in the Policewomen's Bureau, to specialize in the crime prevention activities Ness saw as central to modern law enforcement. Over the next decade, the number of black women employed by the bureau would double, until more than a quarter of its officers and staff—nine out of thirty-three—were African American.

The white press took little notice of Ness's action, but the *Call & Post* used it to encourage more blacks to take the civil service exam for police jobs. A black applicant, David Beasley, came in nineteenth among the next applicants, high enough to be sworn in with the upcoming class of new policemen. The twenty-seven-year-old patrolman praised how Ness got his recruits up to speed by shuffling them around the department for a sense of the work done by various bureaus.

"This all-around experience is invaluable to a man who wants to make his career in the department, as I do," Beasley said.

Still, change would come slowly. The same month Houston and Clark became the city's newest policewomen, a white patrolman accosted Charles White, an African-American attorney employed by the city—shoving him, threatening him with a blackjack, and telling him "to move on" or else be arrested.

White, a Republican ward leader, allowed himself to be arrested without revealing his identity to see how Cleveland cops treated other black men. After refusing to admit to a crime he hadn't committed, White was booked and jailed. Prosecutors quickly dismissed the case against him.

"This is a clear indication," White told the *Call*, "of the treatment which is accorded Negroes at the hands of the local police department."

At Mayor Burton's urging, White told Ness about the false arrest. The Safety Director formally reprimanded the white cop, but let the man keep his job. Instead, reported the *Call & Post*, the officer would be transferred to "some district other than where colored people live."

SOON AFTER SWEARING in his summer crop of rookies, Ness took five aside for a special assignment. A complaint had come in about a large off-track betting joint in the Eighth Precinct, run by dapper gangster Tommy McGinty. The place had operated openly for almost a decade, raking in as much as $500,000 in a given year. Ness told the rookies to blend in among the gamblers and report what they'd seen to precinct captain Adolph Lenahan. They did, but Lenahan did nothing about it.

On July 17, the rookies returned to the gambling joint. Ness had a woman in his office phone the precinct with a complaint, pretending to be the wife of a gambler who'd lost big in McGinty's place.

"Oh," the desk cop said, "you mean that bookie joint down the street."

The call spurred two police officers to raid the casino, but a lookout saw them approach and hit a warning signal. Inside the betting room, the rookies watched as flashing lights alerted the employees to hide all their gambling paraphernalia, cash, and incriminating documents. After the raiders left, the place was up and running again within the hour.

Over the next few days, the Safety Director's office called

the precinct with more anonymous complaints. Ness placed one himself, posing as an ordinary citizen who'd been cleaned out at McGinty's. But the precinct attempted no more raids.

Finally, on July 21, Captain Lenahan showed up for duty "pretty well drunk," according to Matowitz. The chief suspended Lenahan on the spot. A few days would pass before Lenahan sobered up enough to submit his resignation.

With his rookies in place inside McGinty's, Ness led John Flynn and a handful of officers on an impromptu raid that same day. Once again, the lookout saw them coming and hit the warning signal. But when the lights started flashing, the rookies grabbed several employees, keeping them from disposing of any evidence.

Ness burst in, ahead of Flynn and the others. "This is a police raid!"

Seven employees were arrested. Police seized a cache of financial records going back years, which Ness turned over to the Treasury Department.

The spectacle of the Safety Director personally leading his own raids prompted some critics to brand him a "Boy Scout," but most Clevelanders cheered him on.

"If the city had more 'Ness,'" one citizen told the *News*, "it would be a safer place to live in."

THE DAY AFTER Ness raided McGinty's, a seventeen-year-old girl went walking in the woods on Cleveland's West Side and came upon a naked, headless, worm-ridden corpse.

When police arrived, they found the skull a short distance away, near a bundle of clothing, too rotted for any use in identification. Its long hair, and a nearby hobo camp, suggested the dead man had been a transient. Coroner Pearse estimated the victim had died before the tattooed man, but couldn't confirm that decapitation had killed this victim, too.

"The whole thing was so decomposed," Pearse explained, "that it is possible for the head to have dropped off and to have been carried a few yards by a dog or other animal."

But Cleveland's newspapers had no doubts, and their coverage stoked fears even higher.

"Is there somewhere in Cuyahoga County a madman whose strange god is the guillotine?" asked the next day's *News*. "What fantastic chemistry of the civilized mind converted him into a human butcher?"

This growing terror began to cast a pall over the entire city—including that symbol of optimism, the Great Lakes Exposition. In the Expo's Hall of the Great Lakes, a showcase for the region's history and culture, tourists could view the painted death mask of the nameless tattooed man. Police had placed it on display in hopes one of the Expo's millions of visitors might recognize him.

No one ever did.

Nor would the West Side victim ever be named.

Edward Andrassy and Flo Polillo would be the only victims ever definitively identified. The sheer namelessness of the rest remains unique in the history of serial killing. The Butcher didn't just kill his victims, didn't just steal their heads and defile their bodies. He wiped most of them from existence.

And he was just getting started.

S TORSO KILLER NEW INSAN

Couzens Trails in Rep an Ra

MAINE VOTE IS BAD NEWS TO NEW DEAL

Buel Says Election Shows Threat of Republican Victory in November.

ROOSEVELT JUST SMILES

ndicates Result Was About What He Expected.

BY WALKER S. BUEL
Plain Dealer Bureau,
ST. ALBAN INNE,
WASHINGTON, Sept. 15

Maine's election is very bad news
. the New Deal and President
osevelt.

It is definite indication of a Republican trend, a definite threat of
Republican victory in November,
definite forerunner of a Republican
Democratic landslide in Con-

No. 20 for Allen

Allen injured his back in the fifth inning, but was given credit for his twentieth victory yesterday as the Indians walloped Boston, 12 to 3. Hildebrand finished the game. Tuesday hit his sixth and sixth homers. New York defeated Chicago, 2 to 1; Detroit trimmed Philadelphia, 6 to 5, and Washington took a double header from St. Louis, 13 to 7 and 6 to 1. Weather stopped the National League.

(Details on Sport Pages)

WPA WORKERS TO BE EXPO GUESTS

Families, Also, to Attend Saturday as Honor to Garden Builders.

Today's Events.

BUY YOUR OWN MEALS, NESS TELLS ROOKIES

Ten New Patrolmen Told Appointments Are Based on Own Merits.

"DON'T BE OBLIGATED"

Warns "You'll Get No Great Reward for Honesty."

Youth, 16, T   atens Shirley Tem

Associated Press Wirephoto

OUTLAW SITDOWN, PLEA IS UP TO URW

Strikes Hit Akron Plants as Rubber International Weighs Policy Issue.

Plain Dealer Bureau,
220 Ohio Building,
AKRON, O., Sept. 15

SHAKER EXTEN TO RUN CARS

Shuttle Service t
Rd. Expected in 2 W
May Go to Richme

BY JAMES W. MOONEY

Says Fight With Richman Nearly Sank Ocean Plane

NEW YORK, Sept. 15.—(AP)—The

Michael Shuga
Eliot Ness
Capt. Arthur Roth

Ness with Capt. Arthur Roth.

Cleveland Press Collection, Cleveland State University

Det. Peter Merylo.

Cleveland Public Library Photograph Collection

SIX

The Butcher's Meat

Summer 1936

"Firemen have an old saying that any fire can be put out with a pail of water, if it's reached soon enough," Eliot Ness said. "Many men and boys likewise may be saved from lives of crime if the underlying causes are corrected or removed early enough."

Rejecting a focus on coercion and punishment, Ness believed police should find and fix the deeper social problems that turned good kids bad. He hoped the youth of Cleveland would one day look at cops as friendly, big brother figures—much as Ness had his federal agent brother-in-law, Alexander Jamie.

His test case came that summer in Tremont, a depressed neighborhood just south of downtown, perched over the industrial wasteland of the Flats, its eastern edge hugging the Cuyahoga River.

Tremont's residents lived in row houses packed between factory smokestacks and church spires, both catering to the area's many ethnic groups. Waves of immigration had turned Tremont into one of Cleveland's more diverse neighborhoods, pushing out the original Irish and German inhabitants and replacing them with Eastern Europeans, Greeks, and Syrians. New arrivals often hung on to their old-world customs and languages, even as their children embraced American values and attitudes.

"They learned to look down on their parents because they couldn't speak English, or for many other reasons," Ness explained. "There was a breach between their homes and themselves, eternal conflict."

This left Tremont's children adrift, searching for community and purpose. A survey in early 1936 revealed Tremont had the highest juvenile delinquency rate of any Cleveland neighborhood, and among the highest in America. Ten percent of Tremont's two thousand boys between the ages of ten and nineteen had a criminal record.

"When I came in," Ness recalled, "a spot map showed that in almost every house in the Tremont area there was at least one juvenile delinquent."

Tremont had been allowed, Ness felt, to devolve into "a bad slum . . . The area was not politically important because most of the people there were aliens. Consequently, they couldn't vote. Consequently, no money was spent on it. There were no recreation centers, nothing but streets, and dirty ones. The result? More than 40 kid gangs had grown up. Social prestige in the neighborhood depended on how tough a kid could be, how much of a criminal he was."

The youth gangs occupied themselves with everything from car theft and shoplifting to drug dealing and pimping.

Ness began asking for suggestions on how to change the culture in Tremont, heading up a small group of officers sharing ideas twice a week after hours. The standout was Arthur Valentine Roth, a forty-nine-year-old police captain. Gruff and inarticulate, Roth exemplified the beat cop, with his bullet-shaped head, prominent nose, and pronounced double chin.

Roth never forgot his first day on the job, when he'd smiled and said hello to a young girl only to see her flee in fear of his uniform. Roth resolved to do whatever it took to make sure no kid ever had reason to fear the police.

When Roth first joined the force, the automobile had only just arrived on the city's streets; accident rates skyrocketed as drivers and pedestrians struggled to adapt. Roth would visit the hospital rooms of accident victims, including many children. Horrified by the carnage, he began teaching kids how to stay safe on the streets.

He leaned on showmanship, learning magic tricks and ventriloquism, performing with a dog trained to cross with the green light; he made short films with a movie camera he purchased himself. As Roth gave fun, informative presentations at schools around the city, Cleveland's rate of child traffic deaths dropped— some 70 percent over the course of his career. A magazine dubbed him "The Cop Who Saved a Thousand Kids."

Cleaning up Tremont, Roth knew, would pose an even greater challenge. Years before, the Boy Scouts tried to recruit neighborhood kids into a troop. But gangs of older boys made it their mission to squelch the effort, ripping uniforms off anyone who joined. If Ness and Roth were to have any hope of success, they would first have to win over the older boys. A direct appeal wouldn't work, because the Tremont kids didn't trust cops.

One day that summer, Roth and another officer ventured in plainclothes into Tremont. Roth had let his beard grow some and no longer looked like a cop. Finding a central spot, he took out a length of rope and began tying knots. His partner looked on intently. Soon, as boys clustered around Roth, he casually mentioned that Eliot Ness wanted to gather all of Tremont's youth gangs into one big group. A meeting would soon be held to present their plan, and Roth hoped all the gang leaders would attend.

Thanks to Roth, word spread. He and Ness rented space in a neighborhood church and made plans for a big dinner, with only the leaders of the forty-five gangs invited.

"The atmosphere was tense," Ness remembered. "It fairly bristled with emotion. . . . The leaders were sworn enemies of each other. And they sat and glared."

Once the food had been served, Ness and Roth got up to speak. The Safety Director needed no introduction; the boys all knew, from the papers, of his war on Al Capone.

Ness and Roth didn't try to sermonize about "right" and "wrong," nor did they preach any high-minded moral lesson.

"Instead," Ness said, "in their language, we analyzed the

'success' of recent 'jobs.' I cut up the swag, reduced it to figures of hourly wage, how much they actually got per hour after jail terms were thrown in and the gang came in, etc., something they could understand and be impressed with."

He focused on one notorious bandit from the area, whose career salary averaged roughly seventeen cents an hour. Most crooks, in Ness's estimation, did even worse.

By the end of his talk, Ness could sense the boys coming around. He and Roth then went around the room, asking each kid why they thought Tremont had such a serious crime problem.

"In their own crude way," Ness recalled, "they told us what we already knew."

They wanted work, but their reputations—and, in some cases, criminal records—denied them opportunities to make money honestly. And they wanted safe places, such as recreation centers, to spend their free time.

Ness offered the gang leaders a "deal"—if they would help him steer their younger brothers and friends toward these new programs, he'd see that the older boys got the playgrounds and recreation centers they wanted.

The Tremont kids took him up on it.

Over the coming weeks, Ness held more meetings with the gang leaders. Keeping things "low-keyed," as one social worker recalled, he knew how to win the trust of these hardened young boys.

He proposed creating "a crack [Boy] Scout troop" to "make the citizens who've been knocking this district sit up and take notice." The gang leaders, eager "to show up the rest of the town," signed on.

"So," Ness said, "it ended up that we, the police, started a very exclusive 'tough' Scout troop. And we kept it exclusive. Gradually we had every kid in the neighborhood breaking their necks to get into it."

A citizens' group donated some "swanky" uniforms, which these tough Scouts could wear without other boys tearing them off. Ness selected a small group of policemen to serve as scoutmasters. Concerned citizens organized sports teams and music groups, funded the construction of playgrounds, and provided opportunities for travel to parks and day camps outside the city.

Meanwhile, Ness kept meeting with the older boys, recruiting them into a new club: "a super gang" called the South Side Improvement Association. As with the Boy Scout troops, Ness and Roth worked to keep the club "exclusive," generating a wait list. When the question of renting a clubhouse came up, a member asked if the cops might look the other way while the kids cracked a few safes and knocked over a gas station or two—just till they had enough for a decent place.

Ness said he understood where they were coming from, but it wouldn't be fair for the police to encourage certain criminals while punishing others. They'd have to raise the money some other way.

"We asked for one thing," Ness recalled, "to have them prove themselves as leaders. We asked them to put the lid on for 30 days, and keep it on—a challenge to every boy to control his gang."

And for sixty days the juvenile crime rate in Tremont plummeted.

That show of discipline gave Ness what he needed to convince business leaders to take a chance on the South Side Improvement Association. Through his and Roth's efforts, five hundred Tremont kids secured jobs over the next few years.

"Almost without exception," Ness recalled, "they made good."

Under the rules of their association, members had to put at least 10 percent of their earnings into a savings account. That way, if times got tough, they wouldn't be tempted to break the law for a quick buck. Those seeking skilled employment could take night classes from the federal Works Progress Administration.

"Youths who lately had used blackjacks and guns," Ness remembered, "now were taught how to use slide-rules, micrometers, and lathes."

With the Tremont program working, Ness established a new Crime Prevention Bureau (later known as the Juvenile Bureau) with Roth as its head. Working under him were eighteen cops, all scoutmasters. They pored over records of youth crime and visited rough neighborhoods around the city—seeking, as Ness put it, "to find out why a boy was going bad, what could be done about it, and any contributing causes of juvenile delinquency in that area."

The city couldn't afford to furnish the bureau with needed equipment, so Ness turned to an unlikely source: bookmakers.

"They promote crime," Ness said. "We decided they should help prevent it. So, every raid we make on a bookie den these days we enter carefully. We seize and preserve all desks, phones, typewriters, and chairs. We need a lot of furniture. So . . . we've made a lot of raids. Gradually we're getting all we need."

The Crime Prevention Bureau did everything it could to avoid giving young offenders a criminal record.

"As cops," Roth said, "we don't like jails for kids. No member of our Juvenile Bureau wears a uniform. We don't make 'arrests.' . . . We keep the boy in society, under the responsibility of his parents, if they are competent, or some older friend whom he trusts."

By 1939, Ness and Burton claimed, their crime prevention efforts had reduced Tremont's juvenile delinquency by some 60 percent; but surviving statistics paint a more complicated picture. Youth crime in Tremont was in decline before Ness and Roth intervened, since the neighborhood's juvenile population had been falling for years.

A social worker in 1938, adjusting for this change in population, found a more modest drop of about 48 percent; how much of this was due to Ness's efforts is impossible to say. The crime prevention program—though attracting roughly three thousand kids—was still too new for its full impact to be gauged.

But the social worker could already sense a "changed attitude of youth toward the police," which he considered "a substantial factor in the present reduction."

This tolerance extended even to juvenile delinquents who had since grown up. One summer night in 1936, police detectives roused a thirty-eight-year-old man from bed to arrest him. Convicted of burglary more than twenty years earlier, he'd escaped from an Oklahoma reformatory at sixteen and come to Cleveland—where, as the *News* put it, he "found himself."

Now "a respectable citizen" married with two kids, the fugitive had a legitimate job and hadn't even bothered to change his name. But when the superintendent of the reformatory learned the man's whereabouts, he alerted the Cleveland Police.

After the fugitive explained himself, Detective Inspector Charles Nevel "sent the man home with encouraging words" and wrote a letter to the reformatory superintendent, urging the case be dropped.

"Neither his wife nor his children know of his past," Nevel said. "So far as I am concerned, this man's secret is safe. He has earned it."

The Safety Director approved. Holding the man responsible for his youthful crimes, Ness told the *News*, would be "persecution, not prosecution."

Ness worked to keep his crime prevention efforts out of the headlines, not wanting them publicized until he knew they were effective. But he couldn't hide his love for the work. Talking about it, a reporter observed, "made Director Ness' usually inscrutable face light up with—could it be pride and joy?"

A woman who knew him well said Eliot "liked people, and most of all, I think, he liked kids. . . . He had an instinct about children and an understanding of their needs. He enjoyed and loved them."

Not having any of his own seemed to sadden him. On those rare occasions when he had some free time, Ness had a habit of dropping by the home of his close friend and landlord, Robert Chamberlin, to play with Chamberlin's kids. He looked forward to a day when half of the department's efforts might focus on crime *prevention*, not just its detection or suppression.

"Millions have been spent in efforts to cope with the problem of adult crime," Ness declared in 1939. "I think the time is at hand when police officials, teachers, and educators should join to prevent problem children from becoming criminals."

• • •

THROUGHOUT THE SUMMER, Ness kept disappearing for long stretches, gathering evidence of graft. His cops were feeling the heat, in more ways than one. A record-breaking heat wave descended on the Midwest in July, with temperatures approaching one hundred degrees in Cleveland. Ness allowed his officers to ditch their coats, despite objections from Chief Matowitz, who feared crooks might lift the cops' exposed guns.

The Safety Director was relaxed about wardrobe in general. Asked by the *News* if his department would bar women from wearing shorts in public, as had New York City, Ness said, "They may wear all the shorts they want to on the streets."

His assistant, John Flynn, was more expansive, and tactless.

"It's all a matter of health," Flynn said, "and I've always believed the less women wear the healthier they'll be."

Ness and Flynn had been mismatched from the start, their differences growing more pronounced as the summer wore on. The assistant did his best to appease the politicians, leaving his door open to cops and others seeking favors. Given the chance to make appointments, he ignored civil service and promoted friendly Republicans.

"They will keep coming in to see Flynn, who finds it very hard to say no," wrote Phil Porter. "It's one of the easiest words in Ness' vocabulary."

Flynn kept urging Ness to abandon his crusade against police corruption, believing they stood scant chance of winning any convictions. Flynn preferred to work *with* high-ranking officers—even those who took bribes now and then—to clean up major crimes, rather than risk antagonizing the force.

In late July, while Ness was out of town, incommunicado—supposedly on vacation, but likely chasing new leads—Flynn had a brief, backdoor meeting with Captain Michael Harwood, central figure of the graft probe.

Harwood asked to be retired on disability. His doctor, he said, had diagnosed him with a "state of nervous exhaustion" and a laundry list of other ailments.

"I am the most misjudged man in Cleveland," Harwood said. "I never drew a dishonest breath."

Harwood's friends had been trying to sway the Safety Director for weeks, promising the captain's resignation if Ness would only "call off the dogs" and let the man keep his pension. So far, Ness had refused. But now Flynn agreed to pass Harwood's request on to the pension board with his own approval.

Ness learned of the decision the next day and moved at once to undo it. If the board granted Harwood's request before the city brought charges against him, the captain would keep his full, lifetime pension, even if convicted later of corruption.

But Ness had no control over the pension board; he could only plead his case. After an hour of debate, they agreed to withhold their decision until Ness had finished his investigation.

Other officials threw obstacles in Ness's path. The police closed ranks, rigidly adhering to what Clayton Fritchey called "the unwritten law of not exposing a fellow member of the department." In the Fifteenth Precinct, adjacent to Harwood's old domain in the Fourteenth, uniformed cops warned potential witnesses that talking to Ness would be bad for their health.

Ness responded on September 1 by cleaning out the entire precinct, transferring all twenty-two officers to other parts of town. The newspapers applauded him, but Ness saw the transfers only as a stopgap.

"You can't straighten out a crooked cop by transferring him," Ness said. "The thing to do is get rid of him."

For months, in between his other activities, Ness had somehow found time to lead the investigation of a "shakedown racket" at the Northern Ohio Food Terminal. Much of the city's fresh produce passed through the terminal, delivered by farmers who sold it to wholesalers and grocers.

A "gang of racketeers, operating under the guise of a labor union," had moved in, forcing farmers and truckers to pay fees before unloading their fruits and vegetables. Most victims had little choice; after all, they couldn't wait around until their products spoiled. And when people did resist, the racketeers responded with threats, violence, and destruction of vehicles.

Ness's investigators distilled the testimony of nearly one hundred witnesses into an eighty-page report, documenting seventy separate cases of extortion. The Safety Director personally handed it to Prosecutor Cullitan on September 2.

Labor unions, who wielded considerable power in Cleveland, had never warmed to the person they called this "G-Man Eliot Ness." Now they rushed to defend the so-called association at the Food Terminal. And with an election coming up, the Democratic prosecutor had little incentive to antagonize a large voting bloc.

"Cullitan should strike fast and strike hard to break up this evil situation," a newspaper editorialized. But the Food Terminal investigation went nowhere, after evidence showed no violation of any laws on the books.

ON SEPTEMBER 10, just over a week after Ness exposed the Food Terminal racket, a drifter waiting for a freight spotted two white objects floating in a Kingsbury Run creek.

The objects turned out to be the upper and lower halves of a man's torso—head cut off, arms and legs, too, sectioned through the stomach, and emasculated.

Police, tracing the creek to a nearby stagnant pool, some twenty feet deep, probed its depths in search of the missing pieces. Hundreds if not thousands of people stood by watching, on the off chance they might catch a glimpse of a body part. After weeks of fruitless searching, the investigators resorted to draining the pool, but never found the head and hands.

Chief Matowitz put his best detective on the case: Peter Merylo, a forty-one-year-old Ukrainian immigrant on the force since 1919. Thickset with thinning hair, Merylo had racked up more arrests than any cop in town, routinely scoring as the department's best shot. He'd once considered the priesthood, and still approached his job as a righteous mission, a crusade to protect the powerless. He had no patience for the incompetent, and let nothing get in the way of justice, even if it meant bending a rule.

Matowitz couldn't have picked a more dogged detective, but the public wasn't satisfied. Cleveland's madman had killed six times in one year, thrice in roughly three months. Hoboes, presumably the Butcher's meat, began fleeing in droves. Press hysteria reached a fever pitch.

"Terror pervades the neighborhoods of the killings," an editorial declared. "Nobody knows when the blood lust of the butcher may turn upon a child, a friend, a member of the family. . . . Director Ness and Chief Matowitz must assign more men to do the job . . . whatever the number, whatever the effort. . . . The people must be saved from this terror. The slaughter must stop."

Inevitably, Mayor Burton asked Ness to step in. Solving murders, no matter how gruesome, didn't really fall under the Safety Director's purview, but Ness could hardly bow out. He'd already proven his penchant for hands-on crimefighting while allowing the press to anoint him the city's savior.

"He had to do something," Merylo recalled. "The mayor was on his neck; so were the Chamber of Commerce and the Come to Cleveland Committee and some of the people who rode home to Shaker Heights through the Run on the Rapid Transit. But so was the whole town, for that matter. It was getting to be something of a national disgrace, Cleveland's uncaught torso murderer."

The Butcher had preyed on the downtrodden for at least two years—but only now, with the elite riled, did City Hall take a serious interest.

On September 12, Ness announced he was personally taking charge of what the press had come to call "the mystery of the headless dead."

In a show of force, he dispatched fifteen cops to round up every transient in the Run and bring them in for questioning. Then he met with Merylo and the detective's handpicked partner, Martin Zalewski, to ask what they'd discovered so far.

Having just gotten the case himself, Merylo bristled at Ness's demands for results. Nor did he appreciate John Flynn suggesting on nothing but a hunch that the Butcher might be a woman—an idea Merylo found idiotic.

Despite their differences, Ness, Merylo, and Zalewski managed to agree on three possible profiles of the killer.

The Butcher, they believed, might be an escaped mental patient, such as one currently sought in Pennsylvania. Or he might really be "a crazed butcher," as indicated by his evident skill with a knife.

But that same anatomical knowledge suggested another possibility: that the Butcher might be "a maddened doctor, possibly a medical student or hospital orderly." Victim Edward Andrassy had worked as an orderly in the mental ward of Cleveland's City Hospital. Was there some connection?

By the end of the meeting, Merylo had sized up the Safety Director and found him lacking.

"You can't bring up Eliot Ness to Peter," Merylo's wife observed years later. "He starts to get nasty. He did not like the man."

Ness and Merylo were of different worlds, with contrary approaches to law enforcement. Merylo was an old-school cop, a hard-boiled detective who played hunches and ran down leads with the persistence of a migraine headache. To him, Ness seemed a dilettante, an interloper, whose ideas on scientific policing might count in the classroom but not on the street.

The hunt for the Butcher would soon become a contest between Merylo's fevered tenacity and Ness's cool intellectualism. At the outset, neither seemed to stand much chance of success.

...S TORSO KILLER NEW INSAN...

...ouzens Trails in Rep...an Ra...

MAINE VOTE IS BAD NEWS TO NEW DEAL

Buel Says Election Shows Threat of Republican Victory in November.

ROOSEVELT JUST SMILES

Indicates Result Was About What He Expected.

BY WALNER S. BUEL
Staff Corespondent.
WASHINGTON, Sept. 25 — Maine's election is very bad news in the New Deal and President Roosevelt.

It is a certain indication of a Republican trend, a definite threat of Republican victory in November, despite forecasts of a tremendous Democratic membership in Congress, a definite indication of a Republican defeat, especially to the ...

There is one for unmistakable fact in this campaign, the White House is going to impress as a fatal to New Deal began the reelection of President Roosevelt. But Mr. Farlee said, making people confident and common enthusiastic that they realize Roosevelt is not anything the sad can do. Really said the probably ready hoped the Republican relief and broken ... throughout the agricultural ...

November Election in Doubt.

Since the November election was as much in doubt as if ... for Maine voted, except that the two percent saying sent the ... in Maine lost the days of the Populist and Republican candidates said that unless President Roosevelt can half the much laid much he is to blamed for...

Senator Wilson won in 1915 in a election, without a vote of any far state, except Gov. Hamp... by a very margin. But Wilson this year and Gov. Roosevelt ...

The vote and by totally, Ohio expects to overcome the trend used by the Maine trend.

Democrats got the best two position the Maine outcome. There is nothing much about is a Democratic strategist accept ...

One Carries Hint Close to U.S. Vote.

BY JAY G. HAYDEN
Sept. 25 — in the Major campaign STAFF... Sept. 15 — Maine marched back into the Republican ... but with pluralities for the candidates of that party sufficient to give the vote the author edge for their own prophecy.

No. 20 for Allen

Allen injured his back in the 6th inning, but was given credit for his twentieth victory yesterday as the Indians outslugged New York, 12 to 6. Hal Trosky and H.G. blasted homers for the Indians. Earl Averill finished the game, touched for eight hits both and and nine homers. New York defeated Chicago, 7 to 1; Detroit trimmed Philadelphia, 4 and 5, and Washington took a double header from St. Louis, 10 to 7 and 6 to 3.

Weather stopped the National League.
(Results on Sport Pages.)

WPA WORKERS TO BE EXPO GUESTS

Families, Also, to Attend Saturday as Honor to Garden Builders.

Today's Events.

United Rubber Workers Day.
United States Pomeroy Day.
Royal Neighbors of America Day.
National Society of Patriots Day.
City Club Day.
Marvin 1933 Day.
Garden Club of Michigan Day.

Attendance yesterday 35,000
Attendance for 16 days 3,174,956
Days left—12.

The WPA will have its day at the Great Lakes Exposition.

Some of the men closely thought that, since everybody that hiring his day at the exposition, should have a direct invitation to inspect the WPA signs of whose 8500 laborers built the low-cost horticultural Gardens on the grounds.

On the fairs, who should the workers and the boss who among the bricks have been invited to attend the exposition Saturday. They will have some conducted by their own WPA hands.

They will take the whole stadium as a special event. Arrangements have been made with exposition concessionaires to sell them with lunches at prices they are paid.

Such a concession will be in mind for workers because numerous employees have said they wanted to see the WPA-built gardens." Joseph H. Alexander, WPA control administrator.

The invitation, which include members of the workers' families, will be in the form of identification.

Distributed on Page 6, column 3.

Less Sight to Hampton Best
HARRISVILLE, O., Sept. 25 — Charles Gallagher, 61, R.F.D., here was fortunately blinded in a dynamite explosion here today. Gallagher travelled to the explosion, may have lost his life.

Says Fight With Richman Nearly Sank Ocean Plane

NEW YORK, Sept. 25 — (AP) — The Daily News, in a copyrighted dispatch from its staff correspondent at Musgrave Harbor, Newfoundland, says a quarrel over the division of honors on their transatlantic flight Harry Richman and Dick Merrill "almost ended with the flyers in Davey Jones' locker."

Merrill and Richman landed at that battered wings yesterday after a return flight from England.

the auditions. "It's his fight." Ambrose put all my arguments for different points were thrown aside ...

As Richman approaches during the conversation, he and Merrill lodged in opposite directions, the paper

Newspaper Plane Damaged.
ST. JOHNS, Newfoundland, Sept. 25 — (AP) — A newspaper plane flown by the New York Daily News

BUY YOUR OWN MEALS, NESS TELLS ROOKIES

Ten New Patrolmen Told Appointments Are Based on Own Merits.

"DON'T BE OBLIGATED"

Warns "You'll Get No Great Reward for Honesty."

The new patrolmen were sworn into office yesterday by Safety Director Eliot Ness in the office at City Hall with the revolutionary admonition that policemen are expected to pay for their own meals.

"You were here appointed on your own merits and promote you alone at the top of the civil service list and on no other reason." Ness told the recruits. "If anyone made claims to you that he was responsible for your appointment, pay no attention.

"Your advancement is up to you.

"You are expected to be honest and to know that you will get no great rewards for being honest. Don't be obligated to anyone, even in small things.

"When you walk into a restaurant for a meal, pay for it. When you get any marketable commodity useful to you, pay for it. If people have been accustomed to giving you things for nothing prior to your becoming a policeman, I suppose it is all right for you to continue to accept those things.

There Will Be Promotions.

"However, it maybe who have never have you anything from before you went off any one interesting without charge, you can conclude that they are buying your badge and your uniform."

In addition to appointing the ten new patrolmen, Ness promoted Sergt. Augustus B. H. Foley to a lieutenancy and Patrolman Herbert Russel and William H. Miller to sergeancies.

The recruits were:

HENRY L. REHBERGER, 2303 Colonna Avenue S. W.
ADALBERT D. O'HARA, 10255 Kinsman Avenue S. E.
EDWARD FUNDY, 26, 10512 Arps Road S. E.
MARTIN F. EBERLING, 2254 W. 12TH Street
FRANK A CADOC, 24, 4573 E. 140th
ROY J. ERICKSON, 2020 Town Avenue S. E.
EDWARD B. BENKE, 3563 E. 135th Street
CLARENCE G. THOMAS, 7647 Esther Avenue S. E.
JOHN D. KILDUFF, 2234 Arps Street
ELMER J. POUND, 1003 Ansel Road
Cadoc, the nephew of former Capt. Louis J. Cadoc, was appointed to the department a month ago by Jonah J. Lewis, examiner, whereas Pound is the nephew of Mrs. Bess. His appointment was revoked at that time by Ness because Pound and Cadoc were the candidates at the foot of the list.

Says Fight With Richman Nearly Sank Ocean Plane

Youth, 16, Th...atens Shirley Tem...

Associated Press Wirephoto.
Henry Edward Stephens, 16, leucopenia Atlanta boy, accused of threats made against the screen star in ... the letter to the ... of Shirley Temple, child film star, is shown between two federal agents as he was moved from the Atlanta police station to the Federal Building.

OUTLAW SITDOWN, PLEA IS UP TO URW

Strikes Hit Akron Plants as Rubber International Weighs Policy Issue.

From Our Staff Bureau.
727 Ohio Building.
AKRON, O., Sept. 25.

The issue of the sitdown strike in might hang on the more important question before the United Rubber Workers of America at their third international convention, in session here.

Resolutions before the convention Friday are asking that the authorized sitdown be outlawed and another that calls the sitdown, one of the most powerful weapons of organized labor, and asks its incorporation into URW policy.

Adolph Germer, C.I.O. representative here, was asked today, referring to the recent sitdown strike, that it would leave pending introduction of the resolution to next week, if the question should come up at all, ...

"Direct Violation." E. Ward.

"I will think that sitdowns were a direct violation of your policies and your principles." Germer said.

SHAKER EXTE... TO RUN CARS

Shuttle Service ... Rd. Expected in 2... May Go to Richm...

BY JAMES G. MORSE.
First extension of the rapid transit in Shaker Heights connected its two tracks ... this will be started about Xmas has been forecast. Sixty new cars for the line would the Rapid Transit Road on the Shaker Road is to be backed in for Road West on setting along, with it ... For the will be a ... rapid ... along a streetcar ... line with ... in ... Van Arden road has run ... shuttle that is ... service from to Rockwell the east running over this route ... past spring, ... of ...

ATLANTA

ATLANTA, Ga., Sept. 25 — A unemployed youth who said he wanted all of his 16 years in a prison school camp, told federal authorities the index of undone a $125.00 reward for the murder of Shirley Temple.

Another source released his story, Stephens, W. Powell is under court for $1,000 on a direct case on a charge of attempting to collect $1,000 from the child star last June. He said he killed next year.

The youth himself today, flashed a frozen Edward Stephens, sent an order by Federal Bureau prosecutions requested and before as his own recognizance after a hearing before United States Commissioner H. A. Gibson.

This was made until one of the federal men held him in the custody of the federal action council to appear ... besides ...

The boy's note written with his left hand said:

Ness delivering the results of his police corruption probe to County Prosecutor Frank Cullitan, October 5, 1936.
Cleveland Public Library Photograph Collection

Ness with his new assistant, Robert Chamberlin (right).
The Cleveland Police Historical Society, Inc.

SEVEN

Perfect Victims

Fall 1936

Americans in the 1930s faced a deadly epidemic, invisible to most authorities. Since at least the late nineteenth century, the press and police had begun taking notice of murderers who killed repeatedly, in a series, not for personal gain or survival, rather to feed some deeper, primal urge.

In the nearly fifty years since Jack the Ripper terrorized London, a new breed of killer began making the American papers. The public knew of some—H. H. Holmes, Earle "Gorilla Man" Nelson, Albert Fish—but those were just a few who got caught. Barely a hundred miles from Cleveland and a decade before the Butcher, a mysterious "clubber" in Toledo bludgeoned twelve women in two weeks, then disappeared, never to be identified.

In 1929, while Eliot Ness began pursuing Al Capone, police in Weimar Germany hunted Peter Kürten, "Vampire of Düsseldorf," responsible for a string of rapes, murders, and assaults stretching back more than fifteen years. Kürten eventually surrendered to authorities and died by the guillotine, leaving a proud and detailed confession unveiling the psychology of people who kill for sexual pleasure. In 1930, Ernst Gennat, pioneering head of Berlin's homicide squad, coined a new term for such behavior: *serienmörder*. Its English equivalent—"serial murder"—would not enter the mainstream American lexicon for another four decades.

Police still knew next to nothing about what made such killers tick, and even less about how to catch them. Authorities treated each as a unique, isolated incident—a singular monster. No one had yet discerned a recognizable pattern of behavior.

Those killers who did end up behind bars typically did so of their own carelessness or arrogance. Albert Fish, for example, wrote a bragging letter to a victim's mother, and detectives traced the stationery right back. As with H. H. Holmes, the extent of Fish's atrocities didn't become known until after his capture.

Facing a careful, methodical murderer leaving no clues to his identity, the cops remained in the dark. Standard police procedure—seeking a motive by identifying a victim and then questioning his or her friends, relatives, and acquaintances—often proved useless with a killer who murdered strangers for private, perverse reasons.

Even in this context, the Butcher offered a unique challenge. His victims remained mostly nameless, denying police a starting point. Primitive forensic techniques could discern little from body parts washed clean, while scraps of newspaper and ragged clothing found with some victims only served to further confound.

The Butcher displayed an ability to hunt, kill, and dispose of evidence without being seen. Even Jack the Ripper left behind enough eyewitnesses for a rough description. But the Butcher remained faceless and formless, a nameless phantom shrouded in the shadows of Kingsbury Run.

Letters from would-be informants, suggesting how to "crack the case," flooded Ness's office. A twenty-four-year-old wrestler and criminology student showed up, offering to be the Safety Director's eyes and ears in Kingsbury Run. Yet another would-be "decoy" visited the Central Police Station volunteering his services. Police looked him up, found a warrant for sexual assault, and put him behind bars.

The Bureau of Narcotics suggested, according to the *Plain Dealer*, "that the slayer was addicted to narcotics, probably marijuana, which . . . inspires its users with an unreasoning desire to kill."

Seeking a more informed opinion, Coroner Arthur Pearse called a "torso clinic" on the evening of September 15. Ness, Matowitz, and other police officials were joined by experts in psychology, anatomy, and forensic science. At 8 P.M., thirty-four attendees crowded into the ballistics room at headquarters for a discussion—and viewing of victim photos—lasting two and a half hours. The heat had most men in their shirtsleeves and suspenders. Ness, in the front row, kept his jacket on.

Things got off glumly when Detective Sergeant James Hogan, head of homicide, admitted with a pessimistic shrug, "Gentlemen, tonight we're right where we were the day the first body was found."

Then began a debate, working from what they knew of the Butcher's handiwork to fill in what they didn't. They arrived at one of the earliest profiles ever made of a serial killer, possibly the first since Jack the Ripper in 1888. The Butcher, the experts agreed, must be a man, and a big, strong one—capable of carrying a headless corpse down a steep hill, then climbing back up and doing it again. This killer knew the Kingsbury Run area well, likely living near where he left his victims. Although the dismemberments "showed considerable knowledge of anatomy," county pathologist Reuben Straus argued against a trained surgeon, suspecting a hunter or butcher.

As most victims had not been killed where they were found, the clinic attendees felt the Butcher worked in some facility or "laboratory" near the Run. He might befriend his victims, for weeks or even months, before using a large, heavy knife on them.

While the attendees agreed the Butcher was "crazed" and "a pervert," they could label him with no known form of insanity. A mental hospital director said he'd never known a lunatic capable of such complex, long-term planning. The Butcher, they theorized, led a normal life when not pursuing his gruesome hobby. Only decades later would criminologists recognize the ability of some serial killers to hide their true natures behind charming masks.

When tallying the Butcher's victims, the attendees excluded the Lady of the Lake, though subsequent events suggest otherwise. They believed the other six had clearly died by the same hand. The Butcher seemed to choose his prey from society's castoffs— prostitutes and down-and-outers in the Roaring Third and the Flats. Inspector Joseph Sweeney, head of the Detective Bureau, referred to such targets as "perfect victims," whose disappearance would go unnoticed. Later criminologists would describe these as "the less-dead"—living on the fringes, "vulnerable and powerless," slipping from the "less-alive" into the "never-were."

The Butcher knew how to move among them but wasn't necessarily of their world.

"He is of more than ordinary intelligence," a reporter suggested, "perhaps a respected person of a social strata considerably higher than that of his victims."

But even as the attendees came to some agreement on the killer's profile, they could not decide on any strategies for catching him. The best method might be to place people in the Run as bait, a suggestion getting more dark laughter than volunteers.

John Flynn recommended searching every building in the area for the killer's "laboratory," but the feasibility of this suggestion—to say nothing of its legality—went unaddressed. At meeting's end, Detective Hogan could still only shrug.

Throughout, Ness asked few questions and contributed little. He did suggest the Butcher might've cut his victims' heads off purely to prevent identification. This theory couldn't explain the positioning of the first two victims' heads, but it did normalize the killer in a way the Safety Director could understand.

Nothing in Ness's career prepared him for the Butcher. The idea of a murderer who killed solely for satisfaction made no sense to him.

Such a killer challenged his very conception of crime. Sometime later, when asked his opinion on how to protect women from sexual assaults—crimes motivated, like the Butcher's, for gratification and not material gain—Ness fell back on a story from his Chicago days. He recalled listening to a wiretap on the Cicero headquarters of Capone's brother Ralph and overhearing two gangsters bragging about raping a woman who'd spurned their advances. This proved to Ness that both kinds of crime were linked—rapists and racketeers cut from the same cloth.

"Just as one sort of vice leads to another," Ness said, "one sort of crime leads to another. . . . The criminal, you see, has time on his hands. He hasn't respect for one kind of law—be it gambling or bootlegging—and he won't have respect eventually for any kind of law. I would say that any community that had a lot of attacks on women, and a lot of other sex crimes, had a lot of vice and had plenty of undercover gangs and rackets."

This assumption informed Ness's philosophy of law enforcement. He believed removing the conditions giving rise to crime would eliminate lawlessness of all kinds, the way a doctor might bring down a fever by treating the underlying illness.

"In crime, in accident, and in any series of events menacing public safety," Ness wrote, "the cause, the why, is the thing to ferret out. As the pattern evolves, experience and intelligence point to a solution on the basis of those facts, and a course of action becomes crystal clear."

This rational, logical approach worked with rational, logical criminals like Capone. Not with someone like the Butcher—an outlier driven not by logic but by his own private sickness, springing up spontaneously, the "why" not yet understood.

Detective Merylo didn't see the world quite so holistically. He'd worked vice for years, which colored his view of human nature. He saw the Butcher as "a Sex Degenerate" and a necrophile, who cut off his victims' heads so he could better enjoy their bodies. Or perhaps the act of decapitation was satisfying enough; Merylo later theorized "that the MURDERER procure[s] his sexual gratification while watching the blood flow after cutting the jugular vein of his victim."

These ideas hardened in Merylo's mind as he threw light into the dark corners of the city, exposing sexual sadism, forced prostitution, bigamy, rape, and incest. Homosexuality also fit Merylo's idea of perversion, and he would arrest dozens of people for sodomy while hunting for the Butcher. The case became an obsession, consuming his nights, weekends, and days off. He arrested anyone who didn't look quite right, and—in certain quarters of the city—they could usually be found guilty of something.

After the clinic, Ness ordered his detectives to start anew on the murders of Edward Andrassy and the unidentified man found near Jackass Hill. Ness himself questioned one of the boys who'd discovered both bodies. Meanwhile, he sent John Flynn to New Castle, Pennsylvania, to investigate a swamp where headless corpses had been turning up for years. The local authorities believed these to be gang killings, heads removed to prevent identification, and Flynn was inclined to agree.

But Merylo, after making a series of treks to New Castle, came to see this as the work of the same killer. The information he gathered was incomplete and at times inaccurate, pulling his investigation off track. But that didn't stop him from adding these victims—and others—to the Butcher's tally.

The Safety Director—content to let Merylo go his own way—chose instead to confide in David Cowles, the department's thirty-nine-year-old ballistics expert. Bald, rough-hewn, and pudgy, grade school graduate Cowles had taught himself chemistry, turning himself into a scientific policeman in the Ness mold.

One evening, Cowles was summoned to Ness's lakefront apartment. He found Ness with a *Cleveland Press* editor, who explained his paper would underwrite an effort to end the torso murders. The three men determined to hire a handful of undercover detectives with Cowles in charge; he alone would know their names and assignments. His first recruit was a marijuana dealer; soon a couple of rookies, fresh from the academy, were sent undercover as hoboes. Cowles met with them at out-of-the-way places, where they could pass along their intel.

Eventually Cowles learned of a promising suspect: a man police first looked at for Edward Andrassy's murder, even before the killer struck again. Once a successful doctor, this suspect had spiraled into alcoholism; he'd spent much of his life around

Kingsbury Run. His medical training suggested some knowledge of anatomy, if not a practiced surgeon's skill.

Yet police had ruled him out as a possible culprit. The doctor frequently checked himself into a veterans' hospital near Sandusky to dry out. Several of these stays lined up with the estimated death dates of the Butcher's victims, alibiing him for many, if not all, of the murders.

Cowles had no choice but to set the doctor aside and move on to other leads. But he never forgot about him.

WITH THE TORSO case in other hands, Ness got back to the work he knew best.

On October 5, he ordered eight more police officers suspended, then walked into Frank Cullitan's office with a stack of ledgers and an eighty-six-page report—the results of his months-long graft probe.

For more than two hours, Ness sat with Cullitan and Assistant Prosecutor Charles McNamee, going over the documents. Evidence gathered from witnesses, wiretaps, and bank records implicated twenty officers in a massive protection racket. One bent cop, a deputy inspector, had come up for promotion while the investigation was ongoing, and Ness, not wanting to tip his hand, had duly promoted the officer.

According to Clayton Fritchey, Ness's partner on the case, "the rank and file who have taken money were in many cases the victims of an evil system. . . . The department has been so controlled for the last 20 years that it could not breed or attract men of high character."

Honest cops were "sent to the woods," while those who "played ball" and paid for promotions grew powerful. High-ranking officers held raucous parties where new recruits drank and gambled freely, at the expense of crooks they'd shaken down. After "their baptism of corruption," the rookies began squeezing the maximum profit from their precincts. They had little choice.

"When an officer has to lay out large sums of money for promotion," Ness explained, "he is not going to be particular how he gets it back."

During Prohibition, graft had grown out of control. Cops hounded bootleggers for bribes, cracking down hard on missed payments.

"You had to be there exactly at the time they set," a witness recalled. "If you were five minutes late in arriving with the money, there was a raid."

When a bootlegger refused to pay up, police searched his place, found whatever evidence they could, and charged him with a liquor crime. If they didn't find any evidence, they planted some. Then they advised him a trial and a conviction would be very expensive, but for a small fee, the officers' memories would grow hazy.

"How much this graft actually totaled it is impossible to say," Ness told the *Press*, "but it is safe to estimate that it exceeded a million dollars."

Often, cops overestimated just how much a bootlegger could afford. They victimized many small-timers, who could barely make ends meet.

Harwood proved particularly inflexible. When a bootlegger begged him for a break, the captain would reply, "If your business isn't good enough, get out of it and let somebody else make some money."

Such constant police pressure drove out independent operators, allowing the Mayfield Road Mob, the Italian-American branch of the Cleveland Syndicate, to conquer the liquor trade. Eventually, the syndicate grew powerful enough to tell the cops who to raid and who to leave alone.

This shocked Ness more than anything else he uncovered. By exposing these corrupt cops, he hoped to break the collusion between the city's gangsters and policemen.

For three weeks, the grand jury heard testimony from more than sixty witnesses, detailing how police preyed on them during Prohibition.

"Look at my clothes," a witness said, gesturing to his thread-bare attire. "They're the best I have. I'd be a rich man if I had all the money I'd paid those crooked police."

A fifty-six-year-old widow, mother of six, named thirty-seven policemen who'd extorted $10,000 from her and her late husband. She told Ness, "Line them up, director. Line up the police department and I'll show you every crook."

Ness put a twenty-four-hour guard on her home. Apparently, no one noted the irony of such a famous Prohibition agent guarding a bootlegger from the authorities.

As the hearings wore on, the investigation snowballed, with more witnesses stepping up to testify. Cullitan's office refused to halt the parade for any reason.

On October 29, after nearly eighty witnesses testified, the grand jury handed down bribery indictments against eight officers: Captain Harwood, one deputy inspector, two lieutenants, a sergeant, and three patrolmen.

"The testimony displays a calloused brutality and studied intimidation by police officers of many of our foreign-born citizens," the jury's forewoman said, "citizens who were bewildered by many of our laws and easily exploited by the very men they should have been able to trust."

The accused pleaded not guilty and settled in for a fight.

"Betting is brisk downtown on the outcome of the police trials," reported an observer. "Wagering odds favor a majority of acquittals. Sources close to Ness also lean that way."

First up was Michael Harwood, whose trial began December 7. The captain had flaunted his wealth for years, sinking thousands into restaurants and nightclubs. But the indictment charged him only with soliciting a paltry $770 in seven bribes during the late 1920s.

During Cullitan's opening statement, Harwood clenched his fists and glared. His mood did not improve as bootlegger after bootlegger—among them Casper Korce, the saloonkeeper won over by Ness—recounted how they'd paid the captain off.

After four days of testimony, the prosecution rested, and

Harwood took the stand. He denied everything, claiming witnesses conspired to frame him. But his confidence crumbled under Cullitan's merciless cross-examination.

Ness, an observer at the trial, occasionally approached the prosecution's table to whisper to Cullitan. Harwood's attorney objected, requesting that "Mr. Ness either be a spectator or sit at the trial table and participate directly in the trial." But the judge dismissed his complaint, declaring that "Mr. Ness can sit where he pleases."

The Safety Director's continued attendance may have done much to sway the jury to the prosecution's side.

"In the eyes of the jurors he must have appeared as the youthful crusader against corruption," reported the *News*.

Cullitan made Ness the centerpiece of his closing argument, announcing his "admiration for the determination he has shown in his efforts to rid the city of gangsters, mobsters, racketeers and to clean the Police Department of crooks."

Then Cullitan attacked Harwood "as a grasping grafter," while the captain and his daughter openly sobbed. Harwood "besmirched the badge he wore," Cullitan declared. "He brought disgrace on his family, just as all criminals do."

The jurors deliberated until midnight, then broke for the evening and returned the next day. Rumor had one juror insisting on acquittal.

"I don't believe they ever will convict him," John Flynn told reporters. "It would have saved thousands of dollars to have accepted his resignation."

A few minutes later, the verdict came in: guilty on six of seven counts.

Pale, holding back tears, Harwood fought to stay calm. His wife fainted; one of his daughters wept. The soon-to-be-former captain left the room wordlessly.

Another daughter, as she walked out, spotted the Safety Director and spat, "I can thank you, Mr. Ness."

Ness seemed not to have heard. He told reporters he "would rather not comment" on his victory. But he did tell the *News*,

"There is nothing personal about this case. I am fighting for a principle, that's all."

Later that day, Flynn resigned, getting out just in time—Ness and Burton were already planning to fire him. The Safety Director, in a courteous letter, thanked Flynn for staying on through the Harwood trial.

Ness tapped his friend and neighbor, Robert Chamberlin, to fill Flynn's post. The new assistant bore a striking resemblance to the man he'd replaced, both towering, mustached lawyers and former football stars. But Chamberlin's attitude proved refreshingly different. He gladly took over administrative tasks, leaving Ness to pursue his detective work.

The pair became inseparable—as the *Plain Dealer* put it, "the Cleveland safety directorship . . . has become a two-man position."

Ness and Cullitan pursued prosecutions against the other indicted officers in order of descending rank. They'd won five consecutive convictions by spring 1938—"an almost unprecedented record," according to the *Press*. The chief justice of the state supreme court commended them "on the outstanding completeness and care with which this group of cases was prepared."

That March, Fritchey reported "a revolution" taking place among Cleveland's cops.

"Today there is an entirely new high command in the department," Fritchey wrote, "the dictators have been liquidated, the grafters purged."

Ness spoke of his work with much less relish.

"I have had an unpleasant job to do," he said, "but I have done it in the belief that when you work on cancer you begin with a knife."

The irony of his words, in the Butcher's savage shadow, was apparently lost on this civilized detective.

ife Identified a
er; Head Found

of Grisly Discovery on Lonely Country Road

PART TWO

THE UNKNOWNS

Congressman Martin L. Sweeney

*Library of Congress,
Prints and Photographs Division,
Harris & Ewing Collection,
LC-H22-D-6091*

Coroner Samuel Gerber

Cleveland Public Library Photograph Collection

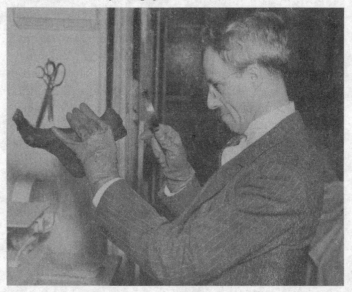

EIGHT

Hero of the Hour

January–July 1937

"This is getting to be a devil of a town," a Cleveland reporter observed in early 1937. "An honest racketeer . . . can't walk the streets any more without police picking him up to 'question' him. And Saturday night, which used to be crime evening, is so sleepy that managing editors curse regularly because there is no news."

The city's crime rate had fallen 15 percent in 1936, to its lowest point in a decade, while felony arrests rose more than 10 percent. But the city's managing editors couldn't complain too much about the dearth of crime news with the hyperactive Safety Director picking up the slack.

"Don't blame us if the name of Eliot Ness continues to be important in the news of the week," wrote the *Press*. "It just can't be helped."

The new year found Ness at the apex of his popularity and influence—"an idolized public figure," an out-of-town reporter wrote, ". . . Cleveland's civic boast to the world and the nation's No. 1 police marvel." The *Press* declared him "a hero of the hour," and the *Plain Dealer* named him "Man of the Year."

Credit for the drop in crime went largely to Ness and the new attitude he'd brought to the force. His police corruption investigation restored the morale of good cops while keeping the rest on their best behavior.

"Everybody who worked for Ness was untouchable," an officer remembered. "We were scared to be bribed—scared of Ness."

The Safety Director seemed to be everywhere; where would he strike next?

"Eliot Ness is such a will-o-the-wisp to reporters," one observed, "that they have to move fast to keep up with him."

At a dull banquet, before the speeches began, he would slip out, then turn up at another event before leaving just as fast.

Work-addicted as he was, he put in sixteen- to twenty-hour days and had yet to take a vacation. His $7,500 annual salary was good money in the Depression, but other cities paid far better. A few tried to woo him away, and private firms made even more lucrative officers. But Ness refused them all.

"Some day I may take one of these jobs," he said. "Right now, however, I want to prove what an honest police force with intelligence and civic pride can do."

In early January, he suspended a police sergeant for beating up an eighteen-year-old honor student mistaken for a robber. That the victim was innocent mattered less to the Safety Director than the barbarity of his interrogation. Ness declared himself "opposed to the third degree methods," and made it clear he wanted no suspects, guilty or innocent, beaten into a confession.

"Intelligence," he told the suspended sergeant, "must supplant brutality."

Meanwhile, Ness kept gathering witnesses and evidence for yet-to-be-tried police corruption cases. A ledger seized in a federal raid on a fancy Cleveland brothel seemed to document payoffs to high police officials, though the madam claimed these were "only names of my friends." Wary of stepping on any federal toes, Ness sought to discuss the case with J. Edgar Hoover on a visit to Washington, D.C., but Hoover appears not to have granted him an audience.

The antigambling campaign continued, though Ness faced resistance from a sluggish department. He came to rely on two "rookie raiders," zealous young patrolmen who dressed like "college boys" and shared the Safety Director's sometimes casual disregard for civil liberties. Operating like the old Untouchables, they shut down bookie joints with or without a warrant, cheerfully harassing both owners and customers. Where police once let casino patrons go free, Ness now ordered his men to photograph, fingerprint, and drag into court anyone on the premises.

Such constant harassment disrupted a major source of illicit revenue. In mid-January, the *Plain Dealer* reported those with the "right connections" could still make bets, but the "lid on gambling was clamped tighter than it had been in Cleveland for at least four years." One bookie complained to the *Press* that Ness's raids had practically driven him out of business.

But the bookies merely had to step across the city line, where Ness held no power and gambling boomed. After Sheriff Honest John Sulzmann's disgrace during the Harvard Club raid, Cuyahoga County voters replaced him with another white-haired, doughy-faced Democrat, Martin L. O'Donnell, who offered little in the way of change.

O'Donnell promised to carry on his predecessor's "home rule" leniency toward gambling and vice. Night after night, the resurrected Thomas and Harvard Clubs enjoyed packed houses while "city gamblers, with a lean and hungry look, cast envious glances at their more prosperous brethren in the suburbs," observed the *Press*.

Mayor Burton faced strong opposition from both Democrats and his own party, who bristled at Ness's rigid, even repressive reforms. His campaign planned to respond by running on Ness's record, holding up the Safety Director as proof of Burton's independence and commitment to good government. But they couldn't count on much help from the apolitical Ness.

Some observers thought Ness's popularity made him politically untouchable.

"So great is his public reputation and so secure his public confidence," noted the *Plain Dealer*, "that it has been suggested that whatever Democrat contends next fall . . . would do well to promise to retain Ness if elected."

ON THE FRIGID afternoon of February 23, a man searching for driftwood along Euclid Beach came across the upper half of a woman's torso—severed at the waist, arms and head missing . . . on practically the same spot where the Lady of the Lake washed up almost two and a half years earlier.

Again, opinions differed as to whether this was the Butcher's work. Unlike the other killings, this woman had not died from decapitation. Investigators couldn't figure out what *had* killed her—or how her body wound up in Lake Erie, or what her name was. The coroner concluded the woman had probably been a mother, but no child or children came forward to claim her.

Detective Orley May showed little doubt that the Butcher had returned: "He gives us one regularly every five months."

The police department's two-man torso detail, Peter Merylo and Martin Zalewski, dug into this latest crime as doggedly—and fruitlessly—as the rest. Two meandering trails of blood near the lakeshore, Merylo decided, marked the route taken by the Butcher and an accomplice. He held to this conviction even after other cops proved the blood came from a wounded dog. The discovery, nearly three months later, of the victim's lower torso, floating in the lake, shed no further light on her death.

And no other pieces of her body ever turned up.

The previous election's Democratic landslide had swept into office a new county coroner: small, pallid, mustached Dr. Samuel R. Gerber, who enjoyed spending time in the morgue and looked it. Gerber threw himself into the torso case, reviewing the evidence and preparing his own report. He chose not to speculate on the Lady of the Lake, who had died "too long ago" and left behind "too few details" to definitely fix her killer. But he firmly believed the rest died by the same hand.

"The possibility of a different operator having entered the series is slight," Gerber wrote. "It is particularly the peculiar dissection of the bodies which groups these seven cases together."

Like the torso clinic, Gerber believed the Butcher to be a big, strong man living near Kingsbury Run, killing in a "laboratory" nearby.

"He is a person of more than average intelligence," Gerber theorized, "with definite professional knowledge of anatomy but not necessarily a man of surgery. . . . In all probability he belongs to a higher social stratum than his victims, but can mingle with vagrants without arousing their suspicion."

The Butcher might be anyone from a medical student to a veterinarian, but was much more likely a doctor, "who performs the crime in the fury of a long drinking bout or derangement following the use of drugs."

Ness assured the city that catching this killer remained "a major priority." Behind the scenes, he asked friendly journalists to rein in their reporting of the killings, if only to bring an end to the worthless tips and dead-end leads pouring in whenever the Butcher made headlines. The new coroner, not shy of the limelight, bristled at Ness's effort to keep the case under wraps. Over the next few months and years, Gerber would use the torso case as a means of self-promotion.

"This has miffed the cops," Phil Porter wrote, "who feel somewhat properly that they have done a lot of hard, though fruitless work . . . and that the coroner was not intended by law to be a detective bureau."

The Associated Press, covering the latest murder, brought national attention to the "sex-mad, surgically skilled maniac" who'd beheaded at least eight people. The piece referred to "Eliot Ness . . . who helped send Al Capone to prison" as the man in charge of Cleveland's police—and, by extension, the unproductive hunt for the Butcher. Ness didn't need that kind of publicity, but the Democrats certainly did. One, in particular, seized on the case in hopes of embarrassing the Safety Director.

BRASH, REBELLIOUS MARTIN L. Sweeney, fifty-one—former mayoral candidate, current Cleveland-area congressman—had "been raising hell" in Ohio politics for years.

Once an outspoken supporter of Franklin Roosevelt, Sweeney disowned the president in 1936, signing on with the insurgent political movement of Father Charles Coughlin, the demagogic "Radio Priest" who would soon become the loudest voice for fascism and anti-Semitism in the United States.

By early 1937, Sweeney had more than earned the enmity of Cleveland's Democratic establishment. But he and the party bosses had a common enemy. "The biggest task facing this community," Sweeney announced that March, "is to defeat Harold H. Burton."

Ten days after the discovery of the latest torso victim, Sweeney appeared with his closest political ally, Sheriff Martin O'Donnell, at a testimonial dinner in their own honor. Red-faced, arms flailing, Sweeney launched into a tirade against Burton, Ness, and President Roosevelt before a large crowd of mostly African-American voters.

"The papers put Mayor Burton in, along with his alter-ego Eliot Ness, the great G-man . . . to clean up the city and give the papers page one stories," Sweeney declared. "But turn to page two and what do you see? Eleven unsolved torso murders in one year!"

Really, police knew of only five torso murders since the previous January, and eight in all. But this white lie to a black crowd mattered less to the *Plain Dealer* than the overall thrust of Sweeney's "gratuitous and shamefully out of order" attack.

"Sweeney adopts the underworld attitude precisely," the paper opined. "Every little crook in the city is saying, aloud or under his breath, why don't Burton and Ness go after the torso murderer or the bank robbers or the assailants of women, instead of spending so much time rooting grafters out of the police department?"

Sweeney—whose name once turned up in the phone records of a Cleveland Syndicate bootleg operation—kept hammering Burton and Ness for prosecuting "policemen who took $25 years ago" while Cleveland's Butcher stalked the streets.

"The built-up Mr. Ness has to go back 10 years to convict police officers," Sweeney said. "And on the evidence of whom? Convicted bootleggers. But I am not going to criticize this, except to ask what an odd procedure, when we have a Jack-the-Ripper in the city!"

MEANWHILE, NESS PURSUED another monstrous killer.

Cleveland had the second worst traffic death rate in the country—this past December, auto accidents had claimed nine lives between Christmas Eve and December 26.

Ness solicited the opinions of sixty prominent Clevelanders and traveled to other big cities to observe how they policed their streets. The *Press* took a page from the Chicago Crime Commission, declaring traffic fatalities "Public Enemy No. 1." On the day the second lady of Lake Erie washed ashore, Ness was out of town on traffic safety tours of Evanston and Milwaukee.

Ness didn't judge a traffic safety program by how many people were pulled over, how many tickets were issued, or how much in fines was collected. He wanted traffic cops to be seen, not hiding behind bushes or billboards, and to treat drivers with respect.

"I think the traffic division ought to have a particular kind of man," he explained, "one with courtesy, tact and personality." But the traffic detail had become "the Siberia of the police department," where inept or politically uncooperative officers got sent.

Rather than lowering standards for some officers, Ness raised qualifications for all, demanding at least a high school diploma—something even the New York Police Department didn't require. He had long wanted a police academy teaching cops forensic science and the rules of evidence while showing them how to better engage with people. So he sent Lieutenant Patrick Lenahan to the FBI's National Police Academy in Washington, D.C., to bring back what he learned.

After receiving a diploma from J. Edgar Hoover himself, Lenahan was placed in charge of the proposed police school. A call went out for "honest-to-goodness college professors, who can teach psychology, evidence, writing of police reports, criminology, fingerprinting, and so forth."

The academy's first class met on April 26 in a small former fire station in the Flats. The blue-uniformed students crammed into desks more suitable for high school students; Lenahan sported a professor's "natty tweeds" as he chalked out equations on the blackboard. Ness supervised from behind a lectern, gazing over the seated students with Mayor Burton in front, as the first two-week course in traffic enforcement and accident investigation began.

The initial graduates were assigned to a new Accident Prevention division as first responders on traffic calls. The city couldn't spare much money for the new squad, so Ness got the Studebaker company to loan them thirteen top-of-the-line President sedans, each painted bright yellow. This eye-catching paint job earned the sedans the nickname "Canary Cars."

"Of course, they can be seen at a distance," Ness said, "and invariably they have the same effect on a motorist that a motorcycle cop viewed at close hand would have—whether he is speeding or not, the car driver generally slows down."

Each Canary Car was a rolling laboratory, packed with photographic and technical equipment, patrolling twenty-four hours a day and speeding to every accident, giving first aid before trying to assess the collision's cause.

The goal was finding and correcting preventable causes of accidents—a new traffic light here, a trimmed hedge there. And by gathering statistics on each collision, no matter how small, the squad revealed previously hidden problems. Thanks to their efforts, Cleveland saw a sharp increase in traffic convictions.

The academy's curriculum would grow to cover every aspect of police work, with lectures by experts from colleges, hospitals, and the department itself on everything from fingerprinting and ballistics to proper care for the mentally ill. Students didn't remain deskbound—they stayed in shape with physical fitness training and tested their detective skills in a "murder room," solving the demise of a hapless dummy named Oscar.

Ness believed each cop should be an athlete, "a doctor of sorts," a crack shot, a "confessor," and "a human relations expert." He encouraged his officers to keep an open mind and a willingness to try new methods and ideas, never forgetting the public they served.

"Don't be badge conscious," he told one graduating class. "The normal reaction to assumption of authority is to feel superior to the man on the street. Remember that the minute you put on a police uniform you have much less liberty than before."

Ness gave rookies his personal phone number. "If anyone asks you for any money at any time, call me immediately," he said. "If you do get asked and don't call me, don't plan on being a police officer for very long."

THANKS TO ITS heavy industry, Cleveland had long been a stronghold for organized labor . . . and a land of opportunity for racketeers maintaining a cancerous presence within many craft unions.

Gangsters avoided the big factories owned by major corporations, where workers might honestly band together for protection against management. Instead, the hoods muscled in on smaller businesses, corralling independent workers into phony unions that only served to fix prices and extort payoffs. Such associations came to control various industries around town, from dry cleaning to barkeeping, but were especially prevalent in the building trades.

No one could erect or remodel any structure in Cleveland without greasing the palms of business agents who threatened walk-offs and vandalism. Even homeowners wanting to paint their own houses had to seek "certificates" from the local Painters' District Council or run the risk of their houses getting sprayed with stain.

This outright extortion all but paralyzed local builders, giving Cleveland a nationwide reputation as a bad place to do business. America's sixth largest city ranked only fifty-seventh for new construction, even in a housing shortage.

By targeting these racketeers, Ness wanted "not only to rehabilitate this city as a business investment site, but . . . to help the union man who has been misguided and who has had to sit back with his hands tied."

New York prosecutor Thomas Dewey had begun a similar crackdown in Manhattan, but corruption kept racketeers well insulated in other cities. J. Edgar Hoover's FBI had the resources for a nationwide cleanup but focused instead on suppressing the activities of leftists and communists within unions—enabling the mob's infiltration of the labor movement.

Decades of political persecution from police and government agents left labor deeply suspicious of law enforcement. In Depression-era battles with management, workers often faced violence and sabotage, inspiring some to respond with gangster-style strong-arm methods.

Early on, Ness had earned labor's enmity by placing Captain John Savage in charge of the police Vandal Squad, which dealt with strikes. A pro-labor paper branded Savage "a brutal, ignorant bully" who "thinks like a Brown Shirt." Even the *Plain Dealer* admitted he displayed "a definite yen for putting pickets in jail."

After the Cleveland Federation of Labor presented the Safety Director with twenty specific instances where Savage had shown anti-union bias, Ness decided to retain him anyway.

"If later evidence indicates that Savage has been unfair in his treatment of labor," Ness said, "at that time the handling of labor situations may be assigned to another officer. . . . But since his principal assignment is to investigate and suppress window smashings, bombings and other kinds of violence, the legitimate labor unions should have no objections."

The decision reflected Ness's lack of political savvy; he saw no problem with Savage's attitudes, so long as the captain got results.

Ness sought Savage's help in early 1937, after a homebuilder complained of extortion. Having put up with such treatment before, the builder finally lost his patience when Harry Barrington, business agent for a local Carpenters Union chapter, slugged him. Savage found several other contractors willing to testify that Barrington had extorted money under threat of strikes and property damage. In April 1937, a grand jury indicted Barrington on five counts of blackmail.

Labor leaders declared full confidence in Barrington's innocence—a poor decision, since he skipped bail and fled the city. Federal agents caught up with the "business agent" in California, where he promised to expose "every building and contracting racket in Cleveland" if sent home to stand trial. But back in Ohio, he changed his mind and pleaded guilty, possibly fearing what a trial might reveal.

Although embarrassing for organized labor, the Barrington affair pointed the way toward reform—like the Cadek and Harwood convictions had for the police department. But the unions still didn't trust Ness or his motives.

"There's more crime and vice in Cleveland than ever," a teamster complained not long after Barrington's indictment, "but Burton and Ness send all their police to picket lines." He suggested the Cleveland Federation of Labor adopt a new, election-year slogan: "Beat Burton; he's no good for the labor movement."

Since March, the Committee for Industrial Organization, recently split off from the American Federation of Labor, had sought union contracts with the nation's leading steel manufacturers. The companies known as "Little Steel"—including Republic Steel, Cleveland's single biggest employer—refused to recognize the CIO, and their intransigence sparked a general strike.

The standoff turned bloody on Memorial Day, when police opened fire on a crowd of unarmed pickets at Chicago's Republic Steel plant, killing ten—all shot in the back. The clash, which soon became known as "the Memorial Day Massacre," challenged Ness's image of a professional, supportive police force.

"A cop is a cop, that's all," a Chicago striker observed. "He's got no soul and no heart for a guy who works for a living."

Strikes at plants in Michigan, Pennsylvania, and Ohio soon spiraled into violence. The CIO and its Steel Workers Organizing Committee shut down four large plants in Cleveland, where workers in the knitting and textile industries were also on strike.

In a fraught and chaotic situation, Burton took no sides, desperate to avoid bloodshed. But a crisis developed in June, with Republic using an airfield leased from the city to fly supplies into plants barricaded by strikers. Tensions rose on the picket lines; one plane's tail was riddled with bullets. Burton had to decide whether to cancel Republic's permit, or let the company continue its airlifts.

The mayor visited the airfield on June 9. As his car pulled up, strikers mistook it for a company vehicle and tried to push it over, before someone shouted, "It's Mayor Burton." Then they hurled invective at Burton as he got out—"Dirty strikebreaker," "Company rat."

"I voted for you once," a striker spat, "but never again."

Ness rolled up in a police car to a chorus of boos.

Behind closed doors, Burton faced divided opinions. The city had no legal right to revoke Republic's permit, his law director advised. But Ness, taking a position that would have surprised his critics, insisted the company had to go. As always, he tried to find the source of the trouble; Republic Steel had turned the airfield into a provocation, making it a threat to public safety. The mayor agreed and chose not to extend their landing rights, forcing them to seek another airport.

Violence finally broke out on June 30—not at the steel plants, but at the Stone Knitting Mills. A jurisdictional dispute turned bloody when AFL members tried to force through a CIO picket line made up largely of women. The scuffle escalated into a melee as mounted police waded in, swinging nightsticks. Four unionists went to the hospital, including the CIO contingent's leader, who visited Ness and Burton in City Hall, eye bandaged, clothes bloodstained.

"I never in my life saw such police brutality," he said.

Burton ordered Ness to investigate police tactics during the fight.

Two days later, Republic ratcheted up the tension, informing Burton of plans to reopen the plants. Fearing another massacre, Burton and Sheriff O'Donnell temporarily forgot their political differences and called on the governor to send in the National Guard. Ness offered up seven hundred policemen.

O'Donnell took charge of the guardsmen and maintained a 1,500-yard "dangerous strike zone" around the plants. Republic reopened for business at 7 A.M. on July 6, and soldiers kept watch as strikebreakers filed past the picket lines. The violence Burton had feared failed to materialize.

At the factories, anyway.

ABOUT AN HOUR and a half before the plants reopened, two National Guardsmen spotted something white floating in the Cuyahoga—the lower part of a man's torso, cut in half, like several previous Butcher victims. More pieces turned up in the river that day and throughout the week—upper half of the torso, wrapped in newspapers and burlap; arms and legs, separated at the joints; but no head. Decapitation had once again caused death. Coroner Gerber noted the same skillful dissection as the other torso murders.

"The killer leaves his signature every time," Gerber remarked.

A new level of brutality marked the body of this latest, nameless victim. The Butcher had chopped off the head with "considerably more hacking than seen in the previous torso cases" and literally disemboweled the corpse, cutting open the abdomen to remove the viscera. He also took the heart.

Perhaps he needed one.

Press columnist Jack Raper, the rare Cleveland newsman who never liked the Safety Director, suggested Ness and Matowitz "persuade the National Guard to remain in town long enough to solve the torso murders."

• • •

WITH THE POWDER keg at Republic failing to ignite, Sheriff O'Donnell withdrew the soldiers less than a week after the plants reopened. On July 17, the day after the final guardsmen left, Burton sent letters of thanks to Ness, O'Donnell, and Matowitz for their service "during the recent emergency arising out of the Republic Steel strike." Ness turned his attention to his labor racketeering investigations.

But scab labor kept crossing the picket lines, and fights with strikers continued. On July 21, after O'Donnell rescinded an order capping the number of strikers allowed near the plant, the picket lines grew. Around three thousand people massed outside Corrigan-McKinney, Republic's biggest plant, and fought to block the strikebreakers from getting inside. Finally, on July 26, a car driven by a Republic loyalist crashed through the line, killing a striker and dragging the body along with it.

The pickets blamed the death on a policeman who'd told strikebreakers to "run over them" if they wouldn't break the line. Police claimed someone had thrown a brick through the car's window, making the driver lose control. Either way, the incident ignited the strikers. They began raining more bricks and stones down on Republic's cars. Another vehicle lost control and swerved into a picket.

Strike leaders did their best to control the scene, marching down the line shouting, "No more bricks! Keep these men in check." But it did nothing to quell the furor, and police wasted little time.

"Drive 'em back!" yelled the officer in charge, as mounted policemen galloped ahead.

A brick hit one rider, knocking him off his horse. He got right back in the saddle, blood flowing down his head, and swung his nightstick, sending at least one striker to the hospital. Other cops fired tear gas into the crowd, clearing a path to the plant.

The strikers regrouped at their headquarters, then marched

on City Hall. A thousand massed on the steps outside Ness's office window, waving a banner that declared: THE POLICE AND MILITIA CAN'T BREAK THIS STRIKE. When Ness stepped onto the balcony to survey the scene, the crowd saw him and booed.

Burton invited twenty strikers inside. They sat around a wide wooden table in his office—the mayor, like the union men, leaned in, bags under his eyes darker and heavier than normal. Ness sat back, stony-faced, with Chamberlin at his side.

The strikers asked Burton to shut down Corrigan-McKinney because the plant had brought in out-of-town strikebreakers to take their jobs. The mayor said he lacked such authority, although he wished Republic would employ local labor. Then the strikers accused John Savage of trying to convince pickets to give up and go back to work; Savage's son, it so happened, worked for Republic Steel.

"No police officer," Burton said, "has any authority to do that."

But even as the mayor tried to resolve the situation, the company prepared to escalate it. At eleven o'clock that night, roughly five hundred Republic loyalists armed with clubs stormed from the plant in a coordinated attack on the pickets. They wore white armbands to distinguish themselves from the union men and fanned out around the neighborhood, sending about a hundred strikers fleeing. Whenever a striker tried to wrest a club from his attacker, Republic's fighters laid into him.

The company men destroyed the union headquarters—turning over tables, smashing chairs, throwing a woman through a window. Mounted police rode about, breaking up fights here and there. But mostly they stayed out of combat—"looking the other way," the strikers said.

The next morning, Burton visited the wrecked headquarters as witnesses described what the "hired gangsters and company thugs" had done to their building. Although Republic insisted "outsiders" started the fight, the company police had indeed directed the assault.

Rather than fix responsibility for the riot, Ness focused on restoring order. He established five-hundred-yard "peace areas" around the entrances to Corrigan-McKinney, allowing no congregating near the plant. His order brought an end to the violence while clearing the way for Republic strikebreakers, effectively handing the company a victory.

A CIO official told Burton and Ness that the union would order its men to go back to work if Republic would promise to welcome returning strikers. On July 29, Burton took the idea before the mayors of several neighboring cities, and together they produced a "very fair" proposal to end the strike. But Republic refused to negotiate. Now that their plants could operate with nonunion labor, all they had to do was wait.

By the end of August, the strike had petered out. Little Steel would refuse to recognize the CIO until the early 1940s, when the federal government finally forced it to during World War II.

Local unionists would not soon forget their defeat . . . nor Ness's role in bringing it about.

24 PAGES   CLEVELAND, WEDNESDAY MORNING, SEPTEMBER 16, 1936   PRICE

LS TORSO KILLER NEW INSAN

Couzens Trails in Rep___an Ra

MAINE VOTE IS BAD NEWS TO NEW DEAL

Buel Says Election Shows Threat of Republican Victory in November.

ROOSEVELT JUST SMILES

Indicates Result Was About What He Expected.

BY WALKER S. BUEL,
Plain Dealer Bureau,
601 Albee Bldg.

WASHINGTON, Sept. 15.— Maine's election is very bad news for the New Deal and President Roosevelt.

It is a definite indication of a Republican trend, a definite threat of Republican victory in November, definite forerunner of a Republican Democratic membership in Congress, a definite indication of a Republican revival, especially in the primary revival.

No. 20 for Allen

Allen blazed his way back to the fifth inning, but was given credit for his twentieth victory yesterday as the Indians whipped Boston, 13 to 7. Hildebrand finished the game; Frankly held him in the sixth and sole homered. New York defeated Chicago, 7 to 1. Detroit trimmed Philadelphia, 4 to 3 and Washington took a double header from St. Louis, 12 to 7 and 6 to 1.

Weather stopped the National League.

(Details on Sport Page.)

WPA WORKERS TO BE EXPO GUESTS

Families, Also, to Attend Saturday as Honor to Garden Builders.

Today's Events.

United Rubber Workers Day.
United Hatters Festivities Day.
Royal Neighbors of America Day.
National Society of Patriots Day.
City Club Day.
Rocks Golf Day.
Garden Clubs of Michigan Day.

Attendance yesterday ......
Attendance to-of day ......
Days left—31

BUY YOUR OWN MEALS, NESS TELLS ROOKIES

Ten New Patrolmen Told Appointments Are Based on Own Merits.

"DON'T BE OBLIGATED"

Warns "You'll Get No Great Reward for Honesty."

Ten new patrolmen were sworn into office yesterday by Safety Director Eliot Ness in the rites at City Hall.

Youth, 16, Th___atens Shirley Tem

OUTLAW SITDOWN, PLEA IS UP TO URW

Strikes Hit Akron Plants as Rubber International Weighs Policy Issue.

Plain Dealer Bureau,
21-A Ohio Building,
AKRON, Sept. 15.

SHAKER EXTE TO RUN CARS

Shuttle Service Rd. Expected in 2 May Go to Rich

BY JAMES G. MOYN

Says Fight With Richman Nearly Sank Ocean Plane

NEW YORK, Sept. 15.—(AP)—The Daily News, in a copyrighted dispatch from a correspondent on the transoceanic flyer Harry Richman and Dick Merrill almost came with the flyers in Davenport.

Russell Lauer below the Lorain-Carnegie Bridge, indicating where he came across the bones that may have belonged to Rose Wallace.

Cleveland Public Library Photograph Collection

A Modern Dracula

June–December 1937

They rose like sentinels above the Flats: eight winged sandstone figures, each more than forty feet tall, watching over a bend in the Cuyahoga. These Art Deco Olympians seemed both ancient and modern—icons of physical perfection with bulging muscles and imposing stares, wearing the laurels of Roman gods. They stood back-to-back in pairs, one with a hay wagon clasped to his bare chest, another a stagecoach, another a motorcar. Each vehicle marked some step in the evolution of transportation, giving the figures their name: the "Guardians of Traffic."

Hewn from the pylons anchoring either end of the Lorain-Carnegie Bridge, which spanned the river with Terminal Tower as its backdrop, the Guardians embodied the city's former faith in progress.

The bridge had been conceived before the Depression, when Clevelanders could still celebrate the technology powering their prosperity; but by the time it opened in 1932, the Guardians seemed more like monuments to a future that would never come. While cars cruised three hundred feet above the river, another world sprawled below, amid the massive warehouses and barren patches of earth where the Butcher was thought to prowl.

Private detectives with the Nickel Plate Railroad, aiding police in their hunt for the killer, often heard of someone living down there. "All the bums used to tell us about him," one detective remembered. "They were all scared of him. He had a nest under the Lorain-Carnegie Bridge."

The investigators sometimes went looking for him, but they only ever found traces: a large footprint, disturbed earth, chicken feathers, and hundreds of pairs of women's shoes, which the invisible man seemed to collect.

"We used to stay down here and lay for him," the detective recalled. "I guess he'd watch us somewheres."

Fourteen-year-old Russell Lauer passed close to the mystery man's makeshift home late in the afternoon of Sunday, June 6. The skinny boy with thick dark hair had gone out to see a movie, only to be drawn to a crowd of people gathered at the river's edge. They'd stopped to watch the Coast Guard drag the depths of the Cuyahoga, searching for a corpse.

Had pieces of another dismembered victim turned up? No—a crewman on a tugboat had gone overboard the night before; his body remained missing.

Losing interest after about twenty minutes, Lauer decided to head home. He cut beneath the bridge through a field called Stone's Levee, dwarfed by the concrete abutments bearing the latticework of steel above. Trash and chunks of slag littered the uneven ground, but something caught Lauer's eye amid the rocks: a small mass near the base of a pylon. Only when Lauer saw a yellow glimmer did he know what he had found.

Gold teeth in a grinning human skull.

Soon, a brace of detectives—among them torso veterans James Hogan and Orley May—gathered under the Guardians' gaze to pick over what looked disturbingly like another victim of Cleveland's Butcher.

Covered in dirt beside the skull lay a tattered burlap bag, its neck tied shut with twine. To one detective, it looked as though the bag hadn't been buried, rather tossed here, left to slowly disappear amid discarded slag and trash. Wrapped within the rotting fabric, police found a collection of bones—the skeletal remains of a torso, without the limbs—and a foot-long chunk of decaying flesh.

A search of the area turned up two pieces of women's clothing: a tasseled woolen cap—once white, since stained by the elements—and the sleeve from a dress. Detectives also found what the *Plain Dealer* called "a tangled mass of black, hair-like material, of the sort stage wigs are made."

Perhaps the most promising clue, apart from the gold bridgework, was an undated scrap of newspaper inside the bag of bones. The text—a theater review—and the advertisements might help detectives pin down when the bag had been filled.

After photographing the scene, police brought their finds to the morgue, where Coroner Gerber examined the bones—"the complete vertebrae, ribs, shoulder blades, hips and skull," according to the *Plain Dealer*.

Finding no marks of trauma that might indicate a cause of death, Gerber remarked that the skeleton "could be a male" and confirmed it belonged to an adult but refrained from estimating the victim's age. A powdered substance permeating the bag proved to be lime, suggesting whoever disposed of the body took pains to make it decompose quickly.

Meanwhile, investigators searched theater bookings for the production, a Ziegfeld Follies–esque revue, mentioned in the newspaper scrap. Finding that the show had run at the Palace Theater in early June of the previous year, they were able to match the clipping with the June 5, 1936, *Plain Dealer*.

To Gerber's eye, the bones looked like they'd been rotting for a full year; he told reporters the burlap bag had been left beneath the bridge "probably within a few days of that date."

June 5 had been the very same day two boys found the head of the unidentified tattooed man in Kingsbury Run. If Gerber estimated correctly, both victims likely died around the same time.

The *Plain Dealer* rushed to list other ways in which this

discovery resembled the Butcher's previous crimes, beginning with the fact that Stone's Levee sat less than a mile from the pool where the bisected torso of another victim had floated into view the previous September.

"The deserted spot is similar to the places chosen for the disposal of six other bodies," the paper observed, "and the unburied skeleton corresponded to the way in which most bodies were left. . . . Lack of injury to the skull in the form of a bullet wound or fracture and dismembering of the body led to the theory that a knife had been the death instrument."

Though a proper autopsy had yet to be performed, the banner headline stretching across the front page of the next day's *Plain Dealer* left little room for doubt: FIND SKELETON, HUNT TORSO CASE LINK.

That same morning, Gerber made a more thorough review of the bones with pathologist Reuben Straus and an anatomist from Western Reserve Medical School, both of whom had taken part in the torso clinic the year before. Their examination determined that the skeleton belonged to an African-American woman roughly five feet in height, around a hundred pounds, and thirty to forty years old.

Straus took a closer look at the mass of hair found with the bones; the presence of rusted hairpins and some flesh told him this was no wig, but what remained of the woman's scalp.

Peering at the vertebrae through a microscope, the doctors saw what they described as "definite knife marks" and "evidence of hacking and cutting." This suggested the woman had been decapitated like the Butcher's other victims, though the remains were too decayed to determine whether her head had been cut off pre- or postmortem—or, indeed, to tell exactly what she had died of. Nor could the autopsy offer a more precise time of death than that suggested by the *Plain Dealer* fragment.

To Gerber, however, the arrival of another "expertly dissected" corpse could mean only one thing. Forgetting his earlier surmise that the bones belonged to a man, the coroner declared this petite black woman to be the Butcher's eighth victim. (He still didn't count the Lady of the Lake, which would have made this number nine.)

If true, this would mean that for the first time since the West Side victim found last July, the Butcher left police a head to identify. And while so far investigators had struggled to put names to rotting faces, the trio of gold teeth on the left side of the woman's upper jaw seemed almost as distinctive as fingerprints.

Still, Gerber told the *Plain Dealer* he doubted the bridgework would ever lead them to the woman's identity. Already detectives had searched missing persons files for women with similar teeth; the only possible match quickly proved a dead end. Nor had any performers from the stage show reviewed in the clipping disappeared while in town. A canvass of Cleveland dentists produced nothing but the opinion that whoever put the crowns in had done a "poor" job.

Then, later that month, a letter arrived pointing police toward a Cincinnati dentist who had inserted such bridgework into the mouth of one Rose Wallace. At first, detectives all but dismissed the tip; but Peter Merylo, never one to ignore a lead, took it upon himself to investigate.

His digging soon confirmed that a black woman by that name, forty years old with roughly the same build as the victim, had disappeared from the Roaring Third on August 21, 1936.

The more Merylo explored Rose Wallace's past, the more she came to resemble what little anyone knew of the other headless bodies. She had been a person of "ephemeral loyalties and peculiar friends," as one journalist put it; a photograph published in the *Press* captures a woman with a crooked smile and a wry glint in her eyes.

She had sometimes worked as a prostitute; the woman in charge of an East Side speakeasy said that Wallace "was hustling for her for about a year." Wallace shared more than a profession with Flo Polillo, the last named torso victim. According to one police informant, "the only man who had ever kept company with her" was an African American known as "One-Armed Willie."

The same person had lived with Polillo for a time; investigators already knew that he had quarreled with Polillo the day before she died. But they hadn't been able to implicate One-Armed Willie in Polillo's murder, and they couldn't link him to Wallace's death, either.

Nevertheless, Merylo kept finding connections between Wallace and Polillo, without ever proving that they had been acquainted. The women moved in the same circles and lived in the same part of town. Both patronized the same dive at East Nineteenth and Scovill, not far from where Wallace lived, and this may have been the spot where Polillo was last seen alive.

Although the final confirmed sighting of her occurred on January 24, 1936—and her autopsy suggested she died sometime that night—another, less reliable report placed her in a bar the following evening, fighting with an unidentified African-American man, before pieces of her body turned up the next morning.

Now, as Merylo began tracing Wallace's last known movements, he found the trail ran right through the very same tavern.

Wallace had been home washing clothes on the afternoon of August 21 when a female friend came by, saying a man wished to meet her at that bar. Without bothering to remove her laundry from the tub, Wallace went to see him, wearing a dress that resembled the sleeve later found under the Lorain-Carnegie Bridge.

Witnesses said Wallace eventually left the bar with someone called Bob, a dark-complected white man; whether this was the same person she had come to see remained unclear. They were said to be on their way to Cleveland's West Side for a party. Not long after, another witness spotted Wallace in a car carrying a trio of white men. There the trail ended, until Wallace's bones—or those of someone who looked much like her—turned up beneath the bridge.

These scraps of information, all seeming to point in the same general direction, gave Merylo the sense of being tantalizingly close to a solution. He latched on to the claim that Wallace had disappeared en route to the West Side. Edward Andrassy came from that part of town; so far only one victim, the naked and decapitated man discovered last July, had been left on that side of the river—and he alone appeared to have died where he was found.

This led Merylo to speculate "that the butcher . . . might be a West Side resident." Rather than operating out of a murder "laboratory" in Kingsbury Run, perhaps he brought his victims to the West Side, killed them there, and disposed of their bodies far from his home base.

That theory, however, rested on the assumption that these bones really did belong to Rose Wallace—and that was impossible to prove without her dentist, who had died fifteen years before.

The following spring, detectives showed a written description of the skeleton to a young man who said he was Wallace's son. Reading those reports convinced the man that he'd found his mother's remains, and Merylo passed this on to reporters as if it were a positive ID. The *Plain Dealer*, likely quoting the detective, claimed that "Merylo and many of his co-workers accept the identification as authentic."

Not quite. Gerber insisted Merylo had it wrong, maintaining this woman died in June—three months before Wallace disappeared.

Eliot Ness, always tight-lipped when it came to the Butcher, expressed his own skepticism, as did others involved in the investigation. In the *Plain Dealer* some months later, Phil Porter called the identification "probably no more than a good guess."

Still, the weight of the evidence—and the fact that Rose Wallace remains otherwise unaccounted for—suggests Merylo may have been right, though it doesn't prove this woman died under the Butcher's blade. The circumstances of Wallace's disappearance, especially the report of her riding off with three unidentified men, do not track with a killer who otherwise gave every indication of working alone in the vicinity of Kingsbury Run.

The condition of the remains made it impossible to determine whether she died by decapitation—the Butcher's primary signature—or whether her body had been dismembered for some other reason, such as disposal or to prevent identification.

Perhaps most crucially, later research would reveal that sexual serial killers rarely murder people of a race different from their own. Every other Butcher victim was white; this one alone was African American. While Merylo may have felt he almost had the complete picture, more likely he was collecting pieces from two very different puzzles.

AFTER THE BARRINGTON indictment, Ness turned to notorious racketeers Donald A. Campbell and John E. McGee. Bellicose and bespectacled, Painters' District Council president Campbell was also business agent for the Glaziers' Union. McGee—"an icicle of a man, with a cold blue eye"—ran the Laborer's District Council. Both had lengthy police records, and neither bothered hiding a mercenary attitude.

Earlier in the decade, McGee had organized a "Protective Barbers' Association," competing with Cleveland's legitimate barbers' union. Barbers who didn't join had their windows smashed; those who withdrew had their shops bombed.

After dodging court charges, McGee joined forces with Campbell and turned the Window Washers' Union into a protection racket; businessmen who didn't pay up found themselves needing new windows. The Glaziers' Union, also under their control, would install new panes only after victims signed on with the window washers.

The racket hinged on painters and glaziers joining a job just before its completion, when a delay would prove costly.

"These people had us just where they wanted us," recalled the Cleveland Arena's manager. "The Arena was ready for opening and a postponement would have cost us a lot of money. We did the only thing we could—we paid the $1,000 demanded."

Campbell and McGee's agents destroyed an estimated ten

thousand windows so fast the extortionists could barely keep up. A racketeer demanding a payoff to replace a broken window found the glass hadn't been smashed yet. He backed off, apologizing for being "two days behind—can't keep up with the 'business.'"

Again, workers were the racket's real victims. Campbell and McGee limited the union's membership to ninety, leaving it shorthanded. When a contractor needed more men, Campbell and McGee offered nonunion labor for a personal kickback. The membership resented this, but the racketeers kept them at bay, fixing union elections.

A few frustrated workers reached out to Ness, but he needed testimony from the businessmen and builders Campbell and McGee had bled, and few were willing to provide any. They were "hopping mad," Ness recalled, but fearful of racketeers and suspicious of police.

Yet the Safety Director, a reporter observed, "somehow or another always gets people to tell him things they hadn't meant to tell him," and he gradually won over the businessmen. The Barrington indictment proved this latest investigation wouldn't be "another whitewash." And Ness promised not to seek an indictment until he found at least thirty willing witnesses.

First to go on record were Vernon and Gordon Stouffer, Cleveland-born brothers who'd built their family's restaurant business into a multistate chain.

McGee had held up work at the Stouffers' new restaurant on Playhouse Square until Vernon made a $1,200 cash payoff. When the restaurant opened, the racketeers came back for more. Vernon refused, and Campbell and McGee responded with two smashed windows and a stench bomb. Furious, the brothers became Ness's key witnesses.

Not trusting his own cops, the Safety Director built a clandestine team of investigators—men in his own mold, clean-cut and closemouthed. These included Keith Wilson, Ness's former aide at the Alcohol Tax Unit; Richard Jones, fellow Sigma Alpha Epsilon fraternity brother; John F. Sawken, fifty-one-year-old former federal agent and private detective; and Thomas Clothey, a soft-spoken, thickset investigator who'd helped Ness's nephew, Wallace Jamie, clean up the St. Paul police.

"Clothey's admiration for Eliot Ness," a reporter observed, "amounts almost to hero worship."

Cleveland's civil service system didn't provide for recruiting undercover men, so Ness skirted the rules by hiring operatives as laborers, secretaries, or clerks. Businessmen—Cleveland's own Secret Six—provided funds. The team worked apart from Ness's City Hall office and answered only to him. They might be seen lunching with Ness in the Hotel Cleveland's Bronze Room, but few knew who they were. An out-of-town journalist saw them as successors to Chicago's Untouchables, christening them the "unknowns."

Through witnesses in Cleveland, Ness and his Unknowns discovered leads taking them to many major cities in the eastern United States. Ness made countless trips himself, supposedly on speaking engagements, research jaunts, or vacations. Sometimes contractors in other cities would meet with him directly. Occasionally he and the Unknowns arranged a seemingly chance meeting on a train or in an airplane.

One lead led to another, and another, as the list of willing witnesses grew. Ness tried to keep the probe a secret, but inevitably it began to leak out. This proved an unexpected blessing, bringing more people forward with tips and testimony almost daily.

This was a dangerous time to attack these rackets, with the labor situation boiling and the Ness name a dirty word among unionists. He received so many death threats he had to take on a bodyguard. Once, as he cruised down Memorial Shoreway between the city and his suburban home, someone took a shot at him.

Nonetheless, Ness usually remained unarmed. He would often wear an empty shoulder holster to give the appearance otherwise, leaving his Smith & Wesson .38 revolver in the bottom drawer of his office filing cabinet.

One day that October, "a small explosion" echoed through City

Hall. Three minutes later, someone burst into Ness's office, shouting about "a wild man loose with a gun on the third floor."

Ness ordered a lockdown—stopping every elevator, posting guards at every entrance. Then he and Robert Chamberlin grabbed guns and tear gas canisters and ran upstairs, with several sweating cops struggling to keep up. When they reached the third floor, they found an expended firecracker.

Ness made a point of appearing unafraid. He'd lived through worse, working undercover in Chicago Heights—where he'd arrested an armed gunman apparently sent to kill him—and the buzz of excitement always seemed to tamp down his anxieties.

But the harassment and stress ate away at Edna. She told one friend she couldn't take it much longer—that she would rather leave Eliot than let her fear get in the way of his work. But she didn't share those feelings with her husband, keeping a brave face around him.

BY EARLY FALL, Ness had enough testimony to take before a grand jury. Burton asked him to wait until after the election, to keep the case out of politics. But local labor leaders knew enough to fear "where the ax will fall next," so they redoubled their efforts to beat Burton anyway.

Ness, as usual, took little interest in the mayoral campaign, but did attend "his first political rally" on September 17. Burton made sure to praise the Safety Director in his stump speech, winning "thunderous applause" from the crowd. Ness displayed "obvious uneasiness," as a columnist described it, delighting reporters covering the event.

The Democrats chose Cuyahoga County engineer John O. McWilliams as their candidate. He faced an uphill battle, as Burton enjoyed wide bipartisan support. The Democrat went on the attack, calling the mayor everything from plutocrat to Nazi sympathizer. Of the Republic Steel strike, McWilliams claimed Burton had "sided with big business to persecute and oppress the common man."

Burton fought back, in his patient and lawyerly way, contending Cleveland had made too much progress for a change of leadership. His opponent reserved his most florid and persistent attacks for Ness. The press, McWilliams said, covered up crime news to create "the myth of the super-sleuth, the great detective who is responsible for the alleged perfection of the Police Department."

McWilliams also cast the shadow of Cleveland's Butcher over the campaign. At a public forum, he presented Burton with a written list of questions that included: "How was it possible during your administration for the torso murderer to continue the most horrible series of crimes ever committed in any city under any administration?"

A forum attendee asked if McWilliams knew of "any particular masterminds" who might succeed where Burton and Ness had so far failed.

"I don't want to be a bit personal," McWilliams said, dodging the question, "but I have the right to appoint you."

The election divided the police department. Most younger cops, hired by Ness, lined up behind Burton. But the old guard, fearing Ness's reforms, supported McWilliams. The latter faction's leader, Andrew Hagan, a former deputy police inspector who'd recently resigned, embodied the old-style politicking Ness meant to purge. Hagan was the natural candidate for Ness's replacement under McWilliams.

On October 11, Hagan released a report whose cherry-picked statistics and anecdotal evidence accused Burton and Ness of turning Cleveland into a "carnival of crime." The *Plain Dealer* noted, however, that "an increase in arrests does not necessarily mean there is more crime. It may well mean that there is less, and that more crooks are really being caught than there were in the days when Andrew Hagan had a hand in the catching."

McWilliams embraced Hagan's figures, as did Congressman Martin Sweeney. "The Hagan report answers Ness," Sweeney told fellow Democrats. "It's the paramount issue with which to rip off Burton's mask."

The party chairman interrupted him. "Isn't it true," he asked, "that [Ness] was a prohibition agent and not a G-man?"

"Yes," Sweeney said. "He was a prohibition agent, and he never caught Capone. His only claim to fame is that in Chicago he and his squad happened to run into a brewery where some old man was tending a still. They found out later that Capone had an interest in it."

The constant if specious criticism drew Ness into a campaign he'd hoped to avoid. A week after Hagan shared his report, Ness released his own, showing a 27 percent drop in crime during Burton's tenure—a sharp decline, the *News* observed, from "when Hagan . . . was considered the unofficial police chief."

Ness insisted his report had nothing to do with politics, but on October 25, he gave a radio talk discrediting Hagan's attacks.

"Note this fact," Ness said, "that during the entire period in which he alleges crime was riding rampant over the city, Andy Hagan made just two arrests, that of a drunk and that of a suspected gambler. The gambler was later released for lack of evidence."

But Hagan didn't let up. In a West Side stump speech, he again invoked the Butcher—"10 headless dead are crying out for vengeance"—adding, "Who will be the next victim of this modern Dracula?" Ness's reforms had failed to keep the city safe, Hagan argued, citing the Butcher as proof.

"I charge that if the police department were allowed to run itself instead of being meddled with by theorists," Hagan declared, "it would solve this crime and reduce the number of traffic accidents."

The Democrats had made a serious miscalculation. In targeting Ness, they allowed Burton to frame the campaign around "one simple, outstanding, important issue"—honesty versus graft. In a radio talk, Burton alluded to the investigation of Campbell and McGee, asking his audience to support the effort with votes.

"I am asking the public not to let Eliot Ness down," he said.

That same day, two Mayfield Road mobsters proved Burton's

point by calling a meeting of several hundred gamblers. "We've got to get rid of Ness," the gangsters reportedly said. "That's why we've got to elect McWilliams."

Meanwhile, Burton's supporters urged voters to uphold Ness's work by reelecting the mayor. A "Women's Committee of the Good Government League"—a thousand citizens strong, according to the *Call & Post*, "represent[ing] all political parties and all nationality groups"—went house-to-house, drumming up support for the mayor.

An African-American member of the group declared, "It is essential that all Cleveland women cast a vote of confidence in Mayor Burton and help keep Safety Director Eliot Ness on the job."

On Election Day, Burton trounced McWilliams by more than thirty-four thousand votes—another record-breaking margin of victory. In Democratic circles, Sweeney took much of the blame, having played major roles in getting McWilliams nominated "and in dictating campaign strategy," according to the *Plain Dealer*, "particularly the attack on Safety Director Eliot Ness."

Burton's reelection, the press said, had given Ness the "go" to complete his labor racket probe.

But first Ness took a rare day off, driving with Chamberlin to the University of Michigan in Ann Arbor. On Saturday, November 6, the two watched their respective alma maters' football teams at Michigan Stadium. The University of Chicago enjoyed a lead until the final minute, when Chamberlin's Wolverines came back to win 13–12. A painful defeat, forgotten that night, when Eliot's brother, Charles, called—their mother had died of a heart attack in the southern Chicago suburb of Roseland.

Seventy-three-year-old Emma Ness had been living with her daughter Effie, who worked as a teacher. A *Press* reporter, earlier that year, found them reluctant to speak of Ness's accomplishments.

Still, the reporter could tell that Emma's youngest son had not disappointed her.

"She doesn't say so," the *Press* observed, "but it's evident that she expected Eliot to do outstanding things."

NESS RETURNED TO Roseland and joined his siblings at Oak Woods Cemetery, where their mother was laid to rest alongside her husband. As with his father's death, Eliot seemed to bury his grief by getting back to work. In mid-November, as he put the finishing touches on his racketeering case, Campbell and McGee stormed into his City Hall office, intent on intimidation.

As Campbell described the meeting, mild-mannered Ness tried to avoid a confrontation; but McGee had other ideas.

"You don't like me," McGee said, "and I don't like you." Referring to Ness's secretary, he went on: "You don't need your girl because I did not come here to confess. I came to say you . . . and the Chamber of Commerce are trying to ruin the labor movement. You are only bluffing about me. You do not have a thing."

"How do you know," Ness asked, "that I have nothing on you?"

"I live my own life," McGee shot back, "and know what I do. Go ahead and do your worst."

The next day, Ness delivered to the county prosecutor's office more than one hundred pages of testimony from roughly sixty witnesses. With Frank Cullitan laid up by a car accident, chief assistant Charles McNamee had a lengthy conference with Ness, after which McNamee called a special grand jury.

Ness finally broke his silence, telling the *Plain Dealer* his investigation had "revealed a situation which was so much worse than I had anticipated that its ramifications left me aghast." He would not attack the labor movement. He only hoped to do for local unions what he had done for the police—purge them of criminals.

"I am against racketeers in labor," Ness said. "I am against racketeers in the Police Department. I am against racketeers."

But at a meeting of the Cleveland Federation of Labor, Campbell insisted "the only thing of which I am guilty is being a good union representative," labeling the case police persecution.

"Bring on your investigations," he said, "bring on your indictments. . . . Let them do their damnedest."

Some unionists echoed Campbell's cries of "persecution," but many labor leaders chose not to come to his defense or McGee's. They remembered Harry Barrington and the police corruption cases, and knew—as did the whole town—that Ness wouldn't seek an indictment unless he really had something.

The grand jury heard testimony for a full month. Ness took extreme precautions, protecting the businessmen who came in to testify. The grand jury issued no subpoenas to help keep witnesses' names secret, and Ness kept them under heavy guard throughout their time in the city.

Despite his personal distaste for guns, he began packing a weapon and rode about town with a sawed-off shotgun in his car. He moved into a downtown hotel suite, never went anywhere alone, and bundled Edna out of town for her own protection.

As Ness pressed on, more and more witnesses came forward. The CIO, once poised as Ness's antagonist, now endorsed his war on rackets; so did the United Auto Workers in Detroit. Letters and telegrams flooded in, many from grateful union workers.

On November 27, forty members of the local builders' union ran McGee and "his henchmen" out of their headquarters and staged a sit-in to "overthrow this dictatorship" and elect a new leader.

"Toward noon several hundred men, their mortar-spattered shoes eloquent of their trade, gathered about the building," reported the *Chicago Daily News.* "There was a polyglot babble of wrongs never righted, of meetings never called, of elections never held, of accounts never rendered.

"There was a tall Scot with a burr, dozens of Irish from dozens of counties with dozens of varieties of the brogue, there were Swedes, Italians, Negroes and Poles, raising their voices in protest against the union leaders."

When informed of the revolt, Ness "looked pleased, but said nothing," according to a reporter. He told the press he'd had nothing to do with the incident and denied giving the rebels a plan of attack.

The city's more experienced newsmen, who'd come to know the Safety Director, just shook their heads. Surely, they thought, it was no "accident" that two of Ness's favorite reporters—Clayton Fritchey of the *Cleveland Press* and Clem Lane of the *Chicago Daily News*—were the only newsmen at the scene. . . .

ON DECEMBER 20, after ninety-seven witnesses had told of a hundred incidents of extortion, the grand jury indicted Campbell, McGee, and two associates, Mose Donley and James McDonnell. Charges focused narrowly on the window-smashing racket, though the testimony turned up many other leads.

Ness promised to keep at it through the holidays, telling the *News* that "our investigation is not through yet."

The indictments put Ness in the headlines more than anything he'd done since Capone days. Newspapers nationwide used his investigation as an example of what might be accomplished in other cities. But not everyone cheered Ness's work.

"Director Ness ought to devote his time to solving the Kingsbury Run murders . . . and leave union leaders like Campbell, Donley, McGee and McDonnell alone," a union supporter wrote to the *News*.

An abrupt decline in the traffic death rate gave Ness further reason to celebrate the holiday season. His department had recently begun a campaign urging drivers and pedestrians to stay safe. As posters and billboards went up, traffic fatalities went down.

But with New Year's Eve looming ahead, Ness launched a special effort to save lives on a potentially deadly night. In the *Plain Dealer*, he warned Clevelanders not to drink and drive, but to rely on taxis or designated drivers if they chose to indulge.

That night, Ness commandeered every available city car—more than three hundred vehicles—and sent policemen out with orders to "prevent accidents." The officers waited outside hotels and big parties, stopping every driver to make sure he or she was sober. They pulled over every car seen speeding or weaving and arrested more than 160 people by the time the sun came up.

Cleveland saw no traffic deaths on New Year's Eve or New Year's Day for the first time since the arrival of the automobile. The "Whoopee Squads," as Ness called them, proved so effective the practice extended to every weekend. Cleveland's traffic death rate continued to decline in the New Year.

S TORSO KILLER NEW INSAN

ouzens Trails in Rep___an Ra

MAINE VOTE IS BAD NEWS TO NEW DEAL

el Says Election Shows Threat of Republican Victory in November.

OSEVELT JUST SMILES

ndicates Result Was About What He Expected.

BY WALKER S. BUEL
Plain Dealer Bureau.
811 Albee Bldg.
WASHINGTON, Sept. 15. ___tion's election is very bad news for the New Deal and President ___evelt.

___rs a definite indication of a Re-___ican trend, a definite threat of ___blican victory in November, ___ance functioning of a coming ___ocratic membership in Con___a definite indication of a Re-___a definite indication of a Re-___n revival, especially in the ___

___it not for longstanding for ___ in this campaign, the Maine ___ might be regarded as a total ___ New Deal hopes for the re-___on of President Roosevelt.

___Factory cases, staring practical ___ers and western combination ___ may re-elect Roosevelt in ___, if anything the east can do ___ yes really knows the po-___ effect of relief and benefit ___ throughout the agricultural

No. 20 for Allen

Allen injured his back in the fifth inning, but was given credit for his twentieth vic-tory yester-day as the Indians out-hiped Bos-ton, 15 to 3. ___ Indfenum finished the game. Tommy ___ hit his 38th and 40th homers. New York defeated Chicago, 7 to 1; De-troit trimmed Philadelphia, 8 to 5, and Washington took a double header from St. Louis, 15 to 7 and 6 to 2.
Weather stopped the Na-tional League.
(Details on Sport Pages)

WPA WORKERS TO BE EXPO GUESTS

Families, Also, to Attend Saturday as Honor to Garden Builders.

Today's Events.

United Rubber Workers Day.
United States Founders Day.
Royal Neighbors of America Day.
National Society of Painters Day.
City Club Day.
Horticultural Day.
Garden Club of Michigan Day.

Attendance yesterday 36,000
Attendance for 95 days 2,593,448
Days left—22.

The WPA will have its day at the Great Lakes Exposition.

Some of the expo workers thought that, since everybody was having his day at the big show, a week to cheer ingratitude to began the WPA, some of whom 31,500 laborers built the Rockefeller Horticultural Garden on the grounds.

So the boys who started the shovels and the boys who swung the picks have been invited to attend the exposition Saturday. They will also count themselves as their own WPA hosts.

They will have the whole exposi-tion a living union Acknowegments have been made with equation encouragement to tell them they have as many honors as they can afford.

"Such a celebration has been in ___ for weeks because numerous employes have said they wanted to see the WPA their gardens," Joseph M. Alexander, WPA district director, says. "The gardens are one of our first projects."

The invitations, which include members of the workers' families, will be in the form of identification cards.

(Continued on Page 8, Column 3)

BUY YOUR OWN MEALS. NESS TELLS ROOKIES

Ten New Patrolmen Told Appointments Are Based on Own Merits.

"DON'T BE OBLIGATED"

Warns "You'll Get No Great Reward for Honesty."

Ten new patrolmen were sworn into office yesterday by safety Di-rector Eliot Ness in his office at City Hall with the revolutionary admoni-tion that patrolmen are expected to pay for their own meals.

"You have been appointed on your own merits and because you stand at the top of the civil service list and for no other reason," Ness told the recruits. "If anyone made claims to you that he was responsible for your appointment, pay no attention.

"Your advancement is up to you.

"You are expected to be honest and to know that you will get no great rewards for being honest. Don't be obligated to anyone, even in small things.

"When you cash into a restau-rant for a meal, pay for it. When you get any questionable commodity useful to you, pay for it. If people have been accustomed to giving you things for nothing prior to your be-coming a policeman, I suppose it is all right for you to continue to ac-cept those things.

"However, if people who have never gave you anything free before can want to give you something without charge, you can conclude that they are buying your badge and your uniform."

In addition to appointing the ten new policemen, Ness promoted Sergt. Augustus F. P. Foley to a lieute-nancy and Patrolmen Herbert Rodel and William M. Miller to sergeancies.

The recruits were:
ELDEN A. FABRECHER, 5361 Thorpe Avenue N. E.
ADELBERT O. O'HARA, 5031 Storrow Avenue S. E.
EDWARD PRICKE, 16, 2605 Acton Road N. E.
RALPH F. HAMLEY, 2517 W. 10th Road N. W.
FRANK J. CADEN, JR., 1275 E. 138th Street.
ROY C. FINCHECK, 3527 Town Av-enue N. W.
RICHARD D. BECKER, 3931 W. 125th Street.
CLARENCE O. TROXEL, 7531 Park Av-enue N. E.
JOHN B. BILSKY, 3601 East Boule-vard S. E.
ELMER J. KLINK, 3205 above address N. E.

Caden, the nephew of former Capt. Lewis J. Caden, was appointed to the department a month ago by John H. Flynn, executive assistant to Ness. His appointment was re-voked at that time by Ness because Flynn had skipped the candidates at the top of the list.

Youth, 16, T____atens Shirley Tem_

OUTLAW SITDOWN, PLEA IS UP TO URW

Strikes Hit Akron Plants as Rubber International Weighs Policy Issue.

Plain Dealer Bureau,
312 Ohio Building,
AKRON, O., Sept. 15.

The issue of the sitdown strike as right loomed as the most important question before the United Rubber Workers of America as their first international convention, in session here.

Resolutions before the convention include one asking that the un-authorized sitdown be outlawed and another that calls the sitdown "one of the most powerful weapons of organized labor" and asks its in-corporation into URW policy.

This last one would put one of the sitdown into the hands of the ex-ecutive council to apply "when justified."

Adolph Germer, Columbus, for In-dustrial Organization organizer, ad-dressed the delegates late today, say-ing he had paid some from a meeting with a group of about sixteen men who wanted to strike and to all, he said, what the URW would do about sitdowns.

"Direct Violation," Is Ward.

"I told them that sitdowns were a direct violation of your policies and past principles," Germer said.
Germer, who claims in surveying the

Associated Press Wirephoto.
Frank Edward Stephens, six-teen-year-old Atlanta boy, arrest-ed in Atlanta yesterday and charged with sending an extor-tion letter to the mother of Shirley Temple, child film star, is shown between two federal agents as he was moved from the Atlanta police station to the Federal Building.

ATLANTA, Ga., Sept. 15.—A mild-mannered youth who told an arrest-ing of his 16 years in a retroac-school salary and federal authori-ties today of grabbing a $5,000 ex-tortion letter to the parents of Shirley Temple, child film star.

Another writers overtook boy, Ster-ling W. Powell, in whose hand of flood in Great Natl. in a charge of attempting to extort $6,000 from the child star last May. He will be tried next year.

The youth caught today, booked as Frank Edward Stephens, was ar-rested by Federal Bureau Investiga-tion operatives and released on his own recognizance after a hearing before United States Commissioner U. S. Griffith.

Stephens, taken into custody at a restaurant where he worked per-diem, signed his own bond of $500. The complainant said it would seal pending investigation at the boy's story that he is an innocent from the Atlanta Boys' Industrial School at Birmingham.

Officials of the Atlanta institu-tion said available records did not on the above group.

Stephens, taken into custody at ___ and said:

"Mrs. Temple

SHAKER EXTEN TO RUN CARS S

Shuttle Service to Rd. Expected in 2 W__ May Go to Richmo

BY JAMES S. MONVERN
First extension of rapid transit in Shaker Heights completed in two weeks, an ers will be started shortly.

What has been termed track east of Warrensville lead on the Shaker Boule__ is to be started an far as ___ fixed. Work on existing p___ stringing trolley wires will them out. For the pre___ will be a single-track exten___ There is a step to up a ___ ahility past the extension ___ another mile to Richmond R__ the near future, with the ex___ trackage to Rockhall Road ___ ready for next spring. ___ bers of the Cleveland Inter___ railway, which owns and op___ the line, last night denied the any suggestion of extension ___ the East

It is intended to operate a service between Green R___ Shaker Square N. 22, in the which the Shaker sch___ heavily served. At the Pr___ engine will transfer to the the N. Warrensville line for half-hour service. The C___ is undecided doing to ext___ lines to

Carries Hint
___ese U. S. Vote.

___FAY (C. HARRY)
___ington, as the above address ___ national Almond, Sec.
LANTA, Me., Sept. 16.—Maine ___ had back into the Republican ___ with plurality of the ___ sufficient to give the "re___" "national" stage the turn ___ prophesy.

___fails, when fully surveyed, ___ confirm two major possibi-___ the certainly shown by the ___ here some of the surest in ___

___ that the election in Novem-___ be one of the closest in ___ history.

___ it will be seen that ___ our election in the east's ___ Crown the urban industrial ___ supporting President ___ and the small towns and ___ tions, backing Gov. Lan-

___ception, the still transi-___ rolled up huge majorities ___ ocratic candidates, but ___ more tenaciously con-___ Republican strength, in ___ villages from the agri-___ ictions, greater both in

Says Fight With Richman Nearly Sank Ocean Plane

NEW YORK, Sept. 15—(AP)—The Daily News is a copyrighted dis-patch from a brief correspondent at Seagrave Harbor, Newfoundland, says a quarrel over the Atlantic be-tween the transoceanic flyers Harry Richman and Dick Merrill "almost ended with the flyers in Dinah's ocean locker."

Merrill and Richman landed in that ocean village yesterday after a return flight from England.
In the course of their dispute, says

the incidents. It's his flight—his plane. All my arguments for en-forced precaution were thrown aside." An abridgeon approached during the conversation, he and Merrill before to appalling directions the pas-

Newspaper Plane Damaged.

ST. JOHN'S, Newfoundland, Sept. 15.—(AP).—A newspaper plane leased by the New York Daily News was slightly damaged tonight when

Ness out on the town with his wife, Edna.

Cleveland Press Collection, Cleveland State University

Don Campbell (right) and John McGee in 1934, at the peak of their power.

Cleveland Public Library Photograph Collection

TEN

Who Will Be Next?

February–May 1938

Ness's plan to drive the rest of the racketeers out of Cleveland hinged largely on the convictions of Campbell and McGee.

Ohio had no set laws against labor racketeering—only decades later would any state have the legal machinery to prosecute such crimes. The case against Campbell and McGee depended on a creative reading of blackmail statutes and would set a precedent.

The defendants arrived in court on Valentine's Day, seemingly confident as jury selection began. McGee winked at courtroom reporters when the first few prospective jurors admitted membership in the American Federation of Labor. Of the men and women selected, one-third either belonged to a union or were married to someone who did. The defense appealed to them as workers, insisting that "labor is on trial in this case," but the prosecution consistently denied it.

Meanwhile, the defense couldn't hide how nervous the Safety Director made them, Campbell's and McGee's eyes following Ness when he first entered the courtroom.

On February 17, the prosecution called Vernon Stouffer, the restaurant magnate who testified to Campbell's pay-off demands and subsequent vandalism. McGee chewed gum, often smiling, eyes roving the ceiling while Campbell took notes.

After Stouffer's testimony, McGee's attorney asked Judge Alva R. Corlett for a mistrial. Ness, he said, was "impressing" the jurors with his presence, and should not be allowed to sit at the trial table with prosecutors. Corlett refused, saying he hoped the jury was "no more impressed by Eliot Ness than anyone else in this courtroom."

That got such a laugh, the judge ejected a dozen or so spectators.

Over the coming days, a parade of witnesses told of shakedowns, bribes, and fixed labor contracts. The defense opened its case on February 25, presenting nine union officials who denied Campbell's involvement in the racket. McGee testified three days later, claiming an income of just $700 during the three-year window-smashing period.

McGee's attorney asked, "From this you had to support your wife and children?"

"Yes," the defendant replied.

Prosecutor Charles McNamee subjected McGee and Campbell to withering cross-examination, but both admitted no wrongdoing. After the defense rested on March 4, the prosecution produced more witnesses refuting Campbell's and McGee's claims.

The defense's closing statement attacked the state's case by smearing the man who'd built it.

"Who is Ness?" McGee's attorney asked. "He's not a lawyer. He's the head of the Police Department. He has tremendous power, a big force of secret police working for him. He came here two or three years ago; he's a politician."

McNamee objected—not even Ness's worst enemies could call him "a politician" with a straight face.

McGee's attorney agreed to replace "politician" with "officeholder." But, he continued, "I never heard of him before he came here. For all I know he may be gone next year." He added, with unintentional irony, "Ness is no more interested in a clean city than we are."

In his closing statement, McNamee hinted at Ness's past accomplishments, referring to Campbell as "the Al Capone of the glass industry" and McGee as "his companion in venal extortion."

McNamee insisted: "These are the men we fight, not labor itself. When they tell you we fight labor, I tell you they lie. This is the first battle in a war on extortionists, and we are enlisted for the duration. Thousands in this city are awaiting your word that the law stands supreme."

The next morning, rumors swirled of a hung jury—that a single holdout was refusing to convict. When the jurors filed back into court at 10:30 A.M., Campbell and McGee wore satisfied smiles. But their faces drained of color after the guilty verdict.

Judge Corlett sentenced them to terms of one to five years in the state penitentiary, and ordered them shipped off to jail that afternoon.

"In all my twenty-five years on the bench," Corlett said, "I've never seen anything like this trial. The defendants attempted to influence the jury, they got husbands and other relatives of the jurors to come into the courtroom and talk with them. These men are dangerous to the community, and there is every reason to fear organized reprisal on the community if they are left at large."

After the gavel fell, Ness approached the bench to thank Corlett.

The conviction made headlines from Chicago to Los Angeles, with Ness written up in *Newsweek* and *Time*.

"From the first day that you joined us," Burton wrote his Safety Director, "you have in a quiet and modest way led the attack on this evil. The conviction of Campbell and McGee marks a major victory in the battle and I believe marks the turning point in our campaign to drive out the rackets."

Ness called the conviction, "Just the first battle in our war on labor racketeering." Then he put his work on hold to take his wife on vacation the next day, March 9, for two weeks in Florida.

• • •

"**THEY ARE DRIVING** down, to an unrevealed destination, for a sun and a swim and a get-acquainted trip," reported the *News*. "Mrs. N. says sorta sadly she spends a lot of evenings alone when the safety director is on a special job."

In this, possibly her only on-the-record comment, Edna hinted at the real reason for the trip: the Nesses' marriage was in trouble.

They had been growing apart at least since Ness's transfer to Cincinnati in 1934, their first extended period of living apart. Once they'd settled in Cleveland, Eliot's sixteen- and twenty-hour workdays often left Edna alone in their tiny cottage, far removed from the city, feeling isolated and abandoned.

She'd always been quiet and something of a homebody, never taking to the social whirl accompanying Eliot's job. Her husband seemed to care more about his career than their marriage, as his actions proved—the death threats he seemed to brush off, the dangerous leads he went off chasing. The Campbell and McGee case, his latest triumph, would lead only to more of the same.

A long time ago, back in Chicago, she'd been part of his thrilling work life. Now that she wasn't, she could no longer stay with him.

On March 28, Ness came back to Cleveland with a frightful sunburn, freckles popping like chicken pox.

"Guess I'm just not the type that tans," he told his colleagues.

His good humor hid the fact that he'd returned without a wife. Edna remained in Florida, where the law allowed people to file for divorce after ninety days' residence.

Ness considered resigning before the divorce went public. But Edna agreed to make regular visits to Cleveland that spring and summer, to help him keep up appearances. In May, a photographer caught them among high society types at the opening of a new theater. In June, the *News* reported them at Municipal

Stadium with seventy thousand others, watching the Cleveland Indians take on the New York Yankees. And in July, the *Press*'s gossip columnist spotted the Nesses dancing in the Vogue Room.

But any hopes of rescuing the marriage didn't survive the fall. The couple divorced in early 1939.

Edna kept her ex-husband's name but never spoke to him again. She returned to Chicago, became a typist, and retreated into quiet obscurity. In the mid-1970s, she moved to a Miami retirement home, taking pains to hide her identity, filling her days with newspapers and television. Edna died, at age eighty-eight, in November 1994. She never remarried, left no family, and received no funeral.

"She had been alone for many years," said her closest friend at the time. "Her greatest wish was not to be known."

AS HIS MARRIAGE crumbled, Ness's campaign to clean up the police department suffered its first major setback. After Michael Harwood's conviction, Ness worked with the county prosecutor's office to convict four other policemen indicted for corruption. But as the accused officers descended in rank, the amounts of their alleged bribes began to dwindle, making it harder to win.

By the time Patrolman Gaylord Stotts—the first low-ranking officer to stand trial—arrived in court in May 1938, the bribes in question seemed paltry, five or ten dollars at a time a decade or more ago. And unlike Harwood, Stotts had left the force a poor man.

Neil McGill, assistant prosecutor on the case, warned Ness against going forward, knowing the jury would sympathize. The Safety Director insisted Stotts be held accountable for his actions.

"We will let the jury have the facts," Ness said.

They did, but the twelve acquitted Stotts anyway, handing Ness his first defeat in a Cleveland courtroom.

"There was no question but that he was guilty," Ness recalled. "So what happened? Well, he walked into court with his wife and nine children arranged like a stepladder. Not only that, but his wife was pregnant. Everybody cried. He was acquitted.

"The thing that really sets me is that I'll swear they weren't even all his kids."

Two more officers, both low-ranking patrolmen like Stotts, had yet to be tried. But McGill dropped the charges seven months after Stotts's acquittal, on Christmas Eve. The pair immediately asked for reinstatement and two years' back pay, but Ness refused. The spirit of the season failed to move him.

"There may be departmental charges against them," he told the *Plain Dealer* on Christmas Day. "We cannot say definitely just yet."

Still, the graft cases had done their part to advance Ness's plan for reform. By mid-1938, his efforts to retrain officers on the force and attract a new breed of recruit had transformed the department. The *Plain Dealer* celebrated these developments in February, saying Ness had replaced the "flatfooted dimwit" of years past with "snappy, alert, studious," and "athletic" cops, "eager and progressive in habits."

The biggest problem remained a crippling lack of manpower. While New York employed more than eighteen thousand cops, Cleveland—with almost one million people—had fewer than fifteen hundred. No precinct felt this more sharply than Cleveland's "Roaring Third," the high-crime area east of downtown.

"We could use fifty more men in this station alone," the captain of that precinct told the *Plain Dealer*. "We can't even make a dent in things. But as badly as we need men, I sometimes think we need equipment more."

The Third had just two four-year-old squad cars—upholstery torn, one windshield cracked—and a fourteen-year-old paddy wagon. Both broke down often. Lack of funds kept the entire department from replacing such "decrepit pieces of tin that may fall apart at any minute," as Phil Porter described them. The problem extended well into the fire department, too.

"I've been whispering about it," Ness admitted, "but it's really true. One of our [fire] trucks won't go up a hill unless it is backed up."

Ness had already worked out a plan to fix these problems, a radical new vision of how policing could operate.

THAT WINTER, CLEVELANDERS had reason to hope the torso killings might be over. For the first time since 1935, the city had gone more than five months without a new headless corpse.

Coroner Samuel Gerber responded to the lull by lending his name to a ghostwritten article on the "Mystery of Cleveland's Headless Cadavers" for *True Detective* magazine. Modest cash prizes were offered to readers with their own solutions, the article concluding in chilling fashion:

> Of the ten victims of which we know, five heads are still missing!
>
> The killer's laboratory has not been uncovered!
>
> And, judging from past experiences, we feel fairly certain that another ghoulish product of this indescribable fiend will be discovered soon by some unsuspecting person.
>
> The question is: Who will be NEXT?

The answer came April 8, when the lower part of a human leg—everything below the knee and above the ankle—was found floating in a storm drain in the Flats. The partial limb belonged to a young, petite woman, who had died within the past few days. A thorough search turned up no other body parts.

Police had little hope of identifying the victim, much less determining her cause of death or even establishing whether she had actually been murdered. Yet the coroner wasted no time announcing that the Butcher had struck again.

"Crude knife marks," Gerber said, "indicate the slayer was in a hurry."

Ness wasn't so sure. In an apparent attempt to tamp down the public's fears, he revealed that Robert Chamberlin—who handled most duties the Safety Director didn't want—had secretly been working the case. Chamberlin suggested the leg might belong to an earlier torso victim, asking for a second opinion on its age.

"I mean no reflection on the coroner," Chamberlin said, "but . . . the time of death is very important and I thought Dr. Gerber wouldn't mind other experts corroborating his findings."

Gerber took this as an insult, with good reason—the previous torso victim had been a man who died roughly ten months ago, and both of his legs were accounted for. Chamberlin seemed to be insinuating Gerber couldn't tell the difference between a fresh limb and one that had decayed for almost a year.

Furious, the coroner turned territorial. When the Safety Director's office sent a pathologist from Western Reserve University to view the leg, Gerber blocked the man from entering.

"Director Chamberlin wanted the leg to conform to the time of a missing person," Gerber told the *Plain Dealer*, "and the facts wouldn't bear that out. I refused to let Chamberlin send in a person to examine the leg because I want someone who is absolutely impartial."

Events soon proved Gerber right. On May 2, more of the body turned up in a burlap bag floating in the Cuyahoga. Again, the decapitated torso had been cut in half and the limbs removed. The arms and head would never be located. But when Gerber looked inside the bag, he found a foot perfectly matching the previously discovered leg.

An autopsy indicated this woman, like at least one other torso victim, had been the mother of multiple children. Her liver and lungs contained large amounts of morphine. Either her killer had drugged her, or she had been addicted—the coroner couldn't say for sure without seeing her arms.

The dismemberment seemed sloppy, hurried, even erratic. The Butcher left deep slashes in each thigh and snapped several ribs, separating the torso. For once, he'd failed to cut the head off cleanly, slicing repeatedly before resorting to ripping the neck apart.

By now, the Butcher had become the subject of the largest manhunt in Cleveland's history. Peter Merylo and Martin Zalewski, the only detectives working the case full-time, had questioned more than fifteen hundred people, arresting roughly three hundred. Police would speak with more than five thousand persons of interest by year's end, turning Cleveland into something of a surveillance state. Every oddball, lowlife, and homosexual became an object of suspicion; displaying a knife in the wrong place could be cause for arrest.

"Don't ever veer from the path of strictly normal behavior in this town," warned the *News*. "One slip, and an inquisitive detective may come visiting."

A dozen new leads came in the mail every day, many worthless. An anonymous tipster urged Ness to look for the Butcher among the "colored hoboes" who "kill each other when they get hungry enough." Thousands more called with their own ideas and opinions.

"I don't even want to think about 'em all," the chief of homicide told the *Press* with a weary head shake.

The investigators, after years of fruitless searching, grew desperate, pursuing ever more eccentric lines of inquiry. Because the Butcher drained his victims of blood, police sought someone with a certain rare blood disease who might need illicit transfusions. The National Guard took aerial photographs of Kingsbury Run, scrutinizing them for hidden pathways that might allow the killer to move about undetected. Some speculated that the Butcher was a collection of murderers who dismembered their victims in similar ways.

Merylo would often gripe about wasting time on such useless leads, but he and Zalewski ran them all down, anyway. The case ate into their weekends, evenings, and vacations. They kept returning to the most miserable parts of the city, probing the lives of wretched, desperate, neglected people.

"I roughly estimate that we have checked approximately 7300 suspects in connection with these crimes," Merylo wrote some years later, "and it is very doubtful whether the real torso killer was ever amongst them."

After the latest victim's discovery, the two detectives got into a heated argument over a minor procedural matter. Zalewski requested a new assignment. Merylo bitterly dismissed him with the hope that his next partner might be more willing to work.

"Them guys," another detective remarked, "have been so close to this thing that they're beginning to suspect each other as the Torso slayer."

Through it all, Ness kept his distance, and the public took note—the Safety Director seemed the only person in the region not actively hunting the Butcher.

Ness, the *News* once observed, "is a bundle of nervous energy, [he] can't sit still and acts as if he has a million things overcrowding his mind at once. . . . His enthusiasm for one case burns rapidly and fades quickly if immediate results are not apparent."

Facing so many other problems, he lacked the patience and the temperament for such a grueling, unending, and seemingly hopeless investigation.

"This killer has great cunning," Ness told a reporter. "He certainly doesn't leave many, if any, clues. About all we have to go on is that one of the victims was a pervert and another was a prostitute. This man seems to specialize in the sort of people nobody is likely to miss."

Which was a big part of the problem.

Whatever their morbid interest in the case, most Clevelanders knew the Butcher would never harm them. He prowled the run-down part of the city, preying on nameless, faceless people—killings easy to dismiss once the headlines faded.

"Nobody took it to heart . . . ," a homicide detective recalled. "Of course, the people in that neighborhood . . . were worried. I remember there was a whorehouse in that area and they lost all their customers."

But downtown businesses didn't suffer, nor did the terror in the Run extend into the suburbs or the posh West Side—where Ness lived. The *Plain Dealer*'s Phil Porter noted this general lack of concern.

"No visible wave of alarm, indignation or surprise appears to have swept the community . . . ," Porter wrote. "In fact, the general attitude seems to be, 'Tsk, tsk. Another torso victim. Too bad, too bad.'

"It is easy to imagine the uproar that would have swept the community if, say, ten industrial leaders or ten members of the baseball team or even ten councilmen had been thus butchered. . . . We would have had posses and hysteria and possibly martial law."

Newspapers as far away as Europe found the killings "a better story" than the hometown press, Porter observed—lurid coverage rebranding Cleveland as "a city in America where a mad killer has cut up ten people." In Germany, Nazi newspapers were using the torso murders to embarrass the United States.

Had Cleveland's elite demanded the Butcher's arrest, much as Chicago's business community did with Capone, Ness would likely have taken a greater interest, sooner. Instead he focused on matters more pressing to civic leaders: driving racketeers out of labor, saving lives in traffic, cleaning up the police department. This made sense statistically—car accidents killed far more Clevelanders than the Butcher ever could. But it left Ness vulnerable to attacks from his political enemies.

"Our delightful Police Department assigns two men to investigate 11 torso murders, while it assigns 28 men to harass union labor," complained an ally of Campbell and McGee's that spring, "and the administration tries to make the public believe it has no designs for tearing down unions."

The looming specter of the Butcher threatened to overshadow the progress Ness had made as Safety Director. Sometime that year, a reporter from the *Philadelphia Ledger* approached Ness, lunching with Toledo's police chief. In town only a few hours, the writer had already gotten an earful about Cleveland's distinguished Safety Director.

Ness agreed to an interview. The reporter began by asking about the Butcher.

"Director Ness refused to become excited over the torso murder question," the *Ledger* reported. "It is said he never is excited about anything."

Not exactly—Ness had admitted, earlier that year, to being "actually excited" about the sharp reduction in traffic deaths his reforms had brought about. After giving a brief rundown of the killings, he moved on to bank robberies.

"Of course," the *Ledger* observed, "Ness wants to catch the torso murderer and his men will get the killer in time. But Ness refuses to become excited."

THE PLAIN DEALE...
24 PAGES   CLEVELAND, WEDNESDAY MORNING, SEPTEMBER 16, 1936   PRICE

...LS TORSO KILLER NEW INSAN...

Couzens Trails in Rep...an Ra...

MAINE VOTE IS BAD NEWS TO NEW DEAL

Ruel Says Election Shows Threat of Republican Victory in November.

ROOSEVELT JUST SMILES

Indicates Result Was About What He Expected.

BY WALKER S. BUEL
Plain Dealer Bureau.
GT JOHN BLDG.,
WASHINGTON, Sept. 15.—Maine's election is very bad news to the new Deal and President Roosevelt.

It is a certain indication of a Republican trend, a definite threat of Republican victory in November, definite forerunner of a continuation Democratic leadership in Congress, a definite indication of a Republican revival, especially in the...

Where it not for unprecedented factors in this campaign, the Maine result might be regarded as a blast for the New Deal hopes for the re-election of President Roosevelt. But two factors enter, making possible confusion and concern manifestation about the New Deal—Roosevelt is shy of anything the can be nobody yet really knows the political effect of relief and unemployment throughout the agricultural...

In November Election in Doubt.
There the November election remains much in doubt, as it is the Maine vote, except that the last seemed many against the new Deal than the days of the first and Democratic candidates looked, and that other President Roosevelt ran both the state and south for is blasted the...

Godfrey Wilcox ran in 1919 in a election, without a vote of support much except New Hampshire's tiny margin. But Wilson the east and Ohio. Roosevelt if it was not to wash Ohio the voters to overcome the trend fixed by the Maine outcome...

Maine Carries Him Close U. S. Vote.

BY FAY G. HAYDEN.
...15 of his King Saxton at...

No. 20 for Allen

Allen figured his best in the fifth inning, but was given credit for his twentieth victory yesterday as the Indians walloped Boston 12 to 3. Trosky finished the game. Trosky's NK SIX 25th and 26th home run... New York defeated Chicago, 6 to 4; Detroit trimmed Philadelphia, 5 to 2, and Washington took a double header from St. Louis, 12 to 7 and 9 to 1.
Washington dropped the National League.
(Details on Sport Pages.)

WPA WORKERS TO BE EXPO GUESTS

Families, Also, to Attend Saturday as Honor to Garden Builders.

Today's Events.

United Rubber Workers Day.
United States Postoffice Day.
Royal Neighbors of America Day.
National Society of Patriots Day.
City Club Day.
Macon (O.) Day.
Garden Club of Michigan Day.

Attendance yesterday ... 38,160
Attendance for 50 days ... 3,939,545
Days left—37.

The WPA will have its day at the Great Lakes Exposition.
Some of the crop crowds thought that, since everybody was having the day at the city show, it would be short impossible to tangle the WPA, some of whom 27,500 laborer and the four-acre Horticultural Garden on the grounds.

So the boys who shared the shovels and the bars who among the picks have been invited to attend the exposition Saturday. They and have been furnished by their own WPA heads.

They will have the week stadium as a dining hall. Arrangements have been made with a exposition concessionaires to sell them not lunches or prices they can afford.

"Such a celebration has been in mind for weeks because numerous employes have said they wanted to see the WPA-built gardens," Joseph H. Alexander, WPA district director, said. "The gardens are one of last first, projects."

The invitations, which include members of the workers' families, will be in the form of certification (Continued on Page 6 Column 1)

Lanes Sight to Dynamite Mine.
BARNESVILLE, O., Sept. 15.—Charles Gavaghan, 60, a WPA worker, was heartstopping blinded in a dynamite explosion here today. Orbit injuries received in the explosion may cost him his life.

BUY YOUR OWN MEALS. NESS TELLS ROOKIES

Ten New Patrolmen Told Appointments Are Based on Own Merits.

"DON'T BE OBLIGATED"

Warns "You'll Get No Great Reward for Honesty."

Ten new patrolmen were sworn into office yesterday by Safety Director Eliot Ness in his office at City Hall with the revolutionary admonition that patrolmen are expected to pay for their own meals.

"You have been appointed on your own merits, and because you stood at the top of the civil service list and paid for on other reasons," Ness told the recruits. "It makes much claims to you that he was responsible for your appointment, pay no attention.

"Your advancement is up to you.

"You are expected to be honest and to know that you can get no great rewards for being honest. Don't be obligated to anyone, even in small things.

"When you walk into a restaurant for a meal, pay for it. When you get any avoidable memorability useful to you, pay for it. If people have been accustomed to giving you things for nothing prior to your becoming a policeman, I suppose it is all right for you to continue to accept those things.

There Is No Exception.
"However, if people who never gave you anything free before not want to give you something without charge, you can conclude that they are buying your badge and your uniform."

In addition to appointing the ten new patrolmen, Ness announced Sergts. Augustus F. J. Foley to a lieutenancy and Patrolmen Herbert Rader and William H. Miller as sergeants.

The recruits sworn:
ELMER A. RUEDIGER 3301 Cedar avenue S. W.
ASHBERT B. O'HARA 13291 Kenyon avenue N. E.
EDWARD FRIDGE JR. 2619 Ames road S. E.
SELVIN P. EUERSLEY 3611 W. 16th street.
FRANK J. CAIRE JR. 4275 E. 176th street.
ROY F. PICHERACK 2603 Penn avenue N. E.
EDWARD E. BECKER, 2003 E. 116th street.
CLARENCE O. TRINKA, 7415 Park avenue S. E.
JOHN E. KRZOS, 2603 Penn avenue S. E.
ELMER J. SLONE, 2901 Ivory road.

Caldell, the nephew of former supt. Leslie J. Caster, was appointed to the department a month ago by John H. Flynn, executive assistant to Ness. His appointment was revoked at once later by Ness, because he found that the department stopped the candidate at the top of the list.

Says Fight With Richman Nearly Sank Ocean Plane

NEW YORK, Sept. 15.—(AP)—The Daily News, in a copyrighted dispatch from a staff correspondent at Musgrave Harbor, Newfoundland, says a quarrel over the Atlantic between the transoceanic flyers Harry Richman and Dick Merrill "almost ended with the drone in Casey James' home."

Merrill and Richman landed at first isolated village yesterday after a raging flight home...

Newspaper Plane Damaged.
ST. JOHNS, Newfoundland, Sept. 15—(U.P.)—A newspaper plane...

Youth, 16, Th...atens Shirley Tem...

Associated Press Wirephoto.
Frank Edward Nephews, sixteen-year-old Atlanta boy, arrested in Atlanta yesterday and charged with sending an extortion letter to the mother of Shirley Temple, child film star, is shown between two federal agents as he was taken from the Atlanta police station to the federal building.

ATLANTA, Ga., Sept. 15.—A mild-mannered youth who said the threat was of no ill intent in a crude school prank, told federal authorities today of sending a $2,000 extortion letter to the mother of Shirley Temple.

Questions before the convention outside say launched the youth, unshackling children he confessed and another that tells the victim, one of the most powerful weapons at seventeen years and seeks Federal protection into city garage.

This text was words get put of the widows into the hands of the extortion menace to apply, "when justified."

Joseph Garner, Committee for Industrial Organization situation, addressed the delegates late today, saying he had just come from a meeting with a group of eleven workers now, and said what the URW would do about sitdowns.

"Direct Violation," Is Ward.
I told them that sitdowns were a direct violation of the agreement and your procedure. Garner said...

OUTLAW SITDOWN, PLEA IS UP TO URW

Strikes Hit Akron Plants as Rubber International Weighs Policy Issue.

Plain Dealer Bureau,
222 Ohio Building,
AKRON, O., Sept. 15.

The issue of the sitdown strike became one of the most important question before the United Rubber Workers of America at their first international convention in session here.

SHAKER EXTE... TO RUN CARS

Shuttle Service to Rd. Expected in 2 May Go to Richm...

BY JAMES C. MONS...
The extension of rapid tracks in Shaker Heights completed in two weeks, be run to Shaker Heights Rapid Transit track, head of Warrensville the line to East Shaker is to be reduced as far Heights. Work on setting emerging trolley wires a along, with it. For the will be a triple track main...

There is said to be a shuttle line the extension another one to Richmond the year later. With the section in Bramard Road goes the next spring, 420 lines of the Cleveland Railway, which soon con the line, last night denied any certainty of commission Green blind.

It is intended to operate service between Green and Shaker Square H. E. when the Shaker rapids bunch service. As the line the mergers are carrying...

Undated portrait of Francis Edward Sweeney, captioned "Doctor X" in the notebook of a Cleveland police detective assigned to the torso murders.

The Cleveland Police Historical Society, Inc.

ELEVEN

Doctor X

Spring–Summer 1938

Ness's reluctance to talk publicly about a case before handing it over to the prosecutor made him seem unconcerned about the torso murders. The public didn't know he'd taken a direct hand in the investigation, which was how he wanted it—for now, anyway. But as criticism mounted, he hinted of his secret hunt for the Butcher.

"We have been doing intensive work for almost a year," Ness told the *Plain Dealer*, "but very quietly. I hope it will lead us to the end of the chain of killings."

A solution was closer than the Safety Director let on. After months of work, when Ness needed it most, David Cowles was closing in on a suspect.

The ballistics expert had stumbled onto a lead while investigating reports of a possible torso murder about fifty miles from Cleveland. In March, a dog near Sandusky discovered a woman's leg, neatly amputated at the knee, and took the prize home to its master. The rest of the body never turned up, but police determined the bizarre discovery had no connection to the Butcher.

While traveling to Sandusky to view the limb, Cowles decided to check up on the down-and-out doctor police had looked at around the time of Edward Andrassy's murder. Investigators had dismissed this suspect because records placed him at the Sandusky Soldiers and Sailors Home, for alcoholism treatment, at the time of the killings. But Cowles decided to visit the facility and make sure the doctor couldn't have slipped out and back to Cleveland.

Right away, Cowles learned the suspect's alibi was worthless. The doctor had admitted himself, so no one took much notice of his comings and goings. He could sign himself in and create an alibi before sneaking away.

Cowles found someone who knew the doctor: Alex Archaki, a convicted burglar living at the facility on work release. The thief not only confirmed Cowles's suspicions, but believed the doctor to be the Butcher.

Archaki met the physician in 1934. The friendly, dapper doctor approached him in a bar and offered to buy him a drink, then began asking questions about Archaki's personal life—whether he lived in Cleveland, whether he was married. Archaki backed off, suspecting the doctor was looking for a sexual partner.

But encountering the medical man some years later at the Soldiers and Sailors Home, Archaki began a sort of partnership with him—supplying the doctor with alcohol in return for prescriptions. Archaki noticed the physician sometimes disappeared for a few days, after which the press would report a new torso murder in Cleveland. Those probing questions in that bar years before now seemed designed to see if Archaki qualified as a potential anonymous victim. The burglar became convinced he'd narrowly escaped losing his own head.

Archaki's story prompted Cowles to take a second look at the suspect. The torso investigators had been watching him for some time, along with countless other medical men. At least twice, they'd lost track of him shortly before another torso murder.

Now they zeroed in.

"Made a quiet investigation," a detective reported, "of some information we received about a Physician whose name we cannot mention at this time."

The *News* got wind of their efforts in early April.

"A once-prominent Clevelander, described as a physician in disrepute with his profession, is under suspicion in Cleveland's 11 unsolved torso murders," the paper disclosed. "The man, said to have discontinued his practice, is middle-aged, has some surgical skill and is described as being a powerfully built, chronic alcoholic with apparent sadistic tendencies."

Both Coroner Gerber and Robert Chamberlin admitted they had the suspect under surveillance, but neither would reveal his name. A policeman working under Cowles kept in his notebook a photo of the suspect labeled: "Doctor X."

Doctor X was Francis Edward Sweeney, forty-four years old. Born in Cleveland to an Irish immigrant family, he grew up near Kingsbury Run. At ten, he lost his mother; his father later died in an asylum, suffering from psychosis.

In the Great War, Sweeney served in France, bringing much-needed medical supplies to the front. After coming back with an unspecified disability—a head injury, perhaps, or poison gas after-effects—he went on to medical school and distinguished himself as a brilliant, dedicated student engrossed in his work, with a robust sense of humor.

He married a beautiful young nurse in 1927 and received his medical degree the following year, returning to begin a practice, and fathering two boys. This offspring of Kingsbury Run was now a heavyset man, almost six feet tall with a long, smooth face, sleepy blue-gray eyes, and prematurely graying reddish-brown hair.

Around 1929, Sweeney evinced signs of his father's psychosis, drinking so heavily the alcohol damaged nerve endings in his hands and feet, leaving him in constant pain. His sour mood and erratic, cruel behavior left his wife claiming her husband "has upon many occasions humiliated her before her friends and has been abusive to her and their children both physically and mentally."

Addiction is now known to factor heavily in the psychology of serial killers. Sexual murders are often committed under the influence of alcohol or other drugs, with the urge to kill itself an addiction—a cycle of violent fantasies ultimately pursued in the real world.

Sweeney's drinking also fueled hallucinations. He would disappear for long stretches without explanation. In late 1933 and early 1934, his wife filed two petitions questioning his sanity; both times he was committed, examined . . . and discharged.

During his commitments, Sweeney stayed in the mental ward of Cleveland's City Hospital—where the Butcher's first named victim, Edward Andrassy, worked off and on as an orderly. This possibly led police to consider Sweeney a suspect.

Serial killers often leave hints of their personality early in their spree; they frequently choose someone they know for an early victim. Alone among the Butcher's victims, Andrassy had rope burns on his wrists, as if he'd tried to free himself, cognizant of what his killer had in store.

Sweeney shared a practice with several other physicians on Broadway Avenue, barely a mile from Kingsbury Run. Next door a funeral parlor handled the city's indigent corpses; the undertaker apparently allowed Sweeney to indulge a "frustrated desire to operate" by practicing on unclaimed bodies. Witnesses would describe Sweeney cutting up corpses in "exactly the same way" the Butcher dismembered his victims.

Sweeney may have pursued his calling in the funeral parlor itself, or at an industrial facility the undertaker owned near Jackass Hill, where the Butcher left Andrassy's corpse. As a private, secluded spot, suitable for the cleaning, draining, and disposing of a large volume of human bodies, this facility seemed ideal—even better than the killer's long-sought "laboratory."

And so close to where the Butcher's victims had been found.

After years of abuse, Sweeney's wife left him in the fall of 1934—around when the Lady of the Lake washed ashore at Euclid Beach. Decades later, FBI profilers, in the first systematic study of serial killers, would label such traumatic events "stressors," often preceding the first in a series of murders, pushing individuals who may have fantasized about killing into finally taking action.

"Anything can be a triggering stressor . . . ," wrote FBI agent John Douglas and author Mark Olshaker. "But the two most common ones, not surprisingly, are losing your job and losing your wife or girlfriend."

Sweeney then entered a period he would later describe as his "truancy in lunacy"—such bizarre plays on words seemingly tickled him. Here he disappears from the written record, his activities and means of support largely a mystery. In early 1938, an acquaintance tried to commit him, saying Sweeney suffered from paranoid delusions of "Federal men after him." That effort failed, but Sweeney's family tried again in April, four days after the Butcher's latest victim turned up.

In both proceedings, doctors found Sweeney's behavior "orderly," "remorseful," and generally improved; they released him, judging him on the mend. Nothing indicated they believed him to be homicidal.

Sweeney's claims of "Federal men" following him may not have been entirely delusional. Wasn't *Eliot Ness* after him? As Cowles and the other investigators pried into Sweeney's history, they watched him. Detectives tracked him around town and kept an eye on his mail. Sweeney seemed to enjoy the attention, even to revel in it. He sent Cowles postcards and clippings for the "Sweeney file." He pranked the detectives following him—he would shake a tail, only to reappear.

"If we're going to be together so often," Sweeney would say, "we might as well be acquainted."

Another time he led a cop into a bar full of black patrons, and spent the night vocally sending drinks to his "white shadow."

Such behavior is now considered typical of serial killers, who often enjoy taunting the authorities. According to Douglas and Olshaker, the "desire to work with the police . . . was to come up over and over again in our serial killer studies. . . . Now, because of what we've learned, we routinely consider the likelihood that a subject will attempt to insinuate himself into the investigation."

Ness could not have known about the characteristics of serial killers, but thanks to Cowles, the Safety Director regarded

Sweeney as an "interesting" suspect. The doctor matched every element of the torso clinic's profile. A large, powerful man, familiar with human anatomy but lacking a practiced surgeon's skill, the doctor had just the right amount of strength and expertise to do the Butcher's work. He'd spent most of his life in the killer's hunting ground, with access to a possible murder "laboratory." Despite serious mental problems, he had a certain ability to conceal or even control them, repeatedly convincing psychiatrists he did not belong in an institution.

But Cowles and his men hadn't turned up anything linking Sweeney to these crimes. This troubled Ness, who boasted Cleveland had "the best ballistics department and scientific laboratory for the detection of crime in the United States." Yet those cutting-edge tools proved useless in analyzing naked body parts and old burlap sacks. The technology to pick up the trace evidence that might have definitively identified the Butcher was decades away.

"We had no evidence whatever," Cowles would admit.

Short of a confession, Ness and Cowles could only hope to catch Sweeney in the act, or perhaps find the collection of heads some believed the Butcher kept as trophies. And the doctor, well aware he was being watched, was clever enough to avoid saying or doing anything incriminating. That left Ness and Cowles with an entirely circumstantial case that would never hold up in court.

Still, they could have arrested Sweeney and questioned him on the record. But Ness hesitated, not wanting to drag in Sweeney's family—especially his siblings, who had done nothing wrong—if he didn't have to. Another member of Sweeney's extended family posed an even more serious concern.

"A relative of his was a congressman," Cowles recalled, "and we had to be very careful how we handled him."

Not just any congressman, either: Martin L. Sweeney, Ness and Burton's chief political antagonist, who had attacked them for failing to find the Butcher. The two Sweeneys were first cousins, if apparently not close. Once the investigation became public, the congressman would surely bellow political persecution, and might even file a lawsuit against Ness. After all, he was known to be litigious, and this was an election year.

In his police corruption and labor racketeering probes, Ness brought only solid cases to court. This gave him an impressive string of convictions and the trust of his community, plus a growing national reputation as a cop who always got his man. A nasty public fight with Congressman Sweeney could undo all that, derailing future investigations and reform efforts. And unless they had hard, incontrovertible evidence—or a confession—the doctor would almost certainly walk.

Quietly, cautiously, Ness came up with a plan that may have been the riskiest of his law enforcement career.

AS A STUDENT of August Vollmer's in Chicago, Ness got to know two of his mentor's other protégés, men with wildly different personalities. John Larson, the elder by more than a decade, was careful, methodical, and scholarly—the first American policeman with a Ph.D. Leonarde Keeler was Ness's age, a born promoter and college dropout. Vollmer delegated this odd couple to perfect an invention of Larson's, which came to epitomize the chief's vision for modern, scientific, professional policing: the lie detector.

As a Prohibition agent, Ness would hang around Northwestern University's crime lab, where Keeler and ballistics expert Calvin Goddard worked. Learning the basics of ballistics from Goddard, Ness also picked up an interest in the polygraph, bringing in bootleggers for a run on the device.

Larson encouraged Ness's interest but warned of the machine's fallibility, considering it of limited law enforcement potential. Keeler, however, publicized the lie detector as a perfect instrument for exploring guilty souls, suggesting the device might one day do away with trial by jury.

After leaving Chicago, Ness kept in touch with both men. In the early 1930s, Keeler rose to national prominence as the

Northwestern lab's polygraph expert before being pushed out over his growing yen for publicity. Larson, meanwhile, kept trying to perfect the technology through his work with the criminal court system in Detroit.

As early as October 1937, Ness sought Larson's help on the torso case, promising to bring him in when they had any real suspects. Now that they had one, he called on both Larson and Keeler. The polygraph remained controversial, its accuracy questionable; test results could never be used in court. But they might point toward actual, solid evidence, or even intimidate Sweeney into admitting his guilt.

Plans for the tests were guarded closely. Tom Clothey, Ness's right-hand man and a member of the Unknowns, helped make necessary arrangements. Dr. Royal Grossman, a psychiatrist employed by the county who'd participated in the torso clinic, agreed to observe the suspect. With a suite secured in the Cleveland Hotel, next to Terminal Tower, Cowles could hold Sweeney away from prying eyes.

Peter Merylo, working the case for almost two years, seems not to have known of Ness's plans. Since Ness and Merylo had clashed from the start, the Safety Director may not have trusted him enough to let him in on the investigation.

The operation echoed the "third degree methods" Ness had fiercely criticized—efforts, by either intimidation or outright violence, to get a suspect to confess.

Before Ness became Safety Director, Cleveland police had regularly held suspects for days without charges, sometimes torturing them by making them stand for up to thirty-six hours or lifting them repeatedly by their genitals. Ness would never condone anything so brutal, but this secret interrogation would be a similar violation of Sweeney's constitutional rights, substituting science for violence. The lie detector offered a kind of "psychological third-degree," as one historian put it.

In early May, Cowles had Sweeney picked up and brought to the hotel suite. The doctor probably didn't need much convincing; he was so drunk, three days would pass before he sobered up enough to answer questions. Given Sweeney's evident delight in taunting police, he may have accepted the invitation just for laughs.

Cowles and two assistants kept watch on Sweeney around the clock, in eight-hour shifts for a week or more. Guards prevented any unauthorized visitors from entering.

Dr. Grossman took note of the suspect's violent mood swings and bizarre delusions. Sweeney seemed to regard the proceedings as a game, parrying probing questions with peculiar jokes. At times he flew into a rage, but never gave anything away.

Eventually, Keeler arrived from Chicago with the magic box that made his name. Despite its reputation, the machine worked only if the test subject believed it did, and Keeler knew just how to maneuver his targets into the right frame of mind. He had an aggressive, almost predatory instinct, and a knack for extracting confessions rivaling the old rubber hoses.

But Sweeney posed a particular challenge.

The lie detector, Keeler often insisted, "does not apply to small children, morons, unethical savages, or insane persons, but for normal civilized persons it is a very reliable guide." Sweeney, lost in his own psychosis, could not be counted on for the increased respiration, jump in blood pressure, and sweaty palms needed by the machine.

Keeler's method included the intimidating process of hooking someone up to the device—strapping a blood pressure cuff to his wrist, wrapping a rubber tube around his chest, and clipping electrodes to the palm of a hand.

He also liked to open with a parlor trick. He would have the suspect pick a playing card, then read through the deck, telling his subject to say "no" each time. Like a magician, Keeler would reveal the chosen card—usually due to the machine picking up the lie, but sometimes because he'd stacked the deck. The trick gave Keeler a baseline and put the subject on edge, priming him for the test.

Keeler probably began with questions about Sweeney's name,

history, and personal details. Then he'd have moved on to the torso murders—asking, in his deep and resonant voice, whether Sweeney had known the victims and whether he had killed them. Sweeney admitted nothing, as Keeler watched the polygraph's styluses draw wavy lines along a scrolling sheet of paper.

Keeler delivered his findings to Ness and the others. In his professional opinion, Sweeney was guilty, no doubt about it.

Otherwise, he declared, "I might as well throw my machine out of the window."

But Ness had an ideal source for a second opinion. Keeler had a lot invested in the lie detector's success and might overstate its accuracy. John Larson—the cautious academic who resented Keeler's efforts to monetize the polygraph—saw the lie detector as a flawed investigative tool. He didn't bully his subjects as Keeler did, and got fewer confessions as a result. These differing philosophies drove a nasty split between the two, turning Larson into Keeler's harshest critic.

Larson arrived on May 11 with two associates, a court psychologist and a Detroit police inspector. Their "little seance," as Tom Clothey described it, carried on well into the night.

Disdaining Keeler's simple, yes/no questioning, Larson used the lie detector to probe his subject's psyche. As the test results spooled through the machine, Larson saw what he would call, with characteristic caution, "disturbances indicative of guilt."

After Larson showed Sweeney the results, the doctor tried "to explain away his reactions" in a manner that, to Larson, "more and more seemed indicative of guilt."

Larson asked if Sweeney would be willing to undergo hypnosis.

"At this point the suspect requested an attorney," Larson recalled, "and refused to go further."

Perhaps reluctantly, Larson had to agree with his rival—Sweeney certainly seemed guilty. But without a confession or any other hard evidence, the investigators couldn't hold the doctor. Because the test had run so late into the night, they decided to release him the following morning.

Larson and an associate packed up and left, driving home so fast a cop stopped them for speeding. (Larson would bristle when accused of trying to put distance between himself and the doctor.) The Detroit police inspector reluctantly stayed behind with the Cleveland detectives. No one felt comfortable going to sleep around this suspect.

Before springing Sweeney, Ness took a moment alone with him. The polygraph sometimes proved too much for its subject; more than one suspect, presented with seemingly scientific proof of guilt, had broken down and confessed. Ness may have hoped for that, especially since Larson's findings seemed to have shaken Sweeney up.

Trying to intimidate the doctor was not Ness's style. He may have attempted to reason with him, if that were possible. But Sweeney refused to confess, knowing full well that lie detector tests could not be used in court.

"I think you did those killings," Ness said.

"You think?" Sweeney replied with a laugh. "Prove it."

The doctor fixed Ness with such a threatening, hateful stare that the Safety Director backed off, moving closer to the door, prepared to call in the other detectives if Sweeney made any move to attack him. But the doctor merely got up and left, having apparently tired of the game.

Ness could do nothing to stop him—at least, nothing legal. When he checked, one shift of guards had left, and their replacements had not yet arrived. To his horror, Ness realized he'd been on his own with a potentially violent lunatic.

For a moment, he felt the same surge of fear as in Chicago Heights, when he'd realized a gangster was preparing to stab him in the back. Threats from racketeers and the occasional potshot would never bother him much, but Francis Sweeney?

Ness had to admit the doctor made him fear for his life.

Still, that didn't necessarily make Sweeney the Mad Butcher. And while the lie detector tests hadn't closed the case, they had changed the rules of engagement. Cleveland police would continue to stalk Sweeney's movements, hoping to deny him any further opportunities to kill. But the doctor now had something else in mind.

Someone else.

From then on, he would be obsessed with Eliot Ness.

LS TORSO KILLER NEW INSAN

Couzens Trails in Rep...an Ra...

MAINE VOTE IS BAD NEWS TO NEW DEAL

Burt Says Election Shows Threat of Republican Victory in November.

ROOSEVELT JUST SMILES

Indicates Result Was About What He Expected.

BY WALKER S. BUEL
Plain Dealer Bureau
614 Albee Bldg.
WASHINGTON, Sept. 15. — Maine's election is very bad news to the New Deal and President Roosevelt.

It is a definite indication of a Republican trend, a definite threat of Republican victory in November. A definite beginning of a Democratic decline, a definite indication of a Republican revival, especially on the agricultural front.

When it put the unprecedented figures in the spotlight, the Maine vote might be regarded as a bitter blow to New Deal hopes for the coming state sweep. Now Hampshire, the Jackpot state, cannot possibly be southern and western combination, but may re-elect Roosevelt in the accompanying the next year definitely the really knows the political effect of relief and lesser items strengthen the agricultural ...

November election in focus. Since the November election in the air in itself is, in itself in Maine going, beyond the ... has her survey series upon the ... that the election the ... land 1936 Presidential ...

No. 20 for Allen

Allen injured his kick in the fifth inning. Not was given credit for the twentieth victory yesterday as the Indians defeated Boston, 15 to 3. Wittenbrand doubled the games Tuesday but his 23rd and 44th homers. New York defeated Chicago, 7 to 4; Detroit trimmed Philadelphia, 6 to 2; and Washington took a double header from St. Louis, 13 up 17 and 6 to 4.

Weather stopped the National League.

(Details on Sport Pages)

WPA WORKERS TO BE EXPO GUESTS

Families, Also, to Attend Saturday as Honor to Garden Builders.

Today's Events.

United Rubber Workers Day.
Buffed Retail Pumpers Day.
Royal Neighbors of America Day.
Northeast Society of Painters Day.
City Club Day.
Marine Corps Day.
Garden Club of Michigan Day.

Attendance yesterday 20,441
Attendance for year 3,032,118
Days left — 19.

The WPA will have its day at the Great Lakes Exposition.

Some of the men who thought that almost everybody was having his day at the exposition woke up to their opportunities to forget the WPA, many of whom WPA laborers had the forename Horticultural Gardens on the grounds.

So the boys who shoved the shovels and the boys who swung the picks have been invited to attend the exposition Saturday. They will have dinner furnished by their own WPA funds.

They will have the when function at a dining hotel. Arrangements have been made, with expansion concessionaires to cut these least to be furnished at prices they can afford.

Such a celebration has been instigated and held for weeks became humorous employees have said a by masters to use the WPA-built gardens through E. Alexander, WPA district director.

"All the gardens are now at full flood bloom," the said.

The invitations, which includes members of the workers' families, will be in the form of certification purchased on Page 5, Column 3.

SHAKER EXTE TO RUN CARS

Shuttle Service to Rd. Expected in 2 May Go to Righ

Sales Fight in Dynamite Blast

BARRESVILLE, O. Sept. 15 — Charles Gallagher, 43, a WPA worker, was permanently blinded in a dynamite explosion here today. Others injured in the explosion may just lose his life.

BUY YOUR OWN MEALS, NESS TELLS ROOKIES

Ten New Patrolmen Told Appointments Are Based on Own Merits.

"DON'T BE OBLIGATED"

Warns "You'll Get No Great Reward for Honesty."

Ten new patrolmen were sworn into office yesterday by Safety Director Eliot Ness in his office at City Hall with the revolutionary admonition that patrolmen are expected to pay for their own meals.

"You have been appointed on your own merits and because you stood at the top of the civil service lists and for no other persons," Ness told the recruits. "If anyone else claims or that he was responsible for your appointment is in an auction.

"Your appointment is up to you. Your are expected to be honest and to know that you will get no great reward for being honest. Don't be obligated to anyone, even in small things.

"Soon you walk into a restaurant for a meal, pay for it. When you get into automobiles prejudicing careful to pay, pay for it. If people have been accustomed to giving you things for nothing prior to your becoming a patrolman, I suppose it is all right for you in starting to do that three things.

Three Win Promotions.

"However, if people who never saw you anyway, free before you want to give you something without charge, you can complete that they are buying your badge and your uniform."

In addition to appointing the ten new patrolmen Ness appointed three as acting patrolmen. Sergeant Augustus K.P. Zoch as a lieutenant and Patrolman Herbert Burke and William H. Miller as sergeants.

The recruits were:

J. JAMES A. KARCHNER (300 Yeoman Avenue S.E.
AGELRENT E. OCARS, 1000 Lorenzo Ave. S.E.
EDWARD FRONIG JR., 2079 were east E.
ALBVIS P. STAHLAV, 951 N. SOM Street.
FRANK A. CADER, JR., 2074 E 19th Street.
JOHN P. FOLKRODE, 2020 Penn Ave.
EDWARD J. HOLMES David E Street.
CLARENCE O. FINSKA, 7012 Penn Ave S.E.
JOHN V. NELSOT, 2015 Sava Avenue S.E.
ELMER J. HLINE, 7007 Juno Road.

Gubala, the nephew of former East Louis J. Gubala, was appointed to the department a month ago, by John H. Flynn, secretary-treasurer to Ness. The appointment was reviewed at that time by Ness because it was feared he had skipped the candidates at the top of the list.

Youth, 16, Th...atens Shirley Te...

OUTLAW SITDOWN, PLEA IS UP TO URW

Strikes Hit Akron Plants as Rubber International Weighs Policy Issue.

Plain Dealer Bureau
304 Ohio Building
AKRON, O., Sept. 15.

The issue of the outlawing outlaw, or "wild" turnout at the most delicate question before the United Rubber Workers of America at three days international convention, is standing here.

Resolutions before the convention involves are asking that the two established sitdown be outlawed and switching that calls the sitdown one of the most powerful weapons of organized labor and needs no restriction into 1936 policies.

This last able would set one of the reasons why the leaders of the union are reluctant to agree to abolishment.

Adolph Germer, Committee for Industrial Organization organizer, addressed the delegates this morning, urging the rank and file to agree with a group of about eighteen advising to a labor man in an aggressive position from the advisory their ... intustrial board ...

"Direct Violation," Is Ward.

... said them that sitdowns were a direct violation of union policies and were principled, Germer said.

The boy's case ...

Shaker Carries Hint Close U.S. Vote.

BY JAY G. HAYDEN.
Sept. 1936 to the both a former Democratic state ... STILLON, Mo. ... Sept. 15 ... which rebel lack the Republican ... but with pluralities for the candidates of that Party ... lightening to give the ... the rather ... sage the force ... the proging ...

Again, when ... confirm two party ... to-pit generally ...

Says Fight With Richman Nearly Sank Ocean Plane

NEW YORK, Sept. 15 — (AP) — The Daily News, in a copyrighted dispatch from a staff correspondent at Musgrave Harbor, Newfoundland, such a quarrel on the Atlantic between the trans-ocean flyers Harry Richman and Dick Merrill "almost ended with the flyers in Davy Jones' locker.

Merrill said Richman landed the plane that failed to operate yesterday after a seven-hour flight from England.

... Newspaper Plane Damaged ...
ST. JOHNS, Newfoundland, Sept. 15 — (U.P.) — A newspaper plane owned by the New York Daily News ...

Burton and Ness with the Cleveland Police Department's
new radio-equipped squad cars, August 1938.
Western Reserve Historical Society

TWELVE

Butcher Paper

Summer 1938

The structure of the Cleveland Police had remained largely unchanged since its founding in 1866, most patrolmen still reporting to one of sixteen precinct stations throughout the city before walking a neighborhood beat.

That system had worked in an era when crime, as Ness explained it, "was a neighborhood affair. The precinct stations were established on the theory the citizen could get—by street car or horse and buggy—to the nearest station, [and] a policeman could be sent out and maybe walk back with a prisoner."

But now that criminals had automobiles—and could speed not just around the city but between states—Ness considered the precinct system obsolete and wanted to scrap it entirely. Police would patrol the city in a new fleet of squad cars, each carrying three officers, two of whom could patrol on foot, giving Clevelanders what they'd come to expect from their neighborhood beat cop. But these motorized units would cover far more ground, able to speed to any emergency.

"Ness," the *Plain Dealer* noted, "is attaching wings to the flat feet of the past."

Where previously police officers had to receive assignments

and file reports at their precinct stations, each car would now have two-way radio and teletype, with officers responding to radio calls and writing reports on typewriters installed in each car.

Cleveland's firefighters already used handheld "pocket radios" to communicate at a fire. Ness wanted to similarly equip police officers, to keep them in touch with their squad cars and with headquarters. His vision anticipated the "2-Way Wrist Radio" adopted by his comic strip doppelgänger, Dick Tracy, almost a decade later—which then seemed so advanced as to be science fiction. Ness even envisioned a time when a central dispatcher could augment an all-points bulletin with a suspect photograph sent wirelessly.

The radio would link all officers to a central station serving as a clearinghouse for information. Ness proposed consolidating crime statistics and reports into a single bureau able to quickly disseminate information, allowing police to take in the city's crime picture at a glance, revealing trouble spots and adjusting patrols accordingly. And by convincing the suburbs to adopt the same equipment, Cleveland's police could share information or set up dragnets countywide.

Ness had long wanted a quicker response to help calls, saying in 1936: "In Detroit they advertise 'A squad at your door within 60 seconds.' We can't say that here."

Clevelanders needing police assistance had to know their precinct number or wait till an operator could connect them. Three decades before the rest of the country would begin to adopt the 911 emergency system, Ness proposed a single city-wide phone number—Main 1234—connecting with the HQ radio room. Central dispatch could send a car even before the caller hung up.

These proposals struck many as fanciful—"the best approximation to be found anywhere," the *News* said, "of what might happen if Buck Rogers joined the cops," a reference to the space-man who shared Dick Tracy's funny pages.

Journalists called the plan "revolutionary," while the *Plain*

Dealer predicted it would "bring the greatest upheaval in the whole history of the police department."

To Ness it just made sense. Each precinct station ate up resources, staffed by cops performing largely clerical tasks. Closing several stations would get those cops back on the streets and increase patrol strength without more hiring.

"Of course it is going to be a great task to sell the public on the new idea," Ness told a reporter, "particularly the merchants who like to have their doors tried every night and the cop on the beat to come in and pass the time of day."

But how could a city too strapped to hire more police officers somehow finance a fleet of brand-new squad cars and four and a half tons of custom-made radio equipment? Ness's plan would increase the PD's budget by about 360 percent. And he couldn't count on the business community—those who'd funded his labor racketeering and police corruption investigations had no interest in buying squad cars.

Instead Ness went to the voters, seeking a small property tax increase. In early 1938, using his heroic reputation as collateral, he began a press blitz to win support for the new system; his reporter friends publicized the sorry state of the department and Ness's vision of its possible future.

On March 1, voters provided the Safety Director an additional $60,000.

Ness pushed for more money from the mayor and the city council. His traffic safety work had lowered city insurance rates significantly while revenue from traffic tickets had gone up. His lobbying brought those dollars back to his department.

Now Ness laid plans for what an official called "the largest and most modern police two-way radio system in the world." He created five police districts of thirty-two patrol zones covered by single squad cars. He hoped for a response time of under a minute, though that would vary from three minutes to a minute and a half.

The new squad cars, thirty-two Ford sedans, arrived that summer. Ness wanted them visible, like the "Canary Cars" driven by the Accident Prevention Bureau, an ongoing reminder of the police presence on city streets. He and Mayor Burton agreed on an eye-popping color scheme: metallic blue on top and bright red below, with a thin stripe of creamy white between.

The *Plain Dealer* said, "If you cannot see them coming a mile away, it will be because you are blind."

Ness also converted twelve panel trucks into "Emergency Mobile Patrol" vehicles doubling as police cruisers, able to carry up to eight cops. Each vehicle bore the red-white-and-blue color scheme, carrying stretchers, inhalators, and other lifesaving equipment.

Decades before the term *paramedic* even existed—when ambulance drivers did little more than get their patients to the nearest doctor—Ness staffed his Emergency Mobile Patrol with officers trained in first aid and hospital procedure.

"We have been criticized by some who say we are doing away with the beat patrolman," Ness told the *Plain Dealer*. "Actually we will have more men on the street than we ever had before."

By year's end, the plan would shutter seven of sixteen precinct stations, putting almost three hundred cops—every able-bodied officer—back on patrol. Ness made no secret of his intention to eliminate all "the soft jobs."

Of course, this raised the ire of the old guard, who appreciated how things used to be. "For years, lieutenants and sergeants have sat at desks, waxed fat and lazy, taking telephone calls and making out reports," observed the *Press*. "Now they'll be out on the street, catching crooks."

Ness could keep tabs on his men, even monitor their movements. Daily roll call was replaced by officers radioing in to central dispatch, their locations tracked on a lighted map. Left unsaid was how this curtailed the ability of high-ranking officers to solicit graft. When the city had been split up into separate precincts, individual captains wielded considerable power and could turn their precincts into fiefdoms, peddling influence and protection for payoffs. Consolidating authority at headquarters did away with that.

"Under the precinct system," Ness said, "we had a precinct captain as coach for every player. Now we'll have one coach for the team—the radio control room."

With so many precinct houses shut down, what might be done with those buildings? Members of the Negro Welfare Association suggested Mayor Burton turn the Fifth Precinct at East Seventy-Ninth and Woodland, near the central neighborhoods where most black Clevelanders lived, into a community recreation center where African-American kids could play, away from the dangers and temptations of the streets.

Crime prevention remained a top Ness priority; the reorganization plan more than doubled Captain Arthur Roth's Juvenile Bureau. The Safety Department repurposed the old Fifth Precinct and five other abandoned stations as after-school centers for youth. These "Boystowns" were patterned after the self-governing "City of Little Men" founded near Omaha by Father Edward Flanagan. Each Boystown elected its own government of young mayors, judges, and police chiefs, providing children with activities meant to keep them out of trouble.

"In sections where a boy's police record had been regarded as a mark of distinction," Ness wrote, "good citizenship is now fashionable."

Father Flanagan's philosophy—"There are no bad boys; there is only bad environment, bad training, bad example, bad thinking"—proved a perfect match for Ness's firm belief "that jails fail to reform people."

Ness spread the Boystown idea through articles, interviews, and lectures given in other cities. He hosted dinners bringing the mayors of each Boystown together with civic leaders and arranging for all members of the program to attend a baseball game at Cleveland Stadium. Within two months of their introduction, Cleveland's Boystowns had a membership of 2,100. By the next year, enrollment had jumped to six thousand.

Ness's reorganization plan epitomized his vision for how a progressive, modern police department should operate. He evangelized at every opportunity, urging other police administrators to follow Cleveland's lead. At home, he came at crime from both sides—employing the latest tools and technologies to catch criminals while engaging with the community to prevent their creation.

LONG BEFORE NESS became Safety Director, the swimming pool at Woodland Hills Park had been a source of racial tension and conflict. At public pools built around the country during the 1920s and 1930s, young men and women mingled with freedom unimaginable a generation earlier, as bathing suits grew smaller and skimpier until men's trunks and the woman's two-piece became the norm. Meanwhile, more and more African Americans were coming north, fleeing the Jim Crow South for industrial cities like Cleveland, only to encounter different kinds of segregation.

With its location near Kinsman Road and East 116th Street, surrounded by neighborhoods transitioning from white to predominately black, the Woodland Hills pool seemed fated to become "a hotbed of discrimination," as the *Call & Post* put it. Mornings were reserved for kids, black children typically swimming without incident. But in the afternoons, when the facility opened to adults, African Americans faced harassment ranging from verbal intimidation to physical assault, while white police officers ignored or dismissed their complaints, instead playing cards or checkers inside.

Shortly before Woodland Hills opened for the summer of 1936, the NAACP sent a formal letter to Mayor Burton, asking that he and Ness "provide proper and adequate protection for such Negro citizens as may desire to make use of these facilities."

Burton met with NAACP representatives and publisher William O. Walker of the *Call & Post*, promising to assign a black lifeguard at Woodland Hills. Ness, attending with other city officials, agreed to an NAACP request for a detail of African-American policemen at the pool. Within the week, Ness stationed more than a dozen cops, black and white, at Woodland Hills.

But even as the mayor promised to keep the pool open to all,

African Americans faced continued discrimination at the Great Lakes Exposition, where dining and dancing were often reserved for whites. That same summer, roughly thirty "disappointed and disgusted" black members of Burton's campaign met to voice their frustrations with his apparent lack of interest in the constituency that helped elect him.

"Mr. Burton will not be acceptable to colored voters if he runs again," an attorney declared. "He promised certain things in the primary, and did not keep his promises. He promised to clean up certain criminal spots, but neither the mayor nor Safety Director Ness has paid any attention to our complaints."

In the summer of 1938, a reporter from the *Call & Post* dropped by Woodland Hills to find at least forty white swimmers and no African Americans, apart from a pair of maintenance workers.

On August 8, African-American postal clerk Raymond Hightower, with his young son and two other eleven-year-old boys, visited Woodland Hills. They "had been swimming for only a short time," Hightower recalled, "before white bathers . . . approached us, called us n——rs, and told us that 'this pool is for white people,'" and to get out or get drowned.

Hightower approached a cop on guard, asking him to "keep a close watch over the children so as to protect them from any violence." The policeman agreed, and Hightower went back to the water. But the white swimmers, half a dozen boys in their late teens, encircled Hightower and the children—"threatening to drown us," the postal clerk remembered, "if we did not leave the pool."

When Hightower went to a white officer for help, he was mocked for his trouble. An African-American policeman on duty went to the gang of teenagers and ordered them to stop. The white boys just splashed him, drenching his clothes.

"When we again entered the pool," Hightower recalled, "nearly fifty white bathers hemmed us in, tripping me into the water, and striking me in the back. Someone must have sent in a riot call, for soon more than a score of policemen were in and about the pool."

After six white youths had been arrested, a white cop asked Hightower scornfully: "Now, do you still want to swim in this pool?"

Hightower did, and he and the children peaceably swam until the clerk was called to a nearby police station to identify the boys. But city prosecutors were reluctant to press charges, urging him to drop the matter to avoid "racial animosity in the future."

Hightower stood his ground, backed up by black community leaders. The prosecutor finally agreed to issue disorderly conduct warrants, charging the teenager who allegedly struck Hightower with an additional count of assault and battery, but refused to charge the boys with assault on a policeman—Burton didn't want "to make an issue of the affair."

The *Call & Post* hoped that convictions might "discourage the continuous program of white bathers to drive Negroes from the pool." But when the first defendant went on trial for assault, he faced an all-white jury, some of whom were on record saying they wouldn't swim with blacks. After Hightower testified he'd been hit from behind, the defense claimed he couldn't positively identify his attacker, and the jury voted to acquit.

The other boys soon pleaded guilty to disorderly conduct and got off with three months' probation.

Police continued to patrol Woodland Hills—including Harrison Hannibal Harney, a rare black officer in plainclothes. The veteran homicide investigator might have put his time and talents to better use elsewhere. But in a city boasting so few black cops, Harney mostly spent his summers guarding the pool.

After the attack on Hightower, some whites went to Ness demanding Harney's transfer.

Soon after, Harney learned he would no longer be guarding Woodland Hills—"his presence at the pool caused resentment among the white bathers, and would possibly lead to trouble if he continued to stay."

In a blistering *Call & Post* editorial, publisher Walker castigated Ness for transferring an officer only doing his duty. "The great G-man who is supposed to have unshackled the police,"

Walker declared, "is revealed as being too prejudiced to unshackle the colored members of the force. . . .

"Since Mr. Ness has been head of the department, not a single Negro officer has received anything like the recognition he has been entitled to. The same old tricks of eliminating Negroes who successfully pass the oral and written examinations, via the physical test, have prevailed with Mr. Ness's approval."

Cleveland—unlike New York, Chicago, and other major cities—continuously failed to promote black cops above the lowest available rank.

Although Ness's later actions would belie these charges of prejudice, the benefits of his reforms were hardly distributed equally. Ness's plan to reorganize the police department privileged, however unconsciously, people like himself—white, male college graduates with aspirations to rise above the middle class. Splitting up the city geographically, Ness assigned more patrol cars to the affluent West Side than the crime-ridden Roaring Third.

As Walker observed, "It takes more than brand new automobiles with all their new . . . gadgets to make a [police] department."

CLEVELAND'S GREAT LAKES Exposition was little more than a memory now. The "magic city on the lake front" had closed the year before, its demolition beginning soon after.

The Expo's founders had hoped their fair would revitalize the area between downtown and Lake Erie, transforming it "from dust bin to beauty spot," as the *Plain Dealer* put it. But as the red, white, and blue pavilions came down, the land reverted to a large public dump.

On Tuesday afternoon, August 16, three African-American men poked through the refuse of that once glorious monument to optimism only to come across a foul-smelling bundle of cloth swarming with flies. Within were the partial remains of a petite woman, about thirty-five years old, dead four to six months.

A police search turned up the rest—including the head. Left

in nine pieces, the ghastly packages had been wrapped in brown paper—butcher's paper—thighs held together with a rubber band, like cuts of meat. A cardboard box, cobbled together from two different food cartons, held the arms and legs.

At the scene, Coroner Gerber viewed the remains, noting the same method of dismemberment as in previous torso killings, speculating the Butcher had held on to this corpse for some time.

"Portions of it were dry and hard, as if preserved, and looked as if they might have been kept in a refrigerator," reported the *Press*. "Also, the boxes that contained her body positively could not have looked as new as they did after four months' exposure to the weather."

News of another torso murder spread, drawing gawkers to the dump like more flies. Around sundown, a spectator noticed a sickening stench and followed it to pieces of a second body, almost entirely decomposed, some bones resting atop a plaster column from the Expo.

Detective Sergeant James Hogan hurried over and grabbed a large can to carry the remains. Looking inside, he saw a human skull—the second victim's missing head.

Puzzling over the bones, Gerber struggled to determine their sex. A woman, he initially thought, probably African American. Finally he concluded this was "a small-boned" white man. In any case, the victim had been dead for seven months to a year.

Gerber felt certain of one thing—these bones bore the same "unmistakable knife marks" as the other torso victims.

That brought the Butcher's tally to twelve or thirteen, depending how you counted. Both had died before the victim whose pieces began turning up back in April. But these bodies apparently arrived in the dump recently—late July at the earliest.

"He's changing his technique," Peter Merylo told the *Press*. "Why, I don't know. But for the first time since the two bodies we found in September 1935, he has left two victims together. And, again changing his method, he left heads of these two."

Also, the Butcher had ventured far outside his comfort zone, leaving bodies downtown, in full view of City Hall—where Eliot

Ness worked—possibly taunting the authorities, the Safety Director in particular.

David Cowles publicly agreed with Gerber that the dismemberment "matched the technique" of the other killings. But privately Cowles and Ness remained unconvinced the Butcher had killed again. After Gerber and his staff finished with the bodies, a Western Reserve University pathologist examined the female remains, offering Ness and Chamberlin a second opinion. With the previous victim, Gerber had been proven right and Ness wrong—but this time the coroner seemed to have made a serious mistake.

The pathologist found the woman's body had not been preserved or refrigerated, rather embalmed. Whoever cut it up might be guilty of grave robbery, not homicide.

An outraged Gerber accused Cowles of a sort of grave robbery himself: stealing those bones for examination. Police nonetheless investigated an embalming school owner, who might have left the bodies as a prank.

Merylo concluded both corpses "were put there by someone with a morbid sense of humor." Ness and Cowles, of course, knew of another possibility—these might be two of the unclaimed, indigent corpses on which Francis Sweeney practiced his unique style of surgery. But even if police could prove Sweeney had cut these bodies up, that wouldn't make him the Butcher. This might be Sweeney's sick joke on the men who had interrogated him.

Detectives seemed guardedly optimistic about identifying the victims. They had heads and hands from both bodies, and clues found with the corpses: a man's blue jacket, a homemade quilt, the cardboard boxes, and fragments of newspaper. But every lead led to another maddening dead end—neither victim would ever be named. The source of the quilt was tracked to a rag shop from which it had apparently been stolen, though no one could figure out why the Butcher would risk taking something so worthless.

The cardboard boxes were traced to the edge of the Flats, the Central Market food stalls southeast of downtown. Nearby, roughly thirty shacks made up a hillside shantytown between Commercial and Canal Roads. Many "forgotten men" scavenged in the area, subsisting on cast-off scraps. Police had long suspected the Butcher stalked victims in such Hoovervilles, which the boxes seemed to confirm.

"Then, too," Ness told the *Press*, "the contents of the stomachs of some of the victims have been mostly fruit and vegetables, indicating they live off refuse picked up around the markets."

On August 17, the *Press* called on civic leaders to put up a $10,000 reward for information leading to "the end of these insane crimes." The torso murders, the paper observed, threatened the "great program" promoting their city through the Expo, aiming to attract new business. The *Press* clearly cared more for Cleveland's reputation than the men and women targeted by the Butcher.

"The nature of the murders, their limited locale and the transient character of the victims, has served to prevent any needless fear on the part of our citizens," they wrote. "But it is uncomfortable to know that Cleveland is the scene of this shuddering horror. Other cities are not likely to realize how remote is this terror from the lives of ordinary Clevelanders. This killer must be caught for the peace of mind of the city, and its good name abroad."

Now that the Butcher posed a threat to the economic elite, the Safety Director had to respond. Public statements and putting more men on the case wouldn't be enough—rumors of Ness's prime suspect had begun to slip out.

In May, the *Press* revealed an unnamed man had been "grilled by federal authorities and police in connection with the murders" and "subjected to lie detector tests." Now the *Plain Dealer* said detectives believed the Butcher "may be a demented surgeon who has lost the right to practice."

But Ness still lacked the evidence to drag Sweeney into court. Identifying the suspect, and openly questioning him, would risk the wrath of the doctor's congressman cousin.

A simple, rational, logical philosophy informed Ness's work as Safety Director: uncover "the cause, the why . . . and a course of action becomes crystal clear." If cars kept colliding at a certain intersection, a new traffic light might be needed. If graft ran rampant in one precinct, the captain and his henchmen had to go.

Here the cause seemed obvious—a crazed killer motivated by madness. But with his prime suspect off-limits, Ness had to find a different reason for why these murders kept happening. So he focused instead on the victims. Cleveland, he reasoned, offered too many targets of opportunity. If the Butcher had fewer hoboes, transients, and homeless to choose from, perhaps the killing would stop.

Each new headless corpse seemed a rebuke to the progress Ness and Burton had made, a ghoulish reminder that much of their city remained mired in misery and poverty even as prosperity returned elsewhere. Clearing out those unfortunates would send a message that Cleveland looked ahead to a brighter future, free of blight and free of the Butcher.

Eliot Ness questions men detained during the shantytown raid, August 18, 1938.
Authors' Collection

The remains of the shantytown in flames the following morning.
Cleveland Press Collection, Cleveland State University

THIRTEEN

Good Riddance

August–September 1938

The Commercial Road Hill shantytown sat both literally and fig-
uratively "in the shadow of the Terminal Tower."

Making way for Cleveland's glorious new skyscraper, the city
had razed a warren of flophouses and slums at downtown's southern edge, where men now sleeping in packing-crate shacks might
once have found a home. With a deepening Depression and a
growing housing shortage, many had no choice but to settle at the
lakefront dump. There they built a "Hoovertown" of modest yet
substantial shanties, constructed with care and displaying ameni-
ties from radio sets to "front porches looking out over the water."

But the city considered this settlement an eyesore, and cleared
it to create space for the Great Lakes Exposition. This pushed
the former residents of Hoovertown into forgotten corners of the
Flats and Kingsbury Run, where no one would come looking for
them. The Expo of tomorrow had driven them into the Butcher's
path today.

Some homeless chose to sleep in the Wayfarer's Lodge, a char-
itable institution with beds costing twenty-five cents or a few
hours' work chopping wood. Often overcrowded, especially in
winter, the Lodge struggled to handle as many as eighteen hundred

souls a night. Those seeking shelter lined up every evening, then underwent a degrading ritual of surrendering their clothes, showering in groups, and submitting to medical exams. The first few hundred received nightshirts to sleep in; the rest slept naked and got their clothes back in the morning.

"I panhandled a day or two and decided to try the Wayfarer's Lodge," an unemployed laborer recalled. "I walked in and looked around and came out. I didn't like the smell of the place and the crowd I saw."

That stench—the "pervading rank smell of stew"—matched the stifling atmosphere.

"More and more homeless men without families are between the Wayfarer's Lodge and the dumps," said the *Press* in 1932. "They resent the wood cutting and the questions of policemen and social workers."

Or, as one squatter put it: "They want us in their soup line, that's all. If we eat without cutting wood for it, it makes them sore."

Setting up a shack in the wild, untamed parts of town represented independence, even rebellion. Shantytown residents elected their own governments, divided up domestic tasks, and lived communally; everyone was expected to contribute scraps of food to a boiling pot of water for the "mulligan stew" all would share.

Though newspapers called them "bums, hoboes and idlers," many worked at least part-time but couldn't afford rent. They took pride in their hovels and tried to keep order among themselves, to avoid unwanted police attention.

As the "mayor" of another Hooverville observed, "If former President Hoover could walk through . . . the little shanty [town] . . . bearing his name . . . he would find it is not inhabited by a bunch of ne'er-do-wells, but by . . . men who are bending every effort to beat back and regain the place in our social system that once was theirs."

From the outside, however, these were miserable vagrants, eking out a precarious existence. Respectable folks venturing into the "jungles" found the lifestyle deplorable. Good food and

potable water were scarce; keeping warm in winter posed dangerous challenges in shacks of highly flammable wood.

"Too large a fire means death by burning," noted the *News*.
"Too small a fire means death by freezing. . . . How can human
beings live under these conditions? The answer can be found in
the vacant stares, the dull eyes of those men who are the living
dead."

This diminishment of shantytown residents made them seem
less than human, already dead before the Butcher might claim
their heads.

Eliot Ness had sympathy, even gullibility, when it came to
hard-luck cases. If a friend asked for a loan of $5, he would hand
over $10.

"For a wayfarer seeking a 'quarter for a bite,'" an acquaintance
recalled, "Ness was the easiest of marks."

Somehow that didn't translate into empathy for Hoovertown
residents. Ness could not see past their shacks—firetraps riddled
with "disease and filth," where perverts and criminals could hide
out undetected. The settlements violated Cleveland's sanitary
laws; as Ness saw it, men camping there "had title neither to the
land nor the buildings in which they had been living."

That meant they had to go.

Also, doing the city fathers' bidding would give Ness an opportunity to seek evidence among the Butcher's prey that might
finally put Sweeney within reach of prosecution. And bringing
scorched earth to the torso killer's Hooverville hunting grounds
might save lives.

He planned it like a Prohibition-era raid. He would meet a
few trusted officers in predawn darkness. No one would know
the details until Ness shared them at the scene. They would
make sure to cover all available escape routes, much like the
Untouchables raiding a Capone brewery. Once again, reporters
and photographers would come along.

At 12:40 A.M. on August 18, a day and a half after the discovery of the latest torso victims, Ness and Robert Chamberlin arrived at a fire station near Commercial Road Hill. They met with

twenty-five police officers and detectives, Cowles among them. Many cops were in shirtsleeves. Ness came impeccably dressed— hatless, shoes shined, a dark suit with gold badge on its lapel.

He explained the plan of action, and the group divided in two, Ness taking charge of one contingent, a sergeant the other. Then they set out in the darkness, carrying flashlights and acetylene lamps, and descended a ramp toward the cluster of thirty shacks. Ness's group passed under the concrete arch of an aging railroad viaduct and took a position at one end of the settlement.

Just after 1 A.M., Ness flashed his light, and the cops moved in. Going methodically from shack to shack, they pounded on each door, wincing at the smells coming from within.

"All right, boys," a cop shouted to the inhabitants, "let's get out!"

Some doors opened, men stumbling into the dark, wearing the mussed and matted clothing they'd slept in. They blinked in the glare of policemen's lamps and the flashes of newsmen's cameras. When knocks got no response, officers smashed down doors and forced occupants out, carrying those too drunk to walk.

An alcoholic stench pervaded, as if this were another brewery raid. The predawn quiet gave way to howling dogs and cursing men. Roughly thirty-five transients formed a line at the base of the viaduct, some black, some white—the shantytown had been segregated, blacks to the south and whites to the north. Police collected names; Ness handled some questioning himself, his neat attire and mirror-polished shoes at odds with the threadbare, baggy clothing of his subjects, at least one with bare feet. Most residents cooperated, but one sneered as the cops went by. Police marked each hut, taking note of who had lived there, so personal effects could be returned.

When the residents had been removed, Ness ordered a fire truck to fix an arc light on the landscape. Cops began a search of each shack for clues, breaking down locked doors. The Safety Director grabbed an ax handle. Another detective found an ax, then threw it at a dog who tried to bite him. Large rats fled some shanties as the cops entered.

Ness would remember the dwellings as the "most miserable hovels he had ever seen in his life." Nothing found inside had any bearing on the torso murders.

A reporter discovered Ness at the center of the settlement, surrounded by cops, seemingly exhausted, his voice quiet and hesitant.

"You see," he said, "if we remove the cause, perhaps we can bring this man out into the open when he looks for his victims."

A detective handed him a bar of chocolate.

Ness hesitated before digging in. "Sure you didn't get this around here, Mac?"

The raiders moved on to a smaller, "higher class" settlement under the Lorain-Carnegie Bridge, banging on doors, rousting ten sleepers. These men were cleaner, and, to a reporter's eyes, "seem[ed] to resent the intrusion more."

A resident complained he'd just landed a job and would be fired if he had to spend the day in jail. If he was telling the truth, Ness said, he could go back to work.

"What's your name?" a detective asked a bleary-eyed drifter.

The man mumbled his response.

"What's that?" the detective said. "How do you spell it?"

"I can't spell," the man replied.

The raiders pressed on, seeking another settlement near the pool where a torso victim had been found floating two years ago. "Scrambling, sliding, falling down the tricky slope," reported the *Press*, "their lights making circles in the dark, they were a weird addition to the weird-enough shapes and shadows that flit through Kingsbury Run."

These men picking their way through dense sumac bushes and rank runoff reminded that reporter "of some movie-style Mississippi man-hunt through swamps and bayous." But word of their intent apparently preceded the raiders, because the men these cops were seeking had vanished. Police managed to arrest only a dozen or so hoboes just off a freight train and bedded down under a railroad overpass.

Around 4 A.M., Ness led his raiders out of the Run. They'd

made sixty-two arrests. Police wagons convoyed the transients to Central Station for questioning and fingerprinting. Should any turn up decapitated, police could now attach a name.

Ness promised more shantytown raids. "We are going to clean out all such places," he told the *Press*. "The men can go to the [Wayfarer's] Lodge. There is ample room for them there."

At least one displaced transient disagreed. "I do not like to stay at the Lodge," he told a reporter. "There are so many men there and so much noise."

Nor did he think much of Ness's rationale for the raids. "The torso murderer—bah! We're not afraid of him."

That afternoon, firemen arrived at Commercial Road Hill to search the vacant shanties. They removed anything of possible value, noting where it came from. The *Press* made a brief inventory: "battered old suitcases, tattered shirts, employment registration slips and two pieces of paper bearing the legend: 'Honorable Discharge from the United States Army.'" Each would be returned after police finished with the owners.

Then firemen wrapped cables around the shacks and used a power winch to pull them down into a pile at the hill's bottom. They doused the wreckage with kerosene and set it alight, as the remaining residents—a few dogs and cats and a single chicken—shrieked, squawked, dashing about. Cockroaches and rats fled the flames.

Despite Ness's promise, the arrested men spent a full day and night in jail before arraignment the following morning. The judge asked each a series of questions: "Have you a job? Any means of support? Any relatives to care for you?"

Fourteen said yes, and the judge turned them over to officials to make sure they weren't lying. The rest could only admit their poverty.

"I have nothing, judge. All I had was a shanty and it's gone."

"I got relatives, judge, but they live in Poland."

"I ain't got no job, judge, but I got money. I got nine cents."

The oldest shantytown resident, Mike Costello, sixty-nine,

recently kicked off relief rolls, had even less; the shantytown man who'd offered him a place to stay now had "nothing, no home, everything's gone."

"I never been in trouble," Costello said, "but I guess I have to plead guilty. I haven't got anything."

At one point, he asked a reporter, "Where can I go now?"

The judge had an answer. To hold them while police checked their fingerprints, he fined forty-eight men court costs. Unable to pay, they went to the workhouse.

The FBI's national fingerprint registry revealed ten arrested men had criminal records, which justified jailing them. The rest were convicted of vagrancy—defined in Cleveland as a man who hadn't sought work despite being capable of manual labor—and sentenced to as much as six months in the workhouse. One man took the verdict philosophically, thanking the judge.

"The other fourteen times I've been there," he said after sentencing, "convince me that autumn in the workhouse is the only place for a man with a poet's soul."

SOME CLEVELANDERS WELCOMED the shantytown raids.

The resolutely Republican *News* admitted that Ness "doesn't have a great chance to catch the torso murderer," yet applauded the removal of "these camps for floaters and degenerates," alluding to "such subnormal male hangouts" where "psychopathic practices" took place.

"Unless these murders are stopped," opined the *News*, "we might someday be known as the home site of 'that phantom killer who cuts off people's heads.' Ill-informed people elsewhere might worry about friends and relatives here. . . . But Director Ness, if he cleans up the 'jungles' where these torso murders without a doubt are born, can strike the most effective blow against any more of them."

The *Press* saw things differently. Previously a staunch Ness ally, assisting his police corruption and labor racketeering investigations, they gave the shantytown raids the usual ink, but with a harsh, unsparing look at the human cost. And they excoriated Ness's "misguided zeal."

"Safety Director Eliot Ness' personally-supervised raid upon the packing box homes underneath the Eagle street ramp may contribute something toward the capture of the torso killer," they editorialized. "We doubt it. . . .

"It is well for all of us to keep in mind that, after all, few men live through choice in such squalor as presented by these jungle camps. If such residents are jobless, that also is probably through no fault of their own. Any single man out of work and hungry knows how hard it is to get any form of public relief.

"That such Shantytowns exist is a sorrowful reflection upon the state of society. The throwing into jail of men broken by experience and the burning of their wretched places of habitation will not solve the economic problem. Nor is it likely to lead to the solution of the most macabre mystery in Cleveland's history."

The *Plain Dealer* joined in, criticizing Ness's "brutal" tactics. Charles Nevel, acting chief of detectives, declared them ineffective.

The men Ness arrested, Nevel told the *Press*, "are the type who would have come in before this and told us if they knew anything about the torso cases." Peter Merylo, never one to hold his tongue, agreed.

Ness remained unfazed, telling the *News* he'd "received numerous phone calls and letters" praising his removal of the shantytowns. He planned to wipe out the rest, promising that "Cleveland no longer will be known as the best hobo stopover in the middle west."

Others had complained of getting "approached and sometimes insulted by vagrants on downtown streets." Ness responded by ordering a police crackdown on panhandlers.

"The whole problem is to be taken care of in the best way we know how," he said. "How we will solve all the angles is yet to be decided, but the shantytowns and junglelands must go. . . . It'll be good riddance."

The Wayfarer's Lodge offered to house the evicted men, but most had no intention of sticking around to be arrested.

"We are not bums," a shantytown spokesman told the *News*. "We have lived here for eight years. We don't bother anyone, but if we have to go, give us a week to get our clothing."

Ness justified the campaign on public safety grounds—these shacks, he said, were firetraps. He ordered eighteen fire wardens to make a "photographic survey" of the area, documenting evidence of health and safety violations.

That was just a cover for their real mission: hunting for the Butcher's "laboratory." Fire wardens didn't need a search warrant to enter a building. By pairing them with a few trusted detectives, Ness could have police inspect every structure in the Roaring Third—a warrantless house-to-house search on a massive scale.

The true purpose of the survey remained a closely guarded secret. Among the six detectives entrusted with the job were Merylo and his old partner, Martin Zalewski. Merylo would not forget the squalor they found in the dark corners of the Roaring Third.

"Big rats ran from under the flooring in some of the huts," he recalled, "the stench . . . nauseating; the meanest flophouse looked good by comparison."

But nothing resembled a killer's workshop. After five days of searching, Charles Nevel broke the story in the press. Few protested the infringement on civil liberties; if anything, newspapers welcomed it as an exposé of how the other half lived. The detectives gave up, having come no closer to the Butcher.

That Ness would order these searches suggests he might not have been convinced of Frank Sweeney's guilt, or perhaps sought an accomplice or evidence against the doctor. But in the midst of the survey, Sweeney confounded investigators once more, applying for readmission to the Sandusky Soldiers and Sailors Home on August 23.

"Life & its—stresses," he wrote on his application, had exacted their "toll" on him.

Sweeney moved back into the hospital two days later. Although the doctor could still check himself in and out at will, the staff would alert Cleveland police whenever he left. The cops would continue to watch him, waiting for him to slip up.

JUST WHEN THE case seemed to have spun from his grasp, Ness received a promising tip from his hometown.

A deputy coroner in Chicago had learned of Emil Fronek, the stevedore and onetime tramp who claimed a mysterious "doctor" drugged him near Kingsbury Run four years before. After the coroner reported the story to the *Chicago Herald and Examiner*, the paper alerted Ness, who dispatched Merylo and another detective to find Fronek.

When they did, Fronek fled in fear, jumping from a moving car and racing down Michigan Avenue. Merylo and his partner caught him, only to be surrounded by Chicago police mistaking them for kidnappers.

In Cleveland, Fronek calmed down and agreed to help. The detectives drove him around the neighborhood near Kingsbury Run till he recognized some landmarks: a pair of churches he'd seen as he wandered toward the doctor's office. This let them narrow their search to a short stretch of Broadway Avenue between East Fiftieth and East Fifty-Fifth Streets.

Merylo and his partner walked Fronek around, trying to jog his memory. But Fronek couldn't find the building where he'd been drugged. That night had been dark, and this was several years ago. Nor did they find anyone who recognized Fronek's description of the doctor.

Though Merylo likely didn't know it, Fronek had led them to the spot where Francis Sweeney practiced medicine in 1934. The house he'd used as an office, with the funeral home next door, sat at 5026 Broadway. Fronek's recollections of the doctor's office matched the layout of Sweeney's building precisely. And although Fronek remembered the doctor being somewhat shorter and slimmer than Sweeney, the rest of his description—a middle-aged man with light, graying hair and a smooth, pale face—closely fit Ness's secret suspect.

While police kept combing the area, interrogating every doctor and searching their offices, Ness met privately with Fronek and listened to the stevedore's story, probing until satisfied it was true. What they discussed exactly is impossible to say. But Ness must have known his prime suspect once practiced on the same street where Fronek encountered his doctor, in a house that greatly resembled the one the stevedore recalled.

And yet, even if Sweeney had drugged Fronek, that would only add another piece of circumstantial evidence to an already circumstantial case. Maybe, if police had some proof linking Sweeney to the actual killings, they could make use of Fronek's story. As of now, they didn't.

"Unquestionably this man has given us some important information," Ness told the *Herald and Examiner.* "I have gone over his story several times with him from beginning to end. I believe he is telling the truth."

Fronek, meanwhile, had grown concerned that he would lose his job if he didn't return home; he promised to come back if needed. Ness let him go.

Apparently, the Cleveland Police never called on Fronek again.

THE LAST OF Cleveland's shantytowns went up in flames on September 9. In just over three weeks, police had destroyed almost one hundred shacks. Of roughly three hundred people evicted, fewer than twelve wound up at the Wayfarer's Lodge. Many others fled, fearing police more than the Butcher. The *News* showed little concern over where they had gone.

"Good riddance," the paper declared, echoing Ness, "and good job."

Ness's campaign to drive out the homeless might have restored the city's honor in the eyes of some, but it did nothing to assuage fears the Butcher might strike again. If anything, the raids only highlighted Ness's failure to catch the killer, and his reputation took a hit from which it would never quite recover.

Though the press remained largely on Ness's side, they would no longer cover him as if he could do no wrong. Most Clevelanders still saw Ness as a hero but not above reproach, and the freedom and trust he had so far enjoyed began to erode.

The Safety Director appeared to be feeling the strain. On September 19, he attended a city council meeting to discuss hiring a new masonry inspector. Councilman Clarence Young, a former vice president of the same painters' union that employed Don Campbell, had a month earlier "sharply criticized" Ness for the shantytown raids.

"The director says he'll do this if we find the money for him," Young said, laying into the Safety Director again. "Well, then, I'd like to find out what he has done with that extra $17,000 in his department for common labor this year."

Young referred to Ness's secret "undercover investigators"—the Unknowns—listed on the public payroll as laborers, clerks, or secretaries. Ness had brushed off similar attacks before, but now, wounded, he lost his characteristic cool.

"Mr. Young has been sharpshooting at my department for a long time," Ness said, "principally because we indicted and convicted officials of a union he was thrown out of the other night."

"That's a lie," Young shot back. "That's a lie, and don't go saying those things around here. I was never thrown out of any union."

The chairman told both men to settle down and abandon such personal attacks.

"I apologize for engaging in personalities," Ness said. "But . . . I'm getting sick and tired of having people come in here and say I don't represent union labor. I want to say right here that honest union labor is back of what I'm doing."

The next day, news of his impending divorce finally hit the papers. When reached for comment, Ness admitted he and Edna had been separated for months.

"We are parting as friends," he told the *Press*.

Cleveland would not let that go so easily. The large Catholic population did not look kindly on divorce. Ness had long sought to keep his personal life out of the public sphere, knowing it might undermine his upstanding image. News of his divorce ended that.

Now, criticism seemed to come from all sides. That same month, *Call & Post* publisher William Walker scathingly accused Ness of racial bias.

"The great G-man," Walker's editorial declared, "is turning out to be just another punk in so far as Negroes are concerned."

Ness was "the only city official who cannot be seen except by a favored few," Walker observed. "He is always out, or in some important conference."

The publisher saw this as self-protection. "Evidently Mr. Ness takes himself too seriously," Walker wrote, "else the aura of mystery that he has built around himself is deliberately done to hide his faults."

But while Ness refused to admit to his flaws in public, he was aware of them in private. He preserved a copy of Walker's editorial in his latest scrapbook, a rare *Call & Post* clipping pasted alongside more glowing coverage from Cleveland's white papers.

Dec. 21,1938

Chief of Police Matowitz,

You can rest easy now as I have came out to sunny California for the winter. I felt bad operating on these people but science must advance. I shall soon astonde the medical profession-- a man with only a D.C.

What did their lives mean in compassion to hundreds of sick x and disease twisted bodies. Just laboratory guinea pigs found on any public street. No one missed them when I failed. My last case was sucessful. I know now the feeling of Pasteur Thoreau and other pioneers.

Right now I have a volunteer who will absolutely prove my theory. They called me mad and a butcherer but the "truth will out".

I have failed but once here. The body has not been found and never will be but the head minus features is buried in a gully on Century Blvd. between Western and Kentury Crenshaw. I feel it is my duty to dispose of the bodies I do .It is God's will not to let them suffer.

X

The letter sent to Chief Matowitz, allegedly from the Butcher, in December 1938.

Cleveland Public Library Photograph Collection

An anti-jaywalking sign put up in 1937, as part of Ness's effort to promote traffic safety.

Authors' Collection

FOURTEEN

Mystery Man

1938–1939

From the outside, the letter could have been a Christmas greeting, one of thousands flooding the mails that holiday season—folded shut without an envelope and closed with Christmas seals, addressed in ink to Police Chief George Matowitz.

But something about it caught the eye of a postal inspector, who rescued it from the dead letter office and brought it to the attention of Peter Merylo and Martin Zalewski. For despite its outward Christmas cheer, the letter's contents—dated December 21, 1938, and rife with misspellings—were anything but festive.

"You can rest easy now," the typewritten message began, "as I have came out to sunny California for the winter. I felt bad operating on those people but science must advance. I shall soon astonde the medical profession—a man with only a D.C.

"What did their lives mean in comparasion to hundreds of sick and disease twisted bodies. Just laboratory guinea pigs found on any public street. No one missed them when I failed."

The letter went on to announce a recent breakthrough, which the writer did not describe but compared to the achievements of pioneering scientist Louis Pasteur and, curiously, the poet Henry David Thoreau. He then said the partial remains of a failed experiment—"the head minus features"—could be found in Los Angeles, "buried in a gully on Century Blvd. between Western and Crenshaw."

"Right now," the writer claimed, "I have a volunteer who will absolutely prove my theory. They called me mad and a butcherer but 'the truth will out'. . . . I feel it is my duty to dispose of the bodies as I do. It is God's will not to let them suffer."

The message was signed: "X."

A Los Angeles postmark confirmed the letter had come from California, and its ravings certainly fit the police profile of a deranged medical man, but nothing in the message claimed any specific knowledge of the torso killings unavailable to newspaper readers. Still, Matowitz sent the LAPD a copy in early January, informing them—based on the reference to "a D.C."—that the killer might be a chiropodist or chiropractor. As soon as detectives laid plans to search the mile-wide area mentioned by the writer, news of the letter hit the Cleveland and L.A. papers.

That same day, January 6, found Merylo and Zalewski keeping busy back in Cleveland, responding to calls from people who thought they'd found a new torso victim. One set of bones, stuck in a sewer pipe, proved to have come from a sheep; another, left in a basement, looked to be the remains of a chicken and sparerib dinner.

Given this steady diet of false leads and even falser hopes, Merylo might be expected to doubt the authenticity of the Matowitz letter. Instead, he told the press he considered it "the best lead yet" amid all the 1,800 letters sent to police about the Butcher. Expressing an optimism bordering on delusion, Merylo informed the *Plain Dealer* "that, whether the Los Angeles police find the head or not, he believes it to be there."

The LAPD found no disembodied head, but they did find some apparently human bones, along with clothes, papers, and photographs belonging to an ex-Marine in his late twenties. When detectives learned the Marine had been missing for about a year, they briefly thought the Butcher might indeed have claimed a California victim. Soon enough, however, they found the missing man in San Francisco—alive and well, the victim only of an acri-monious divorce.

After it became clear that no trace of the Butcher would be found in Los Angeles, Merylo revised his opinion on the letter, branding it a fake. Further sleuthing suggested it had indeed come from a medical man, albeit a quack, with no known connection to the killings.

Nevertheless, this false lead only added to the growing legend of the torso murders, putting the case back on page one. After all, Jack the Ripper owed his name and much of his mystique to the flood of correspondence, supposedly from the killer, sent to London authorities and the press in 1888—most, if not all of it, phony. Fifty years later, Cleveland's Ripper found his voice the same way, through a spurious letter that helped keep him alive in the public mind.

The *Plain Dealer* summarized the speculation swirling around the city that winter: "From the miasmic fog of Cleveland's low-lands the phantom figure of the eerie butcher periodically emerges—and promptly commands the newspaper headlines. Most commonly he is thought to be a man of culture fallen on evil days, a crazed doctor driven by drink or drugs to this some-what unorthodox form of titillation. At intervals he loses his pro-fessional standing and becomes a medical student, or merely a butcher trying his cleaver in a new field; or a Mexican. When he is a Mexican, he is a marijuana addict."

Later that month, Phil Porter dismissed public fears of the Butcher, likening the killings to recent purse snatchings also given page-one coverage in Cleveland.

"The city and suburbs as a whole are not overrun with purse-snatchers," Porter wrote, "any more than most intelligent, alert citizens need worry about the torso murders. If you read Euro-pean newspapers on the subject of the torso killer, you'd think nobody ever ventured out of doors after dark in Cleveland."

Still the legend grew, aided and abetted by media in the United States and abroad—challenging Cleveland's efforts to present it-self as an inviting, forward-thinking city. An article in the January

12 issue of *Ken* magazine, "Cleveland's Rue Morgue," observed that the Butcher had "exploded . . . the myth of scientific crime detection growing out of Conan Doyle and, more latterly, J. Edgar Hoover"—not to mention Eliot Ness.

The killer's apparent ability to confound Ness's progressive new police department seemed to prove "that the 'perfect crime' does not depend upon the cleverness of its execution, but on the selection of a candidate."

That was true in more ways than one. *Ken* detected "a note of blithe irreverence throughout . . . public discussion of this fantastic case, a phenomenon that can only be attributed to the 'mad butcher's' canny precaution to decapitate no one of any standing in the community. . . . There are even those who regard him as a community asset, assuming that anyone who is nameless, homeless, and jobless and becomes as a result, headless, must necessarily have been a New Deal Democrat and a person whose absence need not be deplored."

"LET'S START 1939 right and make it a safer year than any before," Ness said in a special midnight New Year's Eve radio broadcast. "If you have been drinking, don't drive. If you insist on driving, don't go more than twenty miles an hour. Don't spoil your holiday with an accident."

Police were fanning out in what the *Press* called "the largest traffic patrol in the city's history," from Christmas Eve till New Year's Day.

Ness told the *Press*, "We do not want to see those who should be home trimming Christmas trees lying in a hospital or in the County Morgue."

Before 1938, Cleveland's streets had been among the nation's most dangerous, with more than two hundred fatal accidents yearly since at least 1934. After redoubling his efforts in 1938, Ness hoped to earn a National Safety Council distinction—"America's safest big city"—a title almost laughably out of the city's grasp in prior years.

The Safety Director turned to civic leaders to fund a massive public relations effort to scare citizens into safer behavior. Deputy Traffic Commissioner Martin Blecke, heading up the campaign, had an adman's gift for grabbing attention. He began by putting up a signboard on Public Square, with rotating slogans:

"Jeepers, Creepers, Use Your Peepers!"

"Heaven Can Wait—Why Can't You?"

"Driver, Can You Spare a Life?"

Such messages bombarded drivers and pedestrians from hundreds of billboards, and countless radio broadcasts and newspaper articles. Ness's surrogates gave speeches and showed films to citizens' groups, while shocking photos of wrecked automobiles went up in theaters, "where," according to the *Press*, "they would intercept pleasure-seekers with a silent warning like a straight-arm punch."

Though Ness typically had a low tolerance for "stunts," he joined right in. On December 3, Ness and Mayor Burton hosted a memorial service on Public Square for those killed in traffic so far that year. A high school marching band played, church bells tolled, and airplanes soared while the mayor dedicated a collective tombstone.

Of course, Ness preferred more prosaic measures: appointing a city traffic engineer, requiring automobile inspections, and establishing a safety school for traffic violators. He also urged the city to adopt daylight saving time, to brighten the hours when most accidents occurred.

In his New Year's broadcast, Ness reported the "best traffic year in over a decade," exceeding his goal of saving one hundred lives. Fatalities had been cut from 247 in 1937 to 130 in 1938; November saw an eighteen-day stretch with no traffic deaths— the longest lifesaving streak since the city began keeping accident records in 1925.

Cleveland's streets were safer in another way, thanks to Ness reorganizing the police department. Felonies dropped by almost a third, robberies by two-thirds. Car thefts were cut by more than half—"an all-time record for any city of comparable size," according to Chief Matowitz. More than two years had passed since Cleveland's last gang killing, and of fifty-six murders committed in 1938, forty-one had been solved.

In late March, the National Safety Council indeed recognized Cleveland as the country's safest large city, a title shared with last year's winner, Milwaukee. In 1939, Cleveland would win the honor again, but carry the title alone.

"This work," Ness said, "probably is the most important I have ever done."

WHILE TRAVELING TO the West Coast that February, reporter Howard Beaufait of the *News* discovered "that the fame of Eliot Ness [was] well scattered over the map." From Chicago to Los Angeles, people pressed Beaufait to tell them about Cleveland's dynamic young Safety Director. That Ness "was a mild-mannered fellow with a schoolboy complexion" came as a shock to some.

Boarding the train in Chicago for home, Beaufait felt a tap on the shoulder. "It was Eliot Ness himself, smiling, a little shy and impatient. He had the seat next to mine."

On the trip, Beaufait compared the "giant killer" in the papers with the flesh-and-blood man. "There is nothing in the Ness voice to frighten anyone," he wrote. "It is as soft and gentle as southern rain, tinged with eagerness and a dreamy sort of impatience."

When the train rolled through the dingy backyards of Chicago's South Side, Ness appeared "eager and bright-eyed with excitement," glimpsing his old neighborhood.

"As always," Beaufait wrote, "there was something boyish about Mr. Ness, as though a part of him, tucked deep down behind his thoughts, has refused to grow up."

Beaufait struggled to picture Ness speeding through the city in a squad car, siren screaming, toward some "dark and daring errand of justice"—though he knew the Safety Director had done so often.

"He must have looked like a Boy Scout," Beaufait wrote, "in a mad chariot race."

Viktor Schreckengost, a widely respected artist and designer, saw Ness the same way: "I was looking for a big fellow, and here's this quiet guy who never liked to brag, but would just sit back and listen."

The artist took note of the empty shoulder holster Ness wore. "Not the kind of fellow you expected to be a gangbuster at all," Schreckengost said. "In fact, he was the last person you'd think would ever have anything to do with Al Capone."

But the artist saw the other side of Ness when they attended a party in Cleveland Heights and the Safety Director was summoned downtown. Ness asked Schreckengost if he'd like to come along. Then they were in Ness's car going eighty or ninety miles an hour down Euclid Avenue, with other sedans fore and aft.

When they pulled to the curb near Tenth Street, Ness told his passenger to wait by the car. In the dark, terrified and thrilled, Schreckengost stood while Ness went inside for about fifteen minutes. Then the Safety Director emerged.

"No problem," he said. "We got it solved."

They returned to the party, the artist never learning the why of their wild ride.

Ness had a habit of bringing friends along on his exploits. "If something was happening, he'd say 'We'd better go take a look,'" Robert Chamberlin's brother recalled, "and the next thing you know he'd be across town, and whoever happened to be with him went sailing along, too."

Ness's befuddled sidekicks would walk away with a new story to tell, adding to the growing legend. They never knew exactly what had happened, but they always remembered the Safety Director—calm, cool, in command.

Margaret Collins, who joined his staff as a stenographer in 1939, recalled, "He was always the professional, very controlled and polite. Everything was always very proper with him."

But she, too, got swept up in the excitement. Ness called the office one day and told her to get to the hospital to take down a statement from a dying man. Collins grabbed her notepad and rushed into a waiting police car, terrified she might be killed over what this witness had to say. When they arrived, she waited by the car until Ness came out.

"Take her back," Ness told her driver. "He just died."

The news came as a tremendous relief. The young woman had come about as close to Ness's adventures as she cared to get.

OTHER WOMEN WEREN'T so inclined to keep their distance. Marion Hopwood Kelly—wife of reporter Ralph Kelly, Ness's friend at the *Plain Dealer*—would later describe the Safety Director as "the sexiest man I'd ever known." Part of this came from his easy charm, and the knack for flattery he'd picked up in fraternity days.

"He used to say to me, 'I'll never forget the first time that I saw you. You were wearing a red dress,'" Kelly recalled. "I was just so flattered that anybody remembered me for anything."

But there was something else about Ness women found disarming—an air of vulnerability.

"He was not assertive or . . . macho in any way. Not in any way," recalls Natalie Phelps, daughter of another friend. For all the talk of Ness's courage on the job, he gave off a different air in person—"the impression that he needed a strong woman."

He certainly seemed to in early 1939. With his divorce final, and only a cat to come home to, Ness entered a kind of second adolescence. Though just thirty-six, he showed signs of a midlife crisis. His appetite for work seemed to slacken; he grew interested in finding time to unwind.

Ness went "crazy over boats," David Cowles recalled, and bought a sailboat to cruise Lake Erie on lazy summer weekends, often late at night in the company of friends. The water seemed to relax Eliot, offering a sense of shelter and safety.

Sometimes he'd chase that feeling by taking an overnight trip on a palatial steamer running between Cleveland and Detroit. The ships were opulent "floating hotels," appointed like the elegant ocean liners of a bygone age. Onboard, Ness would pass time playing cards, particularly gin rummy, then wander away from the other passengers to walk the decks alone. When the ship arrived, he wouldn't get off, but wait to ride it home again.

Ness's devotion to his work had given him a reputation as a loner, a "mystery man." Now a natural sociability began to emerge, as he threw himself into Cleveland's social whirl. He avoided most nightclubs because of their mob ties, instead attending parties in other people's homes.

Marion Kelly recalled that Ness "would always sit with his back to the wall, facing the door"—a habit he'd picked up in Chicago Heights, when the mob wanted him dead.

"We'd kid him about it and accuse him of seeing too many movies," Kelly said, "but he'd just smile."

His haunts were the Hollenden Hotel's Vogue Room and the Hotel Cleveland's Bronze Room. Both were high-class cousins of the glossy Prohibition-era dine-and-dance joints where music flowed as freely as liquor.

The man who'd once spent his nights shutting down illicit taverns and casinos now stayed out till all hours with trusted reporters. He would sip at cocktails, getting lubricated but never losing control. Despite the drink and the blare of big bands, Ness rarely raised his voice. When he laughed, as he often did, he barely made a sound. Friends took note of his high tolerance for liquor; they never saw him visibly drunk.

Ness admitted to feeling uncomfortable among the city's elite, and at times tried to explode that tension with pranks. The same offbeat sense of humor that had delighted him on liquor raids now led him into elaborate, even dangerous practical jokes.

Once an apparent gangster burst into a bar, gun in hand, and threatened to shoot someone while Ness and a close friend, Dan Moore of the state's securities and exchange commission, were entertaining the governor of Ohio. When the gun-toting actor Ness had hired made his appearance, the governor—fearing bad publicity—fled out the fire escape.

Moore marveled at the boldness behind such a stunt.

"That's just the way Eliot was at that stage of his life," Moore recalled, "a fun-loving guy. . . . He'd do things like invite a seven-foot-tall woman to a party and pair her up on a blind date with the shortest man in the room, just for laughs."

Not everyone appreciated Eliot's sense of humor. Marion Kelly remembered attending a party with around twenty other guests at Ness's apartment. As the revelry neared its end, Ness said he'd had the place bugged. Then he played the recording.

"He managed to pick up quite a lot," Kelly recalled, "and even though it stopped short of scandal, it wasn't a very nice thing to do."

Ness had done to his guests what he so often did to the mob: placed them under surveillance.

He even joked about the hunt for the Mad Butcher. Porter remembered a party where Eliot arrived early to hide a fake leg under the sofa. Once the party was in full swing, he arranged for the discovery of the Butcher's latest "victim," to his evident delight.

Another time, Kelly saw Ness discussing the torso murders with Robert Chamberlin. "Perhaps," Ness said, "somebody without a law-enforcement background, like Marion Kelly here, would see something that the detectives are missing."

So he had all the autopsy reports sent to her. Though an accomplished journalist in her own right, Kelly found nothing in the files that might solve the case.

"On the other hand," she recalled, "I could tell you what any one of the decapitated victims had for dinner the night before being chopped up."

Ness's sense of humor didn't always play well in buttoned-down Cleveland, where people might approve of the Safety Director's on-the-job exploits but not his extracurricular activities. One reporter called him "too handsome and self-centered to be popular with the great bulk of hard-working conservative Clevelanders."

And his need for excitement perhaps impaired his judgment. Though he wanted to avoid mobsters in off-hours, his fondness for the Vogue Room regularly brought him under the same roof as the Cleveland Syndicate, which used the Hollenden as their headquarters.

Nothing got people talking like Ness's familiarity with the opposite sex. In a town where simply winking at the wrong person could start a scandal, the charming, flirtatious Safety Director didn't hide how much he enjoyed the company of good-looking women. He liked to dance, always ready to guide a beauty around the floor. That was more than enough, in some circles, to spread rumors.

But Ness left little record of any romantic attachments outside marriage. Phil Porter recalled that Ness "seemed to have trouble keeping any sort of lasting love life. . . . During his bachelor period, he never lacked for gals who were charmed by his boyishness. But the relationships were short-lived, and one of [the women] said privately that he didn't have the essentials to keep them going."

A close Ness aide insisted the Safety Director became too famous to pursue an affair without risking it going public. But Gus Zukie, a onetime petty crook turned Cleveland cop, claimed to have caught Ness in an unusually compromising position.

Zukie said he and his partner were responding to "a complaint about gambling and noise" in a building behind the Auditorium Hotel.

"When we walked in," Zukie said, "Eliot Ness was there already, sitting on a chair with his chief investigator, Clothey. They were kissing. Ness looked up at us. My partner said, 'Hey, Gus, let's get the hell outta here.' We turned around and walked right out."

Zukie, who had never liked the Safety Director, alleged, "When he was drunk, he was queer."

Like all the other whispers about Ness's private life, Zukie's claims remain nothing more than unsubstantiated rumor. The crook-turned-cop told other tall tales, some easily disproven. But Zukie seems to have reacted negatively to an aspect of Ness's personality that caught many off guard—an indefinable quality unlike the image of a hard-boiled hero.

. . .

WITH THEIR APPEALS exhausted and no governor's pardon forthcoming, Don Campbell and John McGee finally began serving their prison sentences in the fall of 1938. By refusing to overturn these convictions, the state supreme court gave Ohio prosecutors a powerful tool against gangsters preying on labor.

Campbell and McGee's influence, however, remained in Cleveland. The incarcerated Campbell still retained his post as Painters' District Council head in January 1939, sparking an ongoing battle between "old guard" members backing him and a "progressive" faction who wanted him gone. Ness met with representatives from both groups, hoping the dispute wouldn't devolve into more violence. But the old guard leaders refused to stop protecting Campbell.

To the *Plain Dealer*, the problem was simple: "Campbell has enough supporters in the council and of such character that no man who moved to oust the convict president would be safe from personal assault."

Meanwhile, a trio of racketeers—including Maxie Diamond of the Cleveland Syndicate—formed the Cuyahoga Window Cleaning Company, under the presidency of one Sammy Salupo, a twenty-seven-year-old ex-con who'd served time for extorting money from prostitutes. The governor paroled Salupo over objections from Cullitan and the Cleveland Police, after Democratic party and union officials stood up in his defense.

The cops kept tabs on Salupo, however, noting his partnership with Diamond. Realizing he was under surveillance, Salupo brought Diamond to City Hall, barging into Ness's office.

"I'm a legitimate businessman now," Salupo said. "So have your guys lay off."

Ness refused to call off the tail.

Salupo and Diamond faced competition and threats from the original window-smashing racket. But they toughed it out and kept squeezing local businesses, even after a gunman opened fire on their business partner outside his home.

Then, in early August, as Salupo drove through Shaker Heights with his fiancée, he pressed the horn in his car and a bomb went off, killing them both. Soon Diamond and his surviving partner sold their window-washing company to try a safer racket.

The convictions of Campbell and McGee, Cleveland's most notorious racketeers, only paved the way for successors willing to operate more quietly and ruthlessly—often with the connivance of corrupt cops. By fall 1941, the old strong-arm tactics and bribery of witnesses still protected labor racketeers from prosecution.

A county grand jury foreman wrote, "We need laws which will make it possible to deal with modern methods of terrorism, with their professional sluggers, with their unscrupulous lawyers, and with their sub rosa methods of bribery."

Such measures would be slow in coming, until the passage of federal anti-racketeering laws decades later.

IN FALL 1938, an earnest young college student in his final year at Oberlin, fascinated by Ness's exploits in the *Press*, hoped to write a political science paper about the Safety Director. Arnold Sagalyn took a bus to Cleveland, found Clayton Fritchey at the *Press* building, and asked if the reporter would introduce him to Ness.

No one waltzed into Ness's orbit quite so easily. He confided his plans only to a small group of trusted associates and rarely opened up to outsiders.

"His closest aides worship him and unblushingly admit it," wrote the *News*. "[Mayor] Burton sees him about as often as the average citizen."

But Fritchey was about to visit the Safety Director and invited his visitor to tag along. At the meeting, Ness—impressed by the young student's pluck—agreed to a lengthy interview.

Months later, the college student arrived at Ness's office to deliver a copy of his term paper. Sagalyn told Ness how much he'd enjoyed the project, and asked if the Safety Department might have an opening for "an intern-type summer job."

Ness flipped through the paper and asked, "Why don't you just come and work for me full-time?"

Sagalyn remembered reporting for duty on a "special June morning in 1939," primed for adventure. "I was going to be working closely with a man whose exploits I had been avidly following . . . and I felt hyped up, both excited and nervous."

But when Sagalyn arrived at City Hall, a police officer directed him to a small desk and a well-worn chair, to sort through Ness's correspondence.

"I quickly discovered," Sagalyn recalled, "that Eliot's very small staff did not include a personal secretary. . . . So I was, in effect, to become his personal aide and secretary."

But Ness also groomed him for the Unknowns—that "crack team of civilian criminal investigators," as Sagalyn described them, who did most of the Director's undercover work. Ness rotated him through each police department division; though he carried a card as a "Special Policeman in the Department of Public Safety," Sagalyn was on the payroll as a garage worker, a dodge Ness often employed to get his new hires past the frugal city council.

Before long, this young college graduate was working on Ness's most sensitive cases, including the torso murders. His first job was filling in for a detective following Frank Sweeney during one of the doctor's self-authorized furloughs from the Sandusky Soldiers and Sailors Home.

"The elusive Torso Murders suspect knew that Cleveland police detectives were following him," Sagalyn remembered. "He thought it was a game and thoroughly enjoyed outfoxing the series of police detectives who were assigned to track him."

Before Sagalyn traded places with the plainclothesman currently on Sweeney's tail, the detective warned him to be careful.

"This guy can be tricky," he said.

The doctor emerged soon after, and Sagalyn got his first look at his quarry—a "rather ordinary-looking person . . . wearing a green plaid cap and a light tan topcoat." Sweeney glanced around, as if for a familiar detective, then began walking up Euclid Avenue. Sagalyn hung back in a doorway and let the doctor get several yards ahead, always keeping plenty of people between himself and the suspect.

At a nearby trolley stop, Sweeney lounged against a wall before hopping onto a departing streetcar. Sagalyn had no choice but to follow. He managed to catch up with the car and climb on, but he knew the suspect had spotted him.

At the next cross street, Sweeney jumped off the trolley and sprinted to one going in a different direction. This time Sagalyn couldn't keep up—the next streetcar heading that way wouldn't leave for half an hour.

"I had no other means of pursuit," Sagalyn recalled. "I had lost my assigned quarry on my very first surveillance."

He returned to police headquarters, where he found out, to his humiliation, that Sweeney had called in to critique his performance.

"That young kid you had following me wasn't very good," the doctor reported. "If he wants to try again tomorrow, tell him I'll be in the men's department at Higbee's Department Store at 2 P.M."

Despite this initial blunder, Sagalyn earned Ness's trust. "I never talked about him," Sagalyn wrote, "or in any other way revealed anything I heard or saw that might adversely affect or embarrass him."

Ness may have seen himself in Sagalyn, a clean-cut college kid with an interest in turning public service into a profession.

But he wouldn't always choose his confidants so well.

Det. Lt. Ernest Molnar (seated) and Sgt. Peter Allen, posing in blackface after a numbers raid, December 1938.

Authors' Collection

The squad of detectives who conducted Ness's numbers racket probe in 1939. Molnar and Allen stand at center, with Patrolman Claude Lee directly behind Molnar, Patrolman John Henry Jones (in fedora) next to Allen, and Policewoman Virginia Houston sitting at right.

Cleveland Public Library Photograph Collection

FIFTEEN

Right-Hand Man

Fall 1938–Spring 1939

Burly and affable, with "the ruggedness of a tractor and the mobility of a mustang," Detective Lieutenant Ernest Molnar looked like everybody's idea of a flatfoot. He'd studied law at John Carroll University but left without a degree to join the Cleveland Police because, he said, he'd just gotten married and "had to get a job."

For a decade, Molnar rose through the ranks, becoming one of the few officers Ness truly trusted. In February 1937, at thirty-four, he became the department's youngest lieutenant. The next May, Ness chose him to run the vice squad.

"He was one of the smartest lieutenants in the department," recalled Gus Zukie, who served under him. "Molnar knew the game."

Despite a sterling record, Molnar wasn't as untouchable as he appeared. He'd been friends with former police captain Louis Cadek, still serving time for taking bribes. During Ness's ATF days, a federal agent claimed, Molnar often sabotaged the future Safety Director's liquor raids.

But after Ness took charge of the Cleveland Police, his purge of crooked cops left Molnar standing. In 1936, after cleaning out the Fifteenth Precinct, Ness assigned Molnar to help keep it that way. A year later, Ness promoted him and nine other officers, warning them to avoid any "entangling alliances" with criminals.

Molnar raided thirty-seven bookie joints in three days. Over the next few months, his crew racked up a conviction rate of better than 86 percent. The squad became known as "Molnar's Raiders," Cleveland's latest answer to the Untouchables.

"This business is the coming field for a young man," Molnar told the *Plain Dealer*, saying just what Ness wanted to hear.

The Safety Director cemented their partnership as they prepared for Ness's biggest attack on organized crime since Capone—a massive investigation into the gambling racket gripping the city's poorest neighborhoods.

THE NUMBERS RACKET comprised two different kinds of illegal lotteries.

In "policy," players bet on a sequence of numbered balls drawn from a wheel or a box. The game was easy to rig; operators used specially shaped balls or heated ones they didn't want chosen, setting them apart by touch.

In "clearing house," players tried to guess the last three digits of a published number—the closing figures on the New York Stock Exchange, for example. This was much harder to fix, but players got very poor odds—one in a thousand.

Here, as in many other big cities, the numbers racket began and prospered in African-American communities. Most bets were small, usually a few cents, but offered a chance at high reward to people with little else to look forward to.

Some understandably believed the numbers racket exploited the poor. But since the early 1920s, numbers had offered rare opportunities to African-American entrepreneurs. Of the "Big Four" in charge of the Cleveland racket, three were black, running a relatively honest operation and keeping the profits within their community. Police largely ignored them, as did white mobsters, too busy bootlegging to care about penny-ante gambling.

As Prohibition neared its end, however, the Mayfield Road Mob—and their shadowy allies, the Cleveland Syndicate—realized little pennies added up to big money. A single policy operator could take in over $100,000 in a year, making the racket irresistible to chubby, baby-faced "Big Angelo" Lonardo and his short, one-eyed cousin, "Little Angelo" Sciria, survivors of the town's bloody booze wars. Cunning and ruthless, the Mayfield mobsters unleashed a wave of violence in the Roaring Third in the early '30s, fighting to take over the numbers racket.

One of the Big Four was murdered; another left after being shot. The third survived two assassination attempts, went to prison, then signed on "as a fifty-dollar-a-week flunky" for the Mayfield Road Mob. Frank Hoge, the only white member of the Big Four, joined the new regime and stayed prominent in the racket. Those who resisted wound up dead or wounded, their bullet-riddled bodies scattered about the East Side.

By the time Ness became Safety Director, the Mayfield gang had either absorbed or killed off their numbers-game competition. Those remaining ran franchise operations, turning over as much as 40 percent of their take to stay in business. The operators assumed all risk, insulating the mob from any losses. Even if one hit a bad stroke of luck, several players winning big, he still had to give the gang its cut and make up the shortfall. No one questioned the arrangement; bloody memories remained too fresh.

Although the violence had ended, numbers games spilled out into every corner of the city, and the Cleveland Syndicate (through the Mayfield Road Mob) raked in millions, using that money to invade legitimate businesses.

Harold Burton had pledged to crack down on numbers while courting the black vote in 1935. When the new mayor and his young safety director failed to follow up on that promise, some African-American supporters felt betrayed. In February 1936, Burton and Ness attended a mass meeting at the city's leading African Methodist Episcopal Church, where the pastor lambasted both men.

The reverend, reported the *Call & Post*, "challenged Director

Ness to go out as he did in so grandiose a manner to back up Mr. Frank Cullitan at the Harvard and Thomas Clubs and give the people of Cleveland the same kind of protection from the gambling racketeers."

The paper's publisher, William O. Walker, said this "blast on broken pledges . . . nearly jolted Mr. Burton and Director Ness out of their seats."

Walker called out the Burton administration's general indifference toward African Americans. Hadn't Ness declared war on all kinds of illicit gambling—except the numbers racket? This, Walker knew, channeled millions from black hands into white pockets. He met with Ness to press his case, arguing "that as long as Negroes were the big players in numbers and policy . . . they should control them and not have to bow to the Mafia."

WHEN JOHN HENRY Jones joined the Cleveland Police in summer 1916, fewer than six African Americans already wore the badge. A high school graduate from St. Clairsville, Ohio, Jones had come to Cleveland with dreams of being a doctor. But when he learned police were seeking new recruits, he picked up an application and never looked back.

Urbane and debonair, Jones became known in the African-American community as both a trusted, respected cop and a fixture of the black social scene. The *Call & Post* remembered him as "a handsome six-foot-tall 210-pound dark complexioned man who dressed and acted in the suave manner of black detectives on the modern screen."

Jones's skill with his sidearm, "Bertha Mae," earned him the nickname "Deadeye." Like the young Safety Director, he seemed equally at home at a crime scene and a nightclub.

Unlike Ness, Jones's professional opportunities were sharply limited by his skin color. After two decades on the force, he had yet to rise above patrolman, working glorified crossing guard duties outside Cleveland's Central High School.

After a burglary at a prominent African-American attorney's home, the victim's socialite wife went to Ness.

"Why don't you take off that squad of blundering flatfeet and give me just one man, Patrolman John Jones," she said, "and I'll bet you he will locate the missing property and clean up the whole crime. Any moron can escort school kids across the street."

"Not only will I give John Jones a raise if he does so," the *Call & Post* reported Ness saying, ". . . I'll make him a detective."

Jones remembered things differently, claiming Ness phoned him shortly before becoming Safety Director in 1935, saying he had "a special job for you just as soon as I'm sworn in."

Either way, Ness tapped the officer as one of his secret investigators. Then in his forties, Jones became the least known of Ness's Unknowns, working with the Safety Director for four years on cases taking him to eleven states.

A hint leaked out in summer 1936, when the local NAACP leader requested that Jones guard the Woodland Hills pool and Ness had to decline—Jones had been temporarily detailed to the Department of Justice to work a sex-trafficking case.

Now in plainclothes but officially still a patrolman, Jones regularly made headlines in the city's black press alongside his partner and "personal top man," Claude Lee. Fast-talking Lee, "a policeman's policeman," shared both Jones's hatred of vice and his taste for good scotch. Together these "two crack aces of the Cleveland Police Department," as the *Call & Post* described them, racked up arrests for liquor crimes and morals offenses in the black neighborhoods around Central and Scovill Avenues.

The well-publicized pair may have inspired, in part, "Grave Digger" Jones and "Coffin Ed" Johnson in the celebrated crime novels of Chester Himes, small-time armed robber turned mystery writer. Critics and readers of this great African-American author have been largely unaware that New York's Harlem in Himes is really Cleveland's Roaring Third, where the novelist spent his formative years in the 1920s and 1930s.

Jones was also launching a personal crusade. In 1933, he lost a close friend to the numbers war: a small-time policy operator shotgunned to death after refusing to submit to the gang. The patrolman swore to break the mob's hold on the racket, working off-hours to try to find willing witnesses.

"'You won't get anywhere,'" Jones recalled people telling him. "'You're just in for a headache. Nothing ever will come from it because people won't talk.'"

But Jones kept at it. And in 1937, after four years of detective work, the case went to Ness.

The Safety Director had his own reasons for taking down the numbers racket. Businessmen extorted and intimidated by the Mayfield gang convinced Ness the syndicate had to be stopped.

"As long as Cleveland has an underground empire," Ness said, "with tremendous revenues and headed by unscrupulous racketeers, it hangs as a threat over every decent citizen and every decent business."

Molnar assembled a small team to find more witnesses and get their statements. Jones and Lee did much of the legwork, taking them far outside the state. They worked alongside Sergeant Peter Allen, a white officer and Molnar's chief assistant on the vice squad—who, like the lieutenant, was "classified among the department's 'untouchables,'" according to the *Press*.

The other black team member was Policewoman Virginia Houston, whose outstanding civil service score had topped the list of new recruits in 1936. Her work with the Policewomen's Bureau typically involved such cases as illegal abortions and child abuse. After being transferred to Molnar's squad, she joined the other detectives as they crisscrossed the country, gathering testimony against the mob.

BY FALL 1938, the investigators had made enough progress to spark rumors of the Mayfield mob's impending downfall. Pittsburgh gamblers moved in on the Cleveland numbers racket, undercutting the competition with better odds. But the Mayfield gang scared them off with threats of violence.

Molnar's vice squad kept raiding numbers operations, crashing into one policy drawing in late August. The team "had little or no chance to make arrests or secure evidence that might lead to the conviction of the operators," reported the *Call & Post*, "as a crowd estimated at more than 300 made for available exits simultaneously, sweeping the police officers from its path."

On October 1, Jones and Molnar raided a "smoker" at the Central Avenue headquarters of the Ohio State Democratic League. The vice squad interrupted more than three hundred politicos watching dirty movies and ogling two naked women, who were nabbed for nude dancing. Police rounded up Democrats, and forty cop cars took the arrested men to Central Station in shifts. One would be charged for "engaging in an indecent act," having offered himself to the dancers at just the wrong time.

"The raid is said to have been a 'close shave' for many prominent Clevelanders," reported the *Call & Post*, "who were arrested . . . but who escaped formal booking. Nearly two-score of the guests are sporting wrenched backs and sprained ankles . . . having escaped the dragnet by jumping from second story windows."

Later that month, Sergeant Allen raided a policy operation run by Frank Hoge's brothers, which had been taking in $22,000 a day—the "biggest haul in history here against the numbers racket," Molnar told the *Plain Dealer*.

KNOWING COPS ON the gambling beat faced greater temptation than any others, the Safety Director kept an eye on them. Whenever his special surveillance detail discovered a compromised officer, Ness would transfer the offender out of temptation's way. But in fall 1938, he discovered a shocking betrayal: Molnar was taking bribes from Little Angelo Sciria for the names of numbers witness and copies of their affidavits.

Ness's drive to revitalize the police department remained his most visible success. Now the brightest example of that effort— the untouchable officer whom many saw "as Ness' right-hand man"—revealed himself as just another crook.

Ness handled the situation quietly. When he confronted Molnar, the lieutenant did the only thing he could—he confessed. He even handed over $770, claiming it was all the money Sciria had given him.

Previously, Ness had vigorously sought the prosecution of officers suspected of taking far less; but now, at least, he allowed Molnar to remain on the force in a position of trust and authority. What went on between Ness and Molnar is unknown. Most likely, in coming clean, Molnar somehow convinced the Safety Director he could still be trusted.

While Ness the investigator was hardened toward gangsters and racketeers—people he already knew to be guilty—he possessed an alarming blind spot when it came to crooks who hid their criminality, or to people who posed as friends while scheming behind his back, leaving him vulnerable to the treachery of two-timers like Molnar.

Ness revealed the betrayal only to Frank Cullitan, who agreed to keep it secret. The prosecutor took the cash the lieutenant surrendered and stashed it in his desk.

MOLNAR DEMONSTRATED HIS loyalty with a new round of raids in late December 1938, leading seven other cops—five white and two black—to shutter five numbers operations in a single night. The raiders, including Peter Allen and Claude Lee, arrested forty-five people and confiscated ledgers and thousands of betting slips.

Molnar and all the other white raiders slathered their faces in theatrical blackface, supposedly to get past the guards at each door. They claimed Lee had previously tried to enter only to be recognized and turned away, while their half-baked disguises got them in "without trouble or suspicion."

The cops had laughed and joked as they assumed blackface, and Molnar alerted reporters, so photographers would await their return. A front-page photo in the next day's *Plain Dealer* showed the squad posing with their seized evidence, Molnar and the other white cops—most blacked up only to mid-forehead, where their hats would come down—grinning through their makeup.

Lee stood among them, smiling big, while another black officer stood off unhappily to one side. A second photo featured Molnar and Allen, two of Ness's newest Untouchables, "smiling like minstrel end men," as the *Plain Dealer* put it.

Speaking for many in the African-American community, the *Call & Post* branded Molnar's raids a racist publicity grab. By going blackface and targeting African Americans, Molnar's band labeled the numbers game a wholly black problem, ignoring the violent takeover by white gangsters.

Leering, shoe-polished faces on the front page of a major morning paper hardly advertised Ness's vision of a modern, professionalized police force. As local African Americans flooded Ness's office with protests, Chief Matowitz denounced Molnar's racist theatrics, while Ness prohibited use of blackface by his officers.

The numbers raids continued, however, with the conviction in early January of a dozen people arrested in last year's massive roundup.

BY EARLY 1939, Molnar's squad had identified roughly seventy witnesses, plenty for an indictment wrapping up the Mayfield Road Mob leadership. In February, Ness had each witness picked up without warning, often after dark, and brought to a room in a downtown hotel as they had Frank Sweeney last May.

Ness again offered "safety in numbers," promising no one would stand alone against the gang. The successful police corruption and labor racketeering cases, in which no witnesses had been harmed, helped convince the holdouts.

Ness and Cullitan began bringing witnesses before the grand jury, telling how the Mayfield gang had muscled in. Many implicated Lonardo, Sciria, and other leaders by name, while prosecutors offered plenty of documents—"almost a ton of evidence," an official remarked—to back those stories up.

The case dealt not with illegal gambling, but the extortion

of policy operators—the same statutes used against Campbell and McGee. Police kept each witness under guard; investigators made copies of their affidavits, hiding the documents in separate locations.

Twenty-three policy racketeers were indicted on April 26, including such key Mayfield mobsters as Londardo, Sciria, and Frank Hoge. Conspicuously absent were lower-level African-American numbers operators, who usually bore the brunt of police crackdowns while white gangsters escaped arrest.

With two defendants already in jail on unrelated charges, Molnar and Robert Chamberlin led a dragnet of thirty cops, coordinated by Ness's new radio setup, to round up the rest. They tracked down six more defendants, dragging several from bed. Ness went in search of Lonardo and Sciria, but the Angelos were gone.

By the next week, Hoge and two other fugitives had turned themselves in, with a dozen defendants still at large. Clayton Fritchey called the indictments "the most sweeping assault on gangdom in Cleveland's history."

But the gang leaders, including Lonardo and Sciria, remained free. Molnar told the *News* the gangsters had apparently learned of the impending indictments and slipped away. He would "get them all, sooner or later."

But the lieutenant himself had tipped the mobsters off. At his word, a yacht with Sciria and five other defendants set sail for Florida, while Lonardo hid out closer to home—he'd be arrested in the suburbs that June. While police caught up with some of Sciria's companions, Little Angelo remained elusive, having fled to Mexico.

On May 15, with the manhunt in progress, Ness went undercover. To hide his official license plates—"EN-1"—he helped himself to stolen tags held by the police department.

When Patrolman Joseph Prucha—whose memory for license plates earned him the nickname "Camera Eye"—saw the tags on Ness's black Studebaker, he figured he'd spotted a hot car. Prucha forced the sedan to the curb and trained a shotgun on the driver.

"Officer," Ness said, "I am your boss, the Safety Director."

"If you're Eliot Ness," Prucha shot back, "I'm President Roosevelt."

After Ness proved his identity, he didn't hold the incident against Prucha—he wrote him a letter of commendation.

THAT MAY, MOLNAR wrapped up another investigation, breaking up a ring of black marijuana dealers working Cleveland's schools.

Like the numbers case, this one began with a pair of African-American investigators. Around a year before, Virginia Houston had partnered with an anonymous black teacher whose own adolescent son had become a customer. The teacher, working with the police department, enlisted students to buy almost one hundred marijuana cigarettes for use as evidence.

Then Molnar, with three of Ness's black investigators, took over. The young undercover trio bought quantities of the drug while pretending to be marijuana users, compiling evidence and testimony identifying key members of the racket.

The grand jury handed down twelve indictments, and courts delivered twelve convictions. Molnar took much credit for the investigation, posing for a *Call & Post* photo shaking hands with Houston, the cop who really sparked the case.

But rumors of the lieutenant's misconduct persisted. In June, a café owner claimed Molnar "persecuted" him for years "because I refused to put him on my pay roll." Ness ordered a departmental review, but no actionable evidence was found.

Then a woman running a small-time bingo game complained to police that Molnar's squad "picks on the little places that are competing with the big ones that the police don't want to raid." *Press* columnist Jack Raper, always ready to take down the Safety Director, ran with her story.

Both accusations got lost in Ness's latest triumph. The numbers investigation had thrown the Mayfield Road Mob into disarray—decimating its leadership, fueling dissension among policy operators, and bleeding the racket of money.

"There doesn't seem to be any doubt in Cleveland," reported the *Chicago Daily News*, "that most of the 23 named in the bill will go to the penitentiary."

But without certain key defendants, the trials couldn't go forward, leaving a continuing need to protect witnesses. The Mayfield gang was already on the trail of the policy operators, ready to scare them silent, offering as much as $1,000 for information of their whereabouts. The Safety Director sequestered his key witnesses out east, to safely await their days in court.

Meanwhile, Clevelanders, black and white, kept playing the illicit lottery; numbers games ran wide-open, just without their African-American operators splitting the profits with white gangsters. But John Jones and Claude Lee kept up the heat, cracking down on gambling while the indictments they had built awaited trial.

Many African Americans felt the two plainclothes patrolmen deserved more recognition. After the numbers case hit the papers, Ness reportedly approved promoting both to detective, with the rank and pay commensurate with the work they already did. Lee had qualified to become sergeant in 1938, and some boosters hoped to make Jones the police department's first black lieutenant—instead, his rank remained patrolman, bottom rung of the departmental ladder.

In late 1940, an African-American fraternal organization sent Ness a letter urging him to make Lee a sergeant. They reminded Ness that Lee had already earned this promotion, and listed other major cities—New York, Los Angeles, Chicago, Detroit—where black officers rose to even higher ranks.

"One of the outstanding facts of your regime has impressed us greatly," they wrote. "Your fairness in the administration of your office insofar as all groups are concerned. With this thought in mind, and wishing to aid in any way we can to advance a member of our group . . . we would be highly honored if one of our race were elevated to the rank of Sergeant, and placed in charge of a zone car. We regret that so far, not even one Negro is assigned to this branch of the service."

Their plea went unheeded. The following year, when Chief Matowitz promoted two white patrolmen for catching draft dodgers and hit-and-run drivers, the *Call & Post* observed that Jones and Lee still awaited a similar reward.

They would never get it.

Jones and Lee continued their two-man war on the rackets until failing health took Lee out of the fight. In 1952, as his old partner lay in the Cleveland Clinic after a car accident, Jones solicited hundreds of dollars from his fellow officers, asking them to "help make things a little pleasanter for our comrade, Claude Lee." The sidelined detective, who never attained the rank of sergeant, died seven years later at fifty-eight.

Jones never rose higher than detective. In 1947, someone blew up Jones's car in his driveway, shattering the windows of his house and hurling the detective from his bed. Police suspected the bombing had something to do with Jones's continuing fight against the numbers racket.

Jones retired in 1954. He traveled the world, visiting Europe and Africa and even seeking a visa to study how policing in Cleveland compared to the Soviet Union.

"As bad as they say the United States is," Jones reflected six years before his death in 1979, "I'll still take America."

Chester Himes, however, would trade his home country for France and Spain, where he wrote the novels based on the Roaring Third of Jones and Lee.

THE NUMBERS CASE finally went to trial in the summer of 1942, after Sciria was arrested in Mexico City. A few witnesses disappeared in the interim, and indictments against three of the alleged racketeers were dropped. But plenty of small-time numbers operators remained more than willing to testify.

The *Call & Post* noted "the temerity and brazen contempt the nervy little witnesses showed for the accused," recognizing the "long pent up anger" these men and women brought into court. Thanks to this impassioned testimony, the prosecution won convictions against Lonardo, Sciria, and twelve others. Molnar never appeared on the stand, Cullitan choosing not to call him.

"He was too close to the mob," the prosecutor said years later. "We didn't believe we could trust him."

But Molnar hoped to topple the mob, too—for his own reasons. The investigation had demonstrated the Mayfield gang's hold on the numbers racket was weak—a golden opportunity for someone willing and able to grab it.

As future Safety Director Alvin Sutton would explain, Molnar "saw how he could take over control of numbers and get the money rolling his way, now that Ness and Cullitan had smashed up the gang and broken its hold on the games. He moved on the throne."

While Ness and Cullitan worked to keep their case together, Molnar met in secret with three key witnesses they'd hidden out east. He also approached Frank Hoge, offering the policy king a chance to keep running the racket in exchange for a healthy cut. Thereafter, Molnar would raid just as aggressively but leave Hoge's operations alone, driving out the competition. At his trial, Hoge walked for lack of evidence—an outcome that lead investigator Molnar was perfectly positioned to arrange.

The lieutenant's secret agenda would have shocked those who believed his untouchable image. But William Walker saw little difference between the cops and white gangsters still battling over the racket.

"Negro operators who have seen their gambling business taken from them with the full connivance and many times with the help of the police," Walker wrote, "know what the score is. . . . Once the policy and numbers gambling became a million dollar business, certain people decided it was too much money to be flowing into Negro hands."

The numbers trials dropped the curtain on the Mayfield Road Mob, though its remnants would come to capture Cleveland's narcotics traffic. The larger syndicate carried on and prospered, but pressure from Ness, Cullitan, and other Ohio authorities forced them to move their gambling operations elsewhere—most notably to a certain dusty desert town in Nevada . . . Las Vegas.

"Had Cleveland been a city of pantywaist police work, the Cleveland Gang would have stayed in Cleveland," then Safety Director Sutton declared in 1951. "Racketeers may still make their headquarters here, but they have to set up shop somewhere else if they are going to make any money."

This exodus of gangsters cleared the way for Molnar. Under his protection, the numbers racket survived and thrived, grossing some $70 million a year by the late 1940s.

After investigating the lieutenant's activities, Sutton believed Ness had made an honest, if serious and costly, mistake, putting Molnar in charge of the numbers case.

Molnar "worked in Ness's office—right under his eyes," Sutton said. "And Ness never knew."

Frank Dolezal (left) with Sheriff Martin O'Donnell (right).
Cleveland Press Collection, Cleveland State University

SIXTEEN

A New Suspect

Summer 1939

In just over four years, Ness had reformed, reorganized, and modernized the police department, jailed the city's most prominent racketeers, tackled juvenile delinquency, saved countless people from traffic deaths, and dealt a crippling blow to the city's gangsters. Each success raised his public profile.

"He is ambitious for Eliot Ness, admits it and is no hypocrite," observed the *News*. "The publicity spotlight and the crowds' adulation appeal to him."

Some wondered whether Ness might consider running for office—though he stubbornly kept his distance from partisan politics. He'd apparently never voted before 1936 and was known for throwing favor-seeking party hacks out of his office.

"I'm in a Republican administration," he told a reporter. "In a sense I suppose I am considered a Republican. But I hadn't thought of myself as politically aligned in any way."

Still, party officials and admiring citizens hoped Ness might one day run . . . for something. In early 1939, the Republican Party tried to draft him into running for Cuyahoga County sheriff, seeing him as their best chance of taking down Democrat Martin O'Donnell, who continued to offer safe haven to gamblers and gangsters outside city limits. But Ness resisted all encouragement, showing little interest in running for sheriff or anything else.

In 1937, O'Donnell had overseen perhaps the worst prison break in the city's history, and his ongoing failure to close the Thomas and Harvard Clubs prompted a drive to recall him. Ness—despite his distaste for politics—supported that effort, calling the illegal casinos "a playground for known criminals, and . . . a breeding place for crooks."

The recall effort failed, but O'Donnell soon faced a new investigation into Cuyahoga County's illegal gambling. And while Martin Sweeney still backed O'Donnell, the congressman's belligerent behavior and fervent isolationism won the sheriff as many enemies as friends.

With the 1940 election looming, O'Donnell—fearing Ness might swoop in and steal his job—decided to embarrass the Safety Director in the most public way possible. The sheriff would solve the one case Ness seemed unable to crack. . . .

O'Donnell had shown little interest in the torso murders, repeatedly refusing requests for help from the Cleveland Police. The killings, he'd insisted, were a city problem. What changed his mind was a visit from Lawrence J. "Pat" Lyons, a mustached, hard-drinking private eye working the case unofficially since summer 1938.

The Butcher, Lyons believed, could be tracked through connections between the victims. Edward Andrassy, Flo Polillo, and Rose Wallace all patronized a bar frequented by "Frank," a rumored homosexual and former slaughterhouse worker with a "passionate craving for knives." Neighbors had seen Frank with "a man who looked like" Andrassy, as well as a sailor resembling the unidentified tattooed victim. A shaky circumstantial case, perhaps, but Lyons felt certain he had his man.

"Frank" turned out to be fifty-two-year-old Frank Dolezal, a Bohemian immigrant working as a bricklayer. Small and heavyset, Dolezal's otherwise unremarkable looks included large, haunting eyes that bored into everyone he met.

Lyons monitored the man closely in summer 1939, documenting

a sad, lonely life. The bricklayer would get drunk, dress in his best, and go out to pick up men, apparently without much success. The P.I. searched Dolezal's former apartment, finding possible blood-stains in the bathroom. This must be the Butcher's lab! Lyons took samples.

Peter Merylo had already questioned Dolezal twice and in-vestigated him thoroughly before dismissing this possible suspect for not fitting the torso clinic profile, lacking both the necessary physical heft and anatomical knowledge.

Acquaintances described the bricklayer as gentle, gregarious, and generous, though alcohol could throw him into violent rages, revealing a deep depression. Dolezal seemed more a candidate for the Butcher's next victim than the killer himself—isolated, im-poverished, sexually conflicted, he inhabited the same marginal world where the Butcher sought his prey.

But unlike Frank Sweeney, Dolezal had no powerful relatives to protest if he wound up behind bars—the authorities could push him around at will.

Lyons and O'Donnell kept their investigation hidden from po-lice and the Safety Director. In June, however, the private eye blew his own cover, getting drunk and bragging about working on the case. His boasts got back to Merylo. The sheriff, fearing police would steal his lead, arrested Dolezal and, two days later, held a press conference.

"Boys," he announced, "we have a signed confession to one of the torso murders!"

Seemed Dolezal had admitted to killing Flo Polillo. They'd been drinking in his apartment when Polillo attacked him with a knife. Dolezal punched her and she fell back, slamming her head into the bathtub. Believing her dead, the bricklayer chopped her body up to better dispose of it, throwing some pieces into Lake Erie.

The killing had been an accident, Dolezal said, not premed-itated. Dolezal insisted he hadn't killed Andrassy or any of the Butcher's other victims.

The confession rocked the city. Congratulatory messages poured in to O'Donnell from around the nation. Local Democrats celebrated this political coup, though the sheriff denied any ulte- rior motives. Jack Raper, Ness's chief critic at the *Press*, saw it as another crack in the Safety Director's façade.

"It looks much as though," a delighted Raper wrote, "the 'great G-man' myth with which the people of Cleveland have been en- tertained for several years is on its way to the scrap heap."

City detectives, he added (rubbing it in), had twice arrested Dolezal, only to have the sheriff steal their suspect right out from under them.

"We're afraid," Raper wrote, "that after this incident, the newspapers may never again call Ness 'Al Capone's nemesis.'"

Even Eliot's *Plain Dealer* crony Ralph Kelly had to admit O'Donnell—once "the weakest candidate on the county ticket in 1940 and a possible liability to the Democrats in the fall"—had, with Dolezal's arrest, "immeasurably improved" his chances for re- election, dealing a serious blow to Mayor Burton's third-term bid.

"Before the confession Democrats faced the embarrassing dif- ficulty of having few failures with which to tax Ness plausibly," Kelly wrote, "although Congressman Martin L. Sweeney two years ago campaigned vigorously . . . on the Ness-Burton failure to solve the torso murders."

Rumor had it Sweeney might run for mayor himself. But the congressman, who had rarely held his tongue about Ness before his cousin became the prime if secret Butcher suspect, remained conspicuously silent on this latest development. And he would choose not to challenge Burton.

The confession came as relief to the African-American com- munity, since some investigators had thought, according to the *Call & Post*, "a sex-mad Negro was responsible for the deaths of a dozen persons."

"Police had worked in vain for several years in the belief that the murderer was a Negro," the paper reported, "because the butchered remains of the victim's bodies had almost invariably been found in or near sections of the city largely inhabited by members of the Negro 'underworld.'"

Nelle Hackney, a black officer assigned to the Policewomen's Bureau, told the *Call & Post* about an anonymous phone call several months before, asking them to send "Miss Hackney" to a Central Avenue address. She found no one there, in a room of "weird appearance and sinister aspect." Only when she learned of Dolezal's arrest and confession did Hackney realize she'd been summoned to the bricklayer's apartment.

Hackney suspected Dolezal himself had placed the call, but she and other policewomen couldn't agree why. Some speculated he'd meant to confess, while Hackney thought the "pervert" (as the *Call & Post* described him) had been after her head.

"Anyway," concluded the paper, "she was eloquently thankful that Mr. Dolezal was not at home."

THE DAY AFTER Dolezal's confession, reporter Howard Beaufait scored a brief interview with the confessed killer. He found the bricklayer "on the verge of hysteria," fiddling with a handkerchief, his shirt sweat-soaked.

"His eyes are filled with fear," Beaufait wrote, "and he moves his head from side to side in quick, nervous jerks. . . . Now he looks at all men as if they were his enemies. Each stranger who enters his cell brings a threat to his safety."

Beaufait found it hard to imagine this man doing the things he'd been accused of in print. "If he hadn't said so," Beaufait wrote, "you would find it rather preposterous to believe that he could turn his humble home into a slaughter house."

"City Hall privately is skeptical as are a lot of other people," reported the *News*. "Or in other words, is it a 'confession,' solution, or O'Donnell politics?"

Ness refused to air any doubts in public.

"The sheriff is to be commended for his intensive investigation," Ness told the *Plain Dealer*. "The leads he has uncovered will, of course, be followed up to see what possible connection the Polillo case may have with any others. My department and I stand ready to make available to the sheriff any information or facilities that he might feel would be of assistance."

Peter Merylo—furious the sheriff had blundered into his case—pointed out numerous flaws in Dolezal's confession. The bricklayer, he told reporters, had gotten Polillo's time of death wrong, and body parts Dolezal claimed to have dropped in Lake Erie had been left on dry land.

Besides, Merylo pointed out, the lake had been frozen over that night.

"This was my first experience," Merylo wrote, "where a man is making a confession to a murder or any other serious crime, and does not know the details of the crime which he is alleged to have committed."

The sheriff's office soon produced a second confession, then a third—both of which Merylo debunked.

Five days after his arrest, Dolezal sat for a lie detector test, which seemed to suggest he'd truly killed Polillo; but his ragged emotional state compromised it. Briefly separated from the sheriff during the test, Dolezal blurted to police that O'Donnell's men had brutalized him.

"They kept at me until I got crazy," Dolezal said. "They beat me up." The suspect complained of severe pain in his ribs.

That same day, when reporters got another look, Dolezal's face was bruised. The sheriff claimed his prisoner injured himself in a suicide attempt; Dolezal insisted he'd been beaten.

Held without charges for almost a week, Dolezal finally recanted after seeing an attorney, claiming the sheriff's men had tortured him. His interrogation had gone on for roughly forty hours, deputies refusing to give him any real rest. After blindfolding him, they threw him on the cement floor, kicking and punching him. Admitting to Polillo's murder had been the only way to make the ordeal stop.

O'Donnell and his men denied harming their prisoner at all, but the newspapers no longer gave them the benefit of the doubt. "Is the sheriff interested in furthering the ends of justice," asked the *Press*, "or is he interested in making a grandstand play for personal glory and acclaim?"

What little hard evidence O'Donnell's investigators gathered turned out to be worthless. A chemist at Western Reserve University analyzed the stains in Dolezal's bathroom and found them to be "plain dirt," not blood.

At Dolezal's arraignment, the judge charged him with manslaughter instead of murder, ordering him to appear before the grand jury. Unable to pay his $15,000 bond, Dolezal returned to his cell. The case against him seemed destined to evaporate in court, if it even got that far. But Pat Lyons remained convinced they had the Butcher behind bars.

"Sure," he remarked in mid-August, "we got the right man. . . . He will never come out of the County Jail alive."

Ness's newest Untouchable, "Sledgehammer Mike" Blackwell (left, in suit), with the Safety Director and mayor at City Hall, July 15, 1939.
Cleveland Public Library Photograph Collection

Cleveland police battle strikers outside the Fisher Body plant, July 31, 1939.
Authors' Collection

SEVENTEEN

The Right Man?

July–August 1939

Six foot three and two-hundred-plus pounds, Police Captain Michael Blackwell first drew Ness's admiration in 1935, after catching three armed men robbing a jewelry store. When the crooks started shooting, a bullet grazed Blackwell's nose, spraying his face with blood. He returned fire, dropping one bandit and sending the rest fleeing.

Ness soon promoted Blackwell, now counted among Cleveland's "untouchables," dispatching him to drive "the bookies, gamblers and houses of ill-repute out of town." Known for his aggressive raids and immunity to bribes, "Sledgehammer Mike" reportedly bled the local syndicate of a million dollars in a single year.

"His strategy is ruthlessly effective," a journalist wrote. "Keep the racketeers on the jump. Harass them. Wreck their places of business. Frighten their customers."

The *Call & Post* took a dimmer view of Blackwell's tactics—in one ten-day stretch in 1939, the captain "left a trail of broken doors, smashed locks, and wrecked smoke shops" in black neighborhoods while winning only a single conviction.

Blackwell proved "fiercely enthusiastic about his job," putting in the long hours Ness appreciated. Yet he was a family man, "as docile as a kitten" around his wife and two young children. Both sides of Blackwell's personality sprang from a firm moral center fueling a self-righteous, burning rage at obscenity, especially dirty movies.

Arnold Sagalyn remembered him as "a big, brawny, hard-driving, flamboyant Irishman—a self-promoter who loved getting his name in the papers." The captain got his wish that July, after Ness placed him at the center of a boiling labor conflict.

Earlier that summer, the United Auto Workers branch of the CIO declared a strike against General Motors, starting in Detroit and spreading into Ohio, closing the massive Fisher Body works on Cleveland's East Side. Tensions rose in late July as the union resolved to shut down Fisher Body just as production began on the new line of 1940 Chevrolets.

As with the 1937 Republic Steel strike, Ness pledged to preserve order without taking sides. After the union accused Deputy Inspector John Savage of encouraging strikebreakers to cross the picket lines, Ness replaced him with Blackwell.

The battle began early on July 31 when unionists, thought to number between five and six thousand, massed outside the factory's gates. To Blackwell, commanding a one-hundred-man detail, there seemed far more. Many were CIO workers from other factories, ready for a fight in white crash helmets, others bringing heavy clubs disguised as picket signs. From a loudspeaker on a nearby building, a strike leader egged the crowd on and hurled threats at the opposition.

Around 6 A.M., as the first strikebreaker shift arrived, Blackwell approached a union leader.

"We don't want any trouble out here, Steve," the captain said. "We've kept it free of violence for three weeks now and we don't want any."

"We don't want any either," the union leader replied.

But as the first car of strikebreakers approached the factory's gate, picketers surrounded it and started flipping it over. Half a dozen mounted cops galloped in. Strikers responded by throwing bricks and rocks, smashing a car window. More cops dashed toward the skirmish with nightsticks ready. The situation exploded into an all-out melee—"civil war without the bullets," reported the *News*, "but with everything else!"

The strikers fell back and regrouped as more cars arrived.

"Hold your lines!" shouted the loudspeaker wielder directing the mob like a general—pointing out weak spots in the cops' defenses and alerting strikers to approaching scabs.

When the pickets got hold of another car, they turned it over, dragged the occupants out, and beat them. Some threw a match at the gasoline-leaking vehicle, setting its tail alight. Unable to utilize a fire truck, Fire Chief James Granger and his men waded in to douse the blaze with handheld fire extinguishers.

Bricks and pavement chunks rained down on police. Robert Chamberlin, helping direct the plant's defense, felt something slam into his shoulder. Police responded, hurling the missiles right back.

"Pardon me a minute while I throw some rocks," Blackwell told a reporter before doing just that.

Cops with batons subdued brick-throwing strikers; a mounted policeman clubbed a picketer in front of Chamberlin, leaving a two-inch scalp gash.

Blackwell called for reinforcements. The police numbers swelled to more than four hundred, still badly outnumbered. The cops sought shelter behind a factory fence, several drawing their guns despite orders not to open fire "unless [the strikers] storm the plant."

"I heard Captain Blackwell shout 'don't shoot!' at a time when the situation was at white-heat," an eyewitness told the *News*. "It took the greatest amount of self-control not to shoot. I think a few policemen did fire into the air."

Officers lobbed tear gas grenades from the factory's third floor. Some strikers grabbed unexploded canisters and hurled them back.

"Tear gas was everywhere," an eyewitness reported, "and pickets and police alike were crying in the streets."

Firemen turned high-pressure hoses on the strikers. When a hose exploded, workers cheered.

After two hours, the battle ended. Forty-six had been seriously hurt; at least two hundred escaped with minor injuries.

Around 8 A.M., Chief Matowitz asked to meet with union leaders, promising police would throw no more rocks if strikers backed off. A truce followed, but the loudspeaker wielder kept provoking the crowd.

Ness and Burton arrived before 2 p.m. They found the crowd at now between eight and ten thousand. Burton wore a bright white suit and straw boater, standing out like a neon sign. The strikers booed.

As Ness and Burton looked on, another company car tried to force its way through, shoving aside several strikers. Pickets smashed its windows and headlights before mounted police charged in. The cops made three arrests while the crowd hurled catcalls at Ness and the mayor.

In a repeat of the Republic Steel strike, Ness focused on clearing the area. He ordered the loudspeaker silenced, then met with strike leaders, telling them to "clear out of here peacefully or you will be cleared out."

The Safety Director carried a proclamation, signed by himself and the mayor, establishing a five-hundred-yard "riot zone." Only those with "lawful business" would be allowed near the factory. That included a few strikers, but Ness limited their numbers to five pickets at each gate and ten other unionists within the zone— only those, Ness declared, with "a good reason for being there."

To prevent another riot, Ness delayed his order to three A.M. Union leaders called it "a violation of civil liberties" and promised a court fight. Strikers threatened an even bigger riot when the plant opened the next day.

Ness tripled the police presence. Most strikebreakers who had managed to cross the lines bedded down inside the factory, squatters living on canned food stockpiled during the previous major strike. Everyone readied for another battle.

But Ness, going without sleep or a shave, kept trying to build new lines of communication between pickets and police. The next morning, he met with the strikers' attorney, William Corrigan. Although the union refused to concede the legality of Ness's actions, Corrigan agreed they would prevent another riot by helping clear the strike zone. They would go on fighting Ness's proclamation, but peacefully, before a judge.

When the plant reopened, reporters found a scene remarkably calm, children playing baseball across the street. A few strikers passed around the names and addresses of strikebreaking workers, in hopes of taking the picket lines to those doorsteps, but Ness ordered the arrest of anyone involved.

"Such picketing violates every conception of American freedom," he told the *Press*, "and the doctrine that a man's home is his castle."

The renegade strikers soon dispersed.

Union leaders inveighed against Ness and Burton, and followed up on contesting the proclamation in court. But by moving from the streets into a courtroom, they helped Ness prevent bloodshed.

Within days, the UAW reached a tentative agreement; they would ultimately win the concessions they sought. The strike also meant a victory for the city's police, yet another demonstration of progress made under Ness.

"From our personal observation—and our sympathies are normally with labor—the police behaved better than we imagined they could and better than they usually do," opined the *News*. "Detective Captain Michael Blackwell earned credit for this unusual restraint."

JUST OVER THREE weeks after the Fisher Body riot, Pat Lyons's prophecy that Frank Dolezal would not leave jail alive came true.

On August 24, the sheriff's department reported finding their suspect dead in his cell, hanging from a rag-fashioned noose. Deputies, guarding the isolated Dolezal, had stepped briefly out, it seemed, leaving no witnesses to their prisoner's final moments.

But the sheriff saw no mystery in Dolezal's death.

"All I can say is that he must have been afraid to face the grand jury," O'Donnell asserted. "I am sure we had the right man. We did all we could in the case. We got a confession from him, and we were close to tying him up with another of the torso murders."

Dolezal had supposedly hanged himself from a hook five feet seven inches off the floor—a feat for a man five foot eight. A deputy said he'd left the prisoner alone only a short time before finding him strung up and gasping. Yet the doctor, examining Dolezal roughly thirty minutes later, found the body cold. Marks left by the noose should have been broad and faint behind Dolezal's ears, fading rapidly. But photos taken the next day show a thin, deep ligature mark ringing his neck like a collar, as if he'd been garroted, not hanged.

Still, the Democratic coroner seemed to trust the Democratic sheriff. Samuel Gerber ordered no inquest, reversing his decision only after the Cleveland Crime Commission demanded a full investigation.

At the inquest, witnesses repeated Dolezal's claims of being beaten during interrogation. The autopsy revealed Dolezal suffered several broken ribs, almost certainly while in custody. A woman who had previously testified against Dolezal now claimed the sheriff's men got her "drunk as a monkey" before telling her to lie. O'Donnell and his deputies continued to deny any wrongdoing, but their stories didn't always line up.

"We did all we could to keep him from committing suicide," the sheriff insisted. "We treated the man too well."

Gerber chose not to contradict him, returning a verdict of suicide that offered no opinion on how Dolezal broke his ribs.

Ness remained aloof. He must have known O'Donnell arrested Dolezal largely to spite him, but the Safety Director refrained from criticizing the sheriff. Instead, he allowed the legal system to sort out the mess, never expecting Dolezal wouldn't live to see his day in court.

And O'Donnell's actions complicated Ness's efforts to build a case against Frank Sweeney. Arresting the doctor now would seem even more like a political act—retribution not just against Sweeney's cousin, the congressman, but also against a sheriff who'd tried to upstage the competition. Without something solid, Ness would face the same withering scrutiny as O'Donnell.

The following spring, Ness requested an official report from Peter Merylo on allegations that Pat Lyons had admitted to beating Dolezal in custody. Merylo prepared the report, but the matter ended there. Gerber's verdict was allowed to stand, though a review would all but establish Dolezal was no suicide. Whether he was murdered, or perhaps died during another brutal interrogation, remains impossible to say. He became the latest in the line of corpses in the Butcher case, just another marginalized victim.

While the attempt to win some good press at Ness's expense failed, O'Donnell did manage to avoid any serious consequences. The sheriff went on worrying that Ness would run against him in 1940, as did his partner in politics, Congressman Sweeney. But, in late November, Ness put an end to that, announcing in the *Press* he had no plans "to run for sheriff or any other elective office."

With his chief rival on the sidelines, O'Donnell buckled down to defend his post.

"It would be folly to discount the political strength of the present sheriff," observed the *Plain Dealer*. "He has many sources of support, some of them no credit to him or to the community." Such support helped carry him to reelection in November.

But another movement to recall O'Donnell began the following spring, ending in June 1941 with the sheriff's death by a heart attack. To replace him, the county commissioners selected Joseph Sweeney (no relation to the congressman or the doctor), Ness's man in charge of the Detective Bureau.

Finally, Ness had an ally in the sheriff's department.

"With Sweeney as sheriff, you can rest assured there will be no more nonsense about home rule . . . ," Phil Porter predicted. "The gambling gentry will quietly fold up and move into the kinder precincts of Geauga County, or some other spot."

Frank Dolezal had long since disappeared from the headlines. Few would seriously argue he'd been the Butcher, though the public seems to have taken his death as a resolution of sorts. No new torso murders had turned up since August 1938, making it easier to imagine the late sheriff had caught the killer after all. But Coroner Gerber refused to accept that line of thinking.

"The arrest of Dolezal didn't stop the murders," Gerber said years later, "they had already stopped."

Peter Merylo continued to work the case, apparently unaware Ness had his own prime suspect.

In early 1939, before Dolezal's arrest, Merylo received a letter sent from the Sandusky Soldiers and Sailors Home by a resident who suspected another patient, "our Doc," of being the Butcher.

Merylo had always checked out even the most trivial tips, ever fearful of missing the one good lead in a sea of lies and misinformation. But he appears not to have taken the Sandusky missive seriously, filing it away with all the other crank letters and looking elsewhere for the Butcher.

LS TORSO KILLER NEW INSAN

Couzens Trails in Rep........an Ra

MAINE VOTE IS BAD NEWS TO NEW DEAL

Buel Says Election Shows Threat of Republican Victory in November.

ROOSEVELT JUST SMILES

Indicates Result Was About What He Expected.

BY WALKER S. BUEL
Plain Dealer Bureau,
811 Albee Bldg.
WASHINGTON, Sept. 15.—

Maine's election is very bad news for the New Deal and President Roosevelt.

It is a double indication of a Republican trend, a definite threat of Republican victory in November, definite forerunner of a diminution of Democratic membership in Congress, a definite indication of Republican revival, especially in the east.

Even if not for unprecedented factors in this campaign, the Maine vote ought to be regarded as a trend in the New Deal hopes for the election of President Roosevelt. Put the figures aside, making possible southern and western comparison, which may weaken Roosevelt in...

(remainder of column illegible)

No. 20 for Allen

Allen injured his back in the fifth inning, but was given credit for his twentieth victory yesterday as the Indians whipped Boston, 12 to 2. Hildebrand finished the game. Trosky hit his 35th and 40th homers ... New York, defeated Chicago, 7 to 4. Detroit downed Philadelphia, 5 to 6, and Washington took a double header from St. Louis, 15 to 7 and 4 to 1. Weather stopped the National League.

(Details on Sport Pages)

WPA WORKERS TO BE EXPO GUESTS

Families, Also, to Attend Saturday as Honor to Garden Builders.

Today's Events

United Rubber Workers Day.
United States Pemiefion Day.
Naval Reservists of American Day.
National Society of Painters Day.
Club Day.
Haven (O.) Day.
Garden Club at Michigan Bay.

Attendance yesterday 22,600
Attendance for 29 days 1,289,103
Days left—47.

The WPA will have its day at the Great Lakes Exposition.

Most of the expo visitors thought that, since everybody was having his day off his big show, it would be sheer ingratitude to forget the WPA, some of whose 4,700 laborers built the four-acre Horticultural Gardens on the grounds.

So the boys who cleared the streets and the boulevards among the eight have been invited to attend the exposition Saturday. They were made comfortable by their own WPA forces.

They will have the whole stadium as a dining salon. Arrangements have been made with department subcommittees to set their own lunches at prices they can afford. "Such a celebration has been a trend for such tickets something similar to ... have said they wanted to see the WPA with Gardens," Joseph I. Alexander, WPA District director, said. "The Gardens are one of the finest projects."

The attendance, which include members of the laborers' families, will be in the form of benefits to give a job or a future to Cleveland.

(Continued on Page 6, Column 1)

Loses Fight in Dynamite Blast

BARNESVILLE, O., Sept. 15.—Charles Gallagher, 45, a WPA worker, was instantaneously blinded by a dynamite explosion here today. His injuries resulted in the explosion may prove him his life.

BUY YOUR OWN MEALS. NESS TELLS ROOKIES

Ten New Patrolmen Told Appointments Are Based on Own Merits.

"DON'T BE OBLIGATED"

Warns "You'll Get No Great Reward for Honesty."

Ten new patrolmen were sworn into office yesterday by Safety Director Eliot Ness in his office at City Hall with the revolutionary admonition that policemen are expected to pay for their own beers.

"You have been appointed on your own merits and because you stood at the top of the civil service lists and for no other reasons," Ness told the recruits. "If anyone made claims you that he was responsible for your appointment, pay no attention.

"Your advancement is up to you.

"You are expected to be honest and in doing your job you will get no great rewards for being honest. Don't be obligated to anyone, even to small things.

"When you ask take a restaurant for a meal, pay for it. Ness run get any marketable commodity useful to you, pay for it. If people have been accustomed to giving you things for nothing nice to your becoming a policeman, I suppose it is all right for you to continue to accept those things."

There was Precaution

"However, if people who have done you anything free before are eager to give you something without charge, you can conclude that they are buying your badge and your future."

In addition to appointing the ten new patrolmen, Ness promoted Sergeant Anynama F. F. Perry to a lieutenancy and Patrolman Herbert Blades and William M. Miller to sergeancies.

The recruits were:
OWEN J. FAROHER, 2179 Voters Avenue S. E.
BENJAMIN D. EVANS, 8700 Scovill Avenue E. E.
EDWARD PAVLIK, JR., 2916 Aims Road S. E.
MELVIN F. MANLEY, 3311 W. 99th Street.
FRANK A. CADEK, 58, 4826 E. 170th Street.
ROY J. FISCHBACH, 8205 Tioga Avenue S. E.
RICHARD R. BOCKER, 4805 E. 196th Street.
CLARENCE G. TRIMBLE, 7947 Park Avenue S. E.
JOHN W. NEADE, 9472 Shaw Avenue S. E.
ELMER J. MANN, 5050 Joyce Road N. E.

Cadek, the senior of former Capt. Louis F. Cadek, was appointed to the department a month ago by John R. Pugin, executive assistant to Ness. His appointment was revoked at that time by Ness because Pugin had skipped the candidates at the top of the lists.

Youth, 16, T.....atens Shirley Ter...

(WIREPHOTO)

OUTLAW SITDOWN, PLEA IS UP TO URW

Strikes Hit Akron Plants as Rubber International Weighs Policy Issue.

Plain Dealer Bureau,
425 Ohio Building.
AKRON, O., Sept. 15.—

The issue of the sitdown strike is right toward as the first important question before the United Rubber Workers of America at their first international convention is among here.

Resolutions before the convention include one asking that the outlawed sitdown be outlawed and another that asks the sitdown ... The most powerful weapons an organized labor can point to is recognition and URW policies.

Adolph Germer, American Federation of Labor representative, addressed the delegates this today, urging the head and union from a meeting with a group of Akron sitdown men, who wanted to lend jobs at all. He said, and what the URW would do about sitdowns.

"Hirvi Violating," he said.

It was told them that sitdowns were a direct violation of their contracts and their agreements ...

SHAKER EXTE TO RUN CARS

Shuttle Service Rd. Expected in 2 May be Richf...

BY JAMES E. DOY...
First extension of the from Rapid Transit System completed in the few weeks ... will be started next ... What has been termed ... tenth west of Warrensv... Road on the Shaker line ... be turned on for the first. Work on setting the swinging cables when w... ship with R. ... For the will be a single track ove... There is also to be a half ... ... this year the extension ... another mile to Richmond the near future, with the extension to Beachcliff Road ... probably spring, at least as far as the Cleveland In ... Railway, which gives the ... joint ownership of interurban Green Road.

It is intended to operate between Green Shaker Square & ... when the Shaker sidings ... north service. At Richmond ... singers will transfer to buses.

Says Fight With Richman Nearly Sank Ocean Plane

NEW YORK, Sept. 15.—(AP)—The Daily News, in a copyrighted dispatch from a staff correspondent at Musgrave Harbor, Newfoundland, says a quarrel over the Atlantic between the transoceanic flyers Harry Richman and Dick Merrill "almost ended with the plane in Tinker Brook today."

Merrill and Richman landed at that isolated village yesterday after a heavy fight ...

Newspaper Plane Damaged.

ST. JOHN'S, Newfoundland, Sept. 15.—(U.P.)—A newspaper plane...

Evaline McAndrew, the second Mrs. Ness.

Cleveland Public Library Photograph Collection

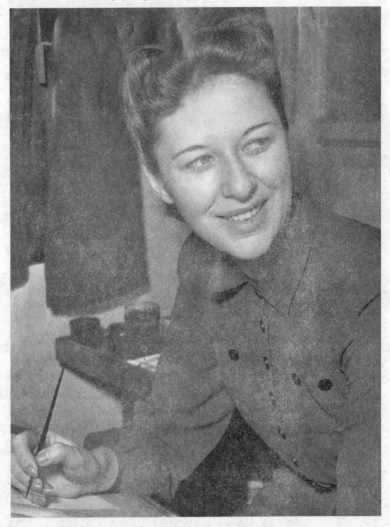

EIGHTEEN

That's the Man

October 1939–July 1940

In mid-October 1939, Ness slipped away from Cleveland and returned with a new bride.

The former Evaline McAndrew, née Michelow, was a twenty-eight-year-old commercial artist lately of New York City. Tall, slim, her long face home to a prominent nose and pronounced chin, Evaline "wasn't beautiful," as a colleague once put it, "but she was wonderful-looking."

Less than eighteen months had passed since Ness and his first wife divorced. He could hardly have picked a more different mate. "Edna was an ordinary, simple person," a friend recalled. "Evaline was striking in appearance, even dramatic."

Like her husband, Evaline was dedicated, driven, often staying at her drawing table late into the evening. "I'm lucky in my profession," she told the *Plain Dealer* after the wedding, "because it's the sort of work that doesn't interfere with being a housewife too."

The couple tied the knot two hundred miles south in Greenup, Kentucky, a hamlet across the river, where they could get married without a blood test. They obscured key details on their marriage license; Eliot put his occupation down as "writer," and Evaline shaved three years off her age. Although each had been married once before, both claimed "single" status, Evaline replacing her parents' surnames with her current married name.

Always averse to making his private life public, Ness waited almost two weeks before alerting the press. Eliot claimed the marriage took place in Chicago and told reporters that Evaline knew his family back home, which appears to be false, feeding rumors of the newlyweds knowing each other in Ness's Chicago days.

"Evaline," a friend speculated, "may have already been in the picture when Eliot and Edna separated."

Really, they had first met on a train several years before, as Evaline remembered it, on a "perfect day in June," while Ness traveled the country by train, gathering labor racketeering evidence.

"Eliot and I talked a lot . . . looked at each other at the same time a lot . . . laughed a lot and kissed a lot when I got off the train," she wrote. "He was married. So was I. I thought that I would never see him again."

Evaline seemed to fall madly in love whenever she felt the need to escape. She'd grown up in the "unbeautiful, factory town" of Pontiac, Michigan, the youngest daughter of a Swedish photographer and Virginian housewife. By Evaline's arrival—"born late," she wrote, "and an unwelcome surprise"—the love had gone out of her parents' marriage, and her once-dashing father now worked at the local Ford plant.

Evaline decided never to fall into a similar trap. Her first brush with marriage—a proposal from a young doctor—ended when she ran away to pursue a passion for art.

"I thought of my mother," Evaline remembered, "washing, ironing, cleaning that one bathroom for six people. . . . I was paralyzed with horror. I knew I couldn't do it."

She married another commercial artist. After they moved to New York, his career took off, hers did not. Evaline grew depressed and quarrelsome, the legacy of what she called her "father's dark Swedish despondency." She left her husband and moved into a flophouse, supporting herself with modeling jobs.

Then Eliot Ness gave her a call. She was thrilled to hear he'd "tracked" her to New York.

"Eliot had many talents," Evaline reflected, "but his 'detective' skill was the one I liked best."

He asked her to dinner, and they met at the elegant Sherry-Netherland Hotel on the Upper East Side. In its ornate lobby, under a ceiling festooned with Italianate frescoes, Ness spread his arms and Evaline fell into them, burying her face in his chest. She called it "the most comforting feeling that I could remember."

Ness said his marriage had collapsed. Evaline said she was collapsing hers.

"Why don't you move to Cleveland," he asked, "where I can see you, touch you, talk to you in the process?"

She soon did, and they married not long after.

"He loved her, no question about that," a friend recalled. "He always called her 'Doll.'"

The local press saw Evaline's work as something of a novelty—NESS' BRIDE TO KEEP HOUSE—AND CAREER, TOO, ran one headline—but Eliot respected and encouraged her calling. He liked to talk with artists about their craft, to probe how they saw the world differently. He also admired independence and self-sufficiency, and was a cat person for just that reason.

"Cats don't have to be walked," Ness explained. "You just open the door and out they go. When they're ready to come back, they come."

A free spirit himself, he seems to have admired those qualities in Evaline.

Eliot didn't hesitate to show off his bride. Edna had always chafed at being married to a public official, but Evaline seemed to revel in it, joining her husband at his favorite nightspots, matching his social circle drink for drink and dance for dance. She even skirted the edges of his working life, attending the trial of a labor racketeer Ness helped expose. Anything but incognito, she sat right down front in a gray dress and matching turban.

"Eliot . . . was in the limelight constantly," she remembered, "and I along with him. I loved it because I felt like a star. But I hated it, too."

She grew to dislike playing the great man's spouse at an endless array of civic functions, making speeches and giving awards to Girl Scouts. She put up with it because Eliot offered a stability she seemed so desperately to crave. She called him "the most controlled man I ever met," and could never quite contain herself the same way.

For a while, the surface held, but hairline cracks soon began to appear. A mutual acquaintance recalled Eliot and Evaline acting "more like . . . best friends or buddies than husband and wife," a mistake Evaline had made in her previous marriage.

THE NESSES MADE their first public appearance October 26, at a rally for Mayor Burton's reelection, the same day Eliot announced their marriage. Though this marked the official opening of Burton's campaign, Ness was the center of attention, the *Plain Dealer* going so far as to call the evening "Ness Night." The speakers, Burton included, focused more on the Safety Director's achievements than the candidate's.

Evaline joined her husband on the podium as the crowd cheered. When Eliot stood to speak, a band played the "Wedding March." It might have been a dry run for the mayoral campaign many Republicans hoped Ness would pursue once Burton inevitably went on to higher office.

Ness spoke out against another choice facing the voters: a proposed amendment to the city charter limiting the mayor's authority over the police and fire departments. The amendment had the support of the Fraternal Order of Police and the Cleveland Fire Fighters Union, who hoped to restrict the influence of elected officials and "take police and firemen out of politics."

But most Clevelanders saw it as "a 'get Ness' proposal" meant to strip the Safety Director of his power. After all, its author and chief proponent was former Deputy Inspector Andrew Hagan, who had tried to discredit Ness during the previous campaign.

The amendment would revert the department to the corruption and politicking of Hagan's reign as the "unofficial chief of police," eliminating Ness's new professional standards.

Hagan's measure drew much support from a growing blue-coated resistance to Ness's reorganization of the police department. Patrolling in cars and not on foot continued to drive crime rates down and save lives; police now regularly picked up burglars or robbers within a few minutes of their offenses. But many cops wistfully recalled comfortably camping out in a precinct station.

A sizable contingent among the rank and file opposed these rapid revisions. They particularly resented Ness's elite, ivory-tower ideas. Streetwise cops would openly mock their boss by asking, "I wonder what a college graduate would do about this?"

But voters rejected Hagan's amendment three to one. "Even in precincts where the vote on candidates for mayor was close and where the amendment was expected to have its greatest support," the *Plain Dealer* reported, "the measure was snowed under."

Burton also won a resounding victory, largely on the strength of Ness's work. "If the Burton administration had accomplished nothing else," wrote the *News*, "its traffic safety record alone would be evidence of rare competence in public office."

The results showed a vast majority of citizens supporting Ness, even if his own police force didn't. With his hold on the department preserved, he wasted no time in exercising it, presiding in late November over a disciplinary hearing for Patrolman Frank Green. A member of the class of new recruits Ness swore in back in 1936, which the *Call & Post* criticized for being entirely white, Green had been suspended for shooting and killing an unarmed black man.

He had walked into an all-black bar one night in May 1939. Off duty and severely drunk, he launched into a racist rant before wandering outside, announcing his intention "to whip all the n——rs on the street."

Twenty-three-year-old Joseph Foreman, who'd followed Green outside, replied, "You're not so tough, I think I could lick you myself."

Foreman may not have known he was challenging a cop—Green wasn't in uniform. A scuffle ensued, and Green pulled a gun, shooting Foreman in the chest and the leg. The patrolman claimed Foreman had "jumped him from the rear," though witnesses and the trajectory of his shots said otherwise.

Foreman lingered in the hospital several days before dying. A superior officer of Green's asked for his badge, but the patrolman preferred to fight, going on suspension while facing a murder charge. The shooting "aroused intense resentment" in the city's African-American community, according to the *Call & Post*, "as well as the fear that Cleveland was in for a series of police brutalities similar to those experienced this year in Washington and Detroit."

Green's trial that September only fed tensions. After hearing the prosecution's evidence, the judge said they'd failed to make their case, taking the charge down from second-degree murder to manslaughter. An all-white jury acquitted Green after four hours of deliberation.

Despite the acquittal, Green remained on suspension pending the Safety Director's decision. At the hearing on November 28, Green and his attorney argued that several attackers had come up behind the patrolman and knocked him down, leaving him no choice but to shoot in self-defense.

The Safety Director conceded that Green may have felt the need to defend himself. But, Ness insisted, the patrolman had shown "poor judgment" by fighting in the first place. That made Green unfit for duty, and Ness dismissed him from the force.

"By his consistent evidence of fairness and reasonableness," the *Call & Post* opined, "Director Ness won the respect of all of our people. Because of these same qualities, the Cleveland police force is gradually being transformed into one of the most respectable in the nation."

Yet that progress was in greater peril than Ness appeared to know. Factions within the department, battling each other for years, now stood united in their hatred of the Safety Director.

. . .

FOLLOWING THE START of World War II in September 1939, Ness knew heavy industry in Cleveland, especially manufacturers of airplane parts and other defense equipment, presented natural targets. Before the United States was drawn into the conflict, Ness was already planning to protect his city from terrorism and sabotage.

In early fall, Lieutenant J. R. Haskin—a young and impulsive reserve officer with the Office of Naval Intelligence—suggested a few preventive measures, deemed inadequate by the concerned Safety Director.

Ness recommended going to industrialists to set up a privately funded spy agency, following the old Secret Six model, gathering tips from informants to pass along to law enforcement. He suggested it be an arm of the Cleveland Safety Council, just as the Secret Six began as part of the Chicago Association of Commerce. Unlike its predecessor, this group would not seek publicity, but avoid it.

Even more secretive than usual, Ness kept his plan from the city's unions. With tensions continuing between labor and law enforcement, Ness didn't trust union members to report suspicious activity, planning instead to put them under surveillance.

"If Eliot had a fault," a friend reflected, "it was what I would call a lack of caution."

The Safety Council embraced the plan and established the Cleveland Industrial Safety Committee. Lieutenant Haskin promised Naval Intelligence support and gave Ness a list of factories with navy contracts—confidential information. Ness and Haskin then invited factory owners to mass meetings in late October and early November for specifics.

The industrialists were to provide the committee with employee lists to be searched for "trustworthy" workers to go undercover. Selecting these informants fell to Thomas Clothey, who resigned as Ness's chief investigator to work for the committee full-time. Yet the navy had not signed off on the idea. Haskin may have led Ness to believe they had, but a reserve officer could hardly speak for the Office of Naval Intelligence.

Ness had strayed once again into the domain of the FBI and its territorial director, J. Edgar Hoover. President Roosevelt had ordered the FBI "to take charge of investigative work in matters relating to espionage, sabotage, and violations of the neutrality regulations." Hoover had forwarded this order "to all law enforcement officials," asking them to send his Bureau any relevant tips.

The Safety Director saw his committee as a complement, not a competitor, to Hoover's efforts. He and Clothey pressed their case with Ed Guinane, Special Agent in Charge of the Cleveland FBI office. FBI memos indicate Guinane did not endorse their plan, nor did he specifically object. This led Ness to assume he had the Bureau's support, along with that of the navy. He had neither.

Soon word of the committee began leaking out—inevitably, as Ness and Haskin had shared their plans with so many industrialists. Haskin accused Guinane of leaking the names; the FBI denied it. The local CIO affiliate responded with predictable outrage.

"Herr Ness and his Gestapo at City Hall are now compiling a list of labor leaders and militant unionists," a union official claimed in mid-October, "who are to be arrested and clapped in jail in the event of war."

"If war comes, we will be on the alert for sabotage, espionage and other forms of subversive activity," Ness responded in the *Press*. "But we are not concentrating on individuals."

Ness's penchant for secrecy and unwillingness to trust outsiders generated wild rumors—that he'd tapped the phones of union men, hired private detectives to stalk them around the city, even established a "radical" squad within the police department (which was closer to the truth). But the Industrial Safety Committee hadn't begun operating yet.

Hoover, safeguarding his Bureau, sent the attorney general a memo criticizing Ness's committee. After a CIO official somehow saw a copy of that memo and revealed Hoover's attitude to the press, the Director made no public comment. His silence mystified Ness, who honestly, if naively, believed the FBI supported his plan.

Ness and Clothey met the special agent in charge of the Cleveland FBI office, offering to give the Bureau any intelligence gathered. Their main concern was that the FBI would begin an investigation only after a sabotage incident, while they hoped to prevent it.

"I'm in charge of the city," Ness said, "and I'm worried about blowing up the down-town section or blowing up some Standard Oil Tanks, which are all along the river, and the protection of the City, primarily."

Ness offered to end the Industrial Safety Committee at once if the FBI could assure him they'd allow no disasters on their watch. The agent refused to give him a definite answer.

The next month, Ness met with a Hoover assistant in Washington, asking why the agency had leaked details of his plan to the CIO. The assistant denied the Bureau had done any such thing.

Hoover, feeling Ness meant to "blame the FBI" for his union difficulties, wanted no part of it. But his Bureau proved willing to use Ness's committee as an intelligence source . . . with the Safety Director assuming all political and legal risks.

Ness went ahead. His secret investigators gathered names of those they found suspicious and passed them along to the FBI. This did nothing to improve Ness's standing with the Bureau, and the effort destroyed whatever goodwill Ness had left with organized labor, which believed he had "set up a spy service to thwart, harass and crush labor unions."

Ness designed the Industrial Safety Committee to operate on "a three-month basis," according to the *Press*, "so that it can be instantly discontinued when the situation created by war ends." When peacetime came, however, and Ness was no longer Safety Director, the police unit he'd established to monitor those tips evolved into a "subversive squad" that would monitor political "radicals" for decades to come.

SINCE FRANK DOLEZAL'S death, Peter Merylo had continued hunting for the Butcher, apparently unaware Ness and David Cowles had their own suspect under surveillance. In February 1940, Cowles gave Merylo a new lead: Francis Sweeney, temporarily checked out of the Sandusky Soldiers and Sailors Home to visit his sister in Cleveland.

Merylo and longtime partner Martin Zalewski, reconciled now, visited Sweeney on February 5. Merylo's report suggests neither man had ever met the doctor, nor had they apparently known his name until Cowles brought him up.

Under lengthy questioning about his personal and professional life, Sweeney couldn't keep still, pacing as he chattered. Merylo got the impression the doctor was full of himself. Both detectives concluded this was probably not the Butcher.

Sweeney "is not the type of person who would associate with perverts or other low type of characters," Merylo reported. "He is inclined to be delicate, even though he weighs 220 pounds. He is . . . rather fat and soft . . . and could not in our opinion fit into the type of person who would mix with the transients around the railroad tracks and swamps."

Merylo had developed his own theory of the case, which all but excluded Sweeney as a suspect. He believed the Cleveland torso murders were linked to similar killings outside the city, especially a series of decapitated bodies found near New Castle, Pennsylvania. The more victims Merylo sought, the more he seemed to find, concluding that Cleveland's Butcher had killed more than thirty people over three decades and as many states.

Only a specific type of individual, Merylo thought, could be responsible for all this carnage: a large, powerful "pervert" who rode the rails, with boxcars his "laboratory." Francis Sweeney did not fit that profile and couldn't have committed the murders in Pennsylvania and elsewhere. So Merylo marked him off.

But others on the case, including David Cowles, were not convinced the Butcher ever killed outside Cleveland. While other murders bore similarities to the Butcher's work, they did not match key details of his modus operandi, the specific signature that grouped his slayings. Moreover, Merylo's theory of a roving murderer contradicted a key point of the torso clinic profile—that the killer displayed enough familiarity with Kingsbury Run to have come from that area.

Merylo's conclusions were based in part on wildly inaccurate information; at other times he ignored inconvenient facts. The deeply flawed profile he followed led him off track, even as the murders became an ever deepening obsession. He spent three weeks that summer posing as a hobo, wandering by train and living among transients from Ohio to Pennsylvania, finding no solid leads. His continuing—and very public—investigation devolved into a diversion, distracting the press and allowing Ness's investigators to work the case in secret.

The Safety Director was convinced the killer had been found. A visiting law enforcement official recalled Ness taking him to a dive bar to point out a patron.

"That's the man," Ness said, "we suspect is the torso murderer."

The official didn't take this seriously, as the alleged killer appeared to be a random drunk. More likely, Ness had singled out his secret suspect.

Eliot Ness trusted his own hunches; an acquaintance recalled him repeatedly advising her to "always go with your gut feeling." That the Kingsbury Run murders stopped when Sweeney checked himself into the hospital, Ness felt, was no coincidence. And when Sweeney was on furlough, Ness kept close tabs on him.

Ness became even more convinced when the doctor began sending him taunting messages and postcards. One featured a photo of a tree marked with an X and the caption "DIG HERE." Investigators found the tree, dug it up, and found nothing. Other messages from Sweeney, which have not survived, apparently included details of the murders that Ness believed could have come only from the Butcher.

A close Ness relative recalled a drunken Sweeney would "call Eliot frequently at his office to taunt him. He'd tell Eliot things that only the killer could know."

None of this was proof beyond a reasonable doubt. Certain he'd caught the killer but unable to prove it, Ness resolved to keep Sweeney off the streets, even if it meant sidestepping due process.

Sweeney's Soldiers and Sailors Home stay ended on July 30, 1940. After that, he was "confined as a mental patient" at a veterans hospital near Battle Creek, Michigan, according to an FBI memo.

Royal Grossman, the court psychiatrist who'd assisted in the secret interrogation of Sweeney, said Ness himself arranged the doctor's commitment. Future Safety Director Alvin Sutton told a similar story—that Ness had gone to Congressman Martin Sweeney, shared his suspicions, and offered him the chance to keep the matter quiet by having his cousin committed.

Years later, when John Larson asked whatever happened to the man he'd polygraphed in 1938, Ness assured him the individual had been taken care of.

"The suspect tested had very powerful contacts," Larson wrote, "and arrangements were made whereby he was placed in a special hospital where he has supposedly been for years."

Word got around the police department of the well-connected doctor who'd escaped arrest because of a lack of evidence, but how much Merylo knew remains unclear. Gus Zukie recalled Merylo telling him of a suspect that could very well have been Sweeney: a nurse, not a doctor, who came from a powerful family.

Merylo "said he knew he was going to run into trouble . . . ," Zukie said, "that eventually he'd be taken off the case because of that nurse."

A male nurse, perhaps?

The detective's daughter recalled her father saying his superiors had told him to "leave it alone," that this suspect might have been guilty but "his family" had had him committed. But Merylo was too wrapped up in his own theory of a nomadic, prolific serial killer to accept Sweeney as a possible Butcher.

After more than six years on the case, Merylo was reassigned in October 1942.

"I will never give up my work on these Torso Murders," he wrote in his final report; "as long as the killer is still at large, he will be arrested." The investigation, Merylo said, had become "a habit with me"—in the addiction sense, possibly.

"Regardless of what my other assignments maybe [*sic*]," Merylo wrote, "I will continue to work on my day[s] off and my vacations as I did in the past." He kept his word, pursuing the case after he retired in 1943 until his death in 1958.

Congressman Sweeney never repeated his earlier criticisms of Ness's failure to catch the Butcher. He committed himself instead to preventing America's entry into World War II. With other isolationist congressmen and senators, Sweeney fell under the sway of a secret Nazi agent, who used elected officials—sometimes with their connivance—to disseminate German propaganda to millions of American voters. The *Plain Dealer* would brand Sweeney "one of Hitler's little helpers in the Congress of the United States."

An apparently unwitting dupe of a fascist foreign power, Sweeney polluted the *Congressional Record* with pro-Nazi statements and material. The British posed a greater threat to America than any of the Axis Powers, he said, calling FDR an "abject failure and a leader whom generations yet unborn will look upon with disdain and contempt." Though Sweeney bristled at being called an anti-Semite, the *Nation* noted he was tightly connected "with groups and individuals who unmistakably represent religious and political bigotry."

In September 1940, Sweeney railed against a conscription bill in the House, deeming it Roosevelt's ruse to drag the country into war. When another congressman called him "a traitor" and "a son of a bitch," Sweeney threw a punch and missed. His critic threw a punch and didn't. An observer called it "the best blow he had heard in his 50 years in the House."

The following year, Sweeney ran for mayor on what Phil Porter called a platform "of more bingo, more Hitler and less newspapers." Unsurprisingly, he failed to secure the Democratic nomination.

His political career imploded in 1942, when he finally lost his seat in Congress. He retreated into his private law practice, dying in 1960.

Although Ness believed he'd closed the torso case, he could never calm the city's fears. The Butcher continued to cast a shadow over Kingsbury Run, setting off a minor panic whenever a potential victim turned up.

The Safety Director swore everyone involved in his investigation to secrecy; decades would pass before Cowles and others revealed their suspect's name. But Ness hadn't heard the last of Frank Sweeney, nor had Cleveland seen the last of its Butcher.

24 PAGES — CLEVELAND, WEDNESDAY MORNING, SEPTEMBER 16, 1936 — PRICE

S TORSO KILLER NEW INSAN

Couzens Trails in Rep___an Ra

MAINE VOTE IS BAD NEWS TO NEW DEAL

_uel Says Election Shows Threat of Republican Victory in November.

OOSEVELT JUST SMILES

dicates Result Was About What He Expected.

BY WALKER S. BUEL
Plain Dealer Bureau,
812 Albee Bldg.
WASHINGTON, Sept. 5.
_aine's election is very bad news for the New Deal and Democratic result.

s a definite indication of a R
_ican trend, A definite threat of _
epublican victory in November.
_hile forecasts of a diminished
Democratic membership in Con-
_s, a definite indication of a Re-
_ican revival, especially in the

_s is not for unprecedented fac-
in this campaign, the Maine _
_ might be regarded as a lead
_to New Deal hopes for the re-
_on of President Roosevelt. But _
_ factors exist, making possible _
_citizens and eastern combination
_s may render Roosevelt to _
_of anything the wind can an-
_ly feel really knows the po-
_effect of relief and bonus _
_tures throughout the agricultu

No. 20 for Allen

Allen injured his back in the fifth inning, but was given credit for his twentieth victory yesterday as the Indians walloped Boston, 12 to 5 Hildebrand finished the game. Trosky hit his 25th and 19th homers.

New York defeated Chicago, 7 to 1; Detroit trimmed Philadelphia, 8 to 4, and Washington took a double header from St. Louis, 13 to 7 and 6 to 5. Weather stopped the National Legacy.

(Details on Sport Pages)

WPA WORKERS TO BE EXPO GUESTS

Families, Also, to Attend Saturday as Honor to Garden Builders.

Today's Events

United Rubber Workers Day.
United States Postoffice Day.
Royal Neighbors of America Day.
National County of Patriots Day.
City Club Day.
Macon (Ga.) Day.
Garden Club of Michigan Day.

(Attendance yesterday 30,385
Attendance to date.........2,288,118
Days left—31.)

BUY YOUR OWN MEALS. NESS TELLS ROOKIES

Ten New Patrolmen Told Appointments Are Based on Own Merits.

"DON'T BE OBLIGATED"

Warns "You'll Get No Great Reward for Honesty."

Ten new patrolmen were given this office yesterday by Safety Director Eliot Ness in his office at City Hall with the revolutionary admonition that patrolmen are expected to pay for their own meals.

Youth, 16, Threatens Shirley Tem

image area

OUTLAW SITDOWN, PLEA IS UP TO URW

Strikes Hit Akron Plants as Rubber International Weighs Policy Issue.

Plain Dealer Bureau,
322 Ohio Building,
AKRON, O., Sept. 15.

The issue of the sitdown strike _ __ght looms as the most important question before the United Rubber Workers of America at their first international convention in session here.

SHAKER EXTEN TO RUN CARS

Shuttle Service to Rd. Expected in 2 W May Go to Richme

BY JAMES G. MOSNE

ATLANTA, Ga., Sept. 15.—A mil_ kidnapped youth was said he spent six of his 16 years in 4 reform school calmly told federal authori-ties today of a plan to abduct 6-year-old Shirley Temple.

Says Fight With Richman Nearly Sank Ocean Plane

NEW YORK, Sept. 16—(AP)—The Daily Item, in a copyrighted dispatch from a staff correspondent at Musgrave Harbor, Newfoundland, says a quarrel over the Atlantic be-tween the transoceanic flyers Harry Richman and Dick Merrill "almost ended with the flyers in Davy Jones' locker."

Merrill and Richman landed at that isolated village yesterday after a return flight from England.

Newspaper Plane Damaged.

ST. JOHNS, Newfoundland, Sept. 15—(U.P.)—A newspaper plane owned by the New York Daily News

Ness upon being named head of the Social Protection Division in 1941.

Cleveland Press Collection, Cleveland State University

NINETEEN

Whatever Became of Eliot Ness?

Summer 1940–1941

I am wondering," reporter Julian Griffin wrote to the *Cleveland Press* in May 1940, "whatever became of Eliot Ness."

Griffin's beat brought him by Ness's office every weekday, yet he hadn't seen the Safety Director in over a month. Such a lengthy absence would once have ignited whispers of another major investigation. But currently, Ness's social calendar seemed to outweigh his caseload.

"Maybe," Griffin suggested, "we should turn in a missing-person report on him."

If so, Ness and Frank Cullitan would have been found meeting in secret with Harry Barrington, the first union official convicted in their labor racketeering probe.

Barrington had gone to prison in 1937 without testifying against partner Albert Ruddy, now president of the Carpenters District Council, thinking Ruddy would get him out of jail. But after more than two years of incarceration, Barrington—seeking early release—gave testimony tying his former partner to extortion, bombing, and murder. Ness and Cullitan couldn't prove the latter, but won indictments for the rest on June 19.

Unlike Campbell, McGee, and the other racketeers Ness had

exposed, Ruddy had an upstanding reputation as a union leader without a hint of criminality. His allies again accused Ness of persecuting unions, a charge Cullitan again refuted.

The Carpenters District Council proved Cullitan's point by distancing itself from its embattled president, publicly refusing to offer Ruddy any moral or financial support.

Throughout the trial, Ness sat with reporters, taking notes and doodling on a legal pad. "He seems neither at work nor at play, neither bored nor excited," wrote Howard Beaufait of the *News*.

Now and then, a whispered order from Ness would send an Unknown slipping out.

"Several of the director's special investigators are in the courtroom most of the time," Beaufait wrote. "They are enigmatic and watch everything that goes on as a cat watches a rat hole." At least one came with a shoulder-holstered gun.

In early October, the jury convicted Ruddy of extortion, the judge giving him four years. The *Press* called it Ness and Cullitan's "most important victory . . . in their cleanup of labor racketeers." The *Plain Dealer* praised Ness for driving out the "dishonest dictatorship" that for at least a decade had dominated the Carpenters District Council.

"Labor now knows, as most Clevelanders have known for a long time," they wrote, "that Ness is one of the best friends honest labor has had in this city."

The *Christian Science Monitor* credited Ness with restoring confidence to local businesses. "People go about now with their heads up," the paper observed. "They move faster and there are more of them on the streets than there were two years ago. There are few empty shops. People are buying, they're going to the theater, patronizing the symphony, doing things. . . . It looks like a happy time in Cleveland."

But not for the criminal classes.

"There is nothing about Ness' appearance to inspire fear," Beaufait wrote. "But the shadowy characters who sometimes drift into the Criminal Courts Building point him out with awe.

'There goes Ness,' they say as though they were indicating Wyatt Erp [*sic*], the two-gun sharpshooter of the gold rush days."

One young man whose father ran an illicit still was called unexpectedly to Ness's office, and couldn't help trembling as he found the Safety Director at his desk. His host ignored him for a moment or two, then looked up.

Ness said, "Your father is using too much sugar."

His visitor left and had the still shut down at once.

Raids were all but unnecessary, if Ness could foil bootleggers with a few mildly threatening words. His work now lacked the danger and excitement that kept him engaged. He couldn't hide that the job had begun to bore him. Ever eager to apply himself to new problems, he seemed restless and hungry. Appearing on a local radio game show, which challenged guests to solve mysteries by asking yes/no questions, he cracked the cases so fast his host quickly ran out of material.

His war on crime was reduced to taking on illegal gaming devices such as pinball machines—the mob had come to rely on the money skimmed from coin-operated games as a major source of illicit income—and periodic crackdowns on commercial bingo parlors.

Ness fought downtown traffic congestion, urging use of public transit, and began an antipollution drive, calling the problem "one of the most serious facing us," searching by plane for factories with belching smokestacks.

In 1940, Catholic leaders pressured Ness to curb the distribution of "obscene" magazines, which they defined as anything "that glorifies crime, [is] predominately sexy, features illicit love or carries disreputable advertising."

Ness didn't share their concerns but tried to quiet the protests by establishing a citizens' committee to study the problem. The group engaged in a flurry of well-publicized activity, then Ness quietly stonewalled them—they met only twice and never accomplished much of anything.

After a few months, the Catholic groups again began to protest.

When the archbishop visited Ness's office, the Safety Director said many Clevelanders found gambling just as offensive as dirty magazines. Some citizens were upset Catholic churches were allowed to operate illegal bingo games.

"If you help me solve this problem by closing down your bingo gambling," Ness said, "I, in return, will strengthen and accelerate my efforts to curb the distribution of obscene literature in Cleveland."

The complaints about obscene literature died away.

His chief focus remained perfecting and promoting the police department's motorization. He gave speeches describing the new system, demonstrating it by calling headquarters to see how long it took a cruiser to arrive. When officers, who once walked beats but now sat in cars all day, began gaining weight, Ness proposed a mandatory physical fitness program.

Many police cars were in worse shape than their drivers. Over a year of constant patrolling had left the vehicles "young in years, but old in miles," an official put it, the average top speed cut nearly in half. The fleet would soon need replacing, but the city didn't have enough money to pay for that. And if the department couldn't keep its cars on the road, Ness would have to scrap the motorized patrol system just as it began to take hold.

Ness also clashed with the City Council over reforming the Policewomen's Bureau. A councilman wanted to eliminate the "useless" bureau, but Ness considered the unit essential, preserving it through a merger with Arthur Roth's Juvenile Bureau. He also eliminated an old rule preventing policewomen from getting married.

Such reforms did not make dramatic headlines. The Safety Director was turning into just another bureaucrat, his heroic aura fading from the spotlight. And the newspapers, who'd long counted on him for good copy, began to tire of Eliot Ness.

This included longtime ally the *Cleveland Press* and its editor, Louis B. Seltzer. A small man, confrontational and profane, Seltzer had established himself as Ohio's leading kingmaker, capable of changing the political fortunes of anyone in the state.

"If he didn't like you," a Ness friend remembered, "you were in trouble."

Now Seltzer's *Press*, which had assisted the Safety Director's secret investigations from police corruption to the torso case, criticized Ness for hiring off-the-books detectives. They began referencing his nightlife activities—alleging, without evidence, that a seedy nightclub received police protection because its owner was Ness's driver's son. To underscore that the Safety Director had never been an FBI agent, *Press* columnist Jack Raper hammered home a taunting new nickname: "Neverwas G-Man Ness."

"Ness," Phil Porter remembered, "was one of the best safety directors who ever held office. . . . But good as he was, he couldn't have attained the public stature that he did without the complete support, indeed, the complete buildup the newspapers gave him. They created the Ness legend and defended him when he was in difficulty."

Without their support, the city would soon find out that its infallible hero was just a man after all.

IN NOVEMBER 1940, Harold Burton won election to the U.S. Senate.

To fill out his mayoral term, Burton chose his hardworking (if unremarkable) assistant law director, Edward Blythin, whose defeat in the next year's election seemed inevitable. Many observers saw him as a placeholder for someone else to run in 1941. With a strong slate of potential Democratic challengers, Republicans could think of only one man popular enough to keep their hold on City Hall: Eliot Ness.

Ness had already entered the political fray, but not on the Republicans' behalf. In October, he'd campaigned for Democrat Frank Cullitan's reelection, declaring "a vote for Cullitan is a vote against crime." This infuriated GOP leaders, whose hopes for defeating the prosecutor evaporated when Ness stood up for him.

But a *Press* columnist took a more cynical view, calling the endorsement "one of the cutest moves in many a day. It firmly established Eliot Ness as an 'independent,' and makes him available to wear that tag in next year's mayoralty race."

The Safety Director did little to discourage such thinking. After Burton made Blythin his successor, Ness told the *Plain Dealer* he'd consider running for mayor, but "a thousand and one things have to be thought over first."

Wiser friends advised him that tackling politics would be a mistake. In the *Plain Dealer*, Phil Porter admitted Ness might well win but could only disappoint as mayor.

"Ness is largely a solo operator," Porter wrote, "an impresario and a detective. As a pursuer of grafters and gatherer of evidence, he has no superior. But he adapts poorly to routine, is impatient with obstacles, and is realistic and somewhat contemptuous about the political mind and method. . . .

"The endless routine of banquets, greetings and dedications would get him down in no time. So would the job of pacifying councilmen and ward leaders. He would be at odds with the political organization continually."

Republicans kept trying to "draft" Ness into the mayoral race, but he refused—he liked his current job.

IN EARLY 1941, Ness went to New York City to pick up the key witness in yet another corrupt labor leader's trial, only to discover the man had disappeared.

Ness spent two of what the *News* called "the most nerve-wracking and exciting days . . . in his war against the rackets," trying to track the witness down. He returned to his Cleveland office looking, a reporter said, "more excited than we'd ever seen him before."

Ness requested privacy, adding, "I'm racing against time."

After the newsmen cleared out, Ness called an investigator friend who worked for New York prosecutor Thomas Dewey. The investigator managed to find the witness, promised protection, and booked him a flight to Ohio. Ness met the man at the airport and got him to court just in time, sealing the racketeer's conviction.

Such dramatic close calls were a drug Ness could never quit.

"The constant excitement of his job is what keeps him there," observed the *News*, "and is one chief reason the mayoralty post has no appeal for Ness."

As such exultant moments became increasingly few, Ness's job grew much more difficult when chief assistant Robert Chamberlin joined the army. Ness replaced him with Tom Clothey, who was fine with bureaucratic drudgery but less effective with the press. Chamberlin had been indispensable as the buffer between his boss and the media; without him, a different side of the Safety Director—impatient, even petty—began to emerge in print.

Shortly after Chamberlin's departure, Ness got into a public tiff with Michael Blackwell, now captain of the vice squad, who claimed the Safety Director had placed "a Communist" in charge of the committee on obscene literature.

Blackwell told the *Press* his boss "might just as well have appointed Stalin" by choosing an attorney who ran the local American Civil Liberties Union chapter. Then a bitter Blackwell complained of Ness transferring his "right-hand man" off the vice squad.

"I'm sick and tired of pouting policemen who spout off every time somebody is transferred," Ness told reporters.

He had enough sense not to discipline Blackwell, long one of the department's "untouchables," yet still revealed a lack of judgment. Ness had already antagonized so many of his police that he could hardly afford to lose any friends.

IN EARLY 1941, Cleveland saw a spike in traffic deaths— more than double the year before. Most victims were middle-aged or older; many were pedestrians killed at night. Ness treated the situation as a major civic emergency, meeting with local leaders— police, industry, education, and organized labor—to brainstorm solutions. He also ordered a crackdown on jaywalking. But the *News* saw these deaths as proof Ness's traffic reforms had begun to fail.

Investigation revealed something more sinister at work. The deaths of so many elderly, indigent people in hit-and-run accidents reminded some police officials of an old "insurance racket" operating in Cleveland's Angle, a poor Irish neighborhood on the Near West Side.

Years before, speculators in the Angle had taken out multiple life insurance policies on older derelicts and chronic alcoholics. Then they plied their victims with bad liquor until they died or met with a fatal accident.

Those accidents often followed a pattern: a drunk person, sent to the store on an errand, wandered into the path of a speeding car. Many victims of this latest spike in traffic deaths had died in much the same way, while walking to or from the grocery store.

Police officials brought their suspicions to Ness. So did Gaspar Corso, a State Insurance Division investigator who'd also noticed a suspicious increase in "boozer" deaths. Ness put several Unknowns on the case.

Working with Corso and Clayton Fritchey, the investigators linked the deaths to the resurgent insurance racket, dubbed by the *Press* "Natural Death Inc." A West Side woman had passed the racket down to her daughter, who formed a gang of mostly female speculators. But the ringleader's indictment and conviction ended the racket, scaring off other would-be investors.

Yet even as the Unknowns worked to expose Natural Death Inc., Ness faced pressure to get rid of these shadowy investigators. In a series of *Press* columns, Jack Raper criticized Ness's "staff of stooges," demanding to know who paid their salaries. The City Council questioned Ness's skirting civil service rules by putting his investigators on the payroll as "laborers."

Ness did his best to explain before a council meeting that January. The "civil service list didn't provide the type of investigators I needed when I came on the job," he said. "And I couldn't use policemen because I was using investigators to investigate the police department."

That failed to convince the Civil Service Commission, which

ordered Ness to disband the Unknowns that spring. Ness did, but worked with the committee to keep most of his so-called "Gestapo" on the job.

One such investigator was just coming into his own as a detective. In March 1941, with Ness's approval, Arnold Sagalyn launched his own investigation into "clip joints," hotels where ruthless women would lure traveling businessmen to rob them. Sagalyn employed a strategy plucked from Ness's playbook: Inspectors would search the hotels for building or fire code violations, where enough problems might be found to pressure the owners into halting the racket.

But when the hotel owners complained to a city councilman, Ness told his protégé to back off. He needed the councilman's vote for new police and fire vehicles.

Ness had to pick his battles carefully these days, as his reforms met increasingly fierce resistance. In early 1941, as he had with the police, he proposed a plan to reorganize and streamline the fire department, challenging the authority of politically influential fire wardens. The fire chief called the plan "a grave mistake," telling the *Plain Dealer* Ness still had a lot to learn about their department's workings.

When these reforms failed to take, Ness castigated fire department officials in a closed-door meeting. Sometime later, working to pass a new levy, he joked that the police and firefighters would happily support the measure if it included a provision removing him.

The Safety Director's unpopularity concentrated in the higher ranks, among older members of the police. Younger officers, hired by Ness, often still thought highly of him. But the city had stopped recruiting in recent years, slowing Ness's efforts to change the department's culture.

In October, Howard Beaufait visited the Cleveland Police Academy—primary symbol of Ness's push for professionalization—to find it vacant and dusty. "Oscar," the oft-murdered dummy upon whom students had practiced their detective skills, lay cobweb covered in a closet. Every man on the force had already graduated from the academy, which would not reopen until there were new police to train.

"Cleveland's experiment in police education and its dream of a new type of police officer," Beaufait wrote, "seems tangled in the same cobwebs as today bind the Academy's 'Oscar.'"

LS TORSO KILLER NEW INSAN

Couzens Trails in Rep___an Ra

MAINE VOTE IS BAD NEWS TO NEW DEAL

Buel Says Election Shows Threat of Republican Victory in November.

OOSEVELT JUST SMILES

ndicates Result Was About What He Expected.

BY WALKER S. BUEL
Plain Dealer Bureau.
417 Alice Bldg.
WASHINGTON, Sept. 15.
Maine's election is very bad news
for the New Deal and President
osevelt.

It is a drastic indication of a Re-
ublican trend, a definite threat of
Republican victory in November,
definite lessening of a Democratic
Democratic membership in Con-
ss, a definite indication of a Re-
blican revival, especially in the

ve's apt to be overestimated far-
in the campaign, the Maine
might be regarded as a fatal
the New Deal hopes for the re-
tion of President Roosevelt. But
a correct case, making possible
wouthern and western combination
ction as most Roosevelt is
y at anything the east can do
dy he really knows the re-
his effort of relief and benevo-
tures throughout the agricultural

overnber Election in Doubt.
oes the November election can
s so much in doubt as it by
the Maine vote, except that
the air and either upon the
Plain Deal the caps of the re-
and 1934 Democratic landslides
ended, and that unless Presi-
Roosevelt can hall the swell
and with in it headed for

ndrous Maine won in 1916 in a
election, without a rate of any
s room, in the best way though
for a clay margin. But Wilson
was won 1916.
The vote and he needs only
experts to overcome the trend
by the Maine vote.
mportant part the hast two year
he landslide' edge into New
e notion" edge the longer
he probably.
result, when fully surveyed,
border lines water predic-
ntion generally made by the
s experts:

that the election in Novem-
be one of the closest in

, that it will be more than
local election in the past, a
between the urban minorities
alus supporting President
and the small towns and
uris, backing Gov. Lan-

nen everyone, the full force
a rollof of high malficium
pie have accumulated into
than other by the side of
in ballots from the agri-

No. 20 for Allen

Allen injured his back in
the fifth inning, but was given
credit for the twentieth victory yester-
day, as the
Indians wal-
loped Bos-
ton, 13 to 2.
Hildebrand
finished the
game. Tro-
sky hit his
25th and
40th homers.
Detroit de-
feated Chicago, 7 to 1; Detroit trimmed Philadelphia,
9 to 6, and Washington took a
double header from St. Louis,
13 to 7 and 6 to 1.
Weather stopped the Na-
tional League.
(Details on Sport Pages)

WPA WORKERS TO BE EXPO GUESTS

Families, Also, to Attend Saturday as Honor to Garden Builders.

Today's Events.

United Rubber Workers Day.
United States Flouride Day.
Royal Neighbors of America Day.
National Society of Patriots Day.
City Club Day.
Boron 60.1 Day.
Garden Club of Michigan Day.
* * *
Attendance yesterday 28,063
Attendance up to date 3,833,443
Days left: 62.
* * *

The WPA will have its day at the
Great Lakes Exposition.
Some of the days wherein though
that, since everyday was having
his day at the exposition, it would be
heir impossible to forget the WPA,
some of whose 12,000 laborers built
the four-acre Horticultural Gardens
on the grounds.
So the men who shovel the
shovels and the men who swung the
picks have been invited to attend
the exposition Saturday. They will
have those furnished by their own
WPA bosses.
They will have the what stadium
it is during also. Arrangements
have been made with exposition
concessionaires to sell trunk and
lunches at prices they feel afford.
Such a celebration has been in-
tend for weeks because numerous
employes have said they wanted
the WPA-built gardens," Joseph
H. Alexander, WPA district director,
said. "The gardens are one of our
first pricesous.
The invitations, which include
members of the workers families,
will be in the form of identification
(Continued on Page 6, Column 2)

BUY YOUR OWN MEALS, NESS TELLS ROOKIES

Ten New Patrolmen Told Appointments Are Based on Own Merits.

"DON'T BE OBLIGATED"

Warns "You'll Get No Great Reward for Honesty."

Ten new patrolmen were sworn
into office yesterday by Safety Director Eliot Ness in the office at City
Hall with the revolutionary admon-
tion that patrolmen are expected to
pay for their own meals.
"You have been appointed on your
own merits and because you stood
at the top of the civil service list
and for no other reason," Ness told
the recruits. "If anyone tells anyone
to him that he was responsible for
your appointment, pay no attention.

"Your advancement is up to you.
"You are expected to be honest
and to know that you will get no
great rewards for being honest.
Don't be obligated to anyone, even
in small things.
"When you walk into a restaurant for a meal, pay for it. When
you get any marketable goods at any
market to you, pay for it. If peo-
have been astonished to giving you
things for nothing prior to your becoming a policeman, I suppose it is
all right for you to continue to accept these things.

Tells Why Promotions.

"However, if people who never
care on, anything free before now
want to give you something without
charge, you can conclude that they
are buying your badge and your
weapon."

In addition to appointing the ten
new policemen, Ness promoted Sergt.
Augustus V. F. Perry to a lieutenancy and Patrolman Herbert Birdel
and William M. Muise to sergeantcies.

The recruits were:
ELMER J. KARCHER, 1407 Virginia
Avenue S. W.
RICHARD O. STARR, 11050 Berwin
Court N.E.
EDWARD PRINTZ, Jr., 1619 Scho-
field S. E.
JAMES W. HEMBAZ, 5341 W. 150th
St.
FRANK J. UMEK, Jr., 4178 E. 131st
St.
ROY F. ZIMMERMAN, 3551 78th Av-
enue N. W.
HOWARD E. BECKER, 2400 E. 123th
St.
CLARENCE D. THOMA, 7557 Park Av-
enue S. E.
JOHN E. FULKES, 2403 Dean Avenue
N. E.
ELMER J. BLOCK, 1007 Juner Boul-
evard.

Cadek, the nephew of former Capt.
Louis J. Cadek, was appointed to
the department a month ago by
John H. Flynn, executive assistant
to Ness. His appointment was revoked at that date by Ness recently
Flynn had slapped the candidates at
the 18th of the list.

Youth, 16, Th___atens Shirley Ten

[photograph]

Acme and Press Wirephoto
Frank Edward Shafer, the
leter-overalls Atlanta boy, escorted to Atlanta fronting) and
charged with sending an extortion letter to the mother of
Shirley Temple (talk box also
is shown because his threat
amusements he was barred from the
Atlanta police station to the
Federal building.

ATLANTA, Ga., Sept 15.—A mild-
mannered youth who said he spent
six of his 24 years in a reform
school asking held federal notions
here today in connection with a $15,000 ex-
tortion letter to the mother of
Shirley Temple.

Another wire-preserved her, through
ing W. Powell, is under bond of
$1,000 at Grant, Neb., on a charge
attempting to extort $2000 from the
child star late this year. He will be
tried next year.

The youth caught today, booked
as Frank Edward Stephens, was accused by Postal Bureau Investigation operatives and related as his
own recognizance after a hearing
before United States Commissioner
E. A. Green.

Stephens, taken into custody at a
restaurant where he worked part-
time, signed his own bond of $500.
The commissioners said it would
avoid hearing investigation of the
case since may be to be punis-
tion the Georgia State Industrial
School at Birmingham.

"Direct Violation" Is Word.
"If is true that whatever may a
direct violation of your policies and
your principles," Green said.
The boy's new writers with his
left, and said.

OUTLAW SITDOWN, PLEA IS UP TO URW

Strikes Hit Akron Plants as Rubber International Weighs Policy Issue.

Plain Dealer Bureau.
310 Ohio Building.
AKRON, O., Sept. 15.

The issue of the sit-down strike (a-
legel) looms as the most important
question before the United Rubber
Workers of America as their first
international convention in session
here.

Resolutions before the conventions are asking that the un-
authorized sitdown be outlawed and
another that calls the actions "one
of the most powerful weapons of
organized labor" and asked for in-
corporation into URW policies.

This last one would put one of the
strikes into the hands of the executive council to apply various
justified.

Adolph Germer, Committee for Industrial Organization organizer, addressed the delegates last night, saying he had just come from a meeting
with a group of Akron rubbermen
who wanted to have some of all, he
said, what the URW could be doing
followers.

SHAKER EXTE TO RUN CARS

Shuffle Service to __ Rd. Expected in 2 W__ May Go to Richm___

BY JAMES C. MOONE
Two extension of rap
tracks in Shaker Heigh
completion in two week
the will be started short
the What low fare exten
Hack east of Warrensvil
Road on the Shaker Rapid
is to be rushed as far as
Road. Work on building
undigging unding steps and
about them, it is for the pr
with the Ambassa Bryan
will be a single-track ex
the Green is said to be a 'st
ability that the extension
tracked from its Richmond
to new tracks, and the
the stop at Brainard Road 1
quare for next spring, aft
future of the Cleveland Rail
Railway), which owns and
the line, and what shuttle s
any certainty of establishin
Green Road.

It is intended to operate 't
Service between Green Ro
Shaker Square A W ill
when the Shaker subway
many years, at the junctio
to the Mayfield line the
is considerable contrib

Says Fight With Richman Nearly Sank Ocean Plane

NEW YORK, Sept. 15—(AP)—The
Daily News, in a copyrighted dispatch from a staff correspondent at
Moneton Harbor, Newfoundland,
says a quarrel over the fueling between the trans-oceanic flyers Harry
Richman and Dick Merrill "almost
ended with the flyers in Davis
Idea" today.

Merrill and Richman landed at
that noised village yesterday after a
return flight from England.

The Newbown, it's the Bight De-
land, all my arguments for different questions were traced,
As Richman approached during the
conversation, he and Merrill looked
at opposite directions, the paper
says.

Newspaper Plane Damaged.
ST. JOHNS, Newfoundland, Sept.
15.—(AP)—A newspaper plane
owned by the New York Daily News

Ness with Mayor Frank Lausche (left) and Federal Security
Administrator Paul McNutt, who oversaw the Social Protection
Division.

Cleveland Public Library Photograph Collection

Nelle Hackney (right) with two other Cleveland policewomen in
1931 press photograph, marked up for newspaper publication.

Cleveland Press Collection, Cleveland State University

TWENTY

The Heat Is On

1941

After sparring with the City Council at Monday night meetings, Ness would often unwind with friends at the new home he shared with Evaline: Vernon Stouffer's boathouse on Clifton Park Lagoon, in the classy West Side suburb of Lakewood.

Cinderblock with a crenellated roof, the squat, boxy building might have been the tower of a medieval castle. Stouffer, the restaurateur whose testimony sent Campbell and McGee to prison, had used the boathouse mostly to host parties, and Eliot and Evaline followed suit, entertaining the city's movers and shakers "in a most sophisticated manner," a reporter recalled, getting "tongues wagging most of the time."

The gossip largely stemmed from Mrs. Ness's unconventional behavior. Marion Kelly recalled seeing the Nesses make the rounds in Cleveland with a tall, strapping woman from Florida, who might have been Evaline's bodyguard. The locals never quite understood the relationship; that the woman had once wedded a dwarf for publicity didn't help.

Once, after Eliot left a boathouse party on an urgent work matter, Evaline went for an impromptu swim in the lagoon. The guests watched in shock as her dress came off and she went in. But some joined the fun.

She transformed the boathouse's top floor into a private art studio. The glassed-in room offered abundant light with views of water on all four sides. Still, the placid surroundings failed to calm Evaline's anxieties.

"She was an interesting, generous, creative person when she was sober," a relative recalled, but "very unpleasant and confrontational when she was drunk."

Eliot, on the other hand, had no trouble holding his liquor. He could drink and dance till all hours, then show up for work fresh and alert. The secret, he told a local prosecutor's wife, was first filling his stomach with saltines and milk.

"That may have been the best part of his life," Evaline said decades later.

Revelry seemed to energize him; visits to nightclubs and boathouse parties made up for thrills lost on the job. His enemies appreciated seeing the former Prohibition agent turning hard-partying playboy, and happily spread rumors that Ness was a drunk.

A new addiction *had* replaced workaholic Ness's appetite for danger—a taste for the good life. He enjoyed spending time with the rich, seeming almost awed by their success. They had the wealth Ness's father had long sought to attain yet never quite did.

As they welcomed Ness into their circle for his prominence and position, he succumbed to their flattery. Stouffer's boathouse gave every appearance of being a perk—whether Ness paid rent remains unconfirmed. The Untouchable who would never take an outright bribe seemingly had no problem accepting a reward from someone whose business he'd saved from racketeers.

The man once content with a $2,500 government salary now lived in Cleveland's most affluent, exclusive suburb, where everybody belonged to the same country club and enjoyed a private beach. Clifton Park had first been developed as a resort area for the elite, with the deepest harbor on Lake Erie hosting huge yachts—including Vernon Stouffer's, which once belonged to the

Duke and Duchess of Windsor. Ness would have seen these vessels, moored at nearby boathouses, as he went to and from work.

Though he pulled down a respectable salary as Safety Director, Ness was hardly in the same class. Combined with the perks of his position, he made just enough to appear affluent, an impression he worked to keep up.

He spent money conspicuously and without hesitation, once sending six women in his office out to get themselves custom-tailored suits. He got a particular kick out of surprising Evaline every so often with a brand-new car. Evaline would sometimes pick her husband up from work at a downtown dock in their seventeen-foot speedboat.

Amid the praise and publicity, the parties and drinking, the new cars and fine clothes, Ness began to lose sight of his purpose, even his identity. He was, at heart, just a cop—a true professional, but a cop. He could never cross over into the elite class.

Around this time, Evaline poked fun at her husband's inflated sense of self with a handmade valentine: "You think you're THE HOTTEST THING in the city—But you're just a SCREW BALL. More's the pity!"

LATE SUMMER 1941, Ness received what he needed most—a fresh challenge. As the federal government geared up for war, the military prepared to protect its fighting force from various threats to health and morale, including sexually transmitted disease.

During the Great War, venereal infections had sidelined more American soldiers than German bullets, taking enough men off the battlefield to fill twenty-three army divisions. The government hoped to avoid a similar situation by establishing the Social Protection Division to stop the spread of VD in the armed forces. When its first director proved unfit, officials sought a replacement.

Since the work involved convincing local law enforcement to crack down on prostitution near military bases, a director well versed in police administration was a must.

Ness had "a breadth of understanding of the problem," an official commented, "and would command the respect not only of police administrators, but of social workers and the public as well."

Ness agreed to take the job if he could stay on as Cleveland's Safety Director. Mayor Blythin arranged to "lend" Ness to the federal government part-time, with trips to Washington, D.C., leaving Tom Clothey in charge. The work helped Ness get out of his rut, presenting new problems to solve while serving the war effort.

Ness would be one of the "dollar-a-year men," as President Roosevelt termed the captains of industry and men of wealth who descended on Washington early in the war to get the new federal bureaucracy going. He couldn't make the same financial sacrifice, but his Safety Director salary kept him solvent.

Some questioned whether Ness could do justice to both jobs. He left Cleveland while trying to push his latest reforms through the City Council, with the police and fire departments in a somewhat disorganized state. On September 11, he returned to argue against a proposal that would raise the salaries of police and firefighters.

"Some of you may think, from what you've read lately, that I may not be here long—that I am going to slough out of the picture," Ness told the City Council. "If that were true, I would not be here today performing this unpleasant duty of opposing your ordinance, saying things you do not want to hear. I want to remain your director of safety a long time, and as long as I am, I want to furnish you intelligent leadership."

But Ness's actions made clear that his priorities were in Washington.

THE SOCIAL PROTECTION job allowed Ness to avoid the fall campaign.

Mayor Blythin ran hard on continuing the policies of his predecessor, warning voters they would lose Ness—whom Blythin called "the most progressive and efficient safety director this city has ever seen"—if they voted Democratic. But Republicans, divided after the fight to succeed Burton, failed to come out in force for their candidate.

Ness made one halfhearted appearance for the mayor, his inaction all but endorsing Democratic challenger Judge Frank Lausche. Talented, charismatic, with unkempt curly hair and a common touch, Lausche had presided over the Albert Ruddy trial. He and Ness were colleagues and friends, with similar views on law enforcement.

"Eliot would tell Frank that he ought to run for mayor," Evaline recalled, "and Frank would insist that Eliot run."

Lausche gave every indication he would keep Ness on as Safety Director. But Ness's numerous enemies—disaffected cops, firefighters, unionists, and Democrats who wanted one of theirs in his post—hoped they could change Lausche's mind.

The Social Protection Division agreed to take Ness on full-time—at a salary of $8,000 a year—if he lost his Cleveland job. But he also turned down lucrative job offers in private business, apparently unconcerned about employment opportunities.

On November 4, Lausche trounced Blythin by more than fifty thousand votes—the largest margin in Cleveland's history. The *Press* called it "the end of the Burton era in Cleveland politics," a prescient prediction. The Democrats held City Hall for years, while Lausche would go on to become Ohio's governor and U.S. senator.

Ness, in Washington, didn't vote. He hadn't requested an absentee ballot, "too busy to do so."

After Lausche delayed announcing his choice for Safety Director, Ness's enemies launched what the *Plain Dealer* called "one of the most poisonous propaganda campaigns ever directed at a good public official in the city." Bombarding Lausche with rumors and slander, they pointed out Ness's frequent absences, accusing him of laziness. They attacked his use of undercover investigators, charging him with bias against unions.

Lausche must have known reappointing Ness would alienate him from a large segment of his party. But in the end, he kept Ness on anyway.

The city's reappointed Safety Director—his six years making him the longest-serving in that post—gave the *News* an interview that sounded like the old Eliot Ness. His first priority would be "to consolidate the gains we've made during the experimental period of the last six years," acknowledging those reforms would be unpopular with the rank and file.

"People resent change," he said. "Improvements bring change. There are folks who start out: 'This guy Ness is crazy . . .' That's part of the job."

He still had much he wanted to do. "I've always felt that if you have a feeling for your job and do it adequately, the future will take care of itself."

THE INCOMING ADMINISTRATION soon began a crackdown on vice in black neighborhoods. Police fanned out around Central and Cedar Avenues, raiding illicit nightclubs and numbers operations, requiring licensed bars to stay open only as late as liquor laws allowed.

Word rippled through the African-American underworld— "the heat is on." Many illicit businessmen closed down as a precaution, counting on the new mayor to let up once he'd proven his sincerity as a reformer—like most new mayors. But others in the neighborhood, led by a particular politician, looked to Ness to keep the lid on.

For some time, City Councilman William O. Walker, publisher of the *Call & Post*, had been battling juvenile delinquency among black Clevelanders. Ness's crime prevention programs had gone a long way toward keeping white kids out of trouble, but hadn't had the same impact on African-American youth.

In 1936, when Ness started working with the boy gangs of Tremont, a similar initiative was promised for black neighborhoods.

More than five years later, Walker and his constituents were still waiting.

Walker lobbied Ness, who called a conference at his City Hall office on December 2. Representatives from the Boy Scouts, Juvenile Court, and police department joined Ness, Walker, and Captain Arthur Roth to discuss reducing black youth crime.

The problem, according to Walker, differed little from what Ness had identified in Tremont: "the increasing tendency of children between the ages of 10 and 14 years to become involved in crime-producing activity that more often than not is leading them into the juvenile correctional institutions." Similar solutions seemed called for—programs keeping kids away from the dangers and temptations of the streets.

But five of six new Boystowns were far from the predominately African-American neighborhoods at the city's center; just one, the old Fifth Precinct at East Seventy-Ninth and Woodland, sat on the edge of where roughly 90 percent of black Clevelanders lived.

The woman from the Juvenile Court argued passionately for building more playgrounds and youth centers in these neglected neighborhoods. A local pastor explained that, while churches and welfare agencies tried to fill the void, children with "bad" reputations often found themselves shut out and in need of other opportunities—like the ones Ness gave the youth of Tremont.

Roth knew too well how these "bad" kids filled their time. On Ness's desk, he put a realistic toy gun, complete with rotating cylinder, as used in recent holdups by juveniles. He also displayed a collection "of vicious looking switchblade knives," confiscated from arrested teenagers.

For two years, Nelle Hackney—the African-American policewoman who'd nearly crossed paths with Frank Dolezal in 1939—had devoted herself to working with youthful offenders in black neighborhoods. Hackney had joined the force in 1931, dealing with everything from rapists to phony fortune-tellers to runaway children.

"Miss Hackney pointed out that beer parlors, pool rooms and houses of prostitution abound in this sector," reported the *Call & Post*, "and lax law enforcement permits scores of teen-age children to frequent these places. Miss Hackney pointed out that the lack of interest of parents in the activities of their children, largely due to economic conditions, was one of the major factors in the increasing crime rate among Negro youngsters."

Walker suggested that Hackney might pursue this full-time as part of a special detail in the central city, to "prevent crime rather than act as arresting agents." Ness liked the idea and asked Hackney to draw up a report on the crime problem and reach out to "responsible interested citizens" for suggestions. But he didn't want her working alone, feeling a male partner "would make the effort doubly effective," according to the *Call & Post*.

Hackney took this in stride. Her sunny demeanor and constant optimism masked a firm dedication to protecting women and children. The *Call & Post* described her as "an advocate of planned parenthood" and a champion "for the advancement of women," who traveled the region giving crime prevention speeches.

The charming Hackney knew how to avoid alienating those with a limited view of what women could or should do. The *Call & Post* assured readers that Hackney "is by no means hard-boiled" and loved cooking and keeping house. Nor did she think that policewomen had any need for guns.

"We can do much more effective work," she said, "in our rightful sphere as women."

Her ideas reflected the "politics of respectability" among the black upper classes, who believed the best path toward racial advancement lay in exceeding the standards of behavior laid down by whites. This approach, despite good intentions, made crime seem endemic to black communities—playing into the prejudiced view of African Americans as inherently inferior, immoral, and criminally inclined.

For Hackney's male partner, the department chose ace investigator John Jones, who shared her views on fighting juvenile delinquency.

"We can't stop children from becoming criminals if they can walk into a bar and drink with hardened criminals," Jones said. "We can't raise good girls and boys with vice running rampant in the community, dope being peddled at the nearest saloon, and disease being spread wholesale from joints that wouldn't be permitted to open their doors in other parts of the city."

Jones took the assignment personally, having "spent the biggest part of my life living in this area and with these people, and I don't see any reason why the Central Area and the East Side should be the dumping-ground for the crime and vice and filth of an otherwise grand city."

Hackney and Jones spent the next few years shuttering unlicensed bars that served minors, racking up arrests for drug possession and carrying knives, and jailing men who sought sex with underage black girls. They drew the ire of high-ranking white officers when the black cops followed leads into their districts—where crime was supposedly under control. When the squad targeted bookie joints downtown and on the affluent white West Side, Jones received at least one threatening phone call.

In the spring of 1944, mounting complaints from white officers prompted Matowitz to transfer Hackney and Jones to a new beat five miles from their previous assignment. The chief praised the "splendid job" they'd done; Jones even got a pay raise, while Hackney had to be content with kind words. But informed African-American observers saw the transfer as "sending them to the sticks."

Ness had been slow to address youth crime among African Americans, his department never lavishing the same resources and attention on black children as on whites. The Boy Scout troops and Boystown clubs Ness celebrated had no real counterparts in the region that arguably needed them most. Instead, black Clevelanders got a belated program focused on locking up predatory adults and wayward kids, minus the socioeconomic uplift that made such a difference in Tremont.

Ness in 1941.

Cleveland Press Collection, Cleveland State University

TWENTY-ONE

EN-3

December 1941–April 1942

As his city reeled from news of the Pearl Harbor attack, Eliot Ness rushed to implement the civil defense plan brewing since 1939. He met with Mayor Lausche, who toured the municipal power plant and found its defenses wanting. Orders went out for additional guards, but Ness had few to spare—a reduced budget precluded hiring four hundred new policemen needed to meet wartime demands.

Earlier that year, he'd sent Arnold Sagalyn to spy on a visiting German couple with ties to the leading domestic Nazi organization, the German-American Bund. Sagalyn slipped into their hotel room at the Hollenden and found correspondence offering German contracts to American factories—a plot to tie up American manufacturers with orders, preventing production of weapons for Britain. Ness passed the intel on to the FBI.

Now the Safety Director placed police patrols around factories with defense contracts, and met with plant representatives to ramp up the antisabotage initiative that had so riled J. Edgar Hoover. That quarrel got lost in the patriotic fervor of the war, Ness assuring the *Plain Dealer* of cooperation between local and federal authorities—the FBI included.

Though evidence of fifth columnists was in short supply, many Americans viewed anyone of Japanese heritage—even American citizens—as a threat. In Cleveland, reports of a car carrying "two suspicious appearing Japs" came in soon after the attack, sending ten police cruisers scurrying about the East Side on a fruitless search for saboteurs.

Federal agents, the public knew, had lists of "potentially dangerous" foreign nationals to arrest in event of war. Some expected the FBI to start filling detention camps.

"All of the seven precinct stations in the city have been set aside for detention purposes should they be needed," Ness said. "We cannot place any person under arrest without arraignment before a United States commissioner, but we will put into effect a plan modeled after the Ellis Island system where immigrants are detained."

Meanwhile, Ness focused on his other wartime priority: the fight against prostitution and venereal disease. America's entry into the war left him increasingly divided between his Safety Director duties and the Social Protection Division.

A week after the attack, the Federal Security Agency, which oversaw the SPD, asked Mayor Lausche to loan them Ness full-time. But the mayor refused to send Ness to D.C., deeming it unfair to leave Cleveland with "a part-time director of the police and fire defenses at this time."

As the *Press* observed, "The safety director's task in Cleveland, always important, is now of emergency proportions. The safeguarding of the huge war industries in this area is a task of great importance from the national as well as the local point of view."

Yet even as Safety Director, Ness pursued his social protection work. After army officials complained of soldiers visiting local vice dens and coming away infected, Ness directed Captain Michael Blackwell and his vice squad to "close up and keep closed" every brothel in town. This did not exclude more respectable establishments.

"If we find any hotel," Ness said, "that allows prostitutes to accompany men patrons to their rooms it can expect to be raided continually until the condition is wiped out."

While Sledgehammer Mike was out living up to his nickname, Ness organized Frank Cullitan and other city officials into the Cleveland Committee on Social Protection, developing a "new four-point policy" to wipe out venereal disease within city limits. Unlike other anti-vice crusaders, who focused on arresting and incarcerating female prostitutes, the committee recognized the role of men in spreading VD—both those who sought sexual services and various illicit entrepreneurs.

"'Customers' at present generally are released by the arresting policeman with a disgusted look or a sharp word," reported the *Plain Dealer*. "After Feb. 20 . . . these men will be taken to Central Police Station and given a physical examination."

Men found free of disease would be released but ordered to attend special classes, like traffic violators, while infected johns would go to the workhouse for treatment. Women still bore the brunt of this crackdown, however—prostitutes would be prosecuted whether infected or not, despite a previous departmental policy of fining and releasing women with clean bills of health. The committee discussed plans for rehabilitating these women, not just incarcerating them, but the details would have to wait. For now, they would get sex workers off the streets.

"The detective bureau will endeavor to get evidence against procurers," Ness said. "Special emphasis will be placed on taxi-cab drivers who direct persons to houses of ill repute."

A legal mechanism was found for cutting telephone service to buildings—whether brothels or hotels—where police made vice arrests. One committee member, a municipal judge, began setting unusually high bail, as much as $3,000, for prostitutes.

On February 19, 1942, Blackwell returned from a search of almost fifty known brothels to report finding zero prostitutes. Recent raids and Ness's impending crackdown had driven sex workers away, perhaps to ply their trade on a street corner or other clandestine location.

The U.S. Army ruled certain nightclubs "off limits" for offering access to prostitutes, overcharging customers, or otherwise threatening the health and morals of America's fighting men. Any soldier found inside could be court-martialed.

The Hot Spot on West Third Street had a particularly "unsavory" reputation, according to Blackwell. Police had been watching the joint due to alleged connections to illicit gambling, and the army had reports of soldiers catching VD from employees. The poorly lit interior had waitresses using flashlights, and the club's "obscene and indecent" striptease shows had already cost the place its liquor license.

The Hot Spot's manager, a Czech immigrant seeking American citizenship, defended his establishment in court, claiming the approval of Safety Director Ness himself—Eliot and Evaline had dropped by the Hot Spot last summer.

"When they were leaving, Mrs. Ness said, 'I enjoyed the show very much,'" the owner testified, "while the director said: 'You've got a nice place here.'"

Ness's after-hours activities again painted him a hypocrite, who patronized the very places he was trying to close as public-health threats. Ness produced a letter he'd sent to immigration officials two weeks earlier, outlining charges against the Hot Spot and describing his visit as an official, if undercover, inspection.

At the *Cleveland Press*, Jack Raper delighted in reprinting Ness's supposed praise of the Hot Spot.

"Of course, we don't know whether or not Ness said it," Raper wrote. "But if he had told us it was a nice place it would have made a deep impression on us. We regard him as an authority on the excellence of night clubs."

NESS CLOSED OUT 1941 with a local holiday tradition: his annual warning about driving under the influence.

"Don't try to drive if you must drink," Ness told *News* readers. ". . . Let's all get together and make this a safe New Year."

The Safety Director would soon run into a power struggle fracturing his department. Although the amendment designed to curtail Ness's reforms had failed in 1939, the high-ranking police- and firemen behind it, led by former Deputy Inspector Andrew Hagan, convinced the state legislature to adopt its key provisions. Their lobbying paid off late in 1941, when the Ohio Supreme Court ruled Cleveland's Safety Department must abide by the new law.

The decision threw out a fundamental Ness reform—requiring a high school education of incoming policemen—and truncated his ability to hire, fire, and promote. After centralizing authority within the Safety Director's office, Ness faced a future in which the real power lay not with City Hall but with precinct captains and department heads.

Ness went before the City Council with a new plan for over-hauling the police and fire departments: rewriting the chain of command, eliminating various high-ranking positions, changing the salary structure, and breaking the police into eight bureaus— detective division, traffic, crime prevention, and so on—each under a single officer appointed by Chief Matowitz.

But many high-ranking police and fire officials refused to surrender what remained of their autonomy. The firefighters' union charged Ness with caring too much about administrative efficiency and too little for the needs of his men.

The Safety Director said the national emergency proved the need to "streamline the police and fire departments" and introduce "business-like management." The fire department's basic structure had barely changed since before the Civil War, leaving it unprepared for the "blitzkrieg problems" of modern warfare. Ness also criticized the officers trying to block his plan, calling them "goldbrickers" and slackers.

Hagan hit back in a City Club speech, threatening a lawsuit from police and firemen against Ness's "illegal and unconstitutional" reforms.

Ness, from the audience, questioned the specifics of Hagan's attacks. Then another in the crowd asked if Hagan considered it "an official duty or merely a social duty for an official of the safety department to visit certain night spots to see whether they were properly conducted?"

As the audience chuckled, Ness tried to defend himself.

"After 15 years of such assignments," he declared, "I assure you that it comes under the heading of work."

Fire Chief James Granger took his displeasure out on Keith Wilson, Ness's longtime aide and former Unknown. Wilson had helped draft the reorganization plan before becoming head of the local civil defense committee. Now Granger retaliated by refusing to cooperate with Wilson in training auxiliary firefighters until Ness got an assurance from the chief that no interdepartmental spat would get in the way of the city's wartime defenses.

Ness faced enough challenges without having a rebellion in the ranks. When he went before the council for a $45,000 increase in the Police Department's budget—a fraction of the nearly three quarters of a million needed to hire enough cops—he was grilled by two councilmen keen on exposing the Safety Director's supposed "Gestapo."

"Where are the undercover men and snoopers," a councilman asked, "that are supposed to be all over town?"

"If you are thinking back to my investigations," Ness replied, "you will find that I did a good deal of that work myself."

While the council considered his proposals, Ness promoted several officers to head the eight new bureaus of his reorganized police department. The *Plain Dealer* applauded Ness's actions, urging the City Council to adopt the rest of his program.

"Perhaps the best testimony in favor of this legislation," the paper added, "is the type of person within and without the departments who is opposing it."

THAT MARCH, NESS'S first article on venereal disease was published, alluding to Al Capone's old nickname by calling prostitution "Military Saboteur Number One."

In the early morning hours of March 3, Eliot called Evaline, who'd worked late into the night, and took her to the Vogue Room to celebrate. They enjoyed a late dinner, had a few drinks, and socialized.

"Then we went to the hotel room of one of my friends," Eliot recalled, "and chatted with him about his farm and other matters for a couple of hours. I had nothing to drink in the room."

Well after 4 A.M., the Nesses finally left the Hollenden, piling into their car and heading west on Bulkley Boulevard, which followed the shoreline toward the Lakewood boathouse. The early-morning hours, like the night preceding them, were cold and wet. A wicked wind came in off the lake, turning light rain into ice.

As Ness took a curve, his car hit a slick spot, lost control, and skidded into an oncoming vehicle.

The impact rocked them, fracturing Eliot's dental plate and throwing Evaline against the side window, knocking her senseless.

"My first thought was for my wife," Eliot recalled, "because I thought she was the most seriously injured."

After reviving her, he checked on the other car. Driver Robert Sims, a twenty-one-year-old machinist, had fractured a kneecap. Ness gave Sims his name and address, then moved his own car up a few hundred yards, out of traffic.

When he got back to the accident scene, Ness planned to take Sims to the hospital with Evaline, but the machinist was gone—a driver had stopped and picked him up. Ness learned from a bystander that Sims had been driven to Fairview Park Hospital. By now, Evaline had recovered enough to insist on going home without seeing a doctor.

At the hospital, Sims gave Patrolman Joseph Koneval a statement, not mentioning Ness's name, but reporting the license plate number of the other car: EN-3.

Around 5 A.M., Ness called the hospital to ask for Sims's contact information. Koneval answered the phone, apparently not identifying himself as a policeman. Ness described himself as "the other man" in the accident.

"I wanted to make sure that the injured man was all right," Ness explained, "but I didn't identify myself. I said that I would have my insurance adjusters on the job in the morning."

Koneval insisted Ness acted more evasively. "He said he would give me his name and information after I had answered his questions," the patrolman reported to his commanding officer. "When I had finished he hung up without saying who he was."

At Central Station, Koneval looked up the license plate number Sims provided. Though Ness's plate was well-known in the department, the patrolman said only then did he realize the other driver was the Safety Director. He chose not to include that fact in his report because Ness had promised over the phone to visit the police station and give his own statement.

But Ness failed to follow up as promised, leaving town for Washington, D.C., apparently on a Social Protection trip. When Sims's father went to Central Station the next day, he was "dumb-founded" to discover the report included only the other driver's license plate number. He checked the number with the Cleveland Automobile Club and managed to track Ness down by phone.

In a tone the elder Sims considered "very nice" and "very courteous," Ness promised to have his insurance company pay for everything.

Ness also called Traffic Commissioner Martin Blecke, asking him to take the official statements from the police records room and "look them over." Blecke did so, arranging to personally handle the rest of the investigation.

Ness apparently hoped to keep the incident out of the papers.

"I don't think he could stand criticism that well," Evaline recalled, "especially when it came to his job. That's why he tried to avoid publicity with the accident."

Years later, a journalist offered another explanation: "Some friends and observers were convinced that Ness had been the passenger in the car and that Evaline was the driver, but they were never able to prove the theory."

Once again, Ness's proclivity for secrecy caused needless controversy. His reforms had created enough enemies within the department to guarantee the story would not stay quiet long.

A *Press* reporter heard about the accident and Blecke's handling of the official report, apparently from a policeman Ness was investigating. When asked for details, the traffic commissioner said, "You'll have to talk to Mr. Ness about it."

After getting Ness's okay, Blecke let the journalist see the accident report. The *Press*, ever eager to embarrass the Safety Director, ran a detailed article on the crash, complete with a photo of Sims in his hospital bed.

The *News* and the *Plain Dealer* covered the story in less depth. Over the following days, the *Press* would run both an editorial and an opinion column chastising Ness's handling of the incident, while the other papers kept the story on their news pages.

Now that he'd been caught, Ness didn't try to duck responsibility, meeting with the mayor March 7.

"It was a very unfortunate thing all the way through," Ness said. "But there was no attempt at evasion in any particular."

Ness's version of events matched Sims's in the important details. He admitted having consumed "several drinks during dinner," but denied alcohol played a role.

"It was very slippery and the thing happened just like that," he told Lausche, snapping his fingers.

Asked if Ness acted negligently, Sims said, "No, it was just a case of slipping on the ice."

Even so, Ness had violated one of his own safe-driving commandments: "If you drink, stay out of traffic." But that mattered less than attempting to keep the mishap quiet.

"If the safety director had called in City Hall reporters Tuesday morning—or even Wednesday morning—and told them he had been involved in an accident, there would not have been one-tenth the publicity," wrote a *Press* columnist.

Lausche declared the matter closed on March 9, saying Ness had "more than paid the penalty" for his misbehavior.

"I have never regretted anything more in my life," Ness told reporters. "I thought I was discharging my duty to the other persons involved. I was very obviously trying to avoid publicity."

Although Ness's political enemies renewed their attempts to push him out of the Safety Department, he probably could have stayed on. But even before the accident, he'd thought of resigning; bored, spent, he no longer found the job fulfilling. Federal officials had repeatedly urged him to work for the Social Protection Division full-time. This embarrassment convinced him.

On March 23, nearly three weeks after the crash, Ness said he would soon resign to "serve wherever the Government designates that I can be of the most use."

A surprised Mayor Lausche supported Ness's decision. Tom Clothey said he, too, would resign and do his part for the war effort.

IN LATE MARCH, police picked up three teenage girls—and then a fourth—for going "on an extended spree involving night club characters," as the *Plain Dealer* described it. Policewomen, including Virginia Houston, uncovered sexual encounters between these white girls and adult men, African Americans among them.

Two of the young women—"all of whom," the *Plain Dealer* hastened to add, "were said to come from families of good reputation"—had picked up a venereal disease, but not from any of the "night club characters," rather a white college student. Police rushed out to arrest him and eight others for contributing to the delinquency of minors. Within two months, a dozen men and the only member of the female quartet older than eighteen would either be convicted or plead guilty.

The scandal, dubbed the "Jitterbug Vice Case" in the press, inflamed simmering racial resentments. The *Call & Post* received reports from black domestic workers employed in white homes, who'd heard variations on "They ought to lynch those N——rs."

Viewing the scandal through a social protection lens, Ness responded to the growing outrage by promising to revoke the liquor licenses of clubs that served the girls and prosecute the men who'd slept with them "to the fullest extent of the law."

"There are two aspects to this case," Ness told the *Plain Dealer.* "One is the threat to the health and morals of minors in the community, and the other involves military and civilian defense and the battle being waged on the venereal front."

The *Plain Dealer* printed rumors, which Ness pledged to investigate, that one young woman had named multiple policemen among her sexual partners, including a high-ranking officer. Michael Blackwell, absurdly, blamed the situation on Ness's new plan to reorganize the police department. The former captain, recently promoted to deputy inspector, had been taken off the vice squad to head up the new patrolmen's bureau. He now claimed the vice situation had markedly deteriorated since he'd begun his new assignment—a month ago.

"I have been told that recently the hoodlum element has been infiltrating back into Cleveland," Blackwell informed the *Plain Dealer*.

Behind closed doors, Ness rebuked Blackwell for disloyalty, saying the department could accomplish nothing "if we get to fighting among ourselves."

Besides, Ness observed, the girls' testimony made it clear their supposed "spree" began before Blackwell left the vice squad.

NESS SPENT HIS last month as Safety Director working to cement his police and fire reforms. After failing to get his reorganization plan through the City Council, he rewrote the department's rules to the same effect. He also proposed a new training program for veteran officers who'd already passed through the police academy.

"Post-graduate courses for police," reported the *News*, "will be the final Ness innovation."

Not quite—during his last week in office, Ness promoted an African-American ambulance driver named Eddie Coleman to police patrolman. Coleman had dreamed for years of becoming a cop, and this "unprecedented transfer," as the *Call & Post* described it, granted his wish, bypassing "the usual training for rookies at the Police Academy."

With time running out, Ness had bent his own rules, recognizing that Coleman's previous duties gave him "as much police training, probably, as he could acquire at the Academy."

At Blackwell's urging, Ness also assigned Coleman and another black patrolman to the squad car detailed to the African-American neighborhoods near Kingsbury Run—the first black cops to man their own patrol car, something the African-American community had wanted for years. But the transfer would not long survive Ness's departure; later that year, the next Safety Director removed Coleman and his partner from their vehicle.

Ness would leave the Cleveland Police Department as racially segregated as he'd found it, with African Americans seriously under represented on the force. By 1946, white officers had reverted to wearing blackface on gambling raids—supposedly, the *Call & Post* reported, because of "the scarcity of Negro officers in the vice department."

David Beasley was promoted to sergeant in 1947, the first black officer to rise above the rank of patrolman in the history of the department. After Ness hired him in 1937, Beasley went on to distinguish himself in the police laboratory, becoming an expert in fingerprinting, ballistics, and other scientific methods of identification.

A week before his resignation took effect, Ness submitted a nineteen-page report to Mayor Lausche, summarizing his time as Safety Director and offering suggestions to his successor. He reflected on the political difficulties hounding him over the past few years, noting that anyone in his position must have "the ability and the courage to say no when no is required," as he himself so frequently did.

"If [a Safety Director] is to operate successfully in the interests of all the people," Ness wrote, "he will soon find himself unpopular with special interests and special groups who seek special favors and privileges."

Ness officially resigned on April 30. The newspapers once welcoming him to City Hall with banner headlines now acknowledged his exit with a few short editorials.

In the *Plain Dealer*, Phil Porter wrote that the exiting Safety Director had brought the Cleveland Police as close to perfection "as any big city is ever likely to [get], and we ought to be grateful to Ness for it."

Even the *Press* managed some qualified words of praise: "Taking Mr. Ness' record as a whole, including all the errors and omissions, we think he is the best safety director Cleveland has ever had, and we have no doubt that, looking backward hereafter, his term of office will gain increasing luster by future comparisons."

Despite efforts to roll back his reforms, Ness left a lasting mark on his city. Even today, Cleveland police patrol in essentially the same pattern Ness laid down in 1938. Arnold Sagalyn credited Ness's cleanup of labor unions with helping enable Cleveland's postwar prosperity. By the mid-1970s, Porter would say, "Ness was way ahead of his time."

As Ness prepared to go to Washington, Clayton Fritchey best summed up his impact on the city: "Cleveland is a different place than it was when Eliot Ness became the safety director. . . . Most people would agree that it is a much better place."

Fritchey compared the Safety Director to Alexander the Great: Both men eventually ran out of worlds to conquer. But Fritchey envisioned a bright future for his friend.

"Now he goes to Washington [to] tackle a big new job," Fritchey wrote, "with the same enthusiasm that he brought to City Hall more than six years ago."

This optimism would prove misplaced. Ness was still a young man, just turned thirty-nine. But, like Al Capone, his glory days were over, the great work of his life behind him, though enduring fame lay ahead.

of Grisly Discovery on Lonely Country Road

PART THREE

PRIVATE SECTOR

Sailor on the USS *Missouri* reading a Social Protection pamphlet authored by Ness, August 1944.

National Archives and Records Administration (80-G-K-4541)

TWENTY-TWO

Social Evil

1942–1944

Eliot Ness and Al Capone—the latter out of prison and in Florida retirement, suffering syphilitic dementia—would spend the war years fighting venereal disease, each in his own way. Sworn in on May 1, 1942, as full-time head of the Social Protection Division, the Untouchable returned to the federal fold to protect fighting men from sexually transmitted disease.

In this time of war, federal officials considered venereal infections a national security matter. Treatments for syphilis and gonorrhea were complicated, imprecise, time-consuming—and ineffective. Every sickened soldier represented lost manpower the country could not afford.

A propaganda campaign about the horrors of venereal disease attempted to scare servicemen into abstinence. But unsettling films couldn't stop more than half of all soldiers from indulging at least once during the war, with an even higher rate among unmarried men.

"The sex act," a medical officer lamented, "cannot be made unpopular."

Instead, the Social Protection Division sought to prevent

servicemen from making contact with willing women—specifically, but not exclusively, prostitutes.

During World War I, state and local governments—at federal urging—enacted anti-prostitution laws mandating medical testing of anyone "reasonably suspected" of carrying a sexually transmitted disease. Such measures, though often phrased in gender-neutral terms, rarely impacted men. And while repressing prostitution as a military imperative ended after the Armistice, the so-called "American Plan" continued in many jurisdictions.

Ness's SPD would push for greater enforcement of existing American Plan laws and urge adoption of new measures. Their single, overriding assumption was that prostitutes, and sexually active women generally, were primarily responsible for spreading venereal disease.

But most soldiers suffering sexually transmitted infections during World War I had caught the clap back home, not from camp followers. And many prostitutes practiced preventive measures likely more effective in checking the spread of VD than the crude medical treatments of the day.

Seeing the sex trade as inevitable, some advocated regulating it, allowing it to operate away from polite society. In the United States, this often meant "red-light districts" where prostitution, while illegal, was ignored or condoned. At higher-end brothels, physicians gave sex workers regular medical checkups while police on the take overlooked or partook.

Through the late nineteenth and early twentieth centuries, such benign neglect sparked a righteous backlash. An unlikely alliance developed between those who blamed prostitutes for the spread of VD (often doctors and public health officials) and moral reformers, typically women seeking to abolish a "social evil" through which males exploited vulnerable females.

Much like Prohibitionists who believed abolishing saloons would eliminate crime, these reformers sought to revise human nature by rewriting the law. They intended to banish brothels while rescuing "fallen" women—not just locking them up and driving them out of business, but reeducating them for a morally upright life . . . if necessary, by force.

In the Progressive Era, tens of thousands of women were detained on the flimsiest of pretenses, subjected to invasive examinations and unwanted, ineffective, even dangerous treatments. A new bureaucracy, straddling public and private spheres, went beyond repressing prostitution into policing promiscuity. Female reformers, working with male officials, advocated "detention houses" for reforming women who engaged in premarital sex.

But when repressing prostitution became federal policy and a military matter, rehabilitating these women fell to a low priority as the needs of fighting men took precedence.

IN THE FIRST decade of the twentieth century, while Ness grew up in Chicago, sensational news stories of innocent girls and young women lured into phony marriages or debased by drugs and alcohol fueled a national "white-slave hysteria."

Progressive reformers added pimps and gangsters to the evils they sought to purge from urban life. Believing poverty and "commercial exploiters" forced vulnerable women into the sex trade, Illinois activists urged their state to create a minimum wage for female workers and children.

This decade-long campaign during Ness's formative years seemingly shaped his view of vice. He would always see sex workers as blameless female victims of unscrupulous, parasitic men, even as his Cleveland work convinced him prostitution threatened public health.

Unlike graft, gambling, and racketeering, prostitution was never Ness's personal priority before WWII. Instead, he delegated that fight to Sledgehammer Mike Blackwell, whose loathing of vice left him immune to the usual temptations. Since other cops would not be so scrupulous, Ness had every reason to avoid giving them duties that, as his mentor August Vollmer warned, uniquely threatened good policing.

Vollmer abhorred prostitution, yet he considered it "apparently inevitable." Red-light districts and wide-open brothels might drive up demand and give criminals safe haven, but trying to shutter them all was a futile endeavor that would only force the sex trade underground.

Ness's SPD, however, hoped to do just that—close all of America's red-light districts and empty the brothels onto the streets—because, they argued, "health and a 'red light district' cannot exist at the same time."

As Ness put it, "Common sense and simple arithmetic proved that prostitutes having as many as 40 to 60 customers each night, as was the rule in houses of prostitution, were able to infect more persons by their tremendous number of contacts than were women who operate clandestinely."

In the many speeches and articles that came with his official duties, Ness described the sex trade as a symptom of defects within the larger community. Many Americans dismissed sex workers as victims of their own failings, but Ness saw them as casualties of men who marginalized and misused them.

"It is unfortunate," Ness said in 1942, "but nevertheless an accurate statement of facts, that prostitutes—and I include all the phases of definition of that term—have been victimized, not only by their exploiters but also by their community. They have been victimized by the very agencies that they should be able to turn to for help."

In a speech before social protection officials in Washington, D.C., Ness framed his argument as an accusation, even an indictment.

"We have been cruel—we have been indifferent—we have been cowards," Ness said. ". . . We have echoed the threat of their exploiters, 'once a prostitute, always a prostitute.' We have hounded them from jail to jail, from town to town and from state to state on the one hand, and have prepared the way for their exploiters . . . on the other. We have ostracized the prostitute—we have deprived her of social status. We have all too frequently refused to recognize her privileges as a person—a person with feeling, a person with certain assets and liabilities."

Convicted prostitutes, he argued, "cannot be helped or saved by confinement in over-crowded, unsanitary jails." Instead, the government should "train as many of these women as possible for employment in our war industries or in other legitimate and gainful occupations."

This attitude set Ness apart from other SPD officials, who often viewed these women as traitors and saboteurs aiding the Axis. But Ness saw this work as the natural sequel to his crime prevention efforts, reflecting his belief that most criminals were the products of circumstance, ready to be reclaimed with help from their community. Central to his vision was a police force that gently guided young female offenders.

"Extreme caution and tact must be exercised," Ness warned. "Guard against entry of her name on a police blotter or even a juvenile court docket."

The work revitalized Ness with the old excitement that had inspired him to enter law enforcement. He'd found a new, wide-open field, ripe for professional reform.

But his ambitions outstripped his resources: a small staff scattered between the Washington headquarters and twelve field offices. Field staffer Marty Lahart, an ex-Untouchable, had been Ness's closest friend on the Capone case. The amiable Lahart and other field reps looked into how local law enforcement dealt with prostitution.

"I got pretty direct with the police, the local mayors," Lahart recalled. "Shut down more houses of prostitution without raids or anything."

Where police refused to cooperate, the feds stood ready to intervene. Congress had passed the May Act in 1941, empowering the secretaries of war and the navy to make prostitution a federal offense in areas around military installations. The FBI could then step in and round up sex workers, with none of Ness's qualms about jailing such women.

By mid-1942, the May Act had only been invoked twice. Hundreds of arrests in North Carolina and Tennessee snagged a disproportionate number of women of color, many not actually prostitutes. Yet the Bureau believed those roundups demonstrated they handled the problem better than the SPD, again treating Ness like an interloper.

Still, Ness proved willing to work with the FBI, though his overtures met with open contempt. J. Edgar Hoover's assistant, Ed Tamm, recalled a high-level meeting where he repeatedly shot down whatever Ness had to say.

"Ness at one point recommended the establishment of a Federal law against prostitution," Tamm reported, "which I ridiculed to the point that he withdrew the suggestion."

The Bureau refused to cooperate with the SPD and investigated Ness's use of paid police consultants, even though the practice was common in other agencies. Representatives from the FBI attended events where Ness and other SPD officials gave talks, and interfered with their efforts to build relationships with local law enforcement.

Ness pushed back, maintaining the social protection program should remain in local hands. He did at times threaten to invoke the May Act, but only to spur local police into action. Privately, he argued against it.

"I felt, having been a police official for a long time," he said, "that if I still were one, I would resent masterminding from Washington."

In fall 1942, Ness met with Police Chief John Woods about cleaning up vice in Norfolk, Virginia. The FBI wanted the May Act invoked, but Ness disagreed. He told Woods the FBI "super-sleuths" had an inflated opinion of themselves. The chief reported the insult to an FBI contact, who added it to Ness's growing federal file.

Unaware of Woods informing on him, Ness later urged the chief to take over as Cleveland's Director of Public Safety. Woods demurred and went straight to the FBI, knowing (as one G-man put it) "that the Bureau does not hold Ness in very high regard and he would do nothing to incur the enmity of the Bureau." A memo reached Hoover, who added a handwritten comment.

"I would be most cautious of anything Ness offers. . . . There is no advice I would give . . . except to beware of Ness."

• • •

NESS CRISSCROSSED THE country, meeting with local police and carrying the SPD's message to health and law enforcement conferences. A Nebraska official noted Ness's grueling schedule, thanking him for a visit in early 1943: "To come into town in the morning, work steadily almost the full day and leave late in the evening requires a great deal of endurance and sacrifice on your part."

Although Evaline often joined him on these trips, she didn't enjoy this nomadic lifestyle. She remembered it as months spent "living in dreary hotels" while Eliot was off in meetings.

Washington, their de facto residence, never seemed like home. The war pushed the city into an unruly growth spurt, bringing thousands of new residents; with an unprecedented housing crisis in D.C. and beyond, most hotels refused to let guests stay longer than three days. Evaline would wind up spending hours on park benches, waiting for a room, while her husband went back to coming up with new ways of inconveniencing lustful soldiers.

Ness plotted his campaign with help from Arnold Sagalyn, the young Oberlin grad who'd worked for him in Cleveland. Once again, Ness relied on a small group of undercover investigators to scope out prostitution in a given area.

"Eliot's approach," Sagalyn recalled, "was to get at the core of the problem by preventing a prostitute from having any physical contact with a serviceman. . . . He designed a systematic, comprehensive program that made it virtually impossible for a prostitute to meet and pick up a serviceman; and if she did succeed, impossible to find and transport him to a hotel or a motel that would give them a room."

Knowing many cabdrivers worked as part-time procurers, Ness arranged to revoke their gas and tire rations, effectively putting them out of business. He also convinced alcoholic beverage distributors not to sell their products to prostitute-friendly bars. Any hotel that failed to respect the SPD's standards could be closed for health violations. In the interests of national security, they were advised to consider "banning women at the bar, whether escorted or unescorted."

After meeting with Ness, authorities in San Antonio, Texas, detained dozens of women on morals charges, subjecting them to "a very poor examination" and jailing those found to be infected.

A Travelers Aid society report noted the spartan conditions these women encountered in custody: "Until a few days ago, there were only ten sheets—now a supply of over one hundred has been received. There are no pillow cases, towels or other toilet necessities. The food is better than that provided for regular prisoners, and girls are permitted to purchase cigarettes, candy, fruit, etc."

Ness meanwhile was focusing on what these arrests revealed about the social circumstances giving rise to the sex trade. Women detained in San Antonio, he noted, mostly were between fourteen and twenty-five and worked in bars or cafés, not as professional prostitutes. Their average earnings of six dollars a week left some in need of extra income, with few employment options besides selling their favors.

A young woman, not yet twenty, married since she was fifteen, now had two children and a husband in the army. Unable to afford rent, she turned to prostitution and soon contracted gonorrhea; police picked her up after a soldier turned her in. When questioned, she didn't blame her customer "because she might have infected many others and she is glad to receive treatment."

Ness used such examples to argue for supplying infected women with medical treatment, counseling, and other forms of care not currently available in many communities.

As the Travelers Aid report noted: "There is no provision for the girl to remain long enough to work out a plan. When the girl is dismissed from the clinic, there is no housing available except that obtained in rooming houses and hotels." The local Catholic Welfare Bureau was "under-staffed and already over-loaded," and the YWCA refused to take in "problem girls."

In African-American communities, statistics showed much

higher VD rates than in white neighborhoods. For years, middle-class blacks had partnered with government authorities in trying to bring those rates down through sex education and community health initiatives.

Many whites took those statistics as proof of their own racial superiority. But Ness and the SPD laid blame for this apparent epidemic on larger systemic problems holding African Americans back—many lived in poverty, lacked access to proper medical care, and had fewer educational opportunities.

Aware many blacks were understandably suspicious of law enforcement, Ness tried to defuse tensions by appointing an African-American advisor between black communities and the authorities.

"We need and will welcome your advice, suggestions and co-operation," Ness told a conference of black leaders in November 1943, "in helping us do our part to achieve the goal of a free America that will be physically healthy, mentally alert and morally sound."

The conference included representatives from the *Chicago Defender* and Howard University, as well as noted educator Mary McLeod Bethune. Their recommendations called for "Negro representation on the Board and staff of organizations . . . concerned with planning and policy making in the field of venereal disease control" and asked the government to train more African-American medical professionals.

But the SPD seemed more interested in having black leaders endorse their policies than in actually addressing their suggestions.

Because the SPD relied on local law enforcement to implement its program, the prejudices of policemen dictated which people—disproportionately working-class women of color—would be locked up. In a single year in Detroit, most of the 861 women detained for possibly having VD were African American—despite blacks amounting to just a tenth of the city's population.

These inequalities remained invisible to the chief architects and prominent supporters of the social protection program, including (as one chronicler put it) "some of the foremost paragons of twentieth-century liberalism."

Eleanor Roosevelt met with Ness on June 9, 1943, at an SPD conference for various women's organizations. Ness and his male colleagues outlined their intention to round up and reform both women who sold sex and those who "had drifted into a kind of promiscuity which was not professional prostitution."

"I think . . . we have decided, that venereal disease is not, strictly speaking, a war problem," Roosevelt said. "It is a peace problem. It is a problem that is with us all the time. . . . And the real roots of the problem lie in the fact that we do not face our community conditions."

The First Lady shared Ness's belief that social factors forced certain women into prostitution. She also believed in the need to educate young people about sex—that when a woman finds herself "caught in something because she doesn't know the facts," her ignorance can only make a bad situation worse.

"It is not just a question of caring for those who are the victims of social diseases," Roosevelt wrote in her newspaper column that week, "it is really a question of removing the conditions which bring about environments where social diseases flourish."

Since most people still avoided the word *sex* in polite conversation, even basic information on the subject was scarce. Ness urged the adoption of scientific sex education programs.

"Schools are important," he said before a congressional hearing on juvenile delinquency. "Teaching the fundamental facts of sex hygiene, including the dangers of venereal disease, are necessary at the junior high-school age. It is true that this should be a function of the parents—but too many parents are ignorant of the facts children need to be taught."

Some saw this as morally irresponsible. A Ness talk in upstate New York drew criticism for ignoring "the moral and religious aspects of the social hygiene problem."

But Ness always avoided any "Holy Joe talk," as he put it. He approached the subject scientifically, with no hint of shame. Only then could the SPD achieve its goal: the eradication of venereal disease. Competent law enforcement, Ness believed, could even eliminate the world's oldest profession.

"When a few people talked about getting rid of prostitution," Ness wrote in 1944, "nearly everyone else ridiculed the idea. . . . More towns are finding out daily that it is possible to get rid of syphilis and gonorrhea."

Ness's optimism and enthusiasm again led him to overreach. He would discover, like many reformers before and since, that his utopian ideas meant something much darker in practice.

THE SPD'S "BLITZ the Brothels" campaign resulted in more than six hundred cities and towns shutting down their red-light districts by early 1944, without any help from the May Act or the FBI. The venereal disease rate in the army and navy dropped to the lowest point in American history, likely due as much to soldiers being given condoms and medication as any SPD efforts.

Arnold Sagalyn recalled a public health officer declaring: "For all practical purposes, the professional prostitute no longer exists in the United States. Instead of having 20 to 40 contacts a day, she now has only one or two because of the difficulty she faces in plying her trade."

The successful repression of prostitution brought unintended— if predictable—consequences. Few police departments had jails big enough to hold all the women they arrested, or facilities where the infected could be treated. And they couldn't build more cells because the war had halted new construction.

A horrified Ness called this "a detention problem of unprecedented proportions," after touring the dark, dank, jam-packed jails he'd helped fill.

"First offenders and girls who are simply in need of medical treatment are being thrust into the same crowded cells with hardened veteran prostitutes," he said. "They are forced to remain in these detention centers for long periods of time, under sanitary conditions that are a throwback to the Dark Ages."

The SPD responded by acquiring roughly thirty camps built for the Civilian Conservation Corps, FDR's New Deal public works program. Abandoned at the end of the CCC, the camps provided space to treat and house infected women with at least a small improvement in living conditions. The SPD intended to offer vocational training that could lead to war-industry jobs.

Yet life in these "Rapid Treatment Centers" differed little from prison. Patients could not refuse medical care or leave if they chose; officials read their mail and monitored their phone calls. Treatment, often requiring drugs now known to be toxic, could last as long as six weeks. Armed guards patrolled camps that sported barbed wire and electrified fences. Some women sought treatment, but most were not there by choice—and few male patients were among them.

Although the feds established most Rapid Treatment Centers, state and local governments operated them according to their prejudices. Often patients were racially segregated; vocational training typically covered domestic tasks and other "women's work," not industrial jobs. Much as he wanted the centers to help women get their lives back on track, Ness justified the existence of these "detention camps," as he called them, on different grounds.

"Unless the needed detention facilities are provided in critical areas soon," he warned, "we face the prospect of having to turn loose thousands of diseased women upon our communities."

Many were not prostitutes at all. Methods of diagnosing VD were far from exact—almost one in four syphilis tests came back with a false positive—and, anyway, authorities didn't need a diagnosis to lock women up. The SPD's first detention hospital, built inside an abandoned hotel in Leesville, Louisiana, treated roughly five hundred patients by 1943—"not more than 5 per cent" of whom were sex workers.

Closing red-light districts hadn't prevented soldiers from having sex—they simply found new partners. Every serviceman diagnosed with VD had to fill out a "contact report" about how he got the disease, and a growing majority blamed their infections on casual "pick-ups" and girlfriends, not prostitutes.

"By most people's standards we were immoral," a soldier re-called, "but we were young and could die tomorrow."

So the country fretted about a strange madness sweeping its youth, the "uniform hysteria" that led many young women to seek a soldier's company. The press called them "good-time Char-lottes," "patriotutes," and "victory girls"—immature, hungry for "excitement," eager to do their part for the war effort.

"In the first place you prevent prostitution," a doctor com-plained to Ness, "in the next place you allow boys to obtain con-traceptives at army stations. Therefore where will they get their sexual gratification?"

Ness could speak about VD with remarkable frankness but seemed tongue-tied when it came to casual sex.

"He always had trouble with the word *whore*," his friend Dan Moore recalled. Eventually, Ness decided on a new euphemism: "women who have a low threshold of sexual approachability."

In 1943, he penned a pamphlet—*What About Girls?*—asking readers to "keep the sex act in its place" by treating women with respect and consideration.

"There is no satisfaction," Ness wrote, "in being always on the receiving end of life. . . . Sordid experiences in brothels, automo-biles, trailers, [and] drab rooming houses do not make good lovers and sweethearts."

Ness reflected on the cruelty of a man who refused to tip a waitress after she spurned his advances. "I guess he never thought that many waitresses make only tips and their meals," he wrote. "Even a buck private's pay, plus clothes, food, and shelter, would be a luxury wage for a lot of the tavern girls."

Elsewhere, Ness observed that "men who say they can't stay away from women" are immature and desperate for attention. "Many promiscuous men conceal a hatred for women," he wrote, "which makes love nothing more than a contemptuous attack."

What About Girls? draws a direct line between the rapid pace of social change and the apparent surge in wartime promiscuity, implying that women had not matured enough to handle their newfound freedoms.

"The promiscuous girl," Ness believed, was "a young experimenter, somewhat lonely—immature in her judgment and, perhaps more important, disassociated from the stabilizing forces of family, the church, or any significant groups which strengthen the individual's integrity and belief in herself."

With America's fathers and brothers off at war and its mothers in factories, Ness felt that responsibility fell to the government. This meant more than detaining and treating infected women, or offering them job training. The SPD considered keeping released women under "modified supervision"—placing them on probation, watching to make sure they didn't fall back into old habits.

"The loss of life of our boys and men in foreign battlefields," Ness told Congress, "is useless slaughter if we are to permit a similar loss of young American girls on native soil. That is what is happening. Disease is taking its toll among teen-age girls."

Ness broadened the SPD's mandate accordingly. His agency urged law enforcement to curb the activities of both prostitutes and promiscuous women, defining the latter as anyone "sexually active despite the lack of sincere emotional content in the relationship"—even those not currently afflicted with VD.

Any unaccompanied female at a bar, hotel, train station, or bus stop became a suspect. Of fourteen hundred women examined for VD in San Francisco between 1943 and 1944, over half were detained on suspicion of promiscuity; just over three hundred were prostitutes.

Women in custody were tested for VD and held until cured if infected. Before penicillin, gonorrhea was difficult to cure and syphilis all but impossible. Women who shared Al Capone's affliction were repeatedly injected with an arsenic compound doing nothing but slowly poisoning them. Some endured terrifying examinations tantamount to sexual assault.

Courts showed little sympathy—states had long quarantined sick people to safeguard public health. Without legal recourse, many women in Rapid Treatment Centers attempted escape, sometimes en masse, a good number succeeding. Other women formed organized resistance.

When Ness made an official visit to Peoria, Illinois, prostitutes gathered to picket his speech. Hawaii's busy sex workers escaped the crackdown for years by going on strike early in the war, declaring themselves "essential to the welfare of the U.S. armed forces." Military police backed off, allowing the brothels to stay open until 1944.

A double standard encouraged soldiers to be sexually adventurous, even aggressive, while women were expected to make themselves available, but not too available, maintaining their virtue while keeping up morale. "You Can't Say No to a Soldier," a popular song advised, even if saying yes meant spending weeks in a detention camp.

Ness knew this approach was unfair and counterproductive. *What About Girls?* lingers on the image of diseased young women crowded into filthy cells.

"These girls were in jail for being the free stuff service men brag about," Ness wrote. "The men may lose some pay; they may not get promoted as fast as they hoped to. But they are getting the best medical care the country can give, in clean, comfortable hospitals."

Ness firmly believed competent policing could change even the most basic aspects of human nature, if it relied on scientific principles. In a 1939 speech, he charted his vision of the past and future of law enforcement.

"In the early days of this country's history," Ness said, "police had only one duty, that of guarding property. Persons guarded themselves." But over time, law enforcement had expanded its authority, until "today we find police embroiled in the most perplexing duty of all—the guiding of social activity."

Ness's work with the SPD took that to its inevitable extreme. He asked police to regulate the most private aspects of American life, even when no crime had been committed. His genuine concern for women and girls victimized by the sex trade had him embracing solutions that victimized them again.

An indignant Arizona resident, outraged by an SPD pamphlet against legalized prostitution, sent Ness a letter in March 1944 insisting the sex trade was inevitable.

"Those damn fools in Washington should have learned that through the lesson the Volstead law taught them. . . . They claim a manpower shortage up there in that crazy house town, so why in hell don't you go to work, Ness, and I mean work. If there ever was an unessential, useless and absolutely worthless . . . endeavor it is what you are doing at the people's expense."

Something in the criticism struck a chord with Ness—the realization, perhaps, that Al Capone's nemesis had failed to learn the lesson of Prohibition. He pasted the letter in the latest of his scrapbooks documenting his exploits. Soon enough, he would take the writer's advice and seek new employment.

S TORSO KILLER NEW INSAN

Couzens Trails in Rep___an Ra

MAINE VOTE IS BAD NEWS TO NEW DEAL

Duel Says Election Shows Threat of Republican Victory in November.

ROOSEVELT JUST SMILES

Indicates Result Was About What He Expected.

BY WALKER S. BUEL
Plain Dealer Bureau.
411 Albee Bldg.
WASHINGTON, Sept. 15

No. 20 for Allen

Allen batted this back in the fifth inning, but was given credit for his twentieth victory yesterday when the Indians walloped Thompson, 12 to 2. Hildebrand boosted the circuit blows by Earl Vosmik 29th and 10th homers.

New York Detroit defeated Chicago, 7 to 1; Detroit trimmed Philadelphia, 4 to 6 and Washington took a double header from St. Louis, 12 to 4 and 8 to 1.

Weather stopped the Boston-Cleveland.

(Details on Sport Pages)

WPA WORKERS TO BE EXPO GUESTS

Families, Also, to Attend Saturday as Honor to Garden Builders.

Today's Events.

BUY YOUR OWN MEALS, NESS TELLS ROOKIES

Ten New Patrolmen Told Appointments Are Based on Own Merits.

"DON'T BE OBLIGATED"

Warns "You'll Get No Great Reward for Honesty."

Youth, 16, Th___atens Shirley Tem

WIREPHOTO

OUTLAW SITDOWN, PLEA IS UP TO URW

Strikes Hit Akron Plants as Rubber International Weighs Policy Issue.

Plain Dealer Bureau.
AKRON, O., Sept. 15

Answered Press Wirephoto.

ATLANTA, Ga., Sept. 15.—A semi-

SHAKER EXTE___ TO RUN CARS

Shuttle Service to ___ Rd. Expected in 2 W___ May Go to Richm___

BY JAMES G. MONN___

Says Fight With Richman Nearly Sank Ocean Plane

NEW YORK, Sept. 15.

Elisabeth Andersen Seaver, the third Mrs. Ness.
Cleveland Press Collection, Cleveland State University

TWENTY-THREE

The Old Restlessness

1944–1946

As the war progressed, Evaline grew more depressed and frustrated.

"I longed for a home," she remembered. "I longed for something to *do*—something more than simply, eternally waiting for a husband to return from *his* activities. I felt useless."

The couple finally found an apartment a few blocks from Dupont Circle. Evaline joined the American Women's Volunteer Services, buying herself a "snappy" uniform and offering her services as a driver. When Eliot found these errands often involved driving officers to and from cocktail parties, he protested. But Evaline needed *something* to fill her time.

"Go to art school," Eliot suggested. "If Renoir could paint through *two* wars, you are allowed to paint through *one*."

Evaline enrolled in classes at the Corcoran Gallery of Art in D.C., where a supportive and dedicated teacher reawakened her love for the medium. She began winning awards and earning the recognition she'd always craved. Her passion deepened into obsession. When not at her easel, she explored Washington's many galleries.

Eliot seemed to resent her newfound enthusiasm. "He said I

was no longer the woman he married," she recalled. "He was right. I wasn't—and what's more, I never wanted to be that woman again."

Once, in class, Evaline sketched a nude woman from life. Captivated by the model, she struck up a conversation after class, and a romance blossomed. With Eliot away—probably giving another talk on female promiscuity—Evaline took their Cadillac and ran off to join her lover in New England.

Her bisexuality came as a shock to Eliot, though he might have thought to question the presence of the tall female who had accompanied them around Cleveland years earlier.

"He was really confused," recalled Dan Moore. "He says, how can you compete with something like that?"

When Ness eventually returned to Cleveland, Evaline refused to join him. On October 9, 1945, after almost a year of separation, Eliot filed for divorce.

In court, Eliot said his wife claimed to have "another person" in her life and wouldn't live with him because she'd gone to study in Maine with an unnamed artist. The real reasons for the divorce remained secret. She did nothing to contest it.

Evaline's career eventually took off. After moving to Bangkok and later Rome, she returned to New York and began illustrating children's books, work that offered a new level of artistic freedom. Not content to interpret the words of others, she began writing her own stories, drawing inspiration from her travels.

In 1967, Evaline won a Caldecott Medal for *Sam, Bangs & Moonshine*, one of sixteen children's books she wrote and illustrated over a long career. By her death in 1986, she'd remarried but continued to write and draw under Eliot's surname.

AFTER TWO YEARS in the federal service, Ness's interest began to wane. The work still offered challenges and affirmation—Ness's scrapbook bulged with newspaper clippings and letters of praise and thanks, and the navy would, after the war, give him a Meritorious Service Citation. But the old restlessness returned.

Ness's close friend Dan Moore chalked it up to a desire for more money. As SPD director, Ness earned a better salary than ever before, but he'd gotten used to a perk-driven standard of living in Cleveland that a government paycheck couldn't achieve. Besides, his fortieth birthday had come and gone—working so hard had lost its appeal.

Moving among Cleveland's elite, he became friendly with wealthy Ohio broker Ralph Rex and his family. Ralph owned a controlling interest in Diebold, the Canton-based manufacturer of safes, locks, and office equipment; his wife, Peggy, Cleveland's "first lady of aviation," had an interest in flight dating back to 1911. Though she never earned her pilot's license, Peggy owned a plane, belonged to aviation organizations, and opened her home to such legendary pilots as Eddie Rickenbacker and Amelia Earhart.

Ralph and Peggy's daughter, Janet, shared her mother's passion. An "aviator and speedboat enthusiast," according to the *Miami Herald*, Janet had been briefly married to a well-known polo player. The family, when not cruising on their yacht, divided their time between Ohio and a Miami Beach winter home. Since the mid-1930s, Ness had socialized with the Rexes on infrequent Florida trips.

After Ralph died in December 1943, Peggy and Janet asked Ness to represent them on Diebold's board. Ness had his business degree and a fanatical honesty about money to recommend him. The Rexes—thirty-four-year-old Janet, in particular—had apparently fallen under the Ness spell, and their closeness spawned rumors that Ness was simultaneously wooing both mother and daughter.

"He was with them all the time," recalled the company's vice president and treasurer. "The daughter, I guess, had a little leaning toward him."

In February 1944, on his way to a conference in Puerto Rico, Ness swung through Miami and joined Janet at Mother Kelly's World Famous Bar. A photographer found them at a table for two, a glass in front of each—hers almost full, his all but empty. Janet looked guardedly over her shoulder, a cigarette between her fingers. Ness wore a goofy smile, eyes half-lidded.

He added the photo to his latest scrapbook with a handwritten comment: "It was 10:30 A.M. and the first drink—and that's my story."

Ness's bond with the Rexes led to Diebold electing him chairman of the board in May 1944 at triple his SPD salary. After briefly trying to hold down both jobs, Ness resigned as SPD director on August 21.

He offered to stay on as an unpaid consultant, believing the work should continue in peacetime. But as the war wound down and penicillin greatly reduced the time it took to treat venereal disease, the SPD became superfluous.

In Washington, Ness lobbied his old boss, Senator Harold Burton, to save the program. Burton was sympathetic, but his colleagues were not. In summer 1946, Congress consigned the SPD to the bureaucratic scrap heap.

DIEBOLD'S SAFE AND vault business had collapsed after the stock market crash, the company's halting efforts to diversify not yet yielding rich returns. Government contracts for armor plating kept Diebold afloat in wartime, with few peacetime prospects. Ness arrived to find small-minded managers squabbling while ignoring postwar possibilities.

Ness did exactly what he'd done with the Cleveland Police, shaking up personnel, clearing out managerial deadwood, and promoting like-minded young men.

Under Ness's leadership, Diebold moved into such new fields as plastics and microfilm, while absorbing its chief competitor and other companies to lock up 50 percent of the vault market. Diebold's financial fortunes turned around; the Rexes saw the value of their shares sextuple. An industrial security firm in Chicago said Ness's first two years as chairman left the business extremely well positioned to take advantage of postwar prosperity.

As in Cleveland, Ness's abrupt arrival and two-fisted management produced great results in a short time, while winning him powerful enemies among those he'd pushed aside.

"In spite of the reputation he had of being extroverted," a company official recalled, "he was sort of bland. He wasn't a very assertive person at that time."

In 1945, Moore offered him a partnership in the Middle East Company, a new import-export firm. Moore, who served in Cairo during the war, saw the eighty million people from Iran to Libya as an untapped market for American industry. The war had toppled some of the region's chief trading partners—Germany, Italy, and Japan—while creating a pent-up demand for consumer goods.

With Diebold on firmer footing, Ness saw promise in the venture and agreed to serve as vice president. This, Moore reflected, "was a wise move, because his days at Diebold were numbered."

After hearing of Eliot's painful split with Evaline, Moore sought to raise his spirits by introducing him to another friend with a failed marriage: Elisabeth Andersen Seaver, thirty-nine, an award-winning sculptress from South Dakota.

Dark haired and apple cheeked, Betty possessed an undeniable elegance. More than one friend would describe her as the most beautiful woman they had ever known. Yet her western upbringing instilled in her a love of hunting, fishing, and getting her hands dirty.

She'd studied at the Cleveland Institute of Art and the Cranbrook Academy near Detroit. In 1936, she achieved local fame for the massive twin statutes adorning a symphony bowl at the Great Lakes Exposition. The twelve-foot figures towered over their five-foot, two-inch creator, who spent four weeks clambering up and down ladders, twelve hours a day, turning two tons of clay into personifications of "Beauty" and "Protection."

Eliot and Betty, who moved in the same circles, had much in common, starting with a shared love of Shakespeare. Like Evaline, Betty was creative and independent; unlike Evaline, she was a traditionalist who'd yet to divorce her husband after living apart from him for years. She appreciated Eliot's prankish humor—his love of surprises and eagerness to deflate puffed-up people.

"When he was reminded, as he was occasionally, of old adventures," Betty recalled, "most of his stories were very funny, and usually on himself. But he was always too busy living in the present to talk much about what was past."

She also liked his reluctance to go with the flow. "He didn't follow routines of others. He was as independent as a cat, and as fastidious—and as tough."

They began seeing a lot of each other in late 1945, around when Eliot filed for divorce and Betty's husband did likewise, but she kept the relationship chaste. On January 31, 1946, three weeks after Betty's divorce became official, they married in a private ceremony in Baltimore.

After a New York honeymoon, the Nesses moved into a six-bedroom home at 10229 Lake Shore Boulevard in Bratenahl, an affluent Cleveland suburb. Eliot's $24,000 Diebold salary allowed hiring a housekeeper/cook, Corrine Lawson, who accommodated Ness's meat-and-potatoes tastes.

"I once asked him, 'How about a tossed salad?'" Lawson recalled. "And he said, 'Well, you go ahead and mix it up, and I'll toss it out the window.'"

Lawson could see the old gangbuster hiding within the middle-aged businessman; she said "he always kept his back to the wall" entering a room. Ness still had his nervous habits: biting his fingernails and flipping a "lucky" coin like a movie gangster.

Despite a .22 rifle stashed in his closet, he retained a dislike of firearms. Betty, a sportswoman, owned two guns, but Eliot demanded she get rid of them. She did, apparently without argument—Lawson never saw the Nesses so much as raise their voices to each other.

"They were so congenial," a family friend recalled. "Betty said one time she had never been so happy in her life as when she was married to him."

But Ness never could escape his restlessness. Like many of his contemporaries—blue- and white-collar war veterans often drowning their depression in liquor—he fell into a comfortable yet empty existence. Though he'd fought a home-front war, he was turning his back on twenty years of stressful excitement, and his drinking habits followed the general trend. His favorite drink—Cutty Sark mixed with soda water—used a brand of scotch founded overseas specifically to be smuggled into America during Prohibition.

No longer Cleveland's top cop, he slipped back into frequenting his favorite nightspots, the Vogue Room and the Bronze Room, which kept tables reserved for him near the exit, where he could duck in and out. At home, the Nesses entertained much as Eliot and Evaline had before the war.

Ness "was a party man," Lawson recalled, ". . . and all the women were just crazy about him."

Less so the men, who seemed to resent his wit and charm. Some called him "the Swede," while others told tales behind his back.

Ness had reached a certain pinnacle—he'd broken into high society, and he'd done it as a businessman. Proof he'd arrived came in January 1946, when *Fortune* magazine profiled Diebold's chief executive: that "slimly handsome young man . . . who instantly commands much attention from both sexes."

The piece outlined how Ness had saved his company and suggested he "could probably be elected Mayor of Cleveland in a walkway." Local Republicans had never stopped urging him to run, but so far Ness showed little interest in taking a job that came with a $9,000 pay cut. For now, he would remain a capitalist.

"Maybe I'll fall flat on my face," he told *Fortune*, "but I'm sure having fun."

Eliot and Betty cast their ballots in the 1947 mayoral election.

Cleveland Public Library Photograph Collection

TWENTY-FOUR

Vote Yes for Ness

1947

On January 27, 1947—two days after Al Capone died in bed at his Miami mansion, pneumonia finishing the work syphilis had begun—the *Cleveland News* introduced readers to an Eliot Ness they'd never seen before.

In his office at the Union Commerce Building, Ness licked his thumb, flipped through a roll of fifty-dollar bills, and signed a stack of paychecks. Then he picked up the phone and told a caller, in a tone of "nervous frenzy," to buy as much steel as possible for $130 a unit.

The former Safety Director, the *News* reported, had fallen "head over heels in business," his days divided between the Diebold chairmanship, the Middle East Company, and the Far East Company, a burgeoning import-export venture in China.

Could he find time in such a hectic schedule to finally run for mayor of Cleveland? Ness would only say the city needed "an administrator" as mayor. But he did admit, after so many apolitical years, to being a Republican.

Cleveland Republicans could use his help, their power having crumbled since the glory days of Mayor Burton. The local GOP was weak and disorganized, its core constituency wealthy professionals who'd flown to the suburbs, leaving behind a working-class and union-friendly electorate whose strong Democratic leanings put any Republican candidate at a disadvantage.

In 1945, Mayor Lausche's handpicked replacement—stocky, bespectacled Thomas A. Burke—easily won his first mayoral race. Former Law Director Burke's popularity sprang from a thriving local economy and the major newspapers' support, which seemingly guaranteed him reelection.

"All he needed to do was coast," recalled the *Plain Dealer*'s Phil Porter, "and that was mostly what he did."

A dozen or so prominent Republicans declined to run against him; initially, Ness felt the same. He liked Burke, even considered him a friend. They went back to that cold January night in 1936 when Burke, then an assistant prosecutor, had joined Ness and Frank Cullitan in their famous Harvard Club raid.

Asked in early 1947 when he planned to announce his mayoral run, Ness replied, "Just as soon as Tom Burke stops being the good mayor he is. And I don't think he'll stop."

But a cadre of mostly big-money Republican donors began working to change his mind, believing he could plausibly run as an "independent," drawing votes from both Democrats and Republicans.

The prodders included two close friends: *Plain Dealer* reporter Ralph Kelly and former Assistant Safety Director Robert Chamberlin. Kelly played on Ness's ego—telling him "he was Superman," according to Porter—while Chamberlin appealed to Ness's loyalty. Chamberlin had made it his postwar mission to revive the local Republican Party, and Ness felt obligated to help the man who'd always backed him up.

Also, police officers young and old told him that "the things I stood for were falling by the wayside," as Ness put it. The city had moved away from his "preventive policing" into a tougher stance on crime under Safety Director William Smith and his assistant, Alvin Sutton—youthful former FBI agents who preferred the quiet grind of law enforcement to splashy raids and headline-grabbing initiatives. Smith, thirty-two, tied Ness's record as Cleveland's youngest Safety Director; two years later, Sutton would break it by assuming the post at thirty-one.

Ness never spelled out which policemen urged him to run, but Ernest Molnar was a likely candidate. A colleague claimed Molnar raised big money for the Ness campaign, and the lieutenant certainly had his reasons to want a change at City Hall.

Molnar's lavish lifestyle—consorting with numbers racketeers, vacationing in Florida, sending his kids to private school out east—fueled rumors of corruption. Mayor Burke had hired Sutton specifically to probe Molnar's suspicious activities; the following year that investigation would finally lead to the lieutenant's conviction for taking $67,500 in bribes. He served four years of a six-decade sentence.

Ness often dropped by Assistant Safety Director Sutton's office as if to relive past glories, only to be reminded the mayor worked just down the hall. Bored and dissatisfied with the business world, he may have seen running for mayor as his shot to get back to the center of civic life. Victory would be a long shot, but he believed the campaign would be "interesting and fun," even if he lost.

"He never planned ahead, which suited me just fine," Betty recalled. "Whatever he did he was doing completely at the time he was doing it."

That lack of foresight horrified Dan Moore, who warned Ness not to throw away an enviable reputation as a police administrator—plenty of cities could use someone with the Untouchable's knowledge and skills. Even if he failed at business, Ness would still have what Moore called "an automatic life work cleaning up everything all over the country."

Only no city would hire a cop with political ambitions.

"But I didn't get anywhere with him at all," Moore recalled.

ON JULY 30, Ness announced his candidacy, declaring that only "a completely non-partisan mayor" could reverse the city's downward spiral.

"When I left Cleveland five years ago to enter the war program," Ness said, "Cleveland was a vibrant, spirited city, interested in accomplishment and improvement. . . . I returned to find it, by comparison, a tired and listless town; its air filled with soot and smoke; its streets dirty and in a most deplorable condition; its transportation system noisy, inadequate and approaching insolvency."

Political observers generally applauded Ness's entry into the race, not because they thought he could win (hardly anyone did) but because they expected him to put up a fight. Until Ness declared, Burke might have waltzed to reelection unopposed, which would be no fun for anyone. Only Phil Porter took note of what the coming slaughter would mean to the candidate.

"Why he decided to run with the odds so completely against him only an accomplished mind reader could tell," Porter wrote. "The best reason I can conjure up is that he is bored at the moment and thinks it might be fun to try."

But if Ness believed the press would back him up as they had a decade earlier, Porter knew better. The free ride was over; memories were too short and fame too fleeting for Ness's Depression-era heroics to mean anything now.

Porter summed it up: "Ness the safety director and Ness the candidate are two different people. . . . He was a sucker to be sold this bill of goods."

To qualify for the race, Ness had to move from suburban Bratenahl into Cleveland proper. He and Betty took an apartment and registered to vote in the city, opening Eliot up to charges of carpetbagging.

Never a brilliant orator, Ness proved dull and uninspiring on the stump. The press still described him as "smooth" and "youthful," but photographs disagreed. Ness's once-trim physique had filled out, his face lined and puffy, heavy bags under his eyes. Beside his attractive young wife, he looked older than his forty-four years. Who could believe this tired-looking man once grabbed headlines with his jujitsu skills?

In the city's African-American wards, Ness campaigned

alongside black City Council candidates. At black churches and before gatherings of Republican Party members, Ness attacked "the Burke Administration for its indifference to the problems of crime, housing and recreation which are most keenly felt in Cleveland's heavily-populated, neglected Negro wards," as the *Call & Post* put it.

"If I am elected," Ness promised, "there will be equal opportunity for jobs for all citizens regardless of race or color."

Although the city's African-American vote traditionally went Republican, Democrats had been making gains since FDR. Ness's campaign tried to reverse that trend by pouring money and resources into Cleveland's black wards. Full-page ads in the *Call & Post* promised this "Independent Republican" would "Make Cleveland Safer by Preventing Crime, rather than by prosecution after crimes are committed," also noting that he "helped materially in the conviction of Al Capone."

Despite its previous ambivalence for the former Safety Director, the *Call & Post* urged readers to vote Ness in the primary: "His whole professional life has been close to the problems we face in our daily struggle. He is young enough to embrace new ideas, progressive thoughts and intelligent action."

Ness struggled to gain similar traction with white voters—despite attempts by Ralph Kelly, who served as his public relations man, to run an active, "news-producing" campaign. To highlight Cleveland's postwar housing shortage, the campaign made much out of Ness's mother-in-law being forced to give up her dog, "Puzzy-Wup," after joining Eliot and Betty in their new apartment. Ness posed for press photographs with the pooch, trying to use its plight as a metaphor for the housing problem, but the absurd spectacle outweighed any point he might hope to make.

"I am beginning to wonder a little about Eliot Ness," a *Press* columnist wrote. "Anything goes in a campaign, I suppose . . ."

In the 1930s, Ness had been the right man at the right time. Now painfully out of step, he seemed the picture of an affluent businessman who thought it might be fun to dabble in politics.

"I am so situated financially that I do not have to worry about a livelihood," Ness told the *Press*. "I have some ideas about public service—and I want to try them."

This stance would win him few friends in so blue-collar a town. "Cleveland voters suspect rich men," observed the *Plain Dealer*. "They don't like their mayors to have fun."

And Betty? In a housing crisis, she told a reporter that their new apartment didn't have nearly enough space for all the furniture they'd collected back in Bratenahl.

Ness's primary asset—donors with deep pockets—only hurt him further. With almost $150,000, Ness had a war chest three times his opponent's. But Clevelanders disliked candidates beholden to "big money," nor did they admire the crowd filling those coffers—men like Tom Girdler, the Republic Steel exec whose tactics inflamed tensions during the 1937 strike.

And many of Ness's biggest donors, living in the suburbs, could only support him with bucks, not ballots. Even Chamberlin, Ness's campaign manager, lived fifty feet outside the city limits.

Within the city, Ness had plenty of enemies. While some cops missed having him in charge, many did not. Local unions had their problems with Burke, but they despised Ness, resolving "to go all out for" his defeat. Cleveland's CIO affiliate decided not to endorse any mayoral candidate while specifically opposing Ness, the "hand-picked candidate of Cleveland Big Business."

A labor leader falsely claimed Ness "ordered police on horses to ride over men and women during the Fisher Body strike of 1939 and ordered others to club defenseless workers." Another union official reminded members of Ness's plan to spy on them at the outset of World War II.

Still, Ness soldiered on. He campaigned tirelessly, even though Burke's record gave him little to run against. So he nitpicked, blaming Burke for everything from the condition of the football stadium to a food shortage supposedly caused by a lack of proper rat control. Burke had been in office too long, he said, running "a ho-hum administration with a philosophy of not getting things done."

Burke seemed content to sit back and let his challenger do the stumping. The mayor ran what the *Plain Dealer* called "an almost listless campaign," figuring if voters weren't already impressed with his record, what could he do about it?

Ness, of course, was most passionate and persuasive on issues of law and order. He might have been running for Safety Director, not mayor. He noted a recent spate of assaults on women, and promised female voters that his administration would keep them safe on the streets. He returned to his old interest in crime prevention and called for more playgrounds and recreational opportunities for youth.

Even out of law enforcement, Ness knew of the growing power of the Cleveland Syndicate, that shadowy organization whose reach extended to Las Vegas.

"It is alleged by mobsters themselves that more Cleveland money goes to finance rackets, semi-legal and illegal activities than in any city in the United States," Ness said. "It is alleged that Cleveland has become the headquarters town of organized gangsters in the United States."

While Ness's battles with the mob were old news, the city hadn't forgotten the one case he could never publicly close: the torso murders. Asked about it on the campaign trail, Ness couldn't hide the frustration he'd kept buried all these years, along with the truth about his secret suspect.

"That case," Ness snapped, "has been solved."

THE MAYORAL PRIMARY in September pitted Ness against Burke and another Democrat, City Councilman Thomas Pucel. The top two candidates, regardless of party, would go on to November's general election.

When Pucel entered the race, Ness and his supporters felt the Democratic vote might be split, helping them peel off supporters in the general. In a radio speech shortly before the primary, Ness urged all Clevelanders to get out and vote. And if they couldn't support him, he asked them to vote for Burke or Pucel.

"It is not believed to be good politics to mention the names of your opponents," Ness explained, "but I am not interested in narrow political rules."

Many voters took his advice. On September 30, Burke carried the primary with more than 72,000 votes, while Ness came in second with just over 47,000. Pucel, meanwhile, came within 12,000 votes of keeping Ness off the ballot.

Call & Post publisher William O. Walker did his best to stay upbeat, noting that Republican support among black voters seemed to be holding.

"Despite the amateurish aspects of his campaign," Walker wrote, "former Safety Director Eliot Ness made a formidable showing. Of the six wards in which he had a clear majority, five were the wards completely dominated by Negro voters."

Gleeful Democrats read a different story in the returns. "The vote shows that Ness is pitifully weak," a former judge told the *Plain Dealer.*

Ness tried to improve his chances by cruising the city in a multicar caravan plastered with placards urging citizens to VOTE YES FOR ELIOT NESS. The candidate and his wife rode in an open convertible behind a truck carrying a uniformed band and a car outfitted with loudspeakers. As the music caught the attention of passersby, the speakers would call out, "For action now, Ness is necessary."

Two African-American City Council candidates joined Ness on the tour, to show solidarity between Republicans, black and white. The caravan focused on the African-American wards, so that Ness could meet as many black voters as possible. The parade would stop while Eliot got out to shake hands with pedestrians and visit local businesses. Betty followed him everywhere, unless the business happened to be a liquor store.

"Every minute we go around," she told the *Plain Dealer*, "I am impressed with the needs of our community. . . . Look at those places in which our colored people live—well-dressed, clean men and women returning to horrible homes. It would be enough to beat me down."

As she spoke, a pedestrian shouted at her husband, "I'll lay you 5-to-1 Burke wins."

Eliot replied with a smile and a wave.

"Almost without exception, the persons the Nesses greet seem flattered by the attention," reported the *Plain Dealer*. "The women, particularly, seem impressed with the affable former safety director. They tell him, with little giggles, that he's better looking than his pictures. Almost invariably, the people inform Ness they are going to vote for him and wish him luck."

This constant stream of flattery altered Ness's view of the race—the more hands he shook, the more he believed he had a chance.

Dan Moore again tried to snap him out it. Moore worked out the mathematics—no matter how many voters Ness personally met, they would only add up to a small fraction of the electorate.

Ness could not be persuaded.

"He thought he could make it work by sheer force of personality," Moore remembered.

As Ness grew desperate, he called on Burke "to disavow Communists and Communist sympathizers" among his supporters. After the mayor offered statistics showing Cleveland's low crime rate, Ness insisted the town had grown more dangerous.

He also latched on to a report of a fireman being skipped over for promotion, alleging Burke had "committed to a policy of monkey business on civil service." Even when a clerical error was shown to be the cause, Ness hinted at malfeasance.

This tactic backfired, damaging Ness's reputation. Newspapers chastised him for his "superficial grasp of the intricate problems of city government" and for using "synthetic" issues to prop up his campaign. To the *Plain Dealer*, Ness no longer seemed the same man who'd battled Al Capone before cleaning up the Dark City.

"The one thing the people of Cleveland had a right to expect of Ness . . . ," they observed, "was competence and thoroughness in any matter requiring investigation. . . . Ness not only uttered a false accusation, but he made a pathetic attempt to make it stand up, after the record had shown the untruth of his allegation."

Burke picked up this thread in his campaign's final weeks, challenging Ness to "show that he, as an ace investigator, has submitted one shred of evidence to support a single charge he has made." The mayor echoed labor's attacks on the secret sabotage prevention plan Ness started during World War II, which Burke equated to the Gestapo. Ness tried to fight back, saying he'd only done his patriotic duty after the U.S. Navy asked him for help.

In early October, Burke announced the FBI would partner with his Safety Department to train a squad of "super-police," thanking Ness's longtime rival, J. Edgar Hoover, for helping set up the plan. The two-week course, undercutting Ness's calls for police reform, began with great fanfare on November 3 . . . one day before the election.

ON ELECTION DAY, November 4, Cleveland saw record-breaking voter turnout despite dark and drizzly weather. The first returns showed Burke with almost 70 percent of the vote, indicating the scale of the defeat to come. Ness's campaign headquarters in the Union Commerce Building grew deathly quiet, only the occasional ringing phone or passing fire engine breaking the silence.

Ness waited until 9:30 to concede defeat. "There are larger things than winning an election," he told his supporters, adding, "The people decided, and I hope they decided correctly."

Burke beat Ness two-to-one: 168,412 votes to 85,990. His 82,000-plus margin added up to the biggest landslide in Cleveland history—surpassing, by 12,000 votes, Harold Burton's 1935 victory. The mayor even held his own in the city's black wards, which Ness carried by only about a thousand votes.

The *Plain Dealer* called it "the most remarkable [showing] ever made by a candidate for major office here"—Burke racked up the numbers while defeating "a man of stature, who had been a political glamour boy."

In a rare show of courtesy for a Cleveland mayoral candidate,

Ness went to Burke's house and congratulated him. "Naturally I am disappointed," he said, "but it is more important that the democratic process has taken place. There were some things I wanted to do in this town."

Burke replied simply, "Nice campaign."

After giving a formal concession speech over a radio setup in Burke's home, Ness stayed to take part in the victory party. He seemed intent on losing himself in the revelry, as he so often did at parties and nightspots around town. But this time he couldn't hide his pain.

His disappointment bled through when he cracked an unusually caustic joke—saying, with a laugh, "Who'd want an honest politician anyway?"

Postcards sent to Ness by Francis Edward Sweeney, 1954–1955.

Western Reserve Historical Society

TWENTY-FIVE

Head Man Ness

1948–1955

When Detroit needed a new police chief, Dan Moore urged a friend in city government to consider Ness, a suggestion warmly received—until officials learned of Ness's run for mayor. They wanted nothing to do with a man seeking higher office.

Eliot "never should have gone into politics," Moore said decades later. "He was a marked man after that."

At least Ness still had his business ventures. He commuted between his home near Cleveland and the Diebold office in Canton. The route took him through small-town Kent, Ohio, where he stopped sometime in 1948 to shop for a new car. He purchased a dark green Mercury coupe decked out with accessories and accouterments, including as much gleaming chrome as its chassis could bear.

Ness paid $2,000, in cash. Impressed, dealer Jack Foyle, in his mid-twenties, remembered Ness counting out the bills. Flush with disposable income, Ness treated money the way Capone once had—something to be spent and not saved.

He took a liking to Foyle and sometimes stopped in Kent for a respite at a hotel bar.

"I would have two drinks," Foyle remembered, "and [Ness] would have twenty-two."

When Ness became a Prohibition agent, he'd chosen a profession with a serious occupational hazard—alcoholism. Now he'd wandered into another line of work with the same risk, where the "three-martini lunch" was "good for business"—an essential lubricant in making deals.

Sometimes Ness would take a page from his late nemesis and, Foyle noted, tip big. Other times, he'd "forgotten" his wallet, leaving his young pal to pick up the tab.

Now and then, Ness shared his Chicago adventures, jokingly calling Foyle "Al Capone." Behind the humor was a depressed, isolated man, broken by his mayoral defeat. Foyle sensed Ness had problems at home and was lingering in Kent to avoid his wife.

"I never saw him actually picking up a woman," Foyle recalled, "but he did a lot of cocktail party talk. He was a very lonesome person."

Finally rising to go, Ness would tell Foyle that Betty would kill him. But the drive posed a more immediate threat. Foyle once had to retrieve Ness from a nearby police station, after an officer pulled him over for driving under the influence.

IN 1949 NESS and Betty adopted a redheaded three-year-old, Robert Warren Ness—Bobby. They doted on their son (some would say spoiled him) and enrolled him in an expensive private school. Eliot loved being a parent, but work kept him on the road.

"He was spread too thin," a friend recalled. "He wanted to spend more time with Betty and Bobby, and they missed him, too. Betty tried to be understanding, but she felt abandoned at times."

Ness frequently traveled to Cincinnati, where he befriended a business associate named Lehman.

"Mr. Ness liked kids," Lehman's son recalled, "and quickly became a favorite visitor at our house. He fascinated me . . . and my

younger sister with his repertoire of magic tricks. He would discover a quarter in my sister's ear, or close his hand on a golf pencil
which then magically disappeared."

Ness rarely talked about his past life with the Lehmans. But
one time at the local country club, the manager recognized the
former fed and barred him from an illicit gambling room. Years
later, when the Lehmans caught the debut of a television series
about a federal agent with the same name as "that nice man who
used to visit," they at first thought it a coincidence. Surely this
Ness and *that* Ness couldn't be the same person!

People who knew Ness during those days found it hard to believe he'd ever been a lawman. He struggled to navigate the corporate world, having lost the courage and discernment of his earlier
career. His trusting nature made him "a lamb among wolves," a
friend said, and "a fall guy for every small bore grafter who came
along," according to another.

But the old detective still lurked within, ready to emerge when
he got one last crack at the mob.

EARLY MORNING APRIL 8, 1950, a dynamite blast ripped
into a house on Sandusky, Ohio's west side. A bomb had been
placed beneath three rooms rented out to an Italian family, the
Barones. The eldest of three children, an eleven-year-old girl, had
been asleep on a living room sofa, above where the bomb went
off—lifting her and it toward the ceiling, then dropping them
through the floor and into the basement.

Police and firefighters found no one else injured, the girl
bruised and shocked but, miraculously, otherwise uninjured—the
heavy sofa bearing the brunt of the blast.

Detective Sergeant Robert Traver and his young protégé,
Detective Hank Jacoby, determined the explosion's source and
learned from the Barones of a possible suspect: Thomas R. Nogare, a onetime family friend, who two years before had publicly
threatened to kill the Barones after his infant daughter fell ill
and died in their care. "Nogare" proved to be an alias for Rocco

Russo, connected with the Terrace Club, an illicit Sandusky casino owned and operated by the Cleveland mob.

As a bustling port city with its share of smuggling and various sailor-oriented vices, Sandusky was hardly immune from organized crime. But as the detectives learned more about the still-at-large Russo, they became convinced he represented something beyond their experience: a soldier of the American Mafia, which law enforcement would come to know as "La Cosa Nostra."

The Sandusky detectives sent a photo of Russo to the Cleveland PD's Bureau of Scientific Investigation, where Detective James Benasek—a criminal identification expert who "never forgot a face"—responded with a report on Russo documenting a thirty-year criminal career. A 1927 murder rap got Russo life in San Quentin, but he'd been deported to Italy in 1945. Immigration officials suspected Russo slipped back into the United States the following year, but they had failed to find him.

Then the cops caught a break—a clueless Russo approached state police to report his wife and young son missing, unaware they had fled to escape his abuse. The troopers arrested him and a man waiting in his car, locking both up in Cleveland, where Detectives Traver and Jacoby questioned Russo at length. The prisoner gave the authorities enough to deport him again, but he denied the bombing, claiming he'd spent that night visiting a brothel outside the city.

Evidence in Russo's car—including a .45-caliber handgun and wire similar to that used in the bombing—strongly suggested he was lying, but detectives needed more to convict. Then the man arrested with Russo was identified as the brother of Frank Brancato, a ranking member of the Cleveland crime family.

Out of his depth, Benasek recommended the detectives bring in someone more familiar with the mob: Eliot Ness. Benasek knew the former Safety Director from the old days and figured he might have some answers to their multiplying questions.

Benasek couldn't hide his admiration for Ness—a guy who "had class, and was lousy with it," despite his drinking. Detective

Jacoby liked to tease the Cleveland cop for parting his graying hair in the middle, like Ness.

When the three detectives met the onetime Untouchable—who agreed to consult unofficially, if they kept his name out of it—Jacoby encountered a "tall and slim" man, with "a deep voice" and dignified bearing. Back in his element for the last time, Ness seemed anything but the bumbling businessman so many encountered in those years.

"My first impression of Ness," Jacoby recalled, "was that he was . . . impeccably dressed and a cultured person. He was conscious of who he was and the impression he made."

Knowing the two detectives came from Sandusky, Ness blurted an apparent non sequitur: "Who is Dago Rose, and where does she get her juice?"

"Dago Rose" turned out to be a Sandusky madam, whose brothel Ness had tried to close in his Social Protection days. She'd managed to duck the crackdown, however, thanks to political pull—or "juice." Jacoby, who sensed this remained "a sore spot" for Ness, would join forces with federal agents two decades later to finally put Dago Rose out of business.

The detectives got to work. Certain names kept popping up, which they hoped Ness could identify based on his knowledge of the Mafia hierarchy.

"Ness was impressed with the amount of intelligence we had developed," Jacoby remembered, "and filled in the blank spots in our investigation. . . . His knowledge of the Mafia and Labor officials was awesome, and a big asset to us."

Ness asked the detectives never to divulge what he told them nor reveal their source. His determination to stay anonymous suggests that—even out of law enforcement the better part of a decade—he still feared mob reprisals.

"He told us quite plainly that we were involved with some pretty 'bad' men," Jacoby recalled, "men who would do anything and stop at nothing to accomplish their assigned objectives. . . . He also told us from now on, we were marked men, and we should be alert."

Ness knew the power and influence of organized crime had only grown since he'd turned in his badge. He impressed upon the detectives "that this menace was the most serious and unquestionably the most dangerous evil that confronted the Country." His words opened up a whole new world for the three detectives—before television coverage of Senator Estes Kefauver's investigation into organized crime would introduce millions of Americans to the Mafia.

Venting his frustration with J. Edgar Hoover, Ness said the Director had "missed the boat" by going after infamous bandits while La Cosa Nostra metastasized like an undiagnosed cancer. "Ness felt that most of the manpower was directed on Public Enemy No. 1, instead of the Mafia," Jacoby recalled. "These guys were stealing peanuts compared to the LCN—millions."

Other, more personal resentments had soured Ness on the FBI Director. He blamed Hoover, at least in part, for his mayoral defeat, though the Bureau's partnership with the Cleveland Police had been only a minor contributing factor. Jacoby also got the impression Ness "was having trouble getting his pension," hinting Hoover may have been the cause.

Ness's Mafia warnings sobered the three detectives. But they went on to New York, tracking down Russo's common-law wife, Jean Ferrare, who agreed to testify against the husband who had terrorized and abused her. She not only linked Russo to the Sandusky bombing but implicated him in other crimes, including a Mafia hit ordered by Frank Brancato. Her testimony, according to Jacoby, was "of considerable assistance to the Cleveland Police Department in solving several crimes suspected of being committed by a large gang under a 'Boss of Bosses.'"

On January 25, 1951, Russo was convicted of bombing the Barones' home. He received a twenty-year sentence but would die behind bars before serving half of it. Jacoby saw this as perhaps the opening wedge in a new crusade against the Mafia.

Ferrare, Jacoby recalled, "had given us information that could be used . . . to put some of them out of business for some time." This included details of "the workings of the Mob, where they held meetings, what cars they used, who some fringe associates were and much more which would prove helpful in both Cleveland and Sandusky in the resolution of several open felony cases."

Traver, the elder detective, advised Jacoby to return to their Sandusky beat. Crippling the Mafia, he said, "wasn't our job, but the FBI's."

Despite misgivings, Jacoby did as told. "It came to me that we would go back to picking up the violent, dangerous, street people," he remembered, "that would make little impact on the overall crime picture. The Mafia investigations would now go to the FBI, and rightly so for it was their jurisdiction."

But Hoover's Bureau remained strangely unwilling to take on the mob—even to acknowledge its existence—perhaps because the Director feared his agents weren't untouchable enough to resist bribes.

"One may well wonder why J. Edgar Hoover concentrated so heavily on the Communist threat and seemed reluctant to even admit to the possibility of a serious threat from Organized Crime," Jacoby observed. "It was almost as though he didn't believe the Mob existed."

That would change in 1957, after police in upstate New York stumbled upon a conference involving the nation's leading crime families. In the 1960s, Attorney General Robert F. Kennedy led a "coordinated drive" on the Cosa Nostra, whose existence and name were confirmed by the Senate testimony of federal informant Joseph Valachi.

This newfound federal interest in the Mafia, however, focused on New York, Chicago, and Las Vegas, while gangsters coming out of Cleveland—especially syndicate boss Moe Dalitz—enjoyed the anonymity of second-tier players. A journalist trying to uncover their operations in 1967 found the mob firmly entrenched in Cleveland, with a strong grip on the police department.

"We gotta live with these people," a cop told him. "They're respectable now."

Exactly what Ness shared with Traver, Benasek, and Jacoby is unknown, but it's clear these three detectives were nibbling at the edges of the Cosa Nostra. Russo's associate Frank Brancato served as a chief lieutenant and enforcer for John Scalish, Cleveland's mob boss in the 1940s.

The reclusive Scalish's cover was blown at the 1957 crime conference, when he was arrested along with Vito Genovese, head of one of New York's infamous five families. Law enforcement wouldn't learn for years that the Genoveses represented Scalish and Cleveland on the nationwide Mafia "Commission" established during Prohibition to carve up territory and settle member disputes.

By Scalish's death in 1976, Cleveland mobsters, through the Commission, were feeding off massive profits made in the city Dalitz helped build: Las Vegas. A major money conduit was Big Angelo Lonardo, central figure convicted in Ness's 1939 numbers investigation.

At large again, the aging Lonardo helped bring to Cleveland hundreds of thousands skimmed from slot machines in two mob-controlled casinos. This flood of untraceable cash lined Lonardo's pockets and, as a journalist put it, "served as seed money for other rackets—loan-sharking, political payoffs, and drug dealing—that multiplied into even greater profits for the Cleveland family."

The feds shut the skim down in 1976—the same year, coincidentally, that Scalish's death kicked off another fierce Cleveland gang war. This time Lonardo again came out on top, becoming local underboss. A few years later, the law caught up with him, winning his conviction for trafficking cocaine. Facing the rest of his life behind bars, Lonardo turned state's evidence, helping the FBI finally cripple what remained of the Cleveland Mafia.

Reflecting on his brief encounter with the Cosa Nostra, forty years later, Jacoby had to wonder how history might have changed if his team had been given the resources to take on the mob in the 1950s. Eliot Ness and the Untouchables, he reflected, "had cut off the head" of the Capone gang, but they couldn't do their job alone.

The Chicago Outfit lived on and grew because the rest of the federal government failed to pick up where Ness left off. Only after Hoover's death would the Bureau truly devote itself to destroying organized crime in Chicago, Cleveland, and around the country.

"The FBI has finally unleashed its power on . . . La Cosa Nostra," Jacoby wrote in 1991. "Ness would have been happy, for it proved him right."

NESS'S IMPORT-EXPORT VENTURE in China, the Far East Company, collapsed when communists seized power in that country. By then, the Middle East Company had also begun to fail. Dan Moore traveled extensively in the region and managed some promising deals, but found Ness and the others at home slow to act. He suggested Ness join him in Turkey, but Betty refused to go and Eliot didn't insist. After Moore took a job with Pan Am, the Middle East Company soon folded.

Ness still had his lucrative position at Diebold but wouldn't for long. Since shaking up the company, Ness had retreated into a passive role, making little effort to build alliances with other executives.

"He came here a couple of times a week," recalled Diebold's vice president, "then maybe he'd miss a week. He didn't fraternize too much down here, and he wasn't really involved in the executive decision making."

This aloofness left Ness unaware of an effort by a financier from New York to take over as chairman of the board. Moore saw the coup coming and tried to warn his friend, but Ness remained perpetually blind to treachery outside the criminal world. When Peggy and Janet Rex sold their stake in the company, his ouster became inevitable.

In spring 1951, the board voted Ness out and the New Yorker in. The other executives, resenting Ness's reforms, felt well rid of him.

The loss of his Diebold paycheck crippled Ness financially. He'd built up no real savings, and his prospects looked bleak. Sometime after his mayoral defeat, Ness called on a friend in

Cleveland who worked in public relations—almost certainly Ralph Kelly.

"I'd regard it as a favor," Ness said, "if you could put me on the payroll for about sixty dollars a week."

Apparently nothing came of it.

Determined to support his wife and son, Ness fell into a succession of short-term jobs and failed business ventures. He worked brief stints at a bookstore and a frozen food company. He cofounded and served as president of a manufacturing firm, the Dorite Company, which quickly failed. He tried to capitalize on his policing expertise by marketing an alarm device and producing a short film on traffic safety for children. Neither venture caught on. He served as a law enforcement consultant for a Republican mayoral candidate and the campaign manager for another. Both lost.

Whenever the Nesses' housekeeper, Corinne Lawson, found him deep in thought, biting his fingernails, he'd "turn on the sunshine" and pretend nothing was wrong. But when the local butcher cut off the Nesses' line of credit, Lawson knew the truth.

David Cowles, the ballistics expert for the Cleveland Police, ran into Ness on a downtown street. Cowles thought his old boss looked practically destitute.

"The last time I saw Eliot," Cowles recalled, "he didn't have two pair of shoes to wear. He was a heavy drinker."

Around this same time, Ness lost a ten-dollar sports bet and covered it with a check, which he had to postdate because his bank account had run dry. Years later, that check would find its way to actor Robert Stack.

"Here's a guy who could have been wealthy if he would have accepted the bribes he was offered," Stack said, "but he stood for something greater, and what kind of thanks did he get? He couldn't even cover a ten-dollar check."

Some part of Ness yearned for a return to law enforcement. In January 1953, he gave a lengthy interview to the *Chicago Sun-Times*, offering advice on how the city could clean up its police department. Ness referred frequently to his time in Cleveland, suggesting his hometown could use help from someone like himself. The following year, Ness traveled to Chicago to appear on a television exposé of police corruption hosted by the crusading alderman Robert Merriam.

But if Ness had hopes of becoming Chicago's top cop, they remained unfulfilled.

Eliot and Betty tried to keep up appearances. They continued to pay Bobby's private school tuition and to employ their housekeeper at a wage far above the standard. They kept throwing parties, too, but Ness was no longer just a social drinker.

Lawson remembered him drinking in his den, joking of researching "an article about alcoholism." She wasn't fooled, and neither were others. When the Nesses tried to move into the exclusive suburb of Shaker Heights, their down payment was rejected.

"They didn't want Mr. and Mrs. Ness to buy," Lawson recalled, "because they drank too much."

IN 1949, A *Harper's* writer working on an article about the Mad Butcher of Kingsbury Run interviewed Samuel Gerber, still county coroner.

"You know, after all these years, I think we still have some parts of those bodies around," Gerber said. "They get tucked away."

The article largely ignored Ness's involvement and concluded with an attempt to profile the Butcher—who, as far as *Harper's* knew, remained unidentified and uncaught.

"It can be argued powerfully," the writer reflected, "that he was the most remarkable murderer of all time."

Who apparently wasn't done yet.

In July 1950, the disarticulated body of a male drifter named Robert Robertson was found scattered in an industrial area on Cleveland's East Side. Everything about the crime, from the character of the victim to the disposal of the corpse, matched the pattern of the torso killings that had stopped almost a dozen years before. Gerber said the body had been cut up in "the Kingsbury technique," but neither he nor the police would say the Butcher had struck again.

"After all," Gerber said, "it's been twelve years."

Once serial murder became a recognized pattern of behavior, however, later generations of law enforcement would discover that uncaught killers tend to slow down as they age into their fifties. Some take lengthy breaks between victims; others stop as a new fixation replaces their murderous addiction.

Had the *Harper's* article inspired a copycat? One thing did distinguish the Robertson case from the earlier murders—witnesses reported that for six weeks before the crime, a heavyset, middle-aged man made repeated visits to the spot where the body would be dumped, apparently to sunbathe. He stopped around the time the victim died.

This "sunbather," as witnesses called him, matched a general description of fifty-six-year-old Francis E. Sweeney.

The doctor's stay in a Michigan veteran's hospital, which Ness apparently helped arrange, had not lasted long. Within a year, Sweeney returned to the Sandusky Soldiers and Sailors Home, living there at least another five years. To his deepening alcoholism he added barbiturate addiction, a habit he fed with his own prescriptions. The drugs further unraveled his mind; surviving letters and correspondence from the early 1950s consist of disjointed phrases and incomprehensible jokes. They suggest a paranoid obsession with Eliot Ness, whom Sweeney associated with an expansive and malignant federal government.

In 1953, Sweeney penned a letter complaining of "Nessism" to J. Edgar Hoover. "[A] Basic principle of our individual freedoms is not at Stake, but, being Prostituted," Sweeney wrote, apparently referring to Ness's work with the Social Protection Division. "Knowing that he is an upriser & upstarter in the Social Reform section . . . (Possibly abolished now since he can no longer twirl the Baton upon the All American Turf.)"

Three years later, Sweeney wrote to a clerk in the Cuyahoga

County probate court, thanking him for sending certain documents from the period of the torso murders. "You have afforded me with the security of Cuyahoga County Court records," Sweeney wrote. "Evidently you are protected . . . from the seeming ever encroaching Federal Octopus or pusses promoting vicious ends by Haunt—Taunt or daunt methods."

Sweeney may have been attempting to clear his name, or at least desiring protection from the man he considered his persecutor.

Ness knew he was Sweeney's obsession—the doctor wrote to him, too. Exactly how long this one-sided correspondence went on is unknown; surviving among Ness's scrapbooks are five postcards and a letter from 1954 and 1955, sent to Ness's business office in the Union Commerce Building, addressed variously to "Eliot Direct-Um Ness," "Eliot Am-Big-U-Ous Ness!" and "Eliot (Head-Man) Ness"—the latter perhaps a reference to Ness's status as Safety Director (and/or the Butcher's head-collecting habit).

With his letter, dated Valentine's Day, 1954, Sweeney sent "a few items for your, Personal Perusal," including a clipping from a newspaper comic strip that featured an Asian man saying: "Revenge is an expensive luxury."

"I trust that we shall meet again," Sweeney wrote, "under more favorable, 'Federal issues'?"

On the postcards, Sweeney scrawled comments and pasted newspaper clippings, including advertisements for "Pansy Plants" and a volume titled *Handbook for Poisoners*. A card from April 1954 includes a publicity photo from the film *Riot in Cell Block 11*, with two prisoners clutching cell bars, including Neville Brand, who—in a disturbing, accidental twist—would later play Capone on TV.

Sweeney captioned the photo: "Who - is - T other–guy? Your Astral - Preeminence? Wah-Hoo.'"

Sweeney signed his name to a couple of the other cards, once referring to himself as Ness's "Paranoidal–Nemesis."

Betty remembered being terrified as her husband received the cards.

"Don't worry about it," Eliot told her. "The guy who is writing these is well out of the way and you don't have to worry about him."

The postcards stopped after about two years, supposedly because their sender died. More likely, this marked Sweeney's final period of forced hospitalization, beginning after the state declared him incompetent in 1956.

The probable Mad Butcher spent his last years in hospitals, dying at age seventy in 1964.

S TORSO KILLER NEW INSAN

Couzens Trails in Re[...]an Ra

MAINE VOTE IS BAD NEWS TO NEW DEAL

[...]uel Says Election Shows Threat of Republican Victory in November.

[...]OOSEVELT JUST SMILES

[...]dicates Result Was About What He Expected.

BY WALKER S. BUEL
Plain Dealer Bureau
811 Albee Bldg.
WASHINGTON, Sept. 15

[...]aine's election is very bad news [...] the New Deal and Franklin [...]oosevelt.

In a definite indication of a Re[...]blican trend, a definite threat of [...] republican victory in November, [...]Maine barometer of a dwindling Democratic membership in Con[...], a definite indication of a Re[...]can revival, especially in the [...]

[...]ere it not for unprecedented far[...] in this campaign, the Maine [...]ight be regarded as a fatal [...] to New Deal hopes for the re[...]ion of President Roosevelt, but [...] factors exist, making possible [...]othern and western combination [...] may re-elect Roosevelt in [...] of anything the rest can do. [...]ody yet really knows this, pa[...] effects of relief and benefit [...] throughout the agricultural

[...]ember Election in Doubt.
[...]re the November election go [...] as much in doubt as is the [...] Maine voted, except that [...] has served notice upon the [...] Hoops that the days of the [...] Democratic prophets are [...]inded, 'one that unless Presi[...] Roosevelt can ride the west [...] south, he is headed for [...]

[...]idrow Wilson won in 1916 in a [...] election, without a vote of [...] a state except New Hamp[...] by a tiny margin. But Wilson [...]he west and the south. Roosevelt [...]he west and he made these [...] expects to overcome the trend [...] up by the Maine vote. [...]ucrats got the lead last pro[...]esday on the Maine returns, [...] vote is nothing good about it [...] a Democratic standpoint except [...]

Continued on Page 4, Column 5

Continued on Page 4, Column 5

[...]ne Carries Hint [...]lose U. S. Vote.

BY JAY G. HAYDEN
[...]ht, 1936, by the Scott-Howard [...]spaper Alliance, Inc.)
[...]TLAND, Me., Sept. 15.—Maine [...]rned back into the Republican [...] but with pluralities for its [...] candidates of that party [...] indicated to give the "na[...]he nation" edge this November [...] prophecy. [...] nevertheless, when fully surveyed, [...] confirms the major predic[...]ngnis generally made by the [...] experts: [...]hat the election in Novem[...] be one of the closest in [...] history. [...]and it will be more than [...] national election in the past, a [...] between the urban industrial [...], supporting President [...], and the small town and [...] farmers, backing Gov. Lan[...]

[...] exception, the bill town [...] rolled up huge majorities [...]andon, while the rural sections [...] farm communities [...] than offset by the side of [...] balloting front the agri[...]

No. 20 for Allen

Allen injured his back in the fifth inning, but was given credit for his twentieth victory yesterday as the Indians walloped Boston, 15 to 2. He triumphed finished the game. Two[...] by hit, his 59th and 60th homers. New York defeated Chicago, 7 to 1; Detroit trimmed Philadelphia, 8 to 5, and Washington took a double header from St. Louis, 15 to 7 and 6 to 1.

Weather stopped the National League.

(Details on Sport Pages)

WPA WORKERS TO BE EXPO GUESTS

Families, Also, to Attend Saturday as Honor to Garden Builders.

Today's Events.

United Rubber Workers Day.
United Surveyors Day.
Boy Scouts of America Day.
National Society of Patders Day.
City Club Day.
Home (R.) Day.
Garden Club of Michigan Day.
* * *
Attendance yesterday 50,460
Attendance for 96 days 2,909,443
Days behind ....

The WPA will have its day at the Great Lakes Exposition.

Many of the expo wizards thought that, since everybody was having his day at the big show, it would be sheer ingratitude to forget the WPA, some of whose 2,356 laborers build the first-ever Horticultural Gardens on the grounds.

So the boys who shoved the shovels and the bars who swung the picks have been invited to attend the exposition Saturday. They will have music furnished by their own WPA bands.

The invitation, which include members of the workers' families, will be in the form of identification cards. It was [...]

Continued on Page 8, Column 3

Continued on Page 8, Column 3

Says Fight With Richman Nearly Sank Ocean Plane

NEW YORK, Sept. 15.—(AP)—The Daily News is a correspondent dispatch from a mail correspondent at Musgrave Harbor, Newfoundland, says a quarrel sent the Atlantic between the transoceanic fivers Harry Richman and Dick Merrill "almost ended with the flyers in Davey Jones' locker."

Merrill and Richman landed at that isolated village yesterday after a return flight from England in the course of a [...]

BUY YOUR OWN MEALS, NESS TELLS ROOKIES

Ten New Patrolmen Told Appointments Are Based on Own Merits.

"DON'T BE OBLIGATED"

Warns "You'll Get No Great Reward for Honesty."

Ten new patrolmen were sworn into office yesterday by Safety Director Eliot Ness in his office as city Hall with the revolutionary admonition that policemen are expected to pay for their own meals.

"You have been appointed on your own merits and deserve you stand at the top of the civil service list and for no other reason," Ness told the recruits. "It angers made others to you that he was responsible for your appointments, pay no attention.

"Your appointment is up to you.

"You are expected to be honest and to know that you will get no great rewards for being honest. Don't be obligated to anyone, even in small things.

"When you walk into a restaurant for a meal, pay for it. When you get any mercantile commodity useful to you, pay for it. If people have been accustomed to giving you things or nothing prior to your becoming a policeman, I suppose it is all right for you to continue to accept these things."

Three Win Promotions.

"However, if people who have given you anything even before you want to give you something without charge, you can conclude that they are buying your badge and your services."

In addition to appointing the ten new policemen, Ness promoted Sergt. Augustus F. F. Foltz to a lieutenant and Patrolman Herbert Biedel and Norman W. Miller to sergeancies.

The recruits were:

ELMER A. BAERTNER, 2571 Vernon Avenue N. E.
CLEVELAND D. O'HARA, 10704 Everton Avenue N. E.
EDWARD PRINZI, JR, 2919 West Road N. E.
MELVIN T. STANLEY, 5614 W. 138th Street.
FRANK J. FABRZ, JR, 4773 E. 154th Street.
ROY J. FISENBACH, 5082 Trent Avenue S. W.
EDWARD A. MESNER, 3485 E. 130th Street.
CLARENCE D. ERIKEL, 3217 Fleet Avenue S. W.
JOHN R. DEISS, 2024 East [...] Avenue N. W.
ELMER J. PLOWE, 1061 Ansel Road N. E.

Cajek, the nephew of former Capt. Louis J. Cajek, was appointed to the department a month ago by John R. Flynn, executive director of Press. His appointment was refused at that time by Flynn because Flynn had shipped the candidates at the top of the list.

Youth, 16, Threatens Shirley Tem[...]

Associated Press Wirephoto.

Film's former star, six-teen-year old Atlanta boy, arrested in Atlanta yesterday and charged with sending an extortion letter to the mother of Shirley Temple, said the plan is shown between two federal agents as he was moved from the Atlanta police station to the Federal Building.

OUTLAW SITDOWN, PLEA IS UP TO URW

Strikes Hit Akron Plants as Rubber International Weighs Policy Issue.

Plain Dealer Bureau.
806 Citle Building.
AKRON, O., Sept. 15.

The issue of the sitdown strike [...] might become as the most important question before the United Rubber Workers of America at their first international convention in session here.

Resolutions before the convention include one asking that the In-ternational sitdown be outlawed and another that calls the sitdown "one of the most powerful weapons of organized labor" and seeks its in-corporation into URW policies.

The last one would set out of the sitdown into the hands of the ex-ecutive board to apply, "when [...] justified."

Adolph Germer, Committee for In-dustrial Organization organizer, ad-dressed the delegates late today, say-ing he had just come from a meeting of a group of Akron railwaymen who wanted to know how of them, he said, what the URW would do about sitdowns.

"Bravo! Vivaléro," is Ward.

"I said them, that sitdowns were a direct violation of your policies and your principles." Germer said.

Germer, who called a national [...]

SHAKER EXTEN[...] TO RUN CARS

Shuttle Service [...] Rd. Expected in 2 W[...] May Go to Richm[...]

BY JAMES C. MAGNIF[...]

First extension of rapid [...] tracks in Shaker Heights [...] completed in two weeks, [...] will be started shortly.

When the new service [...] half east of Warrensville [...] tion, on the Shaker Heigh[...] is to be rushed as fast [...] Road. Work on cutting [...] striking the right of way [...] along with it. For the [...] will be a rapid-transit artery [...]

There is said to be a fair [...] ability that the extension [...] another link in the Kinsman [...] near future, with the [...] relation to Rockside Road [...] queue for next spring, offer[...] trains to the Cleveland fair[...] Highway, a sixth away, and [...] the line, last eight station [...] any certainty of extension [...] Green Road.

It is intended [...]

Newspaper Plane Damaged.

ST. JOHNS, Newfoundland, Sept. 15.—(UP)—A newspaper plane owned by the New York Daily News [...]

Betty in the Nesses' Cleveland home, 1954.

Cleveland Public Library Photograph Collection

Ness with G. Frank Shampanore of the North Ridge Industrial Corporation, 1956.

Cleveland Public Library Photograph Collection

TWENTY-SIX

You Should
Write a Book

1955–1956

In late 1955, an entrepreneur from western Pennsylvania began a new venture.

G. Frank Shampanore, fifty-seven, intended to market a new process for watermarking paper as a fraud preventative. He established two corporations: Guaranty Paper, to protect correspondence or other important documents, and Fidelity Check, to do the same for bank checks.

As president of a holding company, North Ridge Industrial Corporation, Shampanore controlled both subsidiaries. A compact, thickset man with glasses and receding, graying hair, Shampanore had a reputation as "a spell-binder who had made a career of various schemes," a business associate remembered, "but this thing looked so good that he was able to captivate all who came along with his grandiose dreams."

This included his business partner, Joseph Phelps, forty-five, nicknamed "Moose" thanks to a long face and massive frame. New Jerseyite Phelps, a semipro baseball player in his youth, made it through the Depression working the Atlantic City boardwalk.

"Within a few minutes he'd have fifteen people gathered, just from his talking," his daughter Natalie recalls. "And he'd say, 'Hey, let's go in here and have a drink.'"

Phelps, a born salesman, didn't exactly converse; he'd drown his listeners in stories, facts, and sports statistics. His youngest daughter, Linda, remembers him as "a compulsive talker . . . He was trying to be liked, to be someone."

Funding for Phelps and Shampanore's new venture came mostly from tiny Coudersport, Pennsylvania, where the two men met. After setting up an office there, they planned to establish another in Cleveland's Terminal Tower and began seeking a figurehead who could lend their outfit legitimacy.

Eliot Ness had exactly what they were looking for—name recognition in Cleveland, a business pedigree from Diebold, and a law enforcement reputation to promote their fraud-proof checks. His government connections might offer opportunities for lucrative contracts, too.

With his finances in shambles, Ness made an easy target. In late December, Phelps and Shampanore offered to bring him on as president of Fidelity Check—at $7,500 a year (with stock options), a fraction of his Diebold salary, but a lifeline now. Ness signed on in January 1956.

But he struggled to deliver on the promise of his reputation. Most of his old Cleveland contacts declined to get in on the ground floor, so Ness went traveling in search of investors. Phelps usually accompanied him on the road, bonding with the reserved Ness, who often gravitated toward talkative, outgoing personalities. And Dick Tracy fan Phelps got a kick out of knowing an actual G-man.

"Weren't you scared?" Phelps asked about the Capone days.

"Scared? I was scared to death, but I felt it was my duty to do the job."

Phelps loved to associate with famous people; now he bragged of his pal who got Scarface Al. Ness only reluctantly spoke of his past, but Phelps would prod, showing off his partner in front of others.

Seeking press coverage for the company in early 1956, Phelps approached another famous friend, Oscar Fraley, in New York. Phelps asked the slight, sandy-haired syndicated sportswriter to help him connect with "financial writers."

"I said, sure," Fraley recalled. "He said he was bringing a friend with him."

Fraley joined Phelps and Ness in their hotel room at the Waldorf-Astoria. The two old buddies launched into what Fraley called "one of those good old 'long-time-no-see' bull sessions," while Ness sat back, watching.

"Ockie," as friends called Fraley, was prone to leaving wreckage in his wake, and liked to paper over his past with tall tales. Like Ness, he had married three times, but the forty-one-year-old sportswriter's previous marriages had not ended in divorce—Fraley's first wife died in a car accident after he abandoned her, and his second committed suicide after he insisted she have an abortion.

Sometime after midnight, Phelps pointed at his business partner and said, "You'll have to get Eliot to tell you about his experience as a Prohibition agent in Chicago. He's the guy who dried up Al Capone. Maybe you never heard of him, but it's real gangbuster stuff; killings, raids and the works. It was plenty dangerous."

Fraley looked at the quiet businessman with the somewhat doughy face. This guy, a G-man? No way.

Ness merely smiled and said, "It was dangerous."

Eliot began telling stories of the old days, sitting on the floor, his back against the couch. Fraley looked on, spellbound—he knew a good story when he heard it, and this one benefited from being true!

Finally, Ness got to his feet, suggesting they grab some breakfast. Fraley had gotten so wrapped up in Ness's stories that he'd lost track of time—it was 6 A.M.

Fraley remarked, "Someday you should write a book on your experience. You might make some money with it."

Ness said, "I could use it."

Fraley would recall this as a chance meeting leading to an unexpected idea, but Phelps had already been pushing Ness to get his Chicago exploits in print. A Capone book would help promote their business and bring Ness much-needed income.

Phelps asked him, "Why don't you let Fraley write that book for you?"

Ness had turned down opportunities to cash in on his career going back to 1931. Only now, badly needing money, did he actively pursue the possibility. But as with politics, had he waited too long, clinging to his integrity until his moment passed?

Around this time, Ness returned to Chicago and visited newspaper offices, seeking a journalist who might collaborate on a book. No one took him seriously; few even remembered him.

Besides, the story of who "got" Capone had been told over and over. Everyone knew the income tax men had defeated Al Capone, not some group of "Untouchables."

AFTER A SECOND New York meeting, Ness sent Fraley a box of mementos covering his career—scrapbooks, wiretap transcripts, and other documents—which the sportswriter used to bang out a couple of draft chapters. He urged Ness to keep a notebook for jotting down memories as they came to him. From the Cleveland Public Library, Ness checked out an old book on the Chicago gang wars: *The One-Way Ride* by Walter Noble Burns. Within its pages, he could reacquaint himself with the youthful, mythic Capone in all his terrible glory.

On May 6, Fraley sent Ness a copy of the draft chapters, which his agent was already shopping. Fraley reported doing "a helluva lot of research to check facts and figures on Capone, etc., including dates & whatnot," and the early chapters of the published version bear this out. Fraley essentially crafted a nonfiction novel, pulling quotes and details from the historical record to inform his writing.

This melding of truth, fiction, and rearranged facts set the tone for the rest of the book. Ness's memories of that brief period, twenty-five years earlier, were vivid yet spotty and incomplete. He could recall stories and anecdotes, but specific details and the true chronology eluded him.

Fraley would take Ness's memories and shape them into a coherent narrative—supporting them with research, making up dialogue, and providing novelistic touches. He seems to have invented little out of whole cloth—most events described are verifiable—yet Ness worried about its accuracy.

"Don't get scared if we stray from the facts once in a while," Fraley wrote his coauthor. "We've got to make a real gang-buster out of this thing and after all, we have literary license."

BY EARLY JULY, Fraley's agent had a buyer—Julian Messner, Inc.—offering a $1,000 advance. Ness badly needed the money, because his latest business venture was going south.

Selling stock at a dollar a share, North Ridge raised $300,000 in working capital—$80,000 in Coudersport alone. Joe Phelps gave some stockholders his personal guarantee, promising to reimburse them if their shares didn't pay out.

Flush with cash, North Ridge opened a Washington, D.C., office, then filled its Terminal Tower suite with top-of-the-line furniture. On April 9 in Coudersport, Shampanore invited media and dignitaries to view "the first production run of personalized watermark bank checks" at the Pennsylvania plant.

But Shampanore's nephew, young William Ayers—working to perfect the watermarking process—had yet to turn it into something salable.

"We didn't know what our cost was gonna be to produce the thing," Ayers remembered. "We didn't know what our capacity would be. It was just a mess."

Realizing months of laboratory work were needed, Ayers tried to get his uncle to cut back on expenses. But Shampanore just kept spending the investors' money. He burned through secretaries, too, plying them with gifts, cash, and unwanted attention till they went out the door.

Ness and Phelps, sincerely believing in the venture, tolerated Shampanore's behavior for a while. Both men suffered from too much optimism and a desperate need to strike it big.

But Shampanore was misleading them and his investors. He claimed to hold a patent on his watermarking process, though his application had been rejected—a rumor circulated that his magic formula was "nothing more than Johnson's wax." Even Shampanore's show of printing the company's first run of checks had been a sham; the paper running through the press had been blank.

By spring, Phelps had run out of ways to raise money; that July, the company cut costs by moving all operations to Coudersport. While Betty and Bobby stayed in Cleveland, Eliot took up temporary residence in this town of 2,900 tucked away in the Allegheny Mountains. Huge hills ringed the sky, ready to light up in reds and oranges when autumn's leaves turned. Although he'd spent most of his days in big cities, Ness grew to like the languid pace of small-town living.

"You know," he told Phelps, "I wouldn't mind spending the rest of my life here."

As they worked to save North Ridge, Ness and Phelps leaned heavily on each other. Phelps's daughter Natalie, who'd hang around the office above a moldy Main Street storefront, recalls her father "and Eliot kind of slapping each other on the back," as if to say, "Hang in there buddy, it'll be okay."

Phelps kept up his perpetually sunny attitude, though the prospect of financial ruin had him considering suicide. Ness, more melancholic by nature, couldn't hide his growing despair. Natalie would see him staring out the window, radiating gloom like a furnace giving off heat.

LS TORSO KILLER NEW INSAN

Couzens Trails in Re___an R___

MAINE VOTE IS BAD NEWS TO NEW DEAL

Buel Says Election Shows Threat of Republican Victory in November.

ROOSEVELT JUST SMILES

Indicates Result Was About What He Expected.

BY WALKER S. BUEL,
Plain Dealer Bureau.
611 Albee Bldg.
WASHINGTON, Sept. 15.

Maine's election is over and now the New Deal and President Roosevelt...

(remainder of column illegible)

No. 20 for Allen

Allen injured his back in the 6th inning, but was given credit for his twentieth victory yesterday as the Indians managed 8 to 2 ...

BUY YOUR OWN MEALS, NESS TELLS ROOKIES

Ten New Patrolmen Told Appointments Are Based on Own Merits.

"DON'T BE OBLIGATED"

Warns "You'll Get No Great Reward for Honesty."

Ten new patrolmen were sworn into office yesterday by Safety Director Eliot Ness in his office at City Hall with the revolutionary admonition that policemen are expected to pay for their own meals.

WPA WORKERS TO BE EXPO GUESTS

Families, Also, to Attend Saturday as Honor to Garden Builders.

Today's Events.

United Rubber Workers Day.
United States Postoffice Day.
Naval Engineers of America Day.
National Society of Patriots Day.
City Club Day.
Garden Club of Michigan Day.

Attendance yesterday ....
Attendance to date ....
Days left ....

The WPA will have its day at the Great Lakes Exposition.

Youth, 16, T___atens Shirley Te__

WIREPHOTO

OUTLAW SITDOWN, PLEA IS UP TO URW

Strikes Hit Akron Plants as Rubber International Weighs Policy Issue.

Plain Dealer Bureau.
222 Olds Building.
AKRON, O., Sept. 15.

The issue of the sitdown strike is right before the more important question before the United Rubber Workers of America at their first international convention, in session here.

SHAKER EXTE TO RUN CARS

Shuttle Service Rd. Expected in 2 May Go to Rich

BY JAMES G. DOYNE

First extension of its lines in Shaker Heights, completed in two weeks ...

Says Fight With Richman Nearly Sank Ocean Plane

NEW YORK, Sept. 15.—(AP)—The Daily News, in a copyrighted article from a staff correspondent at Musgrave Harbor, Newfoundland, says: All my arguments for different pressure were thrown aside...

Newspaper Plane Damaged.

Ness as he appeared on the back cover of *The Untouchables* (1957).
Authors' Collection

TWENTY-SEVEN

Valuable Citizen

1956–1957

Ness's natural reserve made him almost invisible to his new neighbors—"a man you probably haven't given a second look on the street." This mountain town could be wary of outsiders— "damn flatlanders"—particularly fast-talking, big city types like Phelps with his unending New Jersey patter. While Ness seemed anything but a huckster, his association with Phelps gave some people pause.

Entrepreneur John Rigas, just getting started in the burgeoning business of cable TV, recalls being unimpressed upon first meeting Ness. Phelps had asked Rigas to join Ness and himself at Mackey's, a restaurant on the town square, to talk about investing.

As they drank coffee, Phelps launched into his spiel about Ness's battle with Al Capone. Ness let him talk, obviously uncomfortable. At times he'd try to correct the record: "Well, it wasn't quite like that."

Rigas sensed Ness didn't care to talk about those days. "And even when he described a few of the incidents, it was pretty low-keyed," Rigas recalls. "I never got the impression he was a big hero. It was pretty routine the way he described it."

Still, Rigas didn't quite buy the stories of Ness busting up breweries. He kept thinking, "What's he doing in Coudersport with that kind of resumé and background?"

After all, Ness's poverty was no secret. His 1952 Ford, a black convertible ill suited to western Pennsylvania, had torn upholstery and an empty hole for a rear window. After a heavy snowfall, its roof caved in, filling the interior with snow.

"He'd tell us these things," recalled the principal of Bobby's elementary school, "and we didn't believe him. . . . We thought, if he's so important why is he driving such a beat-up old car?"

Yet Ness projected an aura of decency and trustworthiness that won people over, even if they didn't believe Phelps's blarney. Rigas saw Ness regularly at Mackey's having morning coffee.

"When I came in the restaurant and he'd be sitting there, he didn't have to smile at me, or say, 'Come on over,'" Rigas recalls. "But he did."

Ness rarely if ever brought up investing, and never mentioned Capone. "When you talked to Eliot, he was not a braggart," Rigas says. ". . . He just came across as an honest guy that liked people and had a warm, approachable character."

Rigas didn't put much stock in rumors of Ness's drinking. No one claimed to have seen Ness drunk, at least not to where he grew loud or lost control. Bill Ayers insisted Ness drank "no more than I did or many other people," and that the liquor had no effect on his friend's home or work lives.

But alcohol did help Eliot get through the day. He developed a red nose and a blotchy complexion. When he came home, he'd head for a bottle. Fraley considered him "a big drinker, a borderline alcoholic"; a regular visitor to the Ness house recalled Eliot always with a drink in hand. He partook at the office, too, though Phelps would make him cut it out when they had meetings. Ness knew how to hide his habit, advising a Coudersport resident to drink vodka—it left no odor on the breath.

Ness spent many evenings at the Old Hickory, a large Victorian house converted into a hotel and tavern. Its basement bar catered to the local elite, including professionals who'd invested in North Ridge, who gathered Friday nights to watch boxing on TV.

Phelps would work the room, ready to buy a round even when his family lacked grocery money. He jumped at any opportunity to talk up Ness's past and generate interest in the company. Eliot would go along, reluctantly.

Ness became the Old Hickory's in-house entertainment. A crowd would gather as he sat and fielded questions about places he'd raided and gangsters he'd encountered.

Phelps's teenaged son, Joe Jr., would hang around and listen to Ness until his mother came to fetch him. Ness reminded Joe of Will Kane, the Gary Cooper character in *High Noon*, the 1952 film about an aging, buttoned-down lawman abandoned by the community he'd saved.

Getting these experiences down on paper, Ness found harder. Now that Fraley had a publisher, Ness tried to write his own version of the Capone story. He would show up at Dorothy Wilkinson's home, carrying a vodka bottle and scraps of Guaranty paper. Sitting on the floor with his back against the furniture and a drink resting atop his thigh, he'd jot down memories and give them to Dorothy, a North Ridge secretary, to type up. But the right words often eluded him, and his spelling could be poor.

Ness's twenty-two-page manuscript, like the stories he told at the Old Hickory, stuck close to the facts with few literary flourishes. It reads much like a police report—a flat and sometimes disjointed record of Ness's undercover work in Chicago Heights and his time with the Untouchables. Ness sent it off to Fraley with a cover letter offering to flesh out any parts that seemed too thin.

Fraley, however, would need much more than he could get from Ness in writing. Around the first week of August, he traveled to Coudersport and checked into the Hotel Crittenden. Ness visited Fraley in his room, where—over drinks—the writer tried to coax old memories out of him.

Other times Ness and Fraley would meet at Mackey's, before a window looking on the Potter County Courthouse, with its statue of Justice (sans blindfold). Ness struggled to stay on topic and sometimes spoke of Cleveland, though he never painted himself a hero. He even told Fraley about his secret interrogation of Frank Sweeney and his certainty that he'd found the Butcher—likely the first time he shared that story with anyone but Betty.

On other matters, he proved less forthcoming. He seems not to have told Fraley that at least one Capone squad member turned out to be touchable, and he never discussed his divorces. But Fraley felt the book "had to have some love interest," according to Mrs. Ness, so the final product had Eliot and Betty dating during the Capone investigation, years before they met.

TWO WEEKS AFTER Fraley returned to New York, Ness moved Betty and Bobby to Coudersport. Rain soaked the nighttime streets as they arrived at their new home: the bottom floor of a large Victorian house just off the town square, mere footsteps from a bend in the Allegheny River.

The Nesses filled their home with cats—including one named Pandora and an eight-year-old, black-and-brown tabby called the Judge. They had so many felines that Betty once invited a visitor to keep one.

On Betty's first full day in Coudersport, a local fish warden fined her $25 for fishing without a valid license. The one she'd purchased was for Pennsylvania residents only, and Betty hadn't lived in the state long enough to qualify. Her husband and son were with her, but neither received a ticket—Bobby was a minor and Eliot, "a reluctant fisherman," had been there only as an observer. Initially irritated, Eliot couldn't stop giggling throughout the court proceeding.

The incident made the local paper, the *Potter Enterprise*, which assured its readers: "Mrs. Ness still likes Potter County, we've heard—from no less an authority than Mr. Ness."

Over time, Betty's opinion of Coudersport improved, but only slightly. She compared it to "a Norman Rockwell painting; as wholesome, and just about as boring."

Though Betty joined the local Presbyterian church and spoke

at a women's club on "Sculpturing as a Means of Self Expression," her shy, quiet demeanor kept her from ever fitting in. In public, she was gracious and polite. In private, she resented being dragged to such a backwater, and took her frustrations out on Eliot. As he became better known around town, she grew increasingly hostile toward him.

Eliot enjoyed a closer relationship with his ten-year-old son. Bobby liked to cook and sometimes made his father fried egg sandwiches. They would play together in their backyard or head to a nearby confectionary for homemade chocolates.

Eliot indulged the boy, who seemed to feel he could get away with anything. But when Bobby wanted to go hunting, his father refused.

"I've shot at too many men," he would say. "It isn't fun and I never want to kill anybody or anything again."

Eliot gladly left hunting to the Judge, whose skill at catching rats was much appreciated by the Nesses' neighbors.

In late September, Ness took his Chicago stories to a Rotary Club luncheon, where he spoke more about the workings of Capone's empire—how much money they made, how much beer they brewed—than his own exploits. But he made sure to mention the time he'd thumbed his nose at Scarface by parading a bunch of confiscated trucks past the gang's headquarters. And he added "that the full story of the beginning of the end for Capone would be told in a forthcoming book."

This plug failed to win over a Rotarian, who—before realizing Ness was within earshot—said, "Who the heck does he think he's kidding with a story like that?"

Ness simply smiled and let it go. He had bigger worries.

NESS DID WHAT he could to salvage his business, but only within his tight ethical bounds. Bill Ayers remembered several meetings when Ness flatly rejected proposals he considered dishonorable.

"I have never known a man that had as high a standard as he did," Ayers observed. "They say all men have a price. Well, whatever his price was, it was so high that nobody could pay it."

Ness's scrupulous honesty sparked conflict with Shampanore, who'd hired him for his name and contacts—not to run the company. When Shampanore realized Ness and Phelps "wouldn't dance to his music," as Ayers put it, he fled to Texas and schemed to ruin his former partners. In a letter to Ayers, Shampanore vowed to "blow the thing up and wash it down the sewer before I see the other crowd get control."

That September, Shampanore summoned Ayers to Chicago with a plan to get rid of Ness and Phelps by bankrupting North Ridge. He wanted his nephew to destroy the company from within, promising to treat Ayers well for the sabotage.

Back in Coudersport, Ayers agonized over the decision. He felt a strong sense of loyalty to his uncle, but had come to respect and admire Ness.

"To me," Ayers said, "he was a big man, the greatest I ever met."

Ayers—with few friends in Coudersport and family back in New Jersey—spent many evenings at the Ness home, enjoying Betty's Swedish meatballs, sitting on the floor as he and Eliot drank and listened to Eddy Duchin records. Only later would Ayers realize that Ness, without ever trying to lecture him on ethics, had left an indelible mark.

"A lot of his traits . . . ," Ayers said, "his honesty, his honor, his morals—I see now they rubbed off on me. . . . I'm a much better man than I was before I ever met Eliot Ness, and I give him a lot of that credit."

Ayers called Shampanore and refused to help destroy North Ridge. Instead he offered to broker a peace; but Shampanore would have none of it, sending stockholders libelous letters impugning Ness's character.

These attacks left Ness and Phelps scrambling to keep their company afloat. Phelps took Shampanore's place as president of North Ridge; Ness assumed control of Guaranty Paper. They appealed to the business community for support, claiming their venture could revitalize Coudersport's stagnant economy. While the chamber voted to endorse their work, Shampanore's letters had built a climate of suspicion around North Ridge.

Ness never talked about his troubles when he saw John Rigas at Mackey's. Instead, he offered regular updates on the Capone book. Although Rigas knew Fraley's name from the sports page, he found the project far-fetched.

One time, Ness said he didn't have enough funds to cover a check he'd written Rigas, which amounted to maybe $27. Sadly, anxiously, he asked Rigas not to cash it until it would clear. Rigas agreed. The two men tried to make a joke of it.

"I felt bad for him," Rigas recalls. "I wished I could've helped him."

IN DECEMBER, A Coudersport physician examined Ness and noticed a potentially serious heart murmur. He put Eliot on Miltown—an anxiety-relieving but highly addictive tranquilizer—and sent him to a specialist in a nearby town.

That specialist diagnosed Ness with inactive rheumatic valvular disease, the aftereffect of a childhood bout with rheumatic fever. The disease left scar tissue on the valves of Ness's heart, forcing it to overexert itself. One ventricle had begun to enlarge. The specialist advised Ness to take it easy.

Ness, whose Christian Science upbringing assured him a strong will could overcome any ailment, tried to take the news in stride. He may have told Betty about the diagnosis, but otherwise kept it to himself.

"Looking back at those months," Bill Ayers recalled, "it is obvious to those who knew him that he was working feverishly to 'get his house in order,' both with the business and with his personal life."

All that work helped pull North Ridge out of a death spiral. By early 1957, it appeared the company might make it after all.

"I feel good about things," Ness said that spring, "we are fighting an uphill battle but I'm optimistic."

Meanwhile Shampanore kept undermining Ness and Phelps, sending malicious letters to stockholders and employees, urging the company's board of directors to fire his nephew. Ness and Phelps called a board meeting for April 3, to clear the air and defend their reputations.

Ness told the North Ridge stockholders he'd never encountered a gangster who behaved like Shampanore, promising to sue him for libel if it wouldn't harm the company.

An inebriated board member told Ness to sit down. Ness told him to "behave like a gentleman."

Ayers produced documents proving Shampanore intended to destroy North Ridge, then offered to resign. Ness stood up in his defense, praising Ayers for the work he'd done to give the company a salable product.

"If Ayers leaves, I leave," Ness said.

"He was willing to put himself on the line to protect me," Ayers recalled, "which is something I've never forgotten."

Ness asked for a vote of confidence in Ayers. The board returned it unanimously.

The next day Ness spoke before the annual meeting of the Coudersport Parent-Teacher Association on a favorite topic: juvenile delinquency. Shortly before the speech, he remarked he didn't feel well, then almost collapsed. But he recovered enough to reminisce about his days working with the youth gangs of Tremont.

Coudersport, he warned, "has the potential of a juvenile delinquency problem," and while the town offered many pastimes for young children and adults, "there seems to be a need for organized teen-age activities."

The following Sunday, Ness joined his family at the First United Presbyterian Church. As he entered the building, dizziness overcame him and he collapsed. Several congregants rushed to help, including a doctor who revived him. The reverend tried to make light of it, joking that Ness would do anything to skip a sermon. Ness went home to rest and returned to work within days.

On April 16, three days before his fifty-fourth birthday, Ness went back to his physician for another checkup. The doctor diagnosed him with high blood pressure and suggested he come in for monthly exams.

SOMETIME THAT MONTH, Ness received the final proofs of his memoir. He didn't like what he saw. The minor embellishments seem to have troubled him less than the whole thrust of the book, which placed him squarely in the spotlight.

"He was many times on the verge of chucking the whole project," Ayers recalled, "because the book made him out to be a hero, which he honestly didn't consider himself to be."

Ness knew better than anyone that Capone's conviction had been a team effort. He wanted the credit to go to everyone—not just his own Untouchables, but also the tax investigators.

But he couldn't back out now. His family had no insurance; he and Betty hoped to use whatever they made from the book to send Bobby to college. If Eliot died, he'd leave his family little besides a battered old car and some worthless shares of North Ridge stock. The book would be their inheritance.

By early May, he'd signed off on the proofs.

Ness wasn't the only one having second thoughts. Fraley's editor wanted to lose the scene where Ness turns down a bribe from Capone's henchman.

"It makes him too goody-goody," the editor said. "Nobody's this honest."

But Fraley managed to keep it in. Doubts also arose over the book's working title: *The Untouchables*. Ness worried readers would mistake it for a book about the Indian caste system. The publisher didn't like the title, either, and searched for a suitable replacement, without success.

Over coffee at Mackey's, Ness told John Rigas of his concerns about the book. He made it clear he didn't like seeing his exploits exaggerated.

Then in early May, Ness rushed into the restaurant with

"good news"—they were about to sell the television rights to *The Untouchables*.

Rigas congratulated him, knowing full well what the extra money would mean to Ness's family. But he didn't give it much thought, because the idea of seeing Ness's story on TV seemed highly unlikely.

NESS HAD BIG showbiz hopes for Natalie, Phelps's daughter. She had recently taken up guitar and begun singing country music over the radio.

"Oh, you keep playing that guitar, girl," he'd say. "You've got a beautiful voice. You keep singing."

For Natalie, all of fifteen years old, that encouragement meant the world.

Thursday afternoon, May 16, 1957, Natalie joined Ness and her father at the North Ridge plant, formerly a grocery store on Main Street. As the two men went over financial statements, Phelps asked to take a break, saying he had a headache. Ness replied he felt fine—never better, in fact. They went downstairs and told Bill Ayers they'd finish up their work that evening at Ness's house.

Outside, Phelps asked if Ness wanted a ride home. Ness declined, saying he'd rather walk. Before leaving the Phelpses, he gave Natalie one last bit of encouragement.

"Keep going with that guitar," he said.

Then he headed home.

Muggy, unseasonably warm weather smothered Coudersport. As Ness approached the town square, he began to sweat and took off his coat. He turned left at the Hotel Crittenden, away from home and toward the office of Walter Taylor, editor of Coudersport's newspaper and Potter County's deputy coroner.

Taylor was one of Ness's closest friends here. Some weeks ago, they'd bonded over beers at the Crittenden bar, after realizing they'd almost crossed paths during Ness's glory days in Chicago, when Taylor was still in high school.

On June 9, 1930, as Taylor waited in the Randolph Street Station for a train that would take him home to Indiana, an unknown gunman came up behind another traveler—*Chicago Tribune* reporter Jake Lingle—and shot him in the head. The killing rocked the city, exposing Lingle's corrupt dealings with Capone and other mobsters. Prohibition agent Ness arrived at the crime scene within fifteen minutes, standing maybe five feet from the future small-town journalist.

Now Ness stopped at Taylor's office to ask if his friend wanted to get a "cool one." The newspaperman turned him down—he had a dinner to get to that evening. Eliot turned back toward home, stopping at the corner drugstore to fill a prescription for more Miltown. Down the street, across from the courthouse, sat the Pennsylvania State Liquor Store. Ness entered and chatted pleasantly with the clerk as he purchased some Martini & Rossi gin.

Carrying the bottle and his sedatives, Ness followed the edge of the courthouse square, keeping his head down as if in a hurry. He passed the local funeral home and continued up the block toward the house. As he entered, mopping his sweaty forehead with a handkerchief, he saw his son and said he didn't feel well.

Out in the garden, Betty watched her husband go into the kitchen and turn on the tap, apparently to draw a cool glass of water.

Then she heard a glass shatter.

She called to him, but he didn't respond. The faucet kept running.

Finally, she went inside and found Eliot sprawled on the kitchen floor—dead of a heart attack at fifty-four.

THE MAN ONCE famous for turning down a fortune in bribes died $9,000 in debt. His assets—including the rattletrap car, some shares in the paper company, and what remained of the book advance—amounted to less than $1,000. His checking account contained $273, which wouldn't even cover funeral costs; his wallet held a few worthless paychecks that could never be cashed.

Ness received a brief memorial service in Coudersport, in a small room at the funeral home up the street from his house. Then his body went to Buffalo to be cremated. Betty and Bobby left town in June, never to return.

Joe Phelps served as one of Ness's pallbearers. "Here's the only man I ever met who had no larceny in his heart," Phelps said as he stood over the body, weeping openly. "He was in a different league."

Phelps had lost more than just a friend; without Ness's leadership and name recognition, North Ridge would go bankrupt by the end of the year. After taking his family back to New Jersey, Phelps never stopped trying to pay off his debts in Coudersport.

Some years later, Phelps visited John Rigas and finally repaid money he'd borrowed to cover the North Ridge payroll. Rigas had forgotten all about it; now he realized his initial suspicion of the man had been unwarranted.

Bill Ayers stayed in Coudersport and eventually built a successful printing business from the wreckage of North Ridge.

Four days after his death, Ness received a more elaborate funeral in Cleveland. An honor guard from the Cleveland Police Department came to pay their respects, as did longtime friends Dan Moore, Robert Chamberlin, and Ralph Kelly. Ness's nephew Charles, whom he'd owed $500, sat with Betty and Bobby in the first pew.

The reverend gave a eulogy praising Ness's "community interest, his public service, his courage and integrity, his youthful and vital spirit, his warmth and understanding and his concern for people."

In Chicago, the four major newspapers all ran brief obituaries, each noting in their own way that Ness had "Helped to Send Capone to Prison," as the *Sun-Times* put it.

By then, the people of Coudersport knew all too well the kind of man they'd lost. Hearing of Ness's death, Walter Taylor reported it to the Associated Press. Once the story hit the newswires, telegrams began pouring into Coudersport from all over the country. Government officials, prominent businessmen, and

Hollywood stars all expressed their condolences. Even Eliot's old rival, J. Edgar Hoover, sent the Nesses a note.

Betty particularly cherished the message from Harold Burton, now a Supreme Court justice. Three years earlier, Burton had joined the unanimous ruling in *Brown v. Board of Education* that ended legal segregation in the United States. Now he warmly remembered the man whose exploits helped propel him to Washington.

"I have lost a great and good friend," Burton wrote to Betty. "The nation has lost a valuable citizen. My deepest sympathies to you and your son."

The telegrams kept coming for days. Their volume, and who sent them, stunned Bill Ayers; he'd never imagined Ness was so important.

"He was under great stress in the final months of his life, financially," Ayers observed. "He could've made a phone call and gotten all the help he needed. . . . But he was too proud to take it. He wanted to do it on his own."

Many in town thought of Ness with newfound respect as they came to realize those stories hadn't been tall tales after all.

Ralph Edwards, Betty Ness, and Robert Stack on *This Is Your Life*, November 25, 1960.

Library of Congress, Prints and Photographs Division, New York World-Telegram and the Sun Newspaper Photograph Collection, LC-USZ62-123220

A Modern Myth

Eliot Ness's final hopes and dreams went on sale September 23, 1957—pressed between two red hard covers and wrapped within a dust jacket bearing that unloved title: *The Untouchables*. A dignified studio portrait from Ness's final years dominated the back cover above an author bio reading like an obituary. A brief epilogue from Oscar Fraley summarized Ness's post-Chicago work and noted his death four months before.

"This is his memorial," Fraley wrote, "as well as that of 'The Untouchables.'"

Critics from the *New York Times* to the *Los Angeles Times* greeted the book warmly, praising its vivid and suspenseful story-telling. "It is a matter of well-remembered record that it was the income-tax men who put an end to the fantastic career of Al Capone . . . ," noted one reviewer. "Less well-remembered are the feats of 10 brave, devoted U.S. agents who laid the foundation for his overthrow."

Several publications serialized portions of *The Untouchables* in 1957 and 1958, introducing Ness's story to more and more readers. But not even a late endorsement from famed gossip columnist Walter Winchell, calling the book "a must-read thriller," could push it onto bestseller lists. Eliot's last attempt to provide for his family had, according to Betty, produced a "resounding flop."

THIRTY YEARS HAD passed since Capone ruled Chicago. For older Americans, Prohibition no longer seemed something shameful and better forgotten, but a fading memory of youth. Their Baby Boomer children—too young to know the name "Al Capone," much less "Eliot Ness"—came to the bloody and boozy Roaring Twenties mostly in old movies on late-night TV, an era as remote, colorful, and exciting as Hollywood's Wild West.

In the late 1950s, filmmakers began to revive the gangster genre with a cycle of B-pictures about such Depression-era out-laws as "Baby Face" Nelson, Bonnie Parker, and "Machine Gun" Kelly. In December 1958, the venerated TV anthology series *Playhouse 90* aired "Seven Against the Wall," dramatizing the St. Valentine's Day Massacre. The following March, Allied Artists released a theatrical feature, *Al Capone*, directed by Richard Wil-son, with a charismatic, sinister Rod Steiger in the title role.

Finally, filmmakers were telling Capone's story using his own name. But they still lacked an essential element for creating a modern myth: a hero as compelling as their infamous villain. *The Untouchables* offered that and more—"enough material . . . ," according to the *Los Angeles Times*, "for a half-dozen gangster movies"—and Hollywood noticed. Before Ness's memoir was even published, Warner Bros. had offered Fraley a reported $25,000 for the film rights—money he would split with Betty.

In February 1958, Seven Arts Productions, affiliated with Warner, announced a big-screen adaptation of *The Untouchables*. Producer Ray Stark told the *New York Times* he wanted Richard Widmark—who came to stardom as villainous Tommy Udo in *Kiss of Death* (1947)—to play "one of the Treasury agents" (the book had failed to make Ness a household name). For Capone, Stark had in mind another actor who became a star playing a hoodlum: Edward G. Robinson, whose *Little Caesar* (1931) de-fined the modern movie gangster.

Then, typically, *The Untouchables* slipped quietly into Hollywood's development hell. Later that year the stalled project hit the desk of the president of Desilu Productions.

Desi Arnaz—bandleader Ricky Ricardo on the hit CBS series *I Love Lucy*—had established Desilu in 1950 with his costar wife, Lucille Ball. Nothing else the studio had produced lived up to *Lucy*'s unprecedented success, and most of their TV pilots went unsold. Desilu needed another hit.

Arnaz, despite outstanding debts, went after the Ness-Fraley book; but Stark wouldn't sell the rights apart from a Seven Arts package, and Desilu couldn't afford such a substantial purchase. Arnaz had his legal department look into Stark's option, learning it would expire within six months, after which Desilu bought the rights for $2,500. Only then did Arnaz explain to Ball and studio VP Martin Leeds just why he'd been so eager to acquire the property.

He wanted to play Eliot Ness.

"It seemed insane," Leeds remembered, "but he was the boss. Desi wanted to break out of the Ricky Ricardo stereotype and be accepted as a real actor."

Ball bluntly shut her husband down, his thick Cuban accent among her objections. Arnaz reluctantly gave up trying to play Ness, but he developed "The Untouchables" as a two-part episode of *Westinghouse Desilu Playhouse*, a new anthology series on CBS.

On New Year's Eve, 1958, Arnaz wired Clyde Tolson, J. Edgar Hoover's longtime aide at the FBI, wishing both men a happy 1959 and revealing his interest in adapting Ness's memoir. Arnaz, assuming the real Untouchables had worked for Hoover, asked the Bureau's permission to reference the FBI in the show. And could they help locate the former agents?

The FBI functionary reviewing Arnaz's request suggested the Bureau keep its distance. "The book apparently gives Ness a great deal of credit for the activities of the Government in bringing prohibition violators to justice," he wrote, "even to giving the impression that he was instrumental in sending Al Capone to prison."

Hoover wrote Arnaz saying the Untouchables had never been

FBI agents, and he could not help Desilu locate them. Nor would the term *FBI* be historically accurate, since the Bureau was not known as such before 1935. Unable to contact the real Untouchables for clearance, Desilu gave Ness's team fictitious names.

The next month, when *TV Guide* announced Desilu would be adapting a book cowritten by "former FBI agent Eliot Ness," Hoover ordered the special agent in charge of his Los Angeles field office to monitor the project and inform him of "any reference to the FBI in this production and the attendant publicity."

WRITER PAUL MONASH'S teleplay stayed remarkably faithful to the Ness-Fraley *Untouchables*, despite inevitable dramatic flourishes and a violent final act. Arnaz hired director Phil Karlson, whose 1955 hit film *The Phenix City Story* told a similar true-crime tale, to collaborate with first-time producer Quinn Martin, a former sound cutter married to an *I Love Lucy* writer. Recreating Prohibition-era Chicago raised the show's budget to around $300,000 per episode—leading Leeds to worry *The Untouchables* would sink the company. Allied Artists had paid about the same for their *Capone* film, but this was television.

The money would be well spent, Arnaz knew, if it lent the show a veneer of historical authenticity. With that in mind, he hired Walter Winchell as narrator. Ball objected fiercely—Winchell had almost destroyed her by publicly revealing she'd once registered to vote as a Communist—but this time Arnaz stood firm.

"Walter gave the show a feeling of truth and immediacy," he said. "His machine gun delivery was very, very important to the show."

Success or failure hinged on casting Ness and Capone. The latter, who wouldn't enter until the first episode's cliffhanger, went to Neville Brand. The *Riot in Cell Block 11* star only vaguely resembled Capone but conveyed an animal menace. The producers hired a dialogue coach to tutor Brand in an Italian accent, though Capone was Brooklyn-born.

Arnaz felt the hero shouldn't go to "the obvious cop type," but rather "more of an Alan Ladd type." Desilu approached Van Heflin, who said, "I don't want to be on television every week." Van Johnson stepped up, then dropped out the weekend before the shoot over a salary disagreement.

Second-tier movie star Robert Stack was the last-minute replacement.

"Eliot Ness," Stack remembered, "was a complete stranger to me. This cold-eyed authoritarian was the biggest stretch I was ever asked to perform."

THE FIRST *PLAYHOUSE* installment aired on April 20, 1959, a day after what would've been Ness's fifty-sixth birthday. Betty tuned in alongside her son and a reporter from the *Cleveland Press*, her obvious unease giving way to transparent approval of Stack's performance.

"He has the same quietness of voice," she observed, "the same gentle quality that characterized Eliot. At times, even Stack's small mannerisms are similar. He smiles less, but Mr. Stack has been given less to laugh at than Eliot found in real life."

Even the FBI monitor gave the production high marks: "While the preprogram publicity and schedule announcements kept stating that this was the story of the 'FBI versus Al Capone,' the drama itself makes it clear that the FBI is in no way involved. . . . The drama is well done and is narrated by Walter Winchell in a very effective style."

On April 27, the second episode took more dramatic liberties, with gangsters and G-men trading bullets. Real-life Untouchable Barney Cloonan told the *Chicago American*: "There wasn't any shooting. Nobody got killed, or even wounded. We didn't carry submachine guns—just revolvers and a couple of shotguns."

But in the *Los Angeles Times*, an "old-time police reporter" praised Desilu's Prohibition-era portrayal. "The kids can't understand this," he said. "They think it's fiction. . . . I remember. I lived through it."

Most viewers took the show's accuracy for granted, carried away by its propulsive energy and the striking cinematography borrowed from postwar film noir. The *Chicago Daily News* called it *Desilu Playhouse*'s "best offering of the season," blessed with "good dialog, a rarity in TV these days, and impressive directing by Phil Karlson."

The *Hollywood Reporter* predicted "those who caught the first half won't want to miss the second," and ratings proved them right. The first episode dominated its time slot and the second did even better, netting nearly two-thirds of the viewing public, making it one of the year's top-rated programs. Merged and retitled *The Scarface Mob*, the two-parter "made a hell of a profit," Arnaz said, "when released in theaters around the world" before returning to play in cinemas across the United States.

Having finally delivered the hit his company so sorely needed, Arnaz had no intention of letting Eliot Ness rest in peace. Before the *Playhouse* episodes even aired, he went to CBS chief William Paley about making *The Untouchables* an ongoing series.

"What the hell are you going to do," Paley asked, "after you do Capone?"

"Don't you know how many crooks you had in this country?" Arnaz shot back. "We can go on forever telling the stories about all the gangsters."

But CBS lost the series to rival network (and perennial ratings underdog) ABC, who outbid them for a full season of *Untouchables* episodes budgeted at $110,000 each. Stack agreed to appear as Ness in just eleven of a planned twenty-six episodes while narrating the rest, with fictitious Untouchables making the show more about an organization and an era than one gangbuster's exploits.

But Desilu soon realized just how much the program's success depended on its central character—and its original narrator. Winchell returned as the latter and Stack agreed to stay on for every show, his aversion to TV overcome by a 25 percent stake in the series.

• • •

THE TITLE SEQUENCE of every *Untouchables* episode began with the cover of Ness and Fraley's book, as if what followed came from those pages. Betty told a reporter that the filmmakers had taken her husband's scrapbooks to Hollywood for inspiration, but none of Eliot's non-Capone exploits—in Cleveland or elsewhere—made it into the show.

Desilu instead hired researchers to comb through old newspapers for colorful Depression-era criminals. Screenwriters would soon imagine Ness taking on every gangster from Dutch Schultz and "Mad Dog" Coll to Waxey Gordon and "Legs" Diamond. No longer Chicago Prohibition agents, the Untouchables became generic G-men investigating any federal crime—drug running, white slavery, kidnapping, even Nazi espionage.

The writers were given basic biographical material on the show's central figure, to include "in any story . . . an element of fidelity to the character of Eliot Ness." Stack didn't try to portray the real Ness, basing the character on "three of the bravest men I ever met"—a navy bomber pilot, a stuntman, and war hero/actor Audie Murphy. But he did ask the wardrobe department to clothe him in the long (if unseen) underwear that research suggested Ness wore.

"That's how seriously we take the show," Stack told the *Chicago Daily News*. "But I want to make the point that we're out to entertain the viewers, not to produce documentaries."

The first two *Untouchables* seasons consistently scored high ratings—briefly pushing ABC ahead of the other two networks—and received four Emmys, with one for Stack. The money *The Untouchables* generated kept Desilu afloat. But the show's thrill-ride mix of fact and fiction created intense controversy—especially the second episode, pitting Ness against Ma Barker and her bank-robbing sons.

On January 15, 1935, FBI agents had cornered sexagenarian Kate Barker and son Fred in a house near Ocklawaha, Florida, killing both after an extended gunfight. "Ma Barker and Her Boys," broadcast October 22, 1959, used that battle to frame flashbacks telling how "the most dangerous woman in the U.S. today," as Stack's Ness described her, led her children into a life of crime.

When an ABC affiliate, promoting the upcoming program, reached out to their FBI field office for help, the special agent in charge alerted Director Hoover, who in turn dispatched an "URGENT" wire to the Los Angeles office. Furious that a man the Bureau had long held in contempt would get credit for defeating the Barkers, Hoover demanded an investigation.

The special agent in charge in L.A. met with Arnaz, who apologized for the "terrible goof" and agreed to abandon planned *Untouchables* installments based on such signature FBI cases as John Dillinger, "Pretty Boy" Floyd, and "Baby Face" Nelson. When the special agent suggested the Barker episode not be shown, he was told such drastic action was too late. But Arnaz agreed to make any possible edits to the show.

An all-night reediting session preceded "Ma Barker and Her Boys" going out to ABC affiliates. Changes included a disclaimer provided by the FBI, though Desilu left off the sentence declaring that "Ness and the Treasury Agents featured in tonight's episode had nothing whatsoever to do with this case."

Cartha DeLoach, overseeing the Bureau's publicity department, called Arnaz warning him to avoid future "fraudulent" programs. Arnaz "was told flatly that although we appreciated his friendship and cooperation in the past," DeLoach reported, "the Director wanted him positively to understand that we would refuse to allow usurpation of the FBI cases or perversion of FBI history as . . . 'The Untouchables' had planned."

DeLoach's publicity office continued to monitor *The Untouchables* for any infractions, producing reports on every episode that season. The Bureau received a steady stream of letters from TV viewers, wanting to know more about Eliot Ness, often praising him as an exemplary FBI agent. The Director's office tried to set each correspondent straight—replying that "this Bureau has no connection whatsoever with the television program, 'The Untouchables,'" and that Ness "was never a Special Agent of the FBI"—but it did no good.

In 2016, a *Washington Post* contributor, seeking to describe the FBI's "sterling" reputation, identified two people who personified its history of "unflappable, smart and relentlessly fair" law enforcement: Clarice Starling, the fictional protagonist of *The Silence of the Lambs*, and Eliot Ness. Despite all of Hoover's efforts, his Bureau's public face no longer belonged to the Director, but to the Untouchable he'd always wanted nothing to do with.

SOON AFTER THE *Playhouse* two-parter aired, Capone's widow, son, and sister sued Desilu for appropriating the gangster's image without their consent; the courts dismissed the suit in 1965, finding no legal basis for their claims. Italian-American groups protested the show from the beginning, claiming its use of real and fictional mafiosos defamed their ethnicity.

Senator Thomas J. Dodd, former FBI agent and key Hoover ally in Congress, called *The Untouchables* "one of the goriest and most sadistic series being televised," claiming it inspired young viewers to become criminals. As chairman of the Senate Subcommittee on Juvenile Delinquency, Dodd called Desilu and ABC executives to testify, accusing them of playing up sadism for ratings. The hearings helped turn public opinion against violent TV programs in general and *The Untouchables* in particular, reversing ABC's brief ratings gains.

In 1961, Federal Bureau of Prisons director James V. Bennett protested a two-part *Untouchables* episode broadcast that January in the show's second season. "The Big Train" brought back Neville Brand as Capone, in a story loosely based on the gangster's cross-country transfer from Atlanta Federal Penitentiary to Alcatraz Island. Offended by scenes of corrupt guards doing Capone's bidding, Bennett formally complained to the Federal Communications Commission, threatening to fight license renewals of several

ABC affiliates if they aired the second episode. Each station aired the show anyway.

Desilu again inserted a disclaimer. Nevertheless, the FCC issued a formal letter criticizing ABC, arguing viewers had every reason to take the story as factual because "the only indication as to the origin of the programs was in the video announcement 'based on the book, *The Untouchables*, by Eliot Ness.'"

The constant controversy surrounding *The Untouchables* led Desilu to pull their show away from real history. Later episodes featured fictitious mobsters with generic names inoffensive to any ethnic group. By the fourth season in 1962, Ness's memoir still appeared at the start, but a closing disclaimer denied any resemblance to actual events.

Few audience members would have noticed, much less cared. A documentary aura and newsreel footage lent the show's most ludicrous plots credibility. This illusion of real history had much to do with the rapid-fire narration of Walter Winchell.

"All he has to do is say: 'On the night of Oct. 5, 1931, Eliot Ness went down to the delicatessen,'" a producer remarked, "and people are sure he did."

While the show kept Ness's name alive and made him a modern myth, his credibility and reputation suffered serious damage. In a 1961 article for *Climax* magazine, journalist Anthony Scaduto picked apart the inaccuracies in "The Big Train" and other *Untouchables* episodes to conclude that Ness was nothing but a fraud.

"The saga of the Untouchables has sold so well," Scaduto wrote, "that today millions of Americans will swear Ness was a man of rare genius who combined the wisdom and experience of Sherlock Holmes with the guts and forcefulness of Mike Hammer. . . . According to his own story, however, he never killed an enemy, never even shot anyone."

Scaduto admitted the TV series ignored the most remarkable part of Ness's life: "As Cleveland's underworld scourge, Ness did a fantastic, heroic job. But . . . this phase of his career goes unheralded. As does another—Ness's service during World War II."

Still, Scaduto couldn't forgive Ness for the original sin behind the TV series: the notion that the Untouchables took down Capone. Of course, Ness and Fraley made no such claim; not even the *Desilu Playhouse* two-parter went that far. But many more people watched the series than would ever read the book, and the show's cavalier attitude toward history created the poisonous perception that Ness was a glory hound prone to exaggerate his own exploits.

THE DESILU SERIES counted Ness's widow and son as two loyal fans—for a while.

"I like the program and I wouldn't miss it," Betty wrote in 1961, "even though I no longer know what it will be about."

Although he liked *Maverick* as much as *The Untouchables*, Bobby appreciated how Stack's performance brought back some measure of his father. The boy played "Untouchables" with a close friend—"an Italian boy," his mother said.

"When other children talked about their fathers Bobby, not having one, remained silent," Betty told a reporter. "Now . . . Eliot has come alive and Bobby's friends and teachers ask him about his father and he can talk about him."

Then, in summer 1961, Cleveland's ABC affiliate dropped *The Untouchables*, bowing to "pressure from parents and others." A West Side youth gang had taken the wrong kind of inspiration from the show, calling themselves "the Untouchables" and harassing Betty by phone.

Although Eliot would have hated even indirectly contributing to juvenile delinquency, his widow insisted the show did good, not harm. "I have many, many letters from youngsters who want to grow up to be like Eliot," she said. "They want to be law enforcers. They don't want to be like gangsters!"

Betty earned fewer than two hundred dollars from each new *Untouchables* broadcast. Reruns brought a paltry $28, which went toward her son's education. She worked full-time, first at a high-end clothing store and then in a hospital gynecology ward.

Still, she did her part to promote the series—appearing with Robert Stack on *This Is Your Life* and praising his performance in a *TV Guide* article. More money came from licensing her husband's name on T-shirts, toys, and other products, though Betty insisted she didn't "want cheap comic strips or pulp magazines made of it."

Toy guns, however, seemed to meet with her approval. Young fans of *The Untouchables* could get their hands on tommy guns, revolvers, and sawed-off shotguns, each with Ness's name prominently featured on the packaging—a strange way to remember a man with a distaste for firearms, but in line with Stack's Ness.

Even the bloodiest episodes, Betty felt, honored the memory of her late husband.

"It is fiction," she explained, "the stories are not of what Eliot was doing at that time. But since they are, in spirit, the same—the enforcement of law and order, the fight against exploitation of the law-abiding members of society, the hunting down of criminals—Eliot's admirers should not feel let down."

If the show reflected the real Ness's commitment to public service and professionalism, its sensationalized violence undercut much of what he stood for in life. His signature achievements in Cleveland—fighting juvenile delinquency, reorganizing the police department, promoting traffic safety—stemmed from a deep well of humanity and compassion even for lawbreakers, something rarely found in Stack's portrayal. Viewers saw a quick-trigger lawman simmering with rage, who intimidated and even assaulted suspects.

"Stack's Ness loathes his victims," observed Fletcher Knebel. "Ness liked some, hated none. . . . His gentle ways will soon be swallowed in the legend of a tough gun-toter who never was."

DESILU'S ATTEMPTS TO keep *The Untouchables* on the air by ducking controversy had the opposite effect. Ratings began to slip in the third season, as the producers toned the violence down. The fourth season tried "humanizing" Ness, showing him "as a living, breathing human with faults and imperfections instead of an epic figure of righteous vengeance." But viewers in sufficient numbers failed to tune in.

The Untouchables ceased production the following year, though the series lived on in syndication in the United States and around the world. Its success helped Desilu survive to produce—under new president Lucille Ball—such pop-culture touchstones as *Mission: Impossible* and *Star Trek*, while also serving to keep Ness's memoir in print.

The book became a bona fide bestseller, exceeding one million copies in paperback. The publisher put out a new hardcover edition with Ness's image removed from the back, allowing readers to more easily picture Robert Stack. Little of the proceeds ever found their way to Betty. After the TV series ended, she moved into Corinne Lawson's home, telling her former housekeeper her stay would be temporary; it lasted three years. Depressed, drinking heavily, she subsisted on food stamps as royalty checks dwindled.

In 1961, Betty earned some additional income from lending her husband's scrapbooks to Oscar Fraley for his version of the Cleveland years, *4 Against the Mob*. To the facts Fraley added embellishments, making sure fans of TV's *Untouchables* would recognize their Ness. Describing the Harvard Club raid, for example, Fraley portrays an angry Ness beating up an unarmed prisoner— unthinkable in real life but the kind of thing Robert Stack might do on TV.

4 Against the Mob impressed Harold Burton, who had retired from the Supreme Court in 1958 after being diagnosed with Parkinson's disease.

"Well," Fraley said in 1987, "everything I wrote . . . had to use a lot of license. But years later I got a letter from Burton . . . congratulating me on the accuracy of the account. Haw! Can you believe that?"

In 1962, Fraley—with ex-Untouchable Paul Robsky— published *The Last of the Untouchables*, a ridiculously tricked-up account all but writing Ness out. Even Robsky, who'd left government service after a 1951 drunk driving arrest, said much of the book was fabricated. But it sold some 380,000 copies and was translated into multiple foreign languages.

Fraley's income from these Ness books likely ran into six figures, catapulting him into financial security. He went on to author sports books and ghostwrite celebrity memoirs. But *The Untouchables* remained his most noteworthy success, especially after Hollywood introduced Ness and Capone to a new generation in 1987.

"I wonder if they'd even remember Al Capone if it wasn't for all the *Untouchables* stuff," Fraley mused before his death in 1994.

BETTY MOVED TO California in 1972, while her son stayed behind to pursue a degree in electrical engineering from Cleveland State University. Now caretaker of his father's scrapbooks, Robert loaned them to a local historical society, ensuring a record of Eliot's work would live on even as the city slowly seemed to forget him and America misremembered him.

In 1976, Robert granted an interview to Peter Jedick, a journalist working on a Ness piece for *Cleveland Magazine*. Jedick asked Robert to clear up a mystery: where was his father's final resting place?

"Oh," Robert replied, "he was cremated. Do you want to see his ashes?"

Then he went to a closet and withdrew a cardboard box.

"It seems to me," Jedick reflected, "there should be a more fitting end to the Ness legend than a box of ashes in a clothes closet."

A few months later, in August 1976, Robert died of leukemia at age thirty. Betty succumbed to cancer the following year at seventy-one, surviving her husband by just over twenty years. Both were cremated, and their ashes—along with Eliot's—fell into the care of Robert's widow, who donated Eliot's scrapbooks to the historical society in her late husband's honor.

But she held on to the family's remains for two decades until the time came to lay the Nesses to rest once and for all.

• • •

REBECCA MCFARLAND NEVER knew the leader of the Untouchables had any connection to her hometown until she read
The Dark City (1987), a historical novel by Max Allan Collins
drawing upon Ness's scrapbooks to dramatize his work in Cleveland. Inspired by what she read, McFarland used her position as
a public librarian to research Ness's time as Safety Director and
gave lectures around town to remind locals of this largely forgotten history.

Many who heard her speak wanted to visit the site of Ness's
grave, but McFarland did not know where to send them. Then in
1996, she learned Robert's widow had Eliot's ashes in her garage.
Believing the Untouchable deserved a more fitting resting place,
McFarland decided to give Ness the funeral his family could never
afford.

As a vice president of the Cleveland Police Historical Society,
McFarland corresponded with Ness's daughter-in-law for a year,
proving her good intentions. Robert's widow agreed to turn the
family's remains over to the society if they could be dispersed over
water—Eliot had always taken comfort spending time on Lake
Erie. This required special permission from the site chosen for the
funeral service, the historic Lake View Cemetery on Cleveland's
East Side, where John D. Rockefeller, the Van Sweringen brothers, and President James Garfield were buried. Cemetery officials
agreed to grant the Untouchable this singular honor.

With help from the Cleveland Police Historical Society, the
FBI, and the Treasury Department, McFarland designed the funeral to remind the city that Ness's most important legacy lay in
Cleveland, not Chicago or Hollywood. Ever since the 1987 *Untouchables* film, revisionist historians had stepped up their attacks
on Ness's legacy—leaving "his reputation kicked over like a Prohibition still," as the *Chicago Sun-Times* put it. But the publicity
surrounding the upcoming funeral reintroduced the city to Ness's
achievements as Safety Director.

Despite heavy clouds threatening rain, roughly a thousand people turned out for the memorial service on Wednesday, September 10, 1997. A granite boulder bearing the Nesses' names had been placed near the lake where their ashes would be dispersed, to "stand in perpetuity," according to the Cleveland Police Historical Society, "to honor this great law enforcement officer."

The brass urn containing the ashes of Eliot, Elisabeth, and Robert rode to Lake View Cemetery in a black 1938 Buick accompanied by honor guards, mounted units, and motorcycle officers from the Cleveland Police and Fire Departments. A pipe and drum band from the Chicago Fire Department represented Eliot's birthplace, and another from Pittsburgh represented the state where he died. After driving under the crossed ladders of two fire trucks, the Buick came to a stop near the cemetery's Wade Lake, where local notables gave short speeches remembering Ness.

McFarland delivered the eulogy, emphasizing Eliot's optimism and his willingness to face Cleveland's civic problems. "He firmly believed that each of us has unlimited potential," she said. "He knew that the problems with at-risk youth and crime could be easily solved . . . [and] he keenly recognized the brotherhood of man. That is what community policing was all about to him."

An officer from the honor guard brought the urn into a small blue boat from the police ports and harbor unit, rowing onto the lake while bagpipes played "Amazing Grace." As a horn sounded taps and a rifle salute split the air, he poured the ashes over the side. Then a pair of police helicopters flew overhead, paying final tribute to the former Safety Director.

NESS REMAINS A source of hometown pride for some Clevelanders, who still raise a glass to remember the former Prohibition agent. The Great Lakes Brewing Company, operating out of a 150-year-old tavern on the West Side, sells an amber lager named in his honor and likes to claim that the bullet holes in their bar were meant for frequent patron Ness. No proof of that story has ever come to light (nor likely ever will), but the brew-pub's founders can boast a more direct connection to the Safety Director—their mother once worked as Ness's stenographer. She, for one, doubted he had any connection to the bullet holes, since he so rarely carried a firearm.

Guests of the Hilton Cleveland Downtown, a blue-glass tower added to the skyline in 2016, can enjoy coffee or a cocktail at Eliot's Bar, then take a five-minute walk to City Hall, looking much as it did back when Ness had an office there. His face still greets visitors from a wall plaque, along with other members of "Cleveland's Hall of Fame."

The Great Lakes Exposition is long gone—the Rock & Roll Hall of Fame stands there now. Clevelanders still like to gamble, which they now do legally in a casino right next to Terminal Tower. Away from downtown, some remnants of Ness's time remain—pushed to the side and abandoned, like old photographs you can't bear to look at or part with. A fifteen-minute walk from Terminal Tower to the site of the Canal Road shantytown takes you into a postindustrial landscape that seems never to have recovered from the Depression, massive factories and warehouses haunting the Flats like corporeal ghosts.

An interstate highway has sliced away most of Jackass Hill, thousands of cars passing through every day, with no reminder of the terrible tableau left there in 1935. But turn off the highway onto East Fifty-Fifth Street, crossing first Francis and then Sweeney Avenues, and you find yourself right back in a hunting ground the Butcher would have recognized. Up at the top of Jackass Hill—amid the cracked pavement and boarded-up buildings—thick vegetation blocks your view of the highway, sealing you off into another time.

Not far away, a new housing development presses in on the edge of Kingsbury Run, its pastel-colored houses and neatly regimented streets imposing suburban order on this once-wild spot. Stand at the street's edge and you might be able to see where the Butcher left his tattooed victim, if not for the tangle of trees and shrubs choking the valley side.

Amid snarls of green, an old pedestrian footbridge still crosses the Run, as in Ness's day, but no one's been able to use it for fifty years. Back in the 1960s, African-American children from around Kinsman Road crossed the bridge to attend school in the primarily white neighborhood on the other side, until someone tore the planks out to keep them away. Instead of fixing the bridge, the city closed it off but let it stand, a silent reminder that racial segregation persists long after Harold Burton and his fellow Supreme Court justices voted to kill it in *Brown v. Board*.

In November 2014, the fatal shooting of twelve-year-old Tamir Rice by a Cleveland police officer exposed "stunning systemic police incompetence and indifference," a *Plain Dealer* columnist wrote. The city had never seriously investigated the officer's background before hiring him, and so did not know of evidence suggesting he lacked the temperament and discipline for duty. Ness's successors had fallen far short of the high standards he introduced when Cleveland's police force set a progressive and innovative standard for the nation.

While Ness's legacy lives on in the police academy he founded, his shift toward mobile patrol vehicles may have helped widen the distance between today's officers and the citizens they swear to protect and serve. In the 2000s, as the federal government began to stop funding community policing programs, Cleveland cops retreated from their neighborhood beats into squad cars, acting as occupying soldiers and not the social workers Ness envisioned.

Ness's work remains unfinished—as it always will. Determined to right some wrongs, he remained dangerously ignorant of others. But his dedication to the common good, his willingness to experiment and to challenge conventional wisdom, and his capacity for empathy serve as a model for any public servant. That Hollywood remembered him as a hard-boiled gunman is his blessing and curse, keeping his name alive while blurring the vision of policing he worked so hard to promote.

Ness's name should remind us of the rigorous standards he brought to law enforcement—professionalism, competence, honor, and decency—and a determination to make everyone safer by addressing the systemic root causes of crime. No one, not even Ness, could live up to the legend he left behind, but that image still points to a better, safer future.

In 1992, Peter Jedick suggested naming Cleveland's Justice Center after Ness. That never happened, but the mammoth structure on Ontario Street honors the former Safety Director with exhibits at the Cleveland Police Historical Society Museum. Images and artifacts document the reforms Ness brought to the department, while four death masks of the Butcher's victims look on from an opposite wall. Ness's legacy lies trapped between—his undeniable successes on the one hand, his failure to protect some of his city's most vulnerable on the other.

Under glass in the museum is Ness's service revolver, the nearly ninety-year-old weapon—after so much time in the Safety Director's file cabinet—looking brand-new. Perhaps this is the best memorial to what Eliot Ness stood for, and for everything he thought a police officer should be—the gun he rarely carried, which will never be fired again.

An Informal
Afterword

by Max Allan Collins

This book is not the first time A. Brad Schwartz and I have written about Eliot Ness. Our *Scarface and the Untouchable: Al Capone, Eliot Ness, and the Battle for Chicago* (2018) is an attempt to set the record straight on the real story of its title. But, as you've seen, there's more to the life of the famed (if often misrepresented and unfairly dismissed) Untouchable than bursting into breweries in a truck affixed with a massive steel bumper.

Collaborating with Brad wasn't my first experience writing about Al Capone's nemesis, either. My historical crime novel *True Detective* (1983) began an ongoing saga in which my fictional private eye Nathan Heller tackles the great unsolved crimes and mysteries of the twentieth century. As a fan of *The Untouchables* TV series since the third grade, I had read Ness's biographical book of that title (written with Fraley), and gathered anything I could find about the real man, haunting the local library. So, years later, when it came time to give my Chicago private eye a police contact, using Ness seemed an appropriate, fun idea.

The Heller novels did well enough for an editor to request a spin-off series about Ness—this was 1986, with Brian De Palma's *Untouchables* film in the works—and, thanks to Oscar

Fraley's *4 Against the Mob*, I was aware that Ness, post-Capone, had done important, exciting work in Cleveland. My Heller research associate, George Hagenauer, had relatives there and knew the city well. He suggested we do on-site digging, which took us to (among other places) the Western Reserve Historical Society, where we discovered the oversize, voluminous scrapbooks begun by Ness's mother and continued by him throughout his career. A significant find—and a chilling one—was the postcards the probable Mad Butcher of Kingsbury Run had sent to Ness, taunting and threatening him.

This research gave my four Cleveland books a special if ironic significance: they represented the first time—other than the 1959 two-part *Untouchables* TV pilot—that the actual cases of America's most famous real-life detective were the basis for fictionalized stories about him. *Butcher's Dozen* (1988) was the first book-length treatment of the Torso Killer case. Over the coming years, I became increasingly frustrated when my Ness research turned up in nonfiction books and in rival fictional works (including a graphic novel, a field I work in), without crediting the source. This is a peril that a writer of historical novels faces without recourse.

Ness continued to periodically turn up in Heller novels, with *Angel in Black* (2001) the prime example, as it explores the theory that the Kingsbury Run torso killings were connected to the famous Black Dahlia murder (we do not deal with that theory here). In addition, I wrote a graphic novel, *Scar of the Bat* (2000), which puts Ness and Capone in a Batman "Elseworlds" story.

Although the filmmakers left him out, Ness is a major player in my graphic novel *Road to Perdition* (1998). The success of the 2002 film version inspired me to write a one-man show, *Eliot Ness: An Untouchable Life*, mounted at the Des Moines Playhouse with my friend (now late friend) Michael Cornelison doing a remarkable job as Ness. During its several-week run, I shot a feature version (2005) for Iowa PBS; it's now on DVD, Blu-ray, and several streaming services. This was to be my final statement on Eliot Ness, the culmination of decades of interest and research.

By the time I met Brad Schwartz at a signing at Centuries & Sleuths bookstore in Forest Park, Illinois, the young *Dick Tracy* fan was well steeped in my work on that strip, but also the Heller novels and the four-book Ness-in-Cleveland spin-off series. He was smart and articulate (still is) and we became friends. I can't take much credit for his success, but I did encourage him to revise his college thesis about Orson Welles into an excellent book (*Broadcast Hysteria*), a thesis that had already spawned a PBS special.

Brad traveled from Michigan with his parents (he was still a high school student at the time) to see Mike Cornelison perform in *Untouchable Life*. He also came to Rock Island, Illinois, for the film version's premiere, and began to work on me about collaborating on a Ness biography. My response was, "Absolutely not." I'd said my final word on Ness through the play/feature.

Before I knew it, however, we had put together a book proposal. The project had developed into a dual biography of Capone and Ness, echoing a notion I'd had years before to do their story as a big, fat historical novel. The nonfiction proposal sold and, initially, Brad began work without me—I was busy getting a heart valve replaced.

A note now about our process. Some have assumed, because of Brad's credentials as a historian, that he does the research and I do the writing. No. While Brad has handled recent on-site research, I have done my share using the true-crime (Chicago-centric) library I have assembled in the creation of the Heller saga. On *Scarface and the Untouchable*, Brad wrote rough draft chapters on Ness, while I handled Capone. I did a final draft, but Brad helped polish my Capone chapters. For this book, Brad wrote first draft and I wrote final draft.

How did a second book on Ness come about, and whatever happened to that Capone character? Well, initially we intended to do a single book, that dual Capone-Ness biography. When I returned to the project after my surgery and recovery, the need for the book to focus on Chicago soon became apparent. We had 150,000 words of rough draft, ending with Capone's imprisonment, and knew our editor was looking for 100,000 total. Still, Brad and I felt the second half of Ness's life was at least as interesting as the first, and were hopeful that a Cleveland rest-of-the-story volume might follow.

As for Capone, we considered including his later years here—particularly his Alcatraz stay—but we already had a lengthy story to tell about Ness. Also, the two men had no contact, no interface, after their May 1932 meeting at Dearborn Station when Ness helped ship Capone off to the Atlanta pen.

In my introduction to *Scarface and the Untouchable*, I took on the writers whose supposedly nonfiction books had unfairly reduced and/or mischaracterized Eliot Ness's role in history. I was taken to task for naming names, achieving the rare distinction of generating several major reviews in which the introduction was panned and the book itself praised. While we want to restore Ness to his rightful position, we have presented his uniquely American story in warts-and-all fashion. Our hope has been to share with you the real man—heroic, upright, adventurous, and visionary but, like all real men, flawed.

And now I'll turn this over to my coauthor to thank the many people who have helped us in our efforts.

A Tip of
the Fedora

by A. Brad Schwartz

Peter Hubbard certainly got more than he bargained for back in 2015, when he picked up our proposal for what would become *Scarface and the Untouchable*. Our dedicated, enthusiastic, and thorough editor may bristle at the cliché, but it's never been more accurate—our initial proposal for a single volume covering Al Capone and Eliot Ness from cradle to grave has now spawned two books.

Peter recognized early on that Ness's second act deserved its own book and suggested as much while we still clung to the notion that we could fit this whole saga between two covers. Once we came to our senses and realized that the "battle for Chicago" had to stand alone, we made the difficult decision to set all of our Ness-post-Capone work aside, in the hope that Peter would like what we'd done enough to want that second volume. Fortunately, he did. So, our thanks must first go to Peter, for supporting us through this unexpectedly lengthy process and allowing us to tell this epic story in the way it wanted to be told.

Because most of the research for this book was done while we thought we were working on *Scarface and the Untouchable*, it's difficult to separate both projects for the purpose of thanking those who helped us along the way. This has truly been a single continuous process; no sooner had we corrected the galley proofs of the first volume than we moved right along to assembling the manuscript for the second, before going back to make a few key edits to the paperback edition of *Scarface and the Untouchable* in light of newly discovered information.

So while we designed this book to stand on its own, these acknowledgments necessarily cannot. This serves essentially as an update to the afterword I wrote for *Scarface and the Untouchable*, singling out those people who contributed most to this part of our chronicle without intending to ignore anyone who helped us cover the other portions of this story. None of those who shared their time, knowledge, and expertise have been forgotten; we're grateful to each and every one of them. But the conclusions drawn from this research are necessarily our own, and we take full responsibility for them—as well as any errors that may have slipped through.

Rebecca McFarland was one of the very first people I contacted even before this project went from an idea to an actual job. More than two decades after arranging Ness's funeral, she remains as knowledgeable and dedicated to preserving the memory of Cleveland's Untouchable as ever. From the very beginning, she generously shared her research and answered numerous questions, even after our shared desire to shed new light on Ness's Cleveland career got unavoidably delayed. I hope the result is worth the wait.

In Coudersport, Paul Heimel graciously shared the research he collected writing the first biography of Ness—including, crucially, interviews with people no longer with us. Since the release of *Scarface and the Untouchable*, Paul has advocated for our work by making us a featured part of Coudersport's annual "Eliot Ness Fest," taking place every third weekend in July since 2018. Attending the fest for the past two years and counting, I've enjoyed getting to know the people who joined forces with Paul to make this such a fun event—among them William Brennan, Jared

Empson, Steve Green, Paul Herzig, Bill Pekarski, Deb Plummer, Jennifer Rossman, Sarah Schwab, John and Olga Snyder, and Curt Weinhold.

John Rigas has lent his support to the Eliot Ness Fest by letting us use his Coudersport Theatre as a venue for educational and entertainment programming exploring every aspect of the Untouchable's life. Before that, he kindly sat for an interview to share his memories of watching Ness transform from a forgotten man into a television icon. Natalie Phelps also welcomed me into her home outside Coudersport to offer her uniquely personal perspective on her father's old business partner over a delicious home-cooked meal; her siblings, Joe Jr. and Linda Phelps, provided similar insight through phone interviews.

During my first trip to Coudersport in November 2016, David Castano and Diane Caudell arranged a valuable visit to the Potter County Historical Society, and Doug Bretz granted access to his private collection of Ness-related documents. Chandra Livingston and Brian Welsh offered a tour of the Hotel Crittenden, which has recently been renovated and is now much more inviting than in Ness and Fraley's day.

That first visit largely came about thanks to help from Matthew Pearl, whose deeply researched *Vanity Fair* article on the writing of *The Untouchables* broke new ground in understanding Ness and Fraley's collaboration. Beyond opening doors in Coudersport, Matthew never hesitated to share his own research and became a vocal advocate for *Scarface and the Untouchable* after its publication.

James Jessen Badal remains the premier expert on the Cleveland torso murders, with his three books on the subject—especially *In the Wake of the Butcher,* revised and expanded in 2014—still the go-to works for anyone wanting to learn more about these crimes. We know more about Ness's secret Butcher suspect than he ever wanted us to know—from Frank Sweeney's personal history to the probable location of his murder laboratory—thanks largely to Jim's thorough research, and he kindly answered further questions and shared additional insight over a memorable dinner with me and Rebecca in Tremont.

Our account of Sweeney's secret interrogation benefited greatly from documents shared by historian Ken Alder at Northwestern University, the authority on the lie detector and its mismatched inventors. John Carson, from whom I learned the craft of writing history at the University of Michigan, made the essential introduction.

In a sense, the research for this book began before I was even born, when my coauthor found Ness's scrapbooks at the Western Reserve Historical Society in Cleveland. I've returned many times since, both to study these essential primary sources and explore other related collections, benefitting each time from the help and counsel of the library's archivists and staff, including Ann Sindelar and Chad Malkamaki.

Multiple visits were also made to the Cleveland Police Historical Society Museum, where Emily Vernon helped me access archives containing key primary sources. Special thanks go to Rebecca (again) and Commander Robert Cermak for opening those important doors, and Mazie Adams, now executive director of the society, for essential help late in our process. Elsewhere in Cleveland, important research was made possible by the librarians and staff of the Public Administration Library in City Hall and the Cleveland Public Library, where Brian Meggitt continues to go above and beyond the call of duty in supplying photographs. At the Cleveland State University Library, Lynn Bycko, Donna Stewart, Vern Morrison, and William Barrow helped us access the clippings file and photo archives of the *Cleveland Press*.

The Federal Bureau of Investigation responded to numerous Freedom of Information Act requests in a timely and thorough manner, and their online "Vault" offers a wealth of information on the lives of everyone from Eliot Ness to Desi Arnaz. The Bureau of Alcohol, Tobacco, Firearms, and Explosives shared documents gathered by former staff historian Barbara Osteika, covering the careers of Ness and other Untouchables. Hilary Martinson, who followed the reverse of Ness's path from federal law enforcement to Coudersport, kindly shared insight into the latter during one of my many visits to ATF headquarters.

Vanya Scott welcomed me to the archives of the National Law Enforcement Museum years before it opened to the public, allowing me to access a collection of material shedding key light on Ness's later life and mayoral run. Also in our nation's capital, Melissa Lindberg and the archivists at American University guided me on a productive search through the papers of Arnold Sagalyn.

Like its predecessor, this book depended upon the work done by the National Archives and Records Administration. We're grateful to the archivists and staff at the NARA branches in Chicago and College Park, and to the National Personnel Records Center in St. Louis. Special thanks go to Douglas Bicknese, Director of Archival Operations at NARA Chicago, for sharing our commitment to preserving the record of Ness's career.

Essential research was conducted at the Library of Congress in Washington, D.C.; the Bancroft Library at the University of California, Berkeley; the Lilly Library at Indiana University in Bloomington; the University of Chicago Archives; and the Harold Washington Library Center of the Chicago Public Library. Additional resources were provided by the University of Michigan Library, the Michigan State University Library, the Capital Area District Library, and the Princeton University Library. The librarians, archivists, and staff at each institution are a credit to the profession and a pleasure to work with.

My coauthor and I had the privilege of visiting the Mob Museum in Las Vegas, Nevada, both for research and to talk about our work on the ninetieth anniversary of the St. Valentine's Day Massacre. Our thanks go out to Jonathan Ullman, Geoff Schumacher, Ashley Erickson, and Carolyn Fisher, as well as former Mayor Oscar Goodman for bringing the museum to Vegas in the first place. Lora Kalkman, special assistant to Mayor Carolyn Goodman, made each visit possible.

At Princeton University, Tera Hunter allowed me to deepen my understanding of Ness's work in Cleveland and with the Social Protection Division by exploring the subject in a term paper, and Jeremy Schneider saved us from embarrassment by offering a key piece of information about the history of serial killing. Julian

Zelizer, Martha Sandweiss, and Kevin Kruse remain supportive and encouraging mentors who offer a model for how historians can engage with the public.

While working with Peter, we've been fortunate to have the support and assistance of the whole HarperCollins team—including Liate Stehlik, Nick Amphlett, Christina Joell, Libby Collins, Maureen Cole, Kaitlin Harri, and Molly Gendell. William Ruoto did a beautiful job designing *Scarface and the Untouchable* after that book's acknowledgments had been written, which is why we're thanking him here, and Elina Cohen brought a wonderfully creepy vibe to this volume with her equally impressive design.

Ross Harris of the Stuart Krichevsky Literary Agency guided, protected, and advocated for this project with his trademark sagacity and determination. We're lucky to have Ross, Stuart Krichevsky, and the team at SKLA—especially Hannah Schwartz and Aemilia Phillips—looking out for us. Jason Richman at United Talent Agency continues to be a great friend to our work, and his assistant, Nora Henrie, kept things running smoothly.

I'll join my coauthor in extending special thanks to his wife, Barbara Collins, for editorial assistance on yet another massive manuscript, and to Max's friend and literary agent, Dominick Abel.

One of the unexpected privileges of this project has been building a friendship with Scott Leeson Sroka, the grandson of Untouchable Joe Leeson, and his family—especially Pamela, Ken, Marla, and Eliot. I am continually inspired and encouraged by Scott's passion for history and commitment to public service and feel honored to be accepted as an honorary member of the Leeson clan. A special tip of the hat goes out to Scott's mother, Pamela, for sharing stories and materials from her and her mother's attempts to challenge the way Hollywood misrepresented Ness and Leeson's work—an effort I hope our books have brought closer to completion.

Dennis and Nancy Austin Schwartz also got far more than they bargained for when they introduced their son first to *Dick Tracy* and later *The Untouchables*. They made the partnership at the center of this project a reality, by shuttling my teenage self literally around the country—from Forest Park, Illinois, to the San Diego Comic Con—so I could get to know my favorite author. And they never stopped supporting my desire to know all there is to know about Eliot Ness, beginning with our many trips to Cleveland back when I hadn't yet graduated from high school. They have been with this project every step of the way—joining me in archives and on interviews, reading the earliest drafts and the final manuscript—and allowed Ness to live under their roof far longer than most parents could stand. We couldn't have done it without them.

ABBREVIATIONS

ABBREVIATION	COMPLETE CITATION
ABS	A. Brad Schwartz (Personal Collection)
ASP	Arnold Sagalyn Papers, American University, Washington, DC
BCE	*Buffalo Courier-Express*
CCP	*Cleveland Call and Post*
CDN	*Chicago Daily News*
CEA	*Chicago Evening American* (aka *Chicago's American*)
CG	*Cleveland Gazette*
CHE	*Chicago Herald Examiner*
CN	*Cleveland News*
CP	*Cleveland Press*
CPC	*Cleveland Press* Collection, Cleveland State University, Cleveland, OH
CPD	*Cleveland Plain Dealer*
CPHS	Cleveland Police Historical Society Archives, Cleveland, OH
CST	*Chicago Sun-Times*
CT	*Chicago Tribune*
DMM	David Mamet manuscripts, Lilly Library Manuscripts Collection, Indiana University, Bloomington
ENC	Eliot Ness Clippings from Cleveland Newspapers, 1935–1973; Cleveland Public Library, Cleveland, OH
ENPS	Eliot Ness Papers and Scrapbooks, Western Reserve Historical Society, Cleveland, OH

FBI-DA   Federal Bureau of Investigation file on Desi Arnaz, "FBI Records: The Vault," https://vault.fbi.gov/Desi%20Arnaz (accessed February 22, 2017)

FBI-EN   Federal Bureau of Investigation File on Eliot Ness, "FBI Records: The Vault," https://vault.fbi.gov/Eliot%20Ness (accessed August 12, 2015)

FBI-ENA   Federal Bureau of Investigation Applicant File on Eliot Ness, obtained by ABS through a Freedom of Information Act request, February 3, 2015

FBI-FES   Federal Bureau of Investigation file on Francis Edward Sweeney, obtained by ABS through a Freedom of Information Act request, March 25, 2016

HBP   Harold Hitz Burton Papers, Manuscript Division, Library of Congress, Washington, DC

HHB-EBP   Harold H. Burton–Edward Blythin Papers (MS 3828), Western Reserve Historical Society, Cleveland, OH

KDB   Karl & Doug Bretz (Personal Collection)

LAT   *Los Angeles Times*

MMvDP   Case 60 C 84 (Mafalda Maritote, Mae Capone, and Albert Capone vs. Desilu Productions, CBS, and Westinghouse Electric Corporation); Civil Action Case Files; Record Group 21 (Records of the U.S. District Court, Northern District of Illinois, Chicago); National Archives and Records Administration, Chicago, IL

Ness MS.   Untitled manuscript by Eliot Ness, Roll 1, Folder 2, Eliot Ness Papers and Scrapbooks, Western Reserve Historical Society, Cleveland, OH

NLEM   Collection of the National Law Enforcement Museum, Washington, DC

NYT   *New York Times*

OPF   Official Personnel Folder, National Personnel Records Center, St. Louis, MO

OPF/ATF   Official Personnel Folders from the National Personnel Records Center (St. Louis), held by the Bureau of Alcohol, Tobacco, Firearms and Explosives, Washington, DC

PAL   Public Administration Library, Cleveland, OH

PCHS   Potter County Historical Society, Coudersport, PA

PWH   Paul W. Heimel (Personal Collection)

RM   Rebecca McFarland (Personal Collection)

SPD   Records of the Office of Community War Services, Social Protection Division General Records, 1941–1946; Record Group 215, National Archives and Records Administration, College Park, MD

UCB   Bancroft Library, University of California at Berkeley

WP   *Washington Post*

WRHS   Western Reserve Historical Society, Cleveland, OH

SOURCE NOTES

Epigraph

Chandler, *Simple Art of Murder*, p. 18 ("If there were . . .").

Prologue: Untouchable

CPD, September 19, 1934 ("We did our . . ."). Ness MS., pp. 1–22, in ENPS, Roll 1, Folder 2. Oscar Fraley to Eliot Ness, May 6, 1956, KDB. Application for Letters of Administration, June 11, 1957, PCHS. Statement of Debts and Deductions, June 17, 1957, PCHS. Ness and Fraley, *The Untouchables*, pp. 5–7, 47–65, 70–74, 80–83, 88–95, 105–106, 111–117, 124–125, 140–147, 149, 163–165, 168–178, 185–186, 189–194, 200–209, 220–228, 232–240, 249–253, 255–256, and passim. *Potter Enterprise*, March 22, 1961; November 24, 1971. Fraley, *4 Against the Mob*, pp. 7–10, 128–139, and passim. Oscar Fraley, "The Real Eliot Ness," *Coronet*, July 1961, pp. 26–30 (28, "I've seen too . . . ," "The hell with . . ."; 30, "an attempt to . . ."). "Ockie's Jackpot," *Newsweek*, January 14, 1963, pp. 67–68. Scott Eyman, "An Oscar for Elliot [*sic*] Ness," *Sunshine* (*Fort Lauderdale News*), July 21, 1985, pp. 10, 12, 26. *Star-Gazette*, June 22, 1987, RM. Nickel, *Torso*, pp. 198–204. Fred McGunagle, "Postcard from the Mad Butcher," n.p., March 29, 1989, PWH. Oscar Fraley, interviewed in "Eliot Ness," *Unsolved Mysteries*, directed by Mike Mathis, February 20, 1991, in *Unsolved Mysteries: Strange Legends*, disc 1 (Burbank, CA: Cosgrove/Meurer Productions, 2004), DVD. Jacoby, *Sandusky's Finest*, p. 121. Bergreen, *Capone*, p. 612. *News-Press*, December 7, 1994, RM. Recorded recollections of William Ayers, n.d., PWH. "Bill Ayers," n.d., PWH. "Virginia Kallenborn interview," March 25, 2000, PWH. Heimel, *Eliot Ness*, pp. 264–265, 274. Fred Anderson and Lewis Wilkinson, interviewed in "Eliot Ness," *The Real Untouchables*, written and directed by John Fothergill (Thousand Oaks, CA: Goldhil DVD, 2001), DVD. Frankfurt, *On Bullshit*, pp. 55–56, and passim. "Memory Problems Linked to Cardiovascular Disease," Patient Education Center, https://web.archive.org/web/20170307043603/http://www.patienteducationcenter.org/articles/memory-problems-linked-cardiovascular-disease/ (accessed May 23, 2018). ABS visit to Coudersport, Pennsylvania, November 14–15, 2016. Natalie Phelps, personal interview with ABS, November 15, 2016. John Rigas, personal interview with ABS, November 15, 2016. Joe Phelps Jr., telephone interview with ABS, November 22, 2016. Bardsley, *American Sweeney Todd*, pp. 226–231. Matthew Pearl, "Behind *The Untouchables*: The Making of the Memoir That Reclaimed a Prohibition Era Legend," *Vanity Fair*, December 27, 2017, https://www.vanityfair.com/hollywood/2017/12/the-untouchables -the-making-of-the-memoir-prohibition-era-legend (accessed December 27, 2017). Robert Haru Fisher, "PA's Route 6: Driving Through 'God's Country,'" Frommer's, https://www.frommers.com/trip-ideas/cultural-immersion /pas-route-6-driving-through-gods-country (accessed May 25, 2018). Collins and Schwartz, *Scarface and the Untouchable*, pp. 9–10, 37, 67, 126–134, 162–164, 235–239, 323–324, 352–354, 356–365, 394–395, 420–421 (421, "nemesis"), 473–474, 498–501, 531–532, and passim.

Chapter One: The Dark City

NESS BACKGROUND: Paul Ward, "The Man Who Got Al Capone," *Baltimore Sun Magazine*, March 20, 1932, pp. 7, 9. CEA, c. September 1932, in ENPS, Roll 1, Scrapbook 1, p. 49. CPD, January 23, 1936. *Des Moines Sunday Register*, October 29, 1961 ("He stood just . . ."). Fraley, "Real Eliot Ness," p. 28 ("honesty amounted to . . ."). Powers, *Secrecy and Power*, pp. 223–226. Burrough, *Public Enemies*, pp. 411–412, 436, 518–519, 546. Purvis and Tresniowski, *The Vendetta*, pp. 279–284. Collins and Schwartz, *Scarface and the Untouchable*, pp. 29–43, 61–71, 96–105, 121–135, 155–172, 200–204, 235–239, 259–265, 311–314, 317–329, 349–365, 389–395, 412–415, 417–421, 441–443, 463–469, 473–477, 483–496, 498–501, 508–524, 583, and passim.

NESS IN THE ATU: Transfer Order, March 10, 1934; Arthur J. Mellott to Eliot Ness, August 7, 1934; Service Record Card, n.d., both in Eliot Ness OPF. Eliot Ness to W. Bruce Murray, April 4, 1934 ("Our Unit has . . ."); "Liquor Office Lost to Cincinnati," n.p., n.d.; "Alcohol Tax Unit to Be Abolished," n.p., n.d., all in ENPS, Roll 1, Scrapbook 1. Messick, *Silent Syndicate*, pp. 93–125. Messick, *Secret File*, pp. 26–27. Ness and Fraley, *The Untouchables*, p. 255 ("Moonshine Mountains," "Those mountain men . . . ," "revenooer"). Kellner, *Moonshine*, pp. 119–125, 139–140 (139, "a backwoods industry . . ."). Lender and Martin, *Drinking in America*, pp. 172–173. Heimel, *Eliot Ness*, pp. 143–144. Okrent, *Last Call*, pp. 361–362.

CLEVELAND: CP, December 14, 1935 ("The Dark City"). K. R. McIntire, Memorandum for the Director "Re: Police Corruption in CLEVELAND, OHIO," May 12, 1936, in FBI-EN. Condon, *Cleveland*, pp. 2–4,

192. Porter, *Cleveland*, pp. 5–8, 13, 17–32, 52–53, 72–75, 85–87. Nickel, *Torso*, pp. 5, 12–13, 23–25 (23, "safe," "The fix was . . ."). Rose, *Cleveland*, pp. 872–875, 915, 917–918, 966–967. Miller and Wheeler, *Cleveland*, pp. 113–116, 121–123, 129–131 (129, "city within a . . ."), 134–138, 142. Jones, *Men of Tomorrow*, pp. 38–39. Ricca, *Super Boys*, pp. 3–7, 90–92, 298–306. Badal, *In the Wake*, pp. 6–7.

NESS IN CLEVELAND: CPD, September 19, 1934 ("I am just finding . . ."). "Raids Push Bootleg Prices Up," n.p., October 29, 1934; "$200,000 Still Uncovered in 'Flats' Plant," n.p., n.d.; "Illegal Liquor Flow Believed Halted by Raid," n.p., n.d.; "Says Liquor Violations Are Waning," n.p., n.d.; "U.S.-Ohio Agents Nab 2 Big Stills," n.p., September 12, 1934 [?]; "Blackstone Club Raided and Stripped," n.p., November 16, 1934; "New Raids Due in State War on 'Cut' Liquor," n.p., n.d.; "Federal Agents Wipe Out Club in Tax Action," n.p., n.d. ("They took not . . ."); "Home Liquor Making May Go to High Court," n.p., n.d. ("The federal laws . . ."), all in ENPS, Roll 1, Scrapbook 1. CN, February 4, 1937, in ENPS, Roll 1, Scrapbook 5, p. 136 ("I told him . . ."). CN, May 15, 1941, in ENPS, Roll 3, Scrapbook 11, p. 93. Porter, *Cleveland*, pp. 96, 101–103. Nickel, *Torso*, pp. 5–6. Margaret B. Payton to RM, August 16, 1989, RM. Marilyn Bardsley, "After Chicago," *Eliot Ness: The Man Behind the Myth*, courtTV Crime Library, http://www.crimelibrary.com/gangsters_outlaws/cops_others/ness/4.html (accessed March 11, 2006). Heimel, *Eliot Ness*, p. 145. Record for Robert West Chamberlin, *Ohio, Births and Christenings Index, 1774–1973* (Provo, UT: Ancestry.com Operations, Inc., 2011). RM to ABS, personal email, July 23, 2015. Collins and Schwartz, *Scarface and the Untouchable*, pp. 66–67, 101–102.

EMIL FRONEK: CPD, August 29, 1938 ("He said he . . . ," "All I could . . ."). *Evening Star*, August 29, 1938. *Richmond Times-Dispatch*, August 29, 1938. CHE, n.d., in ENPS, Roll 2, Scrapbook 8, p. 59; ("That's funny . . . ," "a private hospital"). Nickel, *Torso*, pp. 129–130. Badal, *In the Wake*, pp. 29, 236–237, 239–242.

LADY OF THE LAKE: CPD, September 6, 1934. CP, September 7–8, 1934 (September 8, "I'm sure it . . . ," "No surgeon ever . . . ," "so close to . . ."). Nickel, *Torso*, pp. 7–9 (8, "the Lady of . . ."). Badal, *In the Wake*, pp. 22–28.

Chapter Two: An Impossible Mission

KINGSBURY RUN: John T. Flynn, "The Betrayal of Cleveland," *Harper's Magazine*, January 1934, pp. 143–150. CP, September 11, 1936. S. R. Gerber, as told to Oscar A. Bergman and Joseph M. Gambatese, "Mystery of

Source Notes

Cleveland's Headless Cadavers," *True Detective Mysteries*, February 1938, pp. 30–31. William Ritt, "The Head Hunter of Kingsbury Run," in Bayer, *Cleveland Murders*, p. 219. Martin, *Butcher's Dozen*, pp. 55–56. Condon, *Cleveland*, pp. 177, 181–201. Porter, *Cleveland*, pp. 27–31. CPD, January 8, 1989 ("The Run's ugliness . . ."). Nickel, *Torso*, pp. 12–15. Rose, *Cleveland*, pp. 300–301, 318–319. Van Tassel and Grabowski, *Encyclopedia of Cleveland History*, pp. 611, 915–917 (915, "Garden City"). Chernow, *Titan*, pp. 77–79, 101. Marshall, *Shaker Heights*, pp. 44–99. Badal, *In The Wake*, pp. 6–7, 29.

JACKASS HILL MURDERS: CPD, September 24, 1935. William E. Rebout, "Police Reopen Probe of Two Weird Killings," n.p., n.d. [probably CP, May 27, 1936], in ENPS, Roll 1, Scrapbook 2, p. 84 ("to get him . . ."). Gerber, Bergman, and Gambatese, "Mystery of Cleveland's," pp. 30–32. Ritt, "Head Hunter," in Bayer, *Cleveland Murders*, pp. 220–221. Martin, *Butcher's Dozen*, pp. 56–61 (56, "the jugular vein . . ."). Nickel, *Torso*, pp. 14–21 (15, "a dead man . . ."), 216. Bellamy, *Maniac in the Bushes*, pp. 45–48 (48, "I've got a . . ."). Badal, *In the Wake*, pp. 30–48 (35, "That's odd . . ."). James, *Popular Crime*, pp. 168–169, 172. Brady, *Gates of Janus*, p. 190.

NESS'S ATU WORK: "'Grapevine Spreads Word of Federal Agents' Raid Thruout [*sic*] Underworld," n.p., n.d. ("the place looked . . ."); *Lorain Journal*, December 17, 1934; *Akron Times-Press*, December 28, 1934; *Akron Beacon Journal*, December 29, 1934; CPD, December 29, 1934; "75 Witnesses to Face Jury in Cleveland," n.p., n.d.; *Akron Beacon Journal*, December 31, 1934; "Rum Plot Arrests Predicted," n.p., n.d.; *Akron Times-Press*, December 29, 1934; "Held for Reboiling Radiator Alcohol," n.p., n.d.; CN, January 8, 1935; CN, January 10, 1935; CPD, March 16, 1935; *Akron Beacon Journal*, June 26, 1935; CN, July 10, 1935; CPD, July 13, 1935 ("a miniature liquor . . ."); *Akron Times-Press*, July 13, 1935; CPD, September 2, 1935 ("strange noises," "funny smells"); CPD, January 13, 1936 ("a miniature liquor . . ."), all in ENPS, Roll 1, Scrapbook 1. CPD, August 29, 1935; January 9, 1972 ("a real eagle eye"). *Milwaukee Journal*, April 19, 1936, in ENPS, Roll 1, Scrapbook 2. Mark J. Price, "Summit Felt Ness' Touch," *Beacon Journal*, April 7, 2003, http://web.archive.org/web/20030816133031/http://www.ohio.com/mld/beaconjournal/2003/04/07/news/local/5576347.htm (accessed November 22, 2016). Collins and Schwartz, *Scarface and the Untouchable*, pp. 125–126.

ZANESVILLE RAID AND CLEVELAND SYNDICATE: CP, March 12, 1935; CP, March 12, 1935; CP, March 13, 1935 ("more widespread than . . ."); *Akron Beacon Journal*, March 13, 1935; CN, March 13, 1935; CP, March 13, 1935; *Youngstown Telegram*, June 27, 1935 ("the largest ever . . ."); CN, July 10, 1935; "U. S. Men Seize $75,000 Still, Arrest Two Here, n.p.," July 10, 1935 ("the biggest 'still' . . ."); CN, August 22, 1935; CP, August 22, 1935; CP, August 22, 1935, all in ENPS, Roll 1, Scrapbook 1. CPD, January 19, 1936 ("I believe you're . . . ," "I thought I . . . ," "just flunkies"). Messick, *Silent Syndicate*, pp. 93–140. Neff, *Mobbed Up*, pp. 23–24. Porrello, *Rise and Fall of the Cleveland Mafia*, pp. 124–134. Mappen, *Prohibition Gangsters*, pp. 71–72.

NESS'S PROBLEMS WITH ATU: CDT, October 15, 1934, in Federal Bureau of Investigation File on Al Capone, "FBI Records: The Vault," https://vault.fbi.gov/Al%20Capone (accessed August 12, 2015). "U. S. to Increase Ohio Liquor Force," n.p., n.d.; "Fail in Horse Sense; 7 Dry Agents Payless," n.p., n.d.; CN, January 8, 1935; CN, January 15, 1935; CN, February 27, 1935 ("special dispensation"), all in ENPS, Roll 1, Scrapbook 1. CP, December 11, 1935, in ENPS, Roll 1, Scrapbook 2, p. 6. CPD, December 12, 1935, in ENPS, Roll 1, Scrapbook 2, p. 9. CPD, December 12, 1935; November 3, 1966; October 16, 1976. "Ness, Capone's Nemesis, Takes U. S. Job Test," n.p., n.d.; "Last of 'Untouchables' Retires After 47 Years," n.p., April 9, 1972, both in "Newspaper Clippings (photocopies) circa 1930–1970" folder, DMM. *Dallas Morning News*, April 9, 1972. Perry, *Eliot Ness*, pp. 116–117.

DAVIS AND LAVELLE: CN, July 2, 1935, in ENPS, Roll 1, Scrapbook 1 ("a speedboat liquor . . ."). CP, July 22, 1935. CP, December 21, 1935, in ENPS, Roll 2, Scrapbook 2, p. 17. CPD, October 21, 1937, in ENPS, Roll 2, Scrapbook 6, p. 63. William Miller, "Cleveland's Boy Scout and the Racket Patrol," *True*, May 1939, pp. 39–40, in box 374, folder 8, HBP. Messick, *Silent Syndicate*, pp. 136–137. Porter, *Cleveland*, pp. 87–88 (87, "long mysterious trips"), 96–97. Nickel, *Torso*, p. 25. Miller and Wheeler, *Cleveland*, p. 142. Perry, *Eliot Ness*, p. 121.

BURTON: CPD, October 29, 1935; November 3, 1935. CN, October 30, 1935. CN, November 6, 1935; "Burton, Boston Born, Winner in Cleveland," n.p., n.d.; *Boston Globe*, November 5 [?], 1935, all in box 373, folder 12, HBP. "Statement of Harold H. Burton," November 11, 1935, in box 362, folder 7, HBP. K. R. McIntire, Memorandum for the Director "Re: Police Corruption in CLEVELAND, OHIO," May 12, 1936, in FBI-EN ("It is absolutely . . ."). Ralph J. Donaldson, "Old Parties' Power Fades in Cuyahoga," CPD [?], November 27, 1936 [?], in ENPS, Roll 1, Scrapbook 5, p. 88. Stanley High, "Cleveland Versus the Crooks," *Current History*, October 1938, p. 22. "Background Notes on Harold Hitz Burton," October 1945; "From Bowdoin Alumnus, November 1945, issue" ("rock-ribbed New England . . ."); Harry L. Lodge, "The Governmental Services of Harold H. Burton" (thesis, Geneva College,

1948); "A Biography of Justice Harold Hitz Burton," n.d., all in box 372, folder 8, HBP. Condon, *Cleveland*, p. 231. Porter, *Cleveland*, pp. 109–111. Rose, *Cleveland*, p. 923. Kluger, *Simple Justice*, pp. 241–242, 611–613, 660–661.

CHOOSING SAFETY DIRECTOR: Avery, *History of Cleveland*, pp. 377–378. CPD, November 20–21, 1935; December 11, 1935 (December 11, "who this guy . . . ," "Ness is a . . ."). CPD, December 7, 1935, in ENPS, Roll 1, Scrapbook 1 ("I will accept . . ."). CP, December 8, 1935; CPD, December 8, 1935, both in ENPS, Roll 1, Scrapbook 2, p. 1. CN, December 14, 1935; CP, December 14, 1935, both in ENPS, Roll 1, Scrapbook 2, p. 13. CDN, November 30, 1937, "Newspaper clippings (photocopies) circa. 1930–1970" folder, DMM. Miller, "Cleveland's Boy Scout," p. 40. CP, July 1, 1939, in ENPS, Roll 2, Scrapbook 7, p. 15. CPD, September 12, 1939, in ENPS, Roll 2, Scrapbook 7, p. 47 ("quite cynical about . . . ," "a revelation"). Delo E. Mook to Bascom Johnson, July 14, 1941, in Eliot Ness OPF. Fraley, *4 Against the Mob*, pp. 18–20. Porter, *Cleveland*, pp. 96–97 ("Ness would be . . ."). Neff, *Mobbed Up*, p. 21. Potter, *War on Crime*, p. 123. Sagalyn, *A Promise Fulfilled*, p. 45 ("an impossible mission").

NESS CHOSEN, SWORN IN: CPD, December 8, 1935 ("inside track"), in ENPS, Roll 1, Scrapbook 2, p. 1. CN, December 11, 1935, in ENPS, Roll 1, Scrapbook 2, p. 2. CN, December 11, 1935, in ENPS, Roll 2, Scrapbook 2, p. 3. CP, December 11, 1935, in ENPS, Roll 1, Scrapbook 2, p. 6 ("get a look"). CPD, December 12, 1935 ("conservative as possible," "After that I . . ."). CN, December 14, 1935, in ENPS, Roll 1, Scrapbook 2, p. 13.

PRESS, POLITICOS, POLICE REACT: CN, December 11, 1935, in ENPS, Roll 1, Scrapbook 2, p. 4. CP, December 11, 1935, in ENPS, Roll 1, Scrapbook 2, p. 6. CPD, December 12, 1935, in ENPS, in Roll 1, Scrapbook 2, p. 9 ("a scientific policeman . . ."). CPD, December 12, 1935 ("Policemen have seen . . ."). CN, December 12, 1935, in ENPS, Roll 1, Scrapbook 2, p. 10. *Detroit Free Press*, December 12, 1935. CP, December 14, 1935, in ENPS, Roll 1, Scrapbook 2, p. 13. Miller, "Cleveland's Boy Scout," p. 40. Condon, *Cleveland*, pp. 231, 237. Porter, *Cleveland*, pp. 96–98 (97, "a real bombshell," "To say it . . ."). Neff, *Mobbed Up*, p. 21.

MATOWITZ: CPD, December 12, 1935. CN, December 12, 1935, in ENPS, Roll 1, Scrapbook 2, p. 10. CP, December 12, 1935, in ENPS, Roll 1, Scrapbook 2, p. 7 ("I found Mr. . . ."). CPD, December 15, 1935, in ENPS, Roll 1, Scrapbook 2, p. 14. CPD, November 28, 1937, in ENPS, Roll 2, Scrapbook 6, p. 116. CP, April 11, 1940, in ENPS, Roll 2, Scrapbook 7, p. 112 ("a fist like . . ."). Porter, *Cleveland*, pp. 87, 96–97 ("inside chief," "outside chief").

Chapter Three: Showdown

EDNA / NESS'S SECOND DAY: CP, December 11, 1935, in ENPS, Roll 1, Scrapbook 2, p. 6 (YOUNG AND SINGLE). CPD, December 14, 1935 ("That was a . . ."). CN, December 14, 1935 ("I'm certainly not . . ."); CP, December 14, 1935, both in ENPS, Roll 1, Scrapbook 2, p. 13. Nickel, *Torso*, p. 46. Heimel, *Eliot Ness*, p. 155.

POLICE CORRUPTION AND INCOMPETENCE: Elliot H. [*sic*] Ness, "Public Safety and the Three E's: Enforcement—Engineering—Education," *Clevelander*, March 1938, p. 21, in ENPS, Roll 2, Scrapbook 10, p. 136 ("A traffic officer . . ."). CPD, n.d., in ENPS, Roll 1, Scrapbook 2, p. 18. CP, December 19, 1935, in ENPS, Roll 1, Scrapbook 2, p. 17. CPD, January 1, 1936, in ENPS, Roll 1, Scrapbook 2, p. 19. CPD, December 25, 1935, in ENPS, Roll 1, Scrapbook 2, p. 24. CPD, February 1, 1936. *Baltimore Sun*, May 17, 1936, in ENPS, Roll 1, Scrapbook 2, p. 80. CPD, August 5, 1937, ENC ("clean the enemy . . ."). Condon, *Cleveland*, p. 232.

NESS BEGINS CLEANUP: CPD, December 18, 1935, in ENPS, Roll 1, Scrapbook 2, p. 16 ("distinguished service of . . . ," "Other officers testified . . ."). CN, December 17, 1935, in ENPS, Roll 1, Scrapbook 2, p. 15. CN, December 13, 1935, in ENPS, Roll 1, Scrapbook 2, p. 10. CPD, December 18, 1935; CP, December 19, 1935 ("a troubled gaze," "It's getting so . . ."), both in ENPS, Roll 1, Scrapbook 2, p. 17. CP, December 23, 1935, in ENPS, Roll 1, Scrapbook 2, p. 18 ("highest technical intelligence"). CPD, December 24, 1935, in ENPS, Roll 1, Scrapbook 2, p. 23 ("men who have . . ."). CPD, December 25, 1935, in ENPS, Roll 1, Scrapbook 2, p. 24. CN, June 14, 1939, in ENPS, Roll 2, Scrapbook 7, p. 9 ("fair-haired boy").

FLYNN / SEVEN-POINT PROGRAM: CPD, December 29, 1935, in ENPS, Roll 1, Scrapbook 2, p. 21 ("police the police . . ."). CN, n.d.; CPD, January 1, 1936 ("executive assistant"), both in ENPS, Roll 1, Scrapbook 2, p. 19. CPD, January 10–11, 1936. *Kansas City Star*, April 19, 1936, in ENPS, Roll 1, Scrapbook 2, p. 68. CPD, July 31, 1936, in ENPS, Roll 1, Scrapbook 5, p. 24. CPD, August 5, 1936, in ENPS, Roll 1, Scrapbook 5, p. 28. CPD, August 5, 1936, in ENPS, Roll 1, Scrapbook 5, p. 29. CPD, n.d.; untitled editorial, n.p., n.d., both in ENPS, Roll 1, Scrapbook 5, p. 113. CPD, August 7, 1939, in ENPS, Roll 2, Scrapbook 7, p. 42.

ILLEGAL GAMBLING IN CLEVELAND: *Pittsburgh Press*, September 11, 1931 ("Honest John"). CPD, January 11, 1936, in ENPS, Roll 1, Scrapbook

2, p. 28. CPD, January 11, 1936 ("home rule policy"). CP, April 10, 1936, in ENPS, Roll 1, Scrapbook 2, p. 64. K. R. McIntire, Memorandum for the Director "Re: Police Corruption in CLEVELAND, OHIO," May 12, 1936, in FBI-EN. Brian Albrecht, "Whatever Happened to the Gambling Palaces of the Great Depression?" CPD magazine, November 27, 1977, pp. 6, 10, 12 ("Take care of . . . ," "a clean-cut place," "You never had . . ."). Messick, *Silent Syndicate*, pp. 78–79, 90–92, 137–138. Porrello, *Rise and Fall*, p. 134. Burrough, *Public Enemies*, pp. 431–434, 441, 494.

CULLITAN PLANS RAIDS / THOMAS CLUB RAID: CP, January 11, 1936 ("big shots," "a small arsenal"). CPD, January 11, 1936. CPD, January 11, 1936, in ENPS, Roll 1, Scrapbook 2, p. 28. CPD, January 11, 1936, in ENPS, Roll 1, Scrapbook 2, p. 29. CN, January 11, 1936. CN, n.d., in ENPS, Roll 1, Scrapbook 2, p. 36. CPD, January 29, 1936. K. R. McIntire, Memorandum for the Director "Re: Police Corruption in CLEVELAND, OHIO," May 12, 1936, in FBI-EN. CN, July 1, 1939, in ENPS, Roll 2, Scrapbook 7, p. 13. McGill and Perry, *Court Cases of Eliot Ness*, p. 23.

MCNAMEE, CULLITAN, PATTON AT HARVARD CLUB: CN, January 11, 1936 ("You come in . . . ," "You just step . . . ," "two emergency squads," "as soon as . . ."). CPD, January 11, 1936 ("You just step . . . ," "I've tried to . . . ," "as soon as . . ."). CP, January 11, 1936 ("You have your . . . ," "You're talking to . . . ," "We don't want . . . ," "The hell with . . . ," "a steady line . . ."). CPD, January 12, 1936, in ENPS, Roll 1, Scrapbook 2, p. 31. CPD January 15, 1936, in ENPS, Roll 1, Scrapbook 2, p. 34. CN, January 9, 1937, in ENPS, Roll 1, Scrapbook 5, p. 125. *Des Moines Sunday Register*, October 29, 1961. George Condon, "The Last American Hero," *Cleveland Magazine*, August 1987, p. 138.

CULLITAN CALLS FOR HELP: CN, January 11, 1936 ("You ain't going . . . ," "The sheriff says . . ."). CPD, January 11, 1936 ("You ain't going . . . ," "We're in trouble . . . ," "This is the . . ."). CP, January 11, 1936. Albrecht, "Whatever Happened," p. 9. Nickel, *Torso*, p. 48 ("We need help," "Hold everything . . .").

NESS GETS BACKUP: CP, January 11, 1936 ("Prosecutor Cullitan is . . . ," "We can't send . . . ," "The mayor cannot . . . ," "I'll have to . . . ," "To hell with . . . ," "No, we won't . . . ," "as a private . . . ," "I told the . . . ," "I told them I . . ."). CN, January 11, 1936. CPD, January 11, 1936; January 14, 1936 ("You know an . . ."). CPD, January 12, 1936, in ENPS, Roll 1, Scrapbook 2, p. 31. CP, June 15, 1938, in ENPS, Roll 2, Scrapbook 8, p. 24. CPD, June 16, 1938, in ENPS, Roll 2, Scrapbook 8, p. 25. BCE, March 6, 1937, in ENPS, Roll 1, Scrapbook 5, p. 155 ("to inject myself . . ."). Fraley, interviewed in "Eliot Ness," *Unsolved Mysteries*.

NESS RAIDS HARVARD CLUB: CP, January 11, 1936 ("Don't try to . . ."). CN, January 11, 1936 ("I don't think . . ."). CPD, January 11, 1936 ("Let's have a . . . ," "All right . . . ," "We have achieved . . ."); January 14, 1936 ("many tough-looking 'birds,'" "I told our . . . ," "If this affair . . . ," "We are here . . . ," "About the time . . ."). *Baltimore Sun*, May 17, 1936, in ENPS, Roll 1, Scrapbook 2, p. 80. *Des Moines Sunday Register*, October 29, 1961. Condon, *Cleveland*, pp. 232, 234.

The day after the Harvard Club raid, none of Cleveland's newspapers agreed on who breached the casino's front door. CPD, the morning paper, asserted more than once that "Ness shoved open the front door and told Cullitan's constables to finish their job." The two evening papers agreed that Ness led the charge but offered totally different versions of how the door opened. According to CN, "[t]he constables bashed in the unlocked door," while CP claimed that an unnamed "doorman" opened the door from the inside after the raiders pounded on it with nightsticks. A CN photograph of the casino's entrance during the raid (in "S-Cleveland-Clubs-Gambling-Harvard" folder, Cleveland Public Library Photograph Collection) shows police and county officials standing outside a wide-open outer door, while an inner door apparently remains shut. This might explain some of the confusion—Ness may have opened the outer door, leaving Cullitan's forces to enter through the inner door.

We've chosen to follow CPD, because it offers by far the most detailed account of the entrance than either of the other two papers. And despite the differing versions presented the next day by CP and CN, the consensus soon became that Ness opened the door himself (see CP, January 11, 1936, in ENPS, Roll 1, Scrapbook 2, p. 29; *Baltimore Sun*, May 17, 1936, in ENPS, Roll 1, Scrapbook 2, p. 80; CP, January 6, 1941, in ENPS, Roll 3, Scrapbook 11, p. 56).

AFTERMATH OF HARVARD CLUB RAID: CPD, January 11–12, 1936 (January 11, "the city and . . ."; January 12, "as public officials . . ."); January 14, 1936. CPD, January 11, 1936, in ENPS, Roll 1, Scrapbook 2, p. 29. CPD, January 12, 1936, in ENPS, Roll 1, Scrapbook 2, p. 31. CN, January 13, 1936, in ENPS, Roll 1, Scrapbook 2. CN, January 14, 1936, in ENPS, Roll 1, Scrapbook 2, p. 33. Eliot Ness to Henry Sykes, January 14, 1936, CPHS. CPD, January 15, 1936, in ENPS, Roll 1, Scrapbook 2, p. 34 ("Some cops may . . ."). CP, February 14, 1936, in ENPS, Roll 1, Scrapbook 2, p. 52. CN, n.d., in ENPS, Roll 1, Scrapbook 2, p. 36 ("cooked his political . . . ," "a new lease . . ."). Condon, *Cleveland*, p. 235. Burrough, *Public Enemies*, pp. 539–541.

POLILLO MURDER: CPD, January 27, 1936. Gerber, Bergman, and Gambatese, "Mystery of Cleveland's," p. 32. Ritt, "Head Hunter," in Bayer,

Cleveland Murders, pp. 222–223. Martin, *Butcher's Dozen*, pp. 62–68 (62, "some meat was . . ."; 68, "At first we . . ."). Nickel, *Torso*, pp. 51–55. Bellamy, *Maniac in the Bushes*, pp. 67–72. Badal, *In the Wake*, pp. 50–60 (59, "wrenched . . . from the socket").

Chapter Four: The Mad Butcher

NESS AND VOLLMER / SECRET SIX: August Vollmer, "Policemen as Social Workers," *National Police Journal* 4, no. 3 (June 1919), pp. 6, 23, 25 ("Boy gangs may . . ."). August Vollmer, "Aims and Ideals of the Police," *Journal of the American Institute of Criminal Law and Criminology* 13, no. 1 (May 1922), pp. 253–254. CT, May 16, 1929; December 14, 1929. Eliot Ness to August Vollmer, December 16, 1935; Eliot Ness to August Vollmer, January 4, 1936 ("The situation here . . . ," "I am going . . . ," "Racketeering here is . . ."), both in box 24, "Ness, Eliot" folder, August Vollmer Papers, BANC MSS C-B 403, UCB. August Vollmer to Eliot Ness, December 26, 1935, in box 44, "Letters written by Vollmer, Dec. 1935" folder, August Vollmer Papers, BANC MSS C-B 403, UCB. August Vollmer to Eliot Ness, January 17, 1936 ("attempts to put . . ."); August Vollmer to Mrs. Herman Matzen, January 23, 1936 ("the ranks of . . ."), both in box 44, "Letters written by Vollmer Jan.–Feb. 1936" folder, August Vollmer Papers, BANC MSS C-B 403, UCB. CP, January 29, 1936, in ENPS, Roll 1, Scrapbook 2, p. 40. Carte & Carte, *Police Reform*, pp. 2–3, 15–16, 20–36, 41–53, 58–64, 69–74, 77–83, 93, 99–103. Bailey, *Encyclopedia of Police Science*, pp. 412–413. Alder, *Lie Detectors*, pp. xi, 17–23, 63–66, 71–73, 102, 108. Robert Kehlmann, "August Vollmer, Police Chief's Residence," Berkeley Historical Plaque Project, 2012, http://berkeleyplaques.org/e-plaque/august-vollmer/ (accessed September 1, 2016). Collins and Schwartz, *Scarface and the Untouchable*, pp. 200–204, 229–235, 295, 313, 503–508.

NESS CRACKS DOWN ON GAMBLING: CN, January 9, 1936; CP, January 9, 1936, both in ENPS, Roll 1, Scrapbook 2, p. 20. CP, January 18, 1936, in ENPS, Roll 1, Scrapbook 2, p. 36. CP, April 10, 1936, in ENPS, Roll 1, Scrapbook 2, p. 64.

NESS'S VIEWS ON GAMBLING AND LAW: CPD, January 23, 1936 ("I am inclined . . . ," "a situation in . . . ," "that cities which . . . ," "A policeman must . . . "); February 1, 1936. CP, February 1, 1936, in ENPS, Roll 1, Scrapbook 2, p. 42. CP, April 21, 1936, in ENPS, Roll 1, Scrapbook 2, p. 70 ("In passing any . . ."). CN, March 14, 1940, in ENPS, Roll 2, Scrapbook 7, p. 99. Peter Jedick, "Eliot Ness," *Cleveland Magazine*, April 1976, p. 53.

GAMBLERS RETURN / NESS STRIKES BACK: CP, February 14, 1936. CP, February 14, 1936, in ENPS, Roll 1, Scrapbook 2, p. 52. CPD February 15, 1936, in ENPS, Roll 1, Scrapbook 2, p. 53 ("tipoff"). CPD, March 8, 1936, in ENPS, Roll 1, Scrapbook 2, p. 56. CPD, March 9, 1936, in ENPS, Roll 1, Scrapbook 2 p. 57. *Kansas City Star*, April 19, 1936, in ENPS, Roll 1, Scrapbook 2, p. 68. Margaret B. Payton to Rebecca McFarland, August 16, 1989, RM.

GHOST REPORTER: CPD, n.d.; CP, April 3, 1936, both in ENPS, Roll 1, Scrapbook 2, p. 62. CN, April 3, 1936, in ENPS, Roll 1, Scrapbook 2, p. 61. CP, April 9, 1936 ("I've got three . . ."); CPD, April 10, 1936, both in ENPS, Roll 1, Scrapbook 2, p. 63. CP, April 10, 1936, in ENPS, Roll 1, Scrapbook 2, p. 64.

NESS AND PUBLICITY: Viktor Schreckengost and Rebecca McFarland, interviewed in *The Fourteenth Victim: Eliot Ness & the Torso Murders*, produced by Mark Wade Stone (Cleveland: Storytellers Media Group, 2006), DVD. Alder, *Lie Detectors*, pp. 20–21, 27, 65. Sagalyn, *A Promise Fulfilled*, p. 63.

NESS GIVING SPEECHES: CP, January 29, 1936 ("A successful police . . ."); CN, January 29, 1936, both in ENPS, Roll 1, Scrapbook 2, p. 40 ("responded marvelously and . . ."). CPD, February 1, 1936 ("inadequate and demoralized," "to commit six . . ."). CP, February 1, 1936; CN, February 1, 1936 ("off the record," "make no more . . ."), both in ENPS, Roll 1, Scrapbook 2, p. 42. CPD, February 5, 1936, in ENPS, Roll 1, Scrapbook 2, p. 45 ("Not naturally a . . .").

NESS ELUSIVE / PHYSICAL FITNESS: CPD, February 9, 1936; February 12, 1936; February 20, 1936. CP, March [??], 1936, in ENPS, Roll 1, Scrapbook 2, p. 55. CN, April 4, 1936, in ENPS, Roll 1, Scrapbook 2, p. 62. CP, April 23, 1936, in ENPS, Roll 1, Scrapbook 2, p. 70. CP, April 30, 1936, in ENPS, Roll 1, Scrapbook 2, p. 71 ("throw a man . . . ," "quick as a cat"). *Kansas City Star*, April 19, 1936, in ENPS, Roll 1, Scrapbook 2, p. 68. CN, July 22, 1936, in ENPS, Roll 1, Scrapbook 4, p. 10 ("Ness is an . . ."). CCP, August 20, 1936 ("the Brown Condor"). BCE, January 23, 1938, in ENPS, Roll 2, Scrapbook 10, p. 78. BCE, January 26, 1938, in ENPS, Roll 2, Scrapbook 10, p. 79. Jedick, "Eliot Ness," pp. 54–56 (56, "Anything I whisper . . ."). RM to ABS, personal email, August 4, 2016. Phillip Thomas Tucker, "The Legacy of the Brown Condor," *Selamta*, March–April 2016, https://www.selamtamagazine.com/stories/the-legacy-of-the-brown-condor (accessed January 21, 2019).

DICK TRACY CLUB: Vollmer, "Policemen as Social Workers," p. 25 ("into juvenile police"). CN, April 4, 1936, in ENPS, Roll 1, Scrapbook 2, p. 62

("Dick Tracy Detective . . . ," "howling, yelling, whistling . . . ," "spellbound," "You have a . . . ," "enthusiasm was uncontrollable"). Collins and Schwartz, *Scarface and the Untouchable*, pp. 394–395.

GREAT LAKES EXPO AND CENTENNIAL YEAR: CPD, January 1, 1936 ("ought to be . . ."); May 27, 1936. Ritt, "Head Hunter," in Bayer, *Cleveland Murders*, pp. 225–226. Condon, *Cleveland*, p. 235. Porter, *Cleveland*, pp. 94, 106–108. Nickel, *Torso*, pp. 57–59, 74–75. Rose, *Cleveland*, pp. 876–878, 917–918, 925–931. Miller and Wheeler, *Cleveland*, pp. 143–144. Vacha, *Meet Me on Lake Erie*, pp. 1 ("Tin Can Plaza"), 3, 5, 7–12 (8, "Now the country . . ."), 18 ("Incredible to pass . . ."), 30–31, 48–49, 74–92. Capuzzo, *Murder Room*, p. 182 ("city of ivory"). Badal, *In the Wake*, p. 62. Collins and Schwartz, *Scarface and the Untouchable*, pp. 109, 149, 229–230, 524–525.

REPUBLICAN CONVENTION: CP, June 6, 1936 ("bookie and gambling . . . ," "It's going to . . ."). CDN, June 4, 1936, in ENPS, Roll 1, Scrapbook 2, p. 87 ("thinking of a . . ."). CPD, June 7, 1936 ("Voice of Safety"). CP, June 10, 1936, in ENPS, Roll 1, Scrapbook 2, p. 92. CP, June 12, 1936, in ENPS, Roll 1, Scrapbook 2, p. 93. "'Safety's Voice' Clears Visiting Autos' Path," n.p., n.d., in ENPS, Roll 1, Scrapbook 3. CPD, July 12, 1936, in ENPS, Roll 1, Scrapbook 5, p. 4. Jo Chamberlin, "Eliot Ness: The Cosmopolite of the Month," *Cosmopolitan*, August 1940, p. 6. Fraley, *4 Against the Mob*, p. 30. Nickel, *Torso*, p. 62.

THE TATTOOED MAN: CP, June 6, 1936 ("that the workmanship . . . ," "Somewhere in the . . . ," "the opinion of . . ."). CN, June 6, 1936. CPD, June 6–7, 1936 (June 7, "maniac with a . . . ," "While he was . . . ," "That's a maniac's . . ."). Gerber, Bergman, and Gambatese, "Mystery of Cleveland's," p. 32. Ritt, "Head Hunter," in Bayer, *Cleveland Murders*, pp. 223–224. Martin, *Butcher's Dozen*, pp. 68–69. Nickel, *Torso*, pp. 62–64. Bellamy II, *Maniac in the Bushes*, pp. 89–93. Badal, *In the Wake*, pp. frontispiece, 62–68.

Chapter Five: This Is a Raid!

BLACK HAWK RAID: CN, May 29, 1936, in ENPS, Roll 1, Scrapbook 2, p. 85. CPD, June 1, 1936, in ENPS, Roll 1, Scrapbook 2, p. 86 ("Vehovec has made . . ."). CPD, June 7, 1936 ("was plainly a . . . ," "Joe," "Didn't Harwood telephone . . . ," "The matter has . . ."). CP, June 6, 1936, in ENPS, Roll 1, Scrapbook 2, p. 89. CN, June 6, 1936, in ENPS, Roll 1, Scrapbook 2 p. 88. "Ness Testifies at McCarthy Bookie Trial," n.p., July 28, 1936, in ENPS, Roll 1, Scrapbook 3. CP, July 28, 1936, in ENPS, Roll 1, Scrapbook 5, p. 22 ("about 35 men . . . ," "fitted every door").

HARWOOD: CN, June 8, 1936; CP, June 8, 1936, in ENPS, Roll 1, Scrapbook 2, p. 91. CP, June 2, 1936, in ENPS, Roll 1, Scrapbook 2, p. 87.
CPD, August 8, 1936, in ENPS, Roll 1, Scrapbook 5, p. 27. CP, October
5, 1936. CP, October 5, 1936. CP, October 5, 1936, in ENPS, Roll 1,
Scrapbook 3 ("Czar of the 14th"). CP, March 18, 1938, in ENPS, Roll
2, Scrapbook 10, p. 132 ("He consorted openly . . . ," "Big Mike," "Mike
Harwood can't . . ."). McGill and Perry, *Court Cases of Eliot Ness*, pp.
24–25.

CADEK: CP, April 18, 1936, in ENPS, Roll 1, Scrapbook 2, p. 66. CN, April
13, 1936, in ENPS, Roll 1, Scrapbook 2, p. 64. CPD, April 14–16, 1936;
May 22, 1936; May 26–27, 1936. CN, April 14, 1936; CP, April 14, 1936;
CN, April 16, 1936, all in ENPS, Roll 1, Scrapbook 2, p. 65. CP, May 26,
1936; May 29, 1936. CP, October 3, 1936, in ENPS, Roll 1, Scrapbook
3. CP, n.d., in ENPS, Roll 1 Scrapbook 5, p. 82. BCE, March 8, 1937, in
ENPS, Roll 1, Scrapbook 5, p. 155. High, "Cleveland Versus the Crooks,"
pp. 23–24.

Many secondary sources give Ness a major role in the Cadek case (see
Perry, *Eliot Ness*, pp. 153–157), apparently following Fraley (*4 Against the
Mob*, pp. 43–49), who depicted Ness as central to the investigation. But
contemporary news articles make clear that Fritchey turned the results of
his investigation over to Cullitan, not Ness, and that the prosecutor's office
built the case without Ness's help. Only after the indictment did Ness take
a role in the case, trying to use it, according to Fritchey, "as an opening
wedge in a far-reaching investigation of reports that other officials of the
police force have accumulated large sums of money that could not possibly
have been realized through their salaries." Fritchey's later summation of
Ness's police corruption probe makes clear that Ness's investigation began
with Harwood, not Cadek.

(See CN, April 13, 1936, in ENPS, Roll 1, Scrapbook 2, p. 64. CP,
April 14, 1936, in ENPS, Roll 1, Scrapbook 2, p. 65 ("as an opening . . .").
CPD, April 14–15, 1936. CN, April 16, 1936, in ENPS, Roll 1, Scrapbook
2, p. 66. CP, April 18, 1936, in ENPS, Roll 1, Scrapbook 2 p. 66. CP, June
2, 1936, in ENPS, Roll 1, Scrapbook 2, p. 87. CP, October 5, 1936, in
ENPS, Roll 1, Scrapbook 3. Untitled clipping, n.p., n.d., in ENPS, Roll 1,
Scrapbook 5, p. 114.)

NESS AND FRITCHEY INVESTIGATE: CPD, June 24, 1936 ("a severe
attack . . ."); CPD, June 21, 1936; CP, June 22, 1936; CP, June 23, 1936,
in ENPS, Roll 1, Scrapbook 2, p. 96. CPD, July 12, 1936, in ENPS, Roll
1, Scrapbook 5, p. 4. CN, June 20, 1936, in ENPS, Roll 1, Scrapbook 2, p.
95. CPD, July 26, 1936, in ENPS, Roll 1, Scrapbook 5, p. 21. CP, October 5, 1936, in ENPS, Roll 1, Scrapbook 3 ("For three months . . ."). CN,

December 9, 1936, in ENPS, Roll 1, Scrapbook 5, p. 95. NYT, December 17, 1936, in ENPS, Roll 1, Scrapbook 5, p. 111 (see also *Boston Globe* [?], December 17, 1936 [?], in ENPS, Roll 1, Scrapbook 5, p. 111). BCE, March 3, 1937, in ENPS, Roll 1, Scrapbook 5, p. 175 ("worked down through . . ."). CP, October 20, 1937, in ENPS, Roll 2, Scrapbook 6, p. 62 ("treated me decent . . ."). High, "Cleveland Versus," p. 24. Condon, *Cleveland*, pp. 237–238 (238, "Oh, yeah . . . ," "That's right," "Listen, buddy, go . . . ," "I see . . ."). Porter, *Cleveland*, pp. 98–99, 103, 200–203. McGill and Perry, *Court Cases*, p. 25. Jedick, "Eliot Ness," p. 53. Condon, "Last American Hero," p. 138. WP, January 24, 2001, https://www.washingtonpost.com/archive/local/2001/01/24/clayton-fritchey-columnist-and-adviser-to-democrats-dies/b593b0a8-340c-4cd9-972c-9c828d565ecd/ (accessed September 4, 2016). Sagalyn, *A Promise Fulfilled*, pp. 55–56.

NESS AND ROOKIES: CP, January 29, 1936, in ENPS, Roll 1, Scrapbook 2, p. 40. CPD, June 24, 1936; CPD, June 26, 1936, both in ENPS, Roll 1, Scrapbook 2, p. 96. CPD, June 28, 1936 ("be courteous . . ."); CP, June 26, 1936; CN, June 26, 1936, all in ENPS, Roll 1, Scrapbook 5, p. 1. CN, July 22, 1936, ENPS, Roll 1, Scrapbook 4, p. 10. BCE, March 5, 1937, in ENPS, Roll 1, Scrapbook 5, p. 154 ("In Cleveland, the . . . ," "prevent their 'pollution' . . ."). CP, August 21, 1939, RM.

AFRICAN AMERICANS AND THE CLEVELAND POLICE: CCP, July 2, 1936 ("Not a one . . . ," "The blame for . . ."); September 17, 1936; September 24, 1936 ("The question now . . ."); November 5, 1936 ("to move on," "This is a clear. . ."); November 26, 1936 ("some district other . . ."); December 10, 1936; September 23, 1937 ("This all-around . . ."); September 1, 1938; May 25, 1939; June 22, 1946; November 15, 1947; December 8, 1951. CG, June 19, 1937. Van Tassel and Grabowski, *Dictionary of Cleveland Biography*, p. 466. Van Tassel and Grabowski, *Encyclopedia of Cleveland History*, pp. 10–11, 208, 1037–1038.

MCGINTY, RAID, AND AFTERMATH: CP, July 22, 1936, in ENPS, Roll 1, Scrapbook 5, p. 13 ("This is a police . . ."). CN, July 22, 1936, in ENPS, Roll 1, Scrapbook 5, p. 10. CP, July 21, 1936, in ENPS, Roll 1, Scrapbook 5, p. 8. CN, July 22, 1936, in ENPS, Roll 1, Scrapbook 5, p. 12 ("pretty well drunk"). CPD, July 22, 1936, in ENPS, Roll 1, Scrapbook 5, p. 9 ("Oh, you mean . . ."). CPD, July 23, 1936. CPD, July 26, 1936, in ENPS, Roll 1, Scrapbook 5, p. 21. CPD, July 26, 1936. CN, July 29, 1936, in ENPS, Roll 1, Scrapbook 5, p. 22 ("Boy Scout," "If the city . . ."). Joseph Rukenbrod, "Young G-Man Demonstrates How to Clean Up Graft in Big City," Central Press Association, October 7, 1936, in ENPS, Roll 1, Scrapbook 5, p. 76. Messick, *Silent Syndicate*, pp. 161–163.

WEST SIDE VICTIM / DEATH MASK AT EXPO: CN, July 23, 1936 ("Is there somewhere . . ."). CPD, July 23, 1936 ("The whole thing . . ."). Ritt, "Head Hunter," in Bayer, *Cleveland Murders*, p. 227. Martin, *Butcher's Dozen*, pp. 69–70. Nickel, *Torso*, pp. 72–75, 218. Bellamy, *Maniac in the Bushes*, pp. 90–92, 117–120. Vacha, *Meet Me on Lake Erie*, pp. 38, 81. Badal, *In the Wake*, pp. 68, 70–76, 184–185.

Chapter Six: The Butcher's Meat

NESS ON JUVENILE DELINQUENCY: *Milwaukee Journal*, December 13, 1936, in ENPS, Roll 1, Scrapbook 5, p. 104. CPD, February 5, 1937, in ENPS, Roll 1, Scrapbook 5, p. 135. CP, August 4, 1937, in ENPS, Roll 2, Scrapbook 6, p. 39. CPD, December 10, 1937, in ENPS, Roll 2, Scrapbook 10, p. 12. CPD, December 16, 1937, in ENPS, Roll 2, Scrapbook 10, p. 16. CN, December 16, 1937, in ENPS, Roll 2, Scrapbook 10, p. 17. "Ness Outlines War on Crime," n.p., n.d., in ENPS, Roll 2, Scrapbook 10, p. 141. Ness, "Public Safety and the Three E's," pp. 4, 21, in ENPS, Roll 2, Scrapbook 10, pp. 135–136. BCE, February 2, 1938, in ENPS, Roll 2, Scrapbook 10, pp. 80–81. BCE, February 6, 1938, in ENPS, Roll 2, Scrapbook 10, p. 81. CT, July 21, 1939. CHE, July 1939, in "Newspaper clippings (photocopies) circa. 1930–1970" folder, DMM ("Firemen have an . . ."). NYT, August 1 [?], 1939, in ENPS, Roll 2, Scrapbook 7, p. 45. *Townsend National Weekly*, August 18, 1939, in ENPS, Roll 2, Scrapbook 7, p. 42. Carte and Carte, *Police Reform*, pp. 33–36, 92–93. Ruth, *Inventing the Public Enemy*, pp. 15–25, 30–35. Wolcott, *Cops and Kids*, pp. 126–138. Battles, *Calling All Cars*, pp. 106–108, 130–134.

TREMONT AND JUVENILE CRIME: BCE, February 2, 1938, in ENPS, Roll 2, Scrapbook 10, pp. 80–81 ("They learned to . . . ," "When I came . . . ," "a bad slum . . ."). Harold H. Burton, "New Horizons," in *Proceedings*, pp. 38–39. Eliot Ness, "The Participation of Boys," *Phi Delta Kappan*, March 1940, p. 337. W. T. McCullough, "Summary on the Delinquency Problem in the Tremont Area, 1934–1938," n.d., in box 358, folder 1, HBP. Untitled memo, n.d., pp. 1–2, in box 358, folder 2, HBP. *Star-Gazette*, June 22, 1987, RM. Edward M. Miggins, "Between Spires and Stacks: The People & Neighborhoods of Cleveland," in Keating, Krumholz, and Perry, *Cleveland*, p. 188. Van Tassel and Grabowski, *Encyclopedia of Cleveland History*, p. 1015. See also "Ness Outlines War on Crime," n.p., n.d., in ENPS, Roll 2, Scrapbook 10, p. 141. Ness, "Public Safety and the Three E's," pp. 4, 21, in ENPS, Roll 2, Scrapbook 10, pp. 135–136. CDN, June 3, 1938, in ENPS, Roll 2, Scrapbook 8, p. 19. *Townsend National Weekly*, August 18, 1939, in ENPS, Roll 2, Scrapbook 7, p. 42.

ARTHUR ROTH / TYING KNOTS: *Milwaukee Journal*, December 13, 1936, in ENPS, Roll 1, Scrapbook 5, p. 104. BCE, February 2, 1938, in ENPS, Roll 2, Scrapbook 10, pp. 80–81. "Ness Outlines War on Crime," n.p., n.d., in ENPS, Roll 2, Scrapbook 10, p. 141. Ness, "Public Safety and the Three E's," pp. 4, 21, in ENPS, Roll 2, Scrapbook 10, pp. 135–136. CDN, June 3, 1938, in ENPS, Roll 2, Scrapbook 8, p. 19. *Townsend National Weekly*, August 18, 1939, in ENPS, Roll 2, Scrapbook 7, p. 42. Burton, "New Horizons," in *Proceedings*, pp. 38–39. Ness, "Participation of Boys," pp. 337–338. Jo Chamberlin, "The Cop Who Saved a Thousand Kids," *This Week Magazine*, March 1, 1941, pp. 4, 11. Chamberlin, "Eliot Ness," p. 104. *Pittsburgh Press*, June 7, 1950. Record for Arthur Valentine Roth, *U.S., Social Security Applications and Claims Index, 1936–2007* (Provo, UT: Ancestry.com Operations, Inc., 2015).

YOUTH GANG MEETING: BCE, February 2, 1938, in ENPS, Roll 2, Scrapbook 10, pp. 80–81 ("The atmosphere was . . . ," "Instead, in their . . . ," "In their own . . ."). Burton, "New Horizons," in *Proceedings*, pp. 39, 41. CT, July 21, 1939. NYT, August 1 [?], 1939, in ENPS, Roll 2, Scrapbook 7, p. 45. *Townsend National Weekly*, August 18, 1939, in ENPS, Roll 2, Scrapbook 7, p. 42. Ness, "Participation of Boys," p. 338 ("deal"). Chamberlin, "Eliot Ness," p. 104. Untitled memo, n.d., pp. 9–10, in box 358, folder 2, HBP. *Potter Enterprise*, April 18, 1957. *Star-Gazette*, June 22, 1987, RM ("low-keyed").

BOY SCOUTS: CPD, August 16, 1936, in ENPS, Roll 1, Scrapbook 5, p. 35. "Chief Matowtiz Frets as His Brawnies Learn Boy Scouting," n.p., n.d., in ENPS, Roll 1, Scrapbook 5, p. 70. CPD, August 13, 1936. *The Milwaukee Journal*, December 13, 1936, in ENPS, Roll 1, Scrapbook 5, p. 104. CP, January 28, 1937, in ENPS, Roll 1, Scrapbook 5, p. 133. BCE, February 6, 1938, in ENPS, Roll 2, Scrapbook 10, p. 81 ("a crack [Boy] . . . ," "make the citizens . . . ," "to show up . . . ," "So, it ended . . . ," "swanky"). Ness, "Public Safety and the Three E's," pp. 4, 21, in ENPS, Roll 2, Scrapbook 10, pp. 135–136. CDN, June 3, 1938, in ENPS, Roll 2, Scrapbook 8, p. 19. "Ness Outlines War on Crime," n.p., n.d., in ENPS, Roll 2, Scrapbook 10, p. 141. Burton, "New Horizons," in *Proceedings*, pp. 41, 43–44. *A Decade of Progress: Annual Reports for 1936 and 1937* (Cleveland: Cuyahoga County Juvenile Court, 1938), pp. 17–19, in box 358, folder 1, HBP. CT, July 21, 1939. CHE, July 1939, in "Newspaper clippings (photocopies) circa. 1930–1970" folder, DMM. NYT, August 1 [?], 1939, in ENPS, Roll 2, Scrapbook 7, p. 45. *Townsend National Weekly*, August 18, 1939, in ENPS, Roll 2, Scrapbook 7, p. 42. CP, August 21, 1939, RM. Ness, "Participation of Boys," pp. 338–339. Chamberlin, "Eliot Ness," p. 104. Chamberlin, "Cop Who Saved," p. 11. Untitled memo, n.d., pp. 10, 12–16, in box 358, folder 2, HBP. Nickel, *Torso*, p. 127.

SOUTH SIDE IMPROVEMENT ASSOCIATION: Untitled memo, n.d., pp. 10–12, in box 358, folder 2, HBP. BCE, February 2, 1938, in ENPS, Roll 2, Scrapbook 10, pp. 80–81 ("a super gang," "exclusive," "We asked for . . ."). Burton, "New Horizons," in *Proceedings*, pp. 41–42. CT, July 21, 1939. NYT, August 1 [?], 1939, in ENPS, Roll 2, Scrapbook 7, p. 45 ("Almost without exception . . ."). *Townsend National Weekly*, August 18, 1939, in ENPS, Roll 2, Scrapbook 7, p. 42. Ness, "Participation of Boys," p. 338 ("Youths who lately . . ."). Chamberlin, "Eliot Ness," p. 104. Chamberlin, "Cop Who Saved," p. 11.

CRIME PREVENTION BUREAU: CN, August 10, 1936, in ENPS, Roll 1, Scrapbook 5, p. 31. CP, August 12, 1936, in ENPS, Roll 1, Scrapbook 5, p. 33. CPD, August 12, 1936, in ENPS, Roll 1, Scrapbook 5, p. 33. *Milwaukee Journal*, December 13, 1936, in ENPS, Roll 1, Scrapbook 5, p. 104. CP, August 4, 1937, in ENPS, Roll 2, Scrapbook 6, p. 39. CPD, December 10, 1937, in ENPS, Roll 2, Scrapbook 10, p. 12. BCE, February 6, 1938, in ENPS, Roll 2, Scrapbook 10, p. 81 ("to find out . . . ," "They promote crime . . ."). Ness, "Public Safety and the Three E's," pp. 4, 21, in ENPS, Roll 2, Scrapbook 10, pp. 135–136. Burton, "New Horizons," in *Proceedings*, pp. 42–44. George J. Matowitz to Eliot Ness, November 16, 1938, in box 364, folder 8, HBP. Robert W. Chamberlin to Harold H. Burton, February 11, 1939 (see also in box 364, folder 8, HBP); Untitled memo, n.d., pp. 14–15, both in box 358, folder 2, HBP. Ness, "Participation of Boys," p. 339. Chamberlin, "Cop Who Saved," p. 11 ("As cops, we . . ."). W. T. McCullough, "Summary on the Delinquency Problem in the Tremont Area, 1934–1938," n.d., pp. 4–5, in box 358, folder 1, HBP.

STATISTICS / CHANGING ATTITUDES: CN, July 24, 1936, in ENPS, Roll 1, Scrapbook 5, p. 16 ("a respectable citizen," "Neither his wife . . . ," "persecution, not prosecution"). CN, July 25, 1936, in ENPS, Roll 1, Scrapbook 5, p. 21 ("found himself," "sent the man . . ."). *Milwaukee Journal*, December 13, 1936, in ENPS, Roll 1, Scrapbook 5, p. 104. CPD, February 21, 1937, in ENPS, Roll 1, Scrapbook 5, p. 142. CP, January 28, 1937, in ENPS, Roll 1, Scrapbook 5, p. 133. BCE, February 6, 1938, in ENPS, Roll 2, Scrapbook 10, p. 81. Ness, "Public Safety and the Three E's," pp. 4, 21, in ENPS, Roll 2, Scrapbook 10, pp. 135–136. CDN, June 3, 1938, in ENPS, Roll 2, Scrapbook 8, p. 19. Burton, "New Horizons," in *Proceedings*, pp. 43–44. CT, July 21, 1939. NYT, August 1 [?], 1939, in ENPS, Roll 2, Scrapbook 7, p. 45. *Townsend National Weekly*, August 18, 1939, in ENPS, Roll 2, Scrapbook 7, p. 42. W. T. McCullough, "Summary on the Delinquency Problem in the Tremont Area, 1934–1938" n.d., in box 358, folder 1, HBP (4, "changed attitude of . . . ," "a substantial factor . . ."). Chamberlin, "Eliot Ness," p. 104. Nickel, *Torso*, p. 127.

The available statistics are patchy, but they do tend to show an over-all decline in youth crime in Tremont from 1934 to 1939. Much of this reduction, according to McCullough's report (pp. 2–3), occurred before Ness's crime prevention program began. But McCullough also notes that areas near Tremont, which did not benefit from "the special work" initi-ated by Ness and Roth, saw a much shallower drop in male juvenile de-linquency during this period. Cases of "Official Boy Delinquents"—male juvenile offenders brought before the court, instead of being released or warned—jumped up in 1937 both in Tremont and in the rest of the city, possibly because of increased enforcement and reporting or possibly as a by-product of that year's recession. By the following year, juvenile crime of all kinds in Tremont had declined significantly and was on track for further decline in 1939.

(See W. T. McCullough, "Summary on the Delinquency Problem in the Tremont Area, 1934–1938" n.d.; Capt. Arthur Roth, "Juvenile Crime Reports by Precincts: Sept. 1st 1936 to Jan. 1st 1937"; Capt. Arthur Roth, "Juvenile Crime Reports by Precincts: Jan. 1st 1937 to Jan. 1st 1938"; Capt. Arthur Roth, "Juvenile Crime Reports by Precincts: Jan. 1st 1938 to May 31st 1938," all in box 358, folder 1, HBP. Untitled memo ["The following are statistics of Juvenile Delinquency Cases . . ."], n.d.; untitled memo ["Comparison of the report for the Tremont Area . . ."], n.d., both in box 364, folder 8, HBP. Untitled memo, n.d., p. 16, in box 358, folder 2, HBP.)

NESS AND KIDS: BCE, February 6, 1938, in ENPS, Roll 2, Scrapbook 10, p. 81 ("made Director Ness' . . ."). Burton, "New Horizons," in *Proceedings*, pp. 39, 41. CT, July 21, 1939 ("Millions have been . . ."). Elisabeth Ness, "My Husband, Eliot Ness," *TV Guide*, March 11, 1961, p. 7 ("liked peo-ple . . ."). RM, interviewed in *The Fourteenth Victim*. RM to ABS, personal email, October 19, 2016.

HEAT WAVE: CN, July 10, 1936 ("They may wear . . . ," "It's all a . . ."); CN, July 11, 1936, both in ENPS, Roll 1, Scrapbook 3. CP, July 10, 1936, in ENPS, Roll 1, Scrapbook 5, p. 4. Vacha, *Meet Me on Lake Erie*, pp. 79–80.

FLYNN AND HARWOOD: CPD, July 31, 1936, in ENPS, Roll 1, Scrap-book 5, p. 24 ("They will keep . . ."). "Harwood Plea for Pension Rests with Police Board," n.p., July 31, 1936 ("state of nervous . . ."); "Ness Speeds Probe in Harwood Pensions," n.p., August 25, 1936, both in ENPS, Roll 1, Scrapbook 3. CPD, July 31, 1936; CP, July 31, 1936, both in ENPS, Roll 1, Scrapbook 5, p. 25. CP, July 31, 1936; CP, August 1, 1936; CN, August 1, 1936, all in ENPS, Roll 1, Scrapbook 5, p. 26. CPD, August 1–2, 1936; August 25, 1936. CN, August 3, 1936; CP, August 3, 1936; CPD, August 8, 1936, in ENPS, Roll 1, Scrapbook 5, p. 27. CN, August 4, 1936; CPD,

August 4, 1936; CP, August 4, 1936; CPD, August 5, 1936, all in ENPS, Roll 1, Scrapbook 5, p. 28. CP, August 5, 1936; CP, August 8, 1936, both in ENPS, Roll 1, Scrapbook 5, p. 29. CN, August 8, 1936, in ENPS, Roll 1, Scrapbook 5, p. 30. CPD, August 26, 1936; "Hurry, Director," n.p., August 26, 1936, both in ENPS, Roll 1, Scrapbook 5, p. 38. "Strange Aroma," n.p., n.d., in ENPS, Roll 1, Scrapbook 5, p. 39. CP, October 5, 1936 ("I am the most . . ."). CPD, n.d., in ENPS, Roll 1, Scrapbook 5, p. 113 ("call off the dogs"). CN, December 19, 1936, in ENPS, Roll 1, Scrapbook 5, p. 114. Van Tassel and Grabowski, *Dictionary of Cleveland Biography*, p. 368.

FIFTEENTH PRECINCT: CPD, September 2, 1936. CP, September 1, 1936; "Brains and Courage!" n.p., n.d., both in ENPS, Roll 1, Scrapbook 5, p. 41. CP, n.d., in ENPS, Roll 1, Scrapbook 5, p. 43. CP, n.d., in ENPS, Roll 1, Scrapbook 5, p. 44. CP, n.d., in ENPS, Roll 1, Scrapbook 5, p. 63 ("the unwritten law . . ."). "What They Are Saying," n.p., n.d., in ENPS, Roll 1, Scrapbook 5, p. 138 ("You can't straighten . . .").

FOOD TERMINAL RACKET: *Peoples' Press*, January 28, 1936, in ENPS, Roll 1, Scrapbook 2, p. 39. CPD, May 2, 1936, in ENPS, Roll 1, Scrapbook 2, p. 72 ("G-Man Eliot Ness"). CP, July 28, 1936, in ENPS, Roll 1, Scrapbook 5, p. 22. CPD, July 29, 1936. CP, n.p., in ENPS, Roll 1, Scrapbook 5, p. 44 ("shakedown racket," "gang of racketeers . . ."). CN, September 2, 1936, in ENPS, Roll 1, Scrapbook 3. "Grand Jury Probe of Food Terminal Racket Is Asked by Ness," n.p., n.d.; "Cullitan Pledges Study of 'Racket,'" n.p., n.d., both in ENPS, Roll 1, Scrapbook 5, p. 45. "The Real Issue," n.p., n.d.; "Out of Turn," n.p., n.d.; "Cullitan's Move Now," n.p., n.d. ("Cullitan should strike . . ."), all in ENPS, Roll 1, Scrapbook 5, p. 46. CP, September 5, 1936, in ENPS, Roll 1, Scrapbook 5, p. 47. CN, September 29, 1941, in ENPS, Roll 3, Scrapbook 11, p. 115.

NEW BUTCHER VICTIM: CPD, September 13–14, 1936. Martin, *Butcher's Dozen*, pp. 70–71. Nickel, *Torso*, pp. 76–79, 81. Badal, *In the Wake*, pp. 78–84.

PETER MERYLO: CPD, June 7, 1938, in ENPS, Roll 2, Scrapbook 8, p. 19. Martin, *Butcher's Dozen*, pp. 73–74. Nickel, *Torso*, pp. 86–87. Badal, *In the Wake*, pp. 89–95. Badal, *Though Murder*, pp. 15–16. Badal, *Hell's Wasteland*, p. 35.

PUBLIC TERROR / NESS STEPS IN: "Stop This Slaughter," n.p., September 11, 1936, in ENPS, Roll 1, Scrapbook 5, p. 49 ("Terror pervades the . . ."). "Police Find 4th Part of Torso," n.p., n.d., in ENPS, Roll 1, Scrapbook 5, p. 50 ("the mystery . . . ," "a crazed butcher," "a maddened doctor . . ."). CPD, September 13, 1936. Martin, *Butcher's Dozen*, p. 72. Nickel, *Torso*, pp. 78–80. Bellamy, *Maniac in the Bushes*, p. 133. Badal, *In the Wake*, pp. 86–87 ("He had to . . ."), 91–93 (93, "You can't bring . . ."), 95–97, 102–103. Badal, *Though Murder*, pp. 16–17.

Chapter Seven: Perfect Victims

SERIAL KILLING BACKGROUND: Nickel, *Torso*, pp. 4–5, 209–210, 217–218. Sugden, *Complete History*, pp. 95–96, 200–204, 246–248, 333–338, 366–367. Schechter, *Serial Killer Files*, pp. 5–7, 138–147, 180–190, 349, 363–364. Capuzzo, *Murder Room*, pp. 180–181, 185. Badal, *Though Murder*, p. 9. Storer, *Short History*, p. 162. Badal, *In the Wake*, pp. 10, 95, 175, 179. Douglas and Olshaker, *Mindhunter*, pp. 18–19. Dyer, *Lethal Repetition*, p. 19. Vronsky, *Sons of Cain*, pp. 10–14 (13, *serienmörder*, "serial murder"), 24–28, 180–204, 277–278 (278, "Vampire of Düsseldorf"), 280–284. "Peter Kurten," Biography.com, April 16, 2019, https://www.biography.com/crime-figure/peter-kurten (accessed April 25, 2019).

OFFERS OF ASSISTANCE: "Calls Experts in Torso Case," n.p., n.d., in ENPS, Roll 1, Scrapbook 5, p. 51 ("crack the case," "decoy"). CPD, September 13, 1936 ("that the slayer . . .").

TORSO CLINIC: CPD, September 16, 1936 ("torso clinic," "Gentlemen, tonight we're . . . ," "showed considerable knowledge . . . ," "laboratory," "a pervert"). "Calls Experts in Torso Case," n.p., n.d., in ENPS, Roll 1, Scrapbook 5, p. 51. Ben Williamson, "Orders Police Recheck First Torso Murder," n.p., n.d., in ENPS, Roll 1, Scrapbook 5, p. 54 ("crazed," "He is of . . ."). Gerber, Bergman, and Gambatese, "Mystery of Cleveland's," p. 126. Nickel, *Torso*, pp. 82–86 (85, "perfect victims"). Schechter, *Serial Killer Files*, pp. 15, 28–30. Badal, *Though Murder*, pp. 9–10. Badal, *In the Wake*, pp. 86–87, 100–102, 175. Hickey, *Serial Murderers*, pp. 8, 364 ("the less-dead," "vulnerable and powerless," "less-alive," "never-were"). Vronsky, *Sons of Cain*, pp. 236–239.

NESS'S IDEAS ON CRIME: BCE, March 2, 1937, in ENPS, Roll 1, Scrapbook 5, p. 174 ("Just as one . . ."). Ness, "Public Safety and the Three E's," pp. 4, 21, in ENPS, Roll 2, Scrapbook 10, pp. 135–136 ("In crime, in . . .").

MERYLO'S THEORIES: Peter Merylo, "Report on Torso Murders Investigation," March 15, 1943, CPHS ("a Sex Degenerate," "that the MURDERER . . ."). Martin, *Butcher's Dozen*, pp. 73–76. Badal, *In the Wake*, p. 94.

NESS INVESTIGATES / NEW CASTLE: Ben Williamson, "Orders Police Recheck First Torso Murder," n.p., n.d., in ENPS, Roll 1, Scrapbook 5, p. 54. Peter Merylo, "Report on Torso Murders Investigation," March 15,

1943, CPHS. Nickel, *Torso*, pp. 88–89. Badal, *Hell's Wasteland*, pp. xii–xiii, 39–42, 87–89. Badal, *In the Wake*, pp. 97–100, 161–162, 181–182.

DAVID COWLES: David Cowles, transcript of interview by Florence Schwein and Lt. Tom Brown, September 6, 1983, pp. 3–6, CPHS. CPD, January 26, 1988. Cleveland Police Historical Society, *Cleveland Police*, pp. 67, 74. Record for David L. Cowles, *U.S.*, *Social Security Death Index*, *1935–2014* (Provo, UT: Ancestry.com Operations, Inc., 2011). Badal, *In the Wake*, p. 8. Collins and Schwartz, *Scarface and the Untouchable*, pp. 198–200, 203, 228–229, 278–280.

SECRET INVESTIGATION: David Cowles, transcript of interview by Florence Schwein and Lt. Tom Brown, September 6, 1983, pp. 30–34, CPHS. Marilyn Bardsley, "The Kingsbury Run Murders: Eliot Ness Hunts Serial Killer," The Crime Library, http://web.archive.org/web/200012051940 /http://www.dark-horse.com/kingsbury2/kingsbury.htm (accessed August 15, 2016). Marilyn Bardsley, "The Kingsbury Run Murders: Cat and Mouse," The Crime Library, http://web.archive.org/web/20001007082528/http:// crimelibrary.com/kingsbury/kingcat.htm (accessed August 15, 2016). Badal, *In the Wake*, p. 247.

GRAFT PROBE COMPLETE: CN, July 2, 1936, in ENPS, Roll 1, Scrapbook 5, p. 2. CP, October 5, 1936; CN, October 6, 1936; CN, October 14, 1936 ("You had to . . ."), all in ENPS, Roll 1, Scrapbook 3. CP, October 5, 1936 ("the rank and . . . ," "sent to the . . . ," "played ball," "their baptism of . . . ," "When an officer . . . ," "How much this . . ."). CPD, October 6, 1936. CP, October 7, 1936, in ENPS, Roll 1, Scrapbook 5, p. 64 ("If your business . . ."). CP, October 10, 1936, in ENPS, Roll 1, Scrapbook 5, p. 68. Messick, *Silent Syndicate*, p. 10. Porrello, *Rise and Fall of the Cleveland Mafia*, pp. 127–133. Mappen, *Prohibition Gangsters*, pp. 71–72.

GRAND JURY TESTIMONY / INDICTMENTS: "Ex-Officer to Testify in Ness Purge of Million-Dollar Graft," n.p., n.d., in ENPS, Roll 1, Scrapbook 5, p. 63. CP, n.d., in ENPS, Roll 1, Scrapbook 5, p. 66 ("Look at my . . ."). CN, October 7, 1936; CN, October 8, 1936; "Fix That Failed Is Probed As Ex-Bootlegger Tells of Police Double Cross" and "Ness Squelches Police Sale of Bazar Tickets," both n.p., October 10, 1936; CN, October 13, 1936 ("Line them up . . ."); CN, October 14, 1936; CN, October 27, 1936, all in ENPS, Roll 1, Scrapbook 3. CN, n.d.; CPD, October 9, 1936; CP, n.d.; "Grand Jury to Hear Ness Police Charges," n.p., n.d., all in ENPS, Roll 1, Scrapbook 5, p. 65. CPD, October 8, 1936; October 14, 1936; October 22, 1936; October 30–31, 1936. CN, October 9, 1936; October 22, 1936. CPD, n.d., in ENPS, Roll 1, Scrapbook 5, p. 67. CP, October 10, 1936, in ENPS, Roll 1, Scrapbook 5, p. 68. CP, n.d., in ENPS, Roll 1, Scrapbook 5,

p. 69. "Guard Is Posted by Ness over Purge Star," n.p., n.d.; CP, n.d.; "Jury Today Hears 15 in Police Quiz," n.p., n.d; "Fifteen Testify in Ness Purge," n.p., n.d., all in ENPS, Roll 1, Scrapbook 5, p. 71. CP, n.d.; CPD, n.d.; CN, n.d., all in ENPS, Roll 1, Scrapbook 5, p. 74. "U.S. Agents Aid Ness in Hunt for Fugitives," n.p., n.d.; CPD, n.d., in ENPS, Roll 1, Scrapbook 5, p. 70. CP, n.d., in ENPS, Roll 1, Scrapbook 5, p. 64. CN, October 21, 1936, in ENPS, Roll 1, Scrapbook 3 and ENPS, Roll 1, Scrapbook 5, p. 73. CP, n.d.; CPD, October 28, 1936, both in ENPS, Roll 1, Scrapbook 5, p. 75. CN, October 29, 1936 ("The testimony displays . . ."). CP, October 29, 1936, in ENPS, Roll 1, Scrapbook 5, pp. 77–78. LAT, October 30, 1936. WP, October 30, 1936. CP, n.d.; "Not Guilty, Say Eight in Police Purge," n.p., n.d., both in ENPS, Roll 1, Scrapbook 5, p. 81. Jack Kennon, "Politics off the Record," n.p., n.d., in ENPS, Roll 1, Scrapbook 5, p. 88 ("Betting is brisk . . .").

HARWOOD TRIAL: CP, October 5, 1936. CN, October 29, 1936. CN, December 7, 1936; Howard Beaufait, "Harwood Angry as Bribe Trial Evidence Begins," n.p., n.d.; Howard Beaufait, "Two More Say: 'Paid Harwood,'" n.p., December 9, 1936; CN, December 10, 1936; Howard Beaufait, "Harwood Irked by Grilling Says Raids Were Curbed in Mayor Davis' Regime," n.p., December 14, 1936; Howard Beaufait, "Argue to Jury as Harwood and Wife Sob," n.p., December 15, 1936; CN, December 16, 1936 ("There is nothing . . ."), all in ENPS, Roll 1, Scrapbook 3. CP, n.d., in ENPS, Roll 1, Scrapbook 5, p. 91. CPD n.d., in ENPS, Roll 1, Scrapbook 5, p. 92. "Harwood Trial Jury Is Sworn," n.p., n.d.; "Harwood Bribery Trial Is On Today," n.p., n.d., both in ENPS, Roll 1, Scrapbook 5, p. 90. CN, December 11, 1936, in ENPS, Roll 1, Scrapbook 5, p. 100. CP, n.d., in ENPS, Roll 1, Scrapbook 5, p. 93. CN, n.d., in ENPS, Roll 1, Scrapbook 5, pp. 94–95. CPD, December 9, 1936, in ENPS, Roll 1, Scrapbook 5, p. 96 ("Mr. Ness either . . . ," "Mr. Ness can . . ."). "Text of Harwood Trial Testimony," n.p., n.d., in ENPS, Roll 1, Scrapbook 5, p. 97. CN, December 9, 1936, in ENPS, Roll 1, Scrapbook 5, pp. 95–96. CP, December 9, 1936, in ENPS, Roll 1, Scrapbook 5, pp. 97–98. CPD, December 10, 1936, in ENPS, Roll 1, Scrapbook 5, p. 98. CPD, December 10, 1936, in ENPS, Roll 1, Scrapbook 5, pp. 98–99. CN, December 10, 1936, in ENPS, Roll 1, Scrapbook 5, p. 99. CP, December 10, 1936, in ENPS, Roll 1, Scrapbook 5, pp. 99–100. CPD, December 11, 1936, in ENPS, Roll 1, Scrapbook 5, p. 100. CP, December 11, 1936, in ENPS, Roll 1, Scrapbook 5, pp. 100–101. CPD, December 12, 1936; CN, December 12, 1936, both in ENPS, Roll 1, Scrapbook 5, p. 101. CPD, December 13, 1936, in ENPS, Roll 1, Scrapbook 5, pp. 103–104. CP, December 12, 1936, in ENPS, Roll 1, Scrapbook 5, pp. 102–103. CP, December 14, 1936, in ENPS, Roll 1, Scrapbook 5, p. 106. CPD, n.d., in ENPS, Roll 1,

Scrapbook 5, pp. 106–107. Untitled clipping, n.p., n.d., in ENPS, Roll 1, Scrapbook 5, pp. 105–106. CP, December 15, 1936, RM ("admiration for the . . . ," "as a grasping . . . ," "besmirched the badge . . ."). CN, December 15, 1936; CPD, December 16, 1936, both in ENPS, Roll 1, Scrapbook 5, p. 108. Untitled clipping, n.p., n.d., in ENPS, Roll 1, Scrapbook 5, p. 110 ("I don't believe . . ."). CP, December 16, 1936, in ENPS, Roll 1, Scrapbook 5, pp. 108–109 ("I can thank . . . ," "would rather not comment"). CP, December 17, 1936; *Boston Globe*, n.d., both in ENPS, Roll 1, Scrapbook 5, p. 111. CT, December 17, 1936. LAT, December 17, 1936. WP, December 17, 1936. NYT, December 17, 1936. CN, December 19, 1936, in ENPS, Roll 1, Scrapbook 5, p. 114 ("In the eyes . . .").

FLYNN RESIGNS, REPLACED BY CHAMBERLIN: "Ness Writes Flynn on Resignation," n.p., n.d.; CP, December 17, 1936, both in ENPS, Roll 1, Scrapbook 5, p. 112. CPD, n.d., in ENPS, Roll 1, Scrapbook 5, p. 113. CP, December 17, 1936; CN, December 17, 1936, both in ENPS, Roll 1, Scrapbook 5, p. 111. CPD, December 19, 1936. CN, February 4, 1937, in ENPS, Roll 1, Scrapbook 3. CPD, January 2, 1938, in ENPS, Roll 2, Scrapbook 10, p. 27. BCE, January 23, 1938, in ENPS, Roll 2, Scrapbook 10, p. 78. CPD, May 9, 1938, in ENPS, Roll 2, Scrapbook 9, p. 159 ("the Cleveland safety . . ."). CDN, November 27, 1937, in ENPS, Roll 1, Scrapbook 4. CP, August 6, 1940, in ENPS, Roll 3, Scrapbook 11, p. 5. Porter, *Cleveland*, p. 102.

LATER POLICE PROSECUTIONS: CPD, February 6, 1937, in ENPS, Roll 1, Scrapbook 5, p. 136 ("I have had . . ."). CP, February 4, 1938, in ENPS, Roll 2, Scrapbook 10, p. 68 ("an almost unprecedented . . ."). CPD, February 19, 1938, in ENPS, Roll 2, Scrapbook 10, p. 90 ("on the outstanding . . ."). CP, March 18, 1938, in ENPS, Roll 2, Scrapbook 10, p. 132 ("a revolution," "Today there is . . ."). Chamberlin, "Eliot Ness," p. 6. Condon, *Cleveland*, p. 238. Porter, *Cleveland*, p. 99.

Chapter Eight: Hero of the Hour

CRIME DOWN / NESS OMNIPRESENT: "Quiet," n.p., n.d., in ENPS, Roll 1, Scrapbook 5, p. 142 ("This is getting . . ."). "Director," n.p., n.d., in ENPS, Roll 1, Scrapbook 5, p. 134 ("Eliot Ness is . . ."). Robert B. Larkin, "No Unofficial Police Chiefs in Ness' Rule," n.p., n.d., in ENPS, Roll 1, Scrapbook 5, p. 39. CN, December 17, 1936, in ENPS, Roll 1, Scrapbook 5, p. 112 ("a hero of the . . ."). CP, December 18, 1936, in ENPS, Roll 1, Scrapbook 5, p. 114. CP December 26, 1936, in ENPS, Roll 1, Scrapbook 5, p. 116 ("Don't blame us . . ."). CPD, January 2, 1937, in ENPS, Roll 1, Scrapbook 3 ("Man of the Year"). CP, January 6, 1937, in ENPS, Roll 1,

Scrapbook 5, p. 124. CN, January 16, 1937, in ENPS, Roll 1, Scrapbook 5, p. 129. CN, January 18, 1937, in ENPS, Roll 1, Scrapbook 5, p. 130. CP, June 28, 1937, in ENPS, Roll 2, Scrapbook 6, p. 27. CN, January 12, 1937, in ENPS, Roll 1, Scrapbook 5, p. 126. CPD, January 24, 1937, in ENPS, Roll 1, Scrapbook 5, p. 132. BCE, February 28, 1937 ("an idolized public . . ."), both in ENPS, Roll 1, Scrapbook 5, p. 151. CP, March 11, 1937, in ENPS, Roll 1, Scrapbook 5, p. 171. "3500 Laugh at City Club Quips," n.p., April 10, 1937, in ENPS, Roll 1, Scrapbook 5, p. 195. Eliot Ness paycheck, July 30, 1938, CPHS. High, "Cleveland Versus the Crooks," p. 24 ("Some day I . . ."). Jesse Bryant Wilder, "The Last Untouchable," *Northern Ohio Live*, March 1993, p. 117, PWH ("Everybody who worked . . .").

THIRD DEGREE: CN, December 28, 1936; "Youth Charges Police Beating," n.p., December 29, 1936, both in ENPS, Roll 1, Scrapbook 5, p. 117. "Third Degree," n.p., n.d.; "Suspends Officer in 'Beating,'" n.p., December 29, 1936, both in ENPS, Roll 1, Scrapbook 3. CPD, December 28, 1936; CP, December 29, 1936, both in ENPS, Roll 1, Scrapbook 5, p. 118. CP, January 4, 1937 ("opposed to the . . . ," "Intelligence must supplant . . ."); "Lowry Is Laid Off in 'Beating,'" n.p., n.d.; CP, January 5, 1937, all in ENPS, Roll 1, Scrapbook 5, p. 123. CP, January 5, 1937; CN, January 7, 1937; CN, January 8, 1937; "'3rd Degree' Brings Officer's Suspension," n.p., n.d., all in ENPS, Roll 1, Scrapbook 5, p. 124.

BROTHEL RAID: CP, January 13, 1937; CPD, January 14, 1937; CP, January 14, 1937, all in ENPS, Roll 1, Scrapbook 5, p. 127. CN, January 14, 1937; CPD, January 15, 1937 ("only names . . ."); CN, January 15, 1937, all in ENPS, Roll 1, Scrapbook 5, p. 128. CN, January 13, 1937, in ENPS, Roll 1, Scrapbook 5, p. 126. CN, January 16, 1937; CPD, January 16, 1937, both in ENPS, Roll 1, Scrapbook 5, p. 129.

GAMBLING RAIDS: CN, January 9, 1937 ("home rule"); CPD, January 10, 1937; CPD, January 11, 1937; CN, January 12, 1937, all in ENPS, Roll 1, Scrapbook 5, p. 125. "'Clean Out All Bookies,' Ness Orders Police," n.p., January 15, 1937, in ENPS, Roll 1, Scrapbook 3. CPD, January 17, 1937, in ENPS, Roll 1, Scrapbook 5, p. 128 ("right connections," "lid on gambling . . ."). Robert B. Larkin, "City Gamblers Worry; County Joints Do Not," n.p., n.d.; CPD, February 3, 1937 ("rookie raiders," "college boys"), both in ENPS, Roll 1, Scrapbook 5, p. 134 ("home rule"). CP, January 30, 1937, in ENPS, Roll 1, Scrapbook 5, p. 133. CPD, February 5, 1937, in ENPS, Roll 1, Scrapbook 5, p. 135. CP, February 9, 1937, in ENPS, Roll 1, Scrapbook 5, p. 137. CP, February 18, 1937, in ENPS, Roll 1, Scrapbook 5, p. 141. *Buffalo Evening News*, March 11, 1937, in ENPS, Roll 1, Scrapbook 5, p. 172. BCE, March 5, 1937, in ENPS, Roll 1, Scrapbook 5, p. 154. CP, November 12, 1937, in ENPS, Roll 2, Scrapbook 6,

p. 80 ("home rule," "city gamblers, with . . ."). "Cleveland Scene," January 1, 1938, in box 351, folder 1, HBP. Fraley, *4 Against the Mob*, pp. 90–91. Badal, *Though Murder*, pp. 7–8, 146.

UPCOMING ELECTIONS: CPD, January 2, 1937 ("So great is . . ."); I. L. Kenen, "Flynn Eyes Fall Race for Mayor," n.p., January 29, 1937, both in ENPS, Roll 1, Scrapbook 3. CPD, January 24, 1937; CPD, January 24, 1937, both in ENPS, Roll 1, Scrapbook 5, p. 132. CN, March 17, 1937, in ENPS, Roll 1, Scrapbook 5 p. 177. "Your Mayor Reports," c. 1937, in Box 356, Folder 5, HBP. "A Biography of Justice Harold Hitz Burton," n.d., in box 372, folder 8, HBP. See also CPD, January 1, 1937; CP, January 2, 1937, both in ENPS, Roll 1, Scrapbook 5, p. 121. CPD New Year's Day Magazine, January 1, 1937, in ENPS, Roll 1, Scrapbook 5, p. 122. CPD, January 3, 1937; CP, January 4, 1937, both in ENPS, Roll 1, Scrapbook 5, p. 123.

SECOND LADY OF THE LAKE: Gerber, Bergman, and Gambatese, "Mystery of Cleveland's," pp. 126–127. Ritt, "Head Hunter," in Bayer, *Cleveland Murders*, pp. 227–228. Martin, *Butcher's Dozen*, pp. 76–78. Nickel, *Torso*, pp. 98–100 (99, "He gives us . . ."), 103. Bellamy, *Maniac in the Bushes*, pp. 145–148 (147, "He gives us . . ."). Badal, *In the Wake*, pp. 108–114 (110, "He gives us . . .").

CORONER GERBER / NESS AND TORSO PUBLICITY: WP, February 24, 1937 ("sex-mad, surgically . . . ," "Eliot Ness . . ."). CPD, November 4, 1937, in ENPS, Roll 2, Scrapbook 6, p. 78. CPD, January 15, 1939 ("This has miffed . . ."). Untitled clipping, n.p., n.d., in ENPS, Roll 1, Scrapbook 5, p. 142. Ritt, "Head Hunter," p. 228. Martin, *Butcher's Dozen*, pp. 78–79. Nickel, *Torso*, pp. 95, 101–103 (101, "too long ago," "too few details," "The possibility of . . . ," "who performs the . . ."; 103, "a major priority"). Bellamy, *Maniac in the Bushes*, pp. 145–147. Badal, *In the Wake*, pp. 111–112, 176–177 (176, "He is a . . ."; 177, "laboratory").

MARTIN SWEENEY: NYT, July 17, 1936. CPD, March 6, 1937 ("The biggest task . . ."; "policemen who took . . ."); CP, March 6, 1936, both in ENPS, Roll 1, Scrapbook 5, p. 160 ("The papers put . . . ," "The built-up Mr. . . ."). CN, March 6, 1937, in ENPS, Roll 1, Scrapbook 5, p. 158. CPD, March 7, 1937, in ENPS, Roll 1, Scrapbook 5, p. 162 ("gratuitous and shamefully . . . ," "Sweeney adopts the . . ."). "Addresses Given at the Opening of the Burton-for-Mayor Campaign," September 16, 1937, pp. 19–22, in box 362, folder 7, HBP. "The Congress: The Bitter End," *Time*, September 16, 1940, pp. 12–13. *Sweeney v. Caller-Times Pub. Co.*, 41 F. Supp. 163 (1941), p. 163. Will Chasan and Victor Riesel, "Keep Them Out! II. Martin L. Sweeney of Ohio," *Nation*, May 30, 1942, pp. 626–628

(628, "been raising hell"). Messick, *Silent Syndicate*, pp. 122–123. Porter, *Cleveland*, pp. 62–64, 108. Fang, *Those Radio Commentators*, pp. 91–102 (96, "Radio Priest"). Rose, *Cleveland*, p. 872. Van Tassel and Grabowski, *Dictionary of Cleveland Biography*, p. 438. Badal, *Though Murder*, pp. 6–8, 114–115. Hart, *Hitler's American Friends*, pp. 68–71, 74–80, 86–94.

TRAFFIC SAFETY: CPD, December 14, 1935, in ENPS, Roll 1, Scrapbook 2, p. 13 ("I think the . . . ," "the Siberia . . ."). CP, June 26, 1936, in ENPS, Roll 1, Scrapbook 5, p. 1. CP, December 26, 1936 ("Public Enemy No. . . ."); CN, December 26, 1936, both in ENPS, Roll 1, Scrapbook 5, p. 116. CPD, December 27, 1936; December 30, 1936. CP, December 30, 1936, in ENPS, Roll 1, Scrapbook 5, p. 120. CN, January 7, 1937, in ENPS, Roll 1, Scrapbook 5, p. 124. CN, January 15, 1937; CPD, January 15, 1937; CP, January 15, 1937, all in ENPS, Roll 1, Scrapbook 5, p. 128. CN, February 4, 1937, in ENPS, Roll 1, Scrapbook 5, p. 135. CP, February 23, 1937, both in ENPS, Roll 1, Scrapbook 5, p. 145. CP, February 22, 1937, in ENPS, Roll 1, Scrapbook 5, p. 142. CPD, February 23, 1937; CPD, February 24, 1937, both in ENPS, Roll 1, Scrapbook 5, p. 146. CPD, February 24, 1937; CP, February 25, 1937, both in ENPS, Roll 1, Scrapbook 5, p. 147. CP, February 26, 1937, in ENPS, Roll 1, Scrapbook 5, p. 148. CN, October 16, 1937, in ENPS, Roll 2, Scrapbook 6, p. 59. CPD, February 13, 1938, in ENPS, Roll 2, Scrapbook 10, p. 71. "Junior Fire Fighters Program: Radio Script," May 13, 1938, p. 4, in box 351, folder 1, HBP. Eliot Ness, "Cleveland Cashes In," *Public Safety*, September 1938, pp. 26–27, 42, in ENPS, Roll 2, Scrapbook 8, p. 83. *Cincinnati Times*, April [?] 5, 1939, in ENPS, Roll 2, Scrapbook 8, p. 150. *Cincinnati Post*, May 4, 1939, in ENPS, Roll 2, Scrapbook 8. CP, April 3, 1940, in ENPS, Roll 2, Scrapbook 7, p. 106. *Cincinnati Enquirer*, April 18, 1940, in ENPS, Roll 2, Scrapbook 7, p. 109. Eliot Ness, "Don't Keep It a Secret," n.p., n.d., in ENPS, Roll 3, Scrapbook 11, p. 13. "The History of the 'Safety First' Radio Program of the City of Cleveland," n.d., in Box 351, Folder 6, HBP.

POLICE ACADEMY / ACCIDENT PREVENTION: "The Police School," n.p., August 5, 1936, in ENPS, Roll 1, Scrapbook 3. CPD, October 11, 1936, in ENPS, Roll 1, Scrapbook 5, p. 69. "Ness Blames Police Heads for Crime," n.p., n.d.; "Urges Public to Help Police," n.p., n.d., both in ENPS, Roll 1, Scrapbook 5, p. 85. "Courtesy to Be Taught Police at New Department School," n.p., n.d., in ENPS, Roll 1, Scrapbook 5, p. 87. CN, December 23, 1936, in ENPS, Roll 1, Scrapbook 5, p. 115 ("honest-to-goodness . . ."). CPD, January 16, 1937, in ENPS, Roll 1, Scrapbook 5, p. 129. CN, April 14, 1937; CP, April 14, 1937, in ENPS, Roll 1, Scrapbook 5, p. 202. CN, April 26, 1937, in ENPS, Roll 1, Scrapbook 5, p. 206. CP, April 26, 1937, in ENPS, Roll 2, Scrapbook 6, p. 2. CPD May 22, 1937, in ENPS, Roll 2, Scrapbook 6, p. 16. CPD, June 15, 1937, in ENPS, Roll 2, Scrapbook 6, p. 26 ("murder room"). BCE, January 26, 1938, in ENPS, Roll 2, Scrapbook 10, p. 79 ("Canary Cars"). Ness, "Public Safety and the Three E's," pp. 4, 21, in ENPS, Roll 2, Scrapbook 10, pp. 135–136. Gordon Davis, "Police Have College Here," n.p., March 4, 1938, RM (also in ENPS, Roll 2, Scrapbook 10, p. 115) ("natty tweeds"). CDN, June 3, 1938, in ENPS, Roll 2, Scrapbook 8, p. 19 ("Of course, they . . ."). Patrick Lenahan, memo to John R. Sammon, June 3, 1938; John R. Sammon, memo to Edward Donahue, June 3, 1938, both in box 364, folder 8, HBP. *Cincinnati Post*, May 4, 1939, in ENPS, Roll 2, Scrapbook 8, p. 151. Untitled memo, n.d., in box 364, folder 9, HBP. Eliot Ness, "Radio-Directed Mobile Police," *American City*, November 1939, pp. 35–36. CT, December 10, 1939. CN, October 21, 1941, in ENPS, Roll 3, Scrapbook 11, p. 119 ("Oscar"). Carte and Carte, *Police Reform*, pp. 26–30.

NESS REFORMS POLICE: CPD, September 16, 1936. *Canton Repository*, n.d., in ENPS, Roll 2, Scrapbook 6, p. 72 ("a doctor of . . . ," "confessor," "a human relations . . ."). CPD, February 6, 1937, in ENPS, Roll 1, Scrapbook 5, p. 136. CPD, June 15, 1937, in ENPS, Roll 2, Scrapbook 6, p. 26 ("Don't be badge . . ."). Ness, "Public Safety and the Three E's," pp. 4, 21, in ENPS, Roll 2, Scrapbook 10, pp. 135–136. Jedick, "Eliot Ness," p. 53 ("If anyone asks . . ."). Untitled document, n.d., pp. 9–11, in box 1, "Biographical Information on Eliot Ness form files of Cleveland Public Library" folder, ASP.

LABOR RACKETEERING: CP, April 22, 1937, in ENPS, Roll 1, Scrapbook 5, p. 205. CPD, July 16, 1937; CP, July 17, 1937 ("certificates"), both in ENPS, Roll 2, Scrapbook 6, p. 31. CN, July 22, 1937, in ENPS, Roll 2, Scrapbook 6, p. 32. CPD, October 26, 1937, in ENPS, Roll 2, Scrapbook 6, p. 69. *Pittsburgh Press*, November 20, 1937 [?], in ENPS, Roll 2, Scrapbook 6, p. 105. *St. Louis Post-Dispatch*, November 28, 1937. BCE, December 5, 1937, in ENPS, Roll 2, Scrapbook 10, p. 25 ("not only to . . ."). Miller, "Cleveland's Boy Scout," p. 40, in box 374, folder 8, HBP. Neff, *Mobbed Up*, pp. 17–21. Jacobs, *Mobsters, Unions, and Feds*, pp. 1–2, 7–11, 23–34, 76–77, 100–113, 128–130. White, *Last Great Strike*, p. 219.

JOHN SAVAGE: CPD, December 25, 1935, in ENPS, Roll 1, Scrapbook 2, p. 24 ("a definite yen . . ."). CPD, January 16, 1936; CN, January 17, 1936, both in ENPS, Roll 1, Scrapbook 2, p. 35. CP, January 17, 1936; CPD, January 18, 1936 ("If later evidence . . ."), both in ENPS, Roll 1, Scrapbook 2, p. 36. CP, October 29, 1938, in ENPS, Roll 2, Scrapbook 8, p. 85. *Kansas City Star*, April 19, 1936, in ENPS, Roll 1, Scrapbook 2, p. 68. *Union Leader*, August 17, 1939, in ENPS, Roll 2, Scrapbook 7, p. 43 ("a brutal, ignorant . . . ," "thinks like a . . .").

HARRY BARRINGTON: CPD, April 15, 1937, in ENPS, Roll 1, Scrapbook 5, p. 202. CN, April 22, 1937, in ENPS, Roll 1, Scrapbook 5, p. 204 ("There's more crime . . . ," "Beat Burton . . ."). CP, June 8, 1937, in ENPS, Roll 2, Scrapbook 6, p. 22. CPD, August 25, 1937 ("every building and . . ."); CP, August 25, 1937, both in ENPS, Roll 2, Scrapbook 6, p. 42. CN, August 25, 1937, in ENPS, Roll 2, Scrapbook 6, p. 43. CP, October 25, 1937, in ENPS, Roll 2, Scrapbook 6, pp. 67–68. CP, October 25, 1937; CPD, October 26, 1937, both in ENPS, Roll 2, Scrapbook 6, p. 68. CPD, October 26, 1937, in ENPS, Roll 2, Scrapbook 6, p. 69. CDN, November 26, 1937, in ENPS, Roll 1, Scrapbook 4. BCE, December 3, 1937, in ENPS, Roll 2, Scrapbook 10, p. 24. NYT, November 28, 1937. *St. Louis Post-Dispatch*, November 28, 1937. Miller, "Cleveland's Boy Scout," pp. 120–121, in box 374, folder 8, HBP. Jedick, "Eliot Ness," p. 54.

LITTLE STEEL STRIKE: CP, June 9, 1937, in ENPS, Roll 2, Scrapbook 6, p. 23 ("It's Mayor Burton," "Dirty strikebreaker," "Company rat," "I voted for . . ."). CPD, June 10, 1937. CPD, June 13, 1937. C. M. White to Harold H. Burton, July 2, 1937, container 5, folder 6, HHB-EBP. "Addresses of Mayor Harold H. Burton and County Engineer John O. McWilliams at the City Club of Cleveland," October 16, 1937, pp. 40–41, in box 362, folder 8, HBP. *Boston Herald*, November 4, 1937, in box 374, folder 3, HBP. "Cleveland Scene," January 1, 1938, in box 351, folder 1, HBP. *Ohio Guide*, pp. 65–66. Howard Fast, "An Occurrence at Republic Steel," in Leighton, *Aspirin Age*, pp. 383–391 (386, "A cop is . . ."). Miller and Wheeler, *Cleveland*, p. 142. Van Tassel and Grabowski,*Encyclopedia of Cleveland History*, pp. 659, 859. Robert G. Pushkar, "Oldies and Oddities: The Little Steel Strike Airlift," *Air & Space Magazine*, July 2001, http://www.airspacemag.com/history-of-flight/oldies-amp-oddities-the-little-steel-strike-airlift-41977502/?all&no-ist (accessed October 29, 2016). McElvaine, *Great Depression*, p. 295. Hiltzik, *New Deal*, p. 303. White, *Last Great Strike*, pp. 163–164, 178, 219.

STONE KNITTING MILLS / NATIONAL GUARD: CN, June 30, 1937, in ENPS, Roll 2, Scrapbook 6, p. 28 ("I never in . . ."). CN, July 2, 1937; CN, July 5, 1937 ("dangerous strike zone"), both in ENPS, Roll 2, Scrapbook 6, p. 29. C. M. White to Harold H. Burton, July 2, 1937; Harold H. Burton and Martin L. O'Donnell, untitled statement, n.d.; Harold H. Burton to Arthur L. Garfield, July 9, 1937; Nathan Solomon to Harold H. Burton, July 9, 1937, all in container 5, folder 6, HHB-EBP. CPD, July 7, 1937, in ENPS, Roll 2, Scrapbook 6, p. 30. Van Tassel and Grabowski, *Encyclopedia of Cleveland History*, p. 659. White, *Last Great Strike*, pp. 219–220.

LATEST TORSO VICTIM / GUARD WITHDRAWN: CP, July 8, 1937 ("persuade the National . . ."); CN, July 12, 1937, both in ENPS, Roll 2, Scrapbook 6, p. 30. Harold H. Burton to Eliot Ness, July 17, 1937 ("during the recent . . ."); Harold H. Burton to George J. Matowitz, July 17, 1937; Harold H. Burton to Martin L. O'Donnell, July 17, 1937; Harold H. Burton to Robert W. Chamberlin, July 17, 1937; Harold H. Burton to General Frank Henderson, July 17, 1937, all in container 5, folder 7, HHB-EBP. CPD, July 22, 1937, in ENPS, Roll 2, Scrapbook 6, p. 32. CN, July 26, 1937, in ENPS, Roll 2, Scrapbook 6, p. 34. CP, August 25, 1937, in ENPS, Roll 2, Scrapbook 6, p. 42. "Addresses of Mayor Harold H. Burton and County Engineer John O. McWilliams at the City Club of Cleveland," October 16, 1937, pp. 22–23, in box 362, folder 8, HBP. Martin, *Butcher's Dozen*, pp. 81–82. Nickel, *Torso*, pp. 107–110 (109, "The killer leaves . . ."). Van Tassel and Grabowski, *Encyclopedia of Cleveland History*, pp. 659–660. Bellamy, *Maniac in the Bushes*, pp. 187–189. Badal, *In the Wake*, pp. 122–125 (125, "considerably more hacking . . .").

CONFLICT AT REPUBLIC STEEL / NESS AND BURTON MEET STRIKERS: CP, July 26, 1937, in ENPS, Roll 1, Scrapbook 4 ("Drive 'em back," "No police officer . . ."). CT, July 27, 1937. NYT, July 27, 1937 ("No more bricks . . . ," "THE POLICE AND . . ."). Untitled resolution, August 3, 1937, in container 5, folder 7, HHB-EBP. Van Tassel and Grabowski, *Encyclopedia of Cleveland History*, p. 659. White, *Last Great Strike*, pp. 219–220 (220, "run over them").

COMPANY STRIKES BACK: CN, July 27, 1937, in ENPS, Roll 2, Scrapbook 6, p. 34. CP, July 27, 1937, in ENPS, Roll 2, Scrapbook 6, pp. 35–36 ("looking the other . . . ," "hired gangsters and . . . ," "outsiders"). CP, July 27, 1937, in ENPS, Roll 2, Scrapbook 4. CT, July 27, 1937. White, *Last Great Strike*, pp. 220–221.

"PEACE AREAS" / STRIKE ENDS: CP, July 27, 1937, in ENPS, Roll 2, Scrapbook 6, p. 35 ("peace areas"). CT, July 27, 1937. *Atlanta Constitution*, July 28, 1937. Jedick, "Eliot Ness," p. 57. *Ohio Guide*, p. 66. Van Tassel and Grabowski, *Encyclopedia of Cleveland History*, p. 660. White, *Last Great Strike*, pp. 220–222 (222, "very fair").

Chapter Nine: A Modern Dracula

ROSE WALLACE: CPD, June 7, 1936; June 7–8, 1937 (June 7, "a tangled mass . . . ," "the complete vertebrae . . . ," "could be a . . ."; "probably within a . . . ," "The deserted spot . . . ," "FIND SKELETON, HUNT . . ."); April

11, 1938 ("that the butcher . . . ," "Merylo and many . . ."); August 21, 1938 ("probably no more . . ."). Martin, *Butcher's Dozen*, pp. 72 ("All the bums . . . ," "We used to . . ."), 80–81 (80, "poor," "was hustling for . . ."; 81, "the only man . . ."). Nickel, *Torso*, pp. 54, 104–107. Bellamy, *Maniac in the Bushes*, pp. 71, 165–168 (166, "expertly dissected"; 167, "ephemeral loyalties and . . . ," "One-Armed Willie"). Van Tassel and Grabowski, *Encyclopedia of Cleveland History*, pp. 538–539. Schechter, *Serial Killer Files*, p. 345. Douglas and Olshaker, *Mindhunter*, pp. 214, 216. Badal, *In the Wake*, pp. 56, 60, 71–76, 116–121 (118, "definite knife marks," "evidence of hacking . . ."), 178, 185. Vronsky, *Sons of Cain*, p. 23. Erick Trickey, "The Guardians of Traffic," *Cleveland Magazine*, July 17, 2009, https://clevelandmagazine.com/in-the-cle/articles/the-guardians-of-traffic (accessed December 11, 2019). Michael Rotman, "Lorain-Carnegie Bridge," Cleveland Historical, September 24, 2010, https://clevelandhistorical.org /items/show/73 (accessed December 11, 2019).

Though some sources, in 1937 and later, refer to the Lorain-Carnegie Bridge as the "Lorain-Central Bridge" (see CPD, June 7, 1937; Bellamy, *Maniac in the Bushes*, p. 165), we use the more common name to avoid confusion.

NEW NESS INVESTIGATION: CPD, July 22, 1937, in ENPS, Roll 2, Scrapbook 6, p. 32. CN, July 26, 1937, in ENPS, Roll 2, Scrapbook 6, p. 34. CP, August 25, 1937, in ENPS, Roll 2, Scrapbook 6, p. 42. CP, November 17, 1937. *Pittsburgh Press*, November 20, 1937 [?], in ENPS, Roll 2, Scrapbook 6, p. 105. CDN, November 27, 1937, in ENPS, Roll 1, Scrapbook 4 ("an icicle of . . ."). *St. Louis Post-Dispatch*, November 28, 1937.

CAMPBELL AND MCGEE: CP, November 17, 1937 ("Protective Barbers' Association"). CPD, November 17, 1937. *Press*, November 20, 1937 [?], in ENPS, Roll 2, Scrapbook 6, p. 105. CDN, November 26, 1937; CDN, November 27, 1937, both in ENPS, Roll 1, Scrapbook 4. *St. Louis Post-Dispatch*, November 28, 1937 ("These people had . . ."). BCE, December 3, 1937, in ENPS, Roll 2, Scrapbook 10, p. 24 ("two days behind . . ."). Miller, "Cleveland's Boy Scout," p. 121, in box 374, folder 8, HBP. Neff, *Mobbed Up*, pp. 20–21. Neff, *Mobbed Up*, pp. 18–21, 26–27.

NESS INVESTIGATES / STOUFFER BROTHERS: CN, May 7, 1936, in ENPS, Roll 1, Scrapbook 2, p. 74. CPD, May 7, 1936, in ENPS, Roll 1, Scrapbook 2, p. 75. CP, May 25, 1936, in ENPS, Roll 1, Scrapbook 2, p. 84. CP, July 15, 1936 [?], in ENPS, Roll 1, Scrapbook 5, p. 7. CN, February 17[?], 1938, in ENPS, Roll 2, Scrapbook 10, pp. 84–85. CN, September 8, 1937, in ENPS, Roll 2, Scrapbook 6, p. 45. CP, November 17, 1937. CPD, November 17, 1937, ("hopping mad"). CN, November 17, 1937. *Pittsburgh Press*, November 20, 1937 [?], in ENPS, Roll 2, Scrapbook 6, p. 105. NYT,

November 28, 1937. CDN, November 26, 1937, in ENPS, Roll 1, Scrapbook 4. *St. Louis Post-Dispatch*, November 28, 1937. BCE, December 3, 1937, in ENPS, Roll 2, Scrapbook 10, p. 24 ("somehow or another . . . ," "another whitewash"). CT, February 18, 1938. Ben Wickham Jr., "Mother's 'Apple Pie' Puts Stouffers in Big Time," n.p., n.d., in ENPS, Roll 2, Scrapbook 8, p. 94. Van Tassel and Grabowski, *Dictionary of Cleveland Biography*, p. 434. Van Tassel and Grabowski, *Encyclopedia of Cleveland History*, p. 958.

THE UNKNOWNS: CPD, November 17, 1937. NYT, November 28, 1937. BCE, December 3, 1937, in ENPS, Roll 2, Scrapbook 10, p. 24 ("unknowns"). BCE, February 13 [?], 1938, in ENPS, Roll 2, Scrapbook 10, p. 82. CPD, September 20, 1938, in ENPS, Roll 2, Scrapbook 8, p. 64. Ernest C. Davis, "Nemesis of Cleveland Racketeers," *Record of Sigma Alpha Epsilon*, December 1938, p. 389, in ENPS, Roll 2, Scrapbook 8, p. 98. CP, November 25, 1940, in ENPS, Roll 2, Scrapbook 11, p. 44. CN, January 8[?], 1941, in ENPS, Roll 3, Scrapbook 11, p. 49. Howard Beaufait, "Soft Spoken, Acting Safety Chief Packs Punch," n.p., n.d., in ENPS, Roll 3, Scrapbook 11, p. 113 ("Clothey's admiration for . . ."). McGill and Perry, *Court Cases of Eliot Ness*, p. 33. Porter, *Cleveland*, p. 98. Sagalyn, *A Promise Fulfilled*, p. 44, 64. *Cleveland City Directory 1923* (Cleveland: The Cleveland Directory Company, 1923), p. 2298, in *U.S. City Directories, 1822–1995* (Provo, UT: Ancestry.com Operations, Inc., 2011). Record for John F. Sawken, *Ohio, Deaths, 1908–1932, 1938–2007* (Provo, UT: Ancestry.com Operations Inc., 2010).

INVESTIGATION CONTINUES / DANGER BUILDS: CN, September 8, 1937, in ENPS, Roll 2, Scrapbook 6, p. 45. CPD, November 17, 1937. CN, November 17, 1937. *Pittsburgh Press*, November 20, 1937 [?], in ENPS, Roll 2, Scrapbook 6, p. 105. BCE, December 3, 1937, in ENPS, Roll 2, Scrapbook 10, p. 24. Jedick, "Eliot Ness," p. 54. George W. Arruda, "Eliot Ness—Revisited," *Investigator*, May 1988, p. 13, PCHS.

NESS AND GUNS / FIRECRACKER / EDNA: CPD, October 7, 1937, in ENPS, Roll 2, Scrapbook 6, p. 52 ("a small explosion," "a wild man . . ."). Jedick, "Eliot Ness," p. 54. Jedick, *Cleveland*, p. 41. RM to ABS, personal email, November 19, 2016. Collins and Schwartz, *Scarface and the Untouchable*, pp. 9, 67, 163–165, 323–324.

BURTON'S CAMPAIGN: CPD, November 17, 1937. CPD, November 21, 1937, in ENPS, Roll 2, Scrapbook 6, p. 108 ("where the ax . . ."). CN, September 11, 1937, in ENPS, Roll 2, Scrapbook 6, p. 45.

NESS'S FIRST RALLY: CN, September 17, 1937, in ENPS, Roll 2, Scrapbook 6, p. 46. CN, September 21, 1937, in ENPS, Roll 2, Scrapbook 6, p. 48 ("his first political . . . , "thunderous applause," "obvious uneasiness").

MCWILLIAMS RUNS, ATTACKS BURTON AND NESS: "Memorandum of Campaign Topics," September 6, 1937; "Draft of Statement by Mayor Harold H. Burton at Opening of Primary Campaign, September 16, 1937," both in box 350, folder 9, HBP. "Addresses Given at the Opening of the Burton-for-Mayor Campaign," September 16, 1937, in box 362, folder 7, HBP. CPD, September 22, 1937, in ENPS, Roll 2, Scrapbook 6, p. 49. "Addresses of Honorable Harold H. Burton, Mayor of the City of Cleveland, and John O. McWilliams, County Engineer, at the Fortieth Annual Meeting of the Citizens League of Cleveland," October 8, 1937, pp. 6–9, 15–18, 26–28, 33–34; "Addresses of Mayor Harold H. Burton and County Engineer John O. McWilliams at the City Club of Cleveland," October 16, 1937, pp. 9–10, 16–17, 27–29 (27, "sided with big . . ."), 34–39 (34, "the myth of . . ."; 38, "How was it . . ."), 47, 66 ("any particular masterminds," "I don't want . . ."), both in box 362, folder 8, HBP. Joseph B. Keenan to Harold H. Burton, October 14, 1937, in box 362, folder 6, HBP. CN, October 14, 1937, in ENPS, Roll 2, Scrapbook 6, p. 58. CPD, October 17, 1937, in ENPS, Roll 2, Scrapbook 6, pp. 60–61. "Draft of Statement by Mayor Harold H. Burton at Opening of Election Campaign," October 20, 1937; untitled statement, n.d., in box 350, folder 9, HBP. October 21, 1937, in ENPS, Roll 2, Scrapbook 6, p. 63. CPD, October 29, 1937, in ENPS, Roll 2, Scrapbook 6, p. 73. "Cleveland Scene," January 1, 1938, in box 351, folder 1, HBP.

POLICE DIVIDED / ANDREW HAGAN: CP, September 7, 1937, in ENPS, Roll 2, Scrapbook 6, p. 44. CP, October 14, 1937, in ENPS, Roll 2, Scrapbook 6, p. 57. CPD, October 17, 1937, in ENPS, Roll 2, Scrapbook 6, pp. 60–61. "Addresses of Mayor Harold H. Burton and County Engineer John O. McWilliams at the City Club of Cleveland," October 16, 1937, p. 47, in box 362, folder 8, HBP. CPD, February 1, 1942, in ENPS, Roll 3, Scrapbook 11, p. 151.

HAGAN'S REPORT: CPD, October 12, 1937 ("carnival of crime," "Isn't it true . . . ," "Yes. He was . . ."); CP, October 12, 1937, both in ENPS, Roll 2, Scrapbook 6, p. 54 ("The Hagan report . . ."). CPD, October 13, 1937, in ENPS, Roll 2, Scrapbook 6, p. 57 ("an increase in . . ."). CP, October 21, 1937, in ENPS, Roll 2, Scrapbook 6, p. 64.

NESS RESPONDS / HAGAN CRITICIZES: CN, October 19, 1937, in ENPS, Roll 2, Scrapbook 6, p. 62 ("when Hagan . . ."). CP, October 20, 1937, in ENPS, Roll 2, Scrapbook 6, p. 63. CN, October 26, 1937; in ENPS, Roll 2, Scrapbook 6, p. 67 ("Note this fact . . ."). "Ness Fires Back at Hagan on Air," n.p., October 26, 1937; A. C. De Cola, "City Hall Under Hagan's Fire in Torso Murders," n.p., n.d. ("10 headless dead . . . ," "Who will be . . ."), both in ENPS, Roll 2, Scrapbook 6, p. 70. CPD, October 26, 1937, in ENPS, Roll 2, Scrapbook 6, p. 69 ("I charge that . . .").

DEMOCRAT ATTACKS FAIL: "Addresses Given at the Opening of the Burton-for-Mayor Campaign," September 16, 1937, in box 362, folder 7, HBP. CN, October 21, 1937; CPD, October 21, 1937, both in ENPS, Roll 2, Scrapbook 6, p. 63. CPD, October 23, 1937; CP, October 23, 1937, both in ENPS, Roll 2, Scrapbook 6, p. 64. CPD, October 24, 1937, in ENPS, Roll 2, Scrapbook 6, p. 66. CPD, October 26, 1937, in ENPS, Roll 2, Scrapbook 6, p. 70. CCP, October 28, 1937 ("Women's Committee of . . . ," "represent[ing] all political . . . ," "It is essential . . ."); December 8, 1937. CP, October 29, 1937, in ENPS, Roll 2, Scrapbook 6, p. 172 ("We've got to . . ."). "Radio Address of Honorable Harold H. Burton Over Station WGAR, Cleveland," October 28, 1937, in box 350, folder 9, HBP ("one simple, outstanding . . . ," "I am asking . . ."). "Statement by Mayor Harold H. Burton," November 1, 1937, in box 250, folder 10, HBP. CPD, November 30, 1937, in ENPS, Roll 2, Scrapbook 6, p. 122. Record for Carolyn Thornhill in the 1940 U.S. Census.

BURTON REELECTED: CPD, November 3, 1937; CN, November 3, 1937 ("go"), both in ENPS, Roll 2, Scrapbook 6, p. 75. CPD, November 4, 1937, in ENPS, Roll 2, Scrapbook 6, p. 78 ("and in dictating . . ."). *Boston Herald,* November 4, 1937, in box 374, folder 3, HBP. "Cleveland Scene," January 1, 1938, in box 351, folder 1, HBP. High, "Cleveland Versus," p. 24.

NESS IN ANN ARBOR / EMMA NESS DIES: CP, February 23, 1937, in ENPS, Roll 1, Scrapbook 3 ("She doesn't say . . ."). CT, November 7, 1937. CN, November 7, 1937; CN, November 8, 1937, both in ENPS, Roll 2, Scrapbook 6, p. 78. CPD, November 7, 1937; CP, November 8, 1937, both in "Ness, Eliot" microfiche, CPC. Nickel, *Torso,* p. 115.

CAMPBELL AND MCGEE INVESTIGATION ENDS: CPD, November 17, 1937 ("revealed a situation . . ."). CP, November 17, 1937. CN, November 17, 1937. *Pittsburgh Press,* November 20, 1937 [?], in ENPS, Roll 2, Scrapbook 6, p. 105. CPD, November 20, 1937, in ENPS, Roll 2, Scrapbook 6, p. 104. CPD, November 21, 1937, in ENPS, Roll 2, Scrapbook 6, p. 108. CDN, November 26, 1937, in ENPS, Roll 1, Scrapbook 4. CP, November 30, 1937, in ENPS, Roll 2, Scrapbook 6, p. 122. CP, December 2, 1937 ("You don't like . . . ," "You don't need . . . ," "How do you . . . ," "I live my . . ."); CN, December 2, 1937, both in ENPS, Roll 2, Scrapbook 10, p. 9. CPD, December 2, 1937, in ENPS, Roll 2, Scrapbook 10, p. 10. BCE, December 3, 1937, in ENPS, Roll 2, Scrapbook 10, p. 24. *Christian Science Monitor,* March 15, 1938, in ENPS, Roll 2, Scrapbook 10, p. 131.

CP, August 8, 1947, in ENPS, Roll 3, Scrapbook 13 ("I am against . . ."). Collins and Schwartz, *Scarface and the Untouchable*, p. 473.

CAMPBELL AND MCGEE DEFIANT: CPD, November 18, 1937, in ENPS, Roll 2, Scrapbook 6, p. 99 ("the only thing . . . ," "Bring on your . . ."). CP, November 18, 1937, in ENPS, Roll 2, Scrapbook 6, p. 101. CN, November 18, 1937, in ENPS, Roll 2, Scrapbook 6, p. 102. CPD, November 21, 1937, in ENPS, Roll 2, Scrapbook 6, p. 108. NYT, November 28, 1937 ("persecution"). CDN, November 26, 1937, in ENPS, Roll 1, Scrapbook 4. CP, December 2, 1937; CN, December 2, 1937, both in ENPS, Roll 2, Scrapbook 10, p. 9. CPD, December 2, 1937, in ENPS, Roll 2, Scrapbook 10, p. 10. Jedick, "Eliot Ness," p. 56.

GRAND JURY TESTIMONY: Joseph M. Gambatese, "Bring On Indictments, Campbell Cries," n.p., November 18, 1937, in ENPS, Roll 2, Scrapbook 6, p. 99. CP, November 18, 1937, in ENPS, Roll 2, Scrapbook 6, p.100. CN, November 18, 1937, in ENPS, Roll 2, Scrapbook 6, p. 102. CPD, November 19, 1937; CP, November 19, 1937; CPD, November 20, 1937, all in ENPS, Roll 2, Scrapbook 6, p. 104. *Atlanta Constitution*, November 19, 1937. CT, November 19, 1937; November 20, 1937; November 24, 1937. CP, November 23, 1937; CPD, November 23, 1937; CN, November 23, 1937; CN, November 23, 1937; CP, November 24, 1937; CN, November 24, 1937, all in ENPS, Roll 2, Scrapbook 6, p. 109. CPD, November 25, 1937; CN, November 25, 1937, both in ENPS, Roll 2, Scrapbook 6, p. 112. *Detroit Free Press*, November 28, 1937, in ENPS, Roll 2, Scrapbook 10, p. 3. CN, November 30, 1937; CPD, December 1, 1937, both in ENPS, Roll 2, Scrapbook 6, p. 123. CN, December 3, 1937; CP, December 3, 1937, both in ENPS, Roll 2, Scrapbook 10, p. 10. CN, December 8, 1937; CN, December 9, 1937, both in ENPS, Roll 2, Scrapbook 10, p. 11. CPD, December 14, 1937; CN, December 14, 1937; CPD, December 16, 1937, all in ENPS, Roll 2, Scrapbook 10, p. 16. CN, December 16, 1937; CPD, December 17, 1937; CN, December 17, 1937, all in ENPS, Roll 2, Scrapbook 10, p. 17.

NESS IN DANGER: CN, November 23, 1937, in ENPS, Roll 2, Scrapbook 6, p. 109. *St. Louis Post-Dispatch*, November 28, 1937. CDN, November 26, 1937, in ENPS, Roll 1, Scrapbook 4. BCE, December 3, 1937, in ENPS, Roll 2, Scrapbook 10, p. 24.

UNIONS AND WORKERS SUPPORT NESS: CPD, November 20, 1937; CN, November 20, 1937, both in ENPS, Roll 2, Scrapbook 6, p. 104. *Atlanta Constitution*, November 21, 1937. NYT, November 28, 1937. BCE, December 5, 1937, in ENPS, Roll 2, Scrapbook 10, p. 25. Miller, "Cleveland's Boy Scout," p. 40, in box 374, folder 8, HBP.

WORKERS REBEL: CDN November 27, 1937, in ENPS, Roll 2, Scrapbook 4 ("Toward noon several . . ."). CP, n.d.; CPD, November 28, 1937 ("his henchmen"), both in ENPS, Roll 2, Scrapbook 6, p. 117. CN, n.d. ("overthrow this dictatorship"); CPD, November 28, 1937 ("his henchmen"), in ENPS, Roll 2, Scrapbook 6, p. 116. CT, November 28, 1937. CP, November 29, 1937, in ENPS, Roll 2, Scrapbook 6, pp. 120–121. CN, November 29, 1937, in ENPS, Roll 2, Scrapbook 6, p. 120. CP, November 29, 1937; CPD, November 30, 1937, both in ENPS, Roll 2, Scrapbook 6, p. 121. CN, November 29, 1937; CP, November 30, 1937; CPD, December 1, 1937, all in ENPS, Roll 2, Scrapbook 6, p. 123. CN, December 3, 1937; CPD, December 4, 1937; CPD, December 3, 1937, all in ENPS, Roll 2, Scrapbook 10, p. 10. CP, December 6, 1937, in ENPS, Roll 2, Scrapbook 10, p. 11. BCE, December 3, 1937, in ENPS, Roll 2, Scrapbook 10, p. 24 ("looked pleased, but . . . ," "accident").

CAMPBELL AND MCGEE INDICTED: CT, November 28, 1937; December 21, 1937. NYT, November 28, 1937; December 21, 1937. St. Louis Post-Dispatch, November 28, 1937. Detroit Free Press, November 28, 1937, in ENPS, Roll 2, Scrapbook 10, p. 3. BCE, December 3, 1937, in ENPS, Roll 2, Scrapbook 10, p. 24. CN December 20, 1937, in ENPS, Roll 2, Scrapbook 10, pp. 18–19 ("our investigation is . . ."). CP, December 20, 1937, in ENPS, Roll 2, Scrapbook 10, p. 20. CPD, December 21, 1937; CN, December 21, 1937, both in ENPS, Roll 2, Scrapbook 10, p. 21. CN, December 27, 1937, in ENPS, Roll 2, Scrapbook 10, p. 25 ("Director Ness ought . . ."). Jedick, "Eliot Ness," p. 54. Neff, Mobbed Up, p. 25.

TRAFFIC DEATHS DOWN / NEW YEAR'S: CN, December 28, 1937; CN, December 30, 1937, both in ENPS, Roll 2, Scrapbook 10, p. 26. CN, January 1, 1938, in ENPS, Roll 2, Scrapbook 10, p. 27. Ness, "Cleveland Cashes In," pp. 26–27, 42, in ENPS, Roll 2, Scrapbook 6, p. 83 (42, "Whoopee Squads"). BCE, January 23, 1938, in ENPS, Roll 2, Scrapbook 10, p. 78 ("prevent accidents"). CN, March 9, 1938, in ENPS, Roll 2, Scrapbook 10, p. 125. Carl F. Schultz, memo to Harold H. Burton, June 3, 1938; Carl F. Schultz, memo to Eliot Ness, November 26, 1938, both in box 364, folder 8, HBP. Untitled memo, n.d., in box 364, folder 9, HBP.

Chapter Ten: Who Will Be Next?

CAMPBELL AND MCGEE TRIAL: CP, February 14, 1938, in ENPS, Roll 2, Scrapbook 10, p. 73. CP, February 16, 1938, in ENPS, Roll 2, Scrapbook 10, p. 78. CP, February 18, 1938 ("labor is on . . ."); CPD, February 18, 1938 ("impressing," "no more impressed . . ."); CP, February 18, 1938; CN, February 18, 1938, all in ENPS, Roll 2, Scrapbook

10, p. 89. CN, February 14, 1938, in ENPS, Roll 2, Scrapbook 10, p. 72. CN, February 17[?], 1938, in ENPS, Roll 2, Scrapbook 10, p. 84. CP, February 18, 1938, in ENPS, Roll 2, Scrapbook 10, p. 88. CPD, February 19, 1938, in ENPS, Roll 2, Scrapbook 10, p. 90. CP, February 19, 1938, in ENPS, Roll 2, Scrapbook 10, pp. 91–92. CN, February 19[?], 1938, in ENPS, Roll 2, Scrapbook 10, p. 91. *Philadelphia Inquirer,* February 19, 1938, in ENPS, Roll 2, Scrapbook 10, p. 92. CP, February 20[?], 1938, in ENPS, Roll 2, Scrapbook 10, pp. 93–94. CPD, February 20[?], 1938; CP, February 22, 1938, both in ENPS, Roll 2, Scrapbook 10, p. 95. CPD, February 20, 1938, in ENPS, Roll 2, Scrapbook 10, pp. 92–93. CP, February 23, 1938; CP, March 2, 1938; Clayton Fritchey, "$600-a-Month Campbell Pay Shown in Trial," CP, n.d.; Lloyd White, "A. F. of L. Here Supports 4 in Racket Trial," n.p., n.d., all in ENPS, Roll 1, Scrapbook 4. CN, February 23[?], 1938, in ENPS, Roll 2, Scrapbook 10, p. 96. CP, February 23, 1938; CPD, February 24, 1938, both in ENPS, Roll 2, Scrapbook 10, p. 97. CP, February 24, 1938; CPD, February 25, 1938, both in ENPS, Roll 2, Scrapbook 10, p. 98. CN, February 24, 1938, in ENPS, Roll 2, Scrapbook 10, pp. 97–98. CN, February 24, 1938; CN, February 25, 1938, both in ENPS, Roll 2, Scrapbook 10, p. 99. CP, February 25, 1938, in ENPS, Roll 2, Scrapbook 10, pp. 100–101. CPD, February 26, 1938; CN, February 26, 1938, both in ENPS, Roll 2, Scrapbook 10, p. 101. CP, February 26, 1938; CPD, February 27, 1938, both in ENPS, Roll 2, Scrapbook 10, p. 102. CP, February 28, 1938, in ENPS, Roll 2, Scrapbook 10, pp. 102–103. CN, February 28, 1938, in ENPS, Roll 2, Scrapbook 10, p. 103. CPD, March 1, 1938, in ENPS, Roll 2, Scrapbook 10, p. 104 ("From this you . . . ," "Yes"). CP, March 1, 1938, in ENPS, Roll 2, Scrapbook 10, pp. 104–105. CN, March 1, 1938, in ENPS, Roll 2, Scrapbook 10, pp. 105–108. CP, March 2, 1938, in ENPS, Roll 2, Scrapbook 10, p. 109. CN, March 2, 1938, in ENPS, Roll 2, Scrapbook 10, pp. 109–110. CPD, March 2, 1938, in ENPS, Roll 2, Scrapbook 10, pp. 108–109. CPD, March 3, 1938, in ENPS, Roll 2, Scrapbook 10, p. 110. CP, March 3, 1938, in ENPS, Roll 2, Scrapbook 10, p. 111. CN, March 3, 1938, in ENPS, Roll 2, Scrapbook 10, p. 112. CPD, March 4, 1938; CP, March 4, 1938, both in ENPS, Roll 2, Scrapbook 10, p. 113. CPD, March 5, 1938; CN, March 5[?], 1938, both in ENPS, Roll 2, Scrapbook 10, p. 114. CN, March 8, 1938, in ENPS, Roll 2, Scrapbook 10, p. 122. CP, October 29, 1938, in ENPS, Roll 2, Scrapbook 8, p. 85. Jacobs, *Mobsters, Unions, and Feds,* pp. 120–121, 128–130.

CLOSING STATEMENTS: Clayton Fritchey, "Charges Plot to 'Get' McGee and Campbell," CP, n.d., in ENPS, Roll 1, Scrapbook 4 ("Who is Ness . . . ," "officeholder," "I never heard . . . ," "Ness is no . . ."). CN, March 5, 1938, in ENPS, Roll 2, Scrapbook 10, p. 116. CP, March 5, 1938, in ENPS,

Roll 2, Scrapbook 10, pp. 116–117. CPD, March 6[?], 1938; CP, March 7, 1938 ("the Al Capone . . . ," "his companion in . . . ," "These are the men . . ."); CPD, March 8, 1938, all in ENPS, Roll 2, Scrapbook 10, p. 117. CN, March 8, 1938, in ENPS, Roll 2, Scrapbook 10, p. 118. CP, March 8, 1938, in ENPS, Roll 2, Scrapbook 10, p. 119. CPD, March 12, 1938, in ENPS, Roll 2, Scrapbook 10, p. 129.

CAMPBELL AND MCGEE CONVICTED: CN, March 8, 1938, in ENPS, Roll 2, Scrapbook 10, pp. 119–120 ("In all my . . ."). CP, March 8, 1938 ("Just the first . . ."); CP, March 8, 1938; CP, March 8, 1938; CDN, March 8, 1938; *Christian Science Monitor*, March 15, 1938 (also in ENPS, Roll 2, Scrapbook 10, p. 131), all in ENPS, Roll 1, Scrapbook 4. CN, March 8, 1938, in ENPS, Roll 2, Scrapbook 10, pp. 119–122. CP, March 8, 1938, in ENPS, Roll 2, Scrapbook 10, pp. 123–124. CP, March 8, 1938; CN, March 8, 1938, both in ENPS, Roll 2, Scrapbook 10, p. 122. CT, March 9, 1938; March 11, 1938. LAT, March 9, 1938. CP, March 9, 1938, in ENPS, Roll 2, Scrapbook 10, p. 126. CPD, March 9, 1938, in ENPS, Roll 2, Scrapbook 10, pp. 126–127. CP, March 9, 1938, in ENPS, Roll 2, Scrapbook 10, p. 125. Harold Burton to Eliot Ness, March 12, 1938, in ENPS, Roll 2, Scrapbook 10, p. 140 ("From the first . . ."). "Ohio: Without a Song," *Time*, March 21, 1938, p. 17. "Crime in Cleveland," *Newsweek*, March 21, 1938, RM.

ELIOT AND EDNA TO FLORIDA / MARITAL PROBLEMS: CN, March 9, 1938, in ENPS, Roll 2, Scrapbook 10, p. 140 ("They are driving . . ."). CP, March 9, 1938, in ENPS, Roll 2, Scrapbook 10, p. 126. CPD, March 9, 1938, in ENPS, Roll 2, Scrapbook 10, pp. 126–127. CPD, March 17, 1937, in ENPS, Roll 1, Scrapbook 5, p. 177. Jedick, "Eliot Ness," p. 54. Condon, "Last American Hero," p. 139. Heimel, *Eliot Ness*, pp. 145, 181, 204.

ELIOT RETURNS / EDNA STAYS IN FLORIDA: David F. Cavers, "Migratory Divorce," 16 *Social Forces*, p. 97 (1937). CN, March 28, 1938, in ENPS, Roll 2, Scrapbook 10, p. 139 ("Guess I'm just . . ."). CP, September 20, 1938, in "Ness, Eliot" microfiche, CPC. CN, September 20, 1938, in ENPS, Roll 2, Scrapbook 8, p. 64. CP, October 26, 1939 [?]; CN, October 26, 1939, both in ENPS, Roll 2, Scrapbook 7, p. 57. *Evening Independent*, May 23, 1947. Jedick, "Eliot Ness," p. 54. Heimel, *Eliot Ness*, p. 204. Record for Eliot Ness in *Florida, Divorce Index, 1927–2001* (Provo, UT: Ancestry.com Operations Inc., 2005). Perry, *Eliot Ness*, p. 215.

KEEPING UP APPEARANCES / DIVORCE AND EDNA'S LATER LIFE: CN, May 19, 1938, in ENPS, Roll 2, Scrapbook 8, p. 16. CN, June 22, 1938. CP, July 29, 1938, in ENPS, Roll 2, Scrapbook 8, p. 37. CP, September 20, 1938, in "Ness, Eliot" microfiche, CPC. CN, September 20, 1938, in ENPS, Roll 2, Scrapbook 8, p. 64. Life Insurance Policy, October 24, 1938, KDB. CPD, October 27, 1939, ENC. CP, October 26, 1939 [?]; CN, October 26, 1939, both in ENPS, Roll 2, Scrapbook 7, p. 57. *St. Petersburg Times*, November 19, 1994 ("She had been . . ."). Heimel, *Eliot Ness* p. 204.

LATER GRAFT PROSECUTIONS: "Bribe Jury Convicts Burns," n.p., March 11, 1937, in ENPS, Roll 1, Scrapbook 3. CN, March 11, 1937, in ENPS, Roll 1, Scrapbook 5, p. 170. CPD, March 11, 1937, in ENPS, Roll 1, Scrapbook 5, pp. 169–170. CPD, April 10, 1937, in ENPS, Roll 1, Scrapbook 5, p. 190. CP, April 10, 1937; CN, April 10, 1937, both in ENPS, Roll 1, Scrapbook 5, p. 189. CPD, May 23, 1937, in ENPS, Roll 2, Scrapbook 6, p. 17. CP, May 29, 1937; CPD, May 29, 1937, both in ENPS, Roll 2, Scrapbook 6, p. 19. CP, February 3, 1938; CN, February 3, 1938, both in ENPS, Roll 2, Scrapbook 10, p. 66. CN, April 5, 1938; CP, April 5, 1938; CPD, April 6, 1938, all in ENPS, Roll 2, Scrapbook 8, p. 2. CP, April 3 [?], 1938, in ENPS, Roll 2, Scrapbook 8, p. 3.

GAYLORD STOTTS: CPD, October 30, 1936, in ENPS, Roll 1, Scrapbook 5, p. 80. CN, May 1, 1938, in ENPS, Roll 2, Scrapbook 8, p. 6. CP, May 4, 1938; CN, May 4, 1938; CP, May 5, 1938; CN, May 5, 1938; CN, May 6, 1938; CP, May 6, 1938, all in ENPS, Roll 2, Scrapbook 8, p. 8. CP, May 7, 1938, in ENPS, Roll 2, Scrapbook 8, p. 9. Fraley, *4 Against the Mob*, p. 10 ("There was no . . ."). McGill and Perry, *Court Cases of Eliot Ness*, pp. 27–28 (28, "We will let . . .").

McGill remembered this exchange occurring before the mistrial of Lt. John Nebe (whose name he misspells as "Knebe"). But the details he gives ($5 and $10 bribes, a large family) match Stotts exactly, not Nebe. Given McGill's somewhat confused memory at other points, he almost certainly mixed the two cases up.

GRAFT PROSECUTIONS END: CP, December 24, 1938; CPD, December 25, 1938, both in ENPS, Roll 2, Scrapbook 8, p. 100. CPD, December 26, 1938, in ENPS, Roll 2, Scrapbook 8, p. 101 ("There may be . . .").

CULTURE OF DEPARTMENT CHANGING: CPD, February 12, 1938, in ENPS, Roll 2, Scrapbook 10, p. 71 ("flatfooted dimwit," "snappy, alert, studious," "athletic," "eager and progressive . . .").

LACK OF MANPOWER, MATERIEL, AND MONEY: CPD, December 22, 1937, in ENPS, Roll 2, Scrapbook 10, p. 22 ("We could use . . ."). CP, December 16, 1937, in ENPS, Roll 2, Scrapbook 10, p. 16. CPD, December 26, 1937, in ENPS, Roll 2, Scrapbook 10, p. 25 ("decrepit pieces of . . ."). "Burton Makes Air Appeal for Levy," n.p., n.d., in ENPS, Roll 2, Scrapbook 10, p. 55 ("I've been whispering . . ."). CPD, February 6, 1938, in ENPS, Roll 2, Scrapbook 10, p. 68. CP, January 3, 1939, in ENPS, Roll 2, Scrapbook 8, p. 103.

BUTCHER LYING LOW / GERBER ARTICLE: Gerber, Bergman, and Gambatese, "Mystery of Cleveland's," pp. 28–32, 126–128 (128, "Of the ten . . ."). Martin, *Butcher's Dozen*, p. 83. Nickel, *Torso*, pp. 117, 128, 221. Badal, *In the Wake*, p. 18.

LEG FOUND / NESS AND GERBER FEUD: CPD, April 10, 1938 ("Director Chamberlin wanted . . ."). Ritt, "Head Hunter," in Bayer, *Cleveland Murders*, p. 229. Martin, *Butcher's Dozen*, pp. 84–86. Nickel, *Torso*, pp. 122–123, 126. Bellamy, *Maniac in the Bushes*, pp. 213–214. Heimel, *Eliot Ness*, p. 196. Badal, *In the Wake*, pp. 132–136 (134, "Crude knife marks . . ."; 136, "I mean no . . .").

REST OF VICTIM FOUND: Martin, *Butcher's Dozen*, pp. 84–85. Nickel, *Torso*, pp. 124–126. Bellamy, *Maniac in the Bushes*, p. 217. Badal, *In the Wake*, pp. 136–137.

BUTCHER MANHUNT / MERYLO AND ZALEWSKI: *St. Paul Dispatch*, n.d., in ENPS, Roll 2, Scrapbook 8, p. 10. CPD, July 9, 1939; January 8, 1989. Peter Merylo, "Report on Torso Murders Investigation, from Sept. 10, 1936 to Oct. 1, 1942," March 15, 1943, p. 1, CPHS. Ritt, "Head Hunter," in Bayer, *Cleveland Murders*, pp. 234–236. Martin, *Butcher's Dozen*, pp. 57, 83, 86. Nickel, *Torso*, pp. 115–116 (116, "I don't even . . ."), 123. Bellamy, *Maniac in the Bushes*, pp. 136 ("Them guys have . . ."), 216–217, 296–298. Badal, *Though Murder*, p. 163. Badal, *In the Wake*, pp. 9 ("colored hoboes," "kill each other . . ."), 85–86 (85, "Don't ever veer . . ."), 97, 135, 186 ("I roughly estimate . . .").

NESS ALOOF FROM TORSO CASE: CPD, January 16, 1938, in ENPS, Roll 2, Scrapbook 10, pp. 52–53 ("actually excited"). CPD, April 17, 1938 ("No visible wave . . . ," "a better story," "a city in . . ."). *Philadelphia Ledger*, n.d., in box 383, folder 7, HBP (also in ENPS, Roll 2, Scrapbook 8, p. 60) ("Director Ness refused . . . ," "Of course, Ness . . ."). CP, June 2, 1938 ("Our delightful police . . ."); CPD, June 2, 1938, both in ENPS, Roll 2, Scrapbook 8, p. 18. CN, June 2, 1938, in ENPS, Roll 2, Scrapbook 8, p. 15. CN, December 22, 1938, in ENPS, Roll 2, Scrapbook 8, p. 100 ("is a bundle . . ."). Ritt, "Head Hunter," in Bayer, *Cleveland Murders*, p. 232. David Cowles, transcript of interview by Florence Schwein and Lt. Tom Brown, September 6, 1983, pp. 30–34, CPHS. CPD, January 8, 1989 ("Nobody took it . . ."). Bellamy, *Maniac in the Bushes*, p. 218. Nickel, *Torso*, pp. 126, 144. Heimel, *Eliot Ness*, p. 196 ("This killer has . . .").

Chapter Eleven: Doctor X

COWLES FINDS SUSPECT / ARCHAKI AND "DOCTOR X": CPD, April 10, 1938 ("We have been . . ."). Ritt, "Head Hunter," in Bayer, *Cleveland Murders*, p. 233. Martin, *Butcher's Dozen*, p. 83 ("Made a quiet . . ."). John A. Larson, "Sketches: Torso Case, Cleveland," n.d., in box 2, folder 4 ("Correspondence 1938–1940"), John Larson Papers, BANC MSS 78/160cz, UCB. David Cowles, transcript of interview by Florence Schwein and Lt. Tom Brown, September 6, 1983, pp. 30–34, CPHS. Nickel, *Torso*, p. 122. Heimel, *Eliot Ness*, pp. 221–222. Bardsley, "Eliot Ness Hunts." Bardsley, "Cat and Mouse." Badal, *Though Murder*, pp. 125–138 (135, "A once-prominent . . ."; 136–137 "Doctor X"). Badal, *In the Wake*, pp. 103–104, 226–227, 231, 247 ("A once-prominent . . ."). Bardsley, *American Sweeney Todd*, pp. 217, 229–230.

FRANCIS EDWARD SWEENEY: *Official Roster*, p. 17066. SAC, Cincinnati, memo to Director, FBI, October 2, 1952, FBI-FES. John A. Larson, "Sketches: Torso Case, Cleveland," n.d., in box 2, folder 4 ("Correspondence 1938–1940"), John Larson Papers, BANC MSS 78/160cz, UCB. John A. Larson to Richard Jenkins, April 4, 1959, in box 2, folder 4 ("Correspondence—1938–1940"), John Larson Papers, BANC MSS 78/160cz, UCB (a rougher copy in John Augustus Larson Papers, personal collection of Beulah Allen Graham [courtesy of Ken Alder]). David Cowles, transcript of interview by Florence Schwein and Lt. Tom Brown, September 6, 1983, pp. 31–32, CPHS (32, "exactly the same . . ."). Bardsley, "Cat and Mouse." Sagalyn, *A Promise Fulfilled*, p. 50 ("frustrated desire to . . ."). Badal, *Though Murder*, pp. 117–121, 155–157. Cathleen A. Cerny, MD, "Gaylord Sundheim," in Badal, *Though Murder*, pp. 186–187. Cathleen A. Cerny, MD, "Chronology and Summary of Historical Documents Regarding Francis Sweeney, M.D.," in Badal, *Though Murder*, pp. 193–200 (196, "has upon many . . ."; 199, "Federal men after . . . ," "orderly"; 200, "orderly," "remorseful"), 204 ("truancy in lunacy"). Badal, *In the Wake*, pp. 219, 228–231, 239–246, 251–252. Brady, *Gates of Janus*, pp. 195–200. Bardsley, *American Sweeney Todd*, pp. 215–217, 231. Douglas and Olshaker, *Mindhunter*, p. 142 ("stressors," "Anything can be . . ."). Vronsky, *Sons of Cain*, pp. 50–70.

No evidence exists directly placing Andrassy at City Hospital during Sweeney's commitments, as Badal (*In the Wake*, pp. 242–244, 251–252) suggests. Another latter-day student of the case (Brady, *Gates of Janus*, pp. 195–200), however, also theorized that the Butcher probably knew Andrassy from a stay in City Hospital—apparently without knowing of Sweeney's existence. Brady, a convicted multiple murderer, based his analysis on the presence of rope burns on Andrassy's wrists, the Butcher's probable history of mental illness, and his own personal knowledge of the serial killer mind-set.

The transcript of the Cowles interview on file at CPHS contains numerous errors, which have caused multiple misconceptions while filtering through the secondary literature. With regard to Cowles's claim that the suspect (whose name he did not give) cut up indigent bodies in the same way that the Butcher did, whoever transcribed the tape misheard him saying "in the morgue" as "in the war," which misled Badal (*In the Wake*, pp. 243–244) into thinking that Sweeney "dismembered unidentified dead soldiers" during World War I. The actual audio of the interview, which clarifies Cowles's comments significantly, can be heard at Erick Trickey, "Case Closed?" *Cleveland Magazine*, June 19, 2014, http://clevelandmagazine .com/in-the-cle/the-read/articles/case-closed- (accessed December 2, 2016).

INVESTIGATION CONTINUES / NO HARD EVIDENCE: CPD, December 28, 1937, in ENPS, Roll 2, Scrapbook 10, p. 26 ("the best ballistics . . ."). Ness, "Streamlining Protection," p. 92. Martin, *Butcher's Dozen*, p. 99. Fraley, *4 Against the Mob*, pp. 134–137. Fraley, interviewed in "Eliot Ness," *Unsolved Mysteries*. Bardsley, "Cat and Mouse" ("Sweeney file," "If we're going . . ."). Schechter, *Serial Killer Files*, pp. 318–324. Badal, *Though Murder*, pp. 140–141 ("interesting"), 161. Badal, *In the Wake*, pp. 180, 219 ("white shadow"), 235 ("interesting"). Trickey, "Case Closed?" ("We had no . . ."). Bardsley, *American Sweeney Todd*, p. 219. Douglas and Olshaker, *Mindhunter*, pp. 111–112 (111, "desire to work . . ."; 112, "Now, because of . . .").

SWEENEY'S COUSIN / NESS TAKES RISK: CPD, November 21, 1937, in ENPS, Roll 2, Scrapbook 6, p. 108. NYT, November 28, 1937. *Sweeney v. Caller-Times Pub. Co.*, 41 F.Supp. 163 (1941). Fraley, *4 Against the Mob*, pp. 134–137. Jedick, "Eliot Ness," p. 56. Fraley, interviewed in "Eliot Ness," *Unsolved Mysteries*. Bardsley, "Cat and Mouse." Bardsley, "Eliot Ness Hunts." Marilyn Bardsley, "The Kingsbury Run Murders: The Horror Ends," The Crime Library, http://web.archive.org/web/20001021225447 /http://crimelibrary.com/kingsbury/kinghorror.htm (accessed August 15, 2016). Badal, *Though Murder*, pp. 115–121, 143–145. Badal, *In the Wake*, pp. 232, 259. Trickey, "Case Closed?" ("A relative of . . ."). Bardsley, *American Sweeney Todd*, p. 231.

LARSON & KEELER / NESS AND THE LIE DETECTOR: Eliot Ness to John A. Larson, October 30, 1937; and John A. Larson to Chief of Police, Cleveland Police Department, December 7, 1956, both in John Augustus Larson Papers, personal collection of Beulah Allen Graham (courtesy of Ken Alder). Alder, *Lie Detectors*, pp. xi, xiii–xiv, 4, 23–24, 51–52, 55–61,

75–85, 90, 113–117, 119–153, 155–162, 251. Collins and Schwartz, *Scarface and the Untouchable*, pp. 203–204.

PLANNING INTERROGATION / THIRD DEGREE: Hopkins, *Our Lawless Police*, pp. 76–99, 126–127, 140, 189–204, 227–228, 263. CP, January 4, 1937, in ENPS, Roll 1, Scrapbook 5, p. 123 ("third degree methods"). Tom Clothey to John A. Larson, May 16, 1938 in box 2, folder 4 ("Correspondence 1938–1940"), John Larson Papers, BANC MSS 78/160cz, UCB. Tom Clothey to John A. Larson, May 31, 1938, in Box 2, Folder 4 ("Correspondence 1938–1940"), John Larson Papers, BANC MSS 78/160cz, UCB (also in John Augustus Larson Papers, personal collection of Beulah Allen Graham [courtesy of Ken Alder]). Bardsley, "The Horror Ends." Alder, *Lie Detectors*, p. 129 ("psychological third-degree"). Badal, *Though Murder*, pp. 141–142. Badal, *In the Wake*, pp. 218–219, 248–249.

SWEENEY DETAINED, INTERROGATED: David Cowles, transcript of interview by Florence Schwein and Lt. Tom Brown, September 6, 1983, p. 42, CPHS. Bardsley, "The Horror Ends." Badal, *Though Murder*, p. 142. Badal, *In the Wake*, pp. 219–221. Trickey, "Case Closed?"

The poor transcription of Cowles's interview on file with CPHS (cited above) again causes confusion here. According to the written version (p. 42), Cowles claims that he and his assistants "worked with [Sweeney] eight hours a day." Badal (*In the Wake*, p. 220) takes "worked" to mean *interrogated*, and notes that by that standard Cowles and the others subjected Sweeney to "an extraordinary grilling" (220). Perry (*Eliot Ness*, p. 214), apparently following Badal's lead, repeats the claim that Cowles and his assistant "grilled [Sweeney] eight hours a day, day after day," and adds some unfounded speculation: "It couldn't have been pretty: the two policemen didn't mind securing a confession through sheer brutality."

But the audio of the Cowles interview (in Trickey, "Case Closed?") reveals that he actually said they *"lived* with [Sweeney] eight hours a day" (italics ours). In other words, they watched over him in eight-hour shifts until he had sobered up enough for questioning. This makes much more sense than the claim that they brutally interrogated him, because they cannot have held Sweeney against his will without risking the secrecy they sought so carefully to preserve.

KEELER TESTS SWEENEY: David Cowles, transcript of interview by Florence Schwein and Lt. Tom Brown, September 6, 1983, p. 42, CPHS. Bardsley, "The Horror Ends." Alder, *Lie Detectors*, pp. 71, 73, 82–83, 121, 124–127, 129, 156 ("does not apply . . ."). Badal, *In the Wake*, pp. 220–221. Trickey, "Case Closed?" ("I might as . . .").

Our description of this incident was partially informed by film footage of Keeler giving a lie detector test in *Call Northside 777* (1948), directed by Henry Hathaway (Beverly Hills, CA: Twentieth Century Fox Home Entertainment, Inc., 2004), DVD.

LARSON TESTS SWEENEY: Tom Clothey to John A. Larson, May 16, 1938, in box 2, folder 4 ("Correspondence 1938–1940"), John Larson Papers, BANC MSS 78/160cz, UCB ("little seance"). John A. Larson, "Sketches: Torso Case, Cleveland," n.d., in box 2, folder 4 ("Correspondence 1938–1940"), John Larson Papers, BANC MSS 78/160cz, UCB ("disturbances indicative of . . . ," "to explain away . . . ," "more and more . . . ," "At this point . . ."). John Larson to John Favill, May 17, 1938; and John A. Larson to Chief of Police, Cleveland Police Department, December 7, 1956, both in John Augustus Larson Papers, personal collection of Beulah Allen Graham (courtesy of Ken Alder). John A. Larson to Richard Jenkins, April 4, 1959, in box 2, folder 4 ("Correspondence 1938–1940"), John Larson Papers, BANC MSS 78/160cz, UCB (a rougher copy in John Augustus Larson Papers, personal collection of Beulah Allen Graham [courtesy of Ken Alder]). David Cowles, transcript of interview by Florence Schwein and Lt. Tom Brown, September 6, 1983, p. 42, CPHS. Alder, *Lie Detectors*, pp. 76–79, 125–127, 129–136, 146–148, 155–162 (161, "disturbances indicative of guilt"), 204, 251. Trickey, "Case Closed?"

Cowles didn't mention Larson by name but referred to "another man in Detroit who was with some of the courts up there" (Trickey, "Case Closed?"), which is where Larson worked in 1938 (see Alder, *Lie Detectors*, pp. 160–161). According to Cowles, Larson "gave us the same opinion as Keeler did—that [Sweeney] was the man." (Trickey, "Case Closed?").

NESS AND SWEENEY: Fraley, *4 Against the Mob*, pp. 137–138 (137, "I think you . . . ," "You think . . ."). Fred McGunagle, "Postcard from the Mad Butcher," n.p., March 29, 1989, PWH. Bardsley, "Eliot Ness Hunts." Bardsley, "The Horror Ends." Alder, *Lie Detectors*, pp. 2–10, 109–110, 126–129, 132–133. Badal, *Though Murder*, p. 142. Badal, *In the Wake*, p. 220. Collins and Schwartz, *Scarface and the Untouchable*, p. 134.

Chapter Twelve: Butcher Paper

OLD BEAT COP SYSTEM: "Police Force Goes on Wheels in Ness Reorganization," n.p., n.d., in ENPS, Roll 2, Scrapbook 8, p. 35 ("was a neighborhood . . ."). BCE, January 31, 1938, in ENPS, Roll 2, Scrapbook 10, p. 80. Cleveland Police Historical Society, *Cleveland Police*, p. 9, 51.

PUTTING COPS ON WHEELS / RADIO SYSTEM: CPD, January 23, 1936 ("In Detroit they . . ."). CPD, December 16, 1937, in ENPS, Roll 2, Scrapbook 10, p. 16. CN, December 16, 1937, in ENPS, Roll 2, Scrapbook 10, p. 17. BCE, January 31, 1938, in ENPS, Roll 2, Scrapbook 10, p. 80 ("pocket radios," "Of course it . . ."). Harold H. Burton, "Challenging Crime," 1939, pp. 388–389, in box 358, folder 3, HBP. CPD, October 9, 1938, in ENPS, Roll 2, Scrapbook 8, p. 66 ("Ness is attaching . . ."). CDN, June 3, 1938, in ENPS, Roll 2, Scrapbook 8, p. 18. CPD, June 24, 1938, in ENPS, Roll 2, Scrapbook 8, p. 29. LAT, July 31, 1938 ("revolutionary"). "Police Force Goes on Wheels in Ness Reorganization," n.p., n.d., in ENPS, Roll 2, Scrapbook 8, p. 35 ("revolutionary"). *Milwaukee Journal*, August 17, 1938, in ENPS, Roll 2, Scrapbook 8, p. 41. CPD, September 19, 1938; CPD, September 20, 1938 ("bring the greatest . . ."), in ENPS, Roll 2, Scrapbook 8, p. 64. CPD, October 16, 1938, in ENPS, Roll 2, Scrapbook 8, p. 68. CN, October 22, 1938, in ENPS, Roll 2, Scrapbook 9, p. 77. *Canton Repository*, n.d., in ENPS, Roll 2, Scrapbook 6, p. 79. CN, October 24, 1938, in ENPS, Roll 2, Scrapbook 8, p. 82 ("the best approximation . . ."). CP, January 3, 1939, in ENPS, Roll 2, Scrapbook 8, p. 103. "Largest 2–Way Police Radio Installed at Cleveland," *American Police Review*, January–February 1939, in ENPS, Roll 2, Scrapbook 8, p. 102. Ness, "Radio-Directed Mobile Police," pp. 35–36. Fraley, *4 Against the Mob*, pp. 102–103. Carte and Carte, *Police Reform*, pp. 23, 54–57. Maeder, *Dick Tracy*, pp. 112–113 (113, "2-Way Wrist Radio"). Battles, *Calling All Cars*, pp. 1, 3, 147–148, 150–153, 157–158, 162, 164–165. "9-1-1 Origin & History," National Emergency Number Association, https://www.nena.org/?page=911overviewfacts (accessed December 5, 2016).

NESS SEEKS FUNDS, LAYS PLANS: CPD, December 28, 1937, in ENPS, Roll 2, Scrapbook 10, p. 26. "Burton Makes Air Appeal for Levy," n.p., n.d., in ENPS, Roll 2, Scrapbook 10, p. 55. CPD, February 12, 1938, in ENPS, Roll 2, Scrapbook 10, p. 70. Ness, "Public Safety and the Three E's," pp. 4, 21, in ENPS, Roll 2, Scrapbook 10, pp. 135–136. CDN, June 3, 1938, in ENPS, Roll 2, Scrapbook 8, p. 18. "Police Force Goes on Wheels in Ness Reorganization," n.p., n.d., in ENPS, Roll 2, Scrapbook 8, p. 35. Eliot Ness to George J. Matowitz, September 14, 1938, pp. 1–2, in *Reorganization Police Department: Cleveland, Ohio 1938*, Monographs, reel 4.46, PAL. CPD, September 20, 1938, in ENPS, Roll 2, Scrapbook 8, p. 64. CPD, October 9, 1938, in ENPS, Roll 2, Scrapbook 8, p. 66.

CN, October 24, 1938, in ENPS, Roll 2, Scrapbook 8, p. 82. "Largest 2-Way Police Radio Installed at Cleveland," *American Police Review*, January-February 1939, in ENPS, Roll 2, Scrapbook 8, p. 102 ("the largest and . . ."). CP, January 3, 1939, in ENPS, Roll 2, Scrapbook 8, p. 103. "Two Strikes on the Burglar," *F.B.I. Transmitter* [?], August 2, 1939, in ENPS, Roll 2, Scrapbook 7, p. 27. Ness, "Radio-Directed Mobile Police," p. 35. Untitled memo, n.d., in box 358, folder 2, HBP. Porter, *Cleveland*, p. 101. Nickel, *Torso*, p. 151.

NEW SQUAD CARS / EMERGENCY MOBILE PATROL: BCE, January 26, 1938, in ENPS, Roll 2, Scrapbook 10, p. 79 ("Canary Cars"). CN, June 14, 1938, in ENPS, Roll 2, Scrapbook 8, p. 24. CPD, July 1, 1938, in ENPS, Roll 2, Scrapbook 8, p. 30 ("If you cannot . . ."). CN, August 10, 1938, in ENPS, Roll 2, Scrapbook 8, p. 38. *Milwaukee Journal*, August 17, 1938, in ENPS, Roll 2, Scrapbook 8, p. 41. International Trucks advertisement, *Life*, May 22, 1939, p. 29 ("Emergency Mobile Patrol"). Ness, "Radio-Directed Mobile Police," p. 36. CT, December 10, 1939. Nickel, *Torso*, pp. 150–152. Dennis Edgerly, "Birth of EMS: The History of the Paramedic," *Journal of Emergency Medical Services*, October 8, 2013, http://www.jems.com/articles/print/volume-38/issue-10/features/birth-ems-history-paramedic.html (accessed December 6, 2016).

CRITICISMS, COMPLAINTS, AND GRAFT PREVENTION: BCE, January 31, 1938, in ENPS, Roll 2, Scrapbook 10, p. 80 ("the soft jobs"). Eliot Ness to George J. Matowitz, September 14, 1938, pp. 1–2, in *Reorganization Police Department: Cleveland, Ohio 1938*, Monographs, reel 4.46, PAL. George J. Matowitz, "Supplementary Order Relating to the General Duties of Patrol Car Crews," October 1, 1938, p. 4, in *Reorganization Police Department: Cleveland, Ohio 1938*, Monographs, reel 4.46, PAL. "Police Force Goes on Wheels in Ness Reorganization," n.p., n.d., in ENPS, Roll 2, Scrapbook 8, p. 35 ("Under the precinct . . ."). CPD, October 9, 1938, in ENPS, Roll 2, Scrapbook 8, p. 66 ("We have been . . ."). CPD, October 13, 1938, in ENPS, Roll 2, Scrapbook 8, p. 68. CP, October 15, 1938, in ENPS, Roll 2, Scrapbook 8, p. 69 ("For years, lieutenants . . ."). CP, January 3, 1939, in ENPS, Roll 2, Scrapbook 8, p. 103. Eliot Ness, "Streamlining Protection," *Real Detective*, October 1941, p. 4. Nickel, *Torso*, p. 151. Cleveland Police Historical Society, *Cleveland Police*, p. 51. Battles, *Calling All Cars*, p. 162.

JUVENILE BUREAU / BOYSTOWNS: CN, October 12, 1938, in ENPS, Roll 2, Scrapbook 8, p. 66. CP, October 12, 1938, in ENPS, Roll 2, Scrapbook 8, p. 67. CCP, October 27, 1938; February 23, 1939. Robert W. Chamberlin to Harold H. Burton, February 11, 1939, in box 358, folder 2, HBP. CPD, February 13,

Source Notes

1939, in ENPS, Roll 2, Scrapbook 8, p. 113. CN, February 16, 1939, in ENPS, Roll 2, Scrapbook 8, p. 116. "Leaders Glimpse 'Dividends in Good Citizenship' At C. of C. Luncheon for Five Boystown Mayors," n.p., n.d.; and "Mayor Joe Fazekas Steals Show at Boystown Rally," n.p., n.d., both in ENPS, Roll 2, Scrapbook 8, p. 124. CPD, March 8, 1939, in ENPS, Roll 2, Scrapbook 8, p. 125. CP, January 26, 1940, in ENPS, Roll 2, Scrapbook 7, p. 89 ("that jails fail . . ."). BCE, April 7, 1940, in FBI-ENA. Ness, "Participation of Boys," pp. 338–339 (338, "In sections where . . ."). CP, July 5, 1940, in ENPS, Roll 2, Scrapbook 7, p. 129. CP, December 13, 1940, in ENPS, Roll 3, Scrapbook 11, p. 49 ("bad boys"). Jo Chamberlin, "Stopping Crime Before It Starts," *Look Magazine*, n.d., p. 46, in ENPS, Roll 3, Scrapbook 11, p. 59. *Hearings Before a Subcommittee of the Committee on Education and Labor, United States Senate, Seventy-Eighth Congress, First Session*, pt. 1, *Juvenile Delinquency* (Washington, DC: United States Government Printing Office, 1944), p. 84, in box 13, "Sub-Committee on Wartime Health and Education (Pepper Committee)" folder, SPD. Rose, *Cleveland*, p. 953. Van Tassel and Grabowski, *Encyclopedia of Cleveland History*, p. 122. Wiltse, *Contested Waters*, p. 139. Burch and Stimpson, *American Catholic Almanac*, p. 147 ("City of Little . . . ," "There are no . . .").

WOODLAND HILLS POOL: CCP, July 21, 1934; July 25, 1935; August 22, 1935; October 24, 1935; December 26, 1935; June 18, 1936 ("provide proper and . . ."); July 9, 1936; July 16, 1936 ("a hotbed of . . ."); July 23, 1936; September 17, 1936; July 21, 1938; July 28, 1938; August 11, 1938 ("had been swimming . . . ," "keep a close . . . ," "threatening to drown . . . ," "When we again . . . ," "Now, do you . . . ," "to make an . . ."); August 18, 1938; August 25, 1938 ("encouraged colored bathers . . . ," "his presence at . . . ," "unexpected"); September 1, 1938 ("The great G-man . . . ," "Since Mr. Ness . . . ," "It takes more . . ."); September 8, 1938 ("discourage the continuous . . ."); September 15, 1938; September 22, 1938; October 6, 1938; October 13, 1938; December 15, 1938; July 20, 1939; August 2, 1941; August 9, 1941; August 18, 1951; December 6, 1958. CG, July 25, 1936 ("disappointed and disgusted," "Mr. Burton will . . ."); August 1, 1936; August 20, 1938 ("racial animosity in . . ."); August 27, 1938; September 3, 1938; September 17, 1938; October 1, 1938; October 8, 1938. CPD, July 17, 1938. CP, July 14, 1939, in ENPS, Roll 2, Scrapbook 7, p. 17. CPD, July 7, 1940, in ENPS, Roll 3, Scrapbook 11, p. 1. Van Tassel and Grabowski, *Encyclopedia of Cleveland History*, pp. 663, 711–712. Van Tassel and Grabowski, *Dictionary of Cleveland Biography*, p. 178. Wiltse, *Contested Waters*, pp. 87–153. Wolcott, *Race, Riots, and Roller Coasters*, p. 72. Jeff Wiltse, "The Black-White Swimming Disparity in America: A Deadly Legacy of Swimming Pool Discrimination," *Journal of Sport and Social Issues* 48, no. 4 (2014), pp. 366–389.

END OF GREAT LAKES EXPO / NEW BODIES DISCOVERED: CPD, August 17, 1938 ("unmistakable knife marks"). CP, August 17, 1938, in ENPS, Roll 2, Scrapbook 8, p. 38 ("He's changing his . . ."). CP, August 17, 1938, in ENPS, Roll 2, Scrapbook 8, p. 40 ("Portions of it . . . ," "a small-boned"). Peter Merylo, "Report on Torso Murders Investigation, from Sept. 10, 1936 to Oct. 1, 1942," March 15, 1943, p. 3, CPHS. Ritt, "Head Hunter," in Bayer, *Cleveland Murders*, p. 230. Martin, *Butcher's Dozen*, pp. 86–87. Nickel, *Torso*, pp. 132–136. Bellamy, *Maniac in the Bushes*, pp. 243–246. Badal, *In the Wake*, pp. 141–147. Vacha, *Meet Me on Lake Erie*, pp. 45 ("magic city on . . ."), 48, 188 ("from dust bin . . ."), 193–194.

DOUBTS ABOUT VICTIMS: CPD, August 17, 1938 ("matched the technique"). Peter Merylo, "Report on Torso Murders Investigation, from Sept. 10, 1936 to Oct. 1, 1942," March 15, 1943, p. 3, CPHS ("were put there . . ."). David Cowles, transcript of interview by Florence Schwein and Lt. Tom Brown, September 6, 1983, p. 28, CPHS. Bardsley, "The Horror Ends." Badal, *Though Murder*, pp. 158–159. Badal, *Hell's Wasteland*, p. 106. Badal, *In the Wake*, pp. 150–151, 246–247.

INVESTIGATION CONTINUES / CENTRAL MARKET: CP, August 17, 1938, in ENPS, Roll 2, Scrapbook 8, p. 40. CP, August 18, 1938, in ENPS, Roll 2, Scrapbook 8, p. 43 ("Then, too, the . . ."). CPD, August 18, 1938, in ENPS, Roll 2, Scrapbook 8, pp. 41–42. CN, August 18, 1938, in ENPS, Roll 2, Scrapbook 8, p. 42. Harry Volk, "Ness Pushes Drive to Rid City of Hobo Shacks and Jungles," n.p., n.d., in ENPS, Roll 2, Scrapbook 8, p. 47. Martin, *Butcher's Dozen*, pp. 87–89. Nickel, *Torso*, pp. 140–142. Van Tassel and Grabowski, *Encyclopedia of Cleveland History*, pp. 164–165. Badal, *In the Wake*, pp. 142–149.

ELITE DEMAND ACTION / NESS'S PHILOSOPHY: Ness, "Public Safety and the Three E's," p. 21, in ENPS, Roll 2, Scrapbook 10, p. 136 ("the cause, the . . ."). CP, August 17, 1938, in ENPS, Roll 2, Scrapbook 8, p. 39 ("the end of . . . ," "great program," "The nature of . . ."). CPD, August 17, 1938 ("may be a . . ."). Douglas Mueller, "Raiders Rouse Shacktown Men in Hunt for Killer," n.p., n.d., in ENPS, Roll 2, Scrapbook 8, p. 43. Martin, *Butcher's Dozen*, p. 88. Nickel, *Torso*, p. 136. Badal, *In the Wake*, pp. 152, 156–157, 222 ("grilled by federal . . . ," "subjected to lie . . .").

Chapter Thirteen: Good Riddance

SHANTYTOWNS / WAYFARER'S LODGE: CN, August 18, 1938, in ENPS, Roll 2, Scrapbook 8, p. 42 ("in the shadow . . ."). Harry Volk, "Ness Pushes Drive to Rid City Of Hobo Shacks and Jungles," n.p., n.d., in ENPS, Roll 2, Scrapbook 8, p. 47 ("Hoovertown," "bums, hoboes and . . . ," "Too large a . . ."). Van Tassel and Grabowski, *Encyclopedia of Cleveland History*, pp. 65, 536–537. Vacha, *Meet Me on Lake Erie*, p. 1 ("front porches looking . . ."). Kerr, *Derelict Paradise*, pp. 25–26, 28, 42, 52 ("mulligan stew"), 54–65 (55, "I panhandled a . . ."; 56, "pervading rank smell . . . ," "More and more . . ."; 58, "Hoovertown"), 66–69 (66, "They want us . . ."). Shumsky, *Homelessness*, pp. 66–70 (66, "jungles"), 178–188 (181, "If former President . . ."). Badal, *In the Wake*, pp. 6–7, 12. Hickey, *Serial Murderers*, p. 364.

NESS'S SYMPATHY, LACK OF EMPATHY / PLANNING RAID: CP, August 22, 1938 ("had title neither . . ."); CN, August 23, 1938, both in ENPS, Roll 2, Scrapbook 8, p. 47 ("disease and filth"). *Potter Enterprise*, March 22, 1961 ("For a wayfarer . . ."). *Tucson Citizen*, July 17, 1987. Nickel, *Torso*, p. 137. Collins and Schwartz, *Scarface and the Untouchable*, pp. 33–34, 167–169, 352–353, 357, 474–476.

SHANTYTOWN RAIDS: CPD, August 18, 1938, in ENPS, Roll 2, Scrapbook 8, pp. 41–42. CN, August 18, 1938, in ENPS, Roll 2, Scrapbook 8, p. 42. CP, August 18, 1938 ("higher class," "Scrambling, sliding, falling . . . ," "of some movie-style . . ."); CP, August 18, 1938 ("We are going . . ."); Douglas Mueller, "Raiders Rouse Shacktown Men in Hunt for Killer," n.p., n.d. ("All right, boys . . . ," "You see, if . . . ," "Sure you didn't . . . ," "seem[ed] to resent . . . ," "What's your name," "What's that? How . . . ," "I can't spell"), all in ENPS, Roll 2, Scrapbook 8, p. 43. Harry Volk, "Ness Pushes Drive to Rid City of Hobo Shacks and Jungles," n.p., n.d.; CN, August 23, 1938, in ENPS, Roll 2, Scrapbook 8, p. 47 ("most miserable hovels . . ."). "Jail Vagrants in Torso Hunt," n.p., n.d., in ENPS, Roll 2, Scrapbook 8, p. 59. Ritt, "Head Hunter," in Bayer, *Cleveland Murders*, pp. 230–231. Martin, *Butcher's Dozen*, p. 89. Fraley, *4 Against the Mob*, pp. 132–133. Nickel, *Torso*, p. 137. Van Tassel and Grabowski, *Encyclopedia of Cleveland History*, p. 165. Kerr, *Derelict Paradise*, pp. 69–70 ("I do not like . . . ," "The torso murderer . . ."). Badal, *In the Wake*, pp. 152–153.

SHANTYTOWN BURNED / RESIDENTS ARRAIGNED: CP, August 18, 1938, in ENPS, Roll 2, Scrapbook 8, p. 43 ("battered old suitcases . . . ," "Where can I . . ."). "62 Arraigned After Raid on Shantytown," n.p., August 19 [?], 1938, in ENPS, Roll 2, Scrapbook 8, p. 46 ("Have you a . . . ," "I have nothing . . . ," "I got relatives . . . ," "I ain't got . . . ," "nothing, no home . . . ," "I never been . . ."). CPD, August 25, 1938 ("The other fourteen . . ."); Harry Volk, "Ness Pushes Drive to Rid City of Hobo Shacks and Jungles," n.p., n.d., both in ENPS, Roll 2, Scrapbook 8, p. 47. "Jail Vagrants in Torso Hunt," n.p., n.d., in ENPS, Roll 2, Scrapbook 8, p. 59. Van Tassel and Grabowski, *Encyclopedia of Cleveland History*, p. 536.

PRAISE AND CRITICISM OF RAIDS: CN, August 22, 1938, in ENPS, Roll 2, Scrapbook 8, p. 46 ("doesn't have a . . . ," "these camps for . . . ," "such subnormal male . . . ," "psychopathic practices," "Unless these murders . . ."). CP, August 19, 1938, in ENPS, Roll 2, Scrapbook 8, p. 45 ("misguided zeal," "Safety Director Eliot . . ."). CP, August 18, 1938, in ENPS, Roll 2, Scrapbook 8, p. 43 ("are the type . . ."). Harry Volk, "Ness Pushes Drive to Rid City of Hobo Shacks and Jungles," n.p., n.d., in ENPS, Roll 2, Scrapbook 8, p. 47 ("received numerous phone . . . ," "Cleveland no longer will . . . ," "The whole problem . . . ," "We are not . . ."). CN, August 22, 1938, in ENPS, Roll 2, Scrapbook 8, p. 48 ("It'll be good riddance"). CN, August 25, 1938, in ENPS, Roll 2, Scrapbook 8, p. 49. Nickel, *Torso*, p. 139 ("brutal"). Van Tassel and Grabowski, *Encyclopedia of Cleveland History*, p. 269. Kerr, *Derelict Paradise*, p. 69 ("approached and sometimes . . .").

ROARING THIRD SEARCH: CN, August 25, 1938, in ENPS, Roll 2, Scrapbook 8, p. 49 ("photographic survey"). Martin, *Butcher's Dozen*, p. 89. Nickel, *Torso*, pp. 141–143. Badal, *In the Wake*, p. 156 ("Big rats ran . . .").

SWEENEY COMMITS HIMSELF: Bardsley, "The Horror Ends." Badal, *Though Murder*, pp. 120, 122–123 (122, "Life & its . . . ," "toll"). Cerny, "Chronology and Summary," in Badal, *Though Murder*, p. 200. Badal, *In the Wake*, pp. 232–233. Bardsley, *American Sweeney Todd*, p. 230.

FRONEK RETURNS: CPD, August 29, 1938. *Evening Star*, August 29, 1938. *Richmond Times-Dispatch*, August 29, 1938. CHE, n.d., in ENPS, Roll 2, Scrapbook 8, p. 59 ("Unquestionably this man . . ."). Nickel, *Torso*, pp. 128–130. Badal, *In the Wake*, pp. 237–246.

SHANTYTOWNS CLEARED / NESS'S REPUTATION DAMAGED: CN, September 9, 1938, in ENPS, Roll 2, Scrapbook 8, p. 61 ("Good riddance, and . . ."). Nickel, *Torso*, pp. 138–140, 144–145. Kerr, *Derelict Paradise*, p. 70. Badal, *In the Wake*, p. 157.

CITY COUNCIL SPAT: CP, August 22, 1938, in ENPS, Roll 2, Scrapbook 8, p. 47 ("sharply criticized"). CPD, September 20, 1938 ("The director says . . . ," "Mr. Young has . . . ," "That's a lie . . . ," "I apologize for . . ."); CP, September 19, 1938, both in ENPS, Roll 2, Scrapbook 8, p. 64 ("undercover investigators").

NESS DIVORCE REVEALED: CP, September 20, 1938 ("We are parting . . ."); CPD, September 21, 1938, both in "Ness, Eliot" microfiche, CPC. Jedick, "Eliot Ness," p. 54. Nickel, *Torso*, p. 145.

WALKER EDITORIAL: CCP, August 25, 1938; September 1, 1938 ("The great G-man . . . ," "the only city . . . ," "Evidently Mr. Ness . . ."). CCP,

September 1, 1938, in ENPS, Roll 2, Scrapbook 8, p. 60. Collins and Schwartz, *Scarface and the Untouchable*, pp. 9, 38–39.

Chapter Fourteen: Mystery Man

MATOWITZ LETTER / BUTCHER LEGEND: Anonymous letter to George Matowitz, December 21, 1938, in "S–Cleveland–Police Department–Crime–Murder–Torso Murders #1" folder, Cleveland Public Library Photograph Collection ("You can rest . . . ," "What did their . . . ," "the head minus . . . ," "buried in a . . . ," "Right now I . . . ," "X"). CPD, February 2, 1936; November 1, 1938; January 6–8, 1939 (January 7, "the best lead . . . ," "that, whether the . . ."; January 8, "From the miasmic . . ."); January 25, 1939 ("The city and . . ."); May 15, 1939. LAT, January 6–8, 1939. *Sacramento Bee*, January 9, 1939. William Miller, "Cleveland's Rue Morgue," *Ken*, January 12, 1939, pp. 14–15 (14, "exploded . . . ," "that the 'perfect crime' . . . ," "a note of . . . ," "There are even . . ."). Sugden, *Complete History*, pp. xxv, 259–277. Nickel, *Torso*, pp. 147–148. Badal, *In the Wake*, pp. 158–159.

NEW YEAR'S 1939: Ness, "Cleveland Cashes In," pp. 26–27, 42, in ENPS, Roll 2, Scrapbook 8, p. 83. CP, December 24, 1938, in ENPS, Roll 2, Scrapbook 8, p. 100 ("the largest traffic . . . ," "We do not . . ."). CPD, December 31, 1938; CPD, January 1, 1939 ("Let's start 1939 . . ."), in ENPS, Roll 2, Scrapbook 8, p. 101.

TRAFFIC SAFETY CAMPAIGN: CPD, August 5, 1937, in ENPS, Roll 2, Scrapbook 6, p. 39. CP, January 22, 1938, in ENPS, Roll 2, Scrapbook 10, p. 62. BCE, January 30 [?], 1938, in ENPS, Roll 2, Scrapbook 10, pp. 79–80 ("stunts"). CP, May 19, 1938, in ENPS, Roll 2, Scrapbook 8, p. 17 ("where they would . . ."). Ness, "Cleveland Cashes In," pp. 26–27, 42, in ENPS, Roll 2, Scrapbook 8, p. 83. CCP, September 22, 1938; September 29, 1938; February 16, 1939; February 23, 1939. CN, November 29, 1938; CPD, November 29, 1938, both in ENPS, Roll 2, Scrapbook 8, p. 92. CPD, December 2, 1938, in ENPS, Roll 2, Scrapbook 8, p. 94. CP, December 2, 1938; CP, December 3, 1938; CP, December 7, 1938, all in ENPS, Roll 2, Scrapbook 8, p. 95. CN, December 7, 1938, in ENPS, Roll 2, Scrapbook 8, p. 97. CPD, January 1, 1939, in ENPS, Roll 2, Scrapbook 8, p. 101 ("America's safest big city"). CPD, January [?] 4, 1939, in ENPS, Roll 2, Scrapbook 7, p. 5. CN, May 3, 1939, in ENPS, Roll 2, Scrapbook 8, p. 151. "Cleveland Wins Traffic Award: Safest Large City in Country," *Police*, June 1939, pp. 4–9, 30, in ENPS, Roll 2, Scrapbook 9, p. 158 (8, "Jeepers, Creepers, Use . . . ," "Heaven Can Wait . . ."; 9, "Driver, Can You . . ."). CP, September 4, 1940, in ENPS, Roll 3, Scrapbook 11, p. 5.

"The History of the 'Safety First' Radio Program of the City of Cleveland," n.d., in box 351, folder 6, HBP. Untitled memo, n.d., in box 364, folder 9, HBP.

ACCIDENT AND CRIME RATES DROPPING: High, "Cleveland Versus the Crooks," p. 24. CCP, September 22, 1938. CPD, November 25, 1938, in ENPS, Roll 2, Scrapbook 8, p. 91. CN, November 29, 1938, in ENPS, Roll 2, Scrapbook 8, p. 92. CPD, December 2, 1938, in ENPS, Roll 2, Scrapbook 8, p. 94. CP, December 2, 1938, in ENPS, Roll 2, Scrapbook 8, p. 95. CPD, January 1, 1939, in ENPS, Roll 2, Scrapbook 8, p. 101 ("best traffic year . . ."). CP, January 3, 1939, in ENPS, Roll 2, Scrapbook 8, p. 103. CPD, January 11, 1939, in ENPS, Roll 2, Scrapbook 8, p. 105. CP, March 6, 1939, in ENPS, Roll 2, Scrapbook 8, p. 122 ("an all-time record . . ."). CN, March 7, 1939, in ENPS, Roll 2, Scrapbook 8, p. 123. CPD, March 7, 1939, in ENPS, Roll 2, Scrapbook 8, p. 124. "Cleveland Wins Traffic Award," pp. 4–9, 30, in ENPS, Roll 2, Scrapbook 9, p. 158. Untitled memo, n.d., in box 364, folder 9, HBP.

CLEVELAND NAMED SAFEST CITY: CPD, March 31, 1939, in ENPS, Roll 2, Scrapbook 8, p. 133. CN, March 31, 1939, in ENPS, Roll 2, Scrapbook 8, p. 134. Lyle E. Bland, "National Traffic Safety Contest Winners," *Public Safety*, April 1939, pp. 6–7, 48, in ENPS, Roll 2, Scrapbook 9, pp. 156–157. CPD, April 14, 1939, in ENPS, Roll 2, Scrapbook 8, p. 149. CPD, April 15, 1939, in ENPS, Roll 2, Scrapbook 8, p. 150. "Cleveland Wins Traffic Award," pp. 4–9, 30, in ENPS, Roll 2, Scrapbook 9, p. 158. CP, March 29, 1940; CN, March 29, 1940, both in ENPS, Roll 2, Scrapbook 7, p. 102. CN, March 29, 1940; CPD, March 30, 1940, in ENPS, Roll 2, Scrapbook 7, p. 104. CPD, March 30, 1940, in ENPS, Roll 2, Scrapbook 7, p. 103. Fraley, *4 Against the Mob*, pp. 101–105 (105, "This work probably . . .").

NESS FAMOUS / BEAUFAIT: BCE, January 23, 1938, in ENPS, Roll 2, Scrapbook 10, p. 78. CN, February 23, 1939, in ENPS, Roll 2, Scrapbook 8, p. 119 ("that the fame . . . ," "was a mild-mannered . . . ," "It was Eliot . . . ," "giant killer," "There is nothing . . . ," "eager and bright-eyed . . . ," "As always, there . . . ," "dark and daring . . . ," "He must have . . ."). Chamberlin, "Eliot Ness," p. 6.

NESS AND SIDEKICKS / SCHRECKENGOST, CHAMBERLIN, COLLINS: CPD, September 7, 1997 ("I was looking . . . ," "Not the kind . . . ," "No problem . . . ," "If something was . . ."). CPD, February 21, 2000, http://www.cleveland.com/news/index/ssf?/news/pd/cc21ness.html (accessed March 19, 2000), PWH ("He was always . . ."). Viktor Schreckengost, interviewed in *The Fourteenth Victim*. Joe Queenan, "Untouchable" (London: BBC Radio 4, June 14, 2007), http://www.bbc.co.uk/programmes/b007ngfp (accessed

September 25, 2014) ("Take her back . . ."). NYT, February 2, 2008, http://
www.nytimes.com/2008/02/02/arts/design/02schreckengost.html (accessed
December 18, 2016). Rebecca McFarland, "Eliot Ness in Cleveland from the
Cleveland Police Museum," Teaching Cleveland Digital, January 2012, http://
teachingcleveland.org/eliot-ness-in-cleveland-from-the-cleveland-police
-museum/ (accessed December 14, 2016). See also Perry, *Eliot Ness*, p. 235.

NESS AND WOMEN: Condon, "The Last American Hero," p. 139. Bergreen, *Capone*, p. 598 ("the sexiest man . . . ," "He used to . . ."). Natalie Phelps, personal interview with ABS, November 15, 2016 ("He was
not . . . ," "the impression that . . ."). Collins and Schwartz, *Scarface and
the Untouchable*, p. 66.

NESS AND BOATS: High, "Cleveland Versus," p. 22. CPD, June 22, 1938,
in ENPS, Roll 2, Scrapbook 8, p. 29. David Cowles, transcript of interview by Florence Schwein and Lt. Tom Brown, September 6, 1983, p. 40,
CPHS ("crazy over boats"). Neff, *Mobbed Up*, p. 22. RM to ABS, personal
email, July 23, 2015. Dan T. Moore, interviewed by Paul Heimel and Bob
Merten, May 30, 1995, PWH. Heimel, *Eliot Ness*, p. 206. Austin, *Forgotten Landmarks of Detroit*, pp. 189–213 (189, "floating hotels").

NESS NEWLY SOCIAL / ALCOHOL POST-PROHIBITION: CN, De-
cember 22, 1938, in ENPS, Roll 2, Scrapbook 8, p. 100 ("mystery man").
Philip W. Porter, "An Image Retouched," CPD, n.d., in ENPS, Roll 1,
Folder 1. Allen, *Since Yesterday*, pp. 141–143. Porter, *Cleveland*, p. 102.
Jedick, "Eliot Ness," pp. 54–55. Condon, "Last American Hero," p. 139
("would always sit . . . ," "We'd kid him . . ."). Ness MS., p. 7, in ENPS, Roll
1, Folder 2. Nickel, *Torso*, pp. 152–153. Bergreen, *Capone*, p. 598. Grimes,
Straight Up or On the Rocks, pp. 85, 91, 102. Rotskoff, *Love on the Rocks*,
pp. 36–45. Sagalyn, *A Promise Fulfilled*, p. 54. Erick Trickey, "Renaissance
Cleveland Hotel /1918/," *Cleveland Magazine*, November 18, 2011, http://
clevelandmagazine.com/in-the-cle/renaissance-cleveland-hotel-1918- (accessed December 19, 2016). Untitled document ("The following information was obtained from the Cleveland Public Library file on Eliot Ness"),
pp. 13–14, in Box 1 "Cleveland Eliot Ness 1939–1941—Biographical Information on Eliot Ness from files of Cleveland Public Library" folder,
ASP. Collins and Schwartz, *Scarface and the Untouchable*, p. 164.

NESS'S PRANKS: *Des Moines Sunday Register*, October 29, 1961. Condon, "Last American Hero," p. 139 ("Perhaps somebody . . . ," "On the
other . . ."). Bergreen, *Capone*, p. 598 ("He managed to . . ."). Dan T.
Moore, interviewed by Paul Heimel and Bob Merten, May 30, 1995, PWH.
Heimel, *Eliot Ness*, p. 206 ("That's just the . . ."). Untitled document ("The
following information was obtained from the Cleveland Public Library file

on Eliot Ness"), pp. 13–14, in box 1 "Cleveland Eliot Ness 1939–1941—Biographical Information on Eliot Ness from files of Cleveland Public Library" folder, ASP.

RUMORS ABOUT NESS'S ROMANTIC LIFE: CPD, June 18, 1961, ENC ("too handsome and . . ."). *Des Moines Sunday Register*, October 29, 1961. Messick, *Silent Syndicate*, p. 116. Porter, *Cleveland*, p. 102 ("seemed to have . . ."). Jedick, "Eliot Ness," pp. 54–55. Nickel, *Torso*, pp. 152–153. Dan Moore, interviewed in "Eliot Ness: Untouchable," *Biography*, directed by Michael Husain (New York: New Video, 2001), VHS. Perry, *Eliot Ness*, pp. 218–219, 270.

ZUKIE'S CLAIMS: Wilder, "The Last Untouchable," pp. 45–46 (46, "a complaint about . . . ," "When we walked . . . ," "When he was . . ."), 115–116. For Clothey as Ness's chief investigator, see E. A. Tamm, "Memorandum for the File," December 20, 1939, in FBI-EN.

Zukie claimed, for instance, to have taken part in the Harvard Club raid, but his name does not appear in the list of officers Ness brought to the scene (CP, January 11, 1936) and his description of the event doesn't accord at all with the historical record. Zukie also claimed to have been part of the vice squad in the late 1930s, though contemporary evidence places him there no earlier than 1940. At the time of Ness's reorganization of the police department in 1938, Zukie was assigned to the Accident Prevention Bureau. (CPD, March 4, 1954. "Accident Prevention Bureau," in *Reorganization Police Department: Cleveland, Ohio 1938*, Monographs, reel 4.46, PAL.)

CAMPBELL AND MCGEE IN PRISON / LABOR RACKETEERING PERSISTS: CP, October 26, 1938; CPD, October 27, 1938, "More Fitting Costumes," n.p., October 28, 1938; "Oust Campbell as Painters' President," n.p., n.d., all in ENPS, Roll 2, Scrapbook 8, p. 84. CP, October 29, 1938, in ENPS, Roll 2, Scrapbook 8, p. 85. CP, January 19, 1939 ("old guard," "progressive"); CPD, January 20, 1939, both in ENPS, Roll 2, Scrapbook 8, p. 108 ("Campbell has enough . . ."). Neff, *Mobbed Up*, pp. 25–30 (25, "We need laws . . ."; 28, "I'm a legitimate . . ."). Jacobs, *Mobsters, Unions, and Feds*, pp. 9–22, 114–137.

ARNOLD SAGALYN: CPD, September 14, 1936. CN, December 22, 1938, in ENPS, Roll 2, Scrapbook 8, p. 100 ("His closest aides . . ."). Condon, "Last American Hero," p. 138. Sagalyn, *A Promise Fulfilled*, pp. 39–64 (41, "an intern-type summer . . . ," "Why don't you . . ."; 43, "special June morning . . . ," "I was going . . ."; 44, "I quickly discovered . . . ," "crack team of . . ."; 48, "Special Policeman in . . ."; 50, "This guy can . . . ," "rather ordinary-looking person . . ."; 51, "The elusive Torso . . . ," "I had no . . . ,"

"That young kid . . ."; 59, "I never talked . . ."). Collins and Schwartz, *Scarface and the Untouchable*, pp. 70–71.

Although Sagalyn doesn't name the Butcher suspect in his memoirs, he confirmed it was Sweeney in an interview with James Jessen Badal (*In the Wake*, pp. 233, 235).

Chapter Fifteen: Right-Hand Man

MOLNAR BACKGROUND: CN, June 11, 1936, in ENPS, Roll 1, Scrapbook 2, p. 93. CPD, February 12, 1937, in ENPS, Roll 1, Scrapbook 5, p. 138 ("the ruggedness of . . . ," "had to get . . ."). CPD, May 8, 1937, in ENPS, Roll 2, Scrapbook 6, p. 5. CPD, May 12, 1937, in ENPS, Roll 2, Scrapbook 6, p. 7. CP, October 12, 1938, in ENPS, Roll 2, Scrapbook 8, p. 67. CP, January 2, 1941, in ENPS, Roll 3, Scrapbook 1, p. 49. Messick, *Silent Syndicate*, p. 174. Wilder, "Last Untouchable," p. 115 ("He was one . . .").

NESS AND MOLNAR: CP, September 1, 1936, in ENPS, Roll 1, Scrapbook 5, p. 41. CPD, September 2, 1936, in ENPS, Roll 1, Scrapbook 5, p. 42. CPD, February 6, 1937, in ENPS, Roll 1, Scrapbook 5, p. 136 ("entangling alliances"). CPD, February 12, 1937, in ENPS, Roll 1, Scrapbook 5, p. 138 ("This business is . . ."). *Buffalo Evening News*, February 27, 1937, in ENPS, Roll 1, Scrapbook 5, p. 173. CPD, May 8, 1937, in ENPS, Roll 2, Scrapbook 6, p. 5. CPD, May 12, 1937, in ENPS, Roll 2, Scrapbook 6, p. 7. CP, November 12, 1937, in ENPS, Roll 2, Scrapbook 6, p. 80. CP, October 29, 1938, in ENPS, Roll 2, Scrapbook 8, p. 85. CP, August 21, 1939, RM. CPD, March 24, 1948. Neff, *Mobbed Up*, p. 24. Wilder, "Last Untouchable," pp. 46 ("Molnar's Raiders"), 115–117.

NUMBERS RACKET: CN, March 26, 1936, in ENPS, Roll 1, Scrapbook 2, p. 60. CP, October 18, 1938; April 26, 1939. CPD, April 26, 1939. CN, April 26, 1939, in ENPS, Roll 2, Scrapbook 9, p. 142. CDN, April 29, 1939, in ENPS, Roll 2, Scrapbook 9, p. 159. Messick, *Silent Syndicate*, pp. 146–147. McGill and Perry, *Court Cases of Eliot Ness*, p. 30. Miller and Wheeler, *Cleveland*, pp. 121–123. Wilder, "Last Untouchable," p. 116. Porrello, *Rise and Fall of the Cleveland Mafia*, p. 185. Haller, *Illegal Enterprise*, pp. 107–108, 142–143, 236–238.

NUMBERS WAR / MAYFIELD ROAD MOB: CCP, February 13, 1936 ("challenged Director Ness . . . ," "blast on broken . . ."); April 27, 1939; July 4, 1942; July 9, 1949; July 13, 1974 ("that as long . . ."). CP, October 18, 1938 ("Big Four"); April 26, 1939. CPD, October 19, 1938, in ENPS, Roll 2, Scrapbook 9, p. 72. CP, October 19, 1938, in ENPS, Roll 2, Scrapbook 9, pp. 73, 72. CP, October 20, 1938, in ENPS, Roll 2, Scrapbook

9, p. 74. CPD, April 26, 1939. CN, October 19, 1938, in ENPS, Roll 2, Scrapbook 8, p. 70. CN, April 26, 1939, in ENPS, Roll 2, Scrapbook 9, pp. 143–144. CDN, April 29, 1939, in ENPS, Roll 2, Scrapbook 9, p. 159. *Hearings Before a Special Committee to Investigate Organized Crime in Interstate Commerce*, pt. 6, pp. 33–34. Messick, *Silent Syndicate*, pp. 85, 89–92, 174–175. Jedick, "Eliot Ness," p. 56. McGill and Perry, *Court Cases of Eliot Ness*, pp. 29–31. Neff, *Mobbed Up*, pp. 12–14, 23–24. Van Tassel and Grabowski, *Encyclopedia of Cleveland History*, pp. 881–882. Porrello, *Rise and Fall*, pp. 183–186 (186, "as a fifty . . ."), 197–198, 201–202. Mappen, *Prohibition Gangsters*, pp. 71–75. Haller, *Illegal Enterprise*, p. 143.

JOHN JONES AND CLAUDE LEE: CCP, May 30, 1935; July 25, 1935; July 9, 1936; August 20, 1936; May 13, 1937; May 20, 1937; June 3, 1937; July 29, 1937; August 26, 1937; October 14, 1937; November 4, 1937; November 11, 1937; February 10, 1938; June 9, 1938; August 11, 1938; April 13, 1939; September 21, 1939; October 26, 1939; November 16, 1939; July 13, 1940; November 23, 1940; January 4, 1941; September 27, 1941 ("two crack aces . . ."); October 25, 1941; November 8, 1941; November 15, 1941; January 31, 1942; March 28, 1942; April 15, 1944; June 10, 1944; July 15, 1944; November 9, 1946; November 1, 1947 ("Why don't you . . . ," "Not only will . . ."); May 7, 1949; December 8, 1951; June 12, 1954; November 14, 1959 ("a policeman's policeman"); February 5, 1966; March 2, 1968 ("Bertha Mae"); February 24, 1973 ("a handsome six . . . ," "a special job . . . ," "personal top man"); October 20, 1979 ("Deadeye"). CG, August 20, 1938. "Ness Salutes 70 Who Dared Talk to Jury," n.p., April 26, 1939, in ENPS, Roll 2, Scrapbook 9, p. 144 ("'You won't get . . .'"). CPD, April 26, 1939. CN, April 26, 1939, in ENPS, Roll 2, Scrapbook 9, pp. 143–144. CCP, April 27, 1939. Collins, *Murder by the Numbers*, pp. 207–208. Record for John H. Jones, in Ancestry.com and Ohio Department of Health, *Ohio, Death Records, 1908–1932, 1938–2007* (Provo, UT: Ancestry.com Operations, Inc., 2010). Record for John Henry Jones in Ancestry.com, *Ohio, Rutherford B. Hayes Presidential Center Obituary Index, 1810s–2016* (Lehi, UT: Ancestry.com Operations, Inc., 2010). Jackson, *Chester B. Himes*, pp. 48–49, 60, 64–69, 74–76, 111–141, 376–377.

INVESTIGATION BEGINS / MOLNAR BUILDS TEAM: CCP, September 17, 1936; November 26, 1936; December 10, 1936; January 28, 1937; April 1, 1937; October 14, 1937; April 27, 1939; May 25, 1939; November 9, 1946. CP, November 12, 1937, in ENPS, Roll 2, Scrapbook 6, p. 80. "Vice Bureau," in *Reorganization Police Department: Cleveland, Ohio 1938*, Monographs, reel 4.46, PAL. CPD, April 26–27, 1939 (April 26, "As long as . . ."). CP, April 26, 1939. "Ness Salutes 70 Who Dared Talk to Jury," n.p., April 26, 1939, in ENPS, Roll 2, Scrapbook 9, p. 144. CN, April 26,

1939, in ENPS, Roll 2, Scrapbook 9, pp. 143–144. CCP, April 27, 1939; May 25, 1939. CP, August 21, 1939, RM ("classified among the . . .").

PROGRESS AND RAIDS: CN, August 18, 1938, in ENPS, Roll 2, Scrapbook 8, p. 46. CCP, September 1, 1938 ("had little or . . ."); October 6, 1938 ("smoker," "engaging in an . . . ," "The raid is . . ."); January 12, 1939; April 27, 1939. CPD, October 4, 1938, in ENPS, Roll 2, Scrapbook 8, p. 65 ("biggest haul in . . ."). CN, October 19, 1938, in ENPS, Roll 2, Scrapbook 8, p. 70.

MOLNAR TAKES BRIBE, CONFESSES / NESS LETS HIM GO: "Vice Bureau," in *Reorganization Police Department: Cleveland, Ohio 1938*, Monographs, reel 4.46, PAL. CP, October 12, 1938, in ENPS, Roll 2, Scrapbook 8, p. 67. CPD, October 12, 1938, in ENPS, Roll 2, Scrapbook 8, p. 68. CPD, March 24, 1948 ("as Ness' right . . ."); May 7, 1949. Fraley, *4 Against the Mob*, p. 9. Neff, *Mobbed Up*, p. 24. "Moore, Dan for Biography Ness," n.d., p. 4, PWH. Sagalyn, *A Promise Fulfilled*, pp. 48–49. Collins and Schwartz, *Scarface and the Untouchable*, pp. 483–485.

BLACKFACE RAIDS: CPD, December 29, 1938 ("without trouble or . . . ," "smiling like minstrel . . ."). CCP, January 5, 1939; January 12, 1939; December 28, 1939.

MEETING WITNESSES / GRAND JURY: CPD, January 31, 1937, in ENPS, Roll 1, Scrapbook 5, p. 133. CPD, April 26–27, 1939. "Ness Salutes 70 Who Dared Talk to Jury," n.p., April 26, 1939, in ENPS, Roll 2, Scrapbook 9, p. 144 ("safety in numbers"). CP, April 26, 1939. CN, April 26, 1939, in ENPS, Roll 2, Scrapbook 9, pp. 143–144. CCP, April 27, 1939 ("almost a ton . . ."). CDN, April 29, 1939, in ENPS, Roll 2, Scrapbook 9, p. 159. CN, May 9, 1939, in ENPS, Roll 2, Scrapbook 8.

INDICTMENTS, DRAGNET, RAID / ANGELOS ESCAPE: CPD, April 26, 1939; April 27, 1939; June 10, 1939. CN, April 26, 1939, in ENPS, Roll 2, Scrapbook 9, pp. 143–144 ("get them all . . ."). CP, April 26, 1939 ("the most sweeping . . ."). "A Great Day for Cleveland," n.p., April 26, 1939, in ENPS, Roll 2, Scrapbook 9, p. 137. CN, April 28, 1939, in ENPS, Roll 2, Scrapbook 9, p. 146. CCP, April 27, 1939; May 4, 1939; May 18, 1939. CDN, April 29, 1939, in ENPS, Roll 2, Scrapbook 9, p. 159. CP, April 29, 1939, in ENPS, Roll 2, Scrapbook 9, p. 147. CPD, April 30, 1939, in ENPS, Roll 2, Scrapbook 9, p. 148. CP, May 1, 1939, in ENPS, Roll 2, Scrapbook 8, p. 151. *Chicago Defender,* July 15, 1939. CN, October 3, 1939, in ENPS, Roll 2, Scrapbook 7, p. 52. CP, October 13, 1939, in ENPS, Roll 2, Scrapbook 7, p. 54. CP, January 25, 1940, in ENPS, Roll 2, Scrapbook 7, p. 89. CP, September 18, 1940, in ENPS, Roll 3, Scrapbook

11, p. 10. Messick, *Silent Syndicate*, pp. 174–175. Neff, *Mobbed Up*, p. 24. Wilder, "Last Untouchable," p. 117.

"CAMERA EYE" PRUCHA: "Director's Office," in *Reorganization Police Department: Cleveland, Ohio 1938*, Monographs, reel 4.46, PAL. CPD, February 4, 1962 ("Camera Eye," "Officer, I am . . . ," "If you're Eliot . . ."). Steven Nickel, "The Real Eliot Ness," *American History Illustrated*, October 1987, p. 42 ("EN-1").

MARIJUANA INVESTIGATION: CP, May 18, 1939, in ENPS, Roll 2, Scrapbook 9, p. 159. CP, May 19, 1939. CN, July 1, 1939, in ENPS, Roll 2, Scrapbook 7, p. 13. CCP, May 25, 1939; June 3, 1939; June 22, 1939; July 6, 1939; December 28, 1939. CN, July 5, 1939, in ENPS, Roll 2, Scrapbook 7, p. 15. "Grand Jury Asks School Morals Class," CP, July 1939, in ENPS, Roll 2, Scrapbook 7, p. 23. McGill and Perry, *Court Cases of Eliot Ness*, pp. 49–51.

MOLNAR ACCUSED: CN, June 7, 1939 ("persecuted," "because I refused . . ."); CP, June 7, 1939; CPD, June 9, 1939, all in ENPS, Roll 2, Scrapbook 7, p. 8. CP, June 14, 1939; CPD, June 15, 1939, both in ENPS, Roll 2, Scrapbook 7, p. 9. CP, June 1939, in ENPS, Roll 2, Scrapbook 7, p. 8 ("picks on the . . ."). "Molnar Inquiry Is Ordered by Ness," n.p., n.d., in ENPS, Roll 2, Scrapbook 7, p. 45. CPD, March 24, 1948.

MAYFIELD MOB SMASHED: CN, April 26, 1939, in ENPS, Roll 2, Scrapbook 9, pp. 143–144. CP, April 26, 1939. CPD, April 27, 1939; July 23, 1948; August 16, 1948; May 7, 1949. CCP, April 27, 1939; May 4, 1939; November 29, 1941; July 4, 1942. CDN, April 29, 1939 ("There doesn't seem . . ."); CPD, May 9, 1939, both in ENPS, Roll 2, Scrapbook 9, p. 159. CP, May 9, 1939, in ENPS, Roll 2, Scrapbook 9, p. 160. CP, October 13, 1939, in ENPS, Roll 2, Scrapbook 7, p. 54. *Hearings Before a Special Committee to Investigate Organized Crime in Interstate Commerce*, pt. 6, p. 34. Messick, *Silent Syndicate*, pp. 174–175. McGill and Perry, *Court Cases*, pp. 31–32, 40–43. Jedick, "Eliot Ness," pp. 56–57. Porrello, *Rise and Fall*, p. 186.

JONES AND LEE KEEP WORKING, SEEK PROMOTION: CCP, August 11, 1938; April 27, 1939; May 4, 1939; November 9, 1940 ("One of the . . ."); August 9, 1941; October 18, 1941; October 25, 1941; November 8, 1941; November 15, 1941; December 13, 1941; February 7, 1942; February 21, 1942; March 28, 1942; April 24, 1943; July 15, 1944; October 21, 1944; January 20, 1945; January 27, 1945; May 19, 1945; November 9, 1946; December 7, 1946; February 1, 1947; February 8, 1947; March 15, 1947; November 22, 1947; January 4, 1948; February 14, 1948; December 25, 1948; March 19, 1949; April 16, 1949; May 7, 1949; April 22, 1950; September 29, 1950; December 8, 1951; May 3, 1952 ("Help make things . . ."); July 18, 1953; July 25, 1953; December 19, 1953; June 12, 1954; October 23, 1954; July 23, 1955; November 14, 1959; February 5, 1966; February 24, 1973 ("As bad as . . ."); October 20, 1979. CG, November 2, 1940. Jackson, *Chester B. Himes*, pp. 350–377, 472–477.

TRIALS AND CONVICTIONS: CPD, April 27, 1939; July 23, 1948; August 16, 1948 ("He was too . . ."); May 7, 1949. CCP, November 29, 1941; July 4, 1942 ("the temerity and . . . ," "long pent up . . ."). *Hearings Before a Special Committee to Investigate Organized Crime in Interstate Commerce*, pt. 6, p. 34. Messick, *Silent Syndicate*, pp. 174–175. McGill and Perry, *Court Cases*, pp. 31–32, 40–43. Jedick, "Eliot Ness," pp. 56–57. Porrello, *Rise and Fall*, p. 186.

MOLNAR TAKES OVER RACKET: CCP, July 4, 1942; July 27, 1946; November 9, 1946; November 30, 1946; March 6, 1948; April 3, 1948; July 17, 1948; July 24, 1948; July 31, 1948; August 7, 1948; August 28, 1948; December 18, 1948; May 14, 1949; July 9, 1949 ("Negro operators who . . ."); July 30, 1949; August 6, 1949; August 27, 1949; February 4, 1950; June 14, 1952; January 24, 1953; May 2, 1953; June 12, 1954. *Hearings Before a Special Committee to Investigate Organized Crime in Interstate Commerce*, pt. 6, pp. 32–36 (35, "saw how he . . ."; 36, "Had Cleveland been . . ."). CPD, August 16, 1948; February 18, 1949. Albert Q. Maisel, "Return of the Numbers Racket," *Collier's*, January 15, 1949, p. 72. Messick, *Silent Syndicate*, pp. 175–292. Jedick, "Eliot Ness," p. 56. Porrello, *Rise and Fall*, pp. 202–205. Nickel, *Torso*, pp. 176–178. Neff, *Mobbed Up*, p. 24. Wilder, "Last Untouchable," p. 117 ("worked in Ness's . . ."). Mappen, *Prohibition Gangsters*, pp. 216–217.

Chapter Sixteen: A New Suspect

NESS AND POLITICS: CP, March 2, 1936, in ENPS, Roll 1, Scrapbook 2, p. 55. CP, February 23, 1937, in ENPS, Roll 1, Scrapbook 3. CN, July 14, 1938, in ENPS, Roll 2, Scrapbook 8, p. 32. CN, December 22, 1938, in ENPS, Roll 2, Scrapbook 8, p. 100 ("He is ambitious . . ."). CP, January 20, 1939, in ENPS, Roll 2, Scrapbook 8, p. 108. CPD, June 24, 1939, in ENPS, Roll 2, Scrapbook 7, p. 11 ("I'm in a . . ."). CPD, June 25, 1939, in ENPS, Roll 2, Scrapbook 7, p. 11. CP, June 28, 1939, in ENPS, Roll 2, Scrapbook 7, p. 13. CP, July 1, 1939, in ENPS, Roll 2, Scrapbook 7, p. 15. CP, August 24, 1939, in ENPS, Roll 2, Scrapbook 7, p. 40. CN, November 9, 1939, in ENPS, Roll 2, Scrapbook 7, p. 65. "The Next Mayor," n.p., November 10, 1940, in ENPS, Roll 3, Scrapbook 11, p. 39. Condon, "Last American Hero," p. 141.

O'DONNELL UNFIT, IN TROUBLE, FEARS NESS: CP, June 15, 1938 ("a playground for . . ."); CN, June 15, 1938; CP, June 15, 1938, all in ENPS, Roll 2, Scrapbook 8, p. 24. CPD, June 16, 1938, in ENPS, Roll 2,

Scrapbook 8, p. 25. CPD, January 30, 1939, in ENPS, Roll 2, Scrapbook 8, p. 109. E. P. Guinane to J. Edgar Hoover, November 9, 1939, in FBI-ENA. Badal, *Though Murder*, pp. 7–8, 145–147.

Many sources suggest or imply that O'Donnell's interest in the torso case was politically motivated, but Guinane's FBI memo to Hoover (cited above) makes this explicit. According to Guinane, one of O'Donnell's investigators told the FBI that the sheriff's office believed "that Eliot Ness would probably seek the nomination of sheriff on the Republican ticket against Sheriff O'Donnell," and that "Sheriff O'Donnell, in an attempt to discredit Safety Director Ness and gain publicity, began an investigation of the Cleveland unsolved torso murders without consulting the Cleveland police department."

Guinane wrote to Hoover because this investigator had sought to find out whether or not Ness had ever worked as an FBI agent, so as to prepare O'Donnell for the 1940 campaign. He went on to advise Hoover that "it is the intention of Sheriff Martin O'Donnell to take this matter up personally with you or through Congressman Martin Sweeney, who is a close associate of Sheriff O'Donnell." It remains unclear whether O'Donnell or Sweeney ever followed up with Hoover.

LYONS INVESTIGATION / FRANK DOLEZAL: Ritt, "Head Hunter," in Bayer, *Cleveland Murders*, pp. 236–237, 239–240. Martin, *Butcher's Dozen*, p. 90 ("a man who . . ."). Nickel, *Torso*, pp. 154–157, 159–160. Bellamy, *Maniac in the Bushes*, pp. 268–269. Badal, *Though Murder*, pp. 12–14, 18–23, 26–28, 30–31 ("passionate craving . . ."), 33, 37, 53–54, 70. Badal, *In the Wake*, pp. 186–188, 192.

LYONS BLOWS COVER / DOLEZAL CONFESSES: CPD, July 8, 1939. Ritt, "Head Hunter," in Bayer, *Cleveland Murders*, pp. 239–241 (239, "Boys, we have . . ."). Martin, *Butcher's Dozen*, pp. 90–91. Nickel, *Torso*, pp. 154, 157–159. Badal, *Though Murder*, pp. 24–26, 31–35. Badal, *In the Wake*, pp. 188–189.

REACTIONS TO CONFESSION / POLITICAL IMPLICATIONS: Ralph Kelly, "Torso Case Seen As Aid to Sheriff," CPD, n.d., in ENPS, Roll 2, Scrapbook 7, p. 15 ("the weakest candidate . . . ," "immeasurably improved," "Before the confession . . ."). CP, July 8, 1939, in ENPS, Roll 2, Scrapbook 7, p. 13 ("It looks much . . . ," "We're afraid that . . ."). CCP, July 13, 1939 ("a sex-mad Negro . . . ," "Police had worked . . . ," "Miss Hackney," "weird appearance and . . . ," "pervert," "Anyway, she was . . ."). Nickel, *Torso*, pp. 159–160. Bellamy, *Maniac in the Bushes*, p. 270. Badal, *Though Murder*, pp. 56–57, 151–152, 169–170. Badal, *In the Wake*, p. 191.

DOUBTS ABOUT CONFESSION / MERYLO DEBUNKS: CPD, July 8, 1939 ("The sheriff is . . ."). CN, July 10, 1939, in ENPS, Roll 2, Scrapbook 7, p. 15 ("City Hall privately . . ."). Ritt, "Head Hunter," in Bayer, *Cleveland Murders*, pp. 242–243. Martin, *Butcher's Dozen*, pp. 90–91. Nickel, *Torso*, pp. 159–162. Badal, *Though Murder*, pp. 32–33, 37–38 ("on the verge . . . ," "His eyes are . . . ," "If he hadn't . . ."), 165. Badal, *In the Wake*, pp. 191–193 (192, "This was my . . .").

DOLEZAL ABUSED, RECANTS / CASE FALLING APART: Ritt, "Head Hunter," in Bayer, *Cleveland Murders*, pp. 243–246. Martin, *Butcher's Dozen*, p. 91. Nickel, *Torso*, pp. 160–167. Bellamy, *Maniac in the Bushes*, pp. 271–272 (272, "plain dirt"), 274. Badal, *Though Murder*, pp. 35–36, 42–43, 46–50 (48, "They kept at . . ."; 50, "Is the sheriff . . ."), 55, 84–85, 93–94 ("Sure, we got . . ."), 165. Badal, *In the Wake*, pp. 193–197.

Chapter Seventeen: The Right Man?

BLACKWELL: CCP, February 9, 1939 ("left a trail . . ."); August 6, 1949; August 27, 1949. CP, July 13, 1939, in ENPS, Roll 2, Scrapbook 7, p. 16. CP, July 17, 1939, in ENPS, Roll 2, Scrapbook 7, p. 18. CPD, July 18, 1939, in ENPS, Roll 2, Scrapbook 7, p. 20. CPD, July 29, 1939, in ENPS, Roll 2, Scrapbook 7, p. 22. CP, August 21, 1939, RM ("untouchables"). *Springfield Sunday Union and Republican*, July 27, 1941 ("the bookies, gamblers . . . ," "His strategy is . . . ," "fiercely enthusiastic about . . . ," "as docile as . . . "). Wilder, "Last Untouchable," p. 115 ("Sledgehammer Mike"). Sagalyn, *A Promise Fulfilled*, pp. 47–48 (47, "a big, brawny . . .").

UAW STRIKE: CPD, July 10, 1939. CP, July 31, 1939, in ENPS, Roll 2, Scrapbook 7, pp. 23–25. CT, August 1, 1939. *Chicago Examiner*, August 1, 1939, in ENPS, Roll 2, Scrapbook 7, p. 31. NYT, August 1, 1939; August 2, 1939. LAT, August 1, 1939. CCP, August 3, 1939. CPD, August 4, 1939, in ENPS, Roll 2, Scrapbook 7, p. 39.

FISHER BODY BATTLE: CN, July 31, 1939 ("I heard Captain . . . ," "Tear gas was . . . ,"); August 3, 1939 ("civil war without . . ."). CP, July 31, 1939, in ENPS, Roll 2, Scrapbook 7, pp. 23–25 ("We don't want any trouble . . . ," "We don't want any either," "Pardon me a . . ."). *Atlanta Constitution*, August 1, 1939 ("unless [the strikers] . . ."). *Chicago Examiner*, August 1, 1939, in ENPS, Roll 2, Scrapbook 7, p. 31. CT, August 1, 1939. CPD, August 1, 1939, in ENPS, Roll 2, Scrapbook 7, pp. 29–30. *Daily Mirror*, August 1, 1939, in ENPS, Roll 2, Scrapbook 7, p. 30. LAT, August 1, 1939 ("unless [the strikers] . . ."). NYT, August 1, 1939 ("Hold your lines!"). CT, August 1, 1939, in ENPS, Roll 2, Scrapbook 7, p. 33. CP, August 7, 1939, in ENPS, Roll 2, Scrapbook 7, p. 41. Brigadier General Ludwig S. Conelly and Infantry Captain Lester J. Abele, memo to Major General Gilson D. Light, August 9, 1939, in Container 3, Folder 11, HHB-EBP.

FRAGILE PEACE / NESS AND BURTON ARRIVE: CN, July 31, 1939; August 3, 1939. CP, July 31, 1939, in ENPS, Roll 2, Scrapbook 7, pp. 23–25. *Atlanta Constitution*, August 1, 1939. *Chicago Examiner*, August 1, 1939, in ENPS, Roll 2, Scrapbook 7, p. 31. CT, August 1, 1939. CPD, August 1, 1939, in ENPS, Roll 2, Scrapbook 7, pp. 29–30. *Daily Mirror*, August 1, 1939, in ENPS, Roll 2, Scrapbook 7, p. 30. LAT, August 1, 1939. NYT, August 1, 1939. WP, August 1, 1939. Brigadier General Ludwig S. Conelly and Infantry Captain Lester J. Abele, memo to Major General Gilson D. Light, August 9, 1939, in Container 3, Folder 11, HHB-EBP. "Fisher Body Strike photographs," Ohio History Connection Selections, January 7, 2009, http://www.ohiomemory.org/cdm/compoundobject/collection/p267401coll32/id/1808 (accessed January 2, 2017).

NESS'S PROCLAMATION / WORKING TO KEEP THE PEACE: CN, July 31, 1939 ("lawful business"); August 3, 1939. CP, July 31, 1939, in ENPS, Roll 2, Scrapbook 7, pp. 23–25 ("riot zone"). *Atlanta Constitution*, August 1, 1939. *Chicago Examiner*, August 1, 1939, in ENPS, Roll 2, Scrapbook 7, p. 31 ("a good reason . . ."). CT, August 1–2, 1939. CT, August 1, 1939, in ENPS, Roll 2, Scrapbook 7, p. 33. CPD, August 1, 1939, in ENPS, Roll 2, Scrapbook 7, pp. 29–30. CP, August 1, 1939, in ENPS, Roll 2, Scrapbook 7, p. 28. *Daily Mirror*, August 1, 1939, in ENPS, Roll 2, Scrapbook 7, p. 30 ("clear out of . . ."). LAT, August 1–2, 1939. *New York Post*, August 1, 1939, in ENPS, Roll 2, Scrapbook 7, p. 32. NYT, August 1–2, 1939 (August 2, "a violation of . . ."). CPD, August 2, 1939; *Daily Record*, August 3, 1939, both in ENPS, Roll 2, Scrapbook 7, p. 34. CPD, August 2, 1939, in ENPS, Roll 2, Scrapbook 7, p. 35. CP, August 3, 1939, in ENPS, Roll 2, Scrapbook 7, p. 36 ("Such picketing violates . . ."). *Union Leader*, August 3, 1939; CPD, August 4, 1939, both in ENPS, Roll 2, Scrapbook 7, p. 39. Brigadier General Ludwig S. Conelly and Infantry Captain Lester J. Abele, memo to Major General Gilson D. Light, August 9, 1939, in Container 3, Folder 11, HHB-EBP.

STRIKE ENDS / POLICE, NESS, BURTON PRAISED: CPD, August 1–2, 1939, both in ENPS, Roll 1, Scrapbook 4. CN, August 3, 1939 ("From our personal . . ."). CPD, August 4, 1939, in ENPS, Roll 2, Scrapbook 7, p. 39. Brigadier General Ludwig S. Conelly and Infantry Captain Lester J. Abele, memo to Major General Gilson D. Light, August 9, 1939, in Container 3, Folder 11, HHB-EBP.

DOLEZAL DEATH AND INQUEST: CPD, August 25, 1939 ("All I can . . ."). Ritt, "Head Hunter," in Bayer, *Cleveland Murders*, pp. 244–247.

Martin, "Butcher's Dozen," pp. 90–91. Nickel, *Torso*, pp. 163–168. Bellamy, *Maniac in the Bushes*, pp. 271 ("drunk as a . . ."), 273–274 (274, "We did all . . ."). Badal, *Though Murder*, pp. 58–63, 74–78, 82–95, 99–109, 148, 150, 166–169. Badal, *In the Wake*, pp. 197–203, 205–207.

NESS ALOOF / GERBER'S VERDICT STANDS: Nickel, *Torso*, pp. 165–166. Bellamy, *Maniac in the Bushes*, p. 274. Badal, *Though Murder*, pp. 78–91, 99–109, 147–151, 164–166. Badal, *In the Wake*, pp. 201–207.

O'DONNELL LATER LIFE AND DEATH, REPLACED BY JOSEPH SWEENEY: E. P. Guinane to J. Edgar Hoover, November 9, 1939, in FBI-ENA. CP, November 29, 1939, in ENPS, Roll 2, Scrapbook 7, p. 76 ("to run for . . ."). CP, December 3, 1939, in ENPS, Roll 2, Scrapbook 7, p. 77. CPD, December 12, 1939, in ENPS, Roll 2, Scrapbook 7, p. 82. CPD, March 9, 1940, in ENPS, Roll 2, Scrapbook 7, p. 98 ("It would be . . ."). CPD, November 3, 1940; CN, November 7, 1940, both in ENPS, Roll 3, Scrapbook 11, p. 38. CP, May 24, 1941, in ENPS, Roll 3, Scrapbook 11, p. 89. CPD, June 26, 1941, in ENPS, Roll 3, Scrapbook 5, p. 103. CPD, June 28, 1941, in ENPS, Roll 3, Scrapbook 5, p. 105. CN, June 28, 1941, in ENPS, Roll 3, Scrapbook 11, p. 100. CPD, June 29, 1941 ("With Sweeney as . . ."). Badal, *Though Murder*, p. 147.

DOLEZAL'S DEATH MARKS END OF MURDERS: John Bartlow Martin, "Butcher's Dozen: The Cleveland Torso Murders," *Harper's Magazine*, November 1949, pp. 91, 96 ("The arrest of . . ."). Nickel, *Torso*, p. 168. Badal, *In the Wake*, p. 187.

MERYLO KEEPS INVESTIGATING, GETS LETTER: Badal, *In the Wake*, pp. 135, 165–167 (165, "our Doc").

Chapter Eighteen: That's the Man

NESS'S NEW WIFE / SECRET MARRIAGE: CN, October 26, 1939; CP, October 26, 1939, in ENPS, Roll 2, Scrapbook 7, p. 57. CPD, October 27, 1939, ENC ("I'm lucky in . . ."). "Ness Wins Decree from Artist Wife," n.p., n.d., in "Ness, Eliot" microfiche, CPC. *Evening Star*, May 27, 1944, folder 3, NLEM 2012.39.1. Joan Hess Michel, "Evaline Ness, Caldecott Medalist," *American Artist*, June 1967, p. 71. Commire, *Something About the Author*, p. 165. Porter, *Cleveland*, p. 102. Condon, "Last American Hero," p. 139 ("Edna was an . . . ," "Evaline may have . . ."). Nickel, *Torso*, pp. 152, 170. Tucker, *Eliot Ness and the Untouchables*, pp. 31–32. Perry, *Eliot Ness*, p. 190 ("wasn't beautiful, but . . ."). Charles Romans, "'Untouchable' Eliot Ness Married 2nd Wife in Greenup County,"

Daily Independent, January 17, 2017, http://www.dailyindependent.com
/news/untouchable-eliot-ness-married-nd-wife-in-greenup-county/article
_431e7930–dd25–11e6–9cd6–734223f1aaef.html (accessed January 17,
2017) ("writer," "single").

EVALINE MEETS ELIOT / EARLY LIFE: Michel, "Evaline Ness," p. 71
("unbeautiful, factory town"). "Evaline Ness," in Sarkissian, *Something
About the Author*, pp. 223–227 (223, "born late and . . ."; 226, "perfect
day in . . . ," "Eliot and I . . . ," "I thought of . . . ," "tracked," "Eliot had
many . . ."; 227, "father's dark Swedish . . . ," "the most comforting . . . ,"
"Why don't you . . ."). Jedick, "Eliot Ness," p. 54. Heimel, *Eliot Ness*, p.
209. Perry, *Eliot Ness*, p. 227. Terry Trucco, "Renaissance Murals on the
Ceiling: The Sherry-Netherland Lobby Gets a New Old Look," Overnight
New York, June 1, 2014, http://blog.overnightnewyork.com/renaissance
-murals-on-the-ceiling-the-sherry-netherland-lobby-gets-a-new-old-look/
(accessed January 4, 2017).

ELIOT HEAD OVER HEELS / EVALINE TROUBLED: CPD, October 27,
1939, ENC ("NESS' BRIDE TO . . ."). CN, October 2, 1940, in ENPS, Roll
3, Scrapbook 11, p. 23. *Des Moines Sunday Register*, October 29, 1961.
Fraley, *4 Against the Mob*, pp. 9–10 ("Cats don't have . . ."). Jedick, "Eliot
Ness," pp. 54–55 (55, "the most controlled . . ."). "Evaline Ness," in Sarkissian, *Something About the Author*, pp. 226–231 (227, "Eliot . . ."). Condon,
"Last American Hero," p. 139 ("He loved her . . ."). "Schreckengost, Victor
for Biography Ness," n.d., p. 4, PWH. Perry, *Eliot Ness*, pp. 227, 231–233,
269 ("more like . . .").

BURTON RALLY / POLICE-FIRE AMENDMENT: CP, July 15, 1939
("take police and . . . ," "unofficial chief of . . ."); CPD, July 15, 1939, both
in ENPS, Roll 2, Scrapbook 7, p. 17. CPD, July 18, 1939, in ENPS, Roll
2, Scrapbook 7, p. 18. CP, July 18, 1939, in ENPS, Roll 2, Scrapbook 7,
p. 19. CN, July 24, 1939, in ENPS, Roll 2, Scrapbook 7, p. 20. CN, July
26, 1939; CPD, July 26, 1939, both in ENPS, Roll 2, Scrapbook 7, p.
21. "Statement by Mayor Harold H. Burton as to Charter Amendment
Affecting Divisions of Police and Fire," July 27, 1939, in box 347, folder
4, HBP (also in box 356, folder 6, HBP). CPD, August 6, 1939, in ENPS,
Roll 2, Scrapbook 7, p. 39 ("a 'get Ness' . . ."). CP, October 23, 1939; CN,
October 25, 1939, in ENPS, Roll 2, Scrapbook 7, p. 55. Harold H. Burton,
"Statement at Opening of Mayoral Campaign," October 26, 1939, in box
347, folder 5, HBP. CPD, October 27, 1939, ENC ("Ness Night"). CP,
October 29, 1939, in ENPS, Roll 2, Scrapbook 7, p. 60. CN, October 26,
1939, in ENPS, Roll 2, Scrapbook 7, p. 56. CPD, November 2, 1939; CN,
November 9, 1939, in ENPS, Roll 2, Scrapbook 7, p. 65. "Statement by

Mayor Harold H. Burton Broadcast over W.G.A.R. November 6, 1939, 10:55 P.M.," in box 347, folder 6, HBP (also in box 350, folder 11, HBP). CP, January 8, 1940, in ENPS, Roll 2, Scrapbook 7, p. 83. CN, February 6[?], 1940, in ENPS, Roll 2, Scrapbook 7, p. 92.

POLICE RESENT AND RESIST NESS: Philip W. Porter, "The Inside of the News in Cleveland," CPD, n.d., in ENPS, Roll 1, Scrapbook 2, p. 18. Chads O. Skinner, "1938 Sets Mark in Police Progress," n.p., n.d., in ENPS, Roll 2, Scrapbook 8, p. 103 ("I wonder what . . ."). CPD, July 15, 1939; CP, July 15, 1939, both in ENPS, Roll 2, Scrapbook 7, p. 17. CPD, July 18, 1939, in ENPS, Roll 2, Scrapbook 7, p. 18. CP, July 18, 1939, in ENPS, Roll 2, Scrapbook 7, p. 19. CN, July 24, 1939, in ENPS, Roll 2, Scrapbook 7, p. 20. CN, July 26, 1939; CPD, July 26, 1939, both in ENPS, Roll 2, Scrapbook 7, p. 21. CP, August 19 [?], 1939, in ENPS, Roll 2, Scrapbook 7, p. 46. CN, September 20, 1939, in ENPS, Roll 2, Scrapbook 7, p. 47. CN, October 30, 1939, in ENPS, Roll 2, Scrapbook 7, p. 58. CPD, November 27, 1939. CT, December 10, 1939. CP, January 3, 1940, in ENPS, Roll 2, Scrapbook 7, p. 85. CPD, February 16, 1941, in ENPS, Roll 3, Scrapbook 11, p. 74. "Record of the Safety Department in 1939," n.d., in container 6, folder 6, HHB-EBP. Rose, *Cleveland*, p. 980.

SUPPORT FOR NESS / 1939 ELECTION: Paul Havens, "Personalities in Law Enforcement: Eliot Ness," *True Detective Mysteries*, November 1939, pp. 61. CPD, August 6, 1939, in ENPS, Roll 2, Scrapbook 7, p. 39. CN, September 20, 1939, in ENPS, Roll 2, Scrapbook 7, p. 47 ("If the Burton . . ."). CP, October 19, 1939, in ENPS, Roll 2, Scrapbook 7, p. 54. CP, October 23, 1939; CN, October 25, 1939, both in ENPS, Roll 2, Scrapbook 7, p. 55. CPD, October 27, 1939, [as *News*] in ENPS, Roll 2, Scrapbook 7, p. 58. CP, November 1, 1939, in ENPS, Roll 2, Scrapbook 7, p. 62. CP, November 1, 1939; CN, November 1, 1939, both in ENPS, Roll 2, Scrapbook 7, p. 63. CPD, November 5, 1939; CN, November 5, 1939, both in ENPS, Roll 2, Scrapbook 7, p. 65. CPD, November 8, 1939, in ENPS, Roll 2, Scrapbook 7, p. 79 ("Even in precincts . . ."). CN, November 8, 1939, in ENPS, Roll 2, Scrapbook 7, p. 64. CP, November 8, 1939, in ENPS, Roll 2, Scrapbook 7, p. 67. CP, November 8, 1939; CP, November 8, 1939, both in ENPS, Roll 2, Scrapbook 7, p. 68. CPD, November 8, 1939, in ENPS, Roll 2, Scrapbook 7, p. 80.

PATROLMAN GREEN / FOREMAN KILLING AND AFTERMATH: CPD, June 28, 1936; CP, June 26, 1936; CN, June 26, 1936, all in ENPS, Roll 1, Scrapbook 5, p. 1. CPD, June 26, 1936, in ENPS, Roll 1, Scrapbook 2, p. 96. CCP, May 18, 1939 ("to whip all . . . ," "You're not so . . ."); June

1, 1939 ("jumped him from . . ."); September 7, 1939; September 28, 1939; November 30, 1939 ("aroused intense resentment . . ."); December 7, 1939 ("By his consistent . . ."). CG, May 20, 1939; June 3, 1939; June 17, 1939; June 24, 1939; December 2, 1939 ("poor judgment"). *Chicago Defender*, September 30, 1939; December 9, 1939. CN, September 23, 1939, in ENPS, Roll 2, Scrapbook 7, p. 49. CPD, November 29, 1939, in ENPS, Roll 2, Scrapbook 7, p. 75 ("poor judgment").

WWII BEGINS / INDUSTRIAL SAFETY COMMITTEE CONTRO-VERSY AND AFTERMATH: CPD, September 1, 1939. Harold H. Burton, "Statement as to Cooperation of Cities with Federal Bureau of Investigation Pursuant to Request by the President," September 19, 1939, in box 347, folder 5, HBP ("to all law . . ."). L. R. Pennington, Memorandum for Mr. Tamm, April 28, 1939; Author redacted, memorandum, November 8, 1939 ("trustworthy"); R. P. Kramer, memo to E. A. Tamm, November 18, 1939; W. S. Deveraux to J. W. Gregory, November 21, 1939; E. A. Tamm, Memorandum for the Director, December 1, 1939; John Edgar Hoover, Memorandum for the Attorney General, December 4, 1939; E. A. Tamm, Memorandum for the File, December 19, 1939; E. A. Tamm, Memorandum or the File, December 20, 1939 ("I'm in charge . . ."); J. Edgar Hoover to Edwin M. Watson, December 26, 1939; Anonymous, Memorandum, December 26, 1939; Clyde Tolson, Memorandum for the Director, January 11, 1940; Author unclear, memorandum, January 18, 1940; A. Rosen, "Memorandum for E. A. Tamm, January 18, 1940, all in FBI-EN. CP, October 12, 1939, in ENPS, Roll 2, Scrapbook 7, p. 53 ("Herr Ness and . . . ," "If war comes . . ."). CP, November 30, 1939, in ENPS, Roll 2, Scrapbook 7, p. 76 ("radical"). CP, December 15, 1939, in ENPS, Roll 2, Scrapbook 7, p. 84 ("a three-month . . ."). CN, December 16, 1939. CPD, December 17, 1939, in ENPS, Roll 2, Scrapbook 7, p. 82. CPD, December 19, 1939, in "Ness, Eliot" microfiche, CPC. CP, December 19, 1939, in "Ness, Eliot" microfiche, CPC. CN, October 2, 1940, in ENPS, Roll 3, Scrapbook 11, p. 23. CP, November 25, 1940, in ENPS, Roll 3, Scrapbook 11, p. 44. CPD, November 16, 1941, in ENPS, Roll 3, Scrapbook 11, p. 126 ("set up a . . ."). Allen, *Since Yesterday*, pp. 345–346. Jedick, "Eliot Ness," p. 57. Dan T. Moore, interviewed by Paul Heimel and Bob Merten, May 30, 1995, PWH ("If Eliot had . . ."). Van Tassel and Grabowski, *Encyclopedia of Cleveland History*, p. 500. Burrough, *Public Enemies*, pp. 150, 419, 450, 453, 500, 525. Brands, *Traitor to His Class*, pp. 655 ("to take charge . . ."). Erick Trickey, "Eliot Ness vs. J. Edgar Hoover," *Smithsonian*, October 2014, pp. 83–85 (85, "blame the FBI," "subversive squad," "radicals"). Collins and Schwartz, *Scarface and the Untouchable*, pp. 230–235.

MERYLO INTERVIEWS SWEENEY / MERYLO'S THEORIES: CPD, October 16, 1939 ("pervert"); January 8, 1989. Peter Merylo, "Report on Torso Murders Investigation, from Sept. 10, 1936 to Oct. 1, 1942," CPHS. Martin, "Butcher's Dozen," pp. 76, 91–92, 95–96. Nickel, *Torso*, pp. 153–154, 171–175, 185–187. Bellamy, *Maniac in the Bushes*, pp. 293–294. Badal, *Hell's Wasteland*, pp. xii–xiii, 33–83, 85–121 (115, "is not the . . ."). Badal, *In the Wake*, pp. 159–164, 167, 177–178, 252–255.

NESS CONVINCED OF SWEENEY'S GUILT, HAS HIM COMMITTED: SAC, Cincinnati, memo to Director, FBI, October 2, 1953, in FBI-FES ("confined as a . . ."). John A. Larson, "Sketches: Torso Case, Cleveland," n.d., in Box 2, Folder 4 ("Correspondence 1938–1940"), John Larson Papers, BANC MSS 78/160cz, UCB ("The suspect tested . . ."). John A. Larson to Chief of Police, Cleveland Police Department, December 7, 1956, in John Augustus Larson Papers, personal collection of Beulah Allen Graham (courtesy of Ken Alder). John A. Larson to Richard Jenkins, April 4, 1959, in box 2, folder 4 ("Correspondence—1938–1940"), John Larson Papers, BANC MSS 78/160cz, UCB (a rougher copy in John Augustus Larson Papers, personal collection of Beulah Allen Graham [courtesy of Ken Alder]). *Des Moines Sunday Register*, October 29, 1961 ("That's the man . . ."). Fraley, interviewed in "Eliot Ness," *Unsolved Mysteries*. Bardsley, "Eliot Ness Hunts." Transcript of interview with Dan Moore, November 16, 1997, in Fred McGunagle, email to Paul Heimel, July 5, 1999, PWH. Fred McGunagle, email to Paul Heimel, June 20, 1999, PWH. Barbara A. McCoy Giera, email to Paul Heimel, June 15, 2004, PWH ("always go with . . ."). *Cameron County Endeavor*, December 4, 2004, PWH. *Potter Leader-Enterprise*, February 16, 2005, PWH. Cerny, "Chronology and Summary," in Badal, *Though Murder*, pp. 200, 203. Badal, *Though Murder*, p. 145. Sagalyn, *A Promise Fulfilled*, pp. 51–52 (52, "DIG HERE"). Badal, *In the Wake*, pp. 219. Rebecca McFarland, interview with ABS, December 4, 2015. RM, personal emails to ABS, December 10, 2015, and October 23, 2016. Bardsley, *American Sweeney Todd*, pp. 227, 230–231 ("call Eliot frequently . . .").

RUMORS OF SWEENEY / MERYLO'S LATER LIFE: Peter Merylo, "Report on Torso Murders Investigation, from Sept. 10, 1936 to Oct. 1, 1942," March 15, 1943, pp. 10–11, CPHS ("I will never . . . ," a habit with . . . ," "Regardless of what . . ."). CPD, January 8, 1989 ("said he knew . . ."). Nickel, *Torso*, pp. 186–187. Bellamy, *Maniac in the Bushes*, pp. 295–296. Badal, *In the Wake*, pp. 166–167, 216–217, 256–257 (257, "leave it alone," "his family"), 263–264.

Zukie described Merylo's supposed suspect as a nurse, not a doctor, but he might very well have conflated the suspect with Edward Andrassy, one of the Butcher's first victims and a nurse at City Hospital. (James Jessen Badal, personal email to ABS, August 16, 2016.)

CONGRESSMAN SWEENEY'S LATER LIFE: "The Congress: The Bitter End," p. 12 ("a traitor," "the best blow . . ."). CPD, November 30, 1941, in ENPS, Roll 3, Scrapbook 11, p. 134 ("of more bingo . . ."). Chasan and Riesel, "Keep Them Out," pp. 626–628 (626, "one of Hitler's . . .," "abject failure and . . . "; 628, "with groups and . . ."). O. John Rogge, "Nazi Ties in America Exposed," *Jewish Veteran*, December 1946, p. 6. Rogge, *Official German Report*, pp. 153–154, 160–162, 164, 170–171, 262–263. Van Tassel and Grabowski, *Dictionary of Cleveland Biography*, pp. 148, 438. Badal, *Though Murder*, pp. 151–154, 169–170. Joseph E. Persico, "The Day When We Almost Lost the Army," *American Heritage*, Spring 2012, http://www .americanheritage.com/content/day-when-we-almost-lost-army (accessed December 29, 2016) ("a son of . . ."). Albrecht and Banks, *Cleveland in World War II*, pp. 8–9. Hart, *Hitler's American Friends*, pp. 96–115.

BUTCHER'S SHADOW REMAINS / SWORN TO SECRECY: CCP, July 4, 1942. Ritt, "Head Hunter," in Bayer, *Cleveland Murders*, pp. 231–232. Martin, "Butcher's Dozen," pp. 89–90. CPD, January 8, 1989. Nickel, *Torso*, pp. 144–147. Badal, *Though Murder*, pp. 151–154. Aja Romano, "Uncovering the Mad Butcher of Kingsbury Run," *Daily Dot*, November 27, 2012, http://www.dailydot.com/society/mad-butcher-kingsbury-run/ (accessed January 13, 2017). Badal, *In the Wake*, pp. 161, 226. Bardsley, *The American Sweeney Todd*, pp. 227, 229.

Chapter Nineteen: Whatever Became of Eliot Ness?

NESS MISSING: CP, May 22, 1940, in ENPS, Roll 2, Scrapbook 7, p. 121. ("I am wondering . . . ," "Maybe we should . . ."). Fraley, *4 Against the Mob*, p. 149.

BARRINGTON INVESTIGATION, TRIAL, AND CONVICTION: Clayton Fritchey, "Jurors Also Cite Dylinski, Barrington," n.p., n.d.; CPD, June 20, 1940, both in ENPS, Roll 2, Scrapbook 7, p. 131. CPD, June 4, 1940, in ENPS, Roll 2, Scrapbook 7, p. 125. CN, June 4, 1940; CP, June 4, 1940, both in ENPS, Roll 2, Scrapbook 7, p. 126. CPD, June 5, 1940; CP, June 5, 1940, all in ENPS, Roll 2, Scrapbook 7, p. 127. CN, June 19, 1940; CP, June 20, 1940, both in ENPS, Roll 2, Scrapbook 7, p. 132. CPD, June 21, 1940; CPD, June 21, 1940; CP, June 21, 1940; CN, June 21, 1940, all in ENPS, Roll 2, Scrapbook 7, p. 133. CP, September 27, 1940; CN, September 27, 1940, in ENPS, Roll 3, Scrapbook 11, p. 15. CPD, September 28, 1940, in ENPS, Roll 3, Scrapbook 11, pp. 12, 16. CP, September 28,

1940, in ENPS, Roll 3, Scrapbook 11, p. 16. CP, September 28, 1940; CP, October 1, 1940, both in ENPS, Roll 3, Scrapbook 11, p. 17. CP, September 28, 1940, in ENPS, Roll 3, Scrapbook 11, p. 20. CPD, September 28, 1940, in ENPS, Roll 3, Scrapbook 11, p. 14. CN, September 28, 1940; CN, September 30, 1940; CP, October 2, 1940, all in ENPS, Roll 3, Scrapbook 11, p. 19. CN, October 2, 1940, in ENPS, Roll 3, Scrapbook 11, p. 23 ("He seems . . . ," "Several of the . . ."). CN, October 4, 1940; CP, October 4, 1940, both in ENPS, Roll 3, Scrapbook 11, p. 26. CP, October 12, 1940; CN, October 12, 1940; CP, October 12, 1940 ("most important victory . . ."), all in ENPS, Roll 3, Scrapbook 11, p. 32. CP, October 1, 1940, in ENPS, Roll 3, Scrapbook 11, pp. 17–18. CPD, October 2, 1940, in ENPS, Roll 3, Scrapbook 11, p. 18. CP, October 2, 1940, in ENPS, Roll 3, Scrapbook 11, p. 21. CPD, October 2, 1940; CPD, October 2, 1940; CPD, October 2, 1940; CN, October 3, 1940, all in ENPS, Roll 3, Scrapbook 11, p. 24. CP, October 3, 1940, in ENPS, Roll 3, Scrapbook 11, p. 22. CPD, October 3, 1940, in ENPS, Roll 3, Scrapbook 11, pp. 22, 25. CPD, October 4, 1940; CPD, October 4, 1940; CN, October 10, 1940, all in ENPS, Roll 3, Scrapbook 11, p. 25. CP, October 4, 1940; CPD, October 5, 1940, both in ENPS, Roll 3, Scrapbook 11, p. 27. CP, October 5, 1940; "Delay Ruddy Term. Hint He'll 'Talk,'" n.p., n.d., in ENPS, Roll 3, Scrapbook 11, p. 29. CPD, October 5, 1940; CPD, October 6, 1940, both in ENPS, Roll 3, Scrapbook 11, p. 30. NYT, October 6, 1940. CP, October 7, 1940, in ENPS, Roll 3, Scrapbook 11, p. 28. CP, October 10, 1940, in ENPS, Roll 3, Scrapbook 11, p. 31. CPD, October 27, 1940, in ENPS, Roll 3, Scrapbook 11, p. 36 ("dishonest dictatorship," "Labor now knows . . ."). Fraley, *4 Against the Mob*, pp. 149–153. McGill and Perry, *Court Cases of Eliot Ness*, pp. 35–37. Jedick, "Eliot Ness," p. 54. Nickel, *Torso*, pp. 178–179. Heimel, *Eliot Ness*, pp. 214–215.

IMPACT OF NESS'S REPUTATION: CN, October 2, 1940, in ENPS, Roll 3, Scrapbook 11, p. 23 ("There is nothing . . ."). *Christian Science Monitor*, December 31, 1940, in ENPS, Roll 3, Scrapbook 11, p. 62 ("People go about . . ."). Jedick, "Eliot Ness," p. 56 ("Your father is . . .").

NESS BORED AND RESTLESS: CN, May 28, 1941, in ENPS, Roll 3, Scrapbook 11, p. 89. Jedick, "Eliot Ness," p. 57.

NESS AND GAMING MACHINES: "Ness Maps Moving Day for 'Slots,'" CP, n.d.; CP, February 1, 1939; CP, February 2, 1939, all in ENPS, Roll 2, Scrapbook 8, p. 110. CP, February 3, 1939; CN, February 3, 1939, both in ENPS, Roll 2, Scrapbook 8, p. 111. CP, February 2, 1939; "Out They All Go," n.p., n.d., both in ENPS, Roll 2, Scrapbook 8, p. 112. "'Free Game' Pinball Loses Court Test," n.p., n.d., in ENPS, Roll 2, Scrapbook 9, p. 147. CP, May 25, 1940; CN, May 25, 1940; "Mr. Cassidy and the Slots," n.p., n.d.; CP, May 25, 1940, all in ENPS, Roll 2, Scrapbook 7, p. 122. CP, February 25, 1941; CN, February 25, 1941; CP, February 26, 1941, all in ENPS, Roll 3, Scrapbook 11, p. 75. CN, March 1, 1941; CN, March 1, 1941, both in ENPS, Roll 3, Scrapbook 11, p. 76. CPD, March 2, 1941; CP, March 22, 1941, both in ENPS, Roll 3, Scrapbook 11, p. 77. CP, June 11, 1941, in ENPS, Roll 3, Scrapbook 11, p. 99. CN, June 12, 1941; CPD, June 13, 1941, both in ENPS, Roll 3, Scrapbook 11, p. 100. CPD, June 14, 1941, in ENPS, Roll 3, Scrapbook 11, p. 98. Neff, *Mobbed Up*, pp. 26, 30, 34–36. Jacoby, *Sandusky's Finest*, pp. 122, 127.

NESS AND BINGO: "Ness Praised for Prohibiting Bingo," CP, n.d., in ENPS, Roll 2, Scrapbook 8, p. 119. CP, April 24, 1937; CP, April 23, 1937, both in ENPS, Roll 1, Scrapbook 5, p. 205. CN, June 29, 1937, in ENPS, Roll 2, Scrapbook 6, p. 28. CN, November 12, 1937, in ENPS, Roll 2, Scrapbook 6, p. 78. CN, January 19, 1939; CP, January 19, 1939, both in ENPS, Roll 2, Scrapbook 8, p. 107. CN, February 17, 1939, in ENPS, Roll 2, Scrapbook 8, p. 118. "City Outlaws Bingo; Revokes All Permits," n.p., n.d.; CPD, February 18, 1939, both in ENPS, Roll 2, Scrapbook 8, p. 117. CPD, February 18, 1939; CPD, February 19, 1939, both in ENPS, Roll 2, Scrapbook 8, p. 118. "Church Will Face New Bingo Probe," n.p., n.d., in ENPS, Roll 2, Scrapbook 8, p. 125. CPD, January 5, 1940, in ENPS, Roll 2, Scrapbook 7, p. 88. CN, April 12, 1940; CP, April 13, 1940; CN, April 17, 1940; CP, April 17, 1940, all in ENPS, Roll 2, Scrapbook 7, p. 111. CPD, April 16, 1940, in ENPS, Roll 2, Scrapbook 7, p. 112. CP, January 16, 1941, in ENPS, Roll 3, Scrapbook 11, p. 64. CP, February 4, 1941, in ENPS, Roll 3, Scrapbook 11, p. 69. CN, February 8, 1941, in ENPS, Roll 3, Scrapbook 11, p. 68. CPD, February 8, 1941, in ENPS, Roll 3, Scrapbook 11, p. 67. CP, February 20, 1941, in ENPS, Roll 3, Scrapbook 11, p. 66.

NESS AND PUBLIC TRANSIT: CPD, February 9, 1941, in ENPS, Roll 3, Scrapbook 11, p. 74. CP, February 10, 1941, in ENPS, Roll 3, Scrapbook 11, p. 60.

NESS AND AIR POLLUTION: CPD, January 17, 1941 ("one of the . . ."); CP, January 21, 1941, both in ENPS, Roll 3, Scrapbook 11, p. 64. CN, January 21, 1931, in ENPS, Roll 3, Scrapbook 11, p. 65. CPD, January 26, 1941, in ENPS, Roll 3, Scrapbook 11, p. 68. CP, August 15, 1941, in ENPS, Roll 3, Scrapbook 11, p. 110. Fraley, *4 Against the Mob*, p. 10.

OBSCENE MAGAZINES: CP, November 8, 1940 ("that glorifies crime . . ."); CP, November 11, 1940, both in ENPS, Roll 3, Scrapbook 11, p. 38. CP, November 9, 1940, in ENPS, Roll 3, Scrapbook 11, p. 36. CN, November 28, 1940, in ENPS, Roll 3, Scrapbook 11, p. 41. *Catholic Universe Bulletin*, March 5, 1941; *Catholic Universe Bulletin*, April 4, 1941, both in ENPS,

Roll 3, Scrapbook 11, p. 82. *Catholic Universe Bulletin*, March 7, 1941, in ENPS, Roll 3, Scrapbook 11, p. 80. CP, March 10, 1941, in ENPS, Roll 3, Scrapbook 11, p. 86. *Catholic Universe Bulletin*, March 14, 1941, in ENPS, Roll 3, Scrapbook 11, p. 83. Jedick, *Cleveland*, p. 41. Sagalyn, *A Promise Fulfilled*, pp. 57–58 (58, "If you help . . .").

OVERWEIGHT COPS / WORN-OUT CARS: CN, April 24, 1940, in ENPS, Roll 2, Scrapbook 7, p. 114 ("young in years . . ."). "Contemplated Improvements in the Safety Department in 1940," n.d., in container 6, folder 7, HHB-EBP. CP, January 27, 1941, in ENPS, Roll 3, Scrapbook 11, p. 66. CP, December 10, 1941, in ENPS, Roll 3, Scrapbook 11, p. 132. Jedick, "Eliot Ness," p. 56. Dan T. Moore, interviewed by Paul Heimel and Bob Merten, May 30, 1995, PWH.

CLASHING WITH CITY COUNCIL / POLICEWOMEN: CPD, May 23, 1940, in ENPS, Roll 2, Scrapbook 7, p. 121. CP, August 2, 1940, in ENPS, Roll 3, Scrapbook 11, p. 4. CN, September 13, 1940, in ENPS, Roll 3, Scrapbook 11, p. 7. CP, September 21, 1940, in ENPS, Roll 3, Scrapbook 11, p. 11. CN, October 17, 1940, in ENPS, Roll 3, Scrapbook 11, p. 33. CN, October 31, 1940, in ENPS, Roll 3, Scrapbook 11, p. 36. CP, November 13, 1940, in ENPS, Roll 3, Scrapbook 11, p. 40. CP, January 16, 1941, in ENPS, Roll 3, Scrapbook 11, p. 57. CN, January 16, 1941, in ENPS, Roll 3, Scrapbook 11, p. 58. CN, March 11, 1941, in ENPS, Roll 3, Scrapbook 11, p. 85.

PRESS TURNS ON NESS: CP, May 9, 1940, in ENPS, Roll 2, Scrapbook 7, p. 115. CP, May 24, 1940, in ENPS, Roll 2, Scrapbook 7, p. 121. CP, November 19, 1940, in ENPS, Roll 3, Scrapbook 11, p. 41. CP, November 20, 1940, in ENPS, Roll 3, Scrapbook 11, p. 35. CP, November 21, 1940, in ENPS, Roll 3, Scrapbook 11, p. 39 ("Neverwas G-Man Ness"). CP, November 28, 1940, in ENPS, Roll 3, Scrapbook 11, p. 43. CP, November 29, 1940, in ENPS, Roll 3, Scrapbook 11, p. 44. CP, January 6, 1941, in ENPS, Roll 3, Scrapbook 11, p. 56. CP, January 16, 1941, in ENPS, Roll 3, Scrapbook 11, p. 57. CP, January 21, 1941, in ENPS, Roll 3, Scrapbook 11, p. 66. CP, January 22, 1941, in ENPS, Roll 3, Scrapbook 11, p. 64. CP, February 18, 1941; CP, February 20, 1941, both in ENPS, Roll 3, Scrapbook 11, p. 74. CP, March 7, 1941, in ENPS, Roll 3, Scrapbook 11, p. 78. CP, March 8, 1941, in ENPS, Roll 3, Scrapbook 11, p. 85. CP, May 2, 1941, in ENPS, Roll 3, Scrapbook 11, p. 96. CP, May 10, 1941; CP, May 15, 1941, both in ENPS, Roll 3, Scrapbook 11, p. 91. CP, May 13, 1941; CP, May 17, 1941; CP, May 19, 1941, all in ENPS, Roll 3, Scrapbook 11, p. 92. CP, May 16, 1941, in ENPS, Roll 3, Scrapbook 11, p. 95. CP, May 31, 1941, in ENPS, Roll 3, Scrapbook 11, p. 97. CP, January 29, 1942, in ENPS, Roll 3, Scrapbook 11, p. 149. CPD, January 30, 1942; CP, January 30, 1942, both in ENPS, Roll 3, Scrapbook 11, p. 151. CP, January 30, 1942, in ENPS, Roll 3, Scrapbook 11, p. 148. CPD, August

2, 1947, in ENPS, Roll 3, Scrapbook 13 ("Ness was one . . ."). Porter, *Cleveland*, pp. 21, 84, 200–207. Dan T. Moore, interviewed by Paul Heimel and Bob Merten, May 30, 1995, PWH ("If he didn't . . ."). RM to ABS, personal interview and emails, December 4, 8, and 10, 2015.

BURTON TO SENATE / BLYTHIN AS MAYOR: CPD, October 12, 1940, in ENPS, Roll 3, Scrapbook 11, p. 32. CN, November 7, 1940, in ENPS, Roll 3, Scrapbook 11, p. 38. CN, November 12, 1940, in ENPS, Roll 3, Scrapbook 11, p. 40. CPD, November 13, 1940, in ENPS, Roll 3, Scrapbook 11, p. 41. Porter, *Cleveland*, pp. 110, 123.

NESS AS POSSIBLE CANDIDATE: CN, May 21, 1940, in ENPS, Roll 2, Scrapbook 7, p. 120. CPD, May 26[?], 1940, in ENPS, Roll 2, Scrapbook 7, p. 123. CP, August 17, 1940, in ENPS, Roll 3, Scrapbook 11, p. 3. Jack Kennon, "G.O.P. . . . Mayor As Tri . . . Skies," n.p., n.d., in ENPS, Roll 3, Scrapbook 11, p. 7. CPD, October 10, 1940, in ENPS, Roll 3, Scrapbook 11, p. 26. CPD, October 12, 1940, in ENPS, Roll 3, Scrapbook 11, p. 32. CN, November 7, 1940, in ENPS, Roll 3, Scrapbook 11, p. 38. "The Next Mayor," n.p., November 10, 1940; "Off the Record," n.p., November 23, 1940, both in ENPS, Roll 3, Scrapbook 11, p. 39. CP, November 18, 1940; CN, November 19, 1940, both in ENPS, Roll 3, Scrapbook 11, p. 43. CPD, May 5, 1941, in ENPS, Roll 3, Scrapbook 11, p. 96. CPD, January 26, 1941, in ENPS, Roll 3, Scrapbook 11, p. 68. CPD, June 18, 1961, ENC. Jedick, "Eliot Ness" p. 57.

NESS CAMPAIGNS FOR CULLITAN, CONSIDERS MAYORAL RUN: CPD, October 10, 1940, in ENPS, Roll 3, Scrapbook 11, p. 26. CP, October 12, 1940, in ENPS, Roll 3, Scrapbook 11, p. 32 ("one of the . . ."). CN, October 17, 1940, in ENPS, Roll 3, Scrapbook 11, p. 33. CP, November 1, 1940; CN, November 1, 1940 ("a vote for . . ."), in ENPS, Roll 3, Scrapbook 11, p. 36. CPD, November 3, 1940, in ENPS, Roll 3, Scrapbook 11, p. 38. CPD, November 19 [?], 1941, in ENPS, Roll 3, Scrapbook 11, p. 45 ("a thousand and . . .").

NESS WARNED AGAINST RUNNING, DECIDES NOT TO: CN, May 21, 1940, in ENPS, Roll 2, Scrapbook 7, p. 120. CPD, May 26[?], 1940, in ENPS, Roll 2, Scrapbook 7, p. 123. CP, August 17, 1940, in ENPS, Roll 3, Scrapbook 11, p. 3. Jack Kennon, "G.O.P. . . . Mayor As Tri . . . Skies," n.p., n.d., in ENPS, Roll 3, Scrapbook 11, p. 7. CPD, October 10, 1940, in ENPS, Roll 3, Scrapbook 11, p. 26. CPD, October 12, 1940, in ENPS, Roll 3, Scrapbook 11, p. 32 ("Ness is largely . . ."). CN, November 7, 1940, in ENPS, Roll 3, Scrapbook 11, p. 38. "The Next Mayor," n.p., November 10, 1940; "Off the Record," n.p., November 23, 1940, both in ENPS, Roll 3, Scrapbook 11, p. 39. CP, November 18, 1940, in ENPS, Roll 3, Scrapbook 11, p. 43. CN, November 19, 1940, in ENPS, Roll 3, Scrapbook 11, p. 43. CPD, May 5, 1941, in ENPS, Roll 3, Scrapbook 11, p. 96. CPD, January

26, 1941, in ENPS, Roll 3, Scrapbook 11, p. 68. CN, February 11, 1941, in ENPS, Roll 3, Scrapbook 11, p. 71. CPD, June 11, 1941, in ENPS, Roll 3, Scrapbook 11, p. 99. CN, June 12, 1941, in ENPS, Roll 3, Scrapbook 11, p. 100 ("draft"). CP, November 5, 1941, in ENPS, Roll 3, Scrapbook 11, p. 122. CPD, June 18, 1961, ENC. Jedick, "Eliot Ness," p. 57. Porter, *Cleveland*, pp. 103–104. Condon, "Last American Hero," p. 141. See also Nickel, *Torso*, pp. 179–180.

NEW YORK WITNESS: CN (mislabeled "P.D." but credited to CN writer Jack Kennon), March 24, 1941, in ENPS, Roll 3, Scrapbook 11, p. 87 ("the most nerve-wracking . . . ," "more excited than . . . ," "I'm racing against . . . ," "The constant excitement . . ."). Fraley, *4 Against the Mob*, pp. 154–155. McGill and Perry, *Court Cases*, pp. 38–40.

CHAMBERLIN LEAVES, REPLACED BY CLOTHEY: CP, August 6, 1940, in ENPS, Roll 3, Scrapbook 11, p. 5. CP, November 25, 1940, in ENPS, Roll 3, Scrapbook 11, p. 44. CP, November 23, 1940, in ENPS, Roll 3, Scrapbook 11, p. 42. CN, December 12, 1940, in ENPS, Roll 3, Scrapbook 11, p. 48. Nickel, *Torso*, pp. 175–176.

TIFF WITH BLACKWELL: CP, November 18, 1940, in ENPS, Roll 3, Scrapbook 11, p. 44 ("a Communist," "might just as . . . ," "right-hand man"). CP, November 18, 1940, in ENPS, Roll 3, Scrapbook 11, p. 43 ("I'm sick and . . ."). CP, November 23, 1940, in ENPS, Roll 3, Scrapbook 11, p. 42.

RISE IN TRAFFIC DEATHS: CPD, December 25, 1940, in ENPS, Roll 3, Scrapbook 11, p. 52. CN, January 21, 1941, in ENPS, Roll 3, Scrapbook 11, p. 62. CPD, January 28, 1941, in ENPS, Roll 3, Scrapbook 11, p. 68. CN, February 7, 1941, in ENPS, Roll 3, Scrapbook 11, p. 63. CPD, February 8, 1941, in ENPS, Roll 3, Scrapbook 11, p. 67. CN, February 8, 1941; CP, February 10, 1941, both in ENPS, Roll 3, Scrapbook 11, p. 70. CPD, February 13, 1941; CN, February 14, 1941, both in ENPS, Roll 3, Scrapbook 11, p. 72. CP, February 14, 1941; CPD, February 17, 1941, both in ENPS, Roll 3, Scrapbook 11, p. 71. CN, February 14, 1941; Eliot Ness, "Give Them a Chance!" CN, n.d., both in ENPS, Roll 3, Scrapbook 11, p. 73.

NATURAL DEATH INC: Jack Kennon, "Off the Record," n.p., n.d., in ENPS, Roll 3, Scrapbook 11, p. 73 ("insurance racket"). CP, May 27–29, 1941 (May 28, "Natural Death Inc."). CN, May 27, 1941, in ENPS, Roll 3, Scrapbook 11, p. 90. CN, May 29, 1941, in ENPS, Roll 3, Scrapbook 11, p. 89. Jedick, "Eliot Ness," p. 57. Van Tassel and Grabowski, *Encyclopedia of Cleveland History*, p. 41.

UNKNOWNS CRITICIZED, DISBANDED: CP, November 28, 1940, in ENPS, Roll 3, Scrapbook 11, p. 43. CP, November 29, 1940, in ENPS,

Roll 3, Scrapbook 11, p. 44 ("staff of stooges"). CN, January 8[?], 1941, in ENPS, Roll 3, Scrapbook 11, p. 49 ("laborers," "civil service list . . ."). CP, April 30, 1941. Alvin Silverman, "Ness Yields to Pressure for Layoffs," CPD, n.d., in box 1, "Cleveland Eliot Ness 1939–1941—Cleveland Civil Service action dissolving Ness's undercover investigative staff, Apr. 30, 1941" folder, ASP. CP, May 1, 1941, in ENPS, Roll 3, Scrapbook 11, p. 88. CP, May 21, 1941, in ENPS, Roll 3, Scrapbook 11, p. 92. CP, February 24, 1942, in "Ness, Eliot" microfiche, CPC ("Gestapo"). Sagalyn, *A Promise Fulfilled*, p. 64.

CLIP JOINTS: Sagalyn, *A Promise Fulfilled*, pp. 59–60 (59, "clip joints").

FIRE DEPARTMENT REFORMS / CLASH WITH WARDENS: CP, February 4, 1941; CPD, February 5, 1941 ("a grave mistake"), in ENPS, Roll 3, Scrapbook 11, p. 69. CP, February 5, 1941; CPD, February 7, 1941; CPD, February 8, 1941, all in ENPS, Roll 3, Scrapbook 11, p. 67. "All for One, One for All," n.p., February 9, 1941; CPD, February 16, 1941, both in ENPS, Roll 3, Scrapbook 11, p. 74. CN, May 2, 1941, in ENPS, Roll 3, Scrapbook 11, p. 83. CPD, August 25, 1941, in ENPS, Roll 3, Scrapbook 11, p. 111. Nickel, *Torso*, p. 179.

HATRED OF NESS IN HIGHER RANKS / POLICE ACADEMY ABANDONED: CN, October 21, 1941, in ENPS, Roll 3, Scrapbook 11, p. 119 ("Cleveland's experiment in . . ."). CN, December 4, 1941, in ENPS, Roll 3, Scrapbook 11, p. 130. Untitled document, n.d., pp. 9–11, in Box 1, "Biographical Information on Eliot Ness from files of Cleveland Public Library" folder, ASP.

Chapter Twenty: The Heat Is On

LAKEWOOD BOATHOUSE, PARTIES: CPD, June 18, 1961, ENC ("in a most . . . ," "tongues wagging most . . ."). CP, May 25, 1971, ENC. Jedick, "Eliot Ness," pp. 54–55. "Evaline Ness," in Sarkissian, *Something About the Author*, p. 227. Condon, "Last American Hero," p. 139. Neff, *Mobbed Up*, p. 22. *Sun Herald*, February 21, 1991, RM. Jacoby, *Sandusky's Finest*, p. 121. Heimel, *Eliot Ness*, pp. 209–210. Sagalyn, *A Promise Fulfilled*, p. 55. Jim O'Bryan, "Re: $100,000,000 New Development!" posting to The Observation Deck, *Lakewood Observer*, April 13, 2010, http://lakewoodobserver.com/forum/viewtopic.php?t=9082&start=30 (accessed January 13, 2017). Rebecca McFarland, "Eliot Ness in Cleveland from the Cleveland Police Museum," Teaching Cleveland Digital, January 2012, http://teachingcleveland.org/eliot-ness-in-cleveland-from-the-cleveland-police-museum/ (accessed December 14, 2016).

Source Notes

EVALINE'S BEHAVIOR, DRINKING, DEPRESSION: CPD, May 22, 1941. Jedick, "Eliot Ness," pp. 54–55. "Evaline Ness," in Sarkissian, *Something About the Author*, p. 227. Nickel, "Real Eliot Ness," p. 51. Nickel, *Torso*, pp. 152–153, 170, 176. Bergreen, *Capone*, pp. 598–600, 668. Heimel, *Eliot Ness*, p. 209. Sagalyn, *A Promise Fulfilled*, p. 55. Perry, *Eliot Ness*, pp. 231–232 (231, "She was an . . . ," "very unpleasant and . . ."), 234.

NESS'S DRINKING: Chamberlin, "Eliot Ness," p. 104. *Des Moines Sunday Register*, October 29, 1961. Jedick, "Eliot Ness," pp. 54–55 (54, "That may have . . ."). Porter, *Cleveland*, p. 102. Heimel, *Eliot Ness*, p. 209. Linda Rocker, "Fatherly Wisdom Meets Jurisprudence: Manuel 'Manny' Rocker, Prosecutor, Judge, Dad," August 27, 2014, http://lindarocker.com/blog/fatherly-wisdom -meets-jurisprudence-manuel-manny-rocker-prosecutor-judge-dad/ (accessed February 5, 2018). RM to ABS, personal email, December 10, 2015.

NESS ADDICTED TO GOOD LIFE: Eliot Ness, Oath of Office, August 26, 1926, Eliot Ness OPF. CP, June 6, 1941, in ENPS, Roll 3, Scrapbook 11, p. 97. Undated card in ENPS, Roll 3, Scrapbook 11, p. 142 ("You think you're . . ."). Jedick, "Eliot Ness," pp. 54–55. Condon, "Last American Hero," p. 139. *Sun Herald*, February 21, 1991, RM. *Olean Times*, October 7, 1996, PCHS. CPD, February 21, 2000, http://www.cleveland.com /news/index/ssf?/news/pd/cc21ness.html (accessed March 19, 2000), PWH. Becker, *Lakewood*, pp. 7–8, 33–48, 93–104.

NESS JOINS SOCIAL PROTECTION DIVISION: Memorandum, July 20, 1941 ("a breadth of . . ."); Delo E. Mook to Bascom Johnson, July 24, 1941; David L. Robinson Jr. to Raymond F. Clapp, August 14, 1941; Bruce Smith to Raymond F. Clapp, August 18, 1941; "Memorandum—Eliot Ness," August 21, 1941; Press Release ("Office of the Director of the Defense Health and Welfare Service"), September 10, 1941, all in Eliot Ness OPF. CN, September 5, 1941, in ENPS, Roll 3, Scrapbook 11, p. 112. CPD, September 5, 1941 ("lend"); CP, September 5, 1941, both in "Ness, Eliot" microfiche, CPC. CN, November 6, 1941, in ENPS, Roll 3, Scrapbook 11, p. 118. Eliot Ness, "Venereal Disease Control in Defense," *Annals of the American Academy of Political and Social Science*, March 1942, p. 89. Eliot Ness, "Community Policing Vital to Victory," *True Detective*, October 1942, pp. 49, 70. Eliot Ness, "The 'Red Light' District Must Go," *National Sheriff*, September–October 1942, p. 5; *Syracuse Post-Standard*, February 4, 1944, both in ENPS, Roll 3, Scrapbook 12. Porter, *Cleveland*, p. 104. Brinkley, *Washington Goes to War*, pp. 62–63 ("dollar-a-year men"). Brandt, *No Magic Bullet*, pp. 161–166. Hegarty, *Victory Girls*, pp. 12–15, 19. Stern, *Trials of Nina McCall*, pp. 212–213.

Before April 1943, the Social Protection Division was known as the Social Protection Section. The name changed when President Roosevelt signed an executive order replacing the Office of Defense Health and Welfare Services with the Office of Community War Services ("ODHWS Becomes 'Community War Services,'" *Social Hygiene News* [?], 1943, in ENPS, Roll 3, Scrapbook 12). For the sake of simplicity, we refer to the agency as the Social Protection Division throughout.

CRITICISM OF NESS'S ABSENTEEISM: CP, September 12, 1941, in "Ness, Eliot" microfiche, CPC ("Some of you . . ."). *Sweeney Record*, September 27, 1941, in ENPS, Roll 3, Scrapbook 11, p. 115. CP, October 15, 1941, in ENPS, Roll 3, Scrapbook 11, p. 116. CP, December 15–16, 1941, both in ENPS, Roll 3, Scrapbook 11, p. 132. See also Nickel, *Torso*, pp. 179–181.

1941 ELECTION / BLYTHIN VS. LAUSCHE: CP, October 1, 1940, in ENPS, Roll 3, Scrapbook 11, p. 17. CPD, January 5, 1941, in ENPS, Roll 3, Scrapbook 11, p. 57 ("the most progressive . . ."). CPD, January 26, 1941, in ENPS, Roll 3, Scrapbook 11, p. 68. CN, February 11, 1941, in ENPS, Roll 3, Scrapbook 11, p. 71. CP, March 22, 1941, in ENPS, Roll 3, Scrapbook 11, p. 82. CN, May 5, 1941; CP, May 6, 1941, both in ENPS, Roll 3, Scrapbook 11, p. 96. CPD, May 26[?], 1940, in ENPS, Roll 2, Scrapbook 7, p. 123. CPD, June 30, 1941; CP, July 5, 1941, both in ENPS, Roll 3, Scrapbook 11, p. 107. CP, July [??], 1941, in ENPS, Roll 3, Scrapbook 11, p. 106. CPD, October 24, 1941; CP, October 25, 1941; CN, November 6, 1941 ("too busy to . . ."), all in ENPS, Roll 3, Scrapbook 11, p. 118. CP, October 27, 1941, in ENPS, Roll 3, Scrapbook 11, p. 119. CN, October [??], 1941, in ENPS, Roll 3, Scrapbook 11, p. 116. CPD, November 5, 1941; CP, November 5, 1941 ("the end of . . ."), in ENPS, Roll 3, Scrapbook 11, p. 122. CN, November 6, 1941, in ENPS, Roll 3, Scrapbook 11, p. 117. CN, November 7, 1940, in ENPS, Roll 3, Scrapbook 11, p. 38. CCP, November 8, 1941. CP, November 12, 1941; CP, November 15, 1941, both in ENPS, Roll 3, Scrapbook 11, p. 124. CN, November 12, 1940, in ENPS, Roll 3, Scrapbook 11, p. 40. CPD, November 13, 1940, in ENPS, Roll 3, Scrapbook 11, p. 41. CPD, November 16, 1941, in ENPS, Roll 3, Scrapbook 11, p. 126. Jack Kennon, "G.O.P. . . . Mayor As Tri . . . Skies," n.p., n.d., in ENPS, Roll 3, Scrapbook 11, p. 7. Request for Certification, April 8, 1942; George E. Scott to the U.S. Civil Service Commission, April 8, 1942; W. C. Sorrels to Personnel Director, Federal Security Agency, April 8, 1942, all in Eliot Ness OPF. Jack Kennon, "Off the Record," CN, June [?] 12, 1943; Ralph Kelly, "The Inside of the News in Cleveland," n.p., July [??], 1943, both in ENPS, Roll 3, Scrapbook 12. Jedick, "Eliot Ness," p. 57 ("Eliot would tell . . ."). Porter, *Cleveland*, pp. 123–133.

LAUSCHE PRESSURED, REAPPOINTS NESS: CPD, November 16, 1941, in ENPS, Roll 3, Scrapbook 11, p. 126 ("one of the most . . ."). CP,

November 13, 1941, in "Ness, Eliot" microfiche, CPC. CPD, November 11, 1941, both in ENPS, Roll 3, Scrapbook 11, p. 124. CPD, November 30, 1941, in ENPS, Roll 3, Scrapbook 11, p. 134. CPD, February 1, 1942, in ENPS, Roll 3, Scrapbook 11, p. 152. Ralph Kelly, "The Inside of the News in Cleveland," n.p., July [??], 1943, in ENPS, Roll 3, Scrapbook 12. Seltzer, *The Years Were Good*, p. 231. CPD, June 18, 1961, ENC. Porter, *Cleveland*, p. 104. Jedick, "Eliot Ness," p. 57. Nickel, *Torso*, pp. 180–181.

NESS LONGEST-SERVING SAFETY DIRECTOR / OPTIMISM: CP, November 13, 1941, in "Ness, Eliot" microfiche, CPC. CN, November 14, 1941, in ENPS, Roll 3, Scrapbook 11, p. 127 ("to consolidate the . . . ," "People resent change . . . ," "I've always felt . . ."). Condon, "Last American Hero," p. 140.

NEW MAYOR CRACKDOWN: CCP, November 29, 1941; December 6, 1941 ("the heat is . . .").

BLACK YOUTH CRIME / NELLE HACKNEY: CCP, January 16, 1936; January 23, 1936; January 30, 1936; February 6, 1936; March 26, 1936; July 3, 1936; August 13, 1936; December 3, 1936; April 22, 1937; July 22, 1937; October 14, 1937; July 13, 1939; January 18, 1941; May 10, 1941; December 6, 1941 ("the increasing tendency . . . ," "bad," "of vicious looking . . . ," "Miss Hackney pointed . . . ," "prevent crime rather . . . ," "responsible interested citizens . . . ," "would make the . . ."); January 3, 1942; January 24, 1942; January 31, 1942; April 11, 1942; May 30, 1942; October 17, 1942; October 24, 1942; November 21, 1942; January 16, 1943; February 13, 1943; March 6, 1943; March 27, 1943; April 10, 1943; May 1, 1943; July 3, 1943; October 30, 1943; November 6, 1943; December 18, 1943; December 25, 1943; January 22, 1944; February 4, 1944; March 11, 1944; March 25, 1944; April 1, 1944 ("splendid job"); April 8, 1944 ("sending them to . . ."); April 15, 1944; April 29, 1944; May 6, 1944; May 27, 1944; October 28, 1944; April 13, 1946; July 13, 1946; July 20, 1946; August 24, 1946; February 22, 1947; March 1, 1947; March 15, 1947; November 22, 1947; November 29, 1947; January 24, 1948; May 29, 1948; January 29, 1949; March 5, 1949; March 19, 1949; May 7, 1949; November 5, 1949; February 11, 1950 ("We can't stop . . . ," "spent the better . . ."); February 18, 1950 ("an advocate of . . ."); August 25, 1951 ("for the advancement . . . ," "is by no . . . ," "We can do . . ."); May 10, 1952; March 1, 1958; October 26, 1968. Van Tassel and Grabowski, *Encyclopedia of Cleveland History*, p. 122. Wiltse, *Contested Waters*, p. 139. Muhammad, *Condemnation of Blackness*, pp. 1–14 (10, "politics of respectability"), 269–277.

Chapter Twenty-One: EN-3

NESS PREPARES FOR WAR: CPD, December 8, 1941 ("two suspicious appearing . . . ," "potentially dangerous," "All of the . . ."). CPD, February 26, 1942, in ENPS, Roll 3, Scrapbook 11, p. 154. Robinson, *A Tragedy of Democracy*, pp. 7–59. Sagalyn, *A Promise Fulfilled*, pp. 60–63. Albrecht and Banks, *Cleveland in World War II*, pp. 7–8. Hart, *Hitler's American Friends*, p. 18.

FSA ASKS FOR NESS, LAUSCHE REFUSES: CP, December 15, 1941; CP, December 16, 1941 ("The safety director's . . ."); CP, December 17, 1941 ("a part-time . . ."), all in "Ness, Eliot" microfiche, CPC. CP, December 15–16, 1941, both in ENPS, Roll 3, Scrapbook 11, p. 132. CN, December 17, 1941, in ENPS, Roll 3, Scrapbook 11, p. 136.

FIGHTING VD IN CLEVELAND: CPD, January 12, 1942 ("close up and . . . ," "If we find . . ."); February 11, 1942 ("new four-point . . . ," "'Customers' at present . . . ," "The detective bureau . . ."); February 20, 1942. CP, January 12, 1942, in ENPS, Roll 3, Scrapbook 11, p. 148. CP, February 11, 1942, in ENPS, Roll 3, Scrapbook 11, p. 160. CP, February 19, 1942, in ENPS, Roll 3, Scrapbook 11, p. 150. Carter, *Sin and Science*, pp. 5–7.

THE HOT SPOT: *Springfield Sunday Union and Republican*, July 27, 1941. CP, January 29, 1942, in ENPS, Roll 3, Scrapbook 11, p. 149 ("unsavory," "When they were . . ."). CP, January 30, 1942 ("obscene and indecent"); CPD, January 30, 1942, both in ENPS, Roll 3, Scrapbook 11, p. 151 ("off limits"). CP, January 30, 1942, in ENPS, Roll 3, Scrapbook 11, p. 148 ("Of course, we . . .").

NEW YEAR'S BROADCAST: CN, December 30, 1941, in ENPS, Roll 3, Scrapbook 11, p. 137 ("Don't try to . . .").

POLICE-FIRE REORGANIZATION FIGHT: CN, August 29, 1941, in ENPS, Roll 3, Scrapbook 11, p. 111. CPD, November 18, 1941; December 1–2, 1941; February 1, 1942 ("illegal and unconstitutional," "an official duty . . . ," "After 15 years . . ."); February 24–25, 1942 (February 25, "Perhaps the best . . ."); September 15, 1942. CP, December 1, 1941; CN, December 4, 1941; CPD, December 5, 1941, all in ENPS, Roll 3, Scrapbook 11, p. 130. CN, December 1, 1941; CPD, December 10, 1941, both in ENPS, Roll 3, Scrapbook 11, p. 128. CP, December 2, 1941, in ENPS, Roll 3, Scrapbook 11, p. 129. CP, December 3, 1941, in ENPS, Roll 3, Scrapbook 11, p. 133. CP, December 3, 1941; CP, December 13, 1941 ("business-like management," "goldbrickers"); CN, February 24, 1942, all in ENPS, Roll 3, Scrapbook 11, p. 134. CPD, December 4, 1941; CPD, December 7, 1941; CN, December 9, 1941, all in ENPS, Roll 3, Scrapbook 11, p. 131. CN, December 10, 1941; CN, December 13, 1941 ("streamline the police . . . ," "blitzkrieg problems"); CN, December 15, 1941, all in ENPS, Roll 3, Scrapbook 11, p. 132. CP, December 11, 1941; CPD, December 14, 1941; CPD, December 14, 1941; CP, February 24, 1942, all in "Ness, Eliot" microfiche, CPC ("Gestapo," "Where are the . . . ," "If you are . . ."). CP, December 19, 1941, in ENPS, Roll 3, Scrapbook 11, p. 135. CCP, December 20, 1941. CN, January 28, 1942, in ENPS, Roll 3, Scrapbook 11, p. 149. CP, January 30, 1942, in ENPS, Roll 3, Scrapbook 11, p. 151. CP, February 22, 1942; CP, February 24, 1942, both in ENPS, Roll 3, Scrapbook 11, p. 153. CN, February 23, 1942, in ENPS, Roll 3, Scrapbook 11, p. 152. CPD, February 26, 1942; CP, February 26, 1942; "Police Vandal Squad to Bow Out March 12," n.p., n.d., all in ENPS, Roll 3, Scrapbook 11, p. 154.

VD ARTICLE: Ness, "Venereal Disease Control in Defense," p. 89 ("Military Saboteur Number . . ."). CP, March 7, 1942 ("Then we went . . ."). CPD, March 8, 1942. Nickel, *Torso*, p. 181.

CAR ACCIDENT AND AFTERMATH: CP, March 5, 1942, in "Ness, Eliot" microfiche, CPC ("look them over"). CN, March 5, 1942; March 7, 1942 ("the other man," "He said he . . ."). CP, March 5, 1942, in ENPS, Roll 3, Scrapbook 11, p. 157. CN, March 6, 1942, ENC. CP, March 6–7, 1942 (March 6, "EN-3," "dumbfounded," "very nice," "very courteous"; March 7, "My first thought . . . ," "I wanted to . . ."). CPD, March 6, 1942; March 8, 1942. Jedick, "Eliot Ness," p. 91 ("I don't think . . ."). Condon, "Last American Hero," p. 141 ("Some friends and . . ."). Nickel, *Torso*, pp. 181–182. "Kerr, David for Biography Ness," n.d., p. 4, PWH.

ACCIDENT BECOMES PUBLIC / NESS CRITICIZED, APOLOGIZES: CP, November 12, 1937, in ENPS, Roll 2, Scrapbook 6, p. 80 ("If you drink . . ."). CPD, December 27, 1937, in ENPS, Roll 2, Scrapbook 10, p. 25. "Ness Orders War on Drunk Drivers," n.p., n.d., in ENPS, Roll 2, Scrapbook 8, p. 125. CP, April 29, 1939, in ENPS, Roll 2, Scrapbook 9, p. 147. CP, March 5, 1942, in "Ness, Eliot" microfiche, CPC. CP, March 5, 1942, in ENPS, Roll 3, Scrapbook 11, p. 157 ("You'll have to . . ."). CN, March 5, 1942; March 9, 1942 ("more than paid . . . ," "I have never . . ."). CN, March 6, 1942, ENC. CPD, March 6, 1942; March 8, 1942. CP March 6–7, 1942 (March 7, "It was a . . . ," "several drinks during . . . ," "It was very . . . ," "No, it was . . . ," "If the safety . . ."); March 9, 1942 ("more than paid . . . ," "I have never . . ."). Condon, *Cleveland*, p. 103. Jedick, "Eliot Ness," p. 91. Nickel, *Torso*, p. 182.

NESS ANNOUNCES RESIGNATION: CP, March 23, 1942 ("serve wher-ever the . . ."); CP, April 23, 1942, both in "Ness, Eliot" microfiche, CPC. CN, March 23, 1942. CP, March 24, 1942; April 6, 1942; April 27, 1942. CPD, March 24, 1942, in ENPS, Roll 3, Scrapbook 11, p. 155. CPD, April 24, 1942. Jedick, "Eliot Ness," pp. 91–92. Condon, "Last American Hero," p. 141.

"JITTERBUG VICE CASE": CPD, February 24, 1942; February 26, 1942; March 29–31, 1942 (March 29, "on an extended . . . ," "all of whom . . ."; March 30, "to the fullest . . . ," "There are two . . . ," "I have been . . ."; March 31, "if we get . . ."); April 9, 1942; April 12, 1942; April 14–16, 1942; April 18, 1942; May 2, 1942; May 13, 1942. CCP, April 4, 1942 ("Jitterbug Vice Case," "They ought to . . .").

NESS'S FINAL REFORMS, RESIGNATION: CCP, February 4, 1937; Sep-tember 23, 1937; November 9, 1940; March 15, 1941; May 2, 1942 ("un-precedented transfer," "the usual training . . . ," "as much police . . ."); May 9, 1942; September 5, 1942; January 2, 1943; June 22, 1946 ("the scarcity of . . ."); April 26, 1947; May 17, 1946. CP, March 9, 1942, in ENPS, Roll 3, Scrapbook 11, p. 154. CPD, March 12, 1942; CPD, March 28, 1942, both in ENPS, Roll 3, Scrapbook 11, p. 158. CP, April 27, 1942 ("Taking Mr. Ness' . . . ," "Cleveland is a . . . ," "Now he goes . . ."). CPD, March 24, 1942; CPD, March 25, 1942, both in ENPS, Roll 3, Scrap-book 11, p. 155. CPD, April 1, 1942; CN, April 2, 1942 ("Post-graduate courses for . . ."), both in ENPS, Roll 3, Scrapbook 11, p. 162. CN, April 3, 1942, in ENPS, Roll 3, Scrapbook 11, p. 161. CP, April 23, 1942, in "Ness, Eliot" microfiche, CPC. CP, April 24, 1942, in ENPS, Roll 3, Scrapbook 11, p. 159. CPD, April 24–25, 1942 (April 24, "the ability and . . . ," "If [a Safety . . ."). Ralph Kelly, "The Inside of the News in Cleveland," n.p., July [??], 1943, in ENPS, Roll 3, Scrapbook 12. Harry L. Lodge, "The Govern-mental Services of Harold H. Burton," n.p. (thesis, Geneva College, 1948), in box 372, folder 8, HBP. Porter, Cleveland, p. 106 ("Ness was way . . ."). Nickel, Torso, pp. 182–184. Arnold Sagalyn to Anne Kmieck, November 21, 1997, in box 1, "Cleveland–Ness memorial service, 1997" folder, ASP. Heimel, Eliot Ness, p. 232 ("as any big . . ."). RM to ABS, personal email, October 23, 2016.

Chapter Twenty-Two: Social Evil

CAPONE'S DEMENTIA / NESS AS HEAD OF SPD: Declaration of Ap-pointee, May 1, 1942; Oath of Office, May 1, 1942, both in Eliot Ness OPF. Schoenberg, Mr. Capone, pp. 342–353.

VD AS NATIONAL SECURITY THREAT / ANTI-SEX PROPAGANDA: Ness, "Venereal Disease Control in Defense," pp. 89–90. Eliot Ness, "The 'Red Light' District Must Go," *National Sheriff,* September–October 1942, pp. 1, 5, in ENPS, Roll 3, Scrapbook 12. Ness, "Community Policing Vital to Victory," p. 70. Eliot Ness, "The National Program of Social Protection," *Public Welfare* 1, no. 4 (April 1943), p. 115, PWH (also in ENPS, Roll 3, Scrapbook 12). Carter, *Sin and Science,* p. 5. Costello, *Virtue Under Fire,* pp. 84, 86–89. Brandt, *No Magic Bullet,* pp. 161, 163–165 (164, "The sex act . . ."), 169–170. Brinkley, *Washington Goes to War,* p. 230. Hegarty, *Victory Girls,* pp. 15–16. Parascandola, *Sex, Sin, and Science,* pp. 101–103. Lord, *Condom Nation,* pp. 72, 84–85, 89–90. Cari Romm, "During World War II, Sex Was a National-Security Threat," *Atlantic,* October 8, 2015, http://www.theatlantic.com/health /archive/2015/10/during-world-war-ii-sexually-active-women-were-a -national-security-threat/409555/ (accessed February 1, 2017). Stern, *Trials of Nina McCall,* pp. 94–96, 212.

SPD AND AMERICAN PLAN: *Challenge to Community Action* (Washington, DC: Social Protection Division, 1945), pp. 1, 16–17, in box 3, "Evolution of a Government Pamphlet (Challenge to Community Action)" folder, SPD. "Job Description, Director of Social Protection," n.d., in Eliot Ness OPF. Eliot Ness, "Social Protection Division," *Citizens of Tomorrow: A Wartime Challenge to Community Action,* n.d., pp. 26–27, in ENPS, Roll 3, Scrapbook 13. Ness, "Venereal Disease Control in Defense," pp. 91–92. Ness, "'Red Light' District Must Go," p. 5; Eliot Ness, "The VDCO and Social Protection," Office of Defense Health and Welfare Services, Social Protection Section, March 1943; "Promiscuity Called Chief Social Evil," n.p., February 4, 1944, all in ENPS, Roll 3, Scrapbook 12. Ness, "National Program of Social Protection," p. 115, PWH (also in ENPS, Roll 3, Scrapbook 12). Raymond Clapp, "Some Measures Toward Protection Against Prostitution and Toward Redirection of Prostitutes and Promiscuous Women," n.d., in box 2, "Case History" folder, SPD. Coates, Hoff, and Hoff, *Preventive Medicine in World War II,* pp. 162–164. Roy Lubove, "The Progressives and the Prostitute," *Historian* 24, no. 3 (May 1962), pp. 308–330. Brandt, *No Magic Bullet,* pp. 161–163, 165. Abbott, *Sin in the Second City,* p. 45. Hegarty, *Victory Girls,* pp. 19–20, 47–48, 66–68. Stern, *Trials of Nina McCall,* pp. 5–8, 11–12, 42–80 (55, "reasonably suspected"), 94–96, 102, 121 ("American Plan"), 165, 169–171, 180–182, 185, 206–212.

REGULATION OF PROSTITUTION VS. CRUSADE AGAINST SEX TRADE: Lender and Martin, *Drinking in America,* pp. 64–86, 88–133. Abbott, *Sin in the Second City,* pp. 21, 53–54. Okrent, *Last Call,* pp. 1–4, 7–114. Stern, *Trials of Nina McCall,* pp. 11–16 (14, "social evil"; 15, "red-light districts"), 20, 24, 29–31, 42–46, 48–53 (53, "detention houses"), 70–71, 84–85, 100–101, 131–147, 161–169, 179–180, 187–194, 245–246.

NESS AND PROSTITUTION IN CHICAGO AND CLEVELAND: CPD, January 14, 1936. *Springfield Sunday Union and Republican,* July 27, 1941. CP, October 20, 1941, in ENPS, Roll 3, Scrapbook 11, p. 117. Eliot Ness, "Cooperation of Cities in Social Protection Services," *Minnesota Municipalities,* February 1943, pp. 48–49, in ENPS, Roll 3, Scrapbook 12. Lubove, "Progressives and the Prostitute," pp. 308–330 (312, "white-slave hysteria"; 317, "commercial exploiters").

VOLLMER AND PROSTITUTION: Vollmer, *Police and Modern Society,* pp. 89–92 (89, "apparently inevitable").

NESS'S VIEWS ON PROSTITUTION / SPD STRUCTURE AND OPERATIONS: "Mr. Ness at Hot Springs," n.d.; Eliot Ness, "Municipal Responsibility in the Repression of Prostitution," n.d., pp. 5–7; Eliot Ness, "Social Protection in Venereal Disease Control," n.d.; untitled press release, October 23, 1942; Eliot Ness, "Enlisting Local Action in Venereal Disease Control," n.d., p. 4, all in box 12, "Speeches–Ness" folder, SPD. Ness, "Venereal Disease Control in Defense," pp. 91–93. CP, October 20, 1941, in ENPS, Roll 3, Scrapbook 11, p. 117. Eliot Ness, report to Charles P. Taft, November 24, 1941, in box 5, "Historical Materials" folder, SPD. Eliot Ness, "Physical and Moral Weakness," *Christian Register,* September 1942, p. 328[?]; Ness, "'Red Light' District Must Go," pp. 1, 5; Edward J. Kelly, "Techniques for Repressing Unorganized Prostitution: Recommendations of the Special Committee on Enforcement of the National Advisory Police Committee," November–December 1942; Eliot Ness, "Prostitution Must Be Repressed," *South Dakota Peace Officer,* January 1943; Ness, "Cooperation of Cities," pp. 48–50 (48, "health and a . . ."); Eliot Ness, "The VDCO and Social Protection," Office of Defense Health and Welfare Services, Social Protection Section, March 1943, pp. 1, 5; Eliot Ness, "Law Enforcement for Social Protection—A Health Measure," [*Wisconsin*] *Medical Journal,* February 1944 ("Common sense and . . ."); BCE, February 3, 1944; *Syracuse Post-Standard,* February 4, 1944; Eliot Ness, "They Did the Things Which 'Couldn't Be Done,'" *Pulse,* April 1944, pp. 26–27; Eliot Ness, "New Role of the Police," *Survey Midmonthly,* March 1944, pp. 77–78 (see also an early draft (as Eliot Ness, "Law Enforcement—A Delinquency Preventive") in box 5, "Juvenile Delinquency" folder, SPD), all in ENPS, Roll 3, Scrapbook 12. Eliot Ness, "Rehabilitation in the Social Protection Program," September 25, 1942, pp. 2–3, 5–6 (also in box 12, "Speeches–Ness" folder, SPD) (2, "It is unfortunate . . . ," "We have been . . ."; 3, "cannot be helped . . ."; 5, "train as many . . ."); Raymond Clapp, "Some Measures Toward Protection Against Prostitution and Toward Redirection of Prostitutes and Promiscuous Women," n.d.; Marie Duffin, "Adolescence—1944," May 2, 1944, p. 1, all in box 2, "Case History" folder, SPD. Ness, "Community Policing Vital to Victory," p. 70. Ness, "National Program of Social Protection," pp. 116–118, PWH (also in ENPS, Roll 3, Scrapbook 12). United States Treasury Department Personnel Recommendation, August 31, 1943; Service Record Card, n.d.; Application for Federal Employment, August 31, 1945; Application for Federal Employment, November 8, 1952, all in Martin J. Lahart OPF/ATF. CPD, September 5, 1943, "Ness, Eliot" microfiche, CPC. Ness, *What About Girls*, p. 17. Eliot Ness, memo to Regional Social Protection Representatives, January 31, 1944; Eliot Ness, memo to Regional Social Protection Representatives, February 4, 1944, both in box 10, "Regional Letters" folder, SPD. *Hearings Before a Subcommittee of the Committee on Education and Labor, United States Senate, Seventy-Eighth Congress, First Session*, p. 1, *Juvenile Delinquency*, pp. 87, 96, in box 13, "Sub-Committee on Wartime Health and Education (Pepper Committee)" folder, SPD (87, "Extreme caution and . . ."). Martin J. Lahart to Regional Director, Chicago, August 2, 1945, in box 2, "Civil Rights" folder, SPD. Eliot Ness, "Social Protection Division," *Citizens of Tomorrow: A Wartime Challenge to Community Action*, n.d., pp. 26–27, in ENPS, Roll 3, Scrapbook 13. Coates, Hoff, and Hoff, *Preventive Medicine in World War II*, p. 164. *Star Tribune*, May 30, 1965 ("I got pretty . . ."). Lubove, "Progressives and the Prostitute," pp. 320–321. Costello, *Virtue Under Fire*, pp. 84–87. Brandt, *No Magic Bullet*, pp. 162–163. Hegarty, *Victory Girls*, pp. 3–6, 23, 32–35, 45, 48, 50 67, 133. Sagalyn, *A Promise Fulfilled*, p. 71.

MAY ACT / FBI: Eliot Ness, "The Repression of Prostitution in the Social Protection Program," June 30, 1942; Eliot Ness, "Prostitution Jeopardizes Our Manpower," September 17, 1942; Eliot Ness, "The Challenge of Present Social Conditions to the Correctional System," October 21, 1942; Untitled press release, October 23, 1942; Eliot Ness, "Municipal Responsibility in the Repression of Prostitution," n.d.; Eliot Ness, "Social Protection in Venereal Disease Control," n.d.; Eliot Ness, "Enlisting Local Action in Venereal Disease Control," n.d., all in box 12, "Speeches–Ness" folder, SPD. Ness, "Physical and Moral Weakness," p. 328[?]; Eliot Ness, "Prostitution Must Be Repressed," *South Dakota Peace Officer*, January 1943; Eliot Ness, "Law Enforcement for Social Protection—A Health Measure," [*Wisconsin*] *Medical Journal*, February 1944; *Atlanta Constitution*, February 24, 1944, all in ENPS, Roll 3, Scrapbook 12. Ness, "Community Policing Vital to Victory," p. 70. Ness, "National Program of Social Protection," pp. 115–116, PWH (also in ENPS, Roll 3, Scrapbook 12). *Hearings Before a Subcommittee of the Committee on Education and Labor,*

United States Senate, Seventy-Eighth Congress, First Session, p. 1, *Juvenile Delinquency*, p. 85, in box 13, "Sub-Committee on Wartime Health and Education (Pepper Committee)" folder, SPD. Carter, *Sin and Science*, pp. 5–7. Costello, *Virtue Under Fire*, pp. 85–86, 213. Brandt, *No Magic Bullet*, p. 166. Hegarty, *Victory Girls*, pp. 12, 37–40, 185n128. Lord, *Condom Nation*, p. 85. Stern, *Trials of Nina McCall*, p. 215.

FBI VS. NESS/SPD: S. A. Nease, Memorandum for the Director, November 18, 1941; Edward A. Tamm, Memorandum for the Director, February 5, 1942 ("Ness at one . . ."); R. P. Kramer, Memorandum for D. M. Ladd, July 7, 1942; A. Rosen, Memorandum for E. A. Tamm, October 5, 1942 ("super-sleuths"); C. E. Hennrich to the Director of the FBI, October 5, 1942; C. E. Hennrich to the Director of the FBI, October 22, 1942; J. J. McGuire, Memorandum for Mr. Nichols, December 28, 1942; R. F. Cartwright, Memorandum for Mr. Rosen, April 5, 1943; Hugh H. Clegg, Memorandum for the Director, August 7, 1943; Dwight Brantley (SAC St. Louis) to the Director of the FBI, October 13, 1943; L. B. Nichols, Memorandum for Mr. Tolson, November 22, 1943; H. H. Clegg, Memorandum for the Director, December 7, 1943 ("that the Bureau . . . ," "I would be . . ."); H. H. Clegg, memo to Clyde Tolson, April 10, 1944; Mr. Nichols, memo to Mr. Tolson, July 26, 1944; untitled memorandum, n.d., all in FBI-EN. Eliot Ness, Report to Charles P. Taft, November 24, 1941, p. 8; Press Release, Office of Defense Health and Welfare Services, June 30, 1942, both in box 5, "Historical Materials" folder, SPD. Ness, "Venereal Disease Control in Defense," p. 91. Eliot Ness, "The Repression of Prostitution in the Social Protection Program," June 30, 1942; Eliot Ness, "The Challenge of Present Social Conditions to the Correctional System," October 21, 1942, p. 11; Eliot Ness, "Enlisting Local Action in Venereal Disease Control," n.d., p. 10, all in box 12, "Speeches–Ness" folder, SPD. Ness, "'Red Light' District Must Go," p. 5; Ness, "Cooperation of Cities," pp. 48–51, both in ENPS, Roll 3, Scrapbook 12. Ness, "Community Policing Vital to Victory," p. 70. Eliot Ness, "Repression of Prostitution in Wartime," November 28, 1942, in box 8, "Radio Scripts" folder, SPD (also in box 12, "Speeches–Ness" folder, SPD). Ness, "National Program of Social Protection," p. 116, PWH (also in ENPS, Roll 3, Scrapbook 12). *Hearings Before a Subcommittee of the Committee on Education and Labor, United States Senate, Seventy-Eighth Congress, First Session*, pt. 1, *Juvenile Delinquency*, p. 96, in box 13, "Sub-Committee on Wartime Health and Education (Pepper Committee)" folder, SPD ("I felt, having . . ."). Brandt, *No Magic Bullet*, p. 166. Hegarty, *Victory Girls*, p. 32. Parascandola, *Sex, Sin, and Science*, p. 100. Sagalyn, *A Promise Fulfilled*, p. 70.

NESS'S TRAVEL: Midwest Regional Conference on Social Hygiene pamphlet, February 4, 1943; *Greenville News*, March 25, 1943; *Charlotte News*, June 10, 1943; "War Conference: Michigan Association of Chiefs of Police" program, July 12–14, 1943; *Milwaukee Journal*, September 14, 1943; *Tulsa World*, January 11–12, 1944; Convention and War Conference of the Nebraska Sheriffs' and Peace Officers Association program, January 13, 1944; "Al Capone's Nemesis to Be in Syracuse," n.p., January 30, 1944; "Red Lights Out in U.S., Says FSA," n.p., February 2, 1944 [?]; BCE, February 3, 1944; *Syracuse Herald-Journal*, February 4, 1944; *Puerto Rico World Journal*, February 5[?], 1944; Don Warner to Elliott [*sic*] Ness, February 10, 1943 ("To come into . . ."); *Puerto Rico World Journal* [?], February 10, 1944 [?], all in ENPS, Roll 2, Scrapbook 12. CT, November 6, 1943. *Atlanta Constitution*, February 13, 1944.

EVALINE ON THE ROAD, IN WASHINGTON: Jedick, "Eliot Ness," p. 92. "Evaline Ness," in Sarkissian, *Something About the Author*, p. 227 ("living in dreary . . ."). Brinkley, *Washington Goes to War*, pp. xi–xii, 50–82, 105–110, 228–229, 239–246. Heimel, *Eliot Ness*, p. 235.

NESS'S STRATEGY, RESULTS: "Job Description, Director of Social Protection," n.d., in Eliot Ness OPF. Edward J. Kelly, "Techniques for Repressing Unorganized Prostitution: Recommendations of the Special Committee on Enforcement of the National Advisory Police Committee," November–December 1942; Eliot Ness, "How to Curb Prostitution in Hotels," *Southern Hotel Journal*, February 1943, pp. 17–28, 43 ("banning women at . . ."); *Norfolk Ledger-Dispatch*, March 5, 1943; *Winnipeg Tribune*, July 7, 1944; no name to Eliot Ness, July 26, 1944; R. B. Modehouse to Eliot Ness, August 3, 1944; untitled memo, August 23, 1944, all in ENPS, Roll 3, Scrapbook 12. Ness, "National Program of Social Protection," p. 116, PWH (also in ENPS, Roll 3, Scrapbook 12). CPD, September 5, 1943, in "Ness, Eliot" microfiche, CPC. "Biographical Sketch: Eliot Ness," n.d., in box 2, "Biographies" folder, SPD. "Mr. Ness at Hot Springs," n.d., in box 12, "Speeches–Ness" folder, SPD. Ness, "Social Protection Division," pp. 26–27, in ENPS, Roll 3, Scrapbook 13. Coates, Hoff, and Hoff, *Preventive Medicine in World War II*, p. 165. Brandt, *No Magic Bullet*, p. 166. Carter, *Sin and Science*, p. 7. Costello, *Virtue Under Fire*, pp. 84–85, 213–214. Hegarty, *Victory Girls*, pp. 25–30. Sagalyn, *A Promise Fulfilled*, pp. 70–71 (70, "Eliot's approach was . . ."). Stern, *Trials of Nina McCall*, pp. 173, 216.

SAN ANTONIO: Laura Waggoner, "Preliminary Report, Social Protection Study: Girls and Women Apprehended by Police in San Antonio, Texas, for Prostitution and Allied Offenses," June 20, 1942, in box 2, "Case History" folder, SPD (3, "Until a few . . ."). Stern, *Trials of Nina McCall*, pp. 213 ("a very poor . . ."), 229, 234.

NESS'S CONCERNS / LACK OF RESOURCES: Laura Waggoner, "Preliminary Report, Social Protection Study: Girls and Women Apprehended by Police in San Antonio, Texas, for Prostitution and Allied Offenses," June 20, 1942 (3, "There is no . . . ," "under-staffed and . . . ," "problem girls"; 4, "because she might . . ."); Eliot Ness, "Rehabilitation in the Social Protection Program," September 25, 1942 (also in box 12, "Speeches–Ness" folder, SPD), both in box 2, "Case History" folder, SPD.

SPD AND AFRICAN AMERICANS: Eliot Ness, "Statement on the Social Protection Division, Federal Security Agency, for American Social Hygiene Association Negro Conference," n.d. ("We need and . . ."); Eliot Ness, memo to Regional Social Protection Representatives, October 21, 1943; "Abstract of Proceedings of Conference, November 22, 23, 1943, with Negro Leaders on Wartime Problems in Venereal Disease Control," n.d. (6, "Negro representation on . . ."); Eliot Ness, memo to Regional Director, Defense Health & Welfare Services, Chicago, n.d.; Eliot Ness, memo to Mark A. McCloskey, November 30, 1943; Raymond F. Clapp, "Social Protection Statement for American Social Hygiene Association Negro Conference," n.p., all in box 7, "Negro Groups" folder, SPD. Transcript, "Special Meeting of the Executive Committee of the National Advisory Police Committee on Social Protection," November 19, 1943, p. 20, in box 6, "Law Enforcement" folder, SPD. Edward V. Taylor, "The Negro Community's Share in Prevention," September 18, 1944; "A Brief Resume of Correlative Factors in the Incidence and Prevalence of Venereal Disease," n.d.; "Negro and White Syphilis Rates Among First Million Selectees and Volunteers," n.d., all in box 7, "Negro and White VD Rates" folder, SPD. Brandt, No Magic Bullet, p. 157. Christina Simmons, "African Americans and Sexual Victorianism in the Social Hygiene Movement, 1910–40," Journal of the History of Sexuality 4, no. 1 (July 1993), pp. 51–75. Parascandola, Sex, Sin, and Science, pp. 106–107, 127. Hegarty, Victory Girls, pp. 35–36, 61–62, 78–84, 103. Lord, Condom Nation, pp. 33–35, 74–75. Stern, Trials of Nina McCall, pp. 97–98, 215–217, 222–223, 233, 235.

PROGRESSIVE SUPPORT FOR SPD: Albert Deutsch, "Danger! Venereal Disease," Nation, September 22, 1945, pp. 284–285. Anderson, Wartime Women, p. 109. Kluger, Simple Justice, pp. 705–711, and passim. Stern, Trials of Nina McCall, pp. 212–214, 229–230 (229, "some of the . . .").

ELEANOR ROOSEVELT: Atlanta Constitution, June 11, 1943 ("It is not . . ."). Hegarty, Victory Girls, pp. 150 ("caught in something . . ."), 153–154. Stern, Trials of Nina McCall, pp. 220–221 ("had drifted into . . . ," "I think . . .").

NESS AND SEX EDUCATION: Ness, "Venereal Disease Control in Defense," pp. 90–91. Ness, "Community Policing Vital to Victory," p. 70. Ness, "Cooperation of Cities," p. 48; "It's a Moral Problem First," n.p., February 3, 1944 ("the moral and . . ."); Ness, "They Did the Things," pp. 26–27, all in ENPS, Roll 3, Scrapbook 12. R. F. Cartwright, Memorandum for Mr. Rosen, April 5, 1943, FBI-EN. *Hearings Before a Subcommittee of the Committee on Education and Labor, United States Senate, Seventy-Eighth Congress, First Session*, pt. 1, *Juvenile Delinquency*, pp. 86 ("Schools are important . . ."), 88, in box 13, "Sub-Committee on Wartime Health and Education (Pepper Committee)" folder, SPD. Ness, *What About Girls*, p. 29 ("Holy Joe talk"). *Challenge to Community Action* (Washington, DC: Social Protection Division, 1945), pp. 43–44, in box 3, "Evolution of a Government Pamphlet (Challenge to Community Action)" folder, SPD. Eliot Ness, "Enlisting Local Action In Venereal Disease Control," n.d., in box 12, "Speeches–Ness" folder, SPD.

GOAL OF ERADICATING VD: Ness, "Venereal Disease Control in Defense," pp. 90–91. Eliot Ness, "The Repression of Prostitution in the Social Protection Program," July 30, 1942, in box 12, "Speeches–Ness" folder, SPD. Ness, "Physical and Moral Weakness," p. 328[?]; Ness, "The 'Red Light' District Must Go," p. 5; Ness, "Law Enforcement for Social Protection"; Ness, "They Did the Things," pp. 26–27, in ENPS, Roll 3, Scrapbook 12 ("When a few . . ."). Ness, "Community Policing Vital to Victory," p. 70. CPD, September 5, 1943, in "Ness, Eliot" microfiche, CPC. Eliot Ness, memo to Regional Social Protection Representatives, February 4, 1944, in box 10, "Regional Letters" folder, SPD. Carter, *Sin and Science*, p. 8. Parascandola, *Sex, Sin, and Science*, pp. 92–93, 134–135. Lord, *Condom Nation*, pp. 71–73.

PROSTITUTION AND VD IN DECLINE: Ness, "'Red Light' District Must Go," p. 5; Ness, "Physical and Moral Weakness," p. 328[?]; Ness, "How to Curb," pp. 17–28, 43; Eliot Ness to "Sir," 1943; "Promiscuity Called Chief Social Evil," n.p., February 4, 1944; Ness, "They Did the Things," pp. 26–27, all in ENPS, Roll 3, Scrapbook 12. Ness, "Community Policing Vital to Victory," p. 70. Ness, "National Program of Social Protection," p. 116, PWH (also in ENPS, Roll 3, Scrapbook 12). *Atlanta Constitution*, February 1, 1944. CT, February 1, 1944. "Biographical Sketch: Eliot Ness," n.d., in box 2, "Biographies" folder, SPD. Costello, *Virtue Under Fire*, p. 213 ("Blitz the Brothels"). Brandt, *No Magic Bullet*, p. 166, 170. Hegarty, *Victory Girls*, p. 28. Sagalyn, *A Promise Fulfilled*, pp. 71–72 (72, "For all practical . . .").

OVERCROWDED JAILS: Vollmer, *Police and Modern Society*, p. 91. Eliot Ness, "The Challenge of Present Social Conditions to the Correctional System," October 21, 1942, pp. 8–10 (8, "a detention problem . . . ," "First offenders and . . ."); untitled press release, October 23, 1942; Eliot Ness, "Municipal Responsibility in the Repression of Prostitution," n.d., pp. 7–8, all in box 12, "Speeches–Ness" folder, SPD. "U. S. Placing Women in 30 CCC Camps to Cope with Diseases," n.p., n.d.; "Setback Is Feared in Venereal Fight," n.p., October 23 [1942]; Ness, "Cooperation of Cities," p. 50, all in ENPS, Roll 3, Scrapbook 12. CP, October 23, 1942, in "Ness, Eliot" microfiche, CPC. Transcript, "Special Meeting of the Executive Committee of the National Advisory Police Committee on Social Protection," November 19, 1943, p. 6, in box 6, "Law Enforcement" folder, SPD. Ness, *What About Girls*, pp. 23–24, 26. Hegarty, *Victory Girls*, p. 152. Stern, *Trials of Nina McCall*, pp. 217–218.

CCC CAMPS / RAPID TREATMENT CENTERS: CT, August 27, 1942. "U. S. Placing Women in 30 CCC Camps to Cope with Diseases," n.p., n.d. ("detention camps"); Ness, "Cooperation of Cities," p. 50, both in ENPS, Roll 3, Scrapbook 12. Ness, "National Program of Social Protection," p. 118, PWH (also in ENPS, Roll 3, Scrapbook 12). Transcript, "Special Meeting of the Executive Committee of the National Advisory Police Committee on Social Protection," November 19, 1943, pp. 2–3, 24–25, in box 6, "Law Enforcement" folder, SPD. Eliot Ness, "Municipal Responsibility in the Repression of Prostitution," n.d., p. 8; Eliot Ness, "Recent Developments in S.P.," n.d., pp. 2–3; Eliot Ness, "The Challenge of Present Social Conditions to the Correctional System," October 21, 1942, p. 8 ("Unless the needed . . ."), all in box 12, "Speeches–Ness" folder, SPD. *Hearings Before a Subcommittee of the Committee on Education and Labor, United States Senate, Seventy-Eighth Congress, First Session*, p. 1, *Juvenile Delinquency*, p. 97, in box 13, "Sub-Committee on Wartime Health and Education (Pepper Committee)" folder, SPD. Eliot Ness, memo to Regional Social Protection Representatives, February 4, 1944, in box 10, "Regional Letters" folder, SPD ("Rapid Treatment Centers"). "Girls Learn War Work," *Social Protection Bulletin*, June 30, 1944, p. 4, in box 10, "Social Protection Bulletins" folder, SPD. Brandt, *No Magic Bullet*, p. 167. Hegarty, *Victory Girls*, pp. 31–32, 77, 138. Parascandola, *Sex, Sin, and Science*, pp. 119–128. Lord, *Condom Nation*, p. 91. Stern, *Trials of Nina McCall*, pp. 85, 94, 217–219 (218, "not more than . . ."; 219, "women's work").

RISE IN PROMISCUITY / SEXUAL REVOLUTION: Eliot Ness, Report to Charles P. Taft, November 24, 1941, pp. 3–4, in box 5, "Historical Materials" folder, SPD. CT, December 12, 1942 ("pick-ups"). Edward J. Kelly,

"Techniques for Repressing Unorganized Prostitution: Recommendations of the Special Committee on Enforcement of the National Advisory Police Committee," November–December 1942; BCE, February 3, 1944; Ness, "Social Protection Division," pp. 26–27, in ENPS, Roll 3, Scrapbook 13. Office of War Information, Report on Juvenile Delinquency, October 10, 1943, pp. 5–6, in box 5, "Juvenile Delinquency" folder, SPD (5, "uniform hysteria"). Winifred Ferguson, memo to Eliot Ness, October 27, 1943, in box 8, "Prostitution and Promiscuity" folder, SPD. Carter, *Sin and Science*, pp. 6, 8, 99. Anderson, *Wartime Women*, pp. 106, 109–110. Costello, *Virtue Under Fire*, pp. 7–17 (7, "By most people's . . ."), 81–82, 85, 206–207 (207, "patriotutes"), 213, 216, 246. Brandt, *No Magic Bullet*, pp. 165–168 (167, "victory girls," "good-time Charlottes," "In the first . . ."). Meyer, *Creating GI Jane*, pp. 101–103, 117–118, 120. Hegarty, *Victory Girls*, pp. 15–18, 37–38, 46–47, 90–91, 118–119, 131. Parascandola, *Sex, Sin, and Science*, pp. 123–124. Sagalyn, *A Promise Fulfilled*, p. 70. Littauer, *Bad Girls*, pp. 19–23, 26–27 (26, "contact report"), 39–47.

NESS UNCOMFORTABLE / *WHAT ABOUT GIRLS?*: Ness, *What About Girls?* pp. 21–23 (22, "I guess he . . ."), 26–27 (26, "men who say . . ."; 27, "keep the sex . . . ," "There is no . . ."), 30–31 (30, "Sordid experiences in . . . ," "Many promiscuous men . . ."). *Hearings Before a Subcommittee of the Committee on Education and Labor, United States Senate, Seventy-Eighth Congress, First Session*, pt. 1, *Juvenile Delinquency*, p. 89, in box 13, "Sub-Committee on Wartime Health and Education (Pepper Committee)" folder, SPD. Tappan, *Delinquent Girls in Court*, p. 103 ("the promiscuous girl," "a young experimenter . . ."). Heimel, *Eliot Ness*, p. 235 ("He always had . . . ," "women who have . . ."). Collins and Schwartz, *Scarface and the Untouchable*, p. 66.

NESS TARGETS PROMISCUOUS WOMEN: Eliot Ness, "The Challenge of Present Social Conditions to the Correctional System," October 21, 1942; Eliot Ness, "Recent Developments in S.P.," n.d., pp. 2–3, in box 12, "Speeches–Ness" folder, SPD. CT, December 27, 1942. Edward J. Kelly, "Techniques for Repressing Unorganized Prostitution: Recommendations of the Special Committee on Enforcement of the National Advisory Police Committee," November–December 1942; BCE, February 3, 1944; "It's a Moral Problem First," n.p., February 3, 1944; "Promiscuity Called Chief Social Evil," n.p., February 4, 1944; Eliot Ness, "Law Enforcement for Social Protection—A Health Measure," [*Wisconsin*] *Medical Journal*, February 1944; Ness, "Cooperation of Cities," pp. 48–49; Ness, "They Did the Things," pp. 26–27, all in ENPS, Roll 3, Scrapbook 12. Robert F. Ott to Eliot Ness, July 19, 1943; Dorothy C. Lawson to Eliot Ness, November 6, 1943; Charles F. Marden to Eliot Ness, August 14, 1943; Winifred

Ferguson to Eliot Ness, July 12, 1943, all in box 2, "Curfew" folder, SPD. Transcript, "Special Meeting of the Executive Committee of the National Advisory Police Committee on Social Protection," November 19, 1943, pp. 4–5, in box 6, "Law Enforcement" folder, SPD. Office of War Information, Report on Juvenile Delinquency, October 10, 1943, p. 5, in box 5, "Juvenile Delinquency" folder, SPD. Eliot Ness, memo to Regional Social Protection Representatives, February 4, 1944, in box 10, "Regional Letters" folder, SPD. "Policewoman Project," n.d., in box 8, "Films, Scripts, Etc." folder, SPD. *Hearings Before a Subcommittee of the Committee on Education and Labor, United States Senate, Seventy-Eighth Congress, First Session*, pt. 1, *Juvenile Delinquency*, pp. 86, 89, in box 13, "Sub-Committee on Wartime Health and Education (Pepper Committee)" folder, SPD (89, "The loss of . . ."). *Challenge to Community Action* (Washington, DC: Social Protection Division, 1945), pp. 1–3, in box 3, "Evolution of a Government Pamphlet (Challenge to Community Action)" folder, SPD. Carter, *Sin and Science*, pp. 7–8. Anderson, *Wartime Women*, pp. 103–104, 106–108 (108, "modified supervision"). Costello, *Virtue Under Fire*, pp. 206–207, 213–216. Brandt, *No Magic Bullet*, pp. 167–168. Meyer, *Creating GI Jane*, pp. 103–104 (104, "sexually active despite . . ."). Hegarty, *Victory Girls*, pp. 68, 70, 117, 128, 131, 144. Littauer, *Bad Girls*, pp. 20, 37–38. Romm, "During World War II." Stern, *Trials of Nina McCall*, pp. 114–115, 219–220, 222–225, 232.

VD EXAMINATIONS / RESISTANCE EFFORTS: Howard M. Slutes to Eliot Ness, June 17, 1943; Howard M. Slutes and Howard F. Feast to Eliot Ness, July 31, 1943, both in box 2, "Curfew" folder, SPD. Office of War Information, Report on Juvenile Delinquency, October 10, 1943, pp. 1–2; J. Edgar Hoover, Address before the 52nd Annual Meeting of the International Association of Chiefs of Police, December 10, 1945, both in box 5, "Juvenile Delinquency" folder, SPD. Julius M. Kovachy, "Transcript of Court's Decision," March 15, 1945, in box 5, "Historical Materials" folder, SPD. "Fortune Faces," *Fortune*, January 1946, p. 196. Anderson, *Wartime Women*, pp. 104–105, 108–109. Costello, *Virtue Under Fire*, p. 218 ("essential to the . . ."). Brandt, *No Magic Bullet*, p. 167. Hegarty, *Victory Girls*, pp. 20, 53, 138–143, 147–151. Littauer, *Bad Girls*, pp. 47–51. Romm, "During World War II." Stern, *Trials of Nina McCall*, pp. 25, 84, 212, 219, 222–225.

DOUBLE STANDARD: CPD, February 11, 1942, in ENPS, Roll 3, Scrapbook 11, p. 152. Ness, *What About Girls?* pp. 6, 23–24 ("These girls were . . ."). Carter, *Sin and Science*, p. 9. Anderson, *Wartime Women*, pp. 109–111. Costello, *Virtue Under Fire*, pp. 73–82, 86–88. Brandt, *No Magic Bullet*, pp. 164–165, 168–169. Meyer, *Creating GI Jane*, pp. 100–103, 120.

Hegarty, *Victory Girls*, pp. 12–18, 40–41, 45–46, 85–127, 133. Parascandola, *Sex, Sin, and Science*, pp. 7–14. Lord, *Condom Nation*, pp. 87–88. Littauer, *Bad Girls*, p. 44 ("You Can't Say . . .").

NESS'S VISION / GUIDING SOCIAL ACTIVITY: CPD, November 29, 1939, in "Ness, Eliot" microfiche, CPC ("In the early . . . ," "today we find . . ."). CN, March 14, 1940; CP, March 14, 1940, both in ENPS, Roll 2, Scrapbook 7, p. 99. "Mr. Ness at Hot Springs," n.d., in box 12, "Speeches–Ness" Folder, SPD.

NESS AND SPD CRITICIZED: T. E. Mahan to Eliot Ness, March 29, 1944, in ENPS, Roll 3, Scrapbook 12 ("Those damn fools . . ."). *South Carolina Labor Ledger*, June 22, 1945, in box 2, "Civil Rights" folder, SPD.

Chapter Twenty-Three: The Old Restlessness

EVALINE DEPRESSED, TURNS TO ART, LEAVES ELIOT: *Evening Star*, May 27, 1944; "Addresses of People Working with Eliot Ness (Winnie Higgins)," n.d., both in folder 3, NLEM 2012.39.1. "Evaline Ness," in Sarkissian, *Something About the Author*, p. 227 ("I longed for . . . ," "snappy," "Go to art . . . ," "He said I . . ."). Bergreen, *Capone*, p. 600. "Moore, Dan for Biography Ness," n.d., p. 6, PWH ("He was really . . ."). Perry, *Eliot Ness*, pp. 267–268.

NESS'S SECOND DIVORCE: "Mysterious Ness Divorce Papers Restored to Files," n.p., n.d.; "Ness Wins Decree from Artist Wife," n.p., n.d. ("another person"); "Eliot Ness Wins Divorce from Wife," n.p., n.d.; "Ness Papers in Divorce Invisible," n.p., October 19, 1945, all in "Ness, Eliot" microfiche, CPC. CP, October 19, 1945, ENC (also in "Ness, Eliot" microfiche, CPC). Condon, "Last American Hero," p. 142. "Moore, Dan for Biography Ness," n.d., p. 6, PWH. Heimel, *Eliot Ness*, p. 236.

EVALINE'S LATER LIFE: "Evaline Ness," in Sarkissian, *Something About the Author*, pp. 228–231. Michel, "Evaline Ness," pp. 32–37, 71–72. NYT, August 14, 1986, http://www.nytimes.com/1986/08/14/obituaries/evaline-ness-bayard-is-dead-wrote-and-illustrated-books.html (accessed February 6, 2017).

NESS RESTLESS, READY TO ENJOY LIFE: Temporary Appointment, Transfer, Reinstatement, or Promotion, Etc., April 6, 1942; Notice of Resignation or Separation, August 21, 1944, both in Eliot Ness OPF. Ness and Fraley, *The Untouchables*, p. 256. Fraley, "Real Eliot Ness," pp. 26–27. Condon, "Last American Hero," pp. 141–142. "Moore, Dan for Biography Ness," n.d., p.7, PWH. Lingeman, *Noir Forties*, pp. 26–27.

RALPH, PEGGY, AND JANET REX: CPD, August 7, 1927; April 6, 1930; December 7, 1930; September 2, 1931; December 31, 1936; August 5,

1937; February 18, 1939; December 14, 1943; July 22, 1959 ("first lady of . . ."); August 5, 1959. 1930 U.S. Census Records for Ralph, Almeda, and Janet Rex. WP, March 16, 1930. *Canton Daily News*, June 15, 1930. *Sun*, November 16, 1930; December 2, 1930; May 21, 1937. *Philadelphia Inquirer*, January 3, 1932. *Miami Herald*, January 29, 1933; January 11, 1935; March 17, 1935; April 14, 1935; April 15, 1936; June 16, 1936; June 23, 1936; May 17, 1938 ("aviator and speedboat . . ."); February 3, 1939; February 16–17, 1939; July 5, 1941; February 18, 1943. *Evening Star*, August 3, 1937. *Dayton Daily News*, May 13, 1938. *New York Herald Tribune*, February 17, 1939; February 26, 1939. "The Mocamba" photo, n.d., in ENPS, Roll 1, Scrapbook. "Mother Kelly's World Famous Bar" photo, n.d. ("It was 10:30 . . ."); *Puerto Rico World Journal*, February 4–5, 1944; February 9, 1944; Angel W. Martin to Eliot Ness, February 5, 1944; "PR Venereal Disease Parley Stresses Firm Suppression," n.p., n.d., all in ENPS, Roll 3, Scrapbook 12. "Fortune Faces," p. 196. Report on Diebold, Inc., April 24, 1946, pp. 1, 6, PWH. CP, August 8, 1947, in ENPS, Roll 3, Scrapbook 13. NYT, February 7, 1976, https://www.nytimes .com/1976/02/07/archives/ethel-shutta-singer-dies-at-79-had-a-70year -stage-career.html (accessed July 25, 2018). David Cowles, transcript of interview by Florence Schwein and Lt. Tom Brown, September 6, 1983, p. 41, CPHS. Gary Brown, "Ness no door-bus . . . ," *Canton Repository*, n.d., RM ("He was with . . ."). Condon, "Last American Hero," p. 142. Nickel, *Torso*, p. 193. Dan T. Moore, interviewed by Paul Heimel and Bob Merten, May 30, 1995, PWH. "Kerr, David for Biography Ness," n.d., p. 6, PWH. "When Eliot Ness Ran Diebold," ATM Marketplace, March 20, 2003, https://www.atmmarketplace.com/articles/when-eliot-ness-ran-diebold/ (accessed February 6, 2017). Record for Eliot Ness, *Puerto Rico, Passenger and Crew Lists, 1901–1962* (Provo, UT: Ancestry.com Operations, Inc., 2012). "Ralph K. Rex," Find a Grave, January 6, 2012, https://www .findagrave.com/cgi-bin/fg.cgi?page=grGRid=83038456 (accessed February 5, 2017). "Janet Rex," Find a Grave, September 21, 2013, https://www.find agrave.com/cgi-bin/fg.cgi?page=gr&GRid=117439917 (accessed February 5, 2017).

Our identification of the unnamed woman with Ness in the "Mother Kelly's" photo as Janet Rex is based on her appearance in CPD, December 7, 1930; February 18, 1939; and *Dayton Daily News*, May 13, 1938.

NESS JOINS DIEBOLD, LEAVES SPD: R. B. Modehouse to Eliot Ness, August 3, 1944; Mark A. McCloskey to Eliot Ness, August 25, 1944; Paul V. McNutt to Eliot Ness, September 16, 1944; Richard H. Lyle to Eliot Ness, August 29, 1944; John F. Hardy to Eliot Ness, August 29, 1944; Katharine F. Lenroot to Eliot Ness, August 29, 1944, all in ENPS, Roll 3, Scrapbook 12. "Major Operation in Washington," *Social Protection Bulletin*,

September 12, 1944, p. 1, in box 10, "Social Protection Bulletins" folder, SPD. Eliot Ness, memo to Mark A. McCloskey, August 21, 1944; Notice of Resignation or Separation, August 21, 1944, both in Eliot Ness OPF. "Fortune Faces," p. 196. CP, August 8, 1947, in ENPS, Roll 3, Scrapbook 13. "When Eliot Ness Ran Diebold."

END OF SPD: Ness, "Venereal Disease Control in Defense," p. 91. *Kansas City Star*, January 4, 1944, in ENPS, Roll 3, Scrapbook 12. "Policewoman Project," n.d., in box 8, "Films, Scripts, Etc." folder, SPD. Eliot Ness, memo to Watson Miller, May 26, 1945, in box 6, "Social Protection Legislative File" folder, SPD. *Columbia Record*, July 18, 1946. Coates, Hoff, and Hoff, *Preventive Medicine in World War II*, p. 163. Costello, *Virtue Under Fire*, pp. 89, 244–245. Brandt, *No Magic Bullet*, pp. 171–171. Parascandola, *Sex, Sin, and Science*, pp. 134–135. Lingeman, *Noir Forties*, pp. 17–21. Stern, *Trials of Nina McCall*, pp. 227–228, 237–241.

NESS AT DIEBOLD: "Fortune Faces," p. 196. Report on Diebold, Inc., April 24, 1946; James H. Clark to Eliot Ness, April 26, 1946, both in PWH. CP, August 8, 1947, in ENPS, Roll 3, Scrapbook 13. "Who's Who in America 1954–55," n.d., KDB. Gary Brown, "Ness no door-bus . . . ," *Canton Repository*, n.d., RM ("In spite of . . ."). Nickel, *Torso*, pp. 193–194. Heimel, *Eliot Ness*, pp. 236–238. Lingeman, *Noir Forties*, pp. 60–61, 63, 66, 77–85.

MIDDLE EAST COMPANY: "Announcing the Formation and Services of the Middle East Company," n.d., NLEM 2012.39.8. "Fortune Shorts," *Fortune*, January 1946, p. 226. CP, August 8, 1947, in ENPS, Roll 3, Scrapbook 13. "Eliot Ness Weds Third Wife in East," n.p., n.d., in "Ness, Eliot" microfiche, CPC. Dan T. Moore, interviewed by Paul Heimel and Bob Merten, May 30, 1995, PWH. Heimel, *Eliot Ness*, pp. 238–239 (239, "was a wise . . .").

ELISABETH ANDERSEN SEAVER: Grace V. Kelly, "It Takes More Than Inspiration to Become a Sculptor of Repute," n.p., n.d., RM. "Eliot Ness Weds Third Wife in East," n.p., n.d.; CN, January 27, 1947; CN, January 27, 1947, all in "Ness, Eliot" microfiche, CPC. CPD, February 9, 1946, ENC (also in "Ness, Eliot" microfiche, CPC). CP, July 31, 1947, in ENPS, Roll 3, Scrapbook 13. CN, December 15, 1949, ENC. "Who's Who in America 1954–55," n.d., KDB. *Potter Enterprise*, January 24, 1957; January 31, 1957. Ness and Fraley, *The Untouchables*, p. 6. Ness, "My Husband, Eliot Ness," p. 7 ("When he was . . . ," "He didn't follow . . ."). *Des Moines Sunday Register*, October 29, 1961. Nickel, *Torso*, p. 194. Dan T. Moore, interviewed by Paul Heimel and Bob Merten, May 30, 1995, PWH. "Moore, Dan for Biography Ness," n.d., p. 10, PWH. Heimel, *Eliot Ness*, pp. 237–238. Viktor Schreckengost and Marjorie Mutersbaugh, interviewed in *The*

Fourteenth Victim. Record for Elisabeth Ness, *U.S., Social Security Death Index, 1935–2014* (Provo, UT: Ancestry.com Operations Inc., 2011). Vacha, *Meet Me on Lake Erie*, p. 33 ("Beauty," "Protection"). Perry, *Eliot Ness*, pp. 161–163, 273–275. Anonymous Ness acquaintance, personal interview with ABS, November 15, 2016. John Rigas, personal interview with ABS, November 15, 2016. Linda Phelps, personal interview with ABS, November 22, 2016.

NESS'S THIRD MARRIAGE, MOVE TO BRATENAHL: "Fortune Faces," p. 196. "Eliot Ness Weds Third Wife in East," n.p., n.d., in "Ness, Eliot" microfiche, CPC. CPD, February 9, 1946, ENC (also in "Ness, Eliot" microfiche, CPC). CP, July 31, 1947, in ENPS, Roll 3, Scrapbook 13. Ness, "My Husband, Eliot Ness," p. 7. Jedick, "Eliot Ness," p. 94. Van Tassel and Grabowski, *Encyclopedia of Cleveland History*, pp. 124–125. CPD, September 7, 1997 ("I once asked . . . ," "he always kept . . . ," "lucky," "They were so . . ."). Heimel, *Eliot Ness*, p. 240. Perry, *Eliot Ness*, p. 273. "10229 Lake Shore Blvd, Cleveland, OH 44108," Zillow, http://www.zillow.com /homedetails/10229–Lake-Shore-Blvd-Cleveland-OH-44108/33622726 _zpid/ (accessed February 11, 2017).

NESS STILL RESTLESS, HAVING FUN: "Fortune Faces," p. 196 ("slimly handsome young . . . ," "could probably be . . . ," "Maybe I'll fall . . ."). Ness, "My Husband, Eliot Ness," pp. 6–7. Arruda, "Eliot Ness–Revisited," p. 13, PCHS ("the Swede"). CPD, September 7, 1997 ("was a party . . ."). Rebecca McFarland, "Notes From People Who Telephoned in Response to the Article," n.d., RM. Grimes, *Straight Up or on the Rocks*, pp. 109–110, 113. Rotskoff, *Love on the Rocks*, pp. 56–57, 60, 62, 72, 91, 99–102. Lingeman, *Noir Forties*, pp. 60–61. Jeffreys, *Empire of Booze*, pp. 233–234.

Chapter Twenty-Four: Vote Yes for Ness

CAPONE'S DEATH / NESS AS BUSINESSMAN: *Miami Daily News*, January 22–26, 1947. *Miami Herald*, January 23–26, 1947. CN, January 27, 1947, in "Ness, Eliot" microfiche, CPC ("nervous frenzy," "head over heels . . . ," "an administrator"). Heimel, *Eliot Ness*, pp. 241–242. Alphonse Capone, Medical Chart ("Refer To Old File In Safe For Previous Record"), January 21, 1947, in "#2127–Al Capone," RR Auction, http://www.rrauction .com/bidtracker_detail.cfm?IN=2127 (accessed June 13, 2017). ABS tour of 93 Palm Island, Miami Beach, FL, April 19, 2017.

REPUBLICANS WEAKENED / MAYOR BURKE: CN, January 11, 1936. CPD, November 10, 1941, in ENPS, Roll 3, Scrapbook 11, p. 123. CN, January 27, 1947 ("Just as soon . . ."); CPD, July 23, 1947, both in "Ness,

Eliot" microfiche, CPC. CP, July 25, 1947; CPD, August 2, 1947, both in ENPS, Roll 3, Scrapbook 13. CPD, November 6, 1947. Condon, *Cleveland*, p. 243. Porter, *Cleveland*, pp. 133–134 (134, "All he needed . . ."), 136, 140. Jedick, "Eliot Ness," p. 92. Heimel, *Eliot Ness*, p. 246.

NESS TALKED INTO RUNNING: CN, July 2, 1947; CPD, July 23, 1947; CPD, July 31, 1947; CN, July 30, 1947; CP, July 30, 1947 ("independent"). CPD, August 5, 1947, all in "Ness, Eliot" microfiche, CPC. CP, July 28, 1947; CPD, July 28, 1947; CPD, August 2, 1947; CN, August 2, 1947, all in ENPS, Roll 3, Scrapbook 13. Porter, *Cleveland*, p. 104 ("he was Superman"). Jedick, "Eliot Ness," 92. Condon, "Last American Hero," p. 142. Dan T. Moore, interviewed by Paul Heimel and Bob Merten, May 30, 1995, PWH. "Kerr, David for Biography Ness," n.d., p. 5, PWH. Heimel, *Eliot Ness*, p. 246.

POLICE, SUTTON, AND MOLNAR: "Ness Probes Police Alertness," n.p., September 1947 ("preventive policing"); untitled clipping, n.p., n.d.; Jack Small, "Ness Claims Police Climb on His Wagon," n.p., September 2, 1947; CP, September 15 [?], 1947, all in "Ness, Eliot" microfiche, CPC. CPD November 2, 1947 ("the things I . . ."). CCP, March 6, 1948; April 3, 1948; July 17, 1948; July 24, 1948; July 31, 1948; August 7, 1948; August 28, 1948; December 18, 1948; May 14, 1949; July 9, 1949; July 30, 1949; August 6, 1949; February 4, 1950; June 14, 1952; January 24, 1953. CPD, March 24, 1948; July 23, 1948; August 4, 1956. Maisel, "Return of the Numbers Racket," pp. 72–73. *Hearings Before a Special Committee to Investigate Organized Crime in Interstate Commerce*, pt. 6, pp. 36–37. Jedick, "Eliot Ness," p. 92. Wilder, "Last Untouchable," p. 117, PWH. CPD, September 3, 2001, RM. Neff, *Mobbed Up*, p. 24.

NESS BORED, DECIDES TO RUN: Untitled clipping, n.d.; CPD, August 22, 1947, both in ENPS, Roll 3, Scrapbook 13. CPD, August 5, 1947, in "Ness, Eliot" microfiche, CPC ("interesting and fun"). Jedick, "Eliot Ness," pp. 92–93 (92, "He never planned . . ."). Bergreen, *Capone*, p. 603. Dan T. Moore, interviewed by Paul Heimel and Bob Merten, May 30, 1995, PWH. Heimel, *Eliot Ness*, p. 246. Dan Moore, interviewed in "Eliot Ness: Untouchable" ("an automatic life . . . ," "But I didn't . . .").

CAMPAIGN BEGINS / NESS A BAD CANDIDATE: "Ness' Formal Declaration of Candidacy," n.p., n.d. ("a completely non-partisan . . . ," "When I left . . ."); CP, July 30, 1947; CN, July 30, 1947 ("youthful"); CPD, July 31, 1947 ("smooth"); CP, July 31, 1947; CPD, August 5, 1947; Ray Dorsen, "Ness Hits . . . On With . . . ," n.p., n.d., all in "Ness, Eliot" microfiche,

CPC. CN, July 31, 1947; CPD, August 2, 1947 ("Why he decided . . . ,"
"Ness the safety . . ."); CN, August 2, 1947; CPD, August 18[?], 1947;
untitled clipping, n.d.; CPD, September [?] 13, 1947, all in ENPS, Roll 3,
Scrapbook 13. CPD, November 2, 1947. CPD, November 6, 1947. Con-
don, "Last American Hero," p. 142. Dan T. Moore, interviewed by Paul
Heimel and Bob Merten, May 30, 1995, PWH.

AFRICAN-AMERICAN WARDS, SUPPORT FOR NESS: CCP, September 13, 1947; September 20, 1947; September 27, 1947 ("the Burke
Administration . . . ," "If I am . . . ," "Independent Republican," "Make Cleveland Safer . . . ," "helped materially in . . . ," "His whole professional . . .");
October 4, 1947; October 11, 1947; November 1, 1947; November 8,
1947; November 26, 1966. Untitled clipping, n.p., n.d.; Wilson Hirschfeld,
untitled clipping, n.p., n.d., both in "Ness, Eliot" microfiche, CPC.

CAMPAIGN STUNTS: CN, July 30, 1947; CP, July 30, 1947; CPD, July
31, 1947 ("news-producing"); CPD, August 5, 1947; CPD, September 16,
1947 ("Puzzy-Wup"); CP, September 17, 1947 ("I am beginning . . .");
"Calls Burke Regime Idle," CPD n.d., all in "Ness, Eliot" microfiche, CPC.
CP, July 31, 1947; CN, August 2, 1947; CP, August 8, 1947 ("I am so . . .");
CPD, August 9, 1947 ("Cleveland voters suspect . . ."); untitled clipping,
n.d., in ENPS, Roll 3, Scrapbook 13. CPD, June 18, 1961, ENC. Con-
don, *Cleveland*, p. 243. Jedick, "Eliot Ness," p. 92. Arruda, "Eliot Ness–
Revisited," p. 13. Condon, "Last American Hero," p. 142. Nickel, "Real
Eliot Ness," p. 52. Heimel, *Eliot Ness*, pp. 246–247.

RICH DONORS / LABOR UNIONS: CN, August 14, 1947 ("ordered police
on . . ."); CP, August 14, 1947; CPD, August 14, 1947; CN, August 18,
1947, all in ENPS, Roll 3, Scrapbook 13. CP, August 23, 1947, in "Ness,
Eliot" microfiche, CPC. CPD, September 3–4, 1947 (September 4, "to go
all . . ."); September 11, 1947 ("hand-picked candidate . . ."). CP, November 8, 1947, ENC ("big money"). CP, November 29, 1947. Condon, *Cleveland*, p. 243. Jedick, "Eliot Ness," p. 92. Arruda, "Eliot Ness–Revisited,"
p. 13. Condon, "Last American Hero," p. 142. Nickel, "Real Eliot Ness,"
p. 52.

NESS CRITICIZES BURKE, SPEAKS ABOUT CRIME: "Ness' Formal
Declaration of Candidacy," n.p., n.d.; CPD, July 31, 1947; CP, September 1, 1947; CP, September 2, 1947; CP, September 13, 1947 ("It is
alleged . . ."); CP, September 16, 1947; CP, September 23 [?], 1947; CP,
September [2?], 1947; CPD, September 30 [?], 1947; "Ness Probes Police
Alertness," n.p., September 1947; untitled clipping, n.p., n.d. ("a ho-hum
administration . . ."); Wilson Hirschfeld, untitled clipping, n.p., n.d.; Alvin

Silverman, untitled clipping, n.p., n.d.; "Calls Burke Regime Idle," CPD, n.d., all in "Ness, Eliot" microfiche, CPC. CN, July 31, 1947; CN, August 2, 1947; CP, August 7, 1947; CN, August 9, 1947, all in ENPS, Roll 3, Scrapbook 13. CCP, September 13, 1947; September 27, 1947. CPD, September 28, 1947; October 15, 1947; October 17–18, 1947; October 20, 1947; October 25, 1947; October 30–November 1, 1947; November 5–6, 1947 (November 5, "an almost listless . . ."). Nickel, *Torso*, p. 204 ("That case has . . .").

PRIMARY ELECTION: CN, August 11, 1947; CP, August 11, 1947; CN, August 12, 1947; "Not the Next Mayor," n.p., August 12, 1947; CPD, August 12, 1947; CPD August 13, 1947, all in ENPS, Roll 3, Scrapbook 12. CPD, September 28, 1947 ("It is not . . ."); October 1–2, 1947 (October 1, "The vote shows . . ."); November 5, 1947. CT October 1, 1947. NYT, October 1, 1947. LAT, October 2, 1947. WP, October 2, 1947. CCP, October 11, 1947 ("Despite the amateurish . . .").

NESS CARAVAN: CCP, October 25, 1947; November 8, 1947. CPD, October 29, 1947 ("the Eliot Ness caravan," "For action now . . . ," "Every minute we . . . ," "I'll lay you . . . ," "Almost without exception . . ."). Bergreen, *Capone*, p. 603 ("VOTE YES FOR . . ."). Photographs of campaign caravan in NLEM 2012.39.13–26.

NESS CONVINCED HE CAN WIN, DESPERATE: CPD, October 19, 1947 ("to disavow Communists . . ."); October 29–31, 1947 (October 29, "committed to a . . ."); November 2, 1947; September 7, 1997 ("He thought he . . ."). Jedick, "Eliot Ness," p. 92. Dan T. Moore, interviewed by Paul Heimel and Bob Merten, May 30, 1995, PWH. Heimel, *Eliot Ness*, p. 248.

NESS'S REPUTATION DAMAGED / BURKE CRITICIZES: CPD, September 28, 1947 ("superficial grasp of . . ."); October 26, 1947 ("synthetic"); November 2–3, 1947 (November 2, "The one thing . . . ," "show that he . . ."). CP, November 2, 1947. Trickey, "Eliot Ness vs.," p. 104.

FBI TRAINING PROGRAM: CPD, October 7, 1947 ("super-police"); November 4, 1947. Trickey, "Eliot Ness vs.," p. 104.

ELECTION DAY AND NIGHT: CP, November 4–5, 1947. CPD, November 4–5, 1947 (November 5, "There are larger . . . ," "the most remarkable . . . ," "a man of . . . ," "Naturally I am . . . ," "Nice campaign"). CT, November 5, 1947. NYT, November 5–6, 1947. WP, November 5, 1947. CCP, November 8, 1947; November 26, 1966. Condon, *Cleveland*, p. 243. Jedick, "Eliot Ness," p. 92 ("Who'd want an . . .").

Chapter Twenty-Five: Head Man Ness

NESS EXILED FROM LAW ENFORCEMENT: Jedick, "Eliot Ness," pp. 92–93. Dan T. Moore, interviewed by Paul Heimel and Bob Merten, May 30, 1995, PWH ("never should have . . ."). Heimel, *Eliot Ness*, p. 251. Dan Moore, interviewed in "Eliot Ness: Untouchable."

NESS AND FOYLE: Bergreen, *Capone* pp. 610–611 (610, "I would have . . .";611, "Al Capone," "I never saw . . ."). *Olean Times*, October 7, 1996, PCHS. Rebecca McFarland, "Notes from People Who Telephoned in Response to the Article," n.d., RM. Grimes, *Straight Up or on the Rocks*, pp. 10–11. Rotskoff, *Love on the Rocks*, pp. 56–57 (56, "three-martini lunch"; 57, "good for business"), 99–102, 194–199, 201, 204–206, 228–229. Collins and Schwartz, *Scarface and the Untouchable*, pp. 101–102, 582–583.

NESS BECOMES A FATHER: CP, April 20, 1973, in "Ness, Robert Eliot" folder, CPC. Jedick, "Eliot Ness," p. 94. Arruda, "Eliot Ness–Revisited," p. 13, PCHS. Heimel, *Eliot Ness*, p. 245 ("He was spread . . ."). Marjorie Mutersbaugh, interviewed in *The Fourteenth Victim*. Natalie Phelps, personal interview with ABS, November 15, 2016. Joe Phelps Jr., telephone interview with ABS, November 22, 2016. Linda Phelps, telephone interview with ABS, November 22, 2016. RM to ABS, personal email, February 8, 2017.

LEHMAN FAMILY / NESS'S STRUGGLES: *Potter Enterprise*, March 22, 1961 ("a fall guy . . ."). Fraley, "Real Eliot Ness," pp. 26–27 ("a lamb among . . ."). Porter, *Cleveland*, p. 105. Jedick, "Eliot Ness," pp. 55, 94. Mark Lehman, "Eliot Ness—The Man We Thought We Knew," *Cincinnati Magazine*, August 1987, pp. 19–20, PWH ("Mr. Ness liked . . . ," "that nice man . . ."). CPD, September 7, 1997.

SANDUSKY BOMBING / ROCCO RUSSO: CPD, May 17, 1950; January 24–26, 1951; May 19, 1955. Frank Siedel, "0940–The Ohio Story: 'The Memory Detective,'" *The Ohio Story Radio Scripts*, January 5–6, 1953, Ohio Genealogical Society, https://www.ogsarchive.org/items/show /632 (accessed April 10, 2019). Messick, *Silent Syndicate*, pp. 255, 287–288 (287, "La Cosa Nostra," "coordinated drive"), 292 ("We gotta live . . ."). Neff, *Mobbed Up*, pp. 2–3, 200–210 (209, "served as seed . . ."), 243–244, 246–247, 252, 341, 371. Gentry, *J. Edgar Hoover*, pp. 327–330. Jacoby, *Sandusky's Finest*, pp. vii, 1–2, 55–57, 99–128 (105, "never forgot a . . ."; 110, "He told us . . ."; 111, "a sore spot"; 113, "of considerable assistance . . ."; 114, "had given us . . ."; 115, "the workings of . . ."; 119, "Ness felt that . . . ," "wasn't our job . . . ," "It came to . . ."; 120, "was having trouble . . ."; 121, "had class, and . . . ," "tall and slim," "a deep voice," "My first impression . . . ,"

"Who is Dago . . . ," "Ness was impressed . . . ," "He also told . . . ," "missed the boat"; 125, "that this menace . . . ," "One may well . . ."; 128, "had cut off . . . ," "The FBI has . . ."). Bergreen, *Capone*, p. 611. "Notes from People Who Telephoned in Response to the Article," n.d., RM. Russo, *Outfit*, pp. 32–34, 327–330. Bernstein, *Greatest Menace*, pp. 171–175. Capeci, *Complete Idiot's Guide*, pp. 31–46, 100–102, 165, 190–192, 245–247. Raab, *Five Families*, pp. 5, 32–34, 96–100, 109–111, 117–122, 127–138, 277–278. Cressey, *Theft of the Nation*, pp. xxiii–xxv, 1–7. Jim Finckenauer, introduction to Cressey, *Theft of the Nation*, pp. ix–xxii. Trickey, "Eliot Ness vs.," p. 104.

IMPORT-EXPORT VENTURES COLLAPSE: Dan T. Moore, interviewed by Paul Heimel and Bob Merten, May 30, 1995, PWH. Heimel, *Eliot Ness*, pp. 241–245, 252–254.

FORCED OUT OF DIEBOLD: Report on Diebold, Inc., April 24, 1946, p. 7, PWH. CP, August 8, 1947, in ENPS, Roll 3, Scrapbook 13. NYT, April 14, 1951. Gary Brown, "Ness no door-bus . . . ," *Canton Repository*, n.d., RM ("He came here . . ."). Dan T. Moore, interviewed by Paul Heimel and Bob Merten, May 30, 1995, PWH. Heimel, *Eliot Ness*, pp. 237–238, 251, 254–255. "When Eliot Ness Ran Diebold."

NESS BROKE / SHORT-TERM JOBS / BACK IN CHICAGO: Rita and Oscar Bergman, "The Bystanders," n.p., n.d., in ENPS, Roll 1, Scrapbook 4. CN, December 15, 1949, ENC. "Selected Films Available to TV," *Billboard*, September 6, 1952, p. 30. CPD, August 16, 1953; August 25, 1953; September 17, 1955; September 22, 1955; November 29, 1955. CST, January 18, 1953, in "Newspaper clippings (photocopies) circa. 1930–1970" folder, DMM. CT, March 8, 1954. Robert E. Merriam to Eliot Ness, February 23, 1954; Eliot Ness to Robert E. Merriam, March 1, 1954; Robert E. Merriam to Eliot Ness, March 9, 1954; Eliot Ness to Robert E. Merriam, April 7, 1954; Eliot Ness to Robert E. Merriam, April 16, 1954; Robert E. Merriam to Eliot Ness, May 28, 1954, all in box 31, folder 12, Robert E. Merriam Papers, Special Collections Research Center, University of Chicago Library, Chicago, IL. Application for Employment, December 28, 1955, KDB. *Potter Enterprise*, February 2, 1956. Condon, *Cleveland*, p. 243 ("I'd regard it . . ."). Porter, *Cleveland*, p. 105. Jedick, "Eliot Ness," p. 94 ("turn on the . . ."). David Cowles, transcript of interview by Florence Schwein and Lt. Tom Brown, September 6, 1983, pp. 41–42, CPHS ("The last time . . ."). "Robert Stack returning to Eliot Ness role," n.p., n.d., PCHS. Transcript of Robert Stack on *Larry King Live*, November 7, 1991, PWH. Bergreen, *Capone*, pp. 610–612 (611, "an article about . . ."; 612, "They didn't want . . ."). Dan T. Moore, interviewed by Paul Heimel and Bob Merten, May 30, 1995, PWH. Heimel, *Eliot Ness*, pp. 255–256, 282

("Here's a guy . . ."). Rotskoff, *Love on the Rocks*, p. 201. Alder, *Lie Detectors*, p. 245. Oliver, *August Vollmer*, p. 592. Collins and Schwartz, *Scarface and the Untouchable*, pp. 40–43.

BUTCHER RETURNS: Martin, "Butcher's Dozen," pp. 66–67 (67, "It can be . . ."). Martin, *Butcher's Dozen*, pp. 95 ("It can be . . ."), 99 ("You know, after . . ."). CPD, January 8, 1989. Nickel, *Torso*, pp. 190–192 ("the Kingsbury technique," "After all, it's . . ."). Bellamy, *Maniac in the Bushes*, p. 296. Badal, *Though Murder*, pp. 160–161. Badal, *Hell's Wasteland*, pp. 105–106. Badal, *In the Wake*, pp. 169–173 (169, "sunbather"). Hickey, *Serial Murderers*, p. 6. Vronsky, *Sons of Cain*, pp. 68, 69–70.

SWEENEY'S LATER LIFE / TAUNTING NESS: Frank E. Sweeney to J. Edgar Hoover, September 12, 1953, in FBI-FES ("Nessism," "[A] Basic principle . . ."). Unsigned to "Eliot Direct-Um Ness," January 1954; "The American Sweeney" to "Eliot Am-Big-U-Ous Ness!" March 1954 ("Pansy Plants"); unsigned to "Eliot (Head-Man) Ness," April 1954 ("Who - is - T . . ."); unsigned to "Eliot (Esophogotic) Ness," c. 1954; F. E. Sweeney to Eliot Ness, March 1955 (*Handbook for Poisoners*, "Paranoidal - Nemesis"), all in ENPS, Roll 1, Folder 2. Frank E. Sweeney to Eliot Ness, February 14, 1954, in ENPS, Roll 2, Scrapbook 7, p. 4 ("a few items . . . ," "Revenge is an . . . ," "I trust that . . ."). Fraley, *4 Against the Mob*, pp. 138–139 ("Don't worry about . . ."). James Jessen Badal, interviewed in *The Fourteenth Victim*. Cerny, "Gaylord Sundheim," in Badal, *Though Murder*, pp. 187–189. Cerny, "Chronology and Summary," in Badal, *Though Murder*, pp. 200–210 (204, "You have afforded . . ."). Badal, *In the Wake*, pp. 223–225, 233–235, 259. Bardsley, *American Sweeney Todd*, pp. 217–219.

Chapter Twenty-Six: You Should Write a Book

SHAMPANORE AND PHELPS: CN, December 14, 1955; January 30, 1956, KDB. G. F. Shampanore to George C. and Doris Mosch, December 31, 1955, PCHS. G. F. Shampanore to Eliot Ness, January 10, 1956; Verne M. Haight to Eliot Ness, February 7, 1956, both KDB. *Potter Enterprise*, February 2, 1956. "C. of C. Endorses 'Persona-Seal' Checks," n.p., November 15, 1956, PWH. George C. Mosch to J. T. Rutherford, September 26, 1958, PWH. *Asbury Park Press*, April 26, 1959. *Potter Enterprise*, November 24, 1971 ("a spell-binder . . ."). *Potter Leader-Enterprise*, April 7, 1993, PCHS. *News-Press*, December 7, 1994, PWH. Joe Phelps Jr. to Paul Heimel, January 31, 1995, PWH. Recorded recollections of William Ayers, n.d., PWH. Natalie Phelps, personal interview with ABS, November 15, 2016 ("Moose," "Within a few . . ."). Joe Phelps Jr., telephone interview with ABS, November 22, 2016. Linda Phelps, telephone interview with ABS, November 22, 2016 ("a compulsive talker . . .").

NESS JOINS NORTH RIDGE / TRAVELING WITH PHELPS: Application for Employment, December 28, 1955; Eliot Ness to Frank Shampanore, December 29, 1955; G. F. Shampanore to Eliot Ness, December 31, 1955; CN, January 30, 1956; Verne M. Haight to Eliot Ness, February 7, 1956, all KDB. G. F. Shampanore to George C. and Doris Mosch, December 31, 1955, PCHS. *Asbury Park Press*, April 26, 1959 ("Weren't you scared," "Scared? I was . . ."). *Potter Enterprise*, November 24, 1971. Recorded recollections of William Ayers, n.d., PWH. "John Rigas," n.d., PWH. "Bob Merten Talk," May 10, 1993, PWH. Paul W. Heimel, "Agent Eliot Ness Lived His Last Years in Coudersport," *Pennsylvania*, March/April 1996, pp. 32–33, PCHS. "Virginia Kallenborn interview," March 25, 2000, PWH. Heimel, *Eliot Ness*, pp. 193, 223, 260. Natalie Phelps, personal interview with ABS, November 15, 2016.

OSCAR FRALEY / MEETING NESS: NYT, October 20, 1944. *Asbury Park Press*, April 26, 1959 ("Why don't you . . ."). Fraley, "Real Eliot Ness," pp. 26–27 (26, "one of those . . . ," "You'll have to . . . ," "It was dangerous," "Someday you should . . . ," "I could use . . ."). "Ockie's Jackpot," pp. 67–68 (67, "Ockie"). *Potter Enterprise*, November 24, 1971. Eyman, "An Oscar for Elliot [*sic*] Ness," pp. 10, 12. *Tampa Tribune*, August 8, 1987 ("financial writers," "I said, sure . . ."). Record for Oscar Fraley in the Florida Death Index, 1877–1998 (Provo, UT, Ancestry.com Operations, Inc., 2004). Natalie Phelps, personal interview with ABS, November 15, 2016. Joe Phelps Jr., telephone interview with ABS, November 22, 2016. Linda Phelps, telephone interview with ABS, November 22, 2016. Pearl, "Behind *The Untouchables*."

NESS CONSIDERS SELLING HIS STORY: Raymond M. Schwartz to Eliot Ness, June 17, 1931, in ENPS, Roll 1, Scrapbook 1. Bergreen, *Capone*, p. 433. "Tony Berardi: About Eliot Ness and 'The Untouchables'" (1999), 00:08:42, United Archives, http://www.onlinefootage.tv/stock-video-footage/7684/prohibition-tony-berardi-about-eliot-ness-and-the-untouchables (accessed February 7, 2016). Collins & Schwartz, *Scarface and the Untouchable*, pp. 474–475.

NESS AND FRALEY BEGIN BOOK: Oscar Fraley to Eliot Ness, May 6, 1956 ("a helluva lot . . . ," "Don't get scared . . ."); Emily Lou Alford to Eliot Ness, November 20, 1956, both KDB. Application for Letters of Administration, June 11, 1957, PCHS. Fraley, "Real Eliot Ness," pp. 27–28. *Potter Enterprise*, November 24, 1971. Eyman, "An Oscar for Elliot [*sic*] Ness," pp. 10, 12. Schoenberg, *Mr. Capone*, pp. 295–297. Heimel, *Eliot*

Ness, p. 269. John Rigas, personal interview with ABS, November 15, 2016.

BOOK ADVANCE: Fraley, "The Real Eliot Ness," p. 27. Application for Letters of Administration, June 11, 1957, PCHS. Heimel, *Eliot Ness*, p. 269.

NORTH RIDGE STARTS BIG, MOVES TO COUDERSPORT: *Potter County Journal*, April 12, 1956, KDB ("the first production . . ."). *Potter Enterprise*, April 12, 1956; August 2, 1956; August 16, 1956; August 23, 1956; March 22, 1961; November 24, 1971. "Meeting of the Joint Boards of Directors of the North Ridge Industrial Corporation and the Guaranty Paper Corporation," April 3, 1957, PWH. George C. Mosch to J. T. Rutherford, September 26, 1958, PWH. Joseph E. Phelps, "Report to the Pennsylvania Securities Commission," n.d., in ENPS, Roll 1, Folder 1. *Williamsport Sun-Gazette*, March 16, 1961. Nickel, *Torso*, p. 200 ("You know, I . . ."). *Potter Leader-Enterprise*, April 7, 1993, PCHS ("nothing more than . . ."). Joe Phelps Jr. to Paul Heimel, January 31, 1995, PWH. Recorded recollections of William Ayers, n.d., PWH ("We didn't know . . ."). Natalie Phelps, personal interview with ABS, November 15, 2016. Heimel, *Behind the Badge*, pp. 172, 176.

NESS AND PHELPS: Natalie Phelps, personal interview with ABS, November 15, 2016 ("and Eliot kind . . ."). John Rigas, personal interview with ABS, November 15, 2016. Linda Phelps, telephone interview with ABS, November 22, 2016. Heimel, *Behind the Badge*, pp. 178–180. Natalie Phelps, interviewed by PWH at the Coudersport Theatre, Coudersport, PA, July 22, 2018.

Chapter Twenty-Seven: Valuable Citizen

SUSPICION OF OUTSIDERS: *Potter Enterprise*, June 20, 1957; March 22, 1961 ("a man you . . ."). "John Rigas," n.d., PWH. "Bob Merten Talk," May 10, 1993, PWH. Heimel, "Agent Eliot Ness," pp. 32–33, PCHS. "Virginia Kallenborn interview," March 25, 2000, PWH. Natalie Phelps, personal interview with ABS, November 15, 2016 ("damn flatlanders"). John Rigas, personal interview with ABS, November 15, 2016.

JOHN RIGAS: "John Rigas," n.d., PWH ("Well, it wasn't . . ."). "Bob Merten Talk," May 10, 1993, PWH. "Virginia Kallenborn interview," March 25, 2000, PWH. John Rigas, personal interview with ABS, November 15, 2016 ("And even when . . . ," "What's he doing . . ."). Heimel, *Behind the Badge*, p. 180.

NESS DISBELIEVED / FINANCIAL PROBLEMS, HONESTY, AND MODESTY: *Star-Gazette*, June 22, 1987, RM ("He'd tell us . . ."). "Fred

Anderson—For Biography Ness," n.d., PWH. Natalie Phelps, personal interview with ABS, November 15, 2016. John Rigas, personal interview with ABS, November 15, 2016 ("When I came . . . ," "When you talked . . ."). Heimel, *Behind the Badge*, pp. 7–9, 177.

NESS AND ALCOHOL: Eyman, "An Oscar for Elliot [*sic*] Ness," p. 12 ("a big drinker . . ."). *Star-Gazette*, June 22, 1987, RM ("always seemed to . . ."). *Potter Leader-Enterprise*, April 7, 1993, PCHS. "Bill Ayers," n.d., PWH ("no more than . . ."). William Ayers, email to Paul Heimel, July 11, 1999, PWH. Natalie Phelps, personal interview with ABS, November 15, 2016. John Rigas, personal interview with ABS, November 15, 2016. Joe Phelps Jr., telephone interview with ABS, November 22, 2016.

OLD HICKORY: *High Noon* (1952), directed by Fred Zinnemann (Santa Monica, CA: Artisan Entertainment, 2002), DVD. Heimel, *Eliot Ness* p. 264. Fred Anderson, interviewed in "Eliot Ness," *The Real Untouchables*. Natalie Phelps, personal interview with ABS, November 15, 2016. John Rigas, personal interview with ABS, November 15, 2016. Joe Phelps Jr., telephone interview with ABS, November 22, 2016. Heimel, *Behind the Badge*, pp. 7–9. "Eliot Ness's Last Walk," handout distributed by PCHS during the "Eliot Ness Fest" in Coudersport, PA, July 21, 2018, ABS. Natalie Phelps, interviewed by Paul W. Heimel at the Coudersport Theatre, Coudersport, PA, July 22, 2018.

NESS STRUGGLES TO WRITE: Eliot Ness to Oscar Fraley, n.d., in ENPS, Roll 1, Folder 1. Arruda, "Eliot Ness—Revisited," p. 13, PCHS. *Potter Leader-Enterprise*, April 7, 1993, PCHS. "Lewis Wilkinson," n.d., PWH. Lewis Wilkinson, interviewed in "Eliot Ness: Untouchable." Lewis Wilkinson, interviewed in "Eliot Ness," *The Real Untouchables*. Heimel, *Behind the Badge*, p. 188.

FRALEY COMES TO COUDERSPORT / WORKING ON BOOK: *Potter Enterprise*, August 2, 1956; July 18, 1957; March 22, 1961. Fraley, "Real Eliot Ness," pp. 28, 30. *Des Moines Sunday Register*, October 29, 1961 ("had to have . . ."). Fred McGunagle, "Postcard from the Mad Butcher," n.p., March 29, 1989, PWH. Nickel, *Torso*, pp. 201–202. *Potter Leader-Enterprise*, April 7, 1993, PCHS. *News-Press*, December 7, 1994, RM. Heimel, "Agent Eliot Ness," p. 33. "Virginia Kallenborn interview," March 25, 2000, PWH. John Rigas, personal interview with ABS, November 15, 2016. Heimel, *Behind the Badge*, pp. 190–191. Collins and Schwartz, *Scarface and the Untouchable*, pp. 483–485.

NESS FAMILY MOVES TO COUDERSPORT: *Potter Enterprise*, August 16, 1956; March 22, 1961; December 20, 1967 (the Judge); November 24, 1971. "Mary, Paul, and Mike" to "Betty and Eliot," December 12, 1956,

KDB. George C. Mosch to J. T. Rutherford, September 26, 1958, PWH. *Williamsport Sun-Gazette*, March 16, 1961. *Potter Leader-Enterprise*, April 7, 1993, PCHS. *Olean Times*, October 7, 1996, PCHS. Recorded recollections of William Ayers, n.d., PWH. Matthew Pearl, interview with John Domaleski, October 10, 2016 (Pandora). Heimel, *Behind the Badge*, pp. 7–9, 181. ABS, personal email with Matthew Pearl, August 4, 2019.

BETTY IN COUDERSPORT: *Potter Enterprise*, August 23, 1956 ("Mrs. Ness still . . ."); January 24, 1957; January 31, 1957 ("Sculpturing as a . . ."); March 22, 1961. CPD, October 17, 1959 ("a reluctant fisherman"). "Bill Ayers," n.d., PWH. *Potter Leader-Enterprise*, April 7, 1993, PCHS. Heimel, *Eliot Ness*, p. 264 ("a Norman Rockwell . . ."). Bob Frye, "A Famous Crime Fighter's Brush with Fishing Laws," Wild Outdoors, August 28, 2015, http://blog.triblive.com/wild-outdoors/2015/08/28/a-famous-crime -fighters-brush-with-fishing-laws/ (accessed September 4, 2015). John Rigas, personal interview with ABS, November 15, 2016. Anonymous Coudersport resident, personal interview with ABS, November 15, 2016. Natalie Phelps, interviewed by Paul W. Heimel at the Coudersport Theatre, Coudersport, PA, July 22, 2018.

ELIOT AND BOBBY: J. F. Simon to Eliot Ness, November 28, 1956, KDB. *Potter Enterprise*, December 20, 1967. CPD, October 17, 1959. Fraley, "Real Eliot Ness," p. 28. Fraley, *4 Against the Mob*, p. 10 ("I've shot at . . ."). Jedick, "Eliot Ness," p. 94. Nickel, *Torso*, pp. 200–201. "Bob Merten Talk," May 10, 1993, PWH. Heimel, *Eliot Ness*, p. 264. Natalie Phelps, personal interview with ABS, November 15, 2016. John Rigas, personal interview with ABS, November 15, 2016.

ROTARY CLUB: *Potter Enterprise*, September 27, 1956, PCHS ("that the full . . ."). *Pittsburgh Post-Gazette*, September 11, 1997. Heimel, *Eliot Ness*, p. 265 ("Who the heck . . .").

NESS HOLDING COMPANY TOGETHER / CONFLICT WITH SHAMPANORE: "Meeting of the Joint Boards of Directors of the North Ridge Industrial Corporation and the Guaranty Paper Corporation," April 3, 1957, PWH ("blow the thing . . ."). George C. Mosch to J. T. Rutherford, September 26, 1958, PWH. *Potter Enterprise*, November 24, 1971. Jedick, "Eliot Ness," p. 94. Recorded recollections of William Ayers, n.d., PWH ("I have never . . . ," "wouldn't dance to . . ."). *Potter Leader-Enterprise*, April 7, 1993, PCHS. *News-Press*, December 7, 1994, RM.

SHAMPANORE PLOTS AGAINST NESS, ATTACKS COMPANY: "C. of C. Endorses 'Persona-Seal' Checks," n.p., November 15, 1956, PWH. "Meeting of the Joint Boards of Directors of the North Ridge Industrial Corporation and the Guaranty Paper Corporation," April 3, 1957, PWH.

Olean Times, October 7, 1996, PCHS ("To me, he . . ."). *News-Press*, December 7, 1994, PWH. *Potter Enterprise*, November 24, 1971. Jedick, "Eliot Ness," p. 94. Recorded recollections of William Ayers, n.d., PWH ("A lot of . . ."). "Bill Ayers," n.d., PWH. Heimel, *Behind the Badge*, pp. 178–179, 185.

NESS AND RIGAS: "John Rigas," n.d., PWH. "Bob Merten Talk," May 10, 1993, PWH. John Rigas, personal interview with ABS, November 15, 2016 ("I felt bad . . ."). John Rigas, interviewed by Paul W. Heimel at the Coudersport Theatre, Coudersport, PA, July 22, 2018.

NESS'S HEART PROBLEMS: *Potter Enterprise Sportsmen's Special*, November 24, 1971 ("Looking back at . . ."). CP, April 20, 1973, in "Ness, Robert Eliot" folder, CPC. Jedick, "Eliot Ness," p. 55. Nickel, *Torso*, p. 201. "Dr. George Mosch," December 1994, PWH. Heimel, *Eliot Ness*, p. 269. Heimel, *Behind the Badge*, pp. 186–187. Tony Dokoupil, "America's Long Love Affair with Anti-anxiety Drugs," *Newsweek*, January 21, 2009, http://www.newsweek.com/americas-long-love-affair-anti-anxiety -drugs-77967 (accessed February 21, 2017).

NORTH RIDGE RECOVERING / BOARD MEETING: "Meeting of the Joint Boards of Directors of the North Ridge Industrial Corporation and the Guaranty Paper Corporation," April 3, 1957, PWH ("behave like a . . . ," "If Ayers leaves . . ."). *Potter Enterprise*, October 10, 1957 ("I feel good . . ."). George C. Mosch to J. T. Rutherford, September 26, 1958, PWH. *News-Press*, December 7, 1994, PWH. Recorded recollections of William Ayers, n.d., PWH ("He was willing . . ."). Heimel, *Eliot Ness*, pp. 272–274. Heimel, *Behind the Badge*, pp. 191–192.

PTA MEETING: *Potter Enterprise*, April 11, 1957; April 18, 1957 ("has the potential . . . ," "there seems to . . ."); March 22, 1961. Heimel, *Eliot Ness*, p. 274.

NESS AT CHURCH / HIGH BLOOD PRESSURE: *Potter Enterprise*, March 22, 1961. "Bob Merten Talk," May 10, 1993, PWH. "Dr. George Mosch," December 1994, PWH. Heimel, *Eliot Ness*, p. 274.

SECOND THOUGHTS ABOUT BOOK / TV RIGHTS: *Potter County Journal*, May 23, 1957, PCHS. Application for Letters of Administration, June 11, 1957, PCHS. Statement of Debts and Deductions, June 17, 1957, PCHS. Ness and Fraley, *The Untouchables*, p. 256. *Potter Enterprise*, March 22, 1961; November 24, 1971 ("He was many . . ."). Fraley, "Real Eliot Ness," p. 29 ("It makes him . . ."). Nickel, *Torso*, p. 204. Bergreen, *Capone*, pp. 612–613. *News-Press*, December 7, 1994, PWH. "John Rigas," n.d., PWH. "Bill Ayers," n.d., PWH. "Lewis Wilkinson," n.d., PWH. "Virginia

Kallenborn interview," March 25, 2000, PWH. John Rigas, personal interview with ABS, November 15, 2016 ("good news"). Heimel, *Behind the Badge*, pp. 194–196. John Rigas, interviewed by PWH at the Coudersport Theatre, Coudersport, PA, July 22, 2018.

NESS AND NATALIE PHELPS: Natalie Phelps, personal interview with ABS, November 15, 2016 ("Oh, you keep . . ."). Natalie Phelps, interviewed by PWH at the Coudersport Theatre, Coudersport, PA, July 22, 2018.

NESS'S FINAL DAY: G. F. Shampanore to George C. and Doris Mosch, December 31, 1955, PCHS. Ness and Fraley, *The Untouchables*, pp. 149–151. *Potter Enterprise*, October 10, 1957; November 7, 1957; March 22, 1961 ("cool one"); November 24, 1971. Fraley, "Real Eliot Ness," p. 29. Nickel, *Torso*, p. 204. *Potter Leader-Enterprise*, April 7, 1993, PCHS. "Bob Merten Talk," May 10, 1993," PWH. "Dr. George Mosch," December 1994, PWH. Recorded recollections of William Ayers, n.d., PWH. Heimel, *Eliot Ness*, p. 275. Natalie Phelps, personal interview with ABS, November 15, 2016 ("Keep going with . . ."). Heimel, *Behind the Badge*, pp. 196–197. "Eliot Ness's Last Walk," handout distributed by PCHS during the "Eliot Ness Fest" in Coudersport, PA, July 21, 2018, ABS. Collins and Schwartz, *Scarface and the Untouchable*, pp. 270–287.

AFTERMATH OF NESS'S DEATH / FUNERALS AND OBITUARIES: CST, May 17, 1957 ("Helped to Send . . ."). CT, May 17, 1957. CEA, May 17, 1957. CDN, May 17, 1957. CN, May 17, 1957, in ENPS, Roll 1, Folder 2. CN, May 17, 1957; CPD, May 17, 1957; CP, May 17, 1957, all in ENC. CPD, May 21, 1957 ("community interest, his . . ."). *Potter Enterprise*, May 23, 1957; June 6, 1957; June 13, 1957; June 20, 1957; July 18, 1957; October 10, 1957; March 22, 1961 ("Here's the only . . ."); November 24, 1971. Application for Letters of Administration, June 11, 1957, PCHS. Statement of Debts and Deductions, June 17, 1957, PCHS. George C. Mosch to J. T. Rutherford, September 26, 1958, PWH. *Star-Gazette*, June 22, 1987, RM. *Potter Leader-Enterprise*, April 7, 1993, PCHS. Joe Phelps, Jr. to Paul Heimel, January 31, 1995, PWH. Recorded recollections of William Ayers, n.d., PWH. Natalie Phelps, personal interview with ABS, November 15, 2016. John Rigas, personal interview with ABS, November 15, 2016. Joe Phelps, Jr., telephone interview with ABS, November 22, 2016. Linda Phelps, telephone interview with ABS, November 22, 2016. Heimel, *Behind the Badge*, pp. 213–214. ABS visit to Fickinger Funeral Home, Coudersport, PA, July 21, 2018.

CONDOLENCE LETTERS AND TELEGRAMS: Entry for Sunday, May 19, 1957, Harold Burton Diaries, container 3, reel 4, HBP. *Potter Enterprise*,

June 20, 1957; March 22, 1961 ("I have lost . . ."); November 24, 1971. *Olean Times*, October 7, 1996, PCHS. Recorded recollections of William Ayers, n.d., PWH ("He was under . . ."). "Bill Ayers," n.d., PWH. Kluger, *Simple Justice*, pp. 681–682, 684–685, 699–700, 705–711, and passim.

Epilogue: A Modern Myth

UNTOUCHABLES PUBLISHED: Ness and Fraley, *The Untouchables*, pp. 255–256 (256, "This is his . . ."), and passim. *Potter Enterprise*, July 18, 1957; September 19, 1957; October 3, 1957; March 22, 1961 ("resounding flop"). LAT, September 20, 1957. NYT, September 23, 1957; November 3, 1957. *Arizona Republic*, September 29, 1957 ("It is a . . ."). *St. Louis Post-Dispatch*, November 7, 1957; July 16, 1959; December 3, 1957; July 10, 1958 ("a must-read thriller"); August 4–8, 1958. *Democrat and Chronicle*, November 28, 1957. *Advocate-Messenger*, December 26–27, 1957; December 29, 1957; January 2, 1958. *Honolulu Advertiser*, March 30, 1958. CDN, April 21, 1959, in box 14, folder 6 of 8 (part 1 of 5), MMvDP. Vahimagi, *The Untouchables*, pp. 5–6.

PROHIBITION NOSTALGIA AND FILM/TV GANGSTERS: *Baltimore Sun*, April 19, 1959. *Washington Daily News*, April 20, 1959, in FBI-DA. Allsop, *Bootleggers*, pp. xxi, xxiii–xxv. Vahimagi, *The Untouchables*, pp. 5–13, 59–63. Adam Gopnik, "The Forty-Year Itch," *New Yorker*, April 23, 2012, pp. 19–20.

WB BUYS FILM RIGHTS: *Detroit Free Press*, September 6, 1957. LAT, September 20, 1957 ("enough material . . ."); February 4, 1958. NYT, February 20, 1958 ("one of the . . ."). *New York Daily News*, March 12, 1958. Fraley, "Real Eliot Ness," p. 30. Arnaz, *A Book*, p. 299. Collins and Schwartz, *Scarface and the Untouchable*, pp. 443–444, 477–478.

ARNAZ AND DESILU: Arnaz, *A Book*, pp. 40–41. Harris, *Lucy & Desi*, pp. 37–44. Vahimagi, *Untouchables*, pp. 13–14. Kanfer, *Ball of Fire*, p. 67. Sanders and Gilbert, *Desilu*, pp. 9–47, 56–60, 85–169, and passim.

ARNAZ BUYS *UNTOUCHABLES*, WANTS TO PLAY NESS: *Pittsburgh Post-Gazette*, January 16, 1959. NYT, January 29, 1959. *New York Daily News*, January 31, 1959. *Desert Sun*, February 4, 1959. *Cincinnati Enquirer*, March 31, 1959. Arnaz, *A Book*, pp. 299–300. Harris, *Lucy & Desi*, pp. 238–239 (239, "It seemed insane . . ."). Kanfer, *Ball of Fire*, pp. 192–193. Sanders and Gilbert, *Desilu*, pp. 62, 148–151, 155–157, 162–163, 168–169, 173–174, and passim. Tucker, *Eliot Ness and the Untouchables*, p. 98.

ARNAZ CONTACTS FBI: Desi Arnaz to Clyde Tolson, December 31, 1958; M. A. Jones to Mr. Nease, January 2, 1959 ("The book apparently . . ."); J. Edgar Hoover to Desi Arnaz, January 5, 1959; Director, FBI to SAC, Los

Angeles, February 26, 1959 ("former FBI agent . . . ," "any reference to . . ."); SAC, Los Angeles to Director, FBI, March 13, 1959, all in FBI-DA. *Baltimore Sun*, April 19, 1959. Powers, *Secrecy and Power*, pp. 169–173. Gentry, *J. Edgar Hoover*, pp. 190–192.

PLAYHOUSE CASTING AND DEVELOPMENT: *Monroe News-Star*, March 24, 1959. *Morning Call*, March 28, 1959. CST, April 1, 1959; *Variety*, April 21, 1959; CT, December 16, 1959, both in box 14, folder 6 of 8 (part 1 of 5), MMvDP. *Philadelphia Inquirer*, April 5, 1959. *Cincinnati Enquirer*, April 10, 1959; April 17, 1959. "The Scarface Mob," *Westinghouse Desilu Playhouse*, written by Paul Monash, directed by Phil Karlson, April 20, 27, 1959, in *The Untouchables*: Season 1, Volume 1 (Hollywood: Paramount Pictures, 2007), DVD. LAT, April 20, 1959. "The Surprised Mr. Stack," *TV Guide*, December 5, 1959, p. 10, in FBI-DA. *News Leader*, January 15, 1960. *Indianapolis News*, August 27, 1962. Howard R. Gordon, Third Amended and Supplemental Complaint, n.d., p. 5, in box 14, folder 6 of 8 (part 4 of 5), MMvDP. Arnaz, *A Book*, pp. 299–304 (300, "the obvious cop . . . ," "more of an . . ."). Stack and Evans, *Straight Shooting*, pp. 1–2 (2, "Eliot Ness was . . ."); 206–208, 218. *Houston Chronicle*, November 10, 1991, PWH. Harris, *Lucy & Desi*, pp. 239–240. Gabler, *Winchell*, p. 508 ("Walter gave the . . ."). Robert Stack, interviewed by Ed Robertson, *Television Chronicles* 7 (1996), pp. 76–77, PWH. Vahmiagi, *The Untouchables*, pp. 12–21. Kanfer, *Ball of Fire*, pp. 192–194. Sanders and Gilbert, *Desilu*, pp. 76–84, 150, 152, 162, 174–175 (174, "I don't want . . ."). Tucker, *Eliot Ness and the Untouchables*, pp. 98–104.

PLAYHOUSE PREMIERE / REACTIONS AND RATINGS: *Miami News*, April 18, 1959; January 7, 1981. LAT, April 20, 1959. *Lansing State Journal*, April 20, 1959. M. A. Jones to Mr. DeLoach, April 21, 1959, in FBI-DA ("While the preprogram . . ."). CDN, April 21, 1959, in box 14 ("best offering of . . . ," "good dialog, a . . ."); CT, April 21, 1959; *Variety*, April 22, 1959; *Variety*, n.d., all in box 14, folder 6 of 8 (part 1 of 5), MMvDP. *Asbury Park Press*, April 26, 1959. LAT, April 27, 1959 ("old-time police . . . ," "The kids can't . . ."). CST, April 30, 1959. CPD, October 14, 1959. CEA, February 20, 1960 ("There wasn't any . . ."), in "Newspaper Clippings (photocopies) circa. 1930–1970" folder, DMM. CP, October 20, 1960, ENC. Ness, "My Husband, Eliot Ness," pp. 5–6 ("He has the . . ."). *Des Moines Sunday Register*, October 29, 1961. *Indianapolis News*, August 27, 1962. Howard R. Gordon, Third Amended and Supplemental Complaint, n.d., pp. 7–8, 49–50, in box 14, folder 6 of 8 (part 4 of 5), MMvDP. Arnaz, *A Book*, pp. 300, 304 ("made a hell . . ."). *Daily Dispatch*, April 19, 1976. Harris, *Lucy & Desi*, pp. 251, 270–271. Robert Stack on *Larry King Live*, November 7, 1991, PWH. Schoenberg,

Mr. Capone, p. 363. Vahimagi, *The Untouchables*, pp. 16–19 (16, "those who caught . . ."). William Ayers, email to Paul Heimel, July 11, 1999, PWH. Kanfer, *Ball of Fire*, p. 193. Sanders and Gilbert, *Desilu*, p. 175. Tucker, *Eliot Ness and the Untouchables*, pp. 98–104. Borroel, *Story of the Untouchables*, p. 10. Ronald Wilson, "*The Untouchables* (ABC, 1959–63)," in Sabin, *Cop Shows*, pp. 40–41, 196n3.

UNTOUCHABLES BECOMES A SERIES: Desi Arnaz to J. Edgar Hoover, April 29, 1959; J. Edgar Hoover to Desi Arnaz, May 7, 1959; M. A. Jones, memo to Mr. DeLoach, May 18, 1959; C. D. DeLoach, memo to Mr. Tolson, October 17, 1959; W. C. Sullivan, memo to A. H. Belmont, October 30, 1959; *Daily Variety*, December 4, 1959; "Surprised Mr. Stack," pp. 10–11, all in FBI-DA. *News Leader*, January 15, 1960. CDN, May 4, 1960, in box 14, folder 6 of 8 (part 1 of 5), MMvDP. CEA, September 1, 1960, in box 13, folder 2 of 8, MMvDP. *Lawrence Journal-World*, February 3, 1961. Arnaz, *A Book*, pp. 303–304 (303, "What the hell . . . ," "Don't you know . . ."). Stack and Evans, *Straight Shooting*, p. 207. Powers, *G-Men*, pp. 239–242. Robert Stack on *Larry King Live*, November 7, 1991, PWH. Robert Stack, interviewed by Ed Robertson, *Television Chronicles* 7 (1996), pp. 77–80, PWH. Vahimagi, *The Untouchables*, pp. 20–23, 27, 82. Kanfer, *Ball of Fire*, p. 194. Sanders and Gilbert, *Desilu*, pp. 175–176, 183–185, 191, 202–203. Tucker, *Eliot Ness and the Untouchables*, p. 119. Wilson, "*The Untouchables*," in Sabin, *Cop Shows*, pp. 40–41.

TV SHOW RESEARCH AND RATINGS: CPD, October 17, 1959. *News Leader*, January 15, 1960. CDN, May 4, 1960, in box 14, folder 6 of 8 (part 1 of 5), MMvDP ("That's how seriously . . ."). *New York Journal-American*, February 3, 1960; "The New 'Untouchables,'" *Newsweek*, August 8, 1960, both in FBI-DA. CEA, September 1, 1960, in box 13, folder 2 of 8, MMvDP. *Lawrence Journal-World*, February 3, 1961. *Indianapolis News*, August 27, 1962. "'The Untouchables' Starring Robert Stack as Eliot Ness," Character Bible Owned by Writer Nelson Bond, n.d., ABS ("in any story . . ."). Howard R. Gordon, Third Amended and Supplemental Complaint, n.d., pp. 16–33, in box 14, folder 6 of 8 (part 4 of 5), MMvDP. Stack and Evans, *Straight Shooting*, pp. 208–210 (208, "three of the . . ."), 223–230. *Houston Chronicle*, November 10, 1991, PWH. Robert Stack, interviewed by Ed Robertson, *Television Chronicles* 7 (1996), pp. 76–80, PWH. Vahimagi, *The Untouchables*, pp. 22–37. Jonathan J. Cavallero, "Playing Good Italian / Bad Italian in ABC's *The Untouchables*," in Renga, *Mafia Movies*, p. 76. Sanders and Gilbert, *Desilu*, p. 222. Tucker, *Eliot Ness and the Untouchables*, pp. 105–119. Wilson, "*The Untouchables*," in Sabin, *Cop Shows*, pp. 41, 43.

MA BARKER EPISODE AND FBI RESPONSE: SAC, Little Rock, to Director, October 15, 1959; Director, FBI, to SAC, Los Angeles, October 16, 1959 ("URGENT"); C. D. DeLoach, memo to Mr. Tolson, October 16, 1959; SAC, Los Angeles, to Director, FBI, October 17, 1959; C. D. DeLoach, memo to Mr. Tolson, October 17, 1959 ("terrible goof," "Ness and the . . ."); C. D. DeLoach, memo to Mr. Tolson, October 19, 1959 ("fraudulent," "was told flatly . . ."); SAC, Los Angeles, to Director, FBI, October 20, 1959; redacted to J. Edgar Hoover, October 20, 1959; C. D. DeLoach, memo to Mr. Tolson, October 21, 1959; M. A. Jones, memo to Mr. DeLoach, October 23, 1959; J. Edgar Hoover to redacted, October 27, 1959; W. C. Sullivan, memo to A. H. Belmont, October 30, 1959; M. A. Jones, memo to Mr. DeLoach, October 30, 1959; C. D. Deloach, memo to Mr. Tolson, November 3, 1959; M. A. Jones, memo to Mr. DeLoach, November 6, 1959; redacted to John Edgar Hoover, November 12, 1959; W. W. Burke to J. Edgar Hoover, November 12, 1959; M. A. Jones, memo to Mr. DeLoach, November 13, 1959; M. A. Jones, memo to Mr. DeLoach, November 20, 1959; M. A. Jones, memo to Mr. DeLoach, November 27, 1959; M. A. Jones, memo to Mr. DeLoach, December 4, 1959; M. A. Jones, memo to Mr. DeLoach, December 8, 1959; M. A. Jones, memo to Mr. DeLoach, December 11, 1959; M. A. Jones, memo to Mr. DeLoach, December 14, 1959; Clyde Tolson to redacted, December 15, 1959; Clyde Tolson to Desi Arnaz, December 15, 1959; M. A. Jones, memo to Mr. DeLoach, December 17, 1959; redacted to J. Edgar Hoover, December 18, 1959; J. Edgar Hoover to redacted, December 28, 1959; M. A. Jones, memo to Mr. DeLoach, December 28, 1959; M. A. Jones, memo to Mr. DeLoach, January 4, 1960; M. A. Jones, memo to Mr. DeLoach, January 15, 1960; redacted to J. Edgar Hoover, January 20, 1960; M. A. Jones, memo to Mr. DeLoach, January 22, 1960; redacted to J. Edgar Hoover, January 21, 1960; J. Edgar Hoover to redacted, January 28, 1960; John Edgar Hoover to redacted, January 29, 1960 ("this Bureau has . . ."); M. A. Jones, memo to Mr. DeLoach, January 29, 1960; redacted to the Federal Bureau of Investigation, January 29, 1960; John Edgar Hoover to redacted, February 5, 1960 ("was never a . . ."); M. A. Jones, memo to Mr. DeLoach, February 5, 1960; M. A. Jones, memo to Mr. DeLoach, February 12, 1960; M. A. Jones, memo to Mr. DeLoach, February 19, 1960; M. A. Jones, memo to Mr. DeLoach, February 26, 1960; M. A. Jones, memo to Mr. DeLoach, March 4, 1960; M. A. Jones, memo to Mr. DeLoach, March 11, 1960; C. R. Davidson, memo to Mr. Callahan, March 22, 1960; M. A. Jones, memo to Mr. DeLoach, March 25, 1960; M. A. Jones, memo to Mr. DeLoach, April 1, 1960; M. A. Jones, memo to Mr. DeLoach, April 8, 1960; M. A. Jones, memo to Mr. DeLoach, April 15, 1960; M. A. Jones, memo to Mr. DeLoach, April 22, 1960; M. A. Jones, memo to Mr. DeLoach, April 29, 1960; C. D. DeLoach to Mr. Mohr, May 9, 1960; SAC, Los Angeles, to Director, FBI, May 10, 1960; C.

D. DeLoach to Mr. Mohr, May 12, 1960; SAC, Los Angeles, to Director, FBI, May 26, 1960; M. A. Jones, memo to Mr. DeLoach, May 27, 1960; *New York Journal-American*, July 1, 1960; M. A. Jones, memo to Mr. De-Loach, August 4, 1960; C. D. DeLoach, memo to Mr. Mohr, October 11, 1960; M. A. Jones, memo to Mr. DeLoach, October 14, 1960; M. A. Jones, memo to Mr. DeLoach, October 21, 1960; redacted to the FBI, November 3, 1960; John Edgar Hoover to redacted, November 10, 1960; redacted to the FBI, February 9, 1961; John Edgar Hoover to redacted, February 16, 1961; redacted to John Edgar Hoover, March 30, 1961; J. Edgar Hoover to redacted, April 10, 1961, all in FBI-DA. "Ma Barker and Her Boys," *The Untouchables*, written by Jeremy Ross, directed by Joe Parker, October 22, 1959, in *The Untouchables*: Season 1, Volume 1 (Hollywood: Paramount Pictures, 2007), DVD ("the most dangerous . . ."). Arnaz, *A Book*, pp. 304–305. Powers, *G-Men*, pp. xi–xix, 51–64, 94–112, 114, 161–206, 229–230, 238–248. Powers, *Secrecy and Power*, p. 363. Gentry, *J. Edgar Hoover*, pp. 19–40. Vahimagi, *The Untouchables*, p. 23. Burrough, *Public Enemies*, pp. 31–33; 503–509. Strunk, *Wanted Women*, pp. 5–7, 53–68, 73–74. Wilson, "The Untouchables," in Sabin, *Cop Shows*, p. 46. Chris Cillizza, "The FBI Controversy is the Latest Example of How We Don't Believe in Anything Anymore," *Denver Post*, November 3, 2016, https://www.denverpost.com/2016/11/03/fbi-controversy/ (accessed July 2, 2019) ("sterling," "unflappable, smart and . . ."). Jason Linkins, "Fun Fact: Clarice Starling Isn't Real," *Huffington Post*, November 3, 2016, https://www.huffpost.com/entry/learn-a-book-chris-cillizza_n_581b48a3e4b08f9841ada288 (accessed July 2, 2019).

FURTHER CONTROVERSY: CST, August 7, 1959. *Appeal Democrat*, October 24, 1959. *Daily Variety*, December 31, 1959; WP, January 27, 1961; *Broadcasting*, February 6, 1961; *New York Daily News*, February 10, 1961; *Washington Daily News*, March 13, 1961; WP, March 18, 1961; *Daily Variety*, March 20, 1961, all in FBI-DA. CEA, February 29, 1960, in box 14, folder 6 of 8 (part 1 of 5), MMvDP. CST, July 19, 1960; CST, August 19, 1960; CST, February 26, 1961; Ed Sullivan as told to Rolaine A. Hochstein, "Is TV Too Violent for Children?" *Good Housekeeping*, n.d., all in box 13, folder 2 of 8, MMvDP. Howard R. Gordon, Answering Brief of Plaintiff to Defendants' Brief in Support of Motion to Dismiss for Failure to State a Claim, December 21, 1960, in box 13, folder 1 of 8, MMvDP. CT, March 26, 1961. *Simpson's Leader-Times*, July 29, 1961. Howard R. Gordon, Third Amended and Supplemental Complaint, n.d., in box 14, folder 6 of 8 (part 4 of 5), MMvDP. *Mafalda Maritote, Mae Capone, and Albert Capone v. Desilu Productions, CBS, and Westinghouse*, United States Court of Appeals for the Seventh Circuit, no. 14828, April 30, 1965, in box 15, folder 8, MMvDP. Wilson & Day, *Special Agent*, p. 6. Stack and Evans, *Straight Shooting*, pp. 210, 217, 219, 221–222. Hammer, *Illustrated History of Organized Crime*, p. 323. Gentry,

J. Edgar Hoover, pp. 407, 591–593. William Boddy, "Senator Dodd Goes to Hollywood: Investigating Video Violence," in Spigel and Curtin, *Revolution Wasn't Televised*, pp. 161–177. Vahimagi, *The Untouchables*, pp. 1, 28, 31–32, 39–42. Bernstein, *Greatest Menace*, pp. 156–171. Kanfer, *Ball of Fire*, pp. 233–234. Cavallero, "Playing Good Italian," in Renga, *Mafia Movies*, pp. 76–83. Sanders and Gilbert, *Desilu*, pp. 221–222. Tucker, *Eliot Ness and the Untouchables*, pp. 107–108. Wilson, "*The Untouchables*," in Sabin, *Cop Shows*, pp. 40 ("one of the . . .", 43–44, 46. Sifakis, *Mafia Encyclopedia*, pp. 13–14.

"THE BIG TRAIN" CONTROVERSY: "The Big Train," *The Untouchables*, written by William Spier, directed by John Peyser, January 5, 12, 1961, in *The Untouchables*: Season 2, Volume 1 (Hollywood: Paramount Pictures, 2008), DVD. *Broadcasting*, January 16, 1961; WP, January 27, 1961; *New York Herald-Tribune*, January 23, 1961; *Broadcasting*, January 23, 1961, all in FBI-DA Ben F. Waple (Acting Secretary, Federal Communications Commission) to the American Broadcasting Company, Inc., September 27, 1961, in box 14, folder 6 of 8 (part 4 of 5) ("the only indication . . ."); Howard R. Gordon, Third Amended and Supplemental Complaint, n.d., pp. 25–33, both in box 14, folder 6 of 8 (part 4 of 5), MMvDP. Schoenberg, *Mr. Capone*, pp. 330–333. Boddy, "Senator Dodd," in Spigel and Curtin, *Revolution Wasn't Televised*, pp. 175–176. Vahimagi, *The Untouchables*, pp. 37–39. Sanders and Gilbert, *Desilu*, pp. 220–221.

SHOW INCREASINGLY FICTIONALIZED / NESS'S REPUTATION DAMAGED: Ness and Fraley, *The Untouchables*, pp. 5–6, 24, 242–249. *Evening Star*, October 16, 1959; *New York Herald-Tribune*, April 19, 1960; *Daily Variety*, February 2, 1961, all in FBI-DA. "The New 'Untouchables,'" *Newsweek*, August 8, 1960, in FBI-DA ("All he has . . ."). CST, January 22, 1961; Paul Molloy, "Seems Ness Has Nabbed Every Rogue Since Cain," *TV Prevue* (CST), n.d., both in box 13, folder 2 of 8, MMvDP. *Des Moines Sunday Register*, October 29, 1961. Anthony Scaduto, "The Eliot Ness Myth," *Climax*, October 1961, pp. 50–53 (52, "The saga of . . ."), 82–84 (82, "As Cleveland's underworld . . ."). Stack and Evans, *Straight Shooting*, pp. 223–224. Boddy, "Senator Dodd," in Spigel and Curtin, *Revolution Wasn't Televised*, pp. 175–176. Vahimagi, *The Untouchables*, pp. 2, 22, 45, 49–50. Tony Berardi, interviewed in "Eliot Ness," *The Real Untouchables*. Bernstein, *Greatest Menace*, pp. 167–171. Okrent, *Last Call*, pp. 135–136. Cavallero, "Playing Good Italian," in Renga, *Mafia Movies*, p. 77. Sanders and Gilbert, *Desilu*, pp. 221–222. Tucker, *Eliot Ness and the Untouchables*, pp. 108–109. Wilson, "*The Untouchables*," in Sabin, *Cop Shows*, p. 42. Collins and Schwartz, *Scarface and the Untouchable*, pp. 476–477.

BETTY AND BOBBY REACT TO TV SERIES / *UNTOUCHABLES* OFF AIR IN CLEVELAND: CPD, October 17, 1959 ("When other children . . ."); June 30, 1961; July 6–7, 1961; July 9, 1961; July 17, 1961; July 20, 1961 ("the Untouchables"). CP, October 20, 1960, ENC ("Untouchables," "an Italian boy," "want cheap comic . . ."). *Des Moines Sunday Register*, October 29, 1961. Ness, "My Husband, Eliot Ness," pp. 5–7 (6, "I like the . . ."). *Houston Chronicle*, November 10, 1991, PWH. Bergreen, *Capone*, p. 613. Boddy, "Senator Dodd," in Spigel and Curtin, *Revolution Wasn't Televised*, p. 175. Cavallero, "Playing Good Italian," in Renga, *Mafia Movies*, p. 81 ("pressure from parents . . ."). Sanders and Gilbert, *Desilu*, p. 222. Olszewski, *Cleveland TV Tales*, pp. 162–165 (164, "I have many . . ."). Heimel, *Behind the Badge*, pp. 206, 210.

TOY GUNS AND NESS'S LEGACY: M. A. Jones, memo to Mr. DeLoach, November 27, 1959, in FBI-DA. CDN, January 13, 1961, in box 13, folder 2 of 8, MMvDP. Ness, "My Husband, Eliot Ness," pp. 5–6 (6, "It is fiction . . ."). CPD, June 18, 1961, ENC. *Des Moines Sunday Register*, October 29, 1961 ("Stack's Ness loathes . . ."). *The Untouchables* (1987), directed by Brian De Palma (Hollywood: Paramount Pictures, 2004), DVD. "Toy Eliot Ness and the Untouchables Shot Gun," liveauctioneers, April 12, 2015, https://www.liveauctioneers.com/item/35681019_toy-eliot-ness-and-the-untouchables-shot-gun (accessed July 4, 2019). "Toy The Untouchables Detective Set," liveauctioneers, April 12, 2015, https://www.liveauctioneers.com/item/35681021_toy-the-untouchables-detective-set (accessed July 4, 2019). "Toy Untouchables Battery Powered Tommie [*sic*] Gun," liveaucioneers, April 12, 2015, https://www.liveauctioneers.com/item/35681023_toy-untouchables-battery-powered-tommie-gun (accessed July 4, 2019).

UNTOUCHABLES TONED DOWN, CANCELLED / BETTY'S POVERTY: CPD, October 14, 1959. NYT, February 23, 1961. *Simpson's Leader-Times*, July 29, 1961. WP, August 22, 1962 ("humanizing," "as a living . . .") (see also CDN, August 20, 1962, in "Newspaper Clippings (Photocopies) Circa. 1930–1970" folder, DMM). *Indianapolis News*, August 27, 1962. "Who Killed Eliot Ness?" *TV Week*, May 4, 1963. Arnaz, *A Book*, pp. 304–305. Stack and Evans, *Straight Shooting*, pp. 223–224. *Daily Spectrum*, July 1, 1987. Harris, *Lucy & Desi*, pp. 269–273, 276, 324. Bergreen, *Capone*, p. 613. Dan T. Moore, interviewed by Paul Heimel and Bob Merten, May 30, 1995, PWH. CPD, September 7, 1997. Vahimagi, *The Untouchables*, pp. 44–45, 47–52. Heimel, *Eliot Ness*, pp. 284–285. Sanders and Gilbert, *Desilu*, pp. 226–231, 242–251, 266, 269, 279–280, 284–285, 289, 294, 304. Tucker, *Eliot Ness and the Untouchables*, pp. 121–122. Perry, *Eliot Ness*, p. 287. Wilson, "*The Untouchables*," in Sabin, *Cop Shows*, pp. 42–43, 46. Pearl, "Behind *The Untouchables*."

4 *AGAINST THE MOB* / FRALEY LATER LIFE AND CAREER: R. E. Tuttle to Deputy Commissioner, Alcohol Tax Unit, April 12, 1951; "Mr. Cooper" to Dwight Avis, April 12, 1951; Statement of Roger B. Parker, April 12, 1951; Statement of George E. Baker, April 12, 1951; Statement of Arvell L. Perry, April 12, 1951; R. E. Tuttle to Deputy Commissioner, Alcohol Tax Unit, April 20, 1951; Statement of Paul Robsky, April 20, 1951; "Mr. Dapolito" to "Miss Hoke," June 12, 1951, all in Paul W. Robsky OPF/ATF. *Miami News*, April 20, 1959; March 27, 1966; February 4, 1969. NYT, February 11, 1961. Fraley, *4 Against the Mob*, pp. 82–83, and passim. Fraley, "Real Eliot Ness," p. 30. *Indianapolis Star*, February 20, 1963. *Fort Lauderdale News and Sun-Sentinel*, November 15, 1969. Stratton Douthat, "The Last of the Untouchables," *The Floridian* (*Tampa Bay Times*), October 3, 1971, pp. 7, 9. Eyman, "An Oscar for Elliot [*sic*] Ness," pp. 10, 12, 26. *Miami Herald*, April 20, 1986 ("I wonder if . . ."). *Daily Spectrum*, July 1, 1987. *Orlando Sentinel*, July 26, 1987. *Tampa Tribune*, August 8, 1987 ("Well, everything I . . ."). "'Untouchables' Author Dies at 79," Associated Press Worldstream, January 8, 1994. *Times Union*, January 8, 1994. NYT, January 9, 1994. Van Tassel and Grabowski, *Dictionary of Cleveland Biography*, pp. 75–76. Ward, *Deciding to Leave*, pp. 163–164, 289. Pearl, "Behind *The Untouchables*."

NESS'S ASHES / DEATHS OF BOBBY AND BETTY: CP, April 20, 1973, ENC. Jedick, "Eliot Ness," p. 94 and passim. Finding Aid, ENPS. Elisabeth Ness to "Margie," August 22, 1977; Rebecca McFarland to Paul Heimel, July 1, 1997, both PWH. CPD, September 2, 1976; November 5, 1977; December 23, 1992 ("Oh, he was . . . ," "It seems to . . ."); September 7, 1997. Heimel, *Eliot Ness*, pp. 284–285. Record for Elisabeth Ness, *U.S., Social Security Death Index, 1935–2014* (Provo, UT: Ancestry.com Operations, Inc., 2011).

1997 FUNERAL: Van Tassel and Grabowski, *Encyclopedia of Cleveland History*, pp. 626–627. CPD, June 25, 1997; September 5, 1997; September 7, 1997, all RM. John Herrington, "Ness Returns to Cleveland," WMV Web News Cleveland, August 27, 1997, http://www.cleveland.oh.us/wmv_news /jherr34.htm (accessed October 20, 2010) ("stand in perpetuity . . ."). CST, September 4, 1997 ("his reputation kicked . . ."); *Columbus Dispatch*, September 9, 1997; CT, September 10, 1997; John Affleck, "Forty Years After His Death, Eliot Ness' Ashes Dispersed," Associated Press; *Pittsburgh Post-Gazette*, September 11, 1997; September 18, 1997, all in "National Newspaper Coverage, Eliot Ness Event," RM. "Touched by an Untouchable," *People*, September 29, 1997. "Eliot Ness Laid to Rest," *CPHS Newsletter* 1, no. 16 (Fall 1997), pp. 1–2, RM. Robert Cermak, "Gund Foundation and

Contributors to Eliot Ness Memorial Education Fund Give Boost to Museum's Education Programs," *CPHS Newsletter* 1, no. 16 (Fall 1997), pp. 1–2, RM. Rebecca McFarland, "Eulogy delivered at the Memorial ceremony for the Ness family," *CPHS Newsletter* 1, no. 16 (Fall 1997), pp. 4–5, RM (4, "He firmly believed . . ."). "Eliot Ness Ceremony," *The Heritage* 12, no. 2 (Fall 1997), pp. 1–2. Allan May, "Eliot Ness," *The Heritage* 12, no. 2 (Fall 1997), pp. 1, 5. Kris Meldrum Denholm, "Memorial Service for Eliot Ness Held in Cleveland," *Inside ATF*, November 1997, RM. RM, personal email to ABS, August 7, 2019.

NESS'S LEGACY IN CLEVELAND: CPD, December 23, 1992. CPD, June 25, 1997, RM. *Pittsburgh Post-Gazette*, September 18, 1997, in "National Newspaper Coverage, Eliot Ness Event," RM. CPD, July 17, 2011, https://www.cleveland.com/business/2011/07/patrick_conway_the_man_behind.html (accessed July 7, 2019). Julie Johnson, "Pull Up a Stool with Pat Conway," *All About Beer Magazine*, September 1, 2012, http://allaboutbeer.com/article/with-pat-conway/ (accessed July 7, 2019). Danielle Rose and Jim Dubelko, "Sidaway Bridge: A Bridge over Troubled Neighborhoods," Cleveland Historical, April 2, 2016, https://clevelandhistorical.org/items/show/762 (accessed July 7, 2019). Karin Connelly Rice, "Downtown Hilton Glitters with All Things Cleveland," FreshWater, June 14, 2016, https://www.freshwatercleveland.com/devnews/Hilton061416.aspx (accessed July 10, 2019). Lowery, *They Can't Kill Us All*, pp. 73–79 (74, "stunning systemic police . . ."), 90–109. ABS visits to Cleveland, July 18, 2013; December 3, 2015 ("Cleveland's Hall of . . ."); August 1–2, 2016.

Books

Abbott, Karen. *Sin in the Second City: Madams, Ministers, Playboys, and the Battle for America's Soul*. New York: Random House, 2008.

Albrecht, Brian, and James Banks. *Cleveland in World War II*. Charleston, SC: The History Press, 2015.

Alder, Ken. *The Lie Detectors: The History of an American Obsession*. New York: Free Press, 2007.

Allen, Frederick Lewis. *Since Yesterday: The Nineteen-Thirties in America, September 3, 1929–September 3, 1939*. New York: Harper & Brothers, 1940.

Allsop, Kenneth. *The Bootleggers: The Story of Chicago's Prohibition Era*. London: Hutchinson & Co., 1968.

Anderson, Karen. *Wartime Women: Sex Roles, Family Relations, and the Status of Women During World War II*. Contributions in Women's Studies. Westport, CT: Greenwood Press, 1981.

Arnaz, Desi. *A Book*. New York: William Morrow, 1976.

Austin, Dan. *Forgotten Landmarks of Detroit*. Charleston, SC: The History Press, 2012.

Avery, Elroy McKendree. *A History of Cleveland and Its Environs: The Heart of New Connecticut*. Vol. 2, *Biography*. Chicago: Lewis Publishing Company, 1918.

Badal, James Jessen. *Hell's Wasteland: The Pennsylvania Torso Murders*. Kent, OH: Black Squirrel Books, 2013.

———. *In the Wake of the Butcher: Cleveland's Torso Murders*. Rev. ed. Kent, OH: Kent State University Press, 2014.

———. *Though Murder Has No Tongue: The Lost Victim of Cleveland's Mad Butcher*. Kent, OH: Black Squirrel Books, 2010.

Bailey, William G., ed. *The Encyclopedia of Police Science*. 2nd ed. New York: Garland Publishing, 1995.

Bair, Deirdre. *Al Capone: His Life, Legacy, and Legend.* New York: Nan A. Talese, 2016.

Bardsley, Marilyn J. *The American Sweeney Todd: Eliot Ness's Toughest Case.* Chatham, GA: DarkHorse Multimedia, 2017.

Battles, Kathleen. *Calling All Cars: Radio Dragnets and the Technology of Policing.* Minneapolis: University of Minnesota Press, 2010.

Bayer, Oliver Weld, ed. *Cleveland Murders.* New York: Duell, Sloan and Pearce, 1947.

Becker, Thea Gallo. *Lakewood.* Images of America. Charleston, SC: Arcadia Publishing, 2003.

Behr, Edward. *Prohibition: Thirteen Years That Changed America.* New York: Arcade Publishing, 1996.

Bellamy, John Stark II. *The Maniac in the Bushes and More Tales of Cleveland Woe: True Crimes and Disasters from the Streets of Cleveland.* Cleveland: Gray & Company, 1997.

Bergreen, Laurence. *Capone: The Man and the Era.* New York: Simon & Schuster, 1994.

Bernstein, Lee. *The Greatest Menace: Organized Crime in Cold War America.* Amherst: University of Massachusetts Press, 2002.

Borroel, Roger. *The Story of the Untouchables as Told by Eliot Ness.* 2nd rev. ed. East Chicago, IN: La Villita Publications, 2012.

Brady, Ian. *The Gates of Janus: Serial Killing and Its Analysis by the Moors Murderer.* Exp. ed. Port Townsend, WA: Feral House, 2015.

Brands, H. W. *Traitor to His Class: The Privileged Life and Radical Presidency of Franklin Delano Roosevelt.* New York: Anchor Books, 2009.

Brandt, Allan M. *No Magic Bullet: A Social History of Venereal Disease in the United States Since 1880.* Exp. ed. New York: Oxford University Press, 1987.

Brinkley, David. *Washington Goes to War.* New York: Ballantine Books, 1988.

Burch, Brian, and Emily Stimpson. *The American Catholic Almanac: A Daily Reader of Patriots, Saints, Rogues, and Ordinary People Who Changed the United States.* New York: Image, 2014.

Burrough, Bryan. *Public Enemies: America's Greatest Crime Wave and the Birth of the FBI, 1933–34.* New York: Penguin Press, 2004.

Capeci, Jerry. *The Complete Idiot's Guide to the Mafia.* 2nd ed. Indianapolis: Alpha Books, 2004.

Capuzzo, Michael. *The Murder Room: The Heirs of Sherlock Holmes Gather to Solve the World's Most Perplexing Cold Cases*. New York: Gotham Books, 2010.

Carte, Gene E., and Elaine H. Carte. *Police Reform in the United States: The Era of August Vollmer, 1905–1932*. Berkeley: University of California Press, 1975.

Carter, Dyson. *Sin and Science*. New York: Heck-Cattell Publishing Company, 1946.

Chandler, Raymond. *The Simple Art of Murder*. New York: Vintage Books, 1988.

Chernow, Ron. *Titan: The Life of John D. Rockefeller, Sr.* New York: Vintage Books, 1998.

Cleveland Police Historical Society. *Cleveland Police*. Images of America. Charleston, SC: Arcadia Publishing, 2005.

Coates, Col. John Boyd Jr., Ebbe Curtis Hoff, and Phebe M. Hoff, eds. *Preventive Medicine in World War II*. Vol. 5, *Communicable Diseases Transmitted Through Contact or by Unknown Means*. Washington, DC: Office of the Surgeon General, 1960.

Collins, Max Allan. *Bullet Proof*. New York: Bantam Books, 1989.

———. *Butcher's Dozen*. Toronto: Bantam Books, 1988.

———. *The Dark City*. Toronto: Bantam Books, 1987.

———. *Murder by the Numbers*. New York: St. Martin's Press, 1993.

———. "Natural Death, Inc." In *Kisses of Death: A Nathan Heller Casebook*. Norfolk, VA: Crippen & Landru, 2001.

Collins, Max Allan, and A. Brad Schwartz. *Scarface and the Untouchable: Al Capone, Eliot Ness, and the Battle for Chicago*. New York: William Morrow, 2018.

Commire, Anne, ed. *Something About the Author: Facts and Pictures About Contemporary Authors and Illustrators of Books for Young People*. Vol. 1. Detroit: Gale Research, 1971.

Condon, George E. *Cleveland: The Best Kept Secret*. Garden City, NY: Doubleday & Company, 1967.

Costello, John. *Virtue Under Fire: How World War II Changed Our Social and Sexual Attitudes*. Boston: Little, Brown and Company, 1985.

Cressey, Donald R. *Theft of the Nation: The Structure and Operations of Organized Crime in America*. New Brunswick, NJ: Transaction Publishers, 2008.

A Decade of Progress: Annual Reports for 1936 and 1937. Cleveland: Cuyahoga County Juvenile Court, 1938.

Douglas, John, and Mark Olshaker. *Mindhunter: Inside the FBI's Elite Serial Crime Unit*. New York: Pocket Books, 2017.

Dyer, Richard. *Lethal Repetition: Serial Killing in European Cinema*. London: British Film Institute, 2015.

Fang, Irving E. *Those Radio Commentators!* Ames, IA: The Iowa State University Press, 1977.

Fraley, Oscar. *4 Against the Mob*. New York: Popular Library, 1961.

Frankfurt, Harry G. *On Bullshit*. Princeton: Princeton University Press, 2005.

Gabler, Neal. *Winchell: Gossip, Power and the Culture of Celebrity*. New York: Vintage Books, 1994.

Gentry, Curt. *J. Edgar Hoover: The Man and the Secrets*. New York: Plume, 1991.

Grimes, William. *Straight Up or on the Rocks: The Story of the American Cocktail*. Rev. ed. New York: North Point Press, 2001.

Haller, Mark H. *Illegal Enterprise: The Work of Historian Mark Haller*. Edited by Matthew G. Yeager. Lanham, MD: University Press of America, 2013.

Hammer, Richard. *The Illustrated History of Organized Crime*. Philadelphia: Courage Books, 1989.

Harris, Warren G. *Lucy & Desi: The Legendary Love Story of Television's Most Famous Couple*. New York: Simon & Schuster, 1991.

Hart, Bradley W. *Hitler's American Friends: The Third Reich's Supporters in the United States*. New York: Thomas Dunne Books, 2018.

Hegarty, Marilyn E. *Victory Girls, Khaki-Wackies, and Patriotutes: The Regulation of Female Sexuality During World War II*. New York: New York University Press, 2008.

Heimel, Paul W. *Behind the Badge: The Untold Story of Eliot Ness*. Coudersport, PA: Knox Books, 2018.

———. *Eliot Ness: The Real Story*. 2nd ed. Nashville: Cumberland House, 2000.

Hickey, Eric W. *Serial Murderers and Their Victims*. 7th ed. Boston: Cengage Learning, 2016.

Hiltzik, Michael. *The New Deal: A Modern History*. New York: Free Press, 2011.

Hopkins, Ernest Jerome. *Our Lawless Police: A Study of the Unlawful Enforcement of the Law*. New York: Viking Press, 1931.

Jackson, Lawrence P. *Chester B. Himes: A Biography*. New York: W. W. Norton, 2017.

Jacobs, James B. *Mobsters, Unions, and Feds: The Mafia and the American Labor Movement*. New York: New York University Press, 2006.

Jacoby, Hank. *Sandusky's Finest: A Veteran Lawman Remembers— Partners Eliot Ness & Lt. Jim Benasek Investigating the Mafia*. Port Clinton, OH: Henry A. Jacoby, 1991.

James, Bill. *Popular Crime: Reflections on the Celebration of Violence*. New York: Scribner, 2011.

Jedick, Peter. *Cleveland: Where the East Coast Meets the Midwest*. 3rd ed. Cleveland: Fine Line Litho, 1994.

Jeffreys, Henry. *Empire of Booze: British History Through the Bottom of a Glass*. London: Unbound, 2016.

Jones, Gerard. *Men of Tomorrow: Geeks, Gangsters and the Birth of the Comic Book*. New York: Basic Books, 2004.

Kanfer, Stefan. *Ball of Fire: The Tumultuous Life and Comic Art of Lucille Ball*. New York: Vintage Books, 2004.

Keating, W. Dennis, Norman Krumholz, and David C. Perry, eds. *Cleveland: A Metropolitan Reader*. Kent, OH: The Kent State University Press, 1995.

Kellner, Esther. *Moonshine: Its History and Folklore*. New York: Weathervane Books, 1971.

Kerr, Daniel R. *Derelict Paradise: Homelessness and Urban Development in Cleveland, Ohio*. Amherst: University of Massachusetts Press, 2011.

Kluger, Richard. *Simple Justice: The History of Brown v. Board of Education and Black America's Struggle for Equality*. New York: Knopf, 2004.

Leighton, Isabel, ed. *The Aspirin Age: 1919–1941*. New York: Simon & Schuster, 1949.

Lender, Mark Edward, and James Kirby Martin. *Drinking in America: A History*. Rev. ed. New York: The Free Press, 1987.

Lingeman, Richard. *The Noir Forties: The American People from Victory to Cold War*. New York: Nation Books, 2012.

Littauer, Amanda H. *Bad Girls: Young Women, Sex, and Rebellion Before the Sixties*. Chapel Hill: University of North Carolina Press, 2015.

Lord, Alexandra M. *Condom Nation: The U.S. Government's Sex Education Campaign from World War I to the Internet.* Baltimore: Johns Hopkins University Press, 2010.

Lowery, Wesley. *They Can't Kill Us All: Ferguson, Baltimore, and a New Era in America's Racial Justice Movement.* New York: Little, Brown and Company, 2016.

Maeder, Jay. *Dick Tracy: The Official Biography.* New York: Plume, 1990.

Mappen, Marc. *Prohibition Gangsters: The Rise and Fall of a Bad Generation.* New Brunswick, NJ: Rutgers University Press, 2013.

Marshall, Bruce T. *Shaker Heights.* Images of America. Charleston, SC: Arcadia Publishing, 2006.

Martin, John Bartlow. *Butcher's Dozen and Other Murders.* New York: Harper & Brothers, 1950.

McElvaine, Robert S. *The Great Depression: America, 1929–1941.* 25th anniversary ed. New York: Three Rivers Press, 2009.

McGill, Neil W., and William H. Perry. *Court Cases of Eliot Ness.* Fullerton, CA: Sultana Press, 1971.

Messick, Hank. *Secret File.* New York: G. P. Putnam's Sons, 1969.

———. *The Silent Syndicate.* New York: Macmillan, 1967.

Meyer, Leisa D. *Creating GI Jane: Sexuality and Power in the Women's Army Corps During World War II.* New York: Columbia University Press, 1996.

Miller, Carol Poh, and Robert Wheeler. *Cleveland: A Concise History, 1796–1990.* Bloomington: Indiana University Press, 1990.

Muhammad, Khalil Gibran. *The Condemnation of Blackness: Race, Crime, and the Making of Modern Urban America.* Cambridge: Harvard University Press, 2010.

Neff, James. *Mobbed Up: Jackie Presser's High-Wire Life in the Teamsters, the Mafia, and the F.B.I.* New York: The Atlantic Monthly Press, 1989.

Ness, Eliot. *What About Girls?* New York: Public Affairs Committee, 1943.

Ness, Eliot, with Oscar Fraley. *The Untouchables.* New York: Julian Messner, 1957.

Nickel, Steven. *Torso: The Story of Eliot Ness and the Search for a Psychopathic Killer.* Winston-Salem, NC: John F. Blair, 1989.

The Official Roster of Ohio Soldiers, Sailors, and Marines in the World War, 1917–1918. Columbus, OH: F. J. Heer Printing Co., 1926.

The Ohio Guide. American Guide Series. New York: Oxford University Press, 1940.

Okrent, Daniel. *Last Call: The Rise and Fall of Prohibition.* New York: Scribner, 2010.

Oliver, Willard M. *August Vollmer: The Father of American Policing.* Durham, NC: Carolina Academic Press, 2017.

Olszewski, Mike and Janice. *Cleveland TV Tales.* Cleveland: Gray & Company, 2014.

Parascandola, John. *Sex, Sin, and Science: A History of Syphilis in America.* Westport, CT: Praeger, 2008.

Perry, Douglas. *Eliot Ness: The Rise and Fall of an American Hero.* New York: Viking, 2014.

Porrello, Rick. *Rise and Fall of the Cleveland Mafia.* Fort Lee, NJ: Barricade Books, 1995.

Porter, Philip W. *Cleveland: Confused City on a Seesaw.* Columbus: Ohio State University Press, 1976.

Potter, Claire Bond. *War on Crime: Bandits, G-Men, and the Politics of Mass Culture.* New Brunswick, NJ: Rutgers University Press, 1998.

Powers, Richard Gid. *G-Men: Hoover's FBI in American Popular Culture.* Carbondale, IL: Southern Illinois University Press, 1983.

———. *Secrecy and Power: The Life of J. Edgar Hoover.* New York: The Free Press, 1987.

Proceedings: Twenty-Ninth Annual Convention of Rotary International—San Francisco, California, June 19–24, 1938. Chicago: Rotary International, 1938.

Purvis, Alston, and Alex Tresniowski. *The Vendetta: FBI Hero Melvin Purvis's War Against Crime, and J. Edgar Hoover's War Against Him.* New York: PublicAffairs, 2005.

Raab, Selwyn. *Five Families: The Rise, Decline, and Resurgence of America's Most Powerful Mafia Empires.* New York: Thomas Dunne Books, 2005.

Renga, Dana, ed. *Mafia Movies: A Reader.* Toronto: University of Toronto Press, 2011.

Ricca, Brad. *Super Boys: The Amazing Adventures of Jerry Siegel and Joe Shuster—The Creators of Superman.* New York: St. Martin's Press, 2013.

Robinson, Greg. *A Tragedy of Democracy: Japanese Confinement in North America*. New York: Columbia University Press, 2009.

Rogge, O. John. *The Official German Report*. New York: Thomas Yoseloff, 1961.

Rose, William Ganson. *Cleveland: The Making of a City*. Kent, OH: Kent State University Press, 1990.

Rotskoff, Lori. *Love on the Rocks: Men, Women, and Alcohol in Post–World War II America*. Chapel Hill: University of North Carolina Press, 2002.

Ruth, David E. *Inventing the Public Enemy: The Gangster in American Culture, 1918–1934*. Chicago: University of Chicago Press, 1996.

Sabin, Roger, ed. *Cop Shows: A Critical History of Police Dramas on Television*. Jefferson, NC: McFarland & Co., 2015.

Sagalyn, Arnold. *A Promise Fulfilled: The Memoir of Arnold Sagalyn*. Burtonsville, MD: House of Printing, 2010.

Sanders, Coyne Steven, and Tom Gilbert. *Desilu: The Story of Lucille Ball and Desi Arnaz*. Rev. ed. New York: Dey St., 2011.

Sarkissian, Adele, ed. *Something About the Author: Autobiography Series*. Vol. 1. Detroit: Gale Research, 1986.

Schechter, Harold. *The Serial Killer Files: The Who, What, Where, How, and Why of the World's Most Terrifying Murderers*. New York: Ballantine Books, 2004.

Schoenberg, Robert J. *Mr. Capone: The Real—and Complete—Story of Al Capone*. New York: Quill, 1992.

Seltzer, Louis B. *The Years Were Good*. Cleveland: World Publishing Company, 1956.

Shumsky, Neil Larry. *Homelessness: A Documentary and Reference Guide*. Santa Barbara: Greenwood, 2012.

Sifakis, Carl. *The Mafia Encyclopedia*. 2nd ed. New York: Checkmark Books, 1999.

Spigel, Lynn, and Michael Curtin, eds. *The Revolution Wasn't Televised: Sixties Television and Social Conflict*. New York: Routledge, 1997.

Stack, Robert, with Mark Evans. *Straight Shooting*. New York: Macmillan, 1980.

Stern, Scott W. *The Trials of Nina McCall: Sex, Surveillance, and the Decades-Long Government Plan to Imprison "Promiscuous" Women*. Boston: Beacon Press, 2018.

Storer, Colin. *A Short History of the Weimar Republic*. London: I.B. Tauris, 2013.

Strunk, Mary Elizabeth. *Wanted Women: An American Obsession in the Reign of J. Edgar Hoover*. Lawrence: University Press of Kansas, 2010.

Sugden, Philip. *The Complete History of Jack the Ripper*. Rev. ed. New York: Carroll & Graf, 2002.

Tappan, Paul W. *Delinquent Girls in Court: A Study of the Wayward Minor Court of New York*. New York: Columbia University Press, 1947.

Tucker, Kenneth. *Eliot Ness and the Untouchables: The Historical Reality and the Film and Television Depictions*. 2nd ed. Jefferson, NC: McFarland & Co., 2012.

United States. Congress. Senate. Special Committee to Investigate Organized Crime in Interstate Commerce. *Hearings Before the United States Senate Special Committee to Investigate Organized Crime in Interstate Commerce*. 82nd Cong. Part 6, *Ohio–Kentucky*. Washington, DC: United States Government Printing Office, 1951.

Vacha, John. *Meet Me on Lake Erie, Dearie! Cleveland's Great Lakes Exposition, 1936–1937*. Kent, OH: Kent State University Press, 2011.

Vahimagi, Tise. *The Untouchables*. London: British Film Institute, 1998.

Van Tassel, David D., and John J. Grabowski, eds. *The Dictionary of Cleveland Biography*. Bloomington: Indiana University Press, 1996.

———, eds. *The Encyclopedia of Cleveland History*. 2nd ed. Bloomington: Indiana University Press, 1996.

Vollmer, August. *The Police and Modern Society*. Berkeley: University of California Press, 1936.

Vronsky, Peter. *Sons of Cain: A History of Serial Killers from the Stone Age to the Present*. New York: Berkeley, 2018.

Ward, Artemus. *Deciding to Leave: The Politics of Retirement from the United States Supreme Court*. Albany: State University of New York Press, 2003.

White, Ahmed. *The Last Great Strike: Little Steel, the CIO, and the Struggle for Labor Rights in New Deal America*. Oakland: University of California Press, 2016.

Wilson, Frank J., and Beth Day. *Special Agent: A Quarter Century with the Treasury Department and the Secret Service*. New York: Holt, Rinehart and Winston, 1965.

Wiltse, Jeff. *Contested Waters: A Social History of Swimming Pools in America*. Chapel Hill: University of North Carolina Press, 2007.

Wolcott, David B. *Cops and Kids: Policing Juvenile Delinquency in Urban America, 1890–1940*. Columbus: Ohio State University Press, 2005.

Wolcott, Victoria W. *Race, Riots, and Roller Coasters: The Struggle over Segregated Recreation in America*. Politics and Culture in Modern America. Philadelphia: University of Pennsylvania Press, 2012.

Selected Articles

Arruda, George W. "Eliot Ness—Revisited." *Investigator*, May 1988, 8–9, 11–13, PCHS.

Bardsley, Marilyn. *Eliot Ness: The Man Behind the Myth*. courtTV Crime Library, http://www.crimelibrary.com/gangsters_outlaws/cops _others/ness (accessed March 11, 2006).

———. "The Kingsbury Run Murders." The Crime Library, http://web .archive.org/web/200012051940/http://www.dark-horse.com /kingsbury2/kingsbury.htm (accessed August 15, 2016).

Bland, Lyle E. "National Traffic Safety Contest Winners." *Public Safety*, April 1939, 6–7, 48, in ENPS, Roll 2, Scrapbook 9, pp. 156–157.

Chamberlin, Jo. "The Cop Who Saved a Thousand Kids." *This Week Magazine*, March 1, 1941, 4, 11.

———. "Eliot Ness: The Cosmopolite of the Month." *Cosmopolitan*, August 1940, 6, 104.

Chasan, Will, and Victor Riesel. "Keep Them Out! II. Martin L. Sweeney of Ohio." *Nation*, May 30, 1942, 626–628.

"Cleveland Wins Traffic Award: Safest Large City in Country." *Police*, June 1939, 4–9, 30, in ENPS, Roll 2, Scrapbook 9, p. 158.

Condon, George. "The Last American Hero." *Cleveland Magazine*, August 1987, 88–91, 138–142, RM.

"The Congress: The Bitter End." *Time*, September 16, 1940, 12–13.

Deutsch, Albert. "Danger! Venereal Disease." *Nation*, September 22, 1945, 284–285.

Dokoupil, Tony. "America's Long Love Affair With Anti-Anxiety Drugs." *Newsweek*, January 21, 2009, http://www.newsweek.com /americas-long-love-affair-anti-anxiety-drugs-77967 (accessed February 21, 2017).

Douthat, Stratton. "The Last of the Untouchables." *Floridian (Tampa Bay Times)*, October 3, 1971, 5–10.

Edgerly, Dennis. "Birth of EMS: The History of the Paramedic." *Journal of Emergency Medical Services*, October 8, 2013, http://www.jems .com/articles/print/volume-38/issue-10/features/birth-ems-history -paramedic.html (accessed December 6, 2016).

Eyman, Scott. "An Oscar for Elliot [*sic*] Ness." *Sunshine (Fort Lauderdale News)*, July 21, 1985, 10, 12, 26.

Flynn, John T. "The Betrayal of Cleveland." *Harper's Magazine*, January 1934, 142–150.

"Fortune Faces." *Fortune*, January 1946, 196, 198.

"Fortune Shorts." *Fortune*, January 1946, 225–226

Fraley, Oscar. "The Real Eliot Ness." *Coronet*, July 1961, 25–30.

Frye, Bob. "A Famous Crime Fighter's Brush with Fishing Laws." Wild Outdoors, August 28, 2015, http://blog.triblive.com/wild -outdoors/2015/08/28/a-famous-crime-fighters-brush-with-fishing -laws/ (accessed September 4, 2015).

Gerber, S. R., as told to Oscar A. Bergman and Joseph M. Gambatese. "Mystery of Cleveland's Headless Cadavers." *True Detective Mysteries*, February 1938, 28–31, 126–128.

Gopnik, Adam. "The Forty-Year Itch." *New Yorker*, April 23, 2012, 19–20.

Havens, Paul. "Personalities in Law Enforcement: Eliot Ness." *True Detective Mysteries*, November 1939, 61, 117–118.

Heimel, Paul W. "Agent Eliot Ness Lived His Last Years in Coudersport." *Pennsylvania*, March/April 1996, 32–33, PCHS.

High, Stanley. "Cleveland Versus the Crooks." *Current History*, October 1938, 22–24.

Jedick, Peter. "Eliot Ness." *Cleveland*, April 1976, 48–57, 91–94.

Lehman, Mark. "Eliot Ness—The Man We Thought We Knew." *Cincinnati Magazine*, August 1987, 19–20, PWH.

Lubove, Roy. "The Progressives and the Prostitute." *Historian* 24, no. 3 (May 1962), 308–330.

Maisel, Albert Q. "Return of the Numbers Racket." *Collier's*, January 15, 1949, 21–23, 71–73.

Martin, John Bartlow. "Butcher's Dozen: The Cleveland Torso Murders." *Harper's Magazine*, November, 1949, 55–69.

McFarland, Rebecca. "Eliot Ness in Cleveland from the Cleveland Police Museum." Teaching Cleveland Digital, January 2012, http:// teachingcleveland.org/eliot-ness-in-cleveland-from-the-cleveland -police-museum/ (accessed December 14, 2016).

Michel, Joan Hess. "Evaline Ness, Caldecott Medalist." *American Artist*, June 1967, 32–37, 69–72.

"Milestones." *Time*, November 14, 1955, 116.

Miller, William. "Cleveland's Boy Scout and the Racket Patrol." *True*, May 1939, 33–43, 120–121, in box 374, folder 8, HBP.

———. "Cleveland's Rue Morgue." *Ken*, January 12, 1939, 14–15.

Ness, Eliot. "Cleveland Cashes In." *Public Safety*, September 1938, 26–27, 42, in ENPS, Roll 2, Scrapbook 8, p. 83.

———. "Community Policing Vital to Victory." *True Detective*, October 1942, 49, 70.

———. "Cooperation of Cities in Social Protection Services." *Minnesota Municipalities*, February 1943, 48–49, in ENPS, Roll 3, Scrapbook 12.

———. "How to Curb Prostitution in Hotels." *Southern Hotel Journal*, February 1943, 17–28, 43, in ENPS, Roll 3, Scrapbook 12.

———. "The National Program of Social Protection." *Public Welfare* 1, no. 4 (April 1943), 115–118, PWH.

———. "New Role of the Police." *Survey Midmonthly*, March 1944, 77–78, in ENPS, Roll 3, Scrapbook 12.

———. "The Participation of Boys." *Phi Delta Kappan*, March 1940, 337–334.

———. "Public Safety and the Three E's: Enforcement—Engineering— Education." *Clevelander*, March 1938, 4, 21, in ENPS, Roll 2, Scrapbook 10, 135–136.

———. "Radio-Directed Mobile Police." *American City*, November 1939, 35–36.

———. "The 'Red Light' District Must Go." *National Sheriff*, September–October 1942, 1, 5, in ENPS, Roll 3, Scrapbook 12.

———. "Streamlining Protection." *Real Detective*, October 1941, 4, 92.

———. "They Did the Things Which 'Couldn't Be Done.'" *Pulse*, April 1944, 26–27, in ENPS, Roll 3, Scrapbook 12.

———. "Venereal Disease Control in Defense." *Annals of the American Academy of Political and Social Science*, March 1942, 89–93.

Ness, Elisabeth. "My Husband, Eliot Ness." *TV Guide*, March 11, 1961, 5–7.

Nickel, Steven. "The Real Eliot Ness." *American History Illustrated*, October 1987, 42–52.

"Ockie's Jackpot." *Newsweek*, January 14, 1963, 67–68.

Pearl, Matthew. "Behind *The Untouchables*: The Making of the Memoir That Reclaimed a Prohibition Era Legend." *Vanity Fair*, December 27, 2017, https://www.vanityfair.com/hollywood/2017/12/the -untouchables-the-making-of-the-memoir-prohibition-era-legend (accessed December 27, 2017).

Persico, Joseph E. "The Day When We Almost Lost the Army." *American Heritage*, Spring 2012, http://www.americanheritage. com/content/day-when-we-almost-lost-army (accessed December 29, 2016).

Pushkar, Robert G. "Oldies and Oddities: The Little Steel Strike Airlift." *Air & Space Magazine*, July 2001, http://www.airspacemag .com/history-of-flight/oldies-amp-oddities-the-little-steel-strike -airlift-41977502/?all&no-ist (accessed October 29, 2016).

Rogge, O. John. "Nazi Ties in America Exposed." *Jewish Veteran*, December 1946, 6.

Romano, Aja. "Uncovering the Mad Butcher of Kingsbury Run." *Daily Dot*, November 27, 2012, http://www.dailydot.com/society/mad -butcher-kingsbury-run/ (accessed January 13, 2017).

Romm, Cari. "During World War II, Sex Was a National-Security Threat." *The Atlantic*, October 8, 2015, http://www.theatlantic.com /health/archive/2015/10/during-world-war-ii-sexually-active -women-were-a-national-security-threat/409555/ (accessed February 1, 2017).

Scaduto, Anthony. "The Eliot Ness Myth." *Climax*, October 1961, 50–53, 82–84.

Simmons, Christina. "African Americans and Sexual Victorianism in the Social Hygiene Movement, 1910–40." *Journal of the History of Sexuality* 4, no. 1 (July 1993), 51–75.

"Touched by an Untouchable." *People*, September 29, 1997.

Trickey, Erick. "Case Closed?" *Cleveland Magazine*, June 19, 2014, http://clevelandmagazine.com/in-the-cle/the-read/articles/case -closed- (accessed December 2, 2016).

———. "Eliot Ness vs. J. Edgar Hoover." *Smithsonian*, October 2014, 78–85, 104, 107.

Vollmer, August. "Aims and Ideals of the Police." *Journal of the American Institute of Criminal Law and Criminology* 13, no. 1 (May 1922), 251–257.

———. "Policemen as Social Workers." *The National Police Journal* 4, no. 3 (June 1919), 6, 23, 25.

"When Eliot Ness Ran Diebold." ATM Marketplace, March 20, 2003, https://www.atmmarketplace.com/articles/when-eliot-ness-ran -diebold/ (accessed February 6, 2017).

Wilder, Jesse Bryant. "The Last Untouchable." *Northern Ohio Live*, March 1993, 45–46, 115–117, PWH.

Wiltse, Jeff. "The Black-White Swimming Disparity in America: A Deadly Legacy of Swimming Pool Discrimination." *Journal of Sport and Social Issues* 34, no. 4 (2014), pp. 366–389.

Films and Radio

Call Northside 777 (1948). Directed by Henry Hathaway. Beverly Hills, CA: Twentieth Century Fox Home Entertainment, Inc., 2004. DVD.

"Eliot Ness." *The Real Untouchables*. Written and directed by John Fothergill. Thousand Oaks, CA: Goldhil DVD, 2001. DVD.

"Eliot Ness" (February 20, 1991). *Unsolved Mysteries*. Directed by Mike Mathis. In *Unsolved Mysteries: Strange Legends*, Disc 1. Burbank, CA: Cosgrove/Meurer Productions, 2004. DVD.

Eliot Ness: An Untouchable Life (2006). Written and directed by Max Allan Collins. Tulsa, OK: VCI Entertainment, 2007. DVD.

"Eliot Ness: Untouchable." *Biography*. Directed by Michael Husain. New York: New Video, 2001. VHS.

The Fourteenth Victim: Eliot Ness & the Torso Murders. Produced by Mark Wade Stone. Cleveland: Storytellers Media Group, 2006. DVD.

High Noon (1952). Directed by Fred Zinnemann. Santa Monica, CA: Artisan Entertainment, 2002. DVD.

Queenan, Joe. "Untouchable." London: BBC Radio 4, June 14, 2007, http://www.bbc.co.uk/programmes/b007ngfp (accessed September 25, 2014).

The Untouchables: Season 1, Volume 1 (1959–1960). Directed by various. Hollywood: Paramount Pictures, 2007. DVD.

The Untouchables: Season 1, Volume 2 (1960). Directed by various. Hollywood: Paramount Pictures, 2007. DVD.

The Untouchables: Season 2, Volume 1 (1960–1961). Directed by various. Hollywood: Paramount Pictures, 2008. DVD.

The Untouchables (1987). Directed by Brian De Palma. Hollywood: Paramount Pictures, 2004. DVD.

Index

Index

MAX ALLAN COLLINS is a Mystery Writers of America "Grand Master." He is the author of the Shamus-winning Nathan Heller historical thrillers (*Do No Harm*) and the graphic novel *Road to Perdition*, basis of the Academy Award–winning film. His innovative *Quarry* novels led to a Cinemax TV series, and he is coauthor with his wife, Barbara, of the award-winning Trash 'n' Treasures mystery series (*Antiques Fire Sale*, Barbara Allan). He has completed numerous Mickey Spillane mysteries from the late author's files (*Murder, My Love*), and has directed and/or written two feature-length documentaries and six features.

A. BRAD SCHWARTZ is the author of *Broadcast Hysteria: Orson Welles's War of the Worlds and the Art of Fake News*. In 2013, he cowrote a documentary about the *War of the Worlds* broadcast for the PBS series *American Experience*, based in part on research from his senior thesis at the University of Michigan in Ann Arbor. As part of the university's selective screenwriting program, he wrote *Open House*, a murder-mystery/comedy short film that premiered at the Traverse City Film Festival. He is currently a doctoral candidate in American history at Princeton University.

ALSO ABOUT
ELIOT NESS

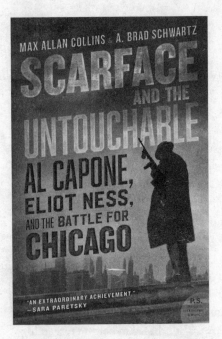

SCARFACE AND
THE UNTOUCHABLE

"Gripping. ... Reads like
a novel."—*Chicago*

"Essential. ... A superior
example [of true
crime]."—*Seattle Times*

"Revolutionizes our
understanding of Al Capone
and Eliot Ness."—Matthew Pearl

Includes 115 photographs and a map of gangland Chicago.

Scarface and the Untouchable draws upon decades of primary source research—including the personal papers of Ness and his associates, newly released federal files, and long-forgotten crime magazines containing interviews with the gangsters and G-men themselves. Collins and Schwartz have recaptured a bygone bullet-ridden era while uncovering the previously unrevealed truth behind Scarface's downfall. Together they have crafted the definitive work on Capone, Ness, and the battle for Chicago.

DISCOVER GREAT AUTHORS, EXCLUSIVE OFFERS, AND MORE AT HC.COM